Lecture Notes in Computer Science

Edited by G. Goos and J. Hartmanis

492

D. Sriram   R. Logcher
S. Fukuda (Eds.)

Computer-Aided Cooperative Product Development

MIT-JSME Workshop
MIT, Cambridge, USA, November 20/21, 1989
Proceedings

Springer-Verlag

Berlin Heidelberg New York London Paris
Tokyo Hong Kong Barcelona Budapest

Volume Editors
Duvvuru Sriram
Robert Logcher
Intelligent Engineering Systems Laboratory
1-253, Department of Civil Engineering
Massachusetts Institute of Technology
Cambridge, MA 02139, USA

Shuichi Fukuda
Department of Management Engineering
Tokyo Metropolitan Institute of Technology
6-6, Asahigaoka, Hino, Tokyo 191, Japan

Workshop Sponsors
Japanese Society of Mechanical Engineers (JSME)
Intelligent Engineering Systems Laboratory at MIT
Bell Atlantic Knowledge Systems, Inc.

CR Subject Classification (1991): I.6, H.2

ISBN 3-540-54008-3 Springer-Verlag Berlin Heidelberg New York
ISBN 0-387-54008-3 Springer-Verlag New York Berlin Heidelberg

Foreword

This volume contains a selection of papers presented at the MIT-JSME Workshop on Cooperative Product Development held at the Massuchusetts Institute of Technology, Cambridge, Mass., U.S.A., November 20/21, 1989. Twenty-eight papers have been selected to appear in this volume. The papers are organized into the following six categories:

- Frameworks, dealing with problem-solving architectures,
- Organizational issues, investigating strategies for organizing engineering activities for effective utilization of computer-aided tools,
- Negotiation techniques, dealing with conflict detection and resolution between various agents,
- Transaction management issues, dealing with interaction issues between the agents and the central communication medium,
- Design methods, dealing with techniques utilized by individual agents,
- Visualization techniques, including user interfaces and physical modeling techniques.

Sponsorship and financial support for the workshop was provided by the Japanese Society of Mechanical Engineers (JSME), the Intelligent Engineering Systems Laboratory at MIT, and the Bell Atlantic Knowledge Systems, Inc. (which markets the LASER knowledge-based programming environment). Joan McCusker (U.S.A.) and Yasuyo Fukuda (Japan) helped with the administrative process. Shamim Ahmed, Keng Lim, and Albert Wong were student volunteers. All this support, and the support of our families, is gratefully acknowledged.

January 1991

D.Sriram
R. Logcher
S. Fukuda

Contents

Negotiation

Transaction Management

Design Methods

Visualization Techniques

Introduction

D. Sriram, R. Logcher, S. Fukuda

Engineering is a collaborative process, where people from various disciplines interact to produce a product. In traditional product development, the lack of proper collaboration between various engineering disciplines poses several problems, as expounded by the following clip from Business Week, April 30, 1990, p. 111 (see Fig. 1 for a typical scenario in the AEC industry).

> The present method of product development is like a relay race. The research or marketing department comes up with a product idea and hands it off to design. Design engineers craft a blueprint and a hand-built prototype. Then, they throw the design "over the wall" to manufacturing, where production engineers struggle to bring the blueprint to life. Often this proves so daunting that the blueprint has to be kicked back for revision, and the relay must be run again - and this can happen over and over. Once everything seems set, the purchasing department calls for bids on the necessary materials, parts, and factory equipment - stuff that can take months or even years to get. Worst of all, a design glitch may turn up after all these wheels are in motion. Then, everything grinds to a halt until yet another so-called engineering change order is made.

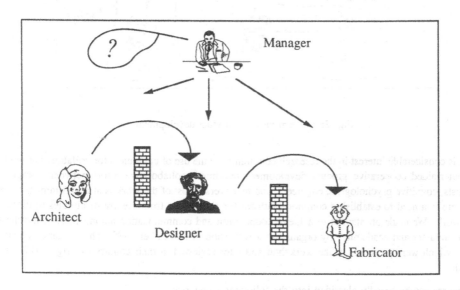

Fig. 1: Over the wall engineering

Several companies have addressed the above problem by resorting to a more flexible methodology, which involves a collaborative effort during the entire life cycle of the product. It is claimed (Business Week,

April 30, 1990) that this approach[1] results in reduced development times, fewer engineering changes, and better overall quality. The importance of this approach has been recognized by the Department of Defense, which initiated a major effort - the DARPA Initiative in Concurrent Engineering with funding in the millions of dollars.

It is conceivable that the current cost trends in computer hardware will make it possible for every engineer to have access to a high performance engineering workstation in the near future. The "over the wall" approach will probably be replaced by a network of computers/users, as shown in Fig. 2, in which we use the term *agent* to denote the combination of a human user and a computer.

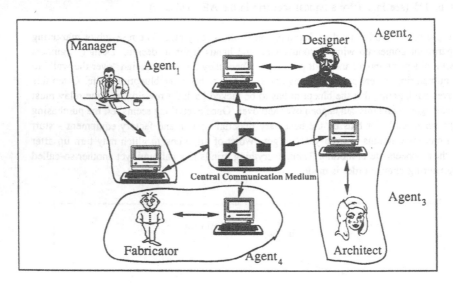

Fig. 2: Modern view of product development

There is considerable interest in the research community in the use of computers for collaborative work. Computer-aided cooperative product development requires a collaborative effort between computer scientists, cognitive psychologists, engineers, and managers. Most of the work is at a preliminary stage and there is a need to establish a common platform for researchers from diverse disciplines to discuss their work. We made an attempt to achieve cooperation and communication among these researchers - from industry and academia - by organizing a workshop in November 1989. This volume contains papers which were presented at the workshop and later reviewed in their country of origin (U.S. and Japan).

The papers can be broadly classified into the following categories:

- **Frameworks**, which deal with problem solving architectures.

- **Organizational Issues**, which investigate strategies for organizing engineering activities for effective utilization of computer-aided tools.

---

[1]The terms Concurrent Engineering, Collaborative Product Development, Cooperative Product Development, Integrated Product Development and Simultaneous Engineering are often used to connote this approach.

- **Negotiation Techniques,** which deal with conflict detection and resolution between various agents.

- **Transaction Management Issues,** which deal with the interaction issues between the agents and the central communication medium.

- **Design Methods,** which deal with techniques utilized by individual agents.

- **Visualization Techniques,** which include user interfaces and physical modeling techniques.

Brief summaries of the papers in this volume are provided below.

Frameworks

Next-Cut: A Second Generation Framework for Concurrent Engineering. Next-Cut consists of a centralized knowledge store, with different agents communicating through this central knowledge medium. The knowledge store embodies both product and process models, depicting the life cycle of the product. Any changes made to this central knowledge store are communicated to the appropriate agents. Although the agents and the central knowledge store reside on a single machine, the architecture is easily extendable to a distributed environment. Next-Cut is implemented in SPE, a LISP-based object-oriented programming environment.

A Blackboard Scheme for Cooperative Problem-Solving by Human Experts. The DARPA DICE project uses the Blackboard approach to achieve communication and coordination. Once the agents agree on a particular design, the design is posted onto a database, which is developed over the ROSE database management system and resides on the computer network. In Next-Cut, the differences in the representation between individual agents and the central knowledge store were not addressed in detail. The interface incompatibilities are addressed in the DARPA DICE project through the use of Wrappers, which provide appropriate translations. The Common LISP environment is being used to develop the DARPA DICE.

An Object-Oriented Environment for Collaborative Engineering Design. In the DARPA DICE framework, the database and the blackboard reside on different computers. This may cause a lot of traffic in the DICE communication channel and thus slow down the system. The MIT DICE project[2] addresses this issue by implementing the blackboard over an object-oriented database management system; thus the blackboard and the object-store are tightly integrated. In addition, the objects in the blackboard have behavior associated with them (this is also the approach followed in Next-Cut). Hence, the need for a sophisticated scheduler (as provided in the DARPA DICE project) is obviated. The MIT DICE project also incorporates comprehensive transaction and version management mechanisms. An initial version of MIT DICE was implemented in Common LISP. Currents versions exist in the OPAL/GEMSTONE and C++/ONTOS environments.

Creativity Support System for Concurrent Product Design. The Creativity Support System (CSS) consists of a domain independent module and a domain dependent module. The system supports various quality improvement schemes used in the industry (e.g., house of quality, Taguchi's method, etc.). These quality improvement schemes are applied to various levels of product refinement throughout the entire life cycle. The domain independent parts of the system have been implemented and integration details are being explored.

---

[2]Although these two projects have similar scope, they are currently being funded by different organizations.

Product Abstraction Evolution by Active Process Facilitators. A framework related to CSS is discussed. Two distinct abstraction activities are identified: interdomain and intradomain. The role of constraints within a design agent and across design agents is discussed.

A Model Integration Framework for Cooperative Design. In the meta-model system for cooperative design, issues involved in the development of a comprehensive knowledge base, which includes the physics of the domain, for the central knowledge store are discussed. Forbes' qualitative process theory is used for the simulation of physical systems. The meta-model system is being implemented in Smalltalk-80.

Towards a Framework for Concurrent Design. A theoretical framework for the cooperative design problem is presented. The notions of conflicts, design operators (or agents), and computational paths for ordering design operators (agents) are presented. Based on the theory, a methodology - TAO graphs - for visualizing, detecting, and avoiding conflicts was developed. An implementation - called FORS - of computational paths (conflict free paths) using TAO graphs is also discussed.

Organizational Issues

Cooperation in Aircraft Design. A study of how aircraft are designed in a large organization, such as Lockheed Aeronautical Systems Company, is presented. Various participants in the design process and the interactions between these participants are identified. The design process is viewed as one of coordinated refinement of models, as assumed by the computer-based framework papers. The negotiation process is considered as being "controlled by an organizationally agreed sequence of commitment steps".

Managing the VLSI Design Process. Significant progress has been made in design automation (DA) research in the VLSI community. The data representation is a fairly well-understood task. However, relatively little effort has been made in the management of various CAD (computer-aided design) tools. In this paper, a model is presented for managing the work of a design team. The model is based "on a task specification language, for encapsulating CAD tool invocations and arranging the sequencing of such invocations to accomplish specific tasks, and a novel activity model, which maintains the history of task innovations and serves as a focus for sharing work results in a cooperative manner". This approach differs significantly from earlier approaches in design integration, such as ULYSSES at CMU.

Towards a Shared Computational Environment for Engineering Design. While most of the Frameworks papers assume a model of the engineering process, the architecture presented here is based on studies conducted from cognitive and social points of view. Emphasis is placed on the various engineering and management models that are typically used in a collaborative design environment.

Organizing the Tasks in Complex Design Projects. A technique for taking an existing design sequence and producing a matrix that reduces potential conflicts between various designers is proposed. This methodology, however, captures all the complex interrelationships between the various design stages.

Negotiation

Knowledge-Based Conflict Resolution for Cooperation Among Expert Agents. The Cooperating Experts Framework (CEF) supports cooperative problem solving among different agents, implemented as knowledge-based systems. Agents in the CEF framework can propose design solutions (proposals), evaluate design solutions, detect conflicts, and respond to conflicts. CEF is implemented over GBB, which is a commercial blackboard-based environment, and provides scheduling and communication support for agents (via the blackboard), a set of conflict resolution strategies (Generate Random Alternatives, Compromise, Generate Constrained Alternatives, Generate Goal Alternatives, Case-based Parameter Set Retrieval, and Revise and Merge Goals), and a set of heuristics to choose the appropriate conflict resolution strategy. The CEF framework is symbol-based, and lacks a rigorous numerical constraint management facility.

Cooperative Negotiation in Concurrent Engineering Design. Negotiation is viewed as a process that happens during the entire product life cycle, and at various levels of design abstraction. This process consists of three tasks: generating a design solution (proposal), iterating on the solution based on the feedback from other agents, and communicating justifications and supporting evidence. The proposed framework, which is being implemented in LISP, for computer-based negotiation incorporates techniques from case-based reasoning, plan generation, argumentation, belief structures, and utility theory.

Evaluating Alternate Connection Designs Through Multiagent Negotiation. The Designer Fabricator Interpreter (DFI) addresses the lack of communication and coordination between structural designers, fabricators, and erectors during the design of beam-column connections. The relationships between the artifact (connection) and the agents are depicted in the form of a dependency network - the DFI relational network. A user/arbitrator specifies an initial design on a blackboard. The structural designer, fabricator, and erector get updated through the DFI relational network. They in turn critique the design and post their views (or alternate solutions) in the blackboard. The arbitrator looks at these different views and starts a negotiation process. DFI is implemented in a frame-based extension of a commercial PROLOG programming environment, and runs on a SUN machine with each agent shown in a separate window.

Transaction Management

Transaction Management in Design Databases. The central communication medium is treated as a database. Several agents can access and modify the database. An inappropriate sequence of operations by agents may lead to loss of data integrity. The entity state transition management scheme facilitates the partial ordering of transactions, which ensures database integrity and aids in concurrency control. A pipe layout design, with an emphasis on theoretical foundations, is used to exemplify the proposed scheme.

A Model of Concurrent, Cooperating Transactions in an Object-Oriented Database. In traditional database management systems (e.g., automated teller machines), correctness and serializability are ensured by a transaction management subsystem which assumes transactions are atomic. However, engineering transactions are not atomic and the serializability condition is too restrictive. The proposed model augments the traditional notions with "programmer-defined correctness criteria", rather than system-defined criteria, and the semantics of a particular application are exploited. A theoretical framework for transaction groups (a collection of cooperating transactions) is developed.

Design Methods

A Prototype of Feature-Based Design for Assembly. A feature is defined as "any geometric or non-geometric attribute of a discrete part whose presence or dimensions are relevant to the product's or part's function, manufacture, engineering analysis, use, etc., or whose availability as a primitive or operation facilitates the design process" (Cunningham and Dixon's paper in the 1988 CIME conference provides an interesting discussion on designing with features). The prototype system, implemented in LISP, provides a framework for feature-based design that takes into account assembly process planning, assembly sequence generation, assembly fixturing assessments, and assembly process costs.

Feature-Based Design for Manufacturability Critique in Concurrent Engineering. Features are extracted from existing BREP solid model descriptions, available from a solid modeling system. These features are input into a manufacturability critic, which evaluates each feature against several rules obtained from manufacturing experts.

Intelligent Suggestive CAD Systems: Research Overview. Boothroyd and Dewhurst's rules for design for assembly are encoded as production rules. During a design session, a user can invoke the production rule-base which provides suggestions on how to alter the design using a set of geometric features specified by the user. Several studies were performed with and without using the suggestive CAD system.

A Method Towards Design Intelligence Modeling. Based on his experience with designing products, the author (who has several patents) discusses a framework for conceptual design. The proposed framework has a design variable generator, a case-based reasoner, and a constraint manager. A prototype has been implemented in PROLOG.

Simultaneous CAE System for Reducing Engine Radiated Noise. The interplay between material selection and performance analysis is discussed.

Expert R&M Design Synthesis: An Enabling Technology for Concurrent Engineering. The ACES tool, implemented in OPS5 and FORTRAN, incorporates knowledge about maintainability, reliability, availability, and support costs. ACES is interfaced to a CAE synthesis program, which provides details about geometry, component weights, material data, etc.

An Artificial Intelligence Approach to Efficient Fusion First Wall Design. In the Fusion Wall design system, implemented in LISP, C, and FORTRAN, the knowledge is stored in the form of objects, rules, and functions. The objects communicate with each other through a message passing scheme. The rules incorporate heuristic design knowledge, while the functions are used for algorithmic analysis. A fuzzy set approach is utilized to handle uncertainties in design.

An Object-Oriented Design Tool Toward CIM for Shipbuilding. The Object-Oriented Design tool (OODT) is similar in scope to the Fusion Wall design system. In OODT, the knowledge base consists of hierarchies of two types of objects: the Design objects (e.g., MainEngine), which contain the structure and constraint knowledge; and the Designer objects (e.g., EngineDesigner), which contain the process knowledge needed to generate values in the Design objects. OODT, implemented in Smalltalk-80, also incorporates a constraint management facility.

Using Design History Systems for Technology Transfer. History systems keep track of the decisions made during the product life cycle. Design history systems are computer-aided systems that enable "the acquisition, manipulation, and presentation of design histories". PTTT, which can be tightly integrated with other DEC software, is a design history system, which was developed for recording the results of the manufacturing process design. PTTT is currently being tested in the wafer process development domain.

Visualization Techniques

ThingWorld: A Multibody Simulation System with Low Computational Complexity. Physical simulation in real time will help the engineer in visualizing and assessing the impacts of engineering designs. For example, a designer can evaluate his design by invoking a physical simulation of a manufacturing process. One main problem with achieving physical simulation in real time is that computational complexity increases exponentially as the problem becomes large. ThingWorld addresses this problem by making the following assumptions: neglect high-order mode shapes in dynamic simulations; represent geometry using implicit functions (e.g., superquadrics); and restrict constraints to be either quadratic energy functions for inexact constraints or linear holonomic functions for exact constraints. Thus, ThingWorld is able to perform complex multibody simulations with linear computational complexity.

A Study on Visualization of Control Software Design. The Tokyo power supply system has three nuclear power plants, 29 thermal power stations, 156 water power plants, 1300 substations, and 18,000 kilometers of power lines. The Tokyo Power Utility company has decided to control the network in an optimal manner utilizing a vast computer networking system. To achieve this goal, there is a need to develop tools for large-scale software development. 3D-Visualization is proposed as a means to coordinate the software development process.

Coded Shape Representation and its Application to Mechanical and Structural Design. The Coded Boundary Representation (CBR) technique, implemented in PROLOG, extends Freeman's work on raster image recognition (see Reference 1 in the paper) to the recognition of vector-based engineering drawings. After the drawing is recognized as belonging to a certain physical model, an analysis is performed on the model.

A list of participants at the workshop is appended at the end of the volume.

Next-Cut: A Second Generation Framework for Concurrent Engineering

D. R. Brown
Mechanical Engineering Department
University of Utah
Salt Lake City, Utah 84112

M. R. Cutkosky
Center for Design Research
Stanford University
Stanford, California 94305

J. M. Tenenbaum
Schlumberger Technologies Corp. and
Computer Science Department
Stanford University
Stanford, California 94305

Abstract *We discuss Next-Cut, a second-generation computational framework for concurrent design and manufacturing. The Next-Cut architecture permits human and computational agents to cooperate in design and manufacturing. The architecture features a central knowledge base that serves both as a shared knowledge base and a medium for information exchange. We review the architecture in Next-Cut, focusing on the central model and the key agents. We then present an example in which the agents interact with each other and with a human designer to prototype or incrementally refine a simple mechanical assembly.*

1. Introduction

In this paper we discuss Next-Cut, an experimental computational framework for Concurrent Engineering. Next-Cut is the successor of First-Cut, an early software environment for concurrent product and process design [Cutkosky and Tenenbaum 90]. Next-Cut incorporates and enhances the strong points of First-Cut and corrects many of its deficiencies. First-Cut taught us that there can be a tight coupling between the design of a part and the design of its process plan. The creation of a part was accomplished through machining-like commands and the designer was restricted at each stage to those operations that could actually be performed on the part. Thus design proceeded literally by constructing a high-level process plan. While First-Cut improved the communication between design and manufacture, experience showed it to be overly rigid for all but detailed design. (It is not always desirable for designers to be intimately concerned with process planning, particularly at the early stages of design.)

Next-Cut allows designers more flexibility to move among the different stages of design and process planning. The approach is to provide a flexible environment in which designers, and system modules, or agents, can jump among different kinds of design problems (e.g., geometric versus functional), working simultaneously with assemblies and components that have reached different levels of completion. Although Next-Cut is not yet complete, it allows the designer to work at a high level where possible and it tries to automatically fill in details and propagate consequences when enough information exists to do so.

Starting at a high level, the designer may wish to pull components from catalogs or on-line design libraries, and combine or modify them to meet functional specifications. If a particular element requires attention, the designer can focus on it and the system will help to refine the design and the accompanying process plan. When part of the design changes, the ramifications for other aspects of the design and for process planning are propagated via simulation, planning, and detection of events (such as interferences). Thus, when the geometry of a feature changes, we simulate the new geometry to establish its effects on an assembly; when a process step changes we simulate the new plan to determine its effects on geometry. This ability to accommodate, and propagate changes for, a continually evolving design is the most important attribute of a system for concurrent design. The need to accommodate incremental changes affects both the representations we use and the design of individual software modules.

In addition to supporting incremental design, Next-Cut attempts to extend the competence of First-Cut in several areas:

• additional manufacturing processes, including assembly and injection molding;

• early stages of design where the representations of designs and processes may be abstract, or incomplete;

• enhanced depth and competence for agents (software modules) so that they make use of physical and geometric reasoning;

• more interaction among modules in detecting and resolving design/manufacturing incompatibilities;

• more modularity and extensibility, making it easier to integrate specialized software modules (e.g., geometric modelers, process planners) many of which will be developed elsewhere.

These extensions will permit Next-Cut to support the design of electromechanical assemblies consisting of catalog parts and machined or injection-molded parts prototyped using the system. The goal we are working towards includes the ability to retrieve designs and associated process plans from a catalog and then to modify either the design or the plan and have the system propagate the consequences.

Before leaving this section we also observe that an important characteristic of a concurrent design environment, and particularly an evolving one like Next-Cut in which some modules may be fairly superficial, is that it is a cooperative man/machine system. Therefore, the human user must have access to all representations and levels of detail and should be able to guide the system, or overrule it where desired. This allows the system to be used on designs which its analysis and planning modules are only partially able to accommodate.

In the rest of this paper we give an overview of the system and describe progress to date on key modules.

2. The Next-Cut Framework

Next-Cut consists of models and modules, as shown in Figure 1. The central model is the main repository of information in the system. The software modules consist of agents and editors, which exchange information through the central model and operate on its objects. Agents are programs that have expertise in specific areas such as fixture design, process planning, geometric reasoning and modeling, and tolerance analysis. They can make modifications to the central representations (e.g., refining a plan) and respond to requests from human users or other agents. "Editors" are intelligent, graphical tools through which people can examine or modify the design and/or process plans, using custom interfaces that support various job-related perspectives (e.g., designer, process engineer). Both agents and editors may also have their own local model of the world that is more specialized than that contained in the central model.

In terms of interaction with the central model, there is no need to distinguish between computer agents and human agents acting through editors. Our goal is to create a virtual design team on which humans, acting through editors, and computerized agents are interchangeable. This approach provides a natural evolutionary path in which editors gradually become agents by adding knowledge and reasoning. However, in the spirit of a cooperative system, the editing function is retained so that human designers can always override automated decisions and take over when problems exceed an agent's competence.

Next-Cut: a Framework for Concurrent Design

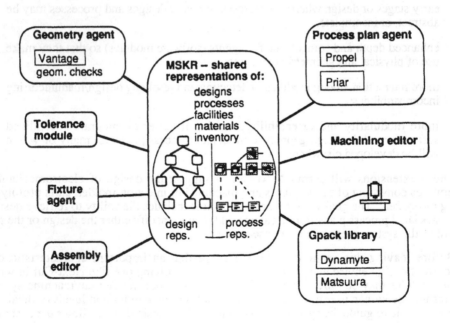

Figure 1: The architecture of Next-Cut showing the central model and its relationship to the surrounding editors and agent modules.

2.1 Notification

Because it is impossible to anticipate all agent interactions, a central issue in a system like Next-Cut is to ensure that modules are automatically invoked when they are needed, rather than by explicit calls. In Next-Cut, this flexibility is accomplished by having the model notify agents of changes that may affect them. In this way, changes made in one agent's local model are reflected in the central model and then passed on to other agents affected by those changes. At the same time, it is necessary for the agents to be somewhat insulated from the shared model for the sake of robustness. Otherwise, the system would signal

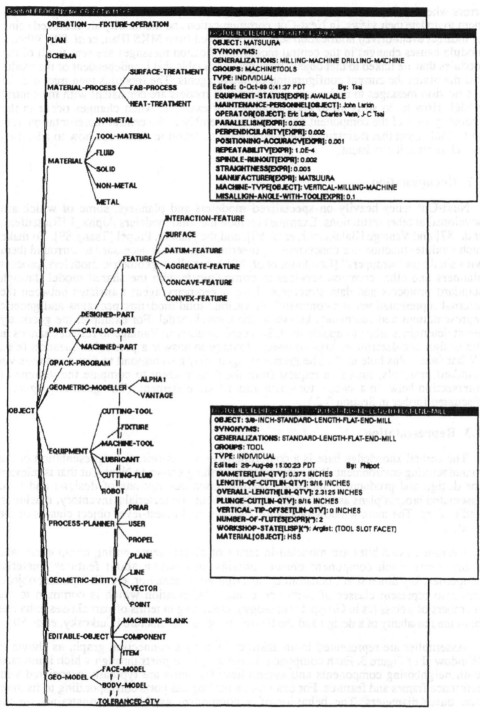

Figure 2: Large window shows a taxonomy of classes near the top level of the central model in Next-Cut. Right windows show typical machine and tooling definitions within the central model.

errors whenever agents or other modules which are not present are sent messages telling them to update their views. In Next-Cut, communication and modularity are achieved using an indirect event-driven notification scheme borrowed from MKS [Pan, *et al*. 89]. When a module causes changes in the central model, notification messages are sent to all of the modules that are linked to that object, through a hash table that is independent of the model and maintains the current configuration of active agents. The modules then may use the notification messages to make sure that their own models are consistent with the central model. How to do so is up to each module. For example, when changes occur in the geometry slots of the component objects of an assembly in the central representation, it is up to each agent that maintains a geometric representation to determine how to adjust its model to make it consistent.

2.2 Encapsulation

Next-Cut relies heavily on specialized modelers and planners, some of which are developed at other institutions. Examples include the solid modelers Alpha_1 [Riesenfeld, *et al*. 87] and Vantage [Balakumar, *et al*. 88], and the planner, Propel [Tsang 89]. To make such modules function in a concurrent engineering system it is necessary to surround them with shells (or "wrappers" [Londono, *et al*. 89]) that allow geometric modelers, process planners and other common services to communicate with the shared model through standard protocols and data structures. Thus a geometry agent translates between the internal representations and commands of various solid modeling packages and generic representations and commands known to the central model. For example, the geometry agent determines when to update the CSG representation in Vantage to reflect changes in the design and determines how to query Vantage to answer a particular question (e.g., "What face is this hole in?"). The geometry agent may also respond to direct requests via standard protocols, such as a request from the fixture agent to compute the volume of intersection between a swept tool-path and a fixture element. (The geometry agent is discussed further in Section 3.2.)

2.3 Representation

The central knowledge base is a comprehensive, object-oriented representation of the manufacturing environment. It encompasses everything known to Next-Cut that is relevant for design and production, including feature-based descriptions of designs and their associated process plans as well as information about raw materials, inventory, machines, and tooling. The main window of Figure 2 shows the highest-level object classes of the model.

Designed assemblies are modeled in terms of objects representing components and connections. Each component object contains information about features, material properties, key dimensions, constraints, descriptions of behavior, etc. Component objects can also represent classes of parts and contain information which is common to the members of a class (as in Group Technology). Designing in terms of part classes enhances both the reusability of a design and the flexibility of its manufacture [Cutkosky, *et al*. 89].

Assemblies are represented in an abstract form by a connection graph, as shown in Window II of Figure 3. Each component in the graph has *ports* through which it interacts with neighboring components and assemblies. The ports are typically associated with reference frames and features. For example, a bearing has ports corresponding to its inner and outer diameters. The behavior of a component establishes constraints on the relationships among quantities at different ports. For example, a bearing has the ability to support (i.e., to transmit) radial forces and angular motion between its inner and outer ports.

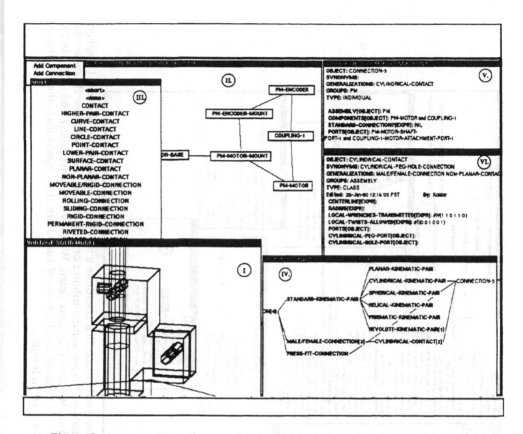

Figure 3: An assembly editor session in which the user has "zoomed in" on a coupling. Window II is the connection graph editor; Window III (partly hidden) is a pull-down menu of connections that can be added to components in Window II; Window IV shows part of a taxonomy of connection types from which *connection-5* between the motor and coupling inherits its kinematic and geometric properties; Windows V and VI allow the user to inspect the details of *connection-5* and one of its parent classes.

The connections between components are also first-class objects with explicit constraints and properties. For example, consider *connection-5* between the motor and coupling objects in Figure 3. As shown in Window IV, this connection inherits properties from *cylindrical-kinematic-pair*, *cylindrical-contact* and *press-fit-connection*, which allow it to establish constraints on form (cylindrical shape), dimensions (mating diameters) and kinematics. Window VI shows some of the properties of the class of *cylindrical-contact* connections. In particular, we notice that the instantaneous degrees of freedom are represented by *wrenches-transmitted* and *twists-allowed* (from screw theory [Roth 84]) in the local coordinate frame.

The above representation of designed assemblies resembles the representations that have been widely used in AI to reason about the structure and function of digital circuits [Singh 85; Davis 84]. In mechanical designs, however, it is also important to represent and reason

14

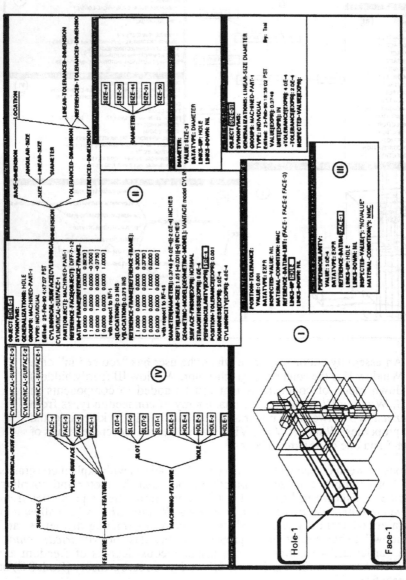

Figure 4: Editor windows of several of the interconnected objects that constitute a machined component. Window I displays the geometric model for graphical interaction. Window II shows some attributes of a feature, *hole-1*. Window III shows the perpendicularity tolerance with respect to *face-1* from Window II in more detail. Window IV shows *hole-1* and *face-1* in the feature taxonomy. Remaining windows show that the diameter and location of *hole-1* are also objects that inherit standard procedures (methods) and are explicitly linked to their parent feature.

about detailed geometry. Accordingly, component, feature, and port objects may have a solid model slot that refers to a corresponding subset of a part's geometric model. The actual solid model representations of features are maintained in external modules (i.e., geometric modelers). The solid models are parameterized and organized so that locational constraints (such as the position and orientation of a shaft port with respect to the base port), dimensions and associated features can be separately extracted or modified. The solid models are kept consistent with the symbolic feature representations in the central model via the notification mechanism.

Figure 4 is a closer look at the coupling component from Figure 3, in terms of its features, dimensions and tolerances. Some of the slots associated with a hole feature object are shown in Window II. The hole has a parent part and surface in addition to its location, dimensions and tolerances. Examining the perpendicularity tolerance, we see that it is another object, as revealed in Window III. The perpendicularity tolerance is with respect to *face-1* and is taken at maximum material condition (MMC). Therefore, *face-1* inherits both from *plane-surface* and from *datum-feature*, as shown in Window IV. Remaining windows show that the hole's location and diameter are also objects with built-in methods for updating their values and with default unit and tolerance slots. Window IV also shows low-level features such as faces and surfaces, which are used for geometric reasoning.

In addition to the objects that represent parts, Next-Cut also maintains objects for representing manufacturing processes. There are objects for machines and tools and also for process steps. A complete process plan for a machined part is represented by a hierarchical tree-like structure known as a *P-graph*, an example of which is shown at the top of Figure 5. At the top level is an ordered sequence of the machine objects used in the part's fabrication. (For the motor-coupling plan shown in Figure 5, there is just one machine). Each machine object, in turn, has a slot containing an ordered list of fixture objects corresponding to the sequence of set-ups on that machine. Continuing down the hierarchy, each fixture object points to the sequence of tool-objects that will be applied in that setup. Finally, each of the tool-objects points to a sequence of detailed process steps (i.e., cuts) to be performed with that tool. As Window III of Figure 5 shows, each process step has explicit preconditions, parent operations and a link to the feature it helps create. There is also a reciprocal link from a part object to the process that makes it, so that a two-way dependency is maintained.

Features and operations may be combined into aggregate features and operations, such as the bolt circle shown in Figure 6. Aggregate features have explicit constraints that govern how they behave and that permit the collection of features to be dimensioned and located with respect to common datum surfaces. Aggregate operations have substeps which are other operations. This aggregation can continue for an arbitrary number of levels. In fact, entire process plans are made as aggregate operations.

The central model also has classes that represent inventory. The part objects described earlier are specifications that define classes of parts. Inventory, on the other hand, describes physical instances of parts: how many are in stock, what is the work-in-process, and what raw materials are available.

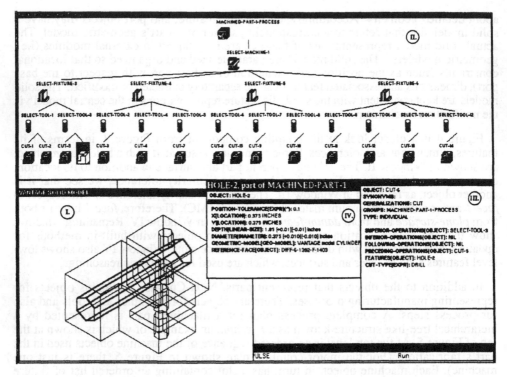

Figure 5: Two interconnected views for working with a machined part: a feature-based CAD view in Window I and a process graph in Window II. *Cut-6* has been selected in the process graph and opened for inspection in Window III. It has an explicit link to the horizontal hole, *hole-2* which it helps to create, and a parent operation *select-tool-3* and precondition, *cut-5*. Therefore, changes to *hole-2* or *cut-5* directly affect *cut-6*. Some of the detailed attributes of *hole-2* are shown in Window IV.

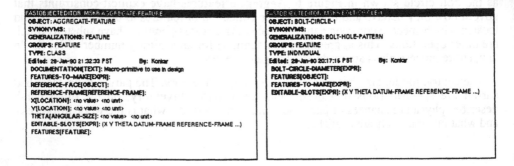

Figure 6: An aggregate operation for making a bolt circle.

3. Modules

As Figure 1 shows, the modules that have been developed in Next-Cut include three editors for design: a machining editor, an assembly editor and injection-molding editor; several autonomous modules for manufacturing, including a process planner, a fixture agent, a tolerance module and a detailed machining module; and a geometry agent that is used for both design and manufacturing. We briefly describe each of these below.

3.1 Design editors

When working in Next-Cut, one pulls up various windows and menus to inspect and modify parts of the design or process plan. Thus, what we call the "assembly editor" or the "machining editor" is basically a set of windows and interaction tools that are relevant for a particular design task. The general philosophy is to allow designers to move among the different views at will and to try to propagate the effects of actions made in one window to the others where possible.

Machining editor

The machining editor provides an environment in which the designer creates machined parts primarily through feature-based design operations, adding or removing features and modifying their attributes, such as dimensions or tolerances. As in First-Cut, this editor reflects manufacturing constraints at a high-level. For example, in the machining editor one can remove material but cannot add it. The editor has two main views, a feature-based geometric model (as shown in Windows I and IV of Figure 5 and a process plan view (as shown in Windows II and III). The designer can work in either of these views, adding features to the graphical representation of the part or editing the accompanying process plan, and inspecting the consequences in the other view.

Assembly editor

The assembly editor provides an environment in which designers can build assemblies from catalog items and machined components. Like the machining editor, the assembly editor provides two principal views: a solid model of the assembly in which graphical interaction can take place and a connection graph, which is an abstract representation of how components interact with each other, as discussed in Section 2.3. At different times, either view may be the more convenient. Thus one can select features and coordinate frames in the graphical window of Figure 3, or one can pull up boxes from an on-line catalog and connect them in the connection diagram, using Windows II and III of Figure 3. The graphical view is then updated (to the extent possible) to reflect the changes in the assembly. In either case, the system automatically takes care of such details as computing the transforms necessary to make connected parts align.

The connection graph is a high-level specification tool that allows the assembly editor to assist the designer in selecting catalog components, determining the geometric configuration of the parts and propagating constraints (e.g., constraints on shape, dimensions, kinematic properties) and filling in details concerning an assembly. For example, the assembly editor will adjust the diameters of a mating hole and shaft to match and can automatically determine the bolting pattern on a plate if a motor with a known hole pattern is connected to it. The assembly editor can also determine and propagate kinematic properties. For example, when a plate is attached to linear bearings that ride on shafts, it can be determined that the plate is able to translate with respect to the shafts (provided that the shafts are parallel) because the linear bearings permit linear motion between their inner and outer ports. Further details on the assembly editor and the constraint propagation methods are provided in [Konkar, *et al*. 90].

Injection molding editor

The injection molding editor is primarily the work of H. Hanada. The injection molding editor is aimed at the preliminary design of injection-molded components, enabling the designer to work in terms of approximate shape, which the editor refines as necessary to assure manufacturability. The designer begins by "sketching" a component using Bezier surfaces. The resulting geometry is interpreted to find wall sections ("slabs") and corners. A rule-based manufacturability analyzer checks for appropriate wall thicknesses, corner radii, etc. and adjusts them if necessary. Gate and parting line locations are also determined. The designer can add features such as ribs and bosses from a menu and can add functional specifications such as identifying surfaces that must have a smooth surface finish or that are load-bearing. The requirement that the component be designed from thin walls is an implicit manufacturability constraint since most injection-molded parts are thin-walled shells due to material cost and shrinkage considerations. Details on the injection molding editor are provided in [Hanada and Leifer 89].

3.2 Manufacturing modules

Planning module

Next-Cut has used the process planner Propel [Tsang 89] for sequence planning. Propel is a rule-based, hierarchical sequence planner that builds upon some of the principles originally developed in GARI [Descotte and Latombe 85]. The approach taken by optimal sequence planners like Propel is inherently time consuming and therefore is primarily useful when a completed design is ready to be released for production and/or evaluated to determine the overall manufacturing cost. Propel is encapsulated by an agent which translates design features into Propel features and which translates the output from Propel into a P-graph, suitable for manipulation by the machining editor.

However, in a system like Next-Cut, it is at least as important to quickly evaluate the ramifications of incremental changes made to a design. While a design is being created and modified, an optimal plan is unnecessary. Indeed it may be undesirable since there is a danger of misleading the designer about manufacturability based on incomplete information. As a result, we have started to develop an incremental process planner that emphasizes plan re-use for rapid replanning [Kambhampati and Cutkosky 90]. Further details on this planner are discussed in Section 5.

Fixture agent

The fixture agent is responsible for producing fixture set-ups to hold the part as it is machined. The fixture agent needs to interact closely with the process planner and the geometry agent (see below). In addition, the fixture agent needs to be able to perform analyses at different levels of detail, depending on the completeness of design and the process plan. For example, if no plan exists then the fixture agent produces preliminary fixture arrangements based purely on geometric checks of accessibility and interference. When a process sequence, or a partial ordering of process steps, is available, the fixture agent uses this information and also checks the kinematics of the fixture arrangement. Work is underway to permit the fixture agent to also perform more detailed force analyses of fixture arrangements [Cutkosky and Lee 89] when there is sufficient information about required tolerances on the part and about expected cutting forces in the process plan.

Tolerance module

Next-Cut currently uses tolerance information in constructing process plans (e.g., in selecting tools and operations) and in the future will use it in design, for conveying functional requirements such as clearance and free-play. There is a taxonomy of tolerance relationships that is used in representing design features. The taxonomy includes reference-tolerances (e.g., locations with respect to a datum surface) and self-tolerances (e.g., diametral tolerances). We are developing a mechanism for statistical tolerance representation and propagation [Frants, et al. 90].

Low-level CNC planning module

Once a high-level process plan has been developed, detailed CNC planning can take place. The detailed plan includes tool selection and tool-path generation. Tool selections are made by a small tool-selection module which uses rules in conjunction with an object-oriented database containing classes of tools (e.g., drills, end mills) and their associated properties. All individual tool descriptions include dimensions, swept areas and active cutting areas, and an indication of the current tool condition (i.e., how worn the tool is). The tool-path computations are performed by a module called Gpack. The heart of Gpack is a library of routines written in Pascal and used in the Stanford student machine shops for high-level CNC programming. Gpack also generates detailed cutter-path simulations for a final visual check of the CNC plan. The detailed CNC plans are converted to machine code and loaded into a vertical-axis CNC machine, along with comment statements telling the operator what tools to load and how to set up the part.

Geometry agent

Geometry information is critical and widely used in Next-Cut. Of course, different solid modeling packages represent geometry in different ways at different levels of detail and with different levels of efficiency. The varied implementation interfaces and data interchange formats associated with different modelers could lead to a lack of modularity, if each module had to deal with them independently. Therefore, we have been developing a geometry agent to standardize the modeling interface.

The geometry agent is an attempt to encapsulate the various functions and data provided by these modelers with a consistent object-oriented interface. For example, instead of dealing directly with Vantage functions for face information and with bounding-box functions for gross feature volumes, we can send a message to a general geometric model and it will field each request appropriately. The advantages of this approach include abstract interfaces to the geometry module that insulate it from changes and message-passing, and that afford a consistent view of the object's geometry, regardless of how the model is implemented. In addition, the geometry agent can choose how to best satisfy a given request, computing and/or caching only as sophisticated a model as is necessary for a particular geometric service. This is important for increasing the responsiveness of the system. Detailed representations include: *geometric-models, spatial-objects*, and *modelers*. *Geometric-models* are an object-oriented abstraction that field a variety of generic messages: display, face/edge/vertex, constituent information requests, etc. Examples of *geometric-models* are abstractions for Vantage faces, Vantage bodies, and bounding boxes. *Spatial-objects* are those objects such as parts, features, tool-paths and fixture elements which are partially described using one or more geometric models. Finally, *modelers* are low-level instances which package information and translate it into the low-level function applications tailored to an external package.

While the geometry agent should not be considered complete, we have had substantial success in freeing the geometry clients in Next-Cut from dependence on the implementation-specific details of a given geometrical modeler. For example, in a recent demo, we used gross bounding box approximations of features, parts, and tool-paths to compute potential geometric interactions, while the general spatial reasoning and CAD input were performed with the aid of the Vantage modeler. Furthermore, this modular design has helped us to port the system to different workstations and operating systems with minimum effort.

4. Example

This section shows a scenario of Next-Cut in use, highlighting the actions and interactions of the various agents as design changes are made and propagated. This scenario is meant to show just one way that the agents might interact. There is no fixed sequence; what happens next depends solely on the actions of the designer and the state of the design.

The action starts with the assembly editor. A designer is modeling a sub-assembly that includes a motor, motor mount, shaft encoder and motor coupling (see Figure 3). The designer builds the assembly using the connection graph, specifying which parts are connected to each other, and through which ports they are connected. In this case, the motor, encoder and motor-mount are standard catalog items, selected on the basis of functional requirements (e.g., required torque or resolution) using the catalog-selection module. The motor coupling is a machined part that has been loaded from an on-line library. The holes at either end of the coupling have been identified as *shaft-ports*.

The designer specifies that the motor-coupling connection (*connection-5* in Figure 3) is a light press fit and the encoder-coupling connection is a *fastenable* connection that can be tightened with a set screw. After the connections have been made, the designer inspects the object that represents the motor coupling and notes the requirements that have been propagated from the adjacent motor and shaft encoder. For example, the hole diameter on the coupling now matches the shaft diameter of the motor with an allowance for a light press fit. If a motor with a different shaft diameter is substituted from the parts catalog, the mating hole on the coupling will change automatically. A closer examination of the connection formed between the motor and the coupling reveals that it forms a cylindrical pair and that it is rigid because of the press fit. In addition, there is a constraint that the motor must be collinear with the coupling.

If a dimension on the motor coupling is changed, the affected agents are notified. For example, the geometry agent, is notified to update the solid model shown in Figures 4 and 5. In some cases the new model can be determined automatically, as when changing the dimensions or location of a feature. In other cases the designer may need to make the alteration manually. For example, if a feature is deleted it may not be clear how to handle the other features that were located with respect to it.

As the geometric features of the motor coupling change, the process planning module is notified that it should generate a new plan. The planner then sends messages to other agents to update the tooling and fixturing and detailed machining choices as necessary. The tooling module responds by selecting the correct tool from its knowledge-base. Similarly, the machining module translates the plan into G-Code, which a Next-Cut machine may execute.

5. Summary

Next-Cut is a prototype computational framework that allows product development teams consisting of humans acting through editors and computer agents to communicate their results into a central knowledge base. The system notifies other agents and editors when changes are made that affect them. The agents also facilitate the integration of application modules by translating between internal representations and those in the central model.

In previous work we have focused on developing a suitable framework for concurrent design [Cutkosky and Tenenbaum 90]. In the future, the power and ease of use that Next-Cut provides will come primarily from enhancements to the modules and representations. To extend the depth and competence of the modules we are concentrating on the following issues:

- development of a new planner — As discussed in Section 3, we are working on the design of a new planner for Next-Cut that emphasizes incremental planning and plan re-use. This planner will rely heavily on geometric reasoning and access to specialists for deeper models of machining, fixturing etc. A number of approaches are being pursued to reduce the problems associated with backtracking, including:

  - maintaining explicit dependencies among design features and process steps. Implicit dependencies (e.g., geometric interferences) will be found through simulation.

  - keeping track of alternative solutions and delaying commitment as long as possible. The planner will use a non-linear plan representation that preserves partial orderings of steps and multiple solutions when suggested by modules (e.g., alternative fixturing arrangements) to minimize the expense associated with replanning. The desire not to overcommit at each stage extends from the designer to the shop floor. The designer should be encouraged to specify ranges of acceptable dimensions, corner radii, etc., and to work with "generic" features to give the planner maximum latitude in planning details. At the other end, detailed planning options (e.g., which of two available CNC mills to use) should be kept open as long as possible to allow for production vicissitudes.

  - exploiting hierarchy where possible. This helps to make the planner faster and to reduce backtracking by working at an abstract level.

  - exploiting external modules, with deep knowledge of processing, spatial reasoning, materials, etc.

- providing all modules with the ability to reason at multiple levels, using deeper models as the design progresses — Examples would include the fixture agent's ability to compute the deformations of parts as they are subjected to clamping and machining forces and the ability of the assembly editor to determine and propagate free-play and compliance in assemblies. These extensions should be added to the primarily geometric computations that Next-Cut makes today. The key issue is knowing what level to reason at. Detailed analyses should be performed when computational cycles permit and the design and plan are sufficiently detailed to justify them.

- increasing the sophistication of the assembly editor and of its representations —
The goal is to allow the designer to work at a high level where possible, with the
system filling in as many details as can be deduced from available information
about mating parts, geometries, behaviors and intended function. Today, Next-
Cut's assembly editor is able to propagate certain geometric and kinematic
constraints, but with richer descriptions of parts, ports and connections it should
be possible to propagate other behavioral and functional constraints (e.g., on
friction, power transmission and structural rigidity) as well. The additional
information contained in the connection graph should also be useful for resolving
ambiguities and retrieving designs from catalogs. For example, the recognition
that an assembly of parts constitutes a way of converting rotary to linear motion
leads to other ways of achieving the same results. Much of the power of
constraint propagation lies in the ability to prune an otherwise large search space.
In current work we are exploring general symbolic methods for constraint
manipulation to realize this potential. As in feature recognition, a considerable
advantage lies in exploiting extra information about the design (e.g., intended
function) and in allowing the designer to guide the process so that we resort to
general simultaneous equation-solving as little as possible.

- providing the ability to recognize standard design and manufacturing features in a
part, as well as sets of features that constitute a partially completed design —
Recognizing features and designs can expedite design, planning and analysis.
Examples include recognizing a significant manufacturing feature (e.g., a flexible
section in a machined part) so that a specialized machining plan can be applied or
a kinematic feature (e.g., a prismatic joint) to simplify kinematic analysis, or a
functional mechanism (e.g., a force-multiplying transmission) to help the
designer identify other solutions from a catalog. A number of standard model-
based recognition techniques from computer vision appear applicable. Moreover,
we have the potential to do even better by exploiting the extra contextual
knowledge we typically have. For example, it is easy to identify slot-like features
in a machined part when we know that they are to be assembled with mating tabs
on another part.

- making Next-Cut into a distributed team design environment — Next-Cut
currently runs on a single high-performance workstation. But there is nothing
inherent in the approach, architecture or communications mechanisms in Next-
Cut that relegates it to single-workstation use. We will be exploring ways to
distribute the "central" knowledge base in Next-Cut across multiple workstations
and permit multiple people to interact with it. For example, imagine the
machining editor with design and process (P-graph) views on separate
workstations, examined by a designer and a manufacturing engineer. The views
are kept consistent from design to processing by invoking process planners and
from process to design by invoking simulations.

5.1 Scaling issues

While it is still too early to say how effectively a system such as Next-Cut can support
concurrent design, it has already become clear that some limitations of the approach must
be addressed before a proof-of-concept system like Next-Cut can be scaled up to support
practical engineering problems. One such issue results from the representations and
propagation mechanisms in Next-Cut, which heavily exploit an object-oriented
programming environment with dynamic binding, multiple inheritance and message
passing. Designs, plans, features, cutting tools, fixtures, solid models and even low-level
entities such as dimensions, tolerances and vectors are all objects. The subject of a design

session becomes a large interconnected web in which various aspects of the design are automatically updated through explicit constraints, planning and simulation procedures. The price that we pay for this convenience is that Next-Cut uses large amounts of memory. For example, after working for approximately 30 minutes on the assembly and coupling design in this paper there were some 3000 frames (data structures) in memory.

For designs of any complexity it will no longer be possible to keep everything resident. When a frame must be updated that is not in memory it must be brought in, at considerable overhead. Moreover, changes to that frame may necessitate additional retrievals, the effects of which can quickly bring the system to a virtual standstill. While many look to object-oriented database technology (i.e. persistent objects) as the answer we are skeptical of such "black box" solutions. The very nature of concurrent engineering requires large, dynamically changing sets of tightly-coupled objects that must be brought out of secondary storage together to perform various tasks. Therefore the system will have to use considerable knowledge to manage memory efficaciously. This is an open research issue.

The management of computational resources presents similar problems. Possible solutions include running lengthy computations in the background (which raises the issue of backtracking) and running the system in distributed fashion on multiple workstations. We will be exploring both of these options in the future.

6. Acknowledgments

Support for this project was provided by DARPA under ONR contract N00014-88-K-0620 with additional support from Schlumberger Technologies, Sun Microsystems, General Motors and Lockheed. The Hyperclass programming environment was provided by Schlumberger Technologies.

We wish to thank the following individuals who have also contributed to the construction of the Next-Cut system: J. Glicksman, J. Pan and B. Hitson of Schlumberger; S-H. Lee, J. Tsai, A. Philpot, R. Konkar, E. Larkin, and S. Kambhampati of the Center for Design Research at Stanford; and H. Hanada from Sekisui Industries. We also thank Prof. Ken Preiss from LeHigh and Ben-Gurion Universities and the reviewers of the first draft for their advice and suggestions.

7. References

[Balakumar, *et al.* 88] P. Balakumar, *et al.* VANTAGE: A Frame-Based Geometric Modeling System. Carnegie-Mellon University Technical Report, 1988.

[Cutkosky and Lee 89] M. R. Cutkosky and S-H. Lee. Fixture Planning with Friction for Concurrent Product/Process Design. *Proceedings of the 1989 NSF Engineering Design Research Conference*, pp. 613–628, June 1989.

[Cutkosky and Tenenbaum 90] M. R. Cutkosky and J. M. Tenenbaum. A Methodology and Computational Framework for Concurrent Product and Process Design. *Mechanism and Machine Theory*, 25(3):365–381, April 1990.

[Cutkosky, *et al.* 89] M. R. Cutkosky, D. Brown and J. M. Tenenbaum. Extending Concurrent Product and Process Design Toward Earlier Design Stages. *Proceedings of the Symposium on Concurrent Product and Process Design*, ASME PED 36:65–72, December 1989.

[Davis 84] R. Davis. Diagnostic Reasoning Based on Structure and Behavior. *Artificial Intelligence*, 24(3):347–410, December 1984.

[Descotte and Latombe 85] Y. Descotte and J-C. Latombe. Making Compromises among Antagonist Constraints in a Planner. *Artificial Intelligence*, 27:183–217, 1985.

[Frants, *et al.* 90] L. Frants, T. O. Binford, J-C Tsai and M. R. Cutkosky. Representation and Propagation of Tolerances for CAD/CAM Systems. *Proceedings of the IFIP WG 5.2 Workshop on Geometric Modeling*, Rensselaer Polytechnic Inst., June 1990.

[Hanada and Leifer 89] H. Hanada and L. J. Leifer. Intelligent Design System for Injection-Molded Parts Based on the Process Function Analysis Method. *Proceedings of the 1989 NSF Engineering Design Research Conference*, pp. 597–612, 1989.

[Kambhampati and Cutkosky 90] R. Kambhampati and M. R. Cutkosky. An Approach Toward Incremental and Interactive Planning for Concurrent Product and Process Design. To be presented at the ASME Symposium on Computer-based Approaches to Concurrent Engineering, November 1990.

[Konkar, *et al.* 90] R. Konkar, M. R. Cutkosky and J. M. Tenenbaum. Towards an Assembly Editor for Concurrent Product and Process Design. *Proceedings of the IFIP WG 5.2 Workshop on Geometric Modeling*, Rensselaer Polytechnic Inst., June 1990.

[Londono, *et al.* 89] F. Londono, K. J. Cleetus and Y. V. Reddy. A Blackboard Scheme for Cooperative Problem-Solving by Human Experts. *Proceedings of the MIT-JSME Workshop on Cooperative Product Development*, pp. 1-30, 1989.

[Pan, *et al.* 89] J. Y-C. Pan, J. M. Tenenbaum and J. M. Glicksman. A Framework for Knowledge-Based Computer-Integrated Manufacturing. *IEEE Transactions on Semiconductor Manufacturing*, SM-2:33–46, 1989.

[Riesenfeld, *et al.* 87] R. F. Riesenfeld, *et al*. DARPA Semi-Annual Technical Report. University of Utah Computer Science Dept. Technical Report, Salt Lake City, April 1987.

[Roth 84] B. Roth. "Screws, Motors, and Wrenches That Cannot Be Bought in a Hardware Store." In *Robotics Research*, edited by P. Brady, pp. 679–693. Cambridge: MIT Press, 1984.

[Singh 85] N. Singh. Exploiting design morphology to manage complexity. Ph.D. diss., Dept. of Computer Science, Stanford University, Stanford, California, 1985.

[Tsang 89] J. P. Tsang. PROPEL: An Expert System for Generating Process Plans. SIGMAN Workshop on Manufacturing Planning, 1989.

A Blackboard Scheme for Cooperative Problem-Solving by Human Experts[*]

F. Londoño, K. J. Cleetus, Y. V. Reddy
Concurrent Engineering Research Center
Drawer 2000
West Virginia University
Morgantown, WV 26506
Phone: (304) 293 - 7226
FAX: (304) 293 - 7541
email: londono@cerc.wvu.wvnet.edu

1. Introduction

This paper describes the development of a blackboard based model for cooperative problem-solving by human experts. The work discussed here is being done as part of the DARPA Initiative in Concurrent Engineering (DICE). A major objective of DICE is the development of an architecture to support a systematic methodology for concurrent engineering.

Cooperative problem-solving is a field receiving wide attention as we pass from the age of the personal computer to that of the networked computer. The presence of cooperating humans on a network raises possibilities for joint working which have yet to be exploited for lack of software. We believe that networks still are ill-utilized because electronic mail, file transfer, remote login, and network file systems (NFS) remain the prime means of computer access to another person's work. These were great advances for their time. However, they deal primarily with the interaction of man and machine and only indirectly with communication between persons. By being indirect, they fail to bring about <u>immediate contact</u> between two or more minds engaged on a problem, and in this respect may be considered inferior to a much older invention, the telephone.

The work described here attempts to assist experts from several domains who need to collaborate intimately in the design of new products. It is presumed that each expert has unique computer-aided tools and human expertise, but a valid new design can only emerge

[*] This work has been sponsored by the Defense Advanced Research Projects Agency, under contract No. MDA972-88-C-0047, for the DARPA Initiative in Concurrent Engineering (DICE).

from the superposition of their individual capabilities. A strong inter-dependency arises in such team-work, and in spite of the best problem partitioning, conflicts will occur if optimization is done in individual domains. Thus, the architecture of the software system defined here facilitates four essential requirements in team-work :

1. Having continuous visibility of the work of peer knowledge workers, insofar as it affects one's work.
2. Providing for coordination by a lead person.
3. Notifying peers of changes, based on their expressed interest.
4. Enabling a new form of cooperative communication for holding meetings on the network.

The set of problems to which the present architecture is applicable is not limited to engineering. It could be used for cooperation between human experts for solving problems in domains as varied as administration, economics, politics, and business. Any problem with the following characteristics can be aided by this approach :

- the number of perspectives is more than one or two;
- a great body of knowledge exists in each perspective among human experts;
- the solution entails a mass of specific details; and
- the essence of problem solving lies in resolving conflicts so as to satisfy multiple goals.

In the rest of this paper we will use the terminology and example of concurrent engineering, which has all the complexity of decision making that can be conceived in any other field, and in addition has a particularly rich representation problem, since the types of data are very diverse.

2. Motivation

Blackboard systems, used by researchers in AI for many years, have natural appeal as an approach for solving partitioned problems by cooperative superposition of contributions from individual domains. Therefore, we have kept the framework of the classical blackboard, but adapted it to cooperation between human experts, instead of automatons with associated knowledge bases. This creates more than a cosmetic change. Indeed, the nature of the blackboard changes completely when human experts are introduced as knowledge sources.

A good review article on blackboard systems by Nii (1986) points to classical papers like one by Hayes-Roth (1985). Some work in distributed artificial intelligence is reported in a collection of papers edited by Huhns (1987), the most significant is entitled "Cooperation through Communication in a Distributed Problem Solving Network" (Lesser, Durfee, and Corkill 1985). This paper well indicates the potential for using communication to coordinate and develop an organization's problem-solving strategy. In addition, a more closely related work is the object-oriented organization of the blackboard model, found within the context of engineering design schemes for cooperation, that appeared in Sriram, Logcher, Groleau, and Cherneff (1988).

We also have followed the blackboard development work reported through blackboard workshops (e. g. Jagannathan, Dodhiawala 1988) and through the compiled papers that were published in Engelmore and Morgan (1988). One of the earliest examples of communication using global visibility as the basis for coordinating team work is the Xerox Colab project described by Stefik (1986). These and other sources suggest several reasons why the blackboard style of problem solving is particularly relevant to human organizations:

- contemporary organizational environments are naturally distributed;
- information is continuously generated, processed, and maintained within the distributed nodes;
- information needs to be integrated by a coordinating agent within the organization;
- many different computers and software platforms are used;
- intramural barriers to information flow are characteristic of large complex organizations; and
- decisions are bound by overall constraints imposed on a project or situation.

We believe that the blackboard model proposed here can be used as an organizational approach to mitigate the worst effects of closet competition within human organizations and to encourage openness. This is because blackboard structures offer a very natural way of integrating information through their global workspace. Human experts appear as knowledge sources who can assume the initiative in proposing product or process changes and improvements. The challenge is really in devising control strategies appropriate to the specific organization.

The product development environment provides a natural arena for the use of our blackboard model. The following characteristics of the problem give the model a special relevance:

- Information is generated by distributed domains of expertise but needs to be integrated in order to arrive at a final product specification. The blackboard provides a good model for integration of information when there is data and domain interdependence.
- The blackboard provides a centralized channel for communication among distributed problem solvers. Different perspectives in the design life cycle can share related information.
- Cooperation among distributed and diverse problem solvers is essential for success. We believe that strong elements of cooperation can be developed within the control strategy of the blackboard.
- A good coordination scheme is fundamental to drive the activities within a human organization. Through integration of the problem solving participants and the data they operate upon, the blackboard control strategy can provide assistance to managers coordinating the operation of the organization.
- A constraint management system can be attached as an automaton to the blackboard to impose external requirements.

Our work is oriented toward engineering design environments, and several issues must be considered in this endeavor. First is the development of an appropriate representation.

This is at the heart of the problem, because it is a situation where multiple perspectives exist. Second, when information flows from one perspective to another, the question arises of the granularity and level of abstraction required for the exchange to be meaningful. In this context there is no surprise in the notion that one should permit knowledge sources to interact with each other, which is contrary to the classical notions in blackboard models. The following sections present the first version of our model for applying the blackboard framework to a product development environment.

3. An Overview

This blackboard, called the DICE Blackboard for Design Evolution (DBB), provides a global workspace to develop the engineering design of a product (Cleetus and Uejio, 1989). The Blackboard supports communication and cooperation between designers; at the project level it also supports the coordination of the designers' activities by the Project Leader (PL). In essence, the Blackboard can be the place where a distributed team of designers agrees as to how a design should look. Reaching consensus through the Blackboard is seen in the following set of transactions.

The design process is begun by posting initial design information onto the globally visible workspace offered by the Blackboard. A *Focus* of the design is stated by the PL, and specific tasks are assigned to each designer. Designers using local and global data perform tasks on their local workstation with tools specific to their domain. All of them develop individual contributions to the solution from the analyses of design alternatives in their domain. Each contribution is placed formally onto the Blackboard as an *Assertion*. The Blackboard accepts assertions and evaluates their conformity to the design requirements. The evaluation of assertions by one designer involves the use of dependency tables to notify other designers of those assertions which could have a bearing on their work. This evaluation may also detect *Conflicts* between domains and the violation of constraints that span across domains. Such conflicts may trigger a *Negotiation* phase coordinated by the PL with the participation of the designers concerned. The Blackboard plays an important role in discovering downstream conflicts that arise from the concerns of experts in manufacturing and maintenance. At the end, agreement should be reached, and the final accepted design of each part must be incorporated (*Signed Off*) into the Product-Process-Organization (PPO) engineering data base as part of the solution. The PPO is the data base or repository of previous design configurations (Kinstrey et al. 1990).

The final solution is maintained in the PPO in the form of linked descriptions of the product, with related design, manufacture, and logistic processes, and the organizational resources. The product design, for example, may be represented by both an assembly tree of parts and a decomposition of functions. The PPO will have the ability to maintain and keep track of different versions for each of the parts in the product structure. Thus, the PPO data base becomes a network structure with multiple relationships among parts stored in it.

The solution of the entire design problem evolves incrementally in the Blackboard. The participation of the designers is opportunistic, but guided over time by the changing Focus expressed in the Blackboard by the PL. The solution is in itself partitioned into different domains to exploit *concurrency* by assigning parallel tasks to several groups of designers.

Concurrency is present in three respects. At the highest level, different domains work on different perspectives of the design in parallel, if at all possible. Furthermore, several parts or components going into the final product may be worked on simultaneously. And finally, within one domain, a group of designers guided by the Project Leader may be working on several different analyses of alternatives.

In sum:

- The Blackboard enables designers to interact and reach consensus about pieces of the design before they are incorporated as part of the solution in the PPO.
- The Blackboard supports communication and cooperation between designers. Decisions, intentions, and actions are shared by designers in the form of assertions on the Blackboard.
- The Blackboard is an assistant to the PL for coordinating the design activities. It provides a place to maintain design focus and also provides the mechanisms by which the PL can develop *tasks*, assign them, and keep track of their progress. Task management on behalf of the PL can be greatly assisted by the Blackboard. It can tell, for example, what tasks remain to be done on a part.
- The Blackboard provides control mechanisms, such as constraints and dependencies, that are helpful in detecting downstream conflicts and guiding the evolution of the design in the right direction.
- The Blackboard operation fits the desired model for concurrency. Different activities can progress in parallel on each designer's workstation with results being shared and integrated through the Blackboard.
- The Blackboard provides continuous visibility of the current status of the design. Designers can view the overall design status through the Blackboard. This visibility is important and assures that everybody who has a say in a part of the design gets to evaluate its acceptability from their perspective.
- The Blackboard provides for the final sign off, which is exercised by the PL. It assists the PL by keeping track of task completion, assuring the acceptance of assertions, and maintaining the skeleton product structure tree through which a new design is integrated into the PPO.

4.   Blackboard Operation

Figure 1 provides an overall view of the design process as it relates to the Blackboard operation. We view the PPO as an entry point to access the Product, Process and Organization information available for the current design activity. While the actual data may be distributed over the DICE network in many databases, the PPO in this figure provides a unique directory through which designers can access any information related to the design.

The Local Object Workspace (LOW) provides a local workspace for users to pursue their own design activities. For example, they may import a piece of the design into their LOW, modify it, and share the results with other designers via the Blackboard.

The Blackboard is a global workspace where designers can interact and reach consensus about solutions they evolve in their LOW's. Pieces of the design are refined in the LOW as a result of interactions mediated by the Blackboard. When pieces of the design have been satisfactorily synthesized, they are incorporated into the PPO.

The Project Lead (PL) is a special overseer who is assigned chief responsibility for the design process. The PL coordinates the design activities with the assistance of the Blackboard.

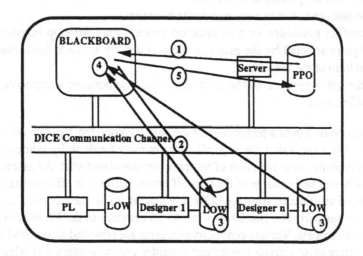

Fig. 1. Blackboard Operation

The sequence of operations in this figure is as follows:

① The design process is begun by putting initial design information onto the Blackboard. This operation is done by the PL and involves several actions.

The PL must identify some nodes in the PPO that represent component parts to be used in the current design. From this point, designers will be able to access these nodes and copy the relevant contents of the nodes (the actual engineering data files, or a header frame containing attribute information for the part) into their LOW's for further processing.

The PL must activate the control structures in the Blackboard. If there is no control information in the blackboard, the PL must import such information from the PPO or develop a strategy in its own LOW.

(2) The PL develops the focus of the design: a collection of tasks is developed from the design specification and the initial information available in the Blackboard. The tasks are formally assigned to the designers.

(3) Using local data, as well as data from the PPO, designers perform their tasks in their own local workspaces with tools specific to their domain. An assertion is a formal statement of the results of local activities performed by the designer. It constitutes the result of a previous task assigned through the Blackboard by the PL.

(4) Assertions are posted on the Blackboard by the designers. Several activities may occur after the posting of assertions :
New tasks can arise as a reaction to the assertion.
A conflict resolution or a negotiation process may develop in which different designers affected by the assertion interact and try to reach consensus about the final form of the assertion.
At the end, agreement will be reached and the assertions are accepted or replaced by a different set.

(5) When the design of a perspective of the part is completed, the sign off process must start. We expect that the sign off process must be done by whoever has major responsibility over the piece of information associated with the assertion. The PL usually will be in charge of the sign off process. The sign off consists of taking the piece of information from the LOW and placing it into the PPO as a new version of a previous part. The Blackboard acts as an assistant to the PL in coordinating the sign off process. Version control mechanisms are provided in the PPO data base.

In supporting these activities, one must consider several matters that relate to the kind of operations, functionality, and flow of transactions expected in the Blackboard to mediate and support cooperative engineering design:

- Representation
- The Project Lead's Capabilities
- Initialization of the Blackboard
- Focus of the Design
- Assertions
- Constraints
- Dependencies
- Maintenance of Versions
- Reasoning With Constraints
- Reasoning With Heuristics
- Negotiation
- Cut and Paste for Viewing only
- Sign Off
- Persistency

We rely on external functions provided by the engineering data base for access to the PPO as required by designers and the Blackboard. In a similar way, communication functions are expected to be provided by modules external to the Blackboard. Interfaces in the Blackboard itself provide for the delivery of tasks to designers, and the acceptance of assertions from designers.

5. Representation

The information represented in the PPO about a part will be diverse: blue prints, dimensions, tables of material characteristics, stress diagrams, description of process operations to realize a part, description of tooling and other resources to manufacture a part, etc. Each part will have different representations from various domain perspectives. Each partial representation will be in the form known to a specific version of a computer-based tool and will be identified by a certain file and path name. Every part in the PPO is assumed to have a **frame-based header** specifying the various representations stored and summarizing the features of the part, as it would be best understood by the designers. Associated with the description of each *part* is a complete collection of nodes organized in a tree hierarchy, whose branches show relationships between the nodes that represent each of the elements of a part (see Fig. 2.)

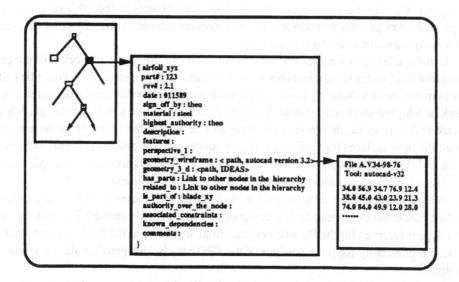

Fig. 2. Information in the PPO

A node like this may be just the root node in a tree where each of the sub-trees can be decomposed in the same way. We assume that when a node is referenced, access is provided to each of the sub-trees that compose the tree. For each of the nodes in the PPO, authority and responsibility levels will be defined for access to the PPO model.

In the following sub-sections, we indicate the requirements from the PPO data base to comply with the operation of the Blackboard.

6. Designers and the PPO

Designers must have access to the direct representation of portions of the design in the PPO. They must be able to select an object in the PPO for which they have authorization. If the designer knows the exact identifier for the object, the request can be sent directly to the PPO. The PPO should support logical searches in the same way as provided by relational database systems in their query language. A designer must be able to establish a logical search for an object or a collection of objects in the PPO. The exact physical location of the objects need not be known to the designer.

The PPO has browsing tools that will allow a designer to traverse its structures in a hierarchical way. When browsing through the PPO, a sub-tree should become visible when the browser reaches the root node of that sub-tree. If a node is selected, the user should be able to explore the node in depth. The user could look at the constraints and dependencies attached to that node, for instance.

The PPO also will allow the creation of copies of its objects when requested by designers. Objects, however, may be linked to other objects in the PPO structure. The copy operation permits components of the structure related to the object to be copied selectively with interaction by the designer.

Usually a designer's requests will focus on leaves of the tree, and work will progress from low level nodes to high level nodes by a process of aggregation. This could be called "bottom-up" design. Nothing, however, prevents the PL from directing a designer to start work at a higher level and proceed downward. That would be top-down design. We are aware that in practice, design is never done all one way or the other. From time to time when the need surfaces for verifying a design concept before proceeding, one will tend to work awhile in bottom-up fashion. Conversely, when concepts are clear and exploration is not needed, design tends to go top-down by progressive refinement.

While designers can access any part of the PPO for read purposes, writing is a different matter. Under no circumstance is a designer allowed to write to the PPO directly. This privilege is reserved for the PL who does the final sign off into the PPO of completed objects. Responsibility for some portions of the PPO may be delegated explicitly to another designer.

Peer approval of an assertion made in the Blackboard by one designer generally indicates that it is valuable as a component of the solution. The sign off process is undergone and a perspective of the part is incorporated into the PPO structure. The sign off is completed by the PL, who in turn will ensure that whichever domain has the highest authority over the part has had its Project Leader sign off too. When all the representations needed to totally specify the part have been incorporated into the PPO, that part is complete and may be readied for manufacturing.

7. The Project Lead

The PL is a designer, having special capabilities, who plays the essential role of guidance and has overall responsibility for decisions made during the design process. The work of the PL has several facets. In addition to coordinating design activities with the assistance of the Blackboard, the PL starts off the design by initializing the Blackboard and developing the focus of the design -- a set of tasks assigned to the designers and published on the Blackboard. The PL intervenes in the negotiation between designers, as needed, to achieve a resolution among conflicting proposals. Because the PL is charged with final responsibility for the product, the PL is required to sign off every part of the design before it is registered as approved in the PPO.

8. Initialization of the Blackboard

The structures in the Blackboard are designed to be independent of the domain of engineering to which the Blackboard is applied. They are general enough that end users of the DICE architecture do not need to modify the structure but only need to initialize it according to their enterprise or industry. Indeed, the generality goes so far as to make it possible to employ this Blackboard for collaborative decision making in any other field besides engineering.

The Blackboard structures are determined by the type of Objects which have to be represented therein:

- Design specifications, in the form of general constraints.
- Tasks developed by the PL as part of the focus of the design.
- Constraints related to components of the product and to the entire product.
- Assertions arriving from the designers.
- Dependencies between designers, for each part. Dependencies will take the general form of tables.
- Heuristics, in the form of rules of design.

During the initialization of the Blackboard, the PL will be able to copy the following kinds of objects from the PPO into the blackboard :

- Design specifications in the form of general constraints that are used to evaluate assertions arriving at the Blackboard.
- General tables of dependencies among the designers.
- Known heuristics for design in the current project. The correct scheduling of assertions and tasks among the designers is an example.

The start-up of the design could be based on the following considerations :

- The PL identifies nodes in the PPO representing component parts that will be used in the current design. The identification consists in creating a skeleton product assembly structure tree of the new design by copying the previous design and doing initial modifications to the nodes based on the new specifications. The PL will then mark the nodes which are to be considered thus making them visible to each of the designers. From then on, designers will be able to access the marked nodes and copy the relevant contents into their local workspaces for further processing.

- Control-related information is placed on the blackboard by the PL, either by explicitly initializing the control data structures of the Blackboard, or by bringing such control information stored in the PPO to the blackboard.

- When the Blackboard structures are filled with the appropriate information, the PL can start developing the Focus of the design. This consists of a collection of tasks developed by the PL, using the specifications and the initial information available in the Blackboard.

9. Focus of the Design

The knowledge about the design available in the blackboard allows the PL to assign and keep track of tasks which can be attacked in parallel by different groups. This problem-solving process must provide continuous visibility of the status of the design to each designer. From time to time it is necessary for the PL to focus the activities of each designer to assure forward movement towards the final state. Completion of assigned tasks must be verified and coordinated by the PL. An initial focus of the design is developed by the PL after a collection of nodes from the PPO is identified and made visible to the designers. This constitutes what we may call the preliminary design. The basic process of developing the focus of the design consists in evaluating the preliminary design against the specifications for the new design. Their divergence will result in a set of tasks that the designers must accomplish so as to bring the preliminary design into harmony with the specifications.

Once a task is developed, a message is sent to notify the designer of a new task; it also will show the designer the pointers to the required tools and data to perform the task. This interactive process is undergone each time the contents of the Blackboard are modified and a new status of the design is reached. Tasks will be assigned in parallel to the different domains, and their completion will be verified and coordinated by the PL.

During the design process, the PL may generate and maintain an agenda of tasks to be performed by different designers (see Fig. 3.):

Focus of the Design			
Agenda of Tasks:			
Task	**Domain**	**Activity**	**Status**
Task # 1	Materials	Select New Material	Completed
Task # 2	Geometry	Develop 3-D Geom.	Pending

Fig. 3. Focus of the Design

The expected actions of the PL and the designers when the focus of the design is being developed are as follows:

- The current status of the design is known through the Blackboard. The PL uses this status and PPO information to develop the focus of the design as a collection of tasks that will drive the design to the next stage.
- Tasks are sent to the designers. The interface from the Blackboard to the designers will allow a pop-up window to appear directly on one of the designer's screens. A dedicated window to provide a direct indication to designers about the focus of the design is desirable. Designers also should have the ability to inquire directly about the focus and related information.
- The Blackboard must maintain complete information about the development and status of the tasks. Specifically, the focus information should be organized for viewing by tasks, by parts, and by domains.

The focus in the Blackboard must keep track of all the developed tasks, their completion, success, results, and so forth. A flavor of this is shown:

Task	**Domain**	**Completion**	**Success**	**Result**
Task xyz	Materials	Yes	Yes	Pointer to file

The Blackboard will keep information by part, showing domains working on those parts:

part_xyz : *List of domains working on it*

The Blackboard will keep track of work done by domains:

domain materials : *List of parts in process*

10. Assertions

Designers work on a segment of the design, guided by the current focus in the Blackboard. They use the special computer-aided tools of their domains in their local workspaces to develop contributions to the design. These contributions are transmitted by the designers as assertions. Assertions state the changes that designers have made in their local workspaces to the objects in focus in the Blackboard.

Consider, for example, that the blueprint of a part is in focus on the Blackboard (see Fig 4.):

- When receiving the task from the PL, the designer obtains the pointer to the blueprint in the PPO. The designer also receives a task statement concerning the work that needs to be done on the blueprint. It is assumed that this designer owns or can obtain the appropriate tools to perform the work at a workstation. Let us assume that the designer will use a computer-aided tool.
- The designer imports a copy of the blueprint from the PPO into the local workspace.
- The designer modifies the blueprint with a computer-aided tool, labels and stores it in the local workspace. The path name and appropriate access rights to this modified blueprint will be available from now on to other designers. Whoever has authority to access it will be able to obtain a copy.
- Globally, the designer asserts the changes to the original blue print. Assertions would be in plain text in this case, stating the grid in which modifications have been done and their nature; besides that, any features modified and in what way would be included. These changes are made visible in the Blackboard so that other designers who may be affected can assent or react to the proposed alterations.

The support mechanism to allow designers to place assertions on the blackboard must be based on the type of transactions and activities performed in each of the domains. The expected assertions by the Cost Modeling designer will employ a different format from the expected assertions of the Geometric Modeling designer. It is proposed to develop a collection of blank forms for each domain which will take into account their possible actions and transactions. Asserting is then reduced to the process of filling a blank form and sending it to the Blackboard. A form may include several kinds of information:

- A part number identifying the object for which the assertion is prepared.
- Specific items related to the assertion. For example, detailed information about changes to a blueprint could be provided.
- Control information, such as the list of designers that should be notified about the proposed changes. This information is extracted directly from the table of dependencies available for that part and for the domain of the designer.

We assume the representation of objects in the PPO is such that objects can be decomposed into low level primitives that can be referenced directly. In the case of a blueprint, a designer may indicate the modification of a drawing by referring through a coordinate system to modifications of the primitives: <line3 in grid C-4 modified to: < new coordinates>>.

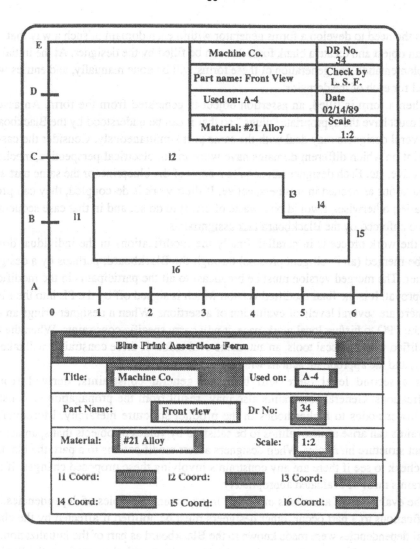

Figure 4.   Asserting About Blue Prints

An assertion must be prepared concerning the modification to this blueprint. The blank forms generator will parse the object, identify its modifiable components, and present the form to be filled by the designer. In this example, we could modify the header of the blueprint or the drawing itself. The new coordinates for line 3 in grid C-4 can be indicated in the entry available for that primitive.

The major assumption here is that objects are decomposable into understandable primitives within each domain. Forms are developed within each domain, indicating the kinds of "things" that designers can state about the objects with which they work. This indicates the need to develop a forms generator within each domain in such a way that it will parse an object and create a blank form that can be filled by the designer. At the initial stage of implementation, the generation of these forms will be done manually, and entries will be defined for each of the domains.

When a form is filled, an assertion object is generated from the form. An assertion object must have the appropriate "plugs," so that it can be understood by the Blackboard.

Several designers may deal with the same part simultaneously. Consider the case of a blueprint on which different domains have work to do: electrical perspective, mechanical perspective, etc. Each designer can acquire a copy of the blueprint for the same part and do modifications as needed in this perspective. If their work is de-coupled, they can proceed in parallel; otherwise, it would be a waste of effort to do so, and in that case sequentiality must be enforced by the Blackboard task assignments.

If the work proceeds in parallel, finally the modifications in the individual domains must be merged (an intelligent process) through the Blackboard, perhaps by a designated designer. The merged version must be broadcast to all the participants in the modification for approval. It is the final modified version which is signed off by the PL into the PPO.

There are several levels of evaluation of assertions. When a designer brings an object from the PPO to his/her local workspace, it will carry specific constraints. When the object is modified with the local tools, an automatic evaluation of these constraints will take place locally, and the appropriate actions will be fired.

At a second level there will be more general constraints, derived from the specifications. General constraints also may result from the propagation of constraints from lower nodes to higher nodes in the product structure hierarchy. Moreover, such constraints can arise as inequalities to be satisfied by values of objects that span across the product structure hierarchy. When designers assert modifications to a part, the blackboard must check to see if there are any constraints involving these proposed changes. If so, the constraints must be evaluated appropriately.

The evaluation of assertions must take into account the tables of dependencies. When modifications to a part occur, other designers must be notified if affected by the changes. Global dependencies were made known to the Blackboard as part of the initialization. Local dependencies and constraints were brought down along with the part from the PPO to the local workspace.

Assertions take the basic format of a form describing the changes a designer makes to the product data. We must consider another form of assertion also. As the design evolves, new control information is defined. New heuristics or rules of design are developed. An example could be the modification and creation of tables of dependencies, or the generation of new constraints about the part being processed. We should be able to assert this control information in such a way that the blackboard can use it as part of its control information. And later it should sign off this information into the PPO to be used in future design activities. Specific forms will be developed so that the designers can assert this kind of control information.

11. Constraints

Constraints play a major role in the design evolution. The form of a constraint should be such as to make it possible to develop an engine to evaluate it.
A frame format for constraints will take the form shown below :

{**constraint_x_y_z**
  attachment : <object_name, property_name>
  condition : <some qualified condition>
  formula : <formula to evaluate the condition>
  parameters : <required parameters in formula>
  actions : <actions if constraint is satisfied or violated>
}

This is a possible general format; the basic idea is that from the constraint we can extract appropriate information to find out whether bounds set on the attributes of some object are satisfied. The constraint also will indicate the actions to be taken when the bound is satisfied, or when it is violated. In general, the action is simply a notification to the designer whose activities fired the constraint to let him/her know of the effect of his/her most recent assertions.

The action may have the same effect as a direct dependency table in which certain designers are notified if the constraint is satisfied. Other designers may be notified if the constraint is violated. More complex actions may get fired with side effects like modification of other objects resulting from the evaluation of a constraint (see below, the section "Reasoning with Constraints").

There are several categories of constraints:

Global Constraints

In this document we refer to global constraints as the overall specifications of the design. For example, in the design of a part a material may be selected beforehand. It could be known that the length of a part must not exceed a certain value. Such global constraints are known from the initial specifications of the design given by the PL. They will be recorded in the PPO at the start. Part of the initialization of the Blackboard will involve the transfer of a copy of these constraints from the PPO. These constraints will get evaluated when the designers assert onto the blackboard and a general engine is being developed for the purpose.

Local Constraints

These constraints are the ones attached to specific parts. They are evaluated locally in the designers' workstations whenever they modify a part carrying a constraint.

Implicit Constraints

In the hierarchy of objects in the PPO, consider, for example, two nodes *a* and *b* joined by a root node *c*. Constraints may exist at the nodes *a* and *b*, but there may be no explicit constraints at the *c* node. However, an implicit constraint could exist on the attributes of *a* and *b*. Typical implicit constraints occur in assembly operations where parts have to mate, though this fact and the constraints implied thereby are not ever made explicit. The evaluation of such an implicit constraint should take place when the sign off is done on nodes *a* and *b*, and they are ready for assembly into part *c*. In the Blackboard scheme, such constraints will be recognized by cooperating experts through the visibility of the design in the Blackboard. But unlike explicit constraints, these ones must be picked up by the experience and insight of human assembly experts.

Constraints are meant to be integrated with the structures stored for a part in the PPO. Therefore, whenever new explicit constraints are developed for a part during the evolution of the design, from existing implicit constraints, they must be incorporated into the PPO during the sign off. This will have the effect of turning the implicit constraints of the past into explicit ones for future design activities, so that they automatically can be enforced without the need of an intelligent agent who carries such information in his/her head.

12. Dependencies

The work done by a designer in his/her domain affects what is done by other designers in their domains. The partition of the design into different domains allows one to assign degrees of responsibility and authority among the design groups over different parts of the design. Information about dependencies must be maintained to resolve the conflicts that arise when several designers work on the same part.

The dependencies are very useful to support the coordination of activities. The tables of dependencies allow the PL to maintain the focus in the blackboard. The evaluation of an assertion on a part for which dependencies are known allows the Blackboard to notify the affected designers. Also, tables of dependency may indicate obligatory sequencing for the assertions on a part by different designers, when work cannot proceed in parallel.

For a given domain, global tables of dependencies are developed over time and get stored in the PPO. These tables of dependency are made available to the Blackboard during the initialization phase. They are used to evaluate assertions. Additionally, each part will carry with it specific dependencies related to the part. When a part is in focus, this specific dependency is read by the Blackboard from the PPO and will be used to moderate any assertions on attributes of that part.

New tables of dependencies can be developed over time as the design evolves. This will constitute new information on the part being worked on that must be signed off into the PPO along with other attributes of the part, so that it can be used in future designs. Tables of dependency are important during the sign off process since they carry information about degrees of responsibility on the part.

A general structure that could be considered for the table of dependencies will relate a part to the sequence of contributions expected from different domains. It will also indicate the owner of the part, or the design group with the highest authority on that part, on whom the responsibility for sign off devolves. For example:

{ **airfoil_34**
   dependencies : aero, mechanical, thermal

chief : aero

}

This is a basic format. Additional information could be considered. For example, basic tasks could be assigned to each designer to indicate the kind of responsibility over the part.

When an assertion arrives at the Blackboard, the evaluation of the assertion will result in the generation of messages to the listed dependent design groups, notifying them about the arrival of the assertion. More complex forms of notification messages can be developed. A notification message could take the form of tasks assigned by a designer to other designers. It also could be a request from a designer to other designers to take some action when the assertion is posted on the Blackboard.

13. Maintenance of Versions

During the exploration of alternative designs, there will be occasions when an interesting potential design is worth storing for future consideration, even if it is not to be incorporated into the current design project. This would be called a *version*. In the same way when a final design of a part is reached, one may choose to store several variants of it, for somewhat different end uses. These too would be called versions of the design.

Versions are maintained by the PPO, and the Blackboard will be able to exercise the versioning mechanism of the engineering data base. When a designer copies an object from the PPO, it is with the intent to modify it in his/her local workspace. This copy will evolve and take a new form. It is a variant of the original copy that must be signed off in the PPO under the new version name when it is accepted. A link to the old copy should be maintained.

At any time it will be possible to select one of the available versions of a given part as a constituent of the final design. Versioning provides the ability to put together broadly similar products for different end-use scenarios. It allows one to explore different design possibilities. For example, variations in cost using different materials may generate different versions of a design. As another example, the deliverable product for a hazardous application will have more reliability constraints than the version for commercial applications.

Versioning results in the creation of a cluster of nodes around an original node. Each of the nodes in the cluster is a different version of the original node. The creation of a new version is triggered when there is consensus that a new acceptable version should be stored for the part under development.

Each version is unique, but we could apply the inheritance concept to store only the information that is different from the original part in the new version number. When retrieving a new version, a merging between its contents and the original copy of the part must be done to extract the total information available for the part. This is equivalent to the general process used in a software version management system like RCS, or the model management used in some simulation systems. The term *context* or *worlds* is used for the analogous operation in knowledge representation systems.

There is no direct versioning mechanism at the Blackboard. The fragments of the design solution are not maintained at the Blackboard. We expect that versioning will be implemented at the PPO by the engineering data base tools. The role of the Blackboard in the maintenance of versions is solely as an assistant to the PL in assuring that consistency is maintained in the PPO. The Blackboard also helps in keeping track of which nodes in the PPO are yet to be finalized. (Recall that some nodes were marked for modification at the beginning during the initialization step and a skeleton was developed to maintain and keep track of the evolving design.)

14. Reasoning With Constraints

Section 11 presented the proposed format to hold the information related to constraints. Constraints were used there in a simple fashion to notify designers of violations. Through more sophisticated means we can provide reasoning capabilities to trigger complex actions from the constraint evaluation and activate the resulting side effects specified. We thus can have a data driven environment in which the modification of values automatically sets off side effect activities.

To develop this scheme of operation the actions slot should be filled incrementally as the design evolves. Designers will have to identify inter-relationships between the different parts in the PPO hierarchy. Side effects that should be invoked must be described. The table of dependencies must also be generalized to include situations in which mere notification is extended to include the assignment of new tasks. It is by capturing such fundamental information that *knowledge of the design process* is entered into the PPO itself. The interactions among designers and their mutual dependencies is the simplest aspect of the design process. However, we intend to go much further and capture side-effect activities also, thus enriching the body of design process knowledge at the command of the PL for future design projects.

15. Reasoning With Heuristics

One of the aims of capturing knowledge of the design process is to influence future design activities with its aid. At the simpler level, this knowledge is captured in terms of the type and sequence of tasks that were done earlier in a given design situation. Other examples of simple design knowledge are the dependencies among domains for various tasks.

Stable design rules can be recognized when the design process is repeated over time. Consider, for instance, the sequentiality of certain activities in the electronics design domain. There is often a natural ordering of domain contributions peculiar to each part of the product being designed. This ordering is made known to the Blackboard by earlier information present in the PPO, or by the PL explicitly stating it, thus ensuring that designers are alerted when it is their turn to take up the design of a part, and make further assertions, once their predecessor in the design chain has finished with it. In the traditional literature on blackboards, this aspect is treated under the heading "scheduling of knowledge sources." The chain is one rule by which designers are stimulated to contribute their domain expertise to the evolving design.

We expect to capture these and other rules of design within the Blackboard, so that the PL may use them to advance the design systematically. The use of heuristics in the Blackboard by the PL allows development of a specific plan of actions that will match what is "common practice" in that field.

It is important to develop a strategy that will capture more heuristics as the design proceeds. We expect that at some point, a designer could suggest a new rule of design in the form of a control assertion. The blackboard is expected to take cognizance of the new rule and use it, if it is approved by the PL. As another example of a heuristic, it could be true that analyses are performed in different domains in a certain sequence for a particular type of problem, and the results should be available together for the PL's consideration, before a design is finalized. Designers develop many such basic rules as they acquire experience. When the Blackboard organization gets refined, the PL will wish to deploy some of these heuristics automatically in the blackboard, to quicken the pace of development in design projects.

16. Conflicts and Negotiation

The posting of assertions on the Blackboard after designers have worked in their LOW's with computer-aided tools raises conflicts, more often than not. This indicates inconsistencies between the actual status of the pieces of the design in the LOW's of different designers, and what it should be to comply with the specified constraints and accord with the assertions of all domains. These temporary inconsistencies are expected in passing, but the process of refining the design will concentrate on removing them. Conflict resolution and negotiation are required steps to achieve this end.

Conflicts are likely to arise when different designers assert on a part. When a conflict occurs, an alert is sent to the designers in conflict and to the PL. The Blackboard plays a key role in detecting conflicts and violations of constraints. It is at once the arena where the conflict is thrown up and where consensus must be reached before the design can be advanced.

Simple conflicts are situations in which designers assert different values for the same attribute of a part. Conflicts also arise when the assertion of one attribute value by a designer makes it impossible for another designer to offer a consistent set of values for other attributes of the part. There can be optimality conflicts, besides, in which the decisions of one designer affect the decisions of another designer in a retrograde way. In general, a situation of conflict is one where it seems temporarily impossible to reach consensus among the domains concerning what a part should look like.

Consider the situation :

Assertion	Who made	Who votes			
		Mechanical	Process	Cost	Project Leader
Length=6.0	Aero	OK	OK	no	Yet to decide

Here is a basic situation of conflict. The Blackboard will alert the PL, who may intervene and solve the problem. The PL could reset the assertion just made by the Aero designer. A new task could be assigned to Cost, requesting for a compromise or re-evaluation with different assumptions. In actual practice, several alternatives may be considered in order to resolve the conflict.

However, it is not necessarily required for the PL to intervene in such a conflict. Quite possibly the individual designers who are alerted to the conflict will be able to find a creative compromise on their own. The intervention of the PL is by choice, or it may be a last resort when the designers decide that the PL's contribution would be important at this stage.

The Blackboard is not always capable of detecting potential conflicts on its own. There is a level of knowledge at which it operates (corresponding to the rules and constraints it has been fed), and beyond that it is for the designers to appreciate when an impasse is reached and an earlier assertion needs re-consideration. The Blackboard is still, however, the medium of communicating the conflict and affording it global visibility.

An environment for cooperation could be developed to support the negotiation phase. Such a utility called *Cooperate* is currently under development (Cleetus and Uejio 1989). It allows text and graphical objects to be visually shared across a network to aid the process of reaching a consensus. Such sharing is vital in the discussion and exchanges which usually precede a resolution of conflicts.

At present we leave it to designers to exploit the *Cooperate* utility in reaching consensus, and offer no further structuring beyond the communication discipline embedded in the utility. It is a future effort to decide whether useful scaffolding might be erected around the negotiation phase. There exist several such useful techniques (e.g. the so-called Delphi technique, sometimes used in management circles) that could be helpful to embed such a structure within *Cooperate*.

17. Cut and Paste for Viewing

This is a mechanism of exchanging graphical information to support the negotiation phase which ensues upon conflict. By exchange of graphical information, we mean the exchange of images or bitmap screens.

Designer A may be interested in having displayed on his/her workstation some results available to another designer in a remote workstation B. The blackboard knows the specific path for the object that holds the information displayed in the remote workstation B. The tools to display that object reside also in the remote workstation.

The object in B is available to A through NFS. The problem is that A does not have the computer-aided tool which can display the object in his/her workstation. A can, however, request B to transmit as a bitmap the desired view. The X-Windows software library has such a capability, and a tool can be fashioned by which part of the picture displayed by the computer-aided tool in workstation B can be cut and transmitted to workstation A for display in the hardware of A (in general, A will have different display characteristics, such as the number of bit planes).

We consider this to be an important utility for cooperative design, particularly useful in the conflict resolution phase, though its invocation need not imply any crisis or conflict. A designer may simply need to look at another designer's graphical analysis or analytic tabulation. Nothing is intended to be done on the analysis by the remote designer, except viewing it. The situation then is that designer B has available on screen the results from the computer-aided tool. B wishes to transmit the results as a *bitmap* to A on a remote workstation for viewing. B pulls down the *Cut and Paste* utility, which is instructed to copy a rectangular region of the current screen and display it on the collaborator's workstation (which must have the mirror image of the utility to grab the transmitted screen bitmap and display it locally), adjusting for any differences in display characteristics.

More sophisticated but cumbersome solutions may involve moving the computer-aided tools to a central place like the Blackboard and providing remote execution capability. A far more expensive solution will duplicate the computer-aided tools on all cooperating workstations which need to view certain perspectives of the design. A more economic approach is to have a single utility on every workstation which can enable the viewing and manipulation of a common graphical format (e. g. IGES) produced by most computer-aided tools.

18. Sign Off

A designer responsible for part of the solution must be alert when accepting assertions posted by other designers. Assertions must be reviewed before acceptance. The common visibility provided by the Blackboard and its mechanism of automatic notification ensures that everybody who has a say in a part of the design, does get to evaluate its acceptability from the relevant angles. As mentioned earlier, the PL assumes full responsibility for the final sign off in the PPO.

The major issue with the sign off task is that of security. The PPO must have extreme protection mechanisms to avoid corruption of its contents by unauthorized updating. The PPO has explicit information as to who has authority over which parts and perspectives of the product structure. This authority information dictates who has the final say in decisions about new objects being consigned to the PPO. The most natural procedure to assure security is for the PL to assume total responsibility over the PPO.

In general, it is expected that earlier information in the PPO is never removed or modified. New designs and revisions to previous designs are only added to the PPO. This procedure implies that a revision system is obligatory to maintain newly generated information in the PPO.

We assume that when the design is started, a new design skeleton is launched. The purpose of the design skeleton is to keep track of the product structure hierarchy for the new design. The design skeleton runs in parallel to the real PPO structure for the previous design. The nodes in the design skeleton maintain headers that point to the nodes in the PPO associated with the previous design. However, the skeleton is not expected to hold any substantive design information initially, i.e., the computer-aided application files which together with the frame-based header and part structure relations constitute the design data, initially are empty.

The design skeleton will allow development and identification of different paths in the structure which can be associated with various possible designs. From the design skeleton, we must be able to reconstruct each of the potential configurations.

The Blackboard can assist in keeping track of the design evolution, if the PL can identify during the initialization the nodes in the PPO that need to be processed by the designers. The sign off procedure, part by part, signifies the completion of tasks. Therefore, task management on behalf of the project lead can be assisted by the Blackboard. It can tell the PL, for example, what are the remaining tasks to be done on a part.

19. Conclusions

In this paper we described a Blackboard scheme for cooperative problem solving by human experts. This scheme has been developed within the framework of the DICE architecture. The important triad for the Blackboard operation is the relationship between Designers, the PPO, and the Blackboard (see Fig. 5). The paper has developed the set of activities and transactions between the triad that are the vital information flows underlying a concurrent engineering environment.

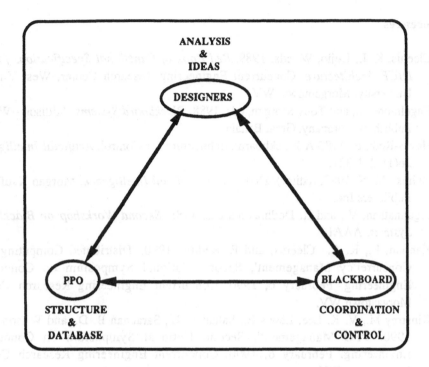

Fig. 5. Major Functions in the Blackboard Scheme

At the time (November 1989) the first version of this paper was written, an initial prototype of the system was under development. The system is more mature now (October 1990), and the prototype has taken a better form. More effort is being focused on its development, integration within the DICE architecture, and scaling for real world use. We plan to report the enhanced state of the system in further publications.

20. Acknowledgments

The following people have contributed either ideas and/or effort to the development and implementation of the current version of the DICE Blackboard system: M. R. Gokhale, D. Nichols, S. Iyer, K. Ashish, R. Ajitsaria and T. C. Woo. In the implementation of the system, we have made use of the communication services provided by the concurrency manager (Kannan, Cleetus and Reddy 1990) developed by the group lead by R. Kannan. We are also indebted to the quality assurance group lead by C. Maheshwari for their continuous support and to the systems support group lead by Alan Butcher for maintaining the computer facilities. Finally, we thank other members of the DICE architecture team and the CERC community for their support and criticism.

References

Cleetus, K. J., Uejio, W. eds. 1989. *Red Book of Functional Specifications for the DICE Architecture*. Concurrent Engineering Research Center, West Virginia University, Morgantown, WV.

Engelmore, R., and Tony Morgan, eds. 1988. *Blackboard Systems*. Addison - Wesley Publishing Company, Great Britain.

Hayes-Roth, B. 1985 A Blackboard Architecture for Control. *Artificial Intelligence,* 26(1): 251-321.

Huhns, M. N. 1987. (editor). *Distributed Artificial Intelligence*, Morgan Kaufmann Publishers Inc.

Jagannathan, V., and R. Dodhiawala eds. 1988. *Second Workshop on Blackboard Systems*. AAAI.

Kannan, R., K. C. Cleetus, and R. Reddy 1990. 'Distributed Computing with Concurrency Management', Second National Symposium on Concurrent Engineering. February 6, 1990. Concurrent Engineering Research Center, Morgantown WV.

Kinstrey M., V. K. Lee, Lewis E., Salant E. L., Sarachan B. D., and Wilson P. R. 1990. 'PPO Management', Second National Symposium on Concurrent Engineering. February 6, 1990. Concurrent Engineering Research Center, Morgantown WV.

Lesser, V. R, E. H. Durfee and D. D. Corkill. 1985. Cooperation through Communication in a Distributed Problem Solving Network, Paper presented at the 5th Workshop on Distributed Artificial Intelligence, December 1985, Sea Ranch California.

Nii, P. H. 1986. Blackboard Systems. *AI Magazine* 7: 38-53, 82-107.

Sriram D., R. D. Logcher, N. Groleau, and J. Cherneff. DICE: An Object Oriented Programming Environment for Cooperative Engineering Design. MIT, 1988.

Stefik M. 1986. The Next Knowledge Medium. *AI Magazine*, 7(1).

An Object-Oriented Framework for Collaborative Engineering Design

D. Sriram, R. Logcher, A. Wong, and S. Ahmed
Intelligent Engineering Systems Laboratory
Dept. of Civil Engineering
1-253, M.I.T., Cambridge, MA 02139

Abstract. Engineering projects, in general, involve a large number of components and the interaction of multiple technologies. The components included in the product are decided in an iterative design process. In each iteration, interfaces and interface conditions among these components are designed with slack to account for potential variations created when the components and interface values become better known. Iteration proceeds towards increasing detail; design personnel may change, and their numbers expand with increasing level of detail. This multi-faceted nature of engineering problems demands considerable coordination between various participants. Lack of coordination may result in several undesirable effects, which may result in a productivity loss.

A computer based system called DICE (Distributed and Integrated environment for Computer-aided Engineering) which is aimed at addressing the coordination and communication problem in engineering, is described in this paper. DICE can be envisioned as a network of computers and users, where the communication and coordination is achieved through a global database and a control mechanism.

The object-oriented methodology seems to provide a natural way to encode engineering product and process models. An implementation of DICE using a commercial object-oriented database management system (GEMSTONE) was developed. Generic objects needed for collaborative work are identified. A detailed description of the prototype - called MagpieBridge - is also provided.

1 Introduction

On July 17, 1981, two skywalks in the lobby of the Hyatt Regency Hotel in Kansas City collapsed. It was cited as the "most devastating structural collapse ever to take place in the United States"; 114 people died and 186 were injured [7]. This was not only a failure of a physical structural system, but also a failure of the process by which most projects in the U. S. are designed and built. The primary objective of our current research is to provide computer based tools which would help during design and construction to avoid errors of the type made in Kansas City.

The Hyatt failure was attributed to a combination of three events. First, in progressing from the preliminary to detailed design, where joint and connection detailing occurs, the design of the hanger to spandrel beam connection was inadequate. Second, in developing shop drawings, the connection detail was changed by the steel fabricator, thereby "compounding an already critical condition." Third, this second error was not caught during approval checking of the shop drawings by the structural engineers. These were all errors of communication and coordination in the design process, errors caused by the structure of the process, lack of tools used in this process, and focus on documenting the product of design while neglecting "process" and "intent" documentation. These problems also exist in other engineering application areas.

Most engineering projects involve a large number of components and the interaction of multiple technologies. The components included in the product are decided in an iterative design process. In each iteration, interfaces and interface conditions among these components are designed with slack to account for potential variations created when the components and interface values become better known. Iteration proceeds towards increasing detail; design personnel may change, and their numbers expand with increasing level of detail.

The problems facing the engineering industry in the U. S. will be highlighted by considering the design and construction[1] of structures. On a single project, interacting design technologies often come from separate firms or functional groups within a firm, and there is little coordination between designers and contractor(s) during design. Because designers find coordination among themselves difficult, they leave this task to construction managers or the contractor. Thus, working drawings, used to inform the contractor of the product, lack detail. Shop or fabrication drawings are required from the contractor to document details, but potential conflicts among trades are often unrecognized until construction begins. Several undesirable effects are caused by this lack of coordination.

1. The construction process is slowed, work stops when a conflict is found.

2. Prefabrication opportunities are limited, because details must remain flexible.

3. Opportunities for automation are limited, because capital intensive high speed equipment is incompatible with work interruptions from field recognized conflicts.

4. Rework is rampant, because field recognized conflicts often require design and field changes.

5. Conservatism pervades design, because designers provide excessive slack in component interfaces to avoid conflict.

6. The industry is unprepared for the advent of automated construction, as the need for experience in design limits choice to available materials placed by hand.

All of these problems decrease productivity. In addition, failures, such as the Hyatt collapse, occur more often then they should. Overcoming these problems requires significant changes to the design process, together with superior *computer integrated design and construction/manufacturing* tools. Those tools must be tailored to the needs of designers who are [4]:

"constantly engaged in searching out various consequences of design decisions [especially those made by others]"

This paper details the development of a prototype system to test new concepts for computer tools to integrate various stages involved in the engineering of a product. The major objectives of this system are to:

1. Facilitate effective coordination and communication in various disciplines involved in engineering.

2. Capture the process by which individual designers make decisions, that is, what information was used, how it was used and what did it create.

3. Forecast the impact of design decisions on manufacturing or construction.

---

[1] Manufacturing in the civil engineering industry is known as *construction*. There are several differences between the construction industry and the manufacturing industry. For example, in manufacturing several hundreds of a single type of product are produced, whereas construction involves the production of one-of-a-kind products. However, the overall engineering process is similar. In this paper the terms manufacturing and construction will be used to denote the *realization or creation of a designed artifact*.

4. Provide designers interactively with detailed manufacturing process or construction planning.

5. Develop intelligent interfaces for automation.

Computer aided tools, which will be collectively called DICE (Distributed and Integrated environment for Computer-aided Engineering), are being currently developed to address the above objectives; a collection of papers reporting similar work at other institutions appears in [5] and [10]. DICE will significantly improve productivity by[2]:

- reducing error in design;

- providing more detailed design;

- providing better manufacturing or construction planning;

- allowing easier recognition of design and manufacturing (construction) problems;

- using manufacturability criteria throughout design; and

- advancing automation.

Lessons from the Hyatt failure show that such tools are required. Had the connection designer had access to the concepts of load transmission underlying the preliminary design, local buckling might have been recognized and the joint details changed. Had the fabricator preparing the shop drawings had access to that information, he would have seen that his change violated the purpose of the connection scheme. Had the shop drawing checker seen all these changes together with their intent, he would have recognized the faults in the design.

Organization of the paper. An overview of the DICE architecture is provided in Section 2. This is followed by a discussion of the object-oriented database requirements of a global database, which supports various engineering transactions, in Section 3. Implementation details of DICE in a commercial object-oriented database management system - GEMSTONE - are addressed in the following sections.

2 Overview of DICE

In Section 1, several objectives for a Distributed Integrated environment for Computer-aided Engineering (DICE) have been enumerated. To achieve these goals, a system architecture based on current trends in programming methodologies, object-oriented databases, and knowledge based systems is proposed. DICE can be envisioned as a network of computers and users, where the communication and coordination is achieved through a global database and a control mechanism (collections of papers reporting similar work at other institutions appear in [5] and [10]). DICE consists of a Blackboard (global database), several Knowledge Modules, and a Control Mechanism. These terms are clarified below.

1. **Blackboard.** The Blackboard is the medium through which all communication takes place. The Blackboard in DICE is divided into three partitions: Solution, Negotiation, and Coordination Blackboards. The Solution Blackboard partition contains the design and construction information generated by various Knowledge Modules; this solution is normally is referred to as the Object-Hierarchy. The Negotiation Blackboard partition consists of the negotiation trace between various engineers taking part in the design and manufacturing (construction) process. The Coordination Blackboard partition contains the information needed for the coordination of various Knowledge Modules.

---

[2]Engineers from several industries that we visited felt that computer aided tools for cooperation and coordination can greatly increase their productivity.

2. **Knowledge Module.** Each Knowledge Module (KM) can be viewed either as: a knowledge based expert system (KBES), developed for solving individual design and construction related tasks, or a CAD tool, such as a database structure, i.e., a specific database, an analysis program, etc., or an user of a computer, or a combination of the above. A KBES could be viewed as an aggregation of Knowledge Sources (KSs). Each KS is an independent chunk of knowledge, represented either as rules or objects. In DICE, the Knowledge Modules are grouped into the following categories: Strategy, Specialist, Critic, and Quantitative. The Strategy KMs help the Control Mechanism in the coordination and communication process. The Specialist KMs perform individual specialized tasks of the design and construction process. The Critic KMs check various aspects of the design process, while the Quantitative KMs are mostly algorithmic CAD tools. The data representation (or language) used in a KM may be different from that used in the BB. Hence, each KM is provided with an interface module which translates the data from the KM to the BB and vice versa.

3. **Control Mechanism.** The Control Mechanism performs two tasks: 1) evaluate and propagate implications of actions taken by a particular KM; and 2) assist in the negotiation process. This control is achieved through the object oriented nature of the Blackboard and a Strategic KM. One of the major and unique difference between DICE and other Blackboard systems is that DICE's Blackboard is more than a static repository of data; DICE's Blackboard is an intelligent database, with objects responding to different types of messages.

A conceptual view of DICE for design and construction is shown in Figure 1; a detailed description of a LISP-based implementation of DICE is provided in [9]. In the DICE framework, any of the KMs can

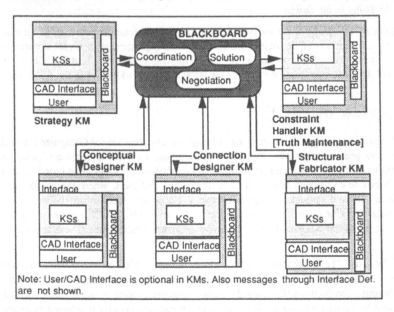

Figure 1: A Conceptual View of DICE for Design and Construction

make changes or request information from the Blackboard; requests for information are logged with the objects representing the information, and changes to the Blackboard may initiate either of the two actions: finding the implications and notifying various KMs, and entering into a negotiation process, if two or more KMs suggest conflicting changes.

3 Blackboard: Object-Oriented Database

The Blackboard is being implemented as an object-oriented database. Encapsulation of data and procedures in objects, inheritance of properties, and abstraction of data are some of the characteristics that makes the object-oriented database an ideal model for encoding engineering information; a detailed discussion on the relevance of object-oriented database mangement systems (OODBMS) for engineering applications is provided in [1].

The Solution BB (SBB) and Coordination BB (COORDBB) partitions are being implemented as a layered object-oriented database, as shown in Figure 2.

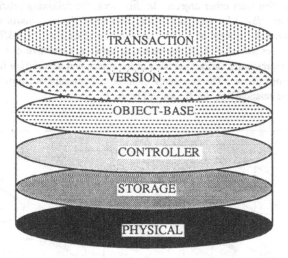

Figure 2: Layered Architecture for DICE BB

The various layers are described briefly below.

1. **Physical Layer.** Data resides in the form of bits on an appropriate storage medium (e.g., magnetic, optical, video disks).

2. **Storage Layer.** Objects are assigned unique identifiers, which are mapped into appropriate areas in the Physical Layer.

3. **Controller Layer.** Grouping of objects, allocation and de-allocation of object buffers, and other storage control activities are achieved at this layer.

4. **Object-base Layer.** Object definition, modification, and other associated activities are included here. The semantics of various nodes and relationships needed for cooperative product development are described in the following section.

5. **Version Layer.** Versions of objects help to keep track of the design evolution and also enhances parallelism of design activities. Various version management facilities are encoded at this layer.

6. **Transaction Layer.** Transaction management layer is responsible for maintaining database integrity, while allowing execution of multiple concurrent transactions by various engineers. This layer supports a transaction framework for collaborative engineering applications.

The object-base, shown in Figure 2, is divided into levels, representing an object-hierarchy (or object-lattice). Each level contains objects that represent certain aspects of the engineering process (design and construction). The SBB does not contain all the information generated by all KMs; only information that is 1) required by more than one KM, and 2) useful in the engineering process is posted on the SBB. For example, the 3D space level will contain objects that represent spaces allocated to structural systems, piping systems, mechanical systems, etc. This level can be reduced to detailed levels, such as system and component levels.

The objects in SBB are connected through relational links; these relationships provide a framework to view the object from different perspectives. Some of the relational links provide means for objects to inherit information from other objects. In this work, the following relationships are used in the SBB: *generalization (IS-A)* for grouping classes into super classes, *classification (INSTANCE-OF)* for defining individual elements of a class, *aggregation (PART-OF, COMPONENT)* for combining components, *alternation (IS-ALT)* for selecting between alternative concepts, *versionization (VERSION-OF)* for representing various versions of an object, and *association* for representing other relationships not outlined above. The semantics of these relationships are provided in [8]. Various planes that depict these relationships are shown in Figure 3.

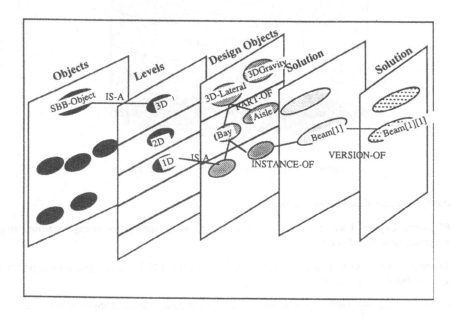

Figure 3: Different Planes in the SBB

The objects also contain justifications, assumptions, creator, time of creation, pointers to multi-media documents, constraints, ownership KM, other concerned KMs, etc. The justification information will provide a designer's rationale and intent for the creation of the object. Assumptions made during design and construction are also stored with the object. For example, the architect, while placing the structural elements, may assume certain spatial characteristics for the HVAC systems. He may record this assumption and the rationale for such an assumption in the objects denoting the appropriate structural elements and the HVAC system. In DICE, *status* facets are associated with data attributes (slots). The *status* facet, for example, can take the following values: *unknown, assumed* and *calculated*. Additional slots needed for the source of data and its change, uses of data, assumptions made, etc., can easily be incorporated.

Associated with these objects are methods which provide a means for: 1) performing some procedural calculations; 2) propagating implications of performing some actions, for example if the status (assumed or actual) or the value for a particular object changes then these changes can be broadcast to all concerned KMs; 3) helping to perform the coordination process. For example, methods can be used as demons to perform the following construction related tasks:

1. **Estimating**, which involves continuous cost forecasting capabilities, from early estimates to detailed costs considering the equipment that will be available. This estimating will start with material and quantity modeling based on building standards for tenant work, and would first be updated with characteristics of the tenant. As layout work proceeds, material and quantity estimates would be updated.

2. **Scheduling**, which is similar in structure to Estimating, and uses much of the quantity data developed from the estimate forecast, passed to it with messages.

3. **Constructibility**, where constant critics look for incompatible materials, space use, construction space needs, equipment requirements, etc.

Knowledge for all of these inputs will come from working with experts on all phases of the project, e.g., owner, designer and constructor.

The top level object in the SBB can be described by the following schema.

```
SBB_Object
     SLOTS:
         name:
         value:
             status:
         created-by:
         justification:
         part-of:
         subpart:
         is-alt:
         version-of:
         version-no:
         owned-by:
         concerned-KMs:
         constraints:
             range: (IS-A CONSTRAINT-OBJECT)
         ------ (and so on)
     METHODS:
         ------ (and so on)
```

It is also conceivable that some slots in SBB objects are of the above type[3].

3.1 Schema Evolution in Engineering Design

Engineering design applications require considerable flexibility in dynamically defining and modifying database schema, i.e., class definitions, inheritance structure of the class lattice and specifications

---

[3]In our current implementation most of the slots in the top level object exist as facets in individual slots.

of instance attributes and methods, without requiring application shutdown. This is because objects associated with a typical design project are specializations of one or more generic SBB objects and the object-hierarchy and design specifications evolve with time. The changes that could be made to the class lattice may be categorized into [3]:

1. Changes to the contents of a node (class or its instances);

2. Changes to an edge (i.e. the relationships between classes); and

3. Changes to a node in a class lattice.

The various types of changes are explained and exemplified in the following sections.

3.1.1   Changes to the contents of a node

1. *Changes to instance and class variables.* An instance variable may be inherited and modified by any instance, while the value of a class variable can be inherited but cannot be changed by the instances or the subclasses. The top level DICE object (SBB_Object) has a number of slots which are inherited by all subclasses and their instances. The various types of changes that the designer may impose on the derived classes and instances are:

   (a) *Add a new instance variable.* A new slot may be added to hold additional design information. For example, the number of beams supporting a floor slab may be added to as an instance variable to the class C_Floor (described in a Section 5.1).

   (b) *Drop an instance variable.* At an advanced stage of the design, some information may become redundant or unnecessary. Hence, the slot holding the information may be deleted to reduce the size of the design object. For example, if a class containing a slot x is made a subclass or component class of another class having a slot containing the same data, then information may be retrieved through inheritance rather than having storage allocated in all individual instances. Thus, slot x may be dropped.

   (c) *Change the name of an instance variable.* Often it may be necessary to identify an instance variable by another name; there may be a name conflict with an inherited variable, or just for the ease of future reference. For example, the user may want to change the *Weight_in_pounds* slot of a Beam object to *Weight*.

   (d) *Change the domain of a variable.* There may be a need to change the type of information (e.g., integer, real, characters etc.) a variable (slot) may store.

   (e) *Change the default value of an instance variable.* This may be necessary if design specifications need to be altered at some stage. For example, after the design of all concrete beams are complete, one may set the default value of the variable *material-type* of all Beam objects to *steel*, so that the designer does not have to set the value for every object s/he instantiates later.

   (f) *Change the inheritance specifications of an instance variable.* This may be necessary if the designer wants to override the information derived for a slot, and specify his/her own specifications. Also, in the case of multiple inheritance, where more than one parent has slots of the same name, the user may choose to inherit the slot from the desired superclass (supertype). For example, assume that Reinforced_Concrete_Beam and Prestressed_Concrete_Beam are superclasses (parents) of T_Beam and the inheritance specification for the default value of the T_Beam's *yield_strength* slot is set to Reinforced_Concrete_Beam. At a later stage this inheritance specification could be changed from Reinforced_Concrete_Beam to Prestressed_Concrete_Beam, so that *yield_strength* would inherit the default value from Prestressed_Concrete_Beam.

(g) *Add a class variable.* This allows addition of new variables that may not have been perceived when the classes where designed. For example, a new variable (slot) *reinforcement_ratio* could be added to a Beam object.

(h) *Drop a class variable.* A variable may be dropped when it is no longer considered necessary for the purposes of design.

(i) *Change the default value of a class variable.* This is necessary if the design specifications have changed at some later stage, and all instances of a class need to be informed about the change.

2. *Changes to methods*, such as:

(a) *Add a new method to a class*, to allow incremental design development; procedures for analysis or design of various sub-components may be added at any time. For example, there may be methods that perform a preliminary cost estimate (especially during preliminary design). Later, methods that perform a detailed cost estimate may be available. These methods can be added to the appropriate design objects.

(b) *Drop an existing method*, when it is no longer useful.

(c) *Change the name of a method*, for the ease of identification or if its functionality has changed.

(d) *Change the source code of a method*, which may be done if there is an error, or if the method is reimplemented to perform some other task.

(e) *Change the inheritance of a method*, which may be done under circumstances similar to that for a variable.

3.1.2 Changes to an edge

These modifications concern changing the hierarchy of classes in the inheritance lattice. They include:

1. *Making a class a superclass of another class.* This is done to abstract the common attributes of several classes into one super class, or to allow the new subclass to inherit several additional attributes from the new superclass. For example, in order to lend graphic abilities to all instances of the class **Beam**, **Beam** could be made a subclass of **Geometric_Obj**, which contains all the procedures for graphic display of objects.

2. *Remove one of the superclasses of a class.* This may be done when certain inherited slots are not perceived necessary, or are in type-conflict with attributes inherited from another superclass.

3. *Change the order of superclasses of a class.* This involves reshuffling the order of the IS-A class hierarchy, and is done to reflect major changes in design specifications.

3.1.3 Changes to a class

The following changes to a class type are supported:

1. *Add a new class*, which is done to introduce a class of new design objects at any stage of the design. For example, a new class T_Beam could be added as a subclass of a Beam object.

2. *Dropping an existing class*, when it is no longer necessary.

3. *Changing the name of a class*, in order to avoid name-conflicts or for ease of identification.

4 Implementation of DICE in GEMSTONE

4.1 Overview

A prototype - called MagpieBridge - was implemented utilizing GEMSTONE, which is a commercial OODBMS marketed by Servio, Inc. (Suite 100, 15220 NW Greenbrier Parkway, Beaverton, OR 97006). A conceptual overview of MagpieBridge is shown in Figure 4. MagpieBridge consists of two specialist KMs: an Architect KM and a Structural Engineer KM. These KMs communicate through the Blackboard. The Blackboard consists of a Critic KM in the form of a Constraint/Consistency module. The Coordination and Negotiation Blackboards do not explicitly exist in MagpieBridge; coordination is provided by the dependency objects. The various class objects needed to realize MagpieBridge are described in the following sections[4].

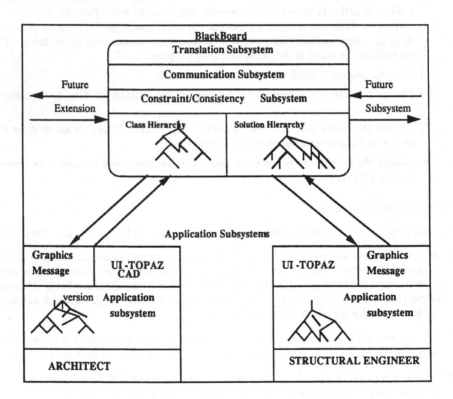

Figure 4: A Schematic View of MagpieBridge

4.2 Local and Shared (Gloabal) Databases: GEMSTONE Dictionaries

In GEMSTONE, access to objects is provided through system dictionaries. The UserGlobals and the Globals are GEMSTONE defined dictionaries available to all users. In addition, we have identified four

---

[4]There are 76 classes in MagpieBridge.

dictionaries: Class_Dictionary, Shared_Classes, Project_Instances, and Shared_Dictionary. For all projects, the Class_dictionary and Shared_Classes dictionaries are used by each participant. The Class_Dictionary stores the local classes and is private to individual users, while the Shared_Classes stores classes of the global database (SBB) and is shared between various users (KMs). For any particular project, two other dictionaries, Project_Instances and Shared_Dictionary maintain reference to instances of local objects and shared objects, respectively. These two dictionaries are different for each project and can be attached and detached depending on the project the user is working on. The symbol list of the user at any time consists of the following dictionaries.

1. UserGlobals
2. Globals
3. Class_Dictionary
4. Shared_Classes
5. Project_instances
6. Shared_Dictionary

4.3   Generic Objects

A set of objects which form the core classes of the SBB partition in the Blackboard and various KMs have been identified; A representative set of these and other domain specific objects in GEM-STONE is described in [11]. The SBB_Object is implemented as a linear set of the following objects: Root_Obj, Geometric_Obj, Box_Obj, Dependency, Versionable_Obj, and Composite_Obj. A partial taxonomy of the generic objects in the Blackboard is shown in Figure 5, and described below.

- **Root_Obj.** All classes are subclasses of this Root_obj. It provides timestamping, ownership stamping, and creation of reference into dictionaries.

Root_Obj
    superclass: Object (from OPAL)
    SLOTS:
    owner:
    date_created:
    date_modified:
    person_modified:
    person_accessible:
    obj_id:
    comment:
    METHODS:
    newwithid: creates object, set obj_id and puts it in
    the dictionary
    update_self: set date_modified, person_modified slots
    ...

- **Root_Objw_doc.** This is a sub_class of root object and is similar to it except that it provides a slot for attaching *document* objects. The documentation system consists of two classes: **Document_Obj**, which incorporates documentation associated with an object, and **Document_Handler**, which provides search mechanisms for document objects.

- **Geometric_Obj.** This object holds the geometric details.

Geometric_Obj
    superclass: Root_Obj
    SLOTS
    loc_geo_model: geometric model of the object in its local frame.
    par_geo_model: geometric model of the object in its parent frame.
    loc_to_par_trans: transformation matrix from local to parent.
    METHODS:
    translate:
    rotate:
    display:
    erase:
    access_methods: several accessing methods for above slots
    .....

- **Box_Object.** This is a subclass of **Geometric_Obj** and models an object as a box. **Box_Object** has been used to describe most of physical objects in the system.

- **Dependency.** The Dependency object checks and keeps a record of the name and the time of various objects which have accessed a particular slot. This information is stored in the *dependents* slot in the form of a list of objects, which are instances of the **Dependency_Rec** object; note that the KM which has modified the slot will exist in the *owner* slot of the **Dependency_Rec** object. When any attribute value (slot's value) is changed a message is sent to all the KMs (or objects) which exist in the appropriate **Dependency_Rec** object. In this manner, the **Dependency_Rec** class helps in consistency maintenance.

Dependency
    superclass: Box_Object
    SLOTS:
    dependents: contains a list of dependency_rec objects which store
    information about the KMs that have accessed a particular object's slot
    METHODS:
    create_dependency_rec: creates a dependency record
    check_dependency: checks if slot of an object has dependency records
    and notifies all dependent objects
    ...

Dependent_Rec
    superclass: Root_Obj
    SLOTS:
    associated_slot: slot which has been accessed

METHODS:
notify: notify the owner of the dependent_rec object

- Versionable_Obj. Versionable_Obj objects define attributes and methods for version control. The Versionable_Obj object allows for the evolution of the object in the form of a version tree as shown in Figure 6. A Version_Set object is used to hold all the versions of an instance and provides different facilities for accessing these instances based on various criteria, such as time.

Versionable_Obj
    superclass: Dependency
    SLOTS:
    preceding_version: holds the preceding version
    succeeding_versions: holds a set of succeeding versions
    the_version_set: holds an instance of the version_set object
    status: if true then versions are created, otherwise not (default is t)
    METHODS:
    derived: derives a new version with name concatenated by a number
    newwithid: creates a new versionable_obj instance
    .....

Version_Set
    superclass: Root_Obj
    SLOTS:
    name: the name of the version set
    ver_array: an array of all versions
    METHODS:
    addlast: add a version
    get_latest_ver: get latest version
    get_ver_f_days: get version which is a certain days old
    ....

- Composite_Obj. Most engineering objects are normally comprised of smaller components. A Composite_Obj class has been defined to deal with the composition of engineering objects. We are currently extending the capabilities of the Composite_Obj class.

Composite_Obj
    superclass: Versionable_Obj
    SLOTS:
    sub_parts: contains all sub_parts of the object
    METHODS:
    sub_part: creates a sub_part relationship
    accessing methods: several accessing methods to access sub_part slots, etc..

Part_Obj

superclass: Root_Obj
SLOTS:
part_of:
METHODS:
newwithid: creates an instance and attaches this to the parent object
access_methods: methods to access slots in parent composite object
....

There are a few objects - called system objects - which are used for maintaining users' information and projects' information; these objects are mostly used by domain KMs. Besides each application has a system object which provides the application specific functions and also provides interface functions to the Blackboard.

- **User_info.** This object stores the user information such as job title, name, post box for receiving communication objects and machine/display address of the machine that the user is logged on.

User_Info

superclass: Root_Obj
SLOTS:
userid: name of the user
display: the display id if the user is logged on a computer; this allows for communication across the network.
title: job title
post_box: post box for receiving communication objects
METHODS:
create_method: creates a user_info object
findbytitle: finds user, given a title
findbyname: find user, given a name
set_display: set the display id of the user during login time
....

- **Project_Obj and Project_Set.** Project objects store information about a particular project. The Project_Set object stores a list of all Project_Obj objects, i.e., a list of all projects the user is working on. The Project_Set object defines functions for changing the current project and loading the appropriate database.

Project_Obj

superclass: Root_Obj
SLOTS:
date_started:
scheduled_completion:
own_ins_dict: the local instance database for the project
(actually it is a key to a dictionary which stores the instances of a project)
shared_ins_dict: the shared instance database for the project
(a dictionary which stores the shared instances of a project)
document_set: the document objects of the project
METHODS:
newwithid: creates a new project

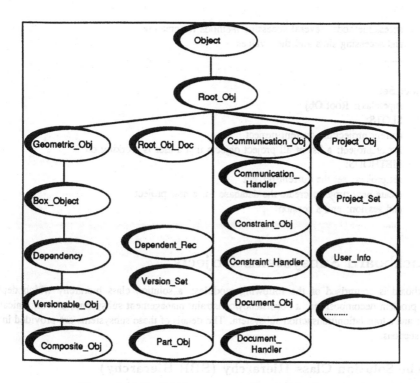

Figure 5: A Partial Taxonomy of Generic Blackboard and KM Objects

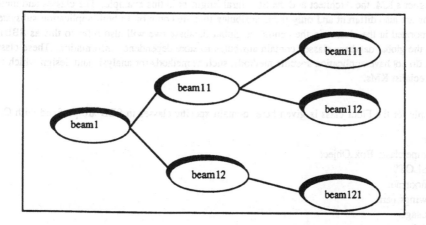

Figure 6: Example of a Version Tree

       access_methods: several accessing methods for creating
       and accessing slots and their values
       ....

Project_Set
       superclass: Root_Obj
       SLOTS:
       current_project:the current project
       list_of_project: a list of all project objects that a user is working on
       METHODS:
       set_project: set the current project
       create_new_project: create the database for a new project
       end_session: end a session
       ....

5   Blackboard Subsystems Objects

The Blackboard is comprised of the following modules: a solution class hierarchy which depicts the global problem decomposition; a consistency/constraint management subsystem; a communication subsystem; and a translation/transaction subsystem. The details of these subsystems are provided in the following sections.

5.1   The Solution Class Hierarchy (SBB Hierarchy)

Knowledge Modules (KMs) depicting individual designers perform design operations and generate the solution in the Solution Blackboard (SBB). This solution is represented by the solution class hierarchy (the actual solution - i.e., the Object-Hierarchy - is an instance of the solution class hierarchy), which is shown in Figure 7 for our application. This global data model is different from the data models of each designer's KM, the Architect and the Structural Engineer in this example. The classes and method definitions are also different and only those attributes that are common to both application subsystems are incorporated in the classes in the central or global database (we will also refer to this as SBB). In addition, the global database classes contain attributes to store dependency information. These classes, however, do not have application specific methods, such as methods for analysis and design which exist in the Specialist KMs.

An example for the Floor class is given here (domain specific classes in SBB are prefixed with C_).

C_Floor
       superclass: Box_Object
       SLOTS:
       floor_no:
       wings_part:
       usage:
       sub_parts:
       METHODS:
       S_retrieve: used by the Structural system object to retrieve a floor
       A_retrieve: used by the Architect's system object to retrieve a floor

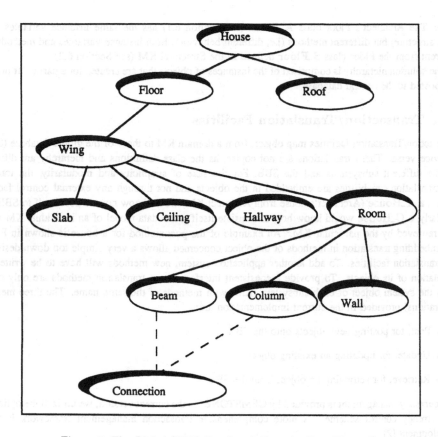

Figure 7: The Global (SBB) Database's Domain Class Hierarchy

Note: The Architect's Floor class A_Floor (see Section 6.1) has the same instance variables (i.e., same structure) but different methods (i.e, different behavior). Both instance variables and methods are different from the Floor class S_Floor defined in the Structural KM (see Section 6.2).

The solution hierarchy is comprised of the instances of objects that are created for a particular project and posted to the central database.

5.2 Transaction/Translation Facilities

Transaction/Translation facilities map objects from a domain KM to those of the global database (SBB) and vice versa. These translations are not copies, as the class definitions and hierarchy are different for the different subsystems and the SBB. For the sake of simplicity and modularity, the transaction/translation capabilities are embedded in the objects and not through any external control facility. Hence, a A_House (Architect's house from Architect KM) would know how to post itself to SBB and similarly, a C_House would know how to translate itself to the data model of an individual KM when it is retrieved by the particular KM.[5] An example of the post method for a house is shown in Figure 8. Embedding translation in methods of the object concerned allows a very simple top down design of the translation facilities. To add another application system, new methods will have to be written for translation of its objects. To provide a consistent interface, these translation methods are only called from the system object of each subsystem (KM) with methods of the same name. The three methods (operations) provided in the current implementation are:

- Post, for posting new objects onto the SBB

- Update, for updating an existing object

- Retrieve, for retrieving an object from the SBB

Concurrency management is provided by GEMSTONE. In the current version, we utilized the optimistic concurrency control scheme. A more comprehensive transaction management framework is under development [2].

5.3 The Constraint/Consistency Subsystem

Utilities for consistency maintenance are needed in any computer-aided cooperative work. Inconsistencies in the global database may occur if either parametric constraints or interaction constraints are violated; a parametric constraint is a constraint on a single object, e.g., *the length of the beam should not be greater than 30 units*, while an interaction constraint is a relationship between two or more objects, e.g., *the sum of the slab depth and the beam depth should not exceed 4 units*. A constraint management facility for handling interaction constraints has been implemented. This is achieved through the Constraint_Obj and the Constraint_Handler objects.

The constraint facility allows a user to specify the constraints as a symbolic relationship between objects. This is then compiled into a method which is checked when a KM accesses the SBB. The constraint system uses the *schema evolution* facility of GEMSTONE, which allows a method to be compiled into a class at run time. If the relationship is not satisfied, the user will be prompted either to abort the transaction or to continue. If s/he chooses to continue, then a Communication object will be sent to the user who has set the constraint. Thereafter, the parties can go through a negotiation phase (we are in the process of developing a negotiation framework). The constraint handler can also be invoked at anytime to check for constraint violations, if required.

---

[5]One might argue that retrieval functions should be associated with domain specific KMs. However, in MagpieBridge we have included the retrieval methods in the SBB objects due to ease of implementation. We are currently addressing this issue in detail.

A_House
category: 'Translation'
method: A_House
post
—hou_obj temp_obj roof_obj tmp_name x y z str aset—
System currentsegment: Shared_segment.
hou_obj := C_House create_a_house: owner address: address usage: usage
      orientation: orientation obj_id: obj_id.
x := pos2 x.
y := pos2 y.
z := pos2 z.
hou_obj dimenx: x y: y z: z.
hou_obj comment: comment.
hou_obj roof_part: roof_obj.
aset := set new.
" just the coordinate points first"
local_model do: [:an_em —temp_obj := an_em post.
aset add: temp_obj.].
hou_obj local_model: aset.
floors_part do: [:an_em —temp_obj := an_em post.
      hou_obj add_a_floor: temp_obj.].
System currentsegment: default_segment.
(Architect_System instance) post_mess: obj_id str1: 'House,' str2: 'House Posted'.
(Architect_System instance) disp: 'House Posted'.

Figure 8: Post Method in Architect KM

The Constraint_Obj and Constraint_Handler objects are described below.

The Constraint_Handler object keeps track of all the constraints associated with an object.

Constraint_Obj
>   superclass: Root_Obj
>   SLOTS:
>   set_of_related_obj: the objects participating in the constraint
>   associated_method: the actual constraint
>   METHODS:
>   check_constraint: checks the constraint by invoking the associated method
>   notify: notifies the appropriate party
>   ....

Constraint_Handler
>   superclass: Root_Obj
>   SLOTS:
>   set_of_con_obj: the set of all constraint_obj objects
>   METHODS:
>   create_con_object: creates a constraint object (constraint_obj)
>   check_constraint: checks a single constraint associated with an Object
>   check_all_constraints: checks all constraints
>   look_all_constraints: look at all constraint objects

The example below shows how a constraint *the sum of the depths of a beam and a slab* is set on two objects - beam1 and slab1 - through the creation of a constraint object.

A_cons_handler create_con_obj: #checkn
method: 'checkn ((beam1 depth) + (slab1 depth) $\leq$ 4)'
rel_obj: #(beam1 slab1) com: 'An example' dict: dictionary_array

5.4   The Communication Subsystem

Communication between members of a team is one of the most important requirement for success of their cooperative work. We have implemented a communication system which facilitates sending of communication objects or messages between different users. Two classes are defined for communication: Communication_Obj, which is instantiated each time a communication is warranted; and Communication_Handler, which manages the communication objects. Each KM will have its own communication handler. The Communication_Handler object has instance variables which hold the incoming and outgoing communication (Communication_Obj) objects. We have also implemented a concept of a post box - implemented as a Post_box object - which is owned by each KM and is attached to the User_info object. All incoming objects are received by the Post_box object. These communication objects are then read by the communication handler (Communication_Handler). The constraint subsystem uses these objects for notification.

Details of the Communication_Obj and the Communication_Handler objects are provided below.

Communication_Obj
>   superclass: Root_Obj
>   SLOTS:

title: the title of the message
receiver: the receiver of the message
associated_obj: any associated object to be sent
category - the category of the message
text: text string
METHODS:
create_com: creates a communication object
....

Communication_Handler
    superclass: Root_Obj
    SLOTS:
    handler_owner: holds an user_info object
    in_stored: stores incoming communication objects
    out_queue: stores outgoing communication object temporarily before sending
    out_stored: stores outgoing communication objects permanently
    pos_in: indicates number of objects in in_stored
    pos_out: indicates number of objects in out_queue
    METHODS:
    create_com: creates a communication_handler object
    read: reads the post box message
    send: sends the last object in the out_queue
    findbyowner: finds communication object with certain owner
    findbytitle: finds communication object with certain title
    ....

6 Architectural and Structural KMs

MagpieBridge is a simple demonstration of the object structure and behavior detailed in the previous section. It contains two KMs for design: an Architect KM and a Structural Engineer KM. It must be noted that the KMs are not comprehensive. These were developed only to demonstrate the functionalities of DICE and should not be construed as depicting actual engineering practice; full scale versions of these KMs are currently under development.

6.1 Architectural KM

The Architect KM defines the classes and required methods which allows an Architect to model the layout and the geometrical properties of a house. A CAD interface could be used by an Architect to specify the layout. However, since we do not have a sophisticated user interface the GEMSTONE interface - called TOPAZ - is used for inputting the Architect's design, which is a preliminary design. In addition, a display facility which allows an architect to display wire frame-models of objects in a 3 dimensional perspective view was developed as a part of this project. After an architect is satisfied with his design, he can post it onto the global database (SBB) for other team members (KMs) to work on.

6.1.1 The Architect's Class Hierarchy

The composition (part-of) class hierarchy of the architect's KM is shown in Figure 9. A few representative classes are described below; domain specific classes in the Architect KM are prefixed with A_

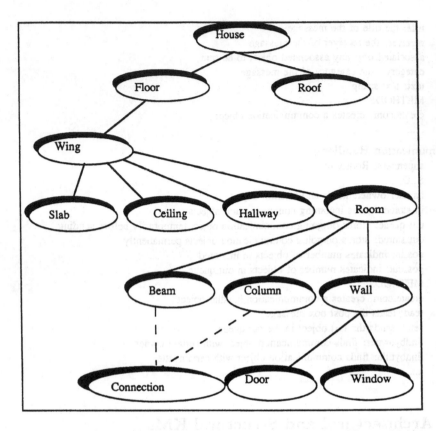

Figure 9: The Architect's Domain Class Hierarchy (Composition)

A comprehensive list of objects is provided in Reference [11].

A_House
    superclass: Box_Object
    SLOTS:
    house_owner:
    address:
    usage:
    color:
    orientation:
    sub_parts: floors_part roof_part
    floors_part:
    roof_part:
    METHODS:
    create_a_house: generates a house design (could be through an interactive CAD tool
    accessing methods: eg . num_of_floors, num_of_rooms,.....
    display:
    ....

A_Roof
    superclass: Box_Object
    SLOTS:
    type:
    material:
    METHODS:
    create_roof:
    accessing methods:
    display:
    ....

A_Beam
    superclass: Box_Object
    SLOTS:
    start: point denoting one end of a beam
    end: point denoting the other end of the beam
    instances: contains all beam instances
    material:
    METHODS:
    accessing methods:

A_Connection
    superclass: Box_Object
    SLOTS:
    pos: a 3-D coordinate point
    beams_connected: a set of beams connected to it
    columns_connected: a set of columns connected to it
    METHODS:
    accessing methods:

6.1.2 The Architect_System Object

The Architect_System object provides the computer-aided design environment for an Architect. All interfaces to the Blackboard are provided through the Architect_System object. Display and communication facilities can also be invoked through the Architect_System object. It also acts as an interface to other system objects' methods such as the functions of User_Info and Project_Obj objects. Its methods are the functionality of the Architect KM.

Architect_System
> superclass: Root_Obj
> SLOTS:
> users: contains a list of user_info objects
> communication_handler:
> project: contains the Project_Set_Obj
> METHODS:
> create: creates and sets instance variables
> post: posts an object to the global database
> update: updates an existing object or a slot, if slot is given as an argument
> retrieve: retrieves an object
> associated_cen_obj:
> send: sends a display message to the message window of the structural engineer KM
> display: displays an object in a 3-d view
> set_view: sets the view point
> zoom:
> ...

6.2 Structural Engineer KM

The Structural Engineer KM retrieves the layout and the dimensions generated by the Architect KM from the Blackboard and designs the structural elements described below.

1. *Slabs.* The area of reinforcing steel necessary for the applied bending moments is determined. This is based on whether the slabs resist the bending moments in one direction or in two directions.

2. *Beams.* The cross section suitable for an applied bending moment acting on the beam is determined. The area modulus is calculated and a section is retrieved from prop_section_tbl, which holds a table of sections and their properties.

3. *Columns.* The cross section for applied compression load acting on the column is determined. The allowable inertia to prevent Eulerian buckling is calculated and a section is retrieved from prop_section_tbl.

6.2.1 The Structural Engineer's Class Hierarchy

The composition (part-of) class hierarchy of the Structural Engineering KM is shown in Figure 10. A few representative set of these classes are described below; domain specific classes in the Structural Engineer KM are prefixed with S_

75

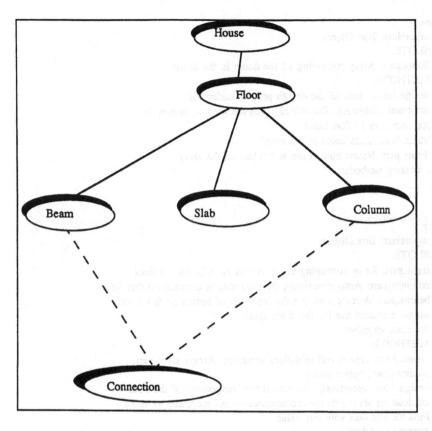

Figure 10: Structural Engineer's Domain Class Hierarchy (Composition)

S_House

> superclass: Box_Object
> SLOTS:
> floors_part: Array containing all the floors in the house.
> METHODS:
> design_house: fires all the design process under the
> structural subsystem. Recursively calls the method *design_floor*
> for each floor in floors_part
> add_a_floor: adds floors to the array
> floors_part. Newer objects are added last on the array.
> accessing methods:
>
> . ...

S_Floor

> superclass: Box_Object
> SLOTS:
> slabs_part: Array containing the instances of slabs on this floor
> columns_part: Array containing the instances of columns on this floors
> beams_part: Array containing the instances of beams on this floor
> usage: predicted use for this floor space.
> floor_no: identifier
> METHODS:
> create_floor: creates and initializes variables (Arrays slabs_part,
> columns_part, beams_part)
> design_floor: recursively designs all the components of the floor
> cal_load_for_slab: gets the recommended load according to usage.
> Fills the slot *load* with this value
> accessing methods: ..
> ....

S_Slender

> superclass: Box_Object
> SLOTS:
> start: starting connection object
> end: ending connecting object
> material
> load:
> section: stores the steel section; currently only steel sections are supported
> METHODS:
> cal_self_weight: calculates the self weight
> accessing methods: ...
> ....

S_Beam

> superclass: S_Slender
> SLOTS:
> METHODS:

design_yourself: designs the beam in the following manner: calculate bending
moment on beam and determine bending stress and required area
modulus; retrieve a section with similar modulus from **prop_section_tbl**
pass_load_to_col: calculates weight of the beam and passes a part of this to an appropriate column
accessing methods: ...

....

Prop_Section_Object
  superclass: Root_Obj
  SLOTS:
  area_mod:
  inertia:
  depth:
  width:
  area:
  section_name: obj_id inherited from root
  METHODS:
  accessing methods: ...
  ....

Prop_Section_Tbl
  superclass: Set (objects in the set are of prop_section_object type)
  SLOTS:
  METHODS:
  get_section_given_mod: finds a section which has a area_mod
  modulus larger than a given modulus
  get_depth_given_inertia: finds a section which has
  inertia larger than a given inertia
  ......
  accessing methods:

6.2.2 The Design Process

The design process starts by sending the message *design_house* to an instance of a S_House.[6] The
method *design_house* of S_House then goes through the following process.

For each *floors_part* of a S_House instance send the *design_floor* message. Sending the *design_floor*
message to a S_floor instance would result in the following set of actions.

  For each slabs_part design_slab
  For each slabs_part pass_load_to_beam
  For each beams_part design_beam
  For each beams_part pass_load_to_col
  For each columns_part design_col
  For each columns_part load_to_down_col

---

[6]This is not a realistic design procedure. We are in the process of developing a computer-aided steel design
system.

Floors in the *floors_part* variable are always sorted in a top-down (descending) order so that the top floors are designed before the bottom ones. Hence, the load is propagated downwards. It can be clearly seen from the pseudo code that the object-oriented implementation allows recursivity and abstraction resulting in simple and natural coding.

6.2.3 The Structural_System Object

The Structural_System object provides general system facilities for a Structural Engineer KM. All interface through the blackboard is provided through the Structural_System object. It also provides communication and display facilities and interface to other system objects, as in the case of the Architect_System object.

Structural_System
      superclass: Root_Obj
      SLOTS:
      users: list of structural engineers
      communication_handler:
      project: instance of Project_Set_Obj
      METHODS:
      create: creates and sets instance variables
      post: posts an object to the global database
      update: updates an existing object or a slot, if slot is given as an argument
      retrieve: retrieves an object
      associated_cen_obj:
      send: sends a display message to the message window of an Architect KM
      display: displays an object in a 3-d view
      design_house: ..
      .....

7 System in Operation

A small, yet representative, example where a two storied (two room) house is planned and designed by an Architect and a Structural Engineer working on two different computers connected over a network is presented in this section.

7.1 Layout by the Architect

Initially, the Architect sets up the project object **Project_Obj**. This is done by sending the *create_project* message to the Architect_system object and making it the current project.

The steps that the Architect follows are:

1. Create an instance of a house (A_House). Information required include the overall dimensions.

2. Create an instance of a floor (A_Floor).

3. Create another instance of the floor (A_Floor) or duplicate the last one.

4. Add the floors as part of the house passing in the floor location and orientation for every floor. A display of the house at this stage will produce an outline of the house and the floors.

5. Create the wings and hallways and add them as parts of the floors.

6. Create the rooms and make them part of the wings.

7. Create the beams, the ducts and the columns for every room

Figure 11 shows a simple three dimensional perspective view of the house being designed, where the house instance is called small_house; Architect can display his design by calling the *display* method of Architect_System.

Figure 12 shows an example when the length of a beam the Architect specifies is too large for economical and structural reasons; knowledge about this exists in the local KMs. A pop-up button asking the Architect whether he wants to abort the transaction is displayed on his screen.

Figure 13 shows the derivation of a new version of window1, which belongs to the A_Window class.

7.2   Posting to the Global Database (SBB)

When the Architect completes the house design, he posts it to the global database (SBB) by sending a *post* message with *small_house* as the argument to the Architect_System object, as shown in Figure 14. Architect_System sends the *post* message to small_house, which is an instance of A_House. The house and its subparts are posted to the SBB through the creation of similar objects in the SBB. The Architect can continue working on his design.

7.3   Retrieving by the Structural Engineer

A message is sent to the Structural Engineer KM[7] informing him that the house has been posted by the Architect; a communication object instance (Communication_Obj) is created and sent to the concerned KMs (in this case, the Structural Engineer KM). Figure 15 shows a message being displayed on the Structural Engineer's message window informing him of the house is being posted and prompting him to check his post box and retrieve the house. The Structural Engineeer retrieves the appropriate objects by using the *retrieve* method of the Structural_System object, as shown in Figure 16.

7.4   Designing by the Structural Engineer

After retrieving the house layout, the Structural Engineer starts designing the house. If the Architect changes any object and posts it in the SBB at any time, a message will be sent to the Structural Engineer if he has retrieved any dependent objects. This can be seen in Figure 17. If this is the case, he has to update his objects too.

The Structural Engineer starts the structural elements design by sending the *design_house* message to the Structural_System object, as shown in Figure 18; also shown in the figure are various browsers available for viewing local and global databases. This initiates the determination of the steel for the slabs and the sections for the beams and the columns.

7.5   Updating the SBB by the Structural Engineer

Updating is achieved by the Structural Engineer through the *update* method of the Structural_System object. During this transaction, interaction constraints (incorporated in the Constraint_Obj) which have been set are checked. If the constraints are not satisfied, the structural engineer is notified, as shown in Figure 19. He has the choice of either aborting the transaction or redesigning the element; redesigning and updating will result in a constraint message being sent to the Architect. Thereafter, the

---

[7]The **Dependency** object holds the information about the appropriate KMs to be notified.

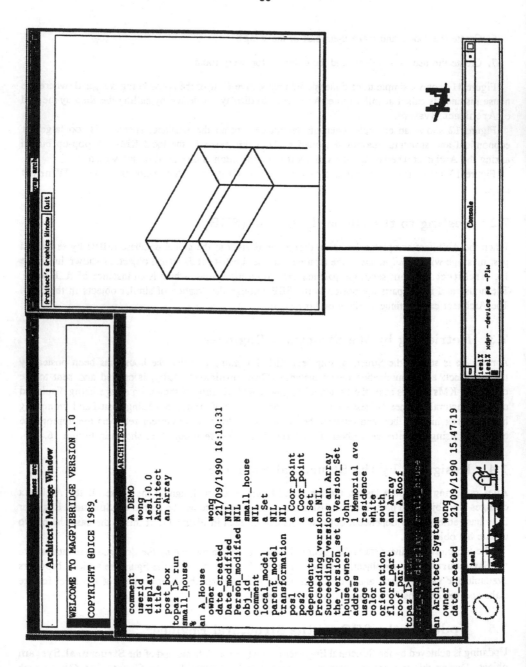

Figure 11: An Initial Screen State of the Architect KM

81

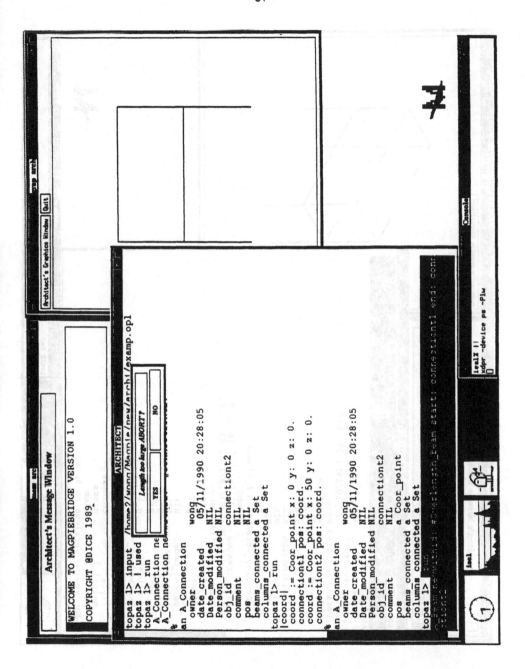

Figure 12: Local Constraint Checking during Design

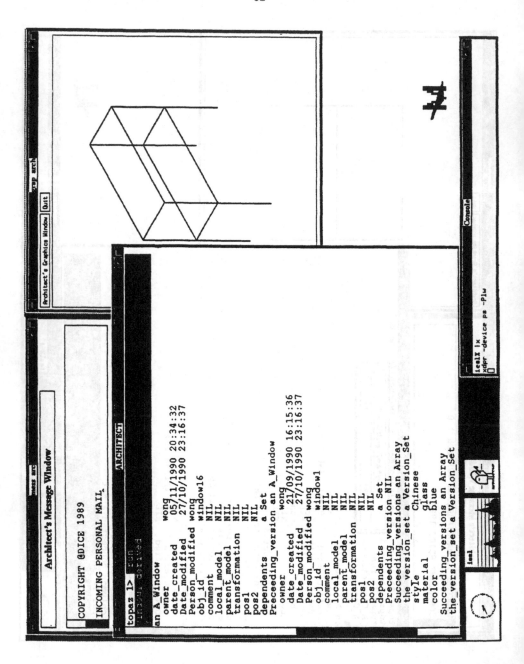

Figure 13: Creating Versions: A new Version of Window1 is Created and Changed

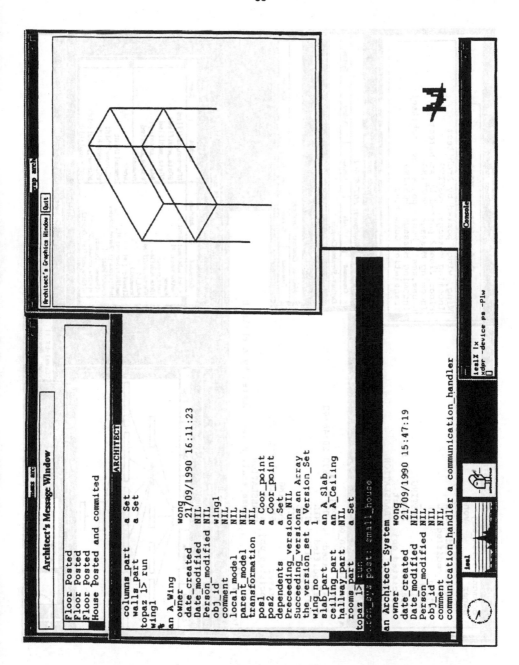

Figure 14: Posting to the Global Database (SBB) - Architect's Screen State

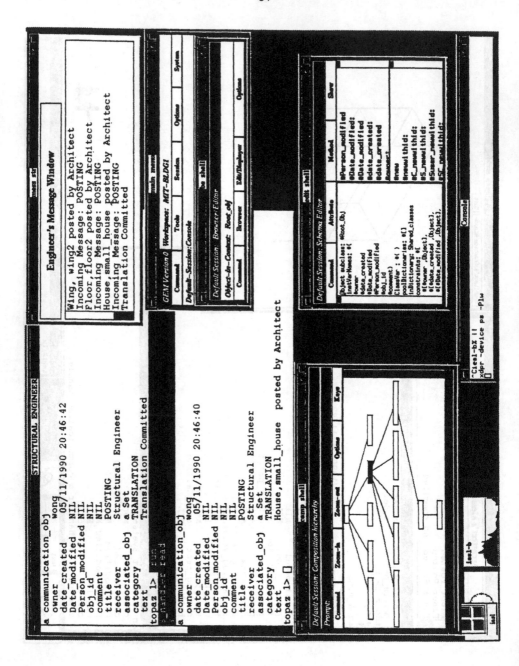

Figure 15: Posting by Architect - Structural Engineer's Screen State (Note the message window and Posting communication object in Structural Engineer's window)

85

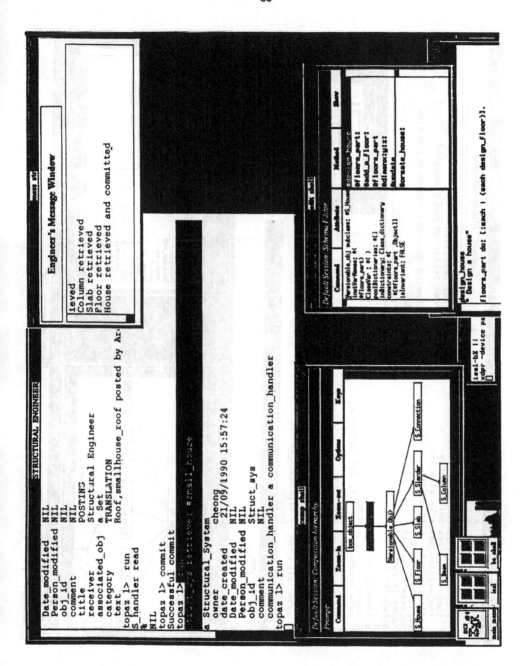

Figure 16: Retrieving from Shared Database (Also seen is part of the class hierarchy and definition of *S_House* and *design_house* methods)

86

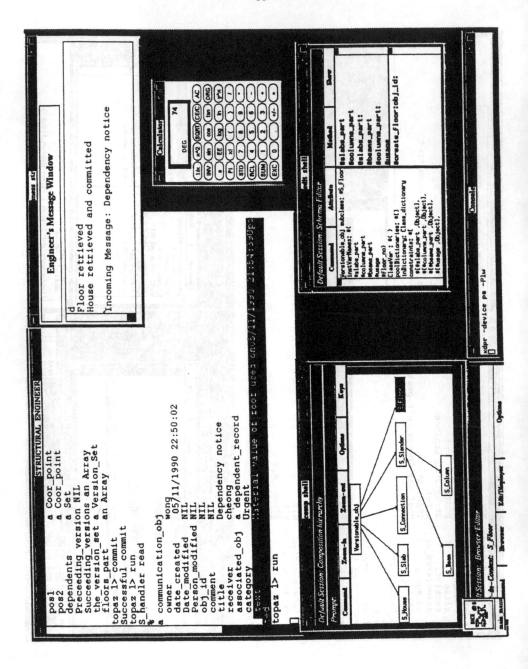

Figure 17: Dependency Notification: Display Message and Communication Object are Sent

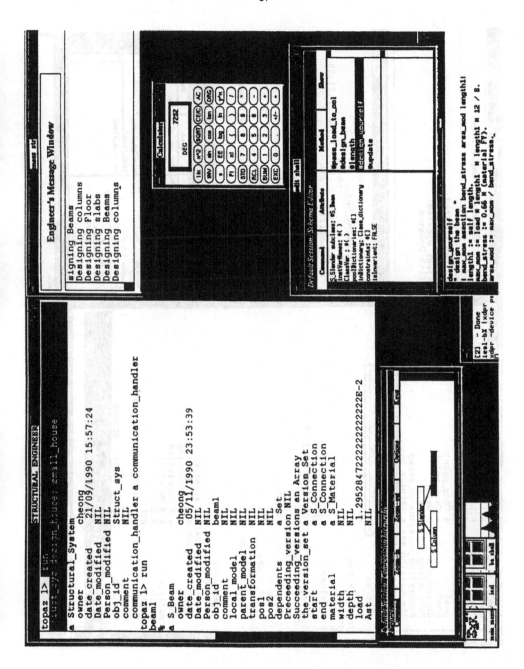

Figure 18: Designing a House

88

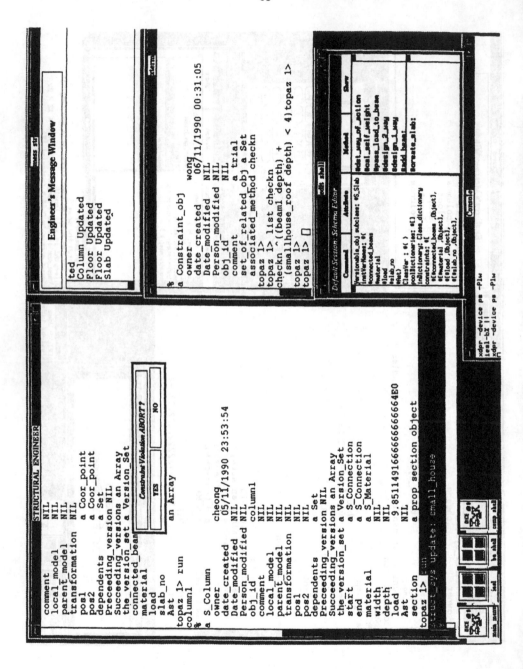

Figure 19: Updating SBB: Constraint Handling through the constraint_handler (The constraint_obj and method are also shown)

Architect can negotiate with the engineer. If everything is satisfied, the design is completed and the construction planning begins.

8   Summary and Current Work

In this paper we have described a computer–based framework called DICE for cooperative product development. An implementation of DICE - called MagpieBridge - in GEMSTONE, which is a commercial object-oriented database management system, was also described. We have identified the following extensions needed for GEMSTONE to handle engineering product development: constraint management, communication, versions, composite objects, and user interfaces. Prototype class objects were implemented in GEMSTONE. The GCI interface was extensively used for user interface development, but was not utilized in the development of KMs.

Our experience with the MagpieBridge prototype has given us considerable insight into the development of computer aided environments for collaborative work. Our current research is focused on the following topics:

1. **Preliminary and Detailed Design Structural Engineering KMs.** Knowledge-based frameworks for preliminary and detailed structural design are currently under development. The preliminary design system - called CONGEN - consists of an inference mechanism, a domain specific knowledge base, and a user interface. Design plans, goals, constraints, objects, and analysis procedures form the knowledge base. The inference mechanism utilizes the knowledge base to generate multiple solution contexts. Four major components of the inference mechanism are: Synthesizer, Evaluator, Geometric Reasoner, and a Constraint Manager. The Synthesizer utilizes a hierarchical refinement strategy. The detailed design system - called DATON - designs various structural elements in conformance with AISC code (currently we are restricting the scope of the detailed design system to steel design). DATON uses GROWLTIGER, an interactive structural analysis package developed at MIT, for performing detailed analysis. Both CONGEN and DATON are being implemented in C++.

2. **Constraint Management.** Constraints are continually being added, deleted and modified throughout the development of a new product. For example, the initial set of specifications may be augmented, changed and/or refined as the design progresses. The resulting constraint set may contain conflicting and/or unrealizable requirements. The management of these constraints throughout the evolving design is a non-trivial task. The constraints are often numerous, complex and contradictory. In complex engineering problem solving, where form, function and physics interact strongly, it is difficult to: 1) keep track of all relevant constraints and parameters, and 2) understand the basic design relationships and tradeoffs. Effective tools for constraint management will facilitate good engineering.

Our framework for constraint management consists of the following components:

   - *Constraint Network Generator.* This module takes a set of constraints and generates a constraint network. The constraint network is reduced to a directed acyclic graph.
   - *Numerical Algorithms.* Various numerical techniques are being incorporated. These include algorithms for solving coupled sets of equations, optimization routines, simulated annealing, etc.
   - *Expert Equation Solver.* This module aids in the selection of appropriate numerical algorithms and in transforming the equations input by the user into a form that could be manipulated by the appropriate program.

3. **Negotiation Framework.** In large engineering projects, conflicts can occur either due to interface constraint violation or due to contradictory modifications of a single object. For example, a HVAC engineer can decide to place pipes at the same location that the architect decided to place a beam. These conflicts can only be detected once the two designs have been generated and sufficient constraint propagation and/or modeling has been performed. Another type of constraint violation occurs when an engineer makes changes to a partial solution generated by another engineer. The two participants may or may not have similar roles in the system. For example, two architects may disagree on the location of the walkway, or the HVAC engineer might want to change the depth of a beam posted by the a structural engineer in order to put some pipes through it. We have identified two types of techniques to address these issues: constraint relaxation and goal respecification. The negotiation framework attempts to provide a computational framework for dealing with constraint violations across disciplines.

4. **A Data Model for SBB.** We are looking into the possibility of generating of the global data model (SBB Object Hierarchy) semi-automatically. In particular, we are concentrating on comprehensive knowledge/data bases for civil engineering.

5. **ONTOS and OBSERVER/ENCORE Implementations.** ONTOS (marketed by Ontologic, Inc., Three Burlington Woods Burlington, MA 01803) is a commercial OODBMS, which supports a direct interface with C++. To alleviate the static nature of C++ program structure, ONTOS provides facilities for programmatic class creation at runtime. The following extensions are being undertaken: version management facilities; inter-client communications; more flexible lock types and deadlock management; composite object management; and graphical user interfaces in a X Window environment.

    OBSERVER is a general purpose object server being developed at Brown Unviersity [6]; OBSERVER provides an implementation mechanism for the Physical, Storage, and Controller layers of DICE's BB. ENCORE is its C-based front end data definition and manipulation language. When fully operational, OBSERVER/ENCORE would be the most powerful public domain OODBMS, since it incorporates most of the advanced object and transaction management features that other commercial systems lack. In addition, the C source code would also be available and may be extended for further enhancements. The following extensions to OBSERVER/ENCORE are being undertaken: extend ENCORE's composite object management facilities to incorporate the rich semantics of the ORION model; develop conflict resolution strategies for multiple inheritance; and add multi-media capabilities.

6. **User Interfaces.** User interfaces are an important part of most software systems. In a computer-supported cooperative work environment, a user interface must facilitate the cooperative process between various groups, besides allowing them to do their individual work. The user interface must therefore facilitate management, visualization and understanding of the design information, allow coordination and monitoring of users' work and provide a medium for systematic decision making.

    The user interface for DICE can be considered as a set of tightly integrated high level tools which provide facilities required for cooperation between various groups. It makes use of multiple windows, menus, graphics and direct interaction techniques to provide a graphical interface with an organizational structure which is easy to comprehend and use.

    The following categories of tools are being incorporated in the DICE user interface:

    (a) *Data management tools for the Blackboard and local databases*, such as: browsers; editors/displayers; querying, data manipulation and presentation facilities; and documentation system.

(b) *Interface tools to Blackboard*, such as: facilities for translation of information between Blackboard and local applications; status checking and monitoring facilities; communication between the Blackboard and the users; and facilities for coordination.

(c) *Communication tools*, such as: electronic message system and electronic conferencing facility/negotiation tool.

(d) *Application specific tools*, which are tailored according to the specific application. For example, an Architect might have a CAD tool for designing the layout of the house.

Details of the above tools can be found in [12].

9 Acknowledgments

The first author would like to acknowledge the support of the NSF PYI Award No. DDM-8957464. Albert Wong is partially supported by the Gleddon Postgraduate Studentship from the University of Western Australia. We would also like to thank the Industrial Affiliate Program of the Intelligent Engineering Systems Laboratory which partially supported the research. Kevin Cheong and Alan Brik were responsible for the implementation of the domain specific KMs.

References

[1] Ahmed, S., Sriram, D., and Logcher, R., *A Comparison of OODBMS for Engineering Applications*, Technical Report No. IESL-90-03, Intelligent Engineering Systems Laboratory, MIT, Cambridge, MA 02139, 1990.

[2] Ahmed, S., Sriram, D., and Logcher, R., *Transaction Management in OODBMS for Collaborative Engineering Applications*, Technical Report No. IESL-90-06, Intelligent Engineering Systems Laboratory, MIT, Cambridge, MA 02139, 1990.

[3] Banerjee, J. et al., Data Model Issues for Object Oriented Systems, *ACM Transactions of the Office Management Systems*, Vol. 5, No. 1, Pages 3-26, January 1987.

[4] Barton, P. K., *Building Services Integration*, E. F. N. Spon, 733 Third Ave., NY 10017, 1983.

[5] *Proceedings of the Second National Symposium on Concurrent Engineering*, Feb. 7-9, 1990, West Virginia University, Drawer 2000, Morgantown, W.Va. 26506, 1990.

[6] Hornick, M. F. and Zdonik, S. B., A Shared Segmented Memory System for an Object-Oriented Database, *ACM Transactions of Office Information Systems*, Vol. 5, No. 1, January 1987.

[7] Marshall, R. D., et al., *Investigation of the Kansas City Hyatt Regency Walkways collapse*, Technical Report Science Series 143, National Bureau of Standards, Washington, D. C., May 1982.

[8] Sriram, D., *Knowledge-Based Approaches for Structural Design*, CM Publications, UK, 1987.

[9] Sriram, D., Logcher, R., Groleau. N., and Cherneff, J. , *DICE: An Object Oriented Programming Environment for Cooperative Engineering Design*, Technical Report IESL-89-03, IESL, Dept. of Civil Engineering, M. I. T., 1989.

[10] Sriram, D., Logcher, R., and Fukuda, S. (Editors) , *Computer Aided Cooperative Product Development*, Proceedings of the MIT-JSME Workshop held at M.I.T., Nov 21-22, 1989, 1-253, M.I.T., Cambridge, MA 02139 [To be published by Springer Verlag].

[11] Sriram, D., Logcher, R., Wong, A., and Ahmed, S., *A Case Study in Computer-Aided Cooperative Product Development*, IESL Technical Report Number IESL-90-01, Intelligent Engineering Systems Laboratory, M.I.T., March 1990.

[12] Wong, A., Sriram, D., and Logcher, R., *User Interfaces for Cooperative Product Development*, In *Proceedings of the Second National Symposium on Concurrent Engineering*, Feb. 7-9, 1990, West Virginia University, Drawer 2000, Morgantown, W.Va. 26506, 1990.

Creativity Support System for Concurrent Product Design

Thomas P. Knight *Steven H. Kim*

Laboratory for Manufacturing and Productivity
Massachussetts Institute of Technology

Abstract. *This paper describes the general architecture of the Creativity Support System, an expert system for assisting users in specific domains requiring creative solutions. The bilevel structure of the system consists of a Domain-Independent Module containing general tools and techniques for creative problem solving, and a Domain-Dependent Module incorporating knowledge specific to particular fields of application. The utility of this approach is illustrated in the realm of concurrent product design by demonstrating a Concurrent Design Advisor within the general architecture of the system. We describe the stages of product design - from product specification to design optimization - as well as the particular techniques incorporated in the Concurrent Design Advisor. By providing these domain-dependent decision rules along with domain-independent creativity tools, the Creativity Support System is designed to guide the user through the entire problem resolution process in the desired domain.*

Acknowledgement

This work was supported in part by the National Science Foundation through grant No. DMC-8817261.

Introduction

Creativity has been defined as the product of resolving difficult problems; it springs from the deliberate selection of options to satisfy a challenging objective. By encoding the decision rules of creative thinkers in specific domains, computer systems can assist in generating solutions to difficult problems [4].

This paper describes the structure of the Creativity Support System, a general purpose architecture to assist in addressing difficult tasks. This general structure is tailored to a package called the Concurrent Design Advisor (CDA), a system for simultaneous synthesis and analysis of products. The CDA focuses the human expertise of a product design group towards creative solutions for satisfying customer needs. Because such activity typifies the creative process, the CDA is shown to be an excellent example of a domain which can be included in the larger, more generic Creativity Support System.

The issues involved in computer-assisted group decision making have a long history. One topic concerns resource allocation and control for project management [8]. However, aside from tools such as Gantt charts and project network diagrams, very few group projects are managed using such computer support systems [7]. The management of product development requires the coordination of many different areas of expertise, organizational departments, and design changes, and hence has proven too complex to be supported by a computer-based approach [12].

The integration of cooperative knowledge-bases, each possessing a unique perspective on the project management task, has proved successful for tackling problems that are beyond the scope of individual experts. This approach recognizes the fact that, to be effective, an organization must make full use of all the knowledge at its disposal [6]. The research in distributed artificial intelligence has led to a constraint-directed negotiation approach for providing extensive coordination between distributed knowledge sources. Such systems provide advantages in speed and reliability, in addition to a conceptually clear, modular structure.

The Creativity Support System, and its domain-dependent modules, have been modeled using the *result-sharing* form of distributed cooperation. That is, its independent knowledge bases assist each other by sharing results as they become available. The CDA, for example, contains knowledge bases which represent the kernel subproblems of product design. The computation performed by each module of the CDA depends on the current structure of the solution as it evolves as a result of the actions of the other modules.

Creativity Support System

System Architecture. The architecture of the Creativity Support System [4] is shown in Figure 1. The structure consists of two primary modules, the Domain-Independent and the Domain-Dependent Modules. The former component contains knowledge independent of the problem domain, while the latter contains information specific to the task at hand.

The Domain-Dependent Module contains a repertoire of the uses to which the CSS may be put. The system also has access to diverse fields or disciplines that may pertain to the problem, such as knowledge of statistical methods, financial accounting, experimental design, or others. Some of this knowledge may reside within the system, while other portions may be available in databases accessed through telecommunication networks. These knowledge bases reflect the need for diversity in addressing difficult problems.

The Case Base contains knowledge of a given problem, including specification of the task and the solution as it develops. For the example of product design, the problem definition is stated in terms of the customer needs, and the ensuring design concepts which satisfy this problem definition are stored in the Case Base.

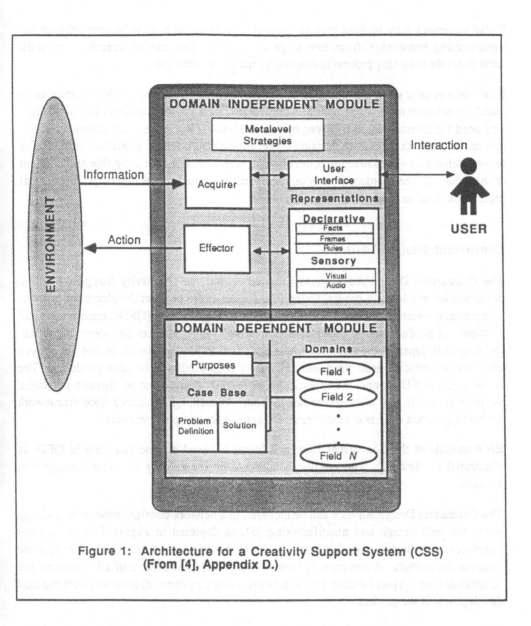

Figure 1: Architecture for a Creativity Support System (CSS) (From [4], Appendix D.)

The Domain-Independent Module contains generic capabilities such as general-purpose strategies and representation techniques. Knowledge is represented and utilized through a set of linguistic and sensory vehicles. Declarative knowledge may be represented through mechanisms such as facts, frames or rules. These may serve as the foundation for linguistic constructs or images such as visual or auditory patterns.

These structures may be manipulated through operators such as inference schema for transforming knowledge from one stage to another. The use of specific operators throughout the reasoning process is directed by metalevel strategies.

New knowledge is sifted and encoded through the acquisition module, which serves as an interface between the environment and the internal base of domain-specific knowledge. The need for externalization is served by two modules. First is the User Interface, which communicates with the human decision maker through audiovisual input and output. The second vehicle for externalization is the effector, which provides for a durable embodiment of the solution. The "hardcopy" may take the form of printed prose, drawings, mechanical prototypes, or other modes of externalization.

Concurrent Design Advisor

The Concurrent Design Advisor, as encoded within the Creativity Support System, possesses knowledge of a general framework for the entire product development process. The process, which has ben called Quality Function Deployment (QFD), encompasses all elements of product design and production after a target market has been identified. Developed in Japan in the late 1970s, this approach to product development has proven effective in reducing lead time and delivering high-quality, low-cost products. The techniques in QFD channel the expertise of marketing, design, and production personnel towards the single goal of customer satisfaction. As such, QFD offers a good framework for helping human experts to reach creative solutions for complex products.

Each module of the Concurrent Design Advisor is based on one key step of QFD, as illustrated in Figure 2. The module is responsible for guiding the user through that process.

The Concurrent Design Advisor can be included in a network configuration of knowledge bases for both design and manufacturing [5], as depicted in Figure 3. The Advisor interfaces with these knowledge bases to obtain the information required to design and produce the product. A complete system would possess knowledge of all resources and constraints (such as part families or available production equipment) involved with the total development of the product.

The main thrust of the Concurrent Design Advisor, however, is the knowledge of the *framework* for product development, not the knowledge of the available resources which constrain that development. In this way, the advisor can rely on the expertise of humans instead of the knowledge bases shown in Figure 3.

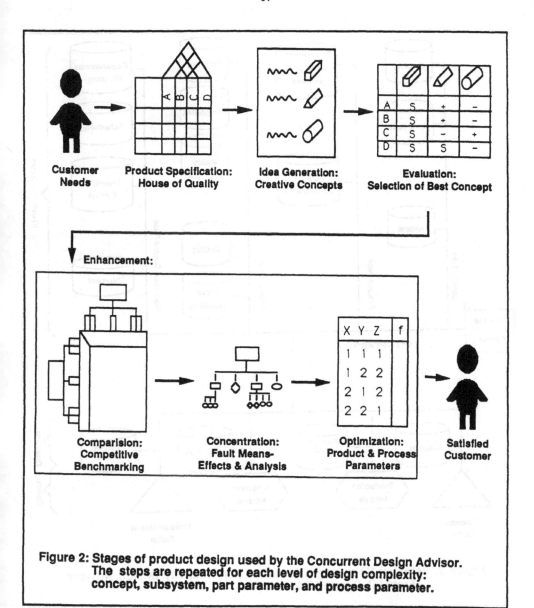

Figure 2: Stages of product design used by the Concurrent Design Advisor. The steps are repeated for each level of design complexity: concept, subsystem, part parameter, and process parameter.

Product Design Process

The crucial element of QFD is the use of multifunctional teams during all phases of product development. By combining the expertise of each field - marketing, design, production, and service - the process is likely to address all relevant issues simultaneously. In this way, the process of "throwing it over the wall" from design to production can be avoided. In effect, this insures that all development work is a technology *pull* from the customer. The concern for quality during this process guards against pushing the product or developing gadgets without considering the customer.

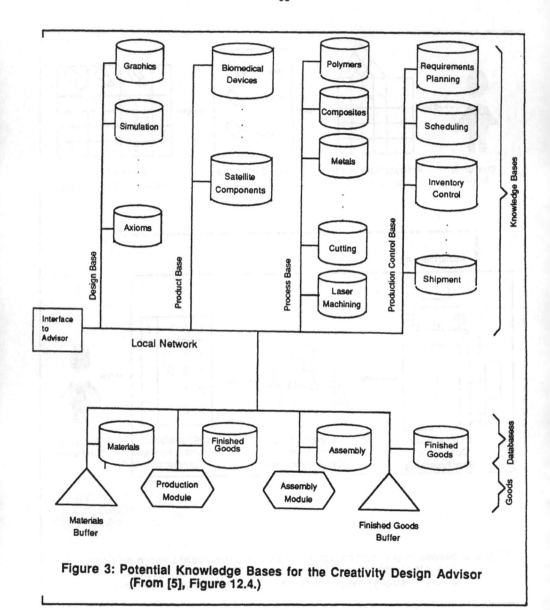

Figure 3: Potential Knowledge Bases for the Creativity Design Advisor (From [5], Figure 12.4.)

The Concurrent Design Advisor is based on the principle of this simultaneous engineering of the product design. It requires, for instance, that all designs be judged according to criteria derived directly from marketing surveys, and that all product specifications are based on production parameters. As such, its main purpose is to help combine the expertise required for concurrent design from several individuals working as a team. To this end, it relies on the following techniques: house of quality, Pugh's Selection and Synthesis Matrix, competitive benchmarking, and the Taguchi Method.

The Concurrent Design Advisor employs the following procedure for product design:

1. Product Specification.
2. Idea Generation.
3. Evaluation.
4. Enhancement.
   a. Comparison
   b. Concentration
   c. Optimization

These steps are repeated four times, once for generating the product concept, and subsequently for subsystem, part parameter, and process parameter designs. The particular techniques incorporated into the Advisor for performing these tasks are described more fully in the following subsections.

Product Specification

The first stage, *product specification*, refers to the identification of the functional requirements and constraints on a design. The technique used by the CDA is the *house of quality*, a planning table for organizing and targeting the needs of the customer. A house of quality illustrating the design of a garage door opener is shown in Figure 4 [1]. The particular form of the house used by the Concurrent Design Advisor is shown in Figure 5.

The rows of the house, called *customer needs*, are taken directly from customer responses. Effort is taken to avoid 'interpreting' these requests before recording them in the house; the responses should be transcribed using the original wording.

The columns of the house, called *design requirements*, are specific engineering measurements that are expected to be achieved in the new product. These parameters, also known as engineering characteristics, simply restate the customer requirements using the engineering expertise of the design team. They serve to guide subsequent design activity in terms of more objective or quantitative terms. During these steps the design team begins to interpret the customer needs; by discussing, debating, and clarifying the functional requirements, the team establishes a common understanding of the goals of the project. As a result, the team will later be able to reach a consensus about the value of various design alternatives.

The *relationship matrix* indicates each area where the design team feels that a relationship exists between the given row (customer need) and column (design requirement). That is, an entry indicates the degree to which achieving the design requirement (column) will have a tendency to satisfy the customer requirement (row). Completing the matrix can indicate that either a column or row should be modified; an empty row indicates that an additional design requirement must be added to satisfy an unfulfilled customer need. An empty

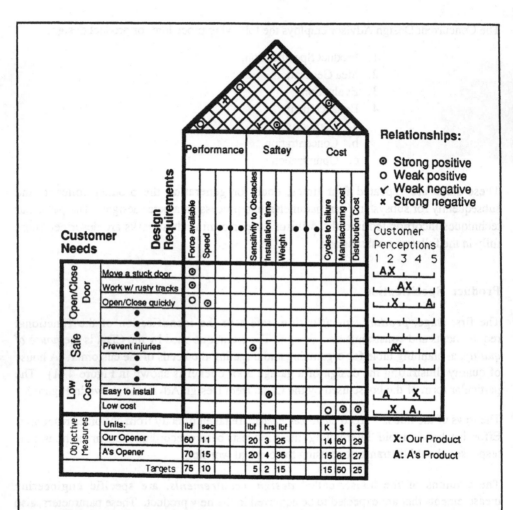

Customer Needs		Design Requirements									Customer Perceptions

Figure 4: The house of quality for the redesign of a garage door opener. Three categories of customer needs have been translated into design requirements, and competitive benchmarking has been used to set design targets. Areas delineated by thick borders define different types of knowledge.

column indicates that the design requirement is not instrumental in meeting a customer need, and hence can be deleted.

Customer perceptions, to the right of the house, graphically display how customers feel about the ability of various products to meet each customer need. This information is useful for identifying aspects of existing designs which must be improved.

Objective measures, located below the house, allow technical competitive benchmarking for each of the design requirements. The performance of competitive products is recorded in

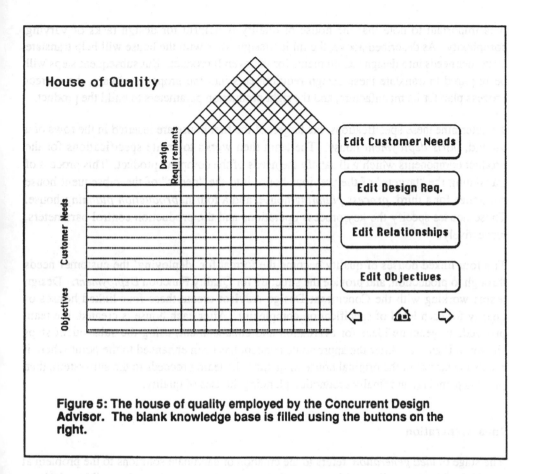

Figure 5: The house of quality employed by the Concurrent Design Advisor. The blank knowledge base is filled using the buttons on the right.

this area, allowing technical comparisons of different products. By comparing this technical evaluation with the customer perceptions, the design team ensures that its technical measurements are accurate indicators of customer satisfaction. Targets are then set for each design requirement which ensures that the product will exceed the performance of competitive products.

The *correlation matrix*, the roof of the house, shows the relationships between pairs of engineering characteristics. Any negative correlation between columns signals that special attention must be given to meet both requirements. For example, decreasing the resistive force which will cause a garage door opener to detect an obstacle and reverse its direction will reduce the maximum force available to move the door over rusty tracks. This observation will compel the design team to consider creative approaches which will allow the product to reach both design goals; for example a sensor strip on the bottom of the door to detect obstructions.

It is important to note that the house of quality is helpful for design tasks of varying complexity. As described above, the initial design work with the house will help translate customer needs into design requirements for the overall product. But subsequent steps will be required to translate these design requirements into the proper hardware, the correct process plan for its manufacture, and the right production parameters to build the product.

To determine these specifications, the targets of the first house are inserted in the rows of a second, *parts deployment* house. The team then works to create specifications for the product components which will satisfy the needs of the complete product. This process of translating the "targets" of the previous house into the "needs" of the subsequent house continues for a third, *process planning* house, and a fourth, *production planning* house. These houses specify the key process operations and the production control parameters, respectively.

The four linked houses of quality become the format for 'deploying' the customer needs through to production, and provide the structure for Quality Function *Deployment*. Design teams working with the Concurrent Design Advisor create these four linked houses of quality for each level of specification complexity. After each house is created, the team proceeds to generate ideas for evaluation and enhancement, using the subsequent steps shown in Figure 2. After the appropriate concept has been enhanced to the point where it meets the targets in the original house of quality, the team proceeds to the subsystem, then process planning, and finally production planning houses of quality.

Idea Generation

The stage of *idea generation* refers to the creation of candidate solutions to the problem at hand. In this phase, directed brainstorming can produce a variety of possible solutions, and the generic creativity enhancement tools encoded in the Creativity Support System are employed to expand and enhance the list of alternatives.

The first phase of group ideation involves brainstorming. Members suggest possible solutions, or components of possible designs, as they are conceptualized. These items are quickly recorded into the Case Base of the CDA in the form of a few descriptive words or quick sketch. Criticism of suggestions is strictly forbidden, and elapsed time is monitored by the CDA.

The ideation stage terminates at the end of the designated time period. More alternatives are sought by producing words, phrases, or pictures that help spark thoughts. The following creativity enhancing utilities encoded in the Creativity Support System are used to create these key words or pictures:[1]

---

[1] A number of these ideas was implemented in a software package called the Creativity Energizer. This was a student project undertaken by Chris Passow at the Massachusetts Institute of Technology in Spring, 1989.

Assumptions are identified to highlight the design constraints which the team members may have been using, whether consciously or unconsciously. The team is asked to list these assumptions, and then speculate on the benefits which would result if each were violated or eliminated. The team can then speculate on methods for removing these constraints.

Resources are considered in order to identify people, equipment, or techniques to aid in the design process. This list includes people who might benefit from the solution, and what they might do to help.

Descriptive words, or *considerations*, are also used to spur thought. These general topics prevent the design team from overlooking possible solutions based on specific properties. Example consideration words include structure, color, function, etc.

Actions which could be performed on existing ideas, called *manipulations*, are used in a similar fashion. By reconsidering previously suggested concepts, the team can create completely different approaches. Manipulation examples include combine, reverse, magnify, shrink, etc.

Parallel worlds are presented to the team in order to consider the role of the product within the context of some fictional or historical 'world'. The team is asked to consider those elements in the parallel world which are related to the problem at hand. As a result, alternative approaches which may be feasible in this 'world' can be generated. Examples of worlds which might spark new ideas include the Old West, mystery stories, etc.

Similarly, *quotations* are used to alter the perspective of the team as it approaches the design problem. Team members must record how the design problem is related to famous quotations chosen to elicit alternative responses.

These six tools produce a variety of creativity triggers which can generate more design alternatives. There is no guarantee that any tool will prove useful with regard to a particular design challenge, but using the entire spectrum is likely to produce some positive results.

This phase culminates with a general grooming of the design alternatives. Criticism is allowed, and the group must determine the feasibility of each concept. A concept should be fleshed out to roughly the same level of detail, and should include a rough sketch of the design. Again, tools within the Creativity Support System are provided to accomplish the deleting, editing and combining which may be necessary to construct the preliminary list of designs considered 'feasible.'

Evaluation

The next step of the process involves the comparative evaluation of the multitude of ideas proposed at the previous stage. The technique used in the CDA is Pugh's selection and synthesis matrix approach. This matrix is a tool for evaluating as many as several dozen alternative concepts against a set of criteria, and allowing for the synthesis of additional

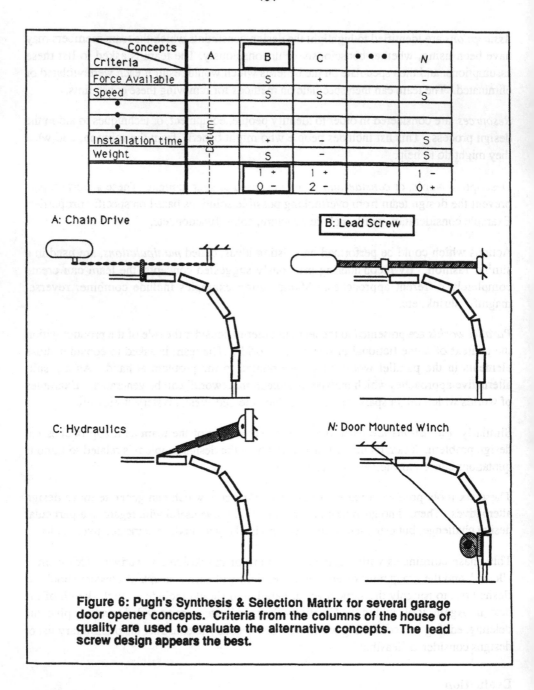

Concepts Criteria	A	B	C	• • •	N
Force Available		S	+		−
Speed		S	S		S
•					
•					
Installation time	Datum	+	−		S
Weight		S	−		S
		1 + 0 −	1 + 2 −		1 − 0 +

A: Chain Drive

B: Lead Screw

C: Hydraulics

N: Door Mounted Winch

Figure 6: Pugh's Synthesis & Selection Matrix for several garage door opener concepts. Criteria from the columns of the house of quality are used to evaluate the alternative concepts. The lead screw design appears the best.

possible concepts [3,10]. Based on the evaluation of the old and new concepts, the "best" idea can be selected.

Figure 6 shows an example of the matrix for the redesign of a garage door opener. The rows of the matrix are taken directly from the columns of the house of quality, and the alternative concepts are arranged in the columns of the matrix. The procedure uses the engineering characteristics from the house of quality as criteria for judging concepts.

The existing (or most promising) concept is chosen as a datum against which all the other concepts are compared. Proceeding horizontally, each concept is judged to be better than, worse than, or the same as the datum in meeting each of the given criteria, and the result recorded in the matrix, using "+", "-", or "S", respectively.

As the team members discuss the strengths and weaknesses of each concept, they will often envision new hybrid concepts; these should be added to the matrix. Often the concept ultimately chosen as best is synthesized during the evaluation process.

After the matrix has been completed, several concepts will prove to consistently under-perform the datum. These concepts can be removed from future consideration. On the other hand, some strong concepts will emerge which consistently outperform the datum. The most promising of these should then be considered as the datum, and the matrix should be updated. Eventually, as poor performers are removed, and new yardsticks are chosen, the 'best' concept will emerge.

This process offers all the design team members a better understanding of the requirements of the product and the candidate solutions, and provides a stimulus to produce other concepts by combining the strong points of older concepts. At the conclusion of the process, the team will have chosen the best concept for meeting the customers needs as listed in the house of quality.

Enhancement

Once the concept has been selected, it must be detailed or fleshed out to ensure that it consistently meets the targets specified in the columns of the house of quality. The *enhancement* phase refers to the elaboration of the basic concept to incorporate effective features.

Competitive benchmarking is a technique for designing the subsystems of a product once a general concept has emerged from the selection phase. The idea behind competitive benchmarking is to learn from analogous products. The design team is required to study the hardware of competing products, and is challenged to either beat these subsystem designs or use them, in their product. This prevents the creation of a product which is "new" but which is no better than an existing design.

The results of competitive benchmarking are useful in Value Analysis/ Value Engineering (VA/VE). This procedure, which is commonly practiced in industry, translates functional requirements of the product into hardware designed to meet these requirements. By placing a monetary value on satisfying functional requirements, the design team is able to specify the value of the corresponding hardware, and hence begin to specify part parameters. The output of VA/VE is often displayed as a bill of materials whose entries are indented according to their position in the functional structure of the overall product.

After focusing on preliminary hardware configurations, it is possible to focus the efforts of the design team towards specific design issues which might cause the product to fail to meet the customer needs. *Fault Means - Effects and Analysis* (FMEA) helps the team to identify the possible failures of the product, and then determine which product parameters would cause such failures. For example, a garage door opener could "fail" to open if the lifting force were insufficient, which would result if the motor power were deficient. After recognizing this, design team would concentrate on optimizing the motor power to prevent this failure. The lowest level in the hierarchy of other possible failures leads the design team to the critical parameters for the design.

At this stage in the design, the basic structure of all the subsystems have been selected, and critical parameters have been identified. All that remains is to optimize these parameters at the component level. A popular tool for efficiently optimizing these parameters has been developed by Taguchi [9,12]. The Concurrent Design Advisor uses knowledge of this procedure to design tests which can be performed on a limited number of prototypes, so that the best values for part parameters can be chosen. The tests are used to determine the *Signal-to-Noise (SN) Ratio* for each prototype parameter; this SN ratio is an indication of how uniformly a product can perform in the face of environmental and production variations.

It is especially important during this phase to ensure that the design is "robust". This means that the design will be able to perform well - i.e. meet the customer's requirements - over the full range of expected operating conditions. In this way, the design team avoids creating a "pampered" product - one that is optimized to perform in only a carefully controlled environment. By optimizing Taguchi's Signal-to-Noise Ratio, the design team minimizes the variation in the performance of the product, ensuring a robust design.

Taguchi's methods of optimization can also be employed to design the required production processes. Again, the Concurrent Design Advisor will incorporate the knowledge to assist the team in designing tests to ensure a reliable process in the face of production variances.

Conclusion and Future Work

The Creativity Support System is potentially suited to many domains requiring innovative solutions. One promising area is product marketing. A Marketing Advisor would encode knowledge of marketing techniques and specific strategies and employ the techniques of *result-sharing* distributed problem solving.

Many other opportunities for tailoring the CSS come to mind. An Investment Advisor, for example, could be added to provide innovative and creative solutions for difficult investment decisions.

However, certain limitations in current technology will have to be overcome before such advisors can begin to automate the group decision process. Improvements in computer-based conferencing systems, coordination theory, and other approaches in distributed artificial intelligence will allow the elements of the CSS to generate creative solutions to problems requiring the integration of human or computer-based expertise.

The effective coordination of human expertise requires the provision of common data and knowledge bases. This coordination is crucial for the successful use of the CSS. While communication systems have been designed which allow computer-based real-time conferencing systems, the development of multi-user applications has been hampered by the high costs of custom programming. More experience is required before common functions can be incorporated into a portable conferencing toolkit [11]. Until real-time conferencing techniques become prevalent, the CDA will depend on traditional group interaction to integrate human expertise, and to act as a bulletin board for displaying these decisions.

These issues apply to the coordination of computer-based expertise as well. Successful conflict negotiation between the results of distributed knowledge bases concerned with the product development domain, for instance, will permit the differing goals and perspectives of each processing node to contribute to the final solution. Innovations in this area will be needed to facilitate the knowledge networking scheme shown in Figure 3. A comprehensive understanding of coordination principles and methods will allow the Creativity Support System to fully support the creative work of interacting human problem solvers.

References

[1] D.P. Clausing & J. R. Hauser, "The House of Quality," *Harvard Business Review* vol. 66, no. 3, May-June 1988, pp 63-73.

[2] J.E. Kelly, Jr. & M.R. Walker, "Critical-Path Planning and Scheduling." *Proceedings of Eastern Joint Computer Conference*, 1959, pp. 160-173.

[3] M. Khan & D.G. Smith, "Overcoming conceptual barriers - by systematic design." *Proceedings of International Conference on Engineering Design*, Harogate, UK, 1989, pp. 605-619.

[4] Steven H. Kim, *Essence of Creativity*. New York: Oxford University Press, 1990.

[5] Steven H. Kim, *Designing Intelligence*. New York: Oxford University Press, 1990.

[6] Susan Lander & Victor R. Lesser, "A Framework for the Integration of Cooperative Knowledge Based Systems." *IEEE International Symposium on Intelligent Control.* A.C. Sanderson, A.A. Desrochers, & K. Valavanis (Eds.), Albany, New York, September 1989, pp. 472-477.

[7] M.J. Liberatore & G.J. Titus, "Management Science Practice in R&D Project Management." *Management Science*, vol. 29, 1983, pp. 962-974.

[8] D.G. Malcolm; J.H. Rosenboom; C.E. Clark; and W. Fazar, "Application of a Technique for Research and Development Program Evaluation." *Operations Research*, vol. 7, number 5, Sept - Oct 1959, pp. 646-669.

[9] Madhav S. Phadke, *Quality Engineering using Robust Design*. Englewood Cliffs, New Jersey: Prentice Hall, 1989.

[10] Stuart Pugh, "Concept Selection - A Method That Works." *Proceedings of WDK5 International Conference on Engineering Design*, Rome, 1981, pp. 497-506.

[11] S. Sarin & I. Grief, "Computer-based Real-time Conferencing Systems." *Computer*, 1985, vol. 18, 1985, pp. 33-45.

[12] Arvind Sathi; Thomas E. Morton; & Steven F. Roth, "Calistro: An Intelligent Project Management System." *AI Magazine*, Winter, 1986, pp. 34-52.

[13] G. Taguchi, *Jikken Keikakuho*, 3rd Edition. Tokyo, Japan: Marzen, vol. 1 and 2, 1977 and 1978 (in Japanese). English translation: G. Taguchi, *System of Experimental Design*, edited by Don Clausing.

Product Abstraction Evolution by
Active Process Facilitators

Mark J. Silvestri
Computervision
A Prime Company

Abstract

This paper provides a framework for concurrent abstract refinement activity for a product throughout its life cycle. Two distinct abstraction activities are discussed: interdomain and intradomain life cycle representation. Product process facilitation by active computer agents provides the vehicle for schema evolution via specialization.

Introduction

Like with the introduction of CAE/CAD/CAM into the engineering, design and manufacturing community, the introduction of product information management techniques involves both a cultural and technical change in the target organization. Evidence for this resides in the fact that most corporations still rely on single department information storage. There are a few corporations at the other end of the spectrum who use status, notification and event triggering tools to provide some control over the advancement of information through a sequential life cycle[2]. ECO/ECN is primarily a manual activity . The major impediments to more pervasive utilization of product process management tools can be grouped into three categories:

- Organizational- Obstacles to information flow are real within the engineering, design and manufacturing community. In part, the problem resides in the fact that various members in the user base rely on different product abstractions within a given product phase and that there are multiple phases in product refinement. Users who have implemented sophisticated product process management solutions have done so as a corporate mission, not random activity.

- Undocumented Process- Most product builders, many of whom are world class competitors, still run their product process via community knowledge, not formal protocol. Indeed, even the

PDES draft proposal only contains a schema placeholder for product life cycle. A particular product process is likely to always be a combination of formal protocols and community knowledge as long as people are involved in its execution.

• Lack of Extensibility & Non-intuitive Interfaces- Because the problem of product process automation is so complex and task specific, it requires a custom solution at each installation. In addition, acquisition of administrative and process information is a bottleneck. Comprehensive and extensible product process definition tools with intuitive interfaces simply don't exist.

This paper provides insight into these issues for an incremental redesign environment. This problem domain allows for the study of the entire product life cycle while allowing for the accumulation of readily applicable experiential knowledge over time. By example, the product design and production tasks for automobiles, appliances and chemical processing plants could conform to this problem domain. Process participants -- people and computer agents-- and their role in abstract refinement will be discussed. A methodology will be presented to coordinate and represent the abstract refinement activity.

Abstractions for Life Cycle Representation

The engineering, design and manufacturing community utilize abstract representations of a product in correspondence to the phase of product refinement that they are engaged. For example, in plant design, natural language specifications; conceptual block diagrams; process and instrumentation diagrams and other schematics; plastic and wood models; and 3-D computer models of various perspectives are ultimately deployed at various phases of the abstract refinement process(Figure 1). The role of these representations is to document and selectively identify incremental advancement toward the goal of finalized artifact specification or actual artifact creation. They reflect a commitment staging toward that end. Commitment staging is so strongly associated to the creation of these abstract representations that virtually all organizations demand paper productions of them as evidence of progress. Geol and Pirolli [9] refer to the use of artificial symbol systems as one of the eight significant invariants in the design task environment. This paper supports the position that the use of artificial symbol systems is a fundamental invariant of design, but relative to the product life cycle as a whole distinguishes between two different forms of abstraction activity: interdomain and intradomain life cycle representation. Interdomain product life cycle representation deals with the phases of product refinement, while intradomain product life cycle representation deals with the functional views within a phase of product refinement.

Between interdomain life cycle representations, there exists intuitive gaps not readily accountable for by formalization. Figure 1 represents this form. In the evolution of representation A to C, numerous commitments occurred for reasons of constraints, experiential knowledge and personal preference.

Interestingly, although the actual transformation function between interdomain life cycle representations is not easily formalized, the product process itself dictates that generically a particular representation will be created and that the transformation will occur. It seems then that a driving function can be initiated based on process phase, independent of but causal to product abstraction specialization. Hence the assertion that active process facilitators can induce product abstraction evolution.

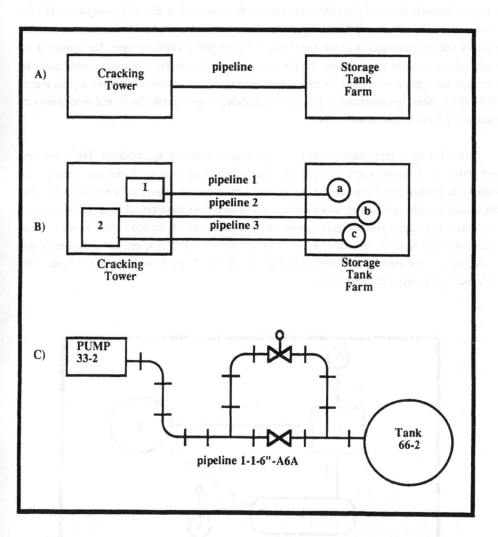

Figure 1. Abstract refinement process A) Conceptual block diagram B) Detailed Conceptual Block Diagram C) Schematic depiction of one of the pipelines in B

Intradomain life cycle representation allows for a more formal treatment. In the PDES Product Structure and Configuration Management model [14], this is referred to as the product item version task view. Although the intent was to support only differing organizational views for a released product, generalization of this notion to other interdomain life cycle representations seems appropriate. Essentially, the constituent leaf nodes remain the same across the various views within an interdomain life cycle representation, but the intradomain abstraction varies at the higher assembly nodes. For example, in Figure 1. (C), for prefabrication purposes, pipeline 1-1-6"-A6A may be broken into two manufacturing spool assembly nodes: pipeline and control station. For field maintenance, the breakdown might be pipeline as the highest assembly node and pipes and components at the next level. In this view, components like the gate valve and tees would be individually depicted so that appropriate quantities of spare parts are stocked; the pipe would be represented as accumulated length for spare part stocking purposes. The content of the intradomain abstractions are equivalent, but the task view is different. Transformations could easily be formalized and applied without an intuitive leap occurring. Use of versioned directed acyclic graphs (VDAGs) for alternate expansions of hierarchical modules is appropriate for formal descriptions of intradomain life cycle representations [24].

Both life cycle representations can be expressed by semantic aggregations. The constituent constructs of a semantic aggregation are: the objects including their attributes and methods, the relationships between the objects, and the explicit constraints upon the objects and the relationships. The latter construct, explicit constraints, adds a semantic net flavor to the more classical hierarchical view of an encapsulated typed aggregation. Figure 2 depicts a typical semantic aggregation which in this example contains objects of type "a", "b" and "c", relationships of type "1" and "2", and explicit constraints of type "x" on object "a" and constraints of type"y" on relationship "2" . Logical operators such as "and", "or", "xor", and "not" qualify inclusion in the set.

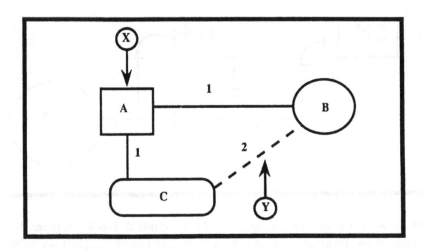

Figure 2. Semantic aggregation

A less abstract description of Figure 2 follows. Object "a", a pipeline, is related to object "b", a pipe, and object "c", a ball valve, by relationship"1", an "is-part-of" relationship. The pipeline which is intended to transport a highly flammable distillate is prevented from penetrating a high voltage zone by constraint "x". Relationship "2" is a connection relationship which has constraint "y" -- mating match, like thread style or sleeve style-- imposed upon it.

Brodie [1] differentiates between three types of constraints for a data model:

• Inherent constraints - those native to the data model; fundamental semantic properties of a
  data model, e.g. unique tuples in a relation.

• Explicit constraints - those that the user imposes on the data model; fundamental to
  database design, e.g. referential integrity relationship for a relational model.

• Implicit constraints - those inferred by explicit and inherent constraints when viewed as
  an entire system. In general, a formal definition of the explicit and inherent
  constraints are required before implicit constraints can be adequately addressed,
  e.g. generation of sub-goals or extending the fact base.

The types of inherent constraints are relative to the DBMS data model, and they are quite different. For most DBMS implementations, expressing explicit constraints is cumbersome or even embedded in the applications utilizing the DBMS. A language for explicit semantic integrity constraints has been proposed to expand the semantic knowledge of a relational database [20]. His later work, POSTGRES, allows for procedures to be embedded in the relations to enforce constraints. In fact,the notion of stored procedures is becoming commonplace in trade journal literature [11]. Taxonomies can be used in conjunction with a relational database for similar purposes [10] However, a convenient language to express explicit constraints in a traditional database environment is still an exception not the norm. Even OODB environments require constraints to be encapsulated as methods and as a consequence, deriving implicit constraints is more difficult.

From the perspective of implementation, Shepherd and Kerschberg [17] provide a treatment of constraints relative to expert database systems. In specific, they propose an architecture that assumes an object-oriented, associative-net knowledge representation which relies primarily on explicit constraints to specify the object behavior.

The conceptual schema and the process blackboard in this paper both support life cycle representations as semantic aggregations(Figure 3). Using a model similar to that of Shepherd and Kerschberg, the process manager blackboard knowledge sources utilize a knowledge interpreter which traverses the net, retrieves the explicit constraints and other knowledge associated to the object nodes and reasons about the constraints implicit in the net.

Multiple knowledge interpreters with differing control strategies and dissimilar inference methodologies will ultimately be deployed. For example, Silvestri [18] proposed a system, dual design partners, with two competing experts machines-- an innovator and a stabilizer. The following excerpt from that paper summarizes the notion:

> One expert machine , the *stabilizer*, would resist change and always present a conservative hypothetical model of the product . Its role would be the facilitator, getting the job done in a fashion as close as possible to the way all previous products have been done . The other expert machine , the *innovator* , would strive for well calculated and justified alternative hypothetical models of the product .

Attachment A profiles these expert machines in greater detail.

That explicit constraints require an interpretative mode of execution is a performance consideration. The important factor is that the explicit constraints are available for reasoning to infer new knowledge. Once instantiated in the databases and knowledgebases of distributed information services, internal schema performance considerations as well as distributed transaction management concerns dictate the storage form.

Example

Consider the following product and process scenario:

A designer specifies that a bar will be attached to a plate by a threaded connection. That is, one end of the bar will be threaded and the plate will have a matching threaded hole. Another designer, after performing FEM analysis specifies a certain material end condition that the mounting plate requires.

A hole of the diameter specified, .625 inches, requires high speed drilling. In order to achieve the material end condition , only low speed drilling and tapping can be performed.

Inherent Constraints

System Data model - Referential integrity is supported in semantic aggregations.

Explicit Constraints

A language external to the data model is available to express application constraint additions to the data model. They are available for implicit constraints to be inferred. For this short example, they would include :

Component mating
When connecting threaded components,
thread type of male must match thread type of female.

Feature processing
Minimum/maximum hole size related to material type related to drill speed related to process characteristics like temperature changes and structure stress.

Parameters to maintain material conditions
For material type *abc* and end condition *xyz*,
process temperature changes must be less than or equal to 15 degrees C.

Implicit Constraints

For this example, the derived implicit constraint might be:
For material type *abc* and material end condition *xyz* , drill holes must be less than or equal to n inches, say .188, in diameter.

This example is not meant to suggest a specific implicit constraint derivation technique, but rather to highlight the value of expressing explicit constraints such that they are available for reasoning. Once derived, an implicit constraint can be added to the knowledgebase with the appropriate truth maintenance linkages.

The system would allow designer #1 to create the component mating relationship of the type "threaded" if designer#1 properly matched the thread types. Designer #2 would be allowed to specify a material end condition attribute for the plate. However at this point, a process sensor would detect a process state change, and the process manager would test for the implied constraint and discover a constraint violation.

Designers#1 and #2 would be advised by the system that the material end condition could not be achieved because the process of making a .625 inch threaded hole changes the temperature by 25 degrees C. Because the implicit constraint is in the knowledgebase, designers#1 and #2 could query what size hole would achieve the material end condition. Further FEM analysis could then be done on the new sizes.

Manufacturing process engineer#1 did not have to enter the cycle to detect and interpret the process plan error due to the implicit constraint checking done by a process specialist on his behalf.

Active Product Process Management

The two different types of product abstractions found in the product life cycle were discussed in the previous section. They were called interdomain and intradomain life cycle representations. The former deals with the phases of the product process; the latter deals with functional views within a phase. This section provides a framework for utilizing active process facilitators to induce product abstraction evolution. The problem domain is confined to an incremental redesign environment in order to realistically achieve product process definition to a granularity worth the formalization investment.

Conceptual Schema

Many researchers [23] are looking towards combining database and AI technology to create expert database systems. Some view databases and knowledgebases as instruments for the same purpose, fact management. At the "knowledge level", databases are knowledgebases which limit the incompleteness expressible in the knowledge representation language [5] The knowledge level perspective is a holistic view which accounts for the entire body of knowledge both explicit and implicit. Indeed, few researchers feel that exploring the difference between "knowledge" and "data" aids in clarifying KBMS issues [4].

The PDES Unification Meta Model(PUMM) is targeted to unify the semantic network and data abstraction approaches to information modeling under a single set of semantic primitives [21]. PUMM will support a "recursive type model", semantic net ; a "unit model",data abstraction ; and a "rule model", declarative and procedural constraints.

At the implementation level, variations on the three schema architecture are most often proposed. In Figure 3, mapping to the internal schema is nested in distributed information services. All persistent information is under the control of distributed information services.

Conceptual Schema Evolution

Schema evolution is via process commitment to product abstraction specialization. At the knowledge level, schema evolution requires selective refinement of the constraint network in order to conform to the specifications derived from sources of product process activity in the context of a product process model which is dynamically influenced by community knowledge.

At the implementation level, mechanisms are required to support specialization relations concerned with slots and slot values like "is-a", "instance-of" and "rcference-of" [16]. VDAGs are applicable.

Process Manager

The process manager is an active agent. Whereas a passive agent only reacts to explicit commands directed to it by administrators and repository users, the active agent additionally reacts to information returned to it by its sensors. Active agent sensors can detect transactions occurring throughout the product process in context of the product process model. The sensors have three components: an information collector which receives the input, a classifier which performs reduction, interpretation and classification of the information, and a transmitter which relays the sensor information to the process manager. A passive agent would only react to explicit commands like Request for Review while the active agent would be able to initiate a Request for Review upon observing the completion of a FEM analysis test.

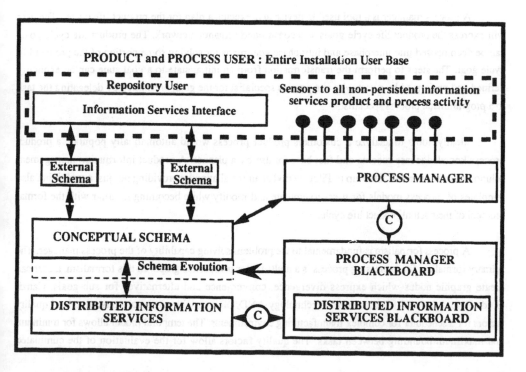

Figure 3. Architecture for Active Product Process Facilitation

The degree to which an process manager can be an active agent is relative to its reasoning capability and the reactivity requirements of the system. There is a predictability-reactivity trade off [7] . At one extreme, if all facts and beliefs relevant to the domain of the process manager can taken together define the world, then any perturbation of the system can have a predicted result. This is the case for a truth maintenance system. However, the reaction time may approach infinity. Brachman & Levesque [5] refer to this as operating at the "knowledge level" as opposed to the "implementation or computation level" which is more concerned with the form of symbolic representation or execution technique deployed. At the other extreme, a system may be highly reactive relative to events as in the case of control theory or operating systems, but incapable of predicting the impact of one event upon another or the system as a whole.

The process manager of this paper possesses characteristics of a plan monitoring/ replanning system. The system requires: a model of its sensors and their capability, and; it must integrate sensor planning with action planning. Planning involves reasoning about future events in the context of the product process model. The focus of the reasoning is to stage a series of commitments in order to advance the solution state. Tools to formalize plan knowledge representation are discussed in the next section.

Process Formalization

A process manager is a tool used to devise and execute a plan for the product life cycle. The user will express the product life cycle goals as a constrained semantic network. The product life cycle goals can be decomposed into interphase and intraphase goal plans for solving some portion of the product life cycle goal. The steps to perform the transformation from an initial state to a goal state can be explicitly defined and performed by a user who is a process specialist for the goal, or implied by delegating the task to a programmatic process specialist.

Ideally, tools to analyze a customers product process would automatically populate a product process knowledgebase schema and fact base for use by a planner. A product information management solution must shorten the "Start-up to Pilot" period at an installation by providing not just a toolkit but also templates of process models for users to emulate and modify while becoming familiar with the formal protocol of their actual product life cycle.

A process formalism is fundamental to the problem solving capability of the process manager. The primary formalism for expressing process is a multi-factor precedence graph. In this formalism, a user can create graphic nodes which express divergence, convergence and alternatives for sub-goals. Canzi, Guida,Poloni & Pozzi [6] combined a technology AND/OR tree with temporal constraints and quality factors for a scheduler for complex manufacturing environments. The temporal model allows for minimum and maximum bounding between tasks. The quality factors allow for the evaluation of the cumulated negative quality impact from OR arcs in the technology tree. This scheme seems generalizable to the entire product process(Figure 4).

Representation interchangeability in the user interface for plan refinement is essential. For example, Waters [22] in reviewing their KBEmacs effort stated that although users devised plans to generate the initial passes of their code, programmers still preferred to edit program text instead of the plans. Changes made via the sub-goal debugger in the native process language must be able to change the plan.

A large collection of process steps and rules will not be randomly clustered together. Instead, a network of process specialists, some explicitly directed by users, will preside over the execution of the product process plan. Brown and Chandrasekaran [3] successfully used process specialists arranged in a hierarchy for routine design. Similarly, Ray [15] supports the development of specialists, process reasoning modules, which have access to deterministic models for parameters in the product process like heat transfer,electrical conductivity and mechanical stress. The process specialists of the process manager in this paper are configured in a semantic network, not a hierarchy(Figure 5).

Process Blackboard

The process manger utilizes a blackboard as the common workspace for product abstraction and process advancement. (Figure 3). The interprocess and intraprocess activity as well as the process specialist activity is instantiated on the blackboard. Nii [12,13] provides a thorough two part review of the blackboard model and working systems which are effectively utilizing it. Dodhiawala, Jagannathan,Baum and Skillman [8] in their report on the first workshop on blackboard systems identify the issues relevant to this technology. A blackboard is a representation mechanism in which transactions are focused through a controller which posts relevant information to a central location for global utilization by applications. The applications which use and manipulate the blackboard data structures are called knowledge sources. This technology assumes cooperating applications, knowledge sources, are collectively utilizing the blackboard to advance the solution state. A blackboard controller determines which knowledge source can execute against the blackboard.

The process manager blackboard implementation style is similar to DICE [19] in that an object oriented model for control is utilized. In this approach, a great deal of controller burden is encapsulated in the objects themselves. The primary differences will be the utilization of semantic aggregations. As a consequence, the explicit constraints are made available for reasoning.

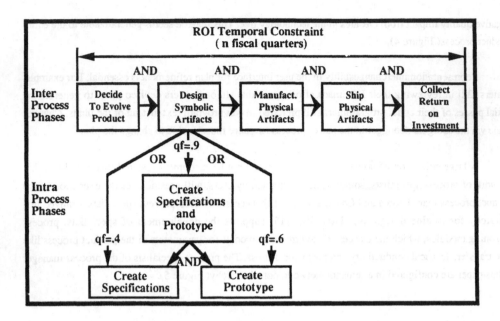

Figure 4. Example Interphase and Intraphase Process Specification. Constraints such as the ROI temporal constraint can be established between process nodes. Quality factors can be associated to the OR arcs.

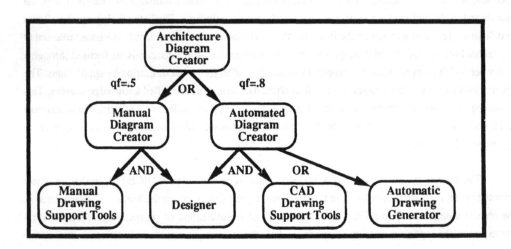

Figure 5. Example Process Specialist Network. Quality factors can be associated to the OR arcs. A plan will result in the superimposition of the process specialist network over the process network in conformance to constraints.

Process Sensors

A process sensor is a probe into the environment of the symbolic artifact support tools like editors, spreadsheet applications, report generators and CAE/CAD/CAM workstation applications. The responsibility of the sensor is to generate information about some product process activity, not to change the physical state. A user customizable toolkit is necessary to:

1) configure process sensors into the process specialist network,

2) create a process sensor(Figure 6)

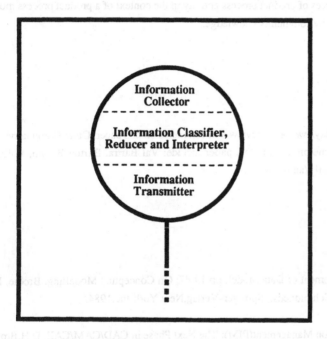

Figure 6. Anatomy of a Process Sensor

In order to create a process sensor, an information collector must be enabled, an information classifier must be enabled and an information transmitter must be linked to one or more process specialists.

Conclusion

This paper provides supporting ideas for the assertion that active process facilitators can induce product abstraction evolution. A framework was developed to sustain a driving function based on process phase, independent of but causal to product abstraction specialization.

Evolution of the intradomain life cycle representations can be accomplished by procedurally forcing standardized intraprocess specific VDAG alternative expansions. This approach supports concurrent engineering within a product process phase.

Evolution of the interdomain life cycle representations is far more complex. Interdomain life cycle representation evolution requires selective refinement of the constraint network in order to conform to the specifications derived from sources of product process activity in the context of a product process model which is dynamically influenced by community knowledge.

Acknowledgements

Many thanks to Chuck Mayhew for his review and comments on this paper. Other Computervision colleagues who struggled with me on ideas in this paper include: Val Bartra, Burton Bloom, William Harrelson, John Senna and Mikhail Vainshtein.

Reference List

[1] Brodie,M.L. On the Development of Data Model, pp.19-47; On Conceptual Modelling. Brodie, M., Mylopoulos,J.and J.W. Schmidt,eds., Springer-Verlag,New York Inc.1984.

[2] Brown, D. Product Information Management(PIM): The Next Phase in CAD/CAM/CAE. D.H.Brown Associates, Inc.1989.

[3] Brown,D.C. and B. Chandrasekaran. Knowledge and Control for a Mechanical Design Expert System. IEEE Computer Magazine, Special Issue, July 1986.

[4] Brodie,M., R. Balzer, G. Wiederhold, R. Brachman, J. Mylopoulos. Knowledge Base Management Systems: Discussions from the Working Group, pp.19-26; Expert Database Systems; Kerschberg,L.,ed., The Benjamin/Cummings Publishing Co.,Inc.1986.

[5] Brachman,R and H. Levesque. What Makes a Knowledgebase Knowledgeable? A View of Databases from the Knowledge Level, pp. 69-78; Expert Database Systems; Kerschberg,L.,ed., The Benjamin/Cummings Publishing Co.,Inc.1986.

[6] Canzi, U. , G. Guida,W. Poloni and S. Pozzi. CRONOS-II. A Knowledge-based Scheduler for Complex Manufacturing Environments. Proceedings from Second International Conference on Data and Knowledge Systems for Manufacturing and Engineering. IEEE 89CH2806-8. pp.76-83. 1989.

[7] Cheeseman, P. Uncertainty and Planning: A Summary. Workshop Report: DARPA Santa Cruz Workshop on Planning , W. Swartout, Editor, AI Magazine. Vol. 9:2. 1988.

[8] Dodhiawala, R. , V. Jagannathan, L. Baum and T. Skillman. Workshop Report: The First Workshop on Blackboard Systems. AI Magazine. Vol. 10:1. 1989.

[9] Geol, V and P. Pirolli. Motivating the Notion of Generic Design within Information Processing Theory: The Design Problem Space. AI Magazine. Vol. 10:1. 1989.

[10] Kostovetsky , A and M. Silvestri . A Taxonomy-Based Knowledge Representation Technique for Extending the Relational Model. Proceedings of the International Symposium of New Directions in Computing , IEEE 85CH2134-5 , pp. 72-79 . 1985.

[11] McGoveran,D. The Power of Stored Procedures. Database Programming and Design. Vol. 2:9. 1989.

[12] Nii , H.P . Blackboard Systems : The Blackboard Model of Problem Solving and the Evolution of Blackboard Architectures , Part One. AI Magazine, 7:2 , pp. 38-53 .1986(a).

[13] Nii , H.P . Blackboard Systems : The Blackboard Model of Problem Solving and the Evolution of Blackboard Architectures , Part Two. AI Magazine,7:3, pp. 82-106. 1986(b).

[14] PDES Product Structure and Configuration Management, ISO TC184/SC4/WG1, Part 44, 1990.

[15] Ray, S. Process Reasoning. Proceedings of the IFIP WG5.7 Working Conference on Information Flow in Automated Manufacturing Systems. 1987.

[16] Reimer, U. A System-Controlled Multi-type Specialization Hierarchy. pp. 173-187. Expert Database Systems; Kerschberg,L.,ed., The Benjamin/Cummings Publishing Co.,Inc. 1986.

[17] Shepherd,A. and L. Kerschberg. Constraint Management in Expert Database Systems, pp. 309-331 . Expert Database Systems; Kerschberg,L.,ed., The Benjamin/Cummings Publishing Co.,Inc. 1986.

[18] Silvestri,M.J. Dual Design Partners in an Incremental Redesign Environment; (in preparation for print) .Tong,C. and D. Sriram, eds.

[19] Sriram,D. and R. Logcher. Cooperative Engineering Design. Knowledge-based System Applications in Engineering Design: Research at MIT. D. Sriram, G. Stephanopoulos, R. Logcher, D. Gossard, N. Groleau, D. Serrano and D. Navinchandra. AI Magazine. Vol 10:3. 1989.

[20] Stonebraker,M. Adding Semantic Knowledge to a Relational Database System, pp.333-353; On Conceptual Modelling. Brodie, M., Mylopoulos,J. and J.W. Schmidt,eds., Springer-Verlag,New York Inc. 1984.

[21] Tyler,J. DRAFT. A Repository of Meta Constructs for Product Data Exchange Specification (PDES). National Institute of Standards and Technology, Md. 1989.

[22] Waters, R.C. KBEmacs: Where's the AI? . AI Magazine , 7:1 , pp. 47-56. 1985.

[23] Workshop Proceedings for Databases in Large AI Systems, eds. F. Golshani and O. Friesen.1988.

[24] Yu,L. and D. Rosenkrantz. Ancestor-Controlled Submodule Inclusion in Design Databases. Proceedings from Second International Conference on Data and Knowledge Systems for Manufacturing and Engineering. IEEE 89CH2806-8. pp.28-37. 1989.

ATTACHMENT A: PROFILE OF TWO COMPETING EXPERT MACHINES IN THE DUAL DESIGN PARTNER ARCHITECTURE

STABILIZER	INNOVATOR
Uses more algorithms than heuristics	Uses more heuristics than algorithms
Algorithms tend to be those used to run well defined subprocesses	Algorithms tend to be those used to support the generation and validation of new hypothetical product models.
Familiar strategies are : Copy and Edit Replay Inference using explicit rules created by humans or induced rules approved by humans	Familiar strategies are : Automated knowledge acquisition and computer learning Conceptual clustering /Knowledge organization Reasoning by analogy Introspection
Typically completes entire tasks and usually without error	Typically completes only a portion of tasks ; requires frequent human feedback to refocus ; results are more error prone.
Operates with approved knowledge	Operates with uncertain knowledge
Compensates for human flaws like fatigue in repetitive tasks.	Compensates for human flaws like early termination of the evaluation of alternative hypothesis.
Dominates the product process	Only occasionally has impact on the product process
When faced with competitive goals, this expert machine tends to order goals as was previously ordered in other product histories.	When faced with competitive goals, this expert machine tends to order goals to defer commitments to impose the fewest restrictions on the form of the design solution.

In general , the innovator expert machine requires less explicit rules and control information than the stabilizer expert machine in order to operate. However, the results of the innovator are potentially more error prone than the stabilizer due to uncertain knowledge. As a consequence, this leads to the requirement for frequent feedback to the innovator from the engineering , design and manufacturing community. Both expert machines employ generalization which inherently improves in accuracy as the sample size increases .

A Model Integration Framework for Cooperative Design

Takeshi Kiriyama, Tetsuo Tomiyama and Hiroyuki Yoshikawa

Department of Precision Machinery Engineering
Faculty of Engineering
The University of Tokyo

Abstract: In a CAD system, a design object is represented by various models from different viewpoints. Maintaining relationships among models is part of the expected tasks for intelligent CAD systems. This paper deals with the integration of models of the design object. First, we examinine the nature of a model and two methods to integrate models are compared, viz. integration of background theories of the models and integration on the description level of the models. Second, we propose a framework named metamodel mechanism as a former approach, which uses knowledge about relationships among background theories. Third, we discuss knowledge representation for the metamodel mechanism. The metamodel represents relationships among models by means of symbolic representation of qualitative physics. Last, an example illustrates the integration of a geometric model and a kinematic model by the metamodel mechanism.

1. Introduction

In design of a mechanical artifact, a designer models a design object from various points of view, creating an *aspect model* corresponding to each view. For instance, a motor used in a mechanism is modeled as a source of torque from the viewpoint of dynamics. The same motor can be modeled as a heat source from a viewpoint of heat problem, and a solid object occupying a space from a viewpoint of geometry. These models, viz. the dynamic model, the heat model, and the solid model, are aspect models representing viewpoints of dynamics, heat transfer, and geometry, respectively.

A CAD (Computer Aided Design) system provides the designer with an environment for creating and evaluating various models of the design object. The models must be compatible with each other, so that information obtained from one model can be reflected in others. Furthermore, the system must be easily extended to incorporate a new model: We would like to plug in a new modeler to an existing CAD system. In order to allow for such pluggable modeling modules, product modeling (Mantyla 1989) was proposed as a framework to maintain relationships among data belonging to various aspect models by having geometric information in its center. However, since product modeling is based on geometric modeling, it is not easy to do so if the new modeler contains non-geometric information. For example, a model used for FEM computations may share information with a geometric model. However, the FEM model often ignores minor shape details and its dimensions are not precise but rough estimations. This implies that the interests and the accuracy of models can be different from each other. Nevertheless, we tend to regard them identical, because they represent the identical object.

Designers cope with this problem by using knowledge about models, i.e., knowledge about physics, engineering, etc., from which they deduce relationships among models. It contrasts with product modeling that uses predetermined relationships among aspects. As a part of the development of an ICAD (Intelligent CAD) system (Akman, ten Hagen, and Veerkamp 1989; ten Hagen and Tomiyama 1987; Yoshikawa and Gossard 1989), we aim at incorporating such knowledge to the system in order to integrate aspect models.

This paper addresses the problem of integrating of aspect models. In Chapter 2, we present a framework for integrating models called the *metamodel mechanism* that derives relationships among models from knowledge about physical laws and maintains consistency among them. The concept of the metamodel was first introduced by Tomiyama and Yoshikawa to explain the evolutionary nature of design processes in (Tomiyama and Yoshikawa 1986). It was later extended to include viewpoints of integrating aspect models in an ICAD environment (Tomiyama et al. 1989). In Chapter 3, we give a more formal theory of the metamodel mechanism and show that qualitative physics can be used as its knowledge representation scheme (Kiriyama et al. 1989). Chapter 4 illustrates the way the metamodel mechanism integrates different aspect models in an example. Chapter 5 gives brief comparisons with related work and Chapter 6 concludes the paper.

2. Integration of Models

2.1. A model and its background theory

In this section, we clarify the relationships among an aspect model, a background theory of an aspect model, and a description. An *aspect model* consists of selected properties of a design object. (For the sake of simplicity, a *model* will be used for an aspect model if the context is clear.) The properties may include attributes, elements, structure (i.e., relationships among elements), and physical phenomena involved in the behavior. These properties are called *concepts* in this paper. And we call a class of concept (e.g. weight, length, force, motion) a concept type. There is a *background theory* behind an aspect model, which defines concept types and relationships among concept types. For example, algebraic geometry is the background theory for a boundary representation model. It defines concept types such as vertex, edge, face, and volume, and relationships among concept types such as a line has two points at both ends. There can be different models for the same design object depending on the background theories. Models of the same design object, such as a kinematic model, a dynamic model, a geometric model, a material model, and an elastic model, are generated by applying their own background theories to the design object.

A *description* is a representation of a model itself denoted by a set of symbols. There can be different *descriptive schemes* for one model, each of which maps the model to a description. For instance, a geometric model can have different data structures due to the differences in the descriptive schemes. Fig. 1 depicts the relationships among a design object, a background theory, and its model.

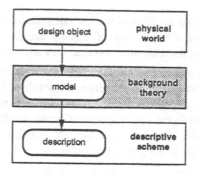

Fig. 1. A design object, a background theory, and its model

2.2. Drawbacks of direct linking among models

Since concepts are not independent of each other but constrained by physical laws, aspect models are related with each other. Relationships among models can be categorized into the following cases.

1. A property is shared by two different models.

2. The same attribute is represented in two models with different accuracy.

3. Properties represented in different models are causally dependent.

4. Attributes are quantitatively constrainted by a physical law.

Models must be kept consistent for these relationships in some way, if they represent a single identical design object. One possible way to maintain the consistency among models is to use relationships constraining properties. Since this method is based on procedures to directly maintain the consistency, we call it *direct linking* among models (see Fig. 2).

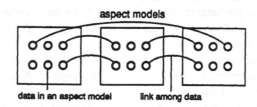

Fig. 2. Direct linking among models

The way product modeling (Mantyla 1989) integrates models falls on this category. It has a set of descriptive schemes for describing different models, and defines transformation rules among descriptive schemes. The direct linking has an advantage about efficiency in updating models. Since all relationships among models are known and fixed beforehand, it requires no reasoning about consistency. However, this architecture is not flexible enough to allow the designer to easily add a new aspect model to a CAD system, because of the following reasons.

1. **Dependence on the descriptive schemes**
   The transformation rules connect not concepts in models but rather descriptions of models. In other words, they define how to update descriptions. Since descriptions depend on the implementation of the CAD system, we cannot assume knowledge about integration of models independently of the descriptions.

2. **Difference in the background theories**
   Each model has its own way to structure the design object, which comes from the difference in the background theories. The transformation rules have also to fill the difference between the background theories besides the descriptive schemes. As a consequence, the rules become complex and difficult to extend.

3. **Integration of models at the surface level**
   A human designer can reason about relationships among models from *deep* knowledge about models themselves. This does not apply to the direct linking, because the transformation rules are not supported by such knowledge. In other word, the rules must be fixed at the time descriptions are made and represent only *surface* relationships. Therefore, maintenance of rules is difficult when extending the system.

These drawbacks result from the problem that the rules represent only surface relationships and are not supported by the knowledge about physics and engineering. To avoid this problem, relationships among models must be reasoned about from the relationships among concepts in the background theories, and therefore we need a knowledge base that defines and contains concepts with respect to the relationships to other concepts. The *metamodel mechanism* aims at integration of models with such a knowledge base and maintains relationships among models (Kiriyama et al. 1989). Integration by the metamodel mechanism contrasts with the integration by direct linking in that the former is integration at the level of the background theories (see Fig. 3) and is based on knowledge about the modeling framework itself, which is missing from the latter.

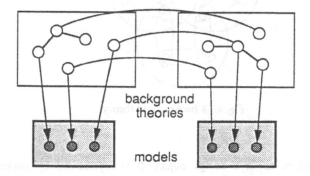

Fig. 3. Integration of models

3. Metamodel

3.1. Definitions of background theories and models

In this chapter, we formally introduce the metamodel mechanism. We begin with defining background theories and models and then defining the metamodel mechanism as an integration of background theories.

Let c_i be a concept and T_i be a unary predicate denoting a concept type. $T_i(c_j)$ represents that c_j belongs to concept type T_i. We use a predicate, R_i, to denote a relationship among concepts such as $R_i(c_1,\dots,c_m)$. L_λ stands for a physical law over a set of concept types $T_\lambda = \{T_1,\dots,T_\kappa\}$ and a set of relationships $R_\lambda = \{R_1,\dots,R_\mu\}$. It constrains relationships among concepts $c_1,\dots,c_m$ belonging to concept types T_λ, such that

$$L_\lambda : R_2(c_{21},\dots,c_{2m}) \wedge \cdots \wedge R_\mu(c_{\mu 1},\dots,c_{\mu m}) \rightarrow R_1(c_{11},\dots,c_{1m}).$$

This means that relationship $R_1(c_{11},\dots,c_{1m})$ holds when $c_1,\dots,c_m$ satisfy the prerequisite relationships in the right hand.

A background theory M is determined by a set of physical laws $L = \{L_\lambda\}$. A physical law L_λ contains a set of concept types T_λ and relationships R_λ, thus a set of physical laws $L = \{L_\lambda \mid \lambda \in \Lambda\}$ form a collection of concept types $T = \bigcup_{\lambda \in \Lambda} T_\lambda$ and relationships $R = \bigcup_{\lambda \in \Lambda} R_\lambda$. Therefore, a background theory consists of sets of concept types T, relationships R, and physical laws L as follows (Fig. 4).

$$M = <T, R, L>.$$

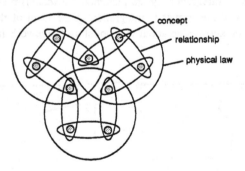

concept

relationship

physical law

Fig. 4. A background theory

An aspect model m about a design object O is represented by concepts and their relationships. It is generated by applying physical laws L of a background theory. For each physical law $L_i \in L$ that is applicable to O, concepts and relationships included in L_i are added to the aspect model m. As a result, m is generated as a pair of concepts c and relationships r satisfying L, such that

$$m = <c, r> ; \ c = \{c_i\}, \ r = \{R_i(c_{i1},\dots,c_{im})\}.$$

Fig. 5 depicts a background theory **M**, a model **m**, and a description **D(m)** about an oscillation model. The background theory defines concepts

T = {position, velocity, acceleration, object, wall, particle, damper, spring, $\cdots$ }

and relationships

R = {connection, weight, elasticModulus, $\cdots$ }.

The model is mapped to a differential equation **D(m)** by the descriptive scheme **D**.

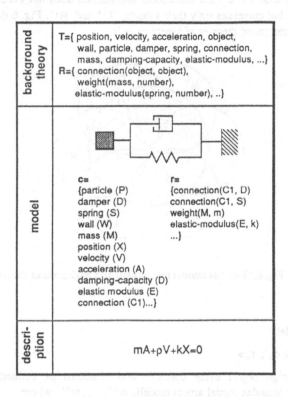

Fig. 5. A model of oscillation

3.2. The metamodel mechanism

There can be different models based on different background theories for the same design object. In the following discussion, *aspect models* are indexed as $m^1, \ldots, m^n$ to distinguish aspects. The metamodel mechanism plays the role of the central background theory that includes all the aspect-dependent background theories.

The *metamodel mechanism* M_o for background theories $M^1, \ldots, M^n$ is defined by

$M_o = < T_o , R_o , L_o >,$

where

$$T_o = T^* \cup T^{1*} \cup \cdots \cup T^{a*},$$

$$R_o = R^* \cup R^{1*} \cup \cdots \cup R^{a*}.$$

T^* and R^* are concept types and relationships that do not belong to any particular background theory, but involved in the physical laws L_o. They are necessary for the metamodel mechanism to integrate background theories. T^{i*} and R^{i*} are subsets of T^i and R^i, respectively. Since T^i and R^i are constrained by L^i, the metamodel mechanism does not necessarily have to know about T^i and R^i, but correlates only their subsets, T^{i*} and R^{i*}. Fig. 6 depicts the metamodel mechanism and background theories of aspect models.

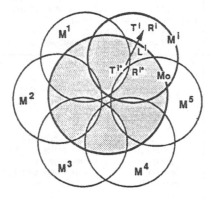

Fig. 6. The metamodel mechanism and background theories

The metamodel

$$m_o = < c_o , r_o >$$

represents the design object using concepts and relationships defined by the metamodel mechanism M_o. It includes partial aspect models, $m^{1*}, \ldots, m^{n*}$, where

$$m^{i*} = < c^{i*}, r^{i*} > ; \quad c^{i*} \subset c^i, \ r^{i*} \subset r^i.$$

An aspect model m^i is generated from the metamodel m_o by a transformation F^i and physical laws L^i. F^i selects concepts and relationships about the aspect model from m_o. m^{i*} is obtained by applying F^i to m_o;

$$F^i(m_o) = m^{i*}.$$

Physical laws L^i in the background theory are used to derive a complete aspect model m^i from m^{i*};

$$m^{i*} \cup L^i \vdash m^i.$$

Fig. 7 illustrates the relationship among the metamodel and aspect models.

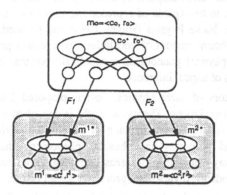

Fig. 7. The metamodel and aspect models

The metamodel mechanism maintains relationships among aspect models as follows. Suppose an aspect model m^i is modified such that $m^{i'} = \langle c^{i'}, r^{i'} \rangle$. Consequently the metamodel m_o is changed to

$$\tilde{m}_o = \langle \tilde{c}_o, \tilde{r}_o \rangle.$$

The metamodel mechanism updates $\tilde{m}_o$ to $m_o' = \langle c_o', r_o' \rangle$ by changing concepts and relationships so that m_o' satisfies L_o. Corresponding to the change of the metamodel, a related aspect model m^i is changed to $m^{i'}$ through m^{i*} as follows.

$$F^i(m_o') = m^{i*},$$

$$m^{i*} \cup L^i \vdash m^{i'}.$$

3.3. Incorporating an aspect model

The metamodel is extended when a new aspect model is added. Suppose that the current metamodel mechanism $M_o = \langle T_o, R_o, L_o \rangle$ integrates models based on the background theories $M^1, \ldots, M^n$, and we add a new background theory

$$M^{n+1} = \langle T^{n+1}, R^{n+1}, L^{n+1} \rangle.$$

Subsets of T^{n+1} and R^{n+1}, viz. T^{n+1*} and R^{n+1*}, are chosen to be concepts and relationships organized by the metamodel mechanism. They are added to T_o and R_o of the metamodel mechanism. Thus T^* and R^* of the metamodel mechanism are extended to correlate T^{n+1*} and R^{n+1*} with the current T_o and R_o. Note that we need modification of the metamodel mechanism only about the relationship between the previous concepts and the newly integrated concepts. Extension of the modeling system will cost more if we use the direct linking, since the direct linking needs to define relationships between each $\langle T^i, R^i \rangle$ and $\langle T^{n+1}, R^{n+1} \rangle$. The metamodel mechanism requires less complexity to incorporate a new background theory, because it only needs new definitions about relationships among $\langle T_o, R_o \rangle$ and $\langle T^{n+1}, R^{n+1} \rangle$.

3.4. Descriptive scheme of the metamodel

The metamodel is represented on a computer by a descriptive scheme. The descriptive scheme of the metamodel is required to be capable of representing concepts and relationships of various aspects. For this purpose, Naive Physics (Hayes 1985) can be used. The approach of naive physics is to establish sufficient amount of vocabulary to represent physical phenomena in the real world. It represents physical phenomena symbolically so that reasoning about physical world is possible by means of logical inference.

As a computable theory of naive physics, Forbus proposed Qualitative Process Theory (Forbus 1984). In Qualitative Process Theory, a world is described by *individuals, individual views, processes*. Individuals are objects existing in the world, individual views are particular states of individuals, and processes are physical phenomena that change the situation. Individuals exist without any prerequisite, whereas individual views and processes can be active only when the prerequite individual views and processes are all active.

As the descriptive scheme for the metamodel, we employ Qualitative Process theory. Individuals are applied to describe concepts about elements of the design object, individual views to concepts about combinations of individuals, and processes to concepts about physical phenomena that appear on the design object. The fact that an individual view or a process becomes active assuming prerequisite individual views or processes represents that a relationships holds among them. Physical laws are represented as definitions of prerequisites of individual views and processes. When a model is modified, validity of activation of individual views and processes are evaluated, and new individual views and processes are created. Thus concepts, relationships, and physical laws are represented using individual views and processes.

4. Implementation of the Metamodel Mechanism

4.1. Integration of a geometric model and a kinematic model

In this chapter, we illustrate integration of the metamodel mechanism with an example (Veerkamp et al. 1990; Xue et al. 1990) about a linear motion mechanism shown in Fig. 8. The mechanism consists of a link with a slot and a slider that can move along the slot. The geometric aspect model m^a of this slider mechanism S models the shapes of the link and the slider. The kinematic aspect model m^k models start and end points of motion, together with the stroke as the distance between the two points. The start and end points are determined by the shape of the slot and the slider, thus the geometric model and the kinematic model have relationships between them.

The two-dimensional geometric model m^a represents S as a collection of faces of the link and the slider, as in Fig. 9. A node in the figure is a concept, and an arc is a relationship between concepts. Each face is associated with its start and end points, and a normal vector.

The kinematic model m^k represents S as a mechanism whose object–in–motion, viz. the slider, performs bounded–linear–motion along the guide, viz. the slot. bounded–linear–motion is associated with start–position, end–position, direction–of–motion, and stroke. Direction–of–motion is a

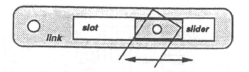

Fig. 8. A slider mechanism

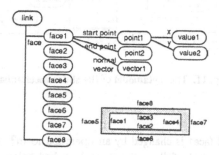

Fig. 9. The geometric model of the slider mechanism

subclass of vector, and stroke is a subclass of distance. The physical laws L^K of the kinematic background theory defines the stroke as the distance between a start–position and an end–position of a bounded–linear–motion. Fig. 10 depicts the kinematic model.

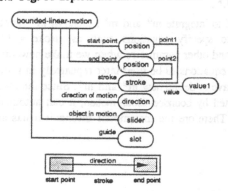

Fig. 10. The kinematic model of the slider mechanism

Fig. 11 illustrates the metamodel m_0 for integrating m^G and m^K. Faces face1, ..., face4 of m^G belong to the slot. The slot delegates the guide of m^K and is regarded as identical to the guide of m^K. The start and end points of the bounded–linear–motion are determined by limit–arrangements between the slot and slider. The positions of the slider in contact with the slot at the two limit–arrangements are the start and the end point of bounded–linear–motion.

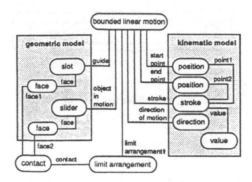

Fig. 11. The metamodel of the slider mechanism

If the start-position of face1 is changed by an operation to m^G, the stroke of m^K must be updated. Calculation of the stroke follows the steps described below. The modification to m^G corresponds to the change in x and y of face1. Limit-arrangement1 has a relationship with contact1, and contact1 is again related with face1. Therefore the metamodel mechanism can deduce that limit-arrangement1 must be updated. Physical laws L_o of the metamodel mechanism define that the position of a limit-arrangement is the position of an object-in-motion whose face is in contact with a face of a guide. By applying L_o to m_o, the metamodel mechanism derives the new start-position from m^G. Then the start-position of m^K is updated and m^K calculates the new stroke with its own physical laws L^K.

If direct linking is used to integrate m^G and m^K, stroke in m^K is related directly to x and y. It means that we have to specify equations such as stroke = $\| point1 - point2 \|$ for calculating stroke from x, y and other parameters when we make new m^G and m^K. This strategy is efficient, once we define equations to be used later repeatedly in routine design. However, it does not help us when we have to define new m^G and m^K. Since the metamodel m_o knows how stroke and x , y are correlated by bounded-linear-motion, it can automatically reason about the relationships among them. Therefore the metamodel mechanism has advantage in integrating models.

4.2. The metamodel system

We implemented a system to embody the metamodel mechanism. The system runs on an object-oriented language Smalltalk-80[1] (Goldberg and Robson 1983). Concept types used by the metamodel mechanism are realized as classes of Smalltalk objects. Concepts are instantiated by the instantiation mechanism of Smalltalk. When a value associated with a concept is changed, the change is informed to relevant concepts by sending messages. If a concept accepts an updating message, the metamodel mechanism takes an action according to the concept type of the concept. Updating relationships of some concepts requires the metamodel mechanism to

---

[1] Smalltalk-80 is a Registered Trademark of Xerox Corp.

refer to aspect models. For instance, the metamodel mechanism asks the geometric model to recalculate limit–position of object–in–motion in order to update the relationship between limit–position and its value.

Fig. 12 shows the metamodel for the slider mechanism above. The graph displayed in the center window is the metamodel. Rectangular nodes are instances of concepts, and arcs are relationships. The lower left and right windows show the geometric model and the kinematic model, respectively. If a user changes a value in the geometric model, it is propagated by the metamodel to the kinematic model.

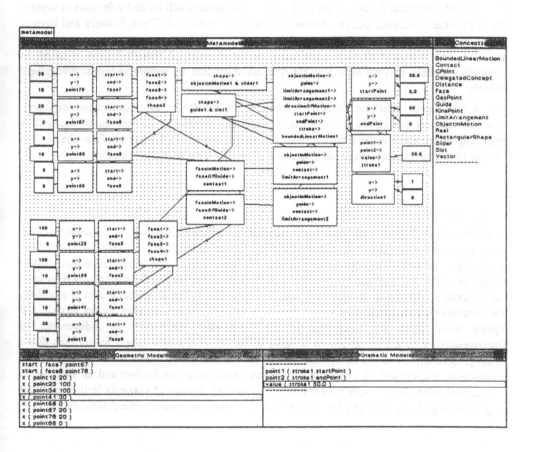

Fig. 12. Implementation of the metamodel mechanism

5. Related Work

There is some work in artificial intelligence related to this research. Murthy developed a design system PROMPT (Murthy and Addanki 1987) that has knowledge to update models of the design object. Modification operators of PROMPT are used to change the structure of the design object, and at the same time operators also change model. According to Murthy, changes of the model are derivable from principal physical laws. Nevertheless, if all modification operators are already known, it is more efficient to associate them with procedures to modify models. The major difference between the metamodel mechanism and PROMPT is that the former does not confine modifications to the design object, whereas the latter allows only restricted operations.

The collection of concepts about elements, structures, and physical phenomena of the metamodel mechanism can be used to qualitatively represent the design object in the conceptual design. If known combinations of concepts are prepared by a CAD system as a standard library, the designer can utilize them to build the qualitative structure and behavior. We call such a combination a *physical feature*. Collection of physical features will be useful in order to support the designer in conceptual design. Edison developed by Dyer *et al.* (Dyer, Flowers, and Hodges 1986) aims at the same goal. The object representation of Edison employs device topology and processes that represent physical phenomena on the devices. Although Edison is based on qualitative models, it is not clear how the qualitative models are related to quantitative aspect models.

A new aspect model can be derived from the metamodel by using qualitative reasoning. The relationships among the derived model and other models are found during qualitative reasoning as prerequisite conditions for the new aspect model. Falkenhainer (Falkenhainer and Forbus 1988), for instance, discusses generation of models by qualitative reasoning.

6. Conclusions

In this paper, we discussed integration of aspect models of the design object. An intelligent CAD system must correlate apsect models not at the level of descriptions but at the level of their background theories. We proposed the metamodel mechanism, that integrates aspect models using knowledge about relationship among their background theories. The metamodel represents aspect models in terms of concepts and their relationships. When an aspect model is modified, the metamodel mehcanism uses knowledge to deduce influences to other aspect models and update them. Since the integration of the metamodel mechanism is independent of implementations of aspect models, it is easier to incorporate a new aspect model than direct linking. Qualitative Process Theory can be used for knowledge representation of the metamodel mechanism. We showed an implementation of the metamodel mechanism and an example of model integration. Future work includes collecting enough amount of concepts (estimated fairly large), and organizing them as a knowledge base for model integration and a design library.

References

Varol Akman, Paul J.W. ten Hagen, and Paul J. Veerkamp (eds.) (1989): *Intelligent CAD Systems II: Implementational Issues*, Springer-Verlag, Berlin.

M.G. Dyer, M. Flowers, and J. Hodges (1986): "Edison: An Engineering Design Invention System Operating Naively," in *Applications of Artificial Intelligence in Engineering Problems*, D. Sriram and R. Adey (eds.), Springer-Verlag, Berlin, pp. 327-341.

B. Falkenhainer and K.D. Forbus (1988): "Setting large Scale Qualitative Models," in *Proceedings of AAAI-88*, pp. 301-306.

K.D. Forbus (1984): "Qualitative Process Theory," *Artificial Intelligence*, 24(3), pp. 85-168.

A. Goldberg and D. Robson (1983): *Smalltalk-80: The language and Its Implementation*, Addison Wesley, Reading, MA.

P. Hayes (1985): "The second naive physics manifesto," in *Formal Theories of the Commonsense World*, J.R. Hobbs and R.C. Moore (eds.), Ablex Publishing, pp. 1-36.

T. Kiriyama, F. Yamamoto, T. Tomiyama, and H. Yoshikawa (1989): "Metamodel; An Integrated Modeling Framework for Intelligent CAD Systems," in *Artificial Intelligence in Design*, J.S. Gero (ed.), Computational Mechanics Publications, Southampton, pp. 429-449.

M. Mantyla (1989): "Directions for Research in Product modeling," in *Computer Applications in Production and Engineering (CAPE´89)*, F. Kimura and A. Rolstadas (eds.), North-Holland, Amsterdam, pp. 71-85.

S.S. Murthy and S. Addanki (1987): "PROMPT: An Innovative design Tool," in *Proceedings of AAAI-87*, pp. 637-642.

Paul J.W. ten Hagen and Tetsuo Tomiyama (eds.) (1987): *Intelligent CAD Systems I: Theoretical and Methodological Aspects*, Springer-Verlag, Berlin.

T. Tomiyama and H. Yoshikawa (1986): "Extended general design theory ," in *Design Theory for CAD, Proceedings of the IFIP WG5.2 Working Conference 1985, Tokyo*, H. Yoshikawa and E.A. Warman (eds.), North-Holland, Amsterdam, pp. 95-130.

Tetsuo Tomiyama, Takashi Kiriyama, Hideaki Takeda, Deyi Xue, and Hiroyuki Yoshikawa (1989): "Metamodel: A key to intelligent CAD systems," *Research in Engineering Design*, 1(1), pp. 19-34.

P.J. Veerkamp, T. Kiriyama, D. Xue, and T. Tomiyama (1990): "Representation and Implementation of Design Knowledge for Intelligent CAD – Theoretical Aspects," in *Proceedings of the Fourth Eurographics Workshop on Intelligent CAD: The Added Value of Intelligence*, pp. 184-205.

D. Xue, T. Kiriyama, P.J. Veerkamp, and T. Tomiyama (1990): "Representation and Implementation of Design Knowledge for Intelligent CAD – Implementational Aspects," in *Proceedings of the Fourth Eurographics Workshop on Intelligent CAD: The Added Value of Intelligence*, pp. 206-226.

H. Yoshikawa and D.C. Gossard (eds.) (1989): *Intelligent CAD, I*, North-Holland, Amsterdam.

TOWARDS A FRAMEWORK FOR CONCURRENT DESIGN

Sarosh N. Talukdar   *Steven J. Fenves*

Engineering Design Research Center
Carnegie Mellon University
Pittsburgh, PA   15213
412-268-8778

ABSTRACT

By a "framework for concurrent design" we mean three things: (1) formal ways of stating the problems of concurrent design, (2) visualization (conceptualization) aids to help devise strategies for solving these problems, and (3) implementation aids to help translate the strategies into working systems.

This paper begins by defining some terms, including "conflict," and "computational path." Next, concurrent design problems are formulated in these terms. Specifically, these problems are shown to be equivalent to finding computational paths that avoid or eliminate conflicts and connect given data-objects to desired data-objects. A class of graphs, called TAO graphs, is developed for visualizing such paths. Finally, a computational environment, called FORS, is described for implementing selected paths.

INTRODUCTION

The design of a complex artifact, such as a car, a bridge or a microelectronic chip, involves a large number of tasks each requiring a different sets of skills. Often, the groups to whom such tasks are assigned work on their assignments at different times and in different places. Nevertheless, their work must be coordinated to take into account the couplings among the tasks. Because of these couplings, decisions made in one task can affect some or all of the others. The decisions made in the early conceptual tasks are of particular concern. These decisions can have profound effects on all the tasks that come later. Often, these effects are deleterious, making it difficult or impossible to perform the later tasks well.

The concurrent design problem can be stated simply as follows: how can the propagation of deleterious effects from one task to another be reduced to tolerable levels? (Henceforth, we will refer to intolerable effects as conflicts or inconsistencies). Strategies for solving the concurrent design problem can be divided into two broad categories:

1. Preventive or look-ahead strategies which seek to anticipate conflicts and avoid them before they occur.
2. Corrective or feedback strategies which allow conflicts to occur and then use backtracking or iteration to eliminate them.

Corrective action is usually more time consuming and therefore, less desirable than preventive action.

Existing techniques for both prevention and correction tend to be people-intensive and cumbersome. Typically, experts from each of the major design areas are assembled into a group that oversees the design project from start to finish. This requires considerable commitments from the experts and powerful mechanisms to transcend the communication barriers that inevitably arise among them.

To help automate prevention and correction processes we propose a visualization aid called a TAO graph. Nodes in this graph denote the declarative portions of design work while directed arcs denote the procedural portions.

We think of the declarative portions of a design as a set of data-objects each containing information on one view or aspect of the artifact being designed. A set of specifications, a set of sketches, a set of blueprints, a parts list, a manufacturing plan, and a prototype are some of the very many different aspects of a car.

Both the inputs and the outputs of design processes can be expressed in terms of aspects and a general form of the design problem is: given the values of certain input aspects and the types of the desired output aspects, find values for the output aspects that are consistent with the inputs and one another. For example, given the specifications of an automobile engine, find or develop blueprints and a manufacturing plan that are consistent with (meet) the specifications and are also consistent with each other.

The procedures by which design problems are solved can be divided into two categories: manual procedures (that are executed through humans) and automatic procedures (that are executed through computers). We visualize both types of procedures as operators that map the contents of one data-object into another (i.e., one aspect into another). Thus, we visualize design activity, both manual and automatic, as tracing paths through TAO graphs. These paths begin at given, input aspects and pass through operators and intermediate aspects to terminate at output aspects. For the activity to be successful, the output aspects must be consistent with one another and the input aspects.

By displaying the different computational paths that link input and output aspects, TAO graphs provide a way for both visualizing design problems and planning strategies for solving them. However, before they can be used, a number of terms such as aspect, operator and consistency, must be more precisely defined. We will suggest definitions for these terms in the immediately following material. The remainder of the paper is devoted to a description of FORS, a programming environment for implementing strategies for solving concurrent design problems.

TERMINOLOGY

Aspects

Let A_1, A_2,---, be sets or spaces and let $a_{i,1}$, $a_{i,2}$,--- be elements or points of A_i, such that $a_{i,j}$ is the j-th instance of the i-th view or feature of an artifact. To illustrate, consider an artifact whose i-th feature is a resistive circuit that is known to have 10 or less nodes. Then $a_{i,1}$, $a_{i,2}$,---, are all the different resistive configurations that are possible with 10 or less nodes and $A_i = \{ a_{i,1}, a_{i,2},--- \}$.

We will refer to the a's as aspects and to the A's as aspect-spaces or data-objects depending on whether we are discussing concepts or programming implementations.

Operators

An operator is a mapping from one aspect-space to another. Thus, the general form of an operator is:

$$O_{i,j} : A_i \rightarrow A_j \quad \text{or} \quad a_j = O_{i,j}(a_i) \tag{1}$$

where A_i is the input-aspect-space of the operator and A_j is its output-aspect-space.

A Taxonomy of Operators

Three dimensions are useful in classifying design operators. They are:

1. Degree of autonomy. This dimension can be used to divide operators into three categories:

-autonomous: operators that act largely on their own volition, for instance, most human designers.

-semiautonomous: operators that will accept commands but can also act on their own volition, for instance, intelligent programs that go looking for tasks when they are not busy with tasks that have been assigned to them.

-non autonomous: operators that do nothing until they are assigned a specific task, for instance, conventional simulation and analysis programs.

2. Effect on information content. This dimension deals with the relative information content and location of an operator's input and output aspects, a_i and a_j. Based on this dimension, operators are divided into four categories (Fig. 1):

-abstractors: a_j has less detail than a_i

-refiners: a_j has more detail than a_i

-translators: a_j and a_i are informational equivalents

-modifiers: a_i and a_j are in the same aspect-space.

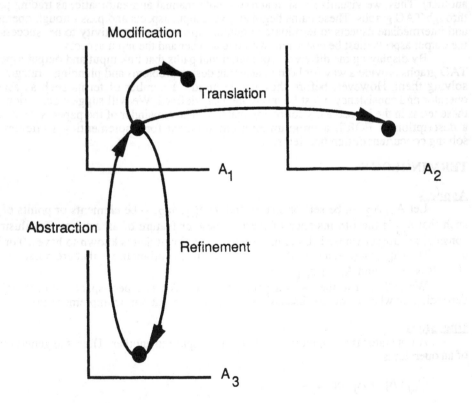

Fig 1: **Four types of operators**
A1 and A2 are informationally equivalent spaces
A3 has more information content than A1

3. Function. This dimension deals with the specific type of transformation performed by an operator. A few of the categories along this dimension are:

Synthesizers : operators that transform specifications into design alternatives;

Analyzers and *simulators* : operators that evaluate the performance or calculate the responses of given alternatives to given stimuli;

Optimizers : operators that improve on design alternatives.

Consistency

Consider two typical aspects: a set of specifications and a set of blueprints. How can one test such aspects for consistency, that is, check to see if the blueprints meet the specifications? In many cases the only practical approach is to transform the blueprints into a physical prototype that is subjected to a number of laboratory tests. In other words, one must select operators to transform the specifications and blueprints into points in a common aspect-space (the space of laboratory experiments) and then check to see if the points are coincident or close. More formally, the ideas involved can be stated as follows:

Aspects a_i and a_j are consistent to degree b, if:

(1) there can be found widely accepted operators $O_{i,k}$ and $O_{j,k}$ that map a_i and a_j into a single space A_k,

(2) there exists a distance metric $\| \cdot \|$ for the space A_k, and

(3) $\| O_{j,k}(a_j) - O_{i,k}(a_i) \| \leq b$ (2)

The selection of the operators and the distance metric imparts a subjective quality to the test that is absent from purer fields, such as mathematical logic, where consistency can be defined objectively. Another difference is that in design it is more convenient to think of consistency as a continuum or fuzzy set rather than as a binary proposition.

Design Tasks

The general design task has the following form:

Given: (1) two aspect spaces, A_{in} and A_{out};

(2) a point (aspect) a_{in} in A_{in};

(3) a consistency threshold b and a test for checking this threshold;

Find: a point a_{out} in A_{out} such that a_{in} and a_{out} are consistent to degree b or better.

Conflicts

Let: AA_{out} be the subset of A_{out} that contains aspects that are consistent with a_{in} to degree b or better. We will say that there is a conflict between the task and its input if AA_{out} is empty. In other words, conflicts are said to occur when there is no solution to a task that is consistent to the required degree with its given input. Such conflicts often occur as the result of the solutions selected for upstream tasks. For instance, the design of the structure of an artifact could make it impossible to manufacture. If allowed to persist, such conflicts result in degradations of quality and performance. Their elimination is the objective of concurrent design.

Computational Paths

By a computational path we mean a partial ordering of operators for solving one or more tasks. To illustrate, consider a simple task that involves solving a pair of nonlinear algebraic equations:

$$x = f(x,y) \qquad (3)$$
$$y = g(x,y) \qquad (4)$$

Let x^*, y^* be a solution to these equations. One iterative algorithm that can be applied to search for this solution is:

$$(P1): \quad x_{n+1} = f(x_n, y_n) \tag{5}$$
$$n,m = 0,1,2,\text{---}$$
$$y_{m+1} = g(x_m, y_m) \tag{6}$$

Another algorithm is:

$$(P2): \quad x_{n+1} = f(x_n, y_+) \tag{7}$$
$$y_{m+1} = g(x_+, y_m) \tag{8}$$

where x_n, y_m are the n-th and m-th approximations to x^*, y^*, and x_+, y_+ are the latest available values of x_n, y_m. Let O_f and O_g be operators for evaluating functions f and g. The partial ordering of these operators corresponding to the two algorithms are shown in Figs. 2 and 3. The first algorithm requires the two operators to be invoked in lock step; every time O_f is invoked O_g must also be invoked. The second algorithm, however, allows the invocations of O_f and O_g to proceed independently (that is, asynchronously). Neither algorithm enjoys a clear superiority over the other; in some cases the first is preferable, in others, the second (Talukdar et al., 1983). In fact, even for this very simple task, there are other partial orderings of operators, each with its own merits, and the number of these orderings increases dramatically if one considers operators besides the two listed above. As we shall see, the problem of designing a good partial ordering of operators for solving this simple task, is in microcosm, the problem of concurrent design.

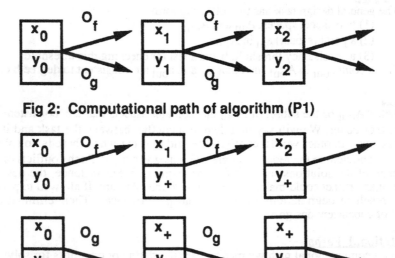

Fig 2: Computational path of algorithm (P1)

Fig 3: Computational path of algorithm (P2)

Design Systems

A design system consists of decision making agents (people and programs) supported by passive resources such as technology bases and laboratories. The agents tend to be arranged in complex hierarchies, that is, structures with multiple levels in which an agent can report to two or more agents in the level above. Some of the agents serve as operators, the others serve as managers. Managers are responsible for setting goals, decomposing large design tasks into smaller tasks and assigning these tasks to operators. As such, the operators occupy the lowest level of the organization.

The purpose of a design systems is to select and implement computational paths for performing given design tasks.

TAO GRAPHS

A TAO graph (the "T" stands for Tao or path in Chinese, the "A" for aspect-space, and the "O" for operator) is an aid for visualizing the capabilities of the lowest level in the organizational structure of a design system, that is, the level in which the operators reside.

A TAO graph is an *and/or* graph whose nodes represent aspect-spaces and whose arcs represent operators. As such, a TAO graph depicts all the paths through a given set of aspect-spaces that are made possible by a given set of operators. Since both aspect-spaces and operators can be aggregated and disaggregated, this perspective can be widened to view the paths for an entire project or narrowed to view an individual task in any desired degree of detail.

The purposes of TAO graphs are (1) to help view available paths and select the best from among them, thereby, aiding in the design of design projects, and (2) to compare the best available paths with desired paths, and thereby, determine how to upgrade an existing design system or design a new design system.

An Example

The Integrated Building Design Environment (IBDE) is a prototype system for the design and construction of high rise, speculative office buildings. IBDE is being assembled to serve as a test bed for the exploration of three sets of issues: (1) the information, control and communication needs of the diverse agents required for the design and construction of a building; (2) the applicability and role of generic tools and design environments in the domain of architectural and civil engineering design; and (3) concurrent design.

IBDE is being developed in two phases. The first phase, which has been completed, involves the integration of seven automatic operators that cover the architectural, structural and foundation design, and the construction planning of high rise buildings. These operators are implemented as knowledge-based systems (KBS's) to facilitate rapid development and modification. While some of the current operators are too limited to serve as models of practical programs, they are comprehensive enough to serve as surrogate experts in exploring the types of design representations and communication mechanisms needed for the concurrent design of buildings and their construction process.

This first phase of IBDE uses the following aspect-spaces:

A1: building owner's targets (area and cost), objectives and constraints
A2: building massing, functional assignments of spaces, vertical circulation area
A3: structural grid: a 3D grid of bays and stories where structural elements can be placed
A4: optimal spatial layout of elevators, stairs, rest rooms etc. occupying the building's core
A5: structural system selection
A6: structural layout and approximate forces acting on structural components
A7: design of structural components

A8: design of foundation components

A9: construction project activities, sequence, costs, durations

A TAO graph of these aspect-spaces and the current complement of operators is shown in Fig. 4. In making available an automatic path that leads all the way from A1, the building's specifications, through several intermediate spaces to a construction plan, IBDE provides a larger scale of design tool integration than any other building design system that we know about. However, notice that there is one and only one path. As we will point out in the next section, concurrent design requires multiple paths and in the second phase of the project, which is now underway, the IBDE team is adding an appropriate set of additional paths.

CONCURRENT DESIGN

Over the last few years, the terms "concurrent design" and "simultaneous engineering," have come to be used for technologies that strive for high quality in a design from several different and often conflicting points of view, such as those taken by the marketers, manufacturers, users, and maintainers of an artifact. Each such group has its own stringent set of specifications that must be met in order for it to consider the artifact to be of high quality. In our terminology this problem can be posed as follows:

Given: a number of design tasks in which each task can have several input aspects, some that are independently specified, others that are computed by previous tasks;

Find: (1) a path to perform each task;

(2) a means for integrating these individual task-paths into a composite path such that all the input and output aspects are consistent (conflict free).

Thus, in essence, the concurrent design problem is one of conflict-free, path integration. As was pointed out earlier, the two basic types of approaches to achieving this sort of integration are preventive and corrective. In the former, conflicts are anticipated and avoided; in the latter, conflicts are allowed to occur and then reduced to tolerable levels through backtracking and iteration. When it is done well, prevention tends to be faster. The difficulties are in the breadth of knowledge required and in the extended horizons over which predictions must be made. To illustrate, consider the IBDE case (Fig. 4). In making massing and space allocation decisions (A->A2), knowledge of all the subsequent design tasks must be brought to bear to predict impacts and potential conflicts to the end of construction planning (A8->A9). As has been pointed out, existing approaches to solving the prevention problem tend to be manual and distributed (a team of experts with a wide enough range of knowledge is assembled to predict and resolve conflicts). Our research has focussed on automating these manual processes. Specifically, we have been investigating the substitution of a team of expert systems, called *critics*, for some or all of the team of human experts. Each critic consists of a simulation, analysis or forecasting program sandwiched between an intelligent pre- and post-processor. The pre-processor is required to:

1. understand the representations used by all the synthesis tasks that might require the services of the critic. For instance, the critic for predicting conflicts with the construction planning task in IBDE (A8->A9 in Fig. 4) must understand the representations used by all the preceding synthesis operations.

2. monitor the progress of these synthesis operations and activate its simulation or forecasting program whenever necessary. For instance, if decisions being made in the A1->A2 operation (Fig. 4) are likely to have effects on construction planning, then the associated critic should activate itself and predict the extent of these effects.

The purpose of the post-processor is to summarize and explain the predicted results.

Thus, a critic is an autonomous operator that contains an analysis or forecasting program augmented with self activation and self explanation capabilities whose collective purpose is the automatic identification of potential downstream conflicts. Once such

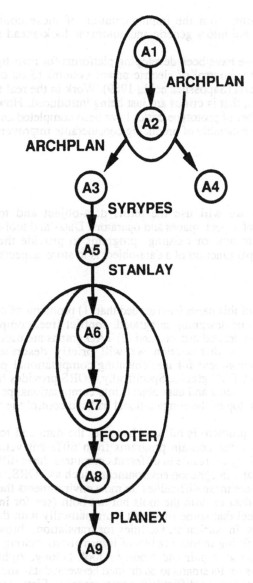

Fig 4. A TAO graph of IBDE

conflicts have been identified they must be resolved. We are in the early stages of developing automatic procedures for conflict resolution.

Ongoing Work

In IBDE, work is now underway to enrich the computational path through the addition of a number of critics and two conflict resolvers, one at the level of spatial conflicts between aspects A3, A4, A5, and the other at the level of construction cost and time conflicts between the owner's targets (A1) and the system's projections (A9). General rules or solutions arising from the implementation of these conflict resolvers may eventually be incorporated into a generic and automatic look-ahead strategy for conflict elimination.

Besides IBDE, we have been developing platforms for investigating critics in two other areas: the real time control of electric power systems (Stoa et al., 1989) and the design of automobile parts (Sapossnek et al., 1989). Work in the real time area is at about the same stage as IBDE, that is critics are just being introduced. However, in the area of automobile parts a number of prototype critics have been completed and from the results of preliminary testing, seem capable of producing considerable improvements in both design time and quality.

FORS

Notation

In this section we will use the terms data-object and tool-object to mean programmed versions of aspect-spaces and operators. Data- and tool-objects are obtained by adding front ends to new or existing programs to provide them with object-like capabilities. The principal function of a data-object is to store aspects; of a tool-object, to transform aspects.

Philosophy

Earlier sections of this paper have argued that (1) problems of concurrent design are equivalent to problems of designing integrated, conflict free, computational paths that connect given aspects to desired aspects; and (2) TAO graphs are useful in visualizing and designing such paths. In this section we will briefly describe FORS (Flexible Organizations), an environment for implementing computational paths that have been designed with the aid of TAO graphs. Specifically, FORS provides facilities to aid in (1) integrating people, tool-objects and data-objects into computational paths; and (2) building control organizations on top of the computational paths to control the flows of information along them.

The integration problem is difficult because the data-and tool -objects that one would like to connect often contain programs from different vendors, are written in different languages and styles, reside in different computers, have different interfaces and use different data formats. Integration environments, such as FORS, provide facilities or "smarts" to help overcome these difficulties. In most environments these smarts tend to be placed either with the data or with the tools but not both (see for instance (Daniell and Director, 1989)). We feel that some smarts fit more naturally with the data, others, more naturally with the tools. In particular, facilities for translation, browsing, detecting and correcting errors, and filling in missing bits of information, belong with the data; while information on how to use, repair and modify a tool, belongs rightfully with the tool. Therefore, FORS allows for its smarts to be divided between data- and tool-objects.

The control problem is difficult for two reasons. First, the control structures required for complex design problems are complex hierarchies (c.f. Section 2.8). However, the experience with automating such hierarchies is limited. In existing design systems automation covers at most the two lowest levels, as in the use of a software structure called a blackboard (Proceedings of the AAAI and Boeing Workshop on Blackboard Systems,1987). All other control is manual.

Second, control structures need to be dynamically adjusted to account for unforeseen contingencies. Invariably, programs will not work as expected, pieces of data will turn up missing, errors will be made, and unforeseen opportunities will appear.

FORS has been designed to allow for the building of complex, dynamically adjustable control structures. However, as yet we have not taken advantage of this capability and its benefits remain to be evaluated.

The following material describes FORS' features in slightly greater detail.

Data-Objects

FORS allows for an expandable library of data-objects. Each of these objects can store one or more aspects and has the facilities to make the aspects available to operators. These facilities include translators (to make aspects available in representation schemes of the operator's choice), error correctors, editors, browsers and default generators (to fill in missing information when necessary). An example is a data-object that is under development for the circuits of electric power networks. When completed, this object will make its contents available in both diagrammatic and tabular forms. Simple errors will be identified and rectified where possible. Typical values of missing information will be supplied when asked for. Both browsing and editing functions will be supported.

To create a new class of data-objects one must develop the mechanisms to support it--representation schemes, translators, etc. This can take a considerable amount of effort. Once the class has been established, however, individual members inherit the support mechanisms and are relatively easy to create.

Tool-Objects

FORS allows for an expandable library of tool-objects. Each of these objects contains a tool or programmed operator that may be written in a number of languages (currently, the list includes: Common Lisp, Fortran-77, C and OPS 5).

Each tool-object also contains a simple template whose contents describe the principal characteristics of the tool, which computer it resides in, how to use it, and which formats it prefers for its input and output data. If the usage patterns and data formats of a new tool are supported by the existing classes of data-objects, then adding the tool to FORS is as simple as filling out the template--a matter of a few minutes. Otherwise, modifications to the classes of data objects are required, and as has already been mentioned, these modifications can require a good deal of effort.

The Interface

FORS has a multi-window interface (Papanikolopoulos, 1989) that has been built on top of DPSK (Cardozo, 1989), a kernel for distributed problem solving, and on a graph display package (Vidovic, 1989). The interface represents each data-object and tool-object by an icon. By arranging these icons to form chains (Fig. 5), the user can create and execute arbitrary computational paths. All the underlying details involved in dealing with a distributed set of heterogeneous computers and programs written in different languages are transparent to the user (provided that the computers are networked and use UNIX).

Automatic Planning and Execution Control

The interface can, of course, be used by people but it can also be used by supervisory programs to construct and modify computational paths. At present, we have only one such program and it is rather simple--given starting and ending data-objects, it identifies all paths that link these objects through available tools. The distributed problem solving facilities that underlie the interface can accommodate much more complicated control structures, including trees and lattices of supervisory programs. The advantages that will accrue from the use of such structures is just beginning to be investigated.

Status and Plans

The basic design, interface and underlying distributed problem solving structure of FORS have been completed. We are proceeding to stock its libraries with objects that will allow the rapid construction of computational paths through a variety of disciplines. Currently, FORS contains about 15 data-objects and 17 tool-objects from the domains of civil, mechanical and electrical engineering. Within a year we expect to add twenty to fifty new objects. These additions will consist primarily of critics and conflict resolvers for the

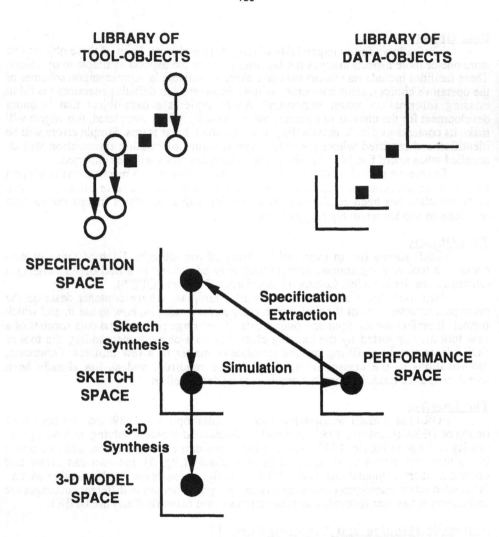

**FIG 5: Constructing and executing computational paths
with the icons in the FORS' Interface**

IBDE project and the other two concurrent design platforms under development, namely, the real time control of power networks and the design of automobile parts.

CONCLUSIONS

This paper has:
1.   defined a set of terms, including aspects, operators, consistency and conflicts, with which to formulate the computational problems of concurrent design;

2.   argued that, good concurrent design is equivalent to constructing integrated, conflict free, computational paths;

3.   suggested that available and desired computational paths be visualized with the aid of TAO graphs whose nodes represent aspect-spaces and whose arcs represent design operators;

4.   described FORS, an integration environment that is being developed for the rapid implementation of integrated, conflict free, computational paths.

As such, the paper provides the beginnings of a framework for handling problems in concurrent design.

REFERENCES

1.   S. N. Talukdar, S. S. Pyo and Ravi Mehrotra, "Distributed Processors for Numerically Intense Problems", Final Report for EPRI Project RP 1764-3, March, 1983.

2.   Petter Stoa, Sarosh Talukdar, Richard Christie, Lily Hou and Nikolaos Papanikolopoulos, "Environments for Security Assessment and Enhancement," presented at the Second Symposium on Expert Systems Applications to Power Systems (ESAPS'89), Seattle, WA, July 17-20, 1989.

3.   Mark Sapossnek, Sarosh Talukdar, Alberto Elfes, Sergio Sedas, Moshe Eisenberger, and Lily Hou, "Design Critics in the Computer-aided Simultaneous Engineering (CASE) Project," Technical Report, EDRC, Carnegie Mellon University, 1989, presented at ASME Winter Annual Meeting, San Francisco, CA., Dec. 11-14, '89.

4.   James Daniell and Steven W. Director, "An Object Oriented Approach to CAD Tool Control Within a Design Framework," Technical Report, EDRC, Carnegie Mellon University, Nov. 18, 1989.

5.   Proceedings of the AAAI and Boeing Workshop on Blackboard Systems: *Implementation Issues*, Seattle, WA, July 1987.

6.   N. Papanikolopolous, "FORS: Flexible Organizations," MS Thesis, Carnegie Mellon University, 1989.

7.   E. Cardozo, "DPSK: A Kernel for Distributed Problem Solving," Ph.D. Thesis, Carnegie Mellon University, 1987.

8.   N. Vidovic, D. Siewiorek, and F. Newberry, "A Graph Based Environment," Technical Report CMUCAD-87, 1987.

Cooperation in Aircraft Design

Alan H. Bond

Manufacturing Engineering Program, University of California
Los Angeles, California 90024

Richard J. Ricci

Automation Systems, Lockheed Aeronautical Systems Company
Burbank, California 91520

Abstract. *We describe how aircraft are designed in a large organization. We discuss the interactions among the different specialist departments during the design process, and the models used by each department. We observe that the main design choices are refinement operations on the design. The overall structure of the organized design process is one of* **coordinated refinement of models.** *We describe how the design negotiation process is controlled by an organizationally agreed sequence of* **commitment steps.** *We briefly discuss design elaboration, for wing design, within one commitment step.*

1 Introduction

The problem of collaborative design. Whereas there is some existing published research on concurrent design requirements and on computer systems for the support of concurrent design, see for example [1] and [2], we know of very little previous work that has reported on existing collaborative design in manufacturing organizations.

We perceive the *problem* as to first *describe* collaborative design, then to *manage* it, i.e., to control action and allocate resources so as to optimize resource use, subject to real-time requirements. As part of this, we can then determine how to support this activity, by changes in *procedure*, *culture* and *computer* support.

Separate models. An illustrative example arises in our work on collaboration in wing section design. Here a stress engineer and a producibility designer interact using a diagram on a CAD system. The stress engineer needs a solution which transmits loads well through the structure, and the designer needs a structure that is easy to fabricate, using, for example, an automatic riveting machine. The criteria used by each specialist are private to them in that they are complex and concerned with their particular technologies.

In the case of the collaboration of a producibility designer and a stress engineer, the producibility designer is concerned with arranging forms and fasteners so that the design realizes (or "sizes") a given layout and function, and is producible, i.e., manufacturable on the machines currently available using techniques and tooling currently in use in the organization. His description concerns the use of the part, and its production. The producibility engineer tries to make joins which are straight, and accessible with known riveting gun types. He also needs to keep rivet spacing constant, or at least to a small number or different rivet spacings.

The stress engineer is concerned with arrangements such that the loads carried in the elements are well formed, in that internal load is transmitted throughout the structure, which satisfies a given external load specification. His description concerns loads, stresses, transmission, and techniques for finding them. The stress engineer works privately with a finite element model which calculates load patterns satisfying differential equations derived from physical principles. These must match the load transmission properties of the sized geometry.

The common language of their collaboration is mainly the shared drawing, that is, geometric elements and their relations. In addition, indications of what is right or wrong with a given geometry, and possibly suggested changes in the geometry.

In aircraft design, there are many other specialists, each with their own technology and language. For example, there are aerodynamicists who use surface models and equations, there are maintainability engineers concerned with access, disassembly and replacement, there are hydraulic engineers, and thermodynamic experts. They do not understand each other's specializations, but they have to collaborate to produce a single design acceptable to all.

The aim of collaboration is to produce a design which is agreed to by each agent. This means that each agent has a justification of the design that he is satisfied with. In organizational practice, it is very important to validate designs. Manufacturing is very much concerned with validation, specification and standardization, as organizational mechanisms. The design must satisfy contractual requirements and must also meet safety and other legal and government-dictated requirements.

2 Interactions among specialists

In this section, we describe the interactions and interfaces among the different specialists and their models.

2.1 Interaction among designer, stress and aerodynamics

We first describe a typical scenario in a preliminary design environment.

At this point in the design, the designer has developed a shape concept with significant detail as far as the location of the vehicle primary systems and vehicle surface components/control surfaces are concerned.

A "bones" diagram determining rib stations, fuselage ring stations, major pressure bulkheads, major joints, and major load carrying members has been developed.

A typical course of action might be as follows. The aero engineer, who has already made previous preliminary runs, now creates a more detailed model and runs the more expensive flow codes to get a better feel of the vehicle performance. He comes back with data which indicate the improvements can be made by modifying certain areas of the vehicle shape.

The designer examines these suggested changes relative to their effect on the packaging of the vehicle systems and the support structure used to hold these systems in place.

The stress engineer examines the designer's changes to the structure needed to fulfill aerodynamic recommendations and runs an upgraded stress finite element model reflecting these changes. The feedback from the FEM analysis is reported to the designer, denoting any trouble areas which may arise.

The three organizations will now sit down together, usually in a meeting to discuss variations of the proposed changes which could alleviate problem areas. Compromises will be suggested. All these organizations will then return to their respective disciplines to make further studies on the recommended compromises. These new studies will necessitate further meetings to reconcile continuing problem areas. This iteration process will continue until all parties are satisfied that they can live with the described changes.

Throughout this process, time and cost of analysis play an important role as to the depth of analysis actually undertaken and the number of iterations allowed. In the end, these two factors are what closes off further development and the development community settles into a "make this work" situation.

2.2 Descriptions of each specialist

2.2.1 Designer

The designer bases his design primarily on the information obtained from the proposal specifications. From this information and previous experience, concepts, etc.,
the designer generates a 3-view cartoon concept which forms the basis of the first
analysis. Thereafter, he/she updates and refines the spatial layouts in interaction
with the technology specialists. Input in received from all other departments and the
designer's task is to constantly resynthesize a good design. The model used is a set
of drawings, on a CAD system, which represent the actual geometry of the aircraft,
as it is estimated so far.

2.2.2 Aerodynamics

The main question being answered by aerodynamics is "Will it fly?". More specifically, estimates of the flight characteristics of the design so far.

Input: The user will query geometry (2D and/or 3D) for specific geometry points
(x,y,z), which will be used to represent the surface shape of the vehicle, and can
be used to demonstrate airflow over the surface.

Model elements: From input data, a 3D quadrilateral grid of points will be developed to represent the airflow system about the vehicle.

Output: Lift, drag, and pressure distribution of the vehicle for a given set of flight
conditions. From the output, the viability of the vehicle to fulfill the flying
requirements will be determined and required changes recommended.

2.2.3 Structures model

The philosophy behind the structures model is that it is created for two basic reasons.
1. To prove, through analysis, the viability of the design (i.e., will the structure fail
to fulfill its strength requirements).
2. To help in the optimization of the design (i.e., reduce weight, reduce cost, reduce
complexity, etc.).
The level of detail varies as the design proceeds toward greater definition and completion.

Input: User will query geometry (2D and/or 3D) for specific geometric points (x,y,z)
which can be used to represent the strength components of the structure. These

include load paths, physical locations, type of loads transferred and strength of load path. The user will also receive external pressure distribution data from the aerodynamics and loads departments.

Model elements: From input data, a "bulk data deck" representing the model is created. This includes:
1. Grid points representing physical locations
2. Connectivity elements representing the physical structure through which the loads pass.
3. Material properties representing the strength and stiffness characteristics of the material of each component.
4. Structural properties representing the physical shape and size of each component.
5. Applied external loads from aerodynamic/loads pressure curves.

Output: Internal loads and configuration deflections. From this output, the viability of the configuration is determined and required changes recommended.

2.2.4 Weights and loads

The weights department is concerned with the total weight and the static weight distribution. Their model contains the following types of information:
1. a lumped model with point masses and moments of inertia.
2. a representation of the 1g loading configuration, i.e., just to lift off the ground.
3. the center of gravity (c.g.)
4. the center of lift (provided by aerodynamics)

In addition to the weights group, there is a loads group which elaborates the dynamic loading cases.

The weights model is generated from several sources including empirical data based on existing aircraft and vendor data on included parts/segments of the airplane, such as engines, radar systems, etc. The loads data is a direct result of combining aerodynamically derived pressure distribution data with flight conditions which impose certain "g" forces and air forces on the vehicle.

The output is the gravitational loading distribution.

2.2.5 Aeromechanics

Aeromechanics are concerned with the dynamic response of the system under given excitation regimes. The model:
1. is an inertia model

2. is generally simpler than a structures model

3. is a stick diagram with lumped masses and stiffnesses.

It is used to generate nodal vibration relationships and vehicle stability characteristics.

The aeromechanics model is derived from the components of the 3-view created by the designer (determines stiffnesses) and the 1g weights developed by the weights group. Mathematical stimuli are applied to the resulting model to determine system vibration and stability characteristics. The outputs contain vibration amplitudes throughout the vehicle, for each flight condition, which are used as multipliers for inertial effects on applied structural loads.

2.2.6 Mission analysis

There may sometimes be a separate mission analysis specialist, who evaluates and optimises the concept design relative to the design constraints of speed, range, payload, maneuvrability, etc., for each mission defined in the customer requirements. Mission analysis may suggest changes to improve satisfaction of needs and reduce cost.

2.2.7 Reliability and maintainability

Separate analysis is nowadays carried out for reliability, maintainability and supportability (r & m). This concerns the ability to maintain the aircraft under specified field conditions and with given technical support capability. The aim is to control life cycle costs.

2.2.8 Radar imaging

This technology determines detectability by radar. The model consists of panelized data used to represent the vehicle shape. The model must be extremely accurate and dense (number of elements) in order to accurately find true reflectance values.

2.2.9 Thermodynamic analysis

This model is concerned with heat absorption, conductance and emittance throughout the vehicle, and how these affect the structural, environmental and reliability characteristics of the aircraft.

3 Overall structure of the design process

Interacting specialists During conceptual design, the initial cartoon is refined up to the point of a fairly detailed layout. During this process, the specialized models are constructed in their initial forms, and then also refined so as to reflect and to incorporate the changes and progression of the central design. This is diagrammed in Figure 1.

Coordinated refinement of models The process of refinement, where each specialist refines his model, and works to keep his model up to date with the central model, is depicted in Figure 2. This also shows the input of specification changes, and their distribution to the relevant specialists.

Changing teams Further, the sets of experts involved gradually changes as the design proceeds. Some leave and some join the dance, see Figure 3.

4 Model refinement

A model may be changed to correct it, but most of the changes are in the *refinement* of the model. We give some examples of refinement:

Envelope to more detailed geometry The initial model specifies an approximate volume, which can be an envelope or a bounding cuboid for the refined model.

More exact numerical estimates e.g., fuel capacity 15,000 gals is a representation of an interval such as [14,000 - 16,000]. A more exact estimate might be 15,500 gals which might at this level of refinement correspond to the interval [15,250 - 15,750].

Single to multiple elements The mapping from the initial model, which lumps elements into abstract elements, may not be a direct expansion of each element into several more detailed elements. We have depicted a lumped model with 4 elements being expanded into a more detailed model with 14 elements. We also show that single element expansions have to be merged to produce a refinement, and that additional elements may be added during this process.

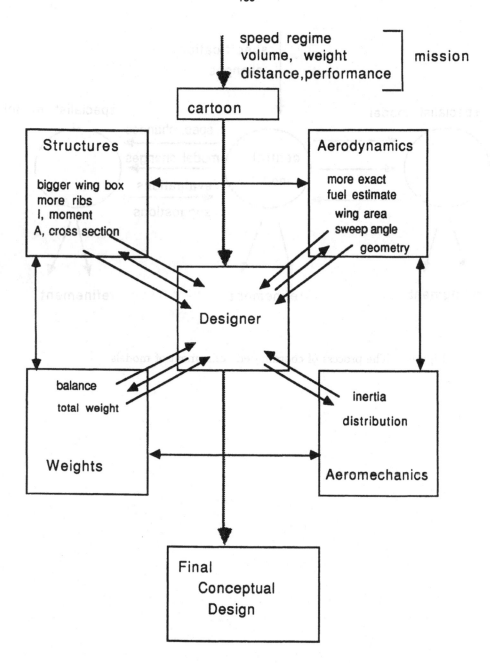

Figure 1: Conceptual Design

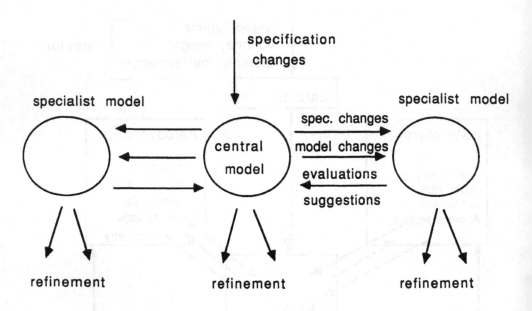

Figure 2: The process of coordinated refinement of models

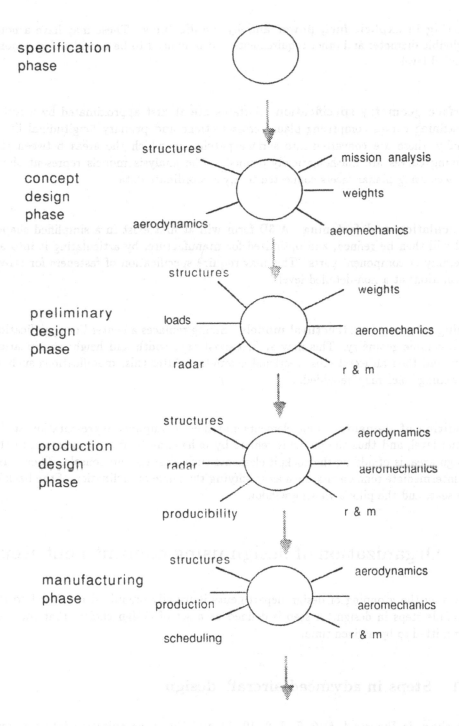

specification
phase

concept
design
phase

structures

mission analysis

weights

aerodynamics

aeromechanics

preliminary
design
phase

structures

weights

loads

aeromechanics

radar

r & m

production
design
phase

structures

aerodynamics

radar

aeromechanics

producibility

r & m

manufacturing
phase

structures

aerodynamics

production

aeromechanics

scheduling

r & m

Figure 3: **Changing teams of specialists**

Putting in explicit fuel, power and hydraulic lines These may have a non-negligible diameter and other requirements and may need to be considered at a non-detailed level.

Surface geometry specification Surfaces are at first approximated by a series of defining curves comprising planar cross-sections and primary longitudinal lines. Finally, these are converted into surface patches in which the areas between the defining curves are mathematically defined. The analysis models represent these surfaces using planar facets connected to x,y,z coordinate data.

Articulation and fastening A 3D form will at first exist in a simplified shape, and will then be refined, and optimized for manufacture, by articulating it into an assembly of component parts. This may require specification of fasteners for stress calculations at a non-detailed level.

Sizing of parts for structural models Sizing replaces a center line specification by a volume geometry. This may at first exist as a width and height specification only, and then an exact cross sectional geometry. After this, modifications such as lightening holes may be added.

Addition of elements Some elements may have a simplified representation at the initial level, and thus the model is refined by enhancing them. An example, in the design area, is of adding the cockpit elements such as seats and console. There may be intermediate refinements, such as specifying the angle of inclination of the back of the seat, and the pilot's viewing window.

5   Organization of design using commitment steps

The way the grouping of design departments is usually organized is related to the schedule steps in design. A step is defined as a set of design choices that must be committed to by a given time.

5.1   Steps in advanced aircraft design

We show, in Figures 4, 5, 6, 7, 8, 9, 10, 11 and 12, an organization into six steps sometimes used in aircraft design. These steps are:

1. Initial design parameters

2. Generate data/ preliminary point design

3. Parametric and trade-off analysis

4. Detail point design studies

5. Refine selected configuration

6. Design and build prototype

Within each step, and for each goal, we indicate which of the many available computer support tools are used. These tool are listed in the following section.

5.2 Commitment steps

We summarize the above six steps in Figure 13.

The concept of commitment step

As diagrammed in Figure 14, the notion of commitment step is that a set of joint commitments is made by all the design agents at the end of each step. These are public commitments to best estimates for decision choices. These estimates are then used by all agents during the next step.

Estimates and decisions must form an adequate sequence

Each step produces estimated results within intervals that are sufficient to allow every agent in the following step to achieve its goals, viz., estimated results within the accuracy or interval required for the end of the next step. Thus, for agents a,b,c and d, if after step i they have produced results in intervals I_i^a, I_i^b, I_i^c and I_i^d, and if they have private results P_i^a, P_i^b, P_i^c, and P_i^d, then P_i^a and $\{I_i^b, I_i^c \text{ and } I_i^d\}$ as input for agent a should be sufficient to allow the computation of P_{i+1}^a and I_{i+1}^a, and P_i^b and $\{I_i^b, I_i^c \text{ and } I_i^d\}$ as input for agent b should be sufficient to allow the computation of P_{i+1}^b and I_{i+1}^b, and so on.

The public estimated results are the context for design action

The public estimated results, at the end of step i, are the context for design action in step i+1.

$$I_i^a\}$$
$$I_i^b\} \text{ and } P_i^a\} \longrightarrow P_{i+1}^a\} \text{ and } I_{i+1}^a\}$$
$$I_i^c\}$$
$$I_i^d\}$$

Customer	Generate requirements.
Project management	From customer requirements and advanced technology assessment, coordinate configuration concept.
Design and systems	Generate baseline drawings, general arrangement, inboard profile (support tool - CADAM)
Loft	
Aerodynamics	Wing proportions - (a) W/S chord length/surface area, (b) thickness/chord length, (c) Aspect Ratio. Empennage size. Thrust to weight ratio T/W.
Propulsion	Engine selection, range of cycle parameters. Engine installation criteria.
Weights	Approx gross weight. Approx empty weight.
Structures	Evaluate configuration for (1) load paths for low cost light weight structures, and (2) reasonable and consistent design parameters.
Aeromechanics	Provide criteria guidelines. Participate in design: (1) evaluation for loads (2) aeroelastic and flutter effects (support tool - loads programs).
Materials and producibility	
Model specifications	
Laboratories	
Engineering shop	
Flight test	
Other disciplines	

Figure 4: Step 1 - Initial design parameters

Customer	Give approval at design review.
Project management	Change configuration concept, revise design parameters, do design review.
Design and systems	Update general arrangement, update inboard profile, find wetted areas and area distribution, functional systems considerations (1) flight controls (2) fuel (3) hydraulic (4) electrical (5) avionics (6) environmental control (6) weapons. (Uses CADAM support tool). (May use Asset support tool). Produce updated baseline drawings, general arrangements, inboard profile.
Loft	
Aerodynamics	Determine (1) eppennage scaling data (2) drag data (3) low speed lift data (4) control surface sizes. (Uses aerodynamic programs)
Propulsion	Determine (1) parametric installed engine, performance data versus (a) overall pressure ratio (b) bypass ratio (c) turbine entry temperature (2) Local flow field conditions (3) inlet and exhaust nozzle performance data (4) Scaling data (5) Installed engine weigh data (6) Performance and weight scaling (7) Initial structural temperatures. (Uses propulsion programs).
Weights	Determine (1) component weight relationships (2) payload and operating equipment weights (3) effects of configuration peculiar items (4) C.G. location and limits (5) Fuel volume relationships. (use mass distribution tool)
Structures	Define structural design criteria. Perform trade-off studies to define (1) basic structural concepts (2) material usage. Provide effects on asset weight equations due to (a) structural technology (b) structural arrangements (c) structural design requirements.
Aeromechanics	Provide parametric basic loads. Participate in design evaluation. Preliminary aerolelastic assessment. (use loads programs, detailed loads programs and aeroelastic program)
Materials and producibility	
Model specifications	
Laboratories	
Engineering shop	
Flight test	
Other disciplines	

Figure 5: Step 2 - Generate data/ preliminary point design

Customer	
Project management	Determine trade-off matrix.
	Do design evaluation.
Design and systems	Study power plant size, wing and eppenage size,
	fuselage size, basic airframe geometry,
	controls and avionics.
	(may use CADAM).
	May do Asset study (Asset tool).
Loft	
Aerodynamics	Study maneuvrability,
	acceleration, rate of climb,
	ceiling, off-design mission capability,
	range/fuel consumption,
	optimum thrust to weight (T/W) ratio.
	(use aerodynamic programs).
Propulsion	Study engine cycle and size,
	lift engine size.
	(use propulsion programs).
Weights	Study gross weight,
	empty weight, structural weight,
	systems and subsystems weight,
	propulsion weight, fuel volume available,
	fuel required, effects of advanced technology,
	effects of configuration changes,
	maximum take-off weight.
	(use mass distribution program).
Structures	Determine structural component/material matrix.
	Provide parametric basic loads.
Aeromechanics	Participate in design evaluation.
	Parametric aerolastic assessment.
	(use detailed loads programs and aeroelasticity program)
Materials and producibility	Study engineering costs
	Study acquisition of
	(1) production material and labor,
	(2) tooling, (3) spares
	Study operational costs:
	(1) maintenance, (2) replenish spares,
	(3) fuel and oil, and (4) pay and allowances.
	Produce estimate of total system cost.
Model specifications	
Laboratories	
Engineering shop	
Flight test	
Other disciplines	Acoustics - side line noise,
	flyover noise, and footprint noise.

Figure 6: Step 3 - Parametric and trade-off analysis

Customer	Give approval at end of step.
Project management	Select detail point designs, design review, and revise design parameters.
Design and systems	From configuration design, generate preliminary concepts, i.e., general arrangements and inboard profiles. Update general arrangements and inboard profiles, consider configuration peculiar items (e.g., radar, weapons, payload), determine wetted areas, and areas distribution. Make layouts for (1) flight controls system (2) powerplant installation (3) structural arrangement (4) landing gear (5) crew station (6) fuel system (7) hydraulic system (8) electrical system (9) avionics system (10) environmental control system (11) weapons system (12) miscellaneous equipment (13) mechanisms. (uses CADAM). Produce updated concept drawings, including general arrangements, inboard profiles, and layouts.
Loft	Develop loft surface. (uses CADAM).
Aerodynamics	Determine (1) drag build up (2) maneuver envelope V-N diagram (3) control surface size (4) primary mission performance analysis (5) airport performance (6) flight envelope (7) (8) C.G. range, loadability (9) preliminary failure analysis. (uses aerodynamic programs and transonic analysis).
Propulsion	Refine (1) engine selection (2) installed performance data (3) inlet and nozzle size and installation configuration. Determine: (1) Fuel system sizing requirements (2) Initial auxiliary system requirements and definition. Refine structural temperatures. Determine transient temperature and histories of structural components. (Uses propulsion programs and detailed propulsion programs).
Weights	Determine (1) group weight statement (2) preliminary mass distribution and moment of inertia data (3) C.G. travel analysis. Do trade-off studies, effects of advanced technology on (1) materials (2) type of construction (3) active controls (4) propulsion. (Uses mass distribution program).

Figure 7: Step 4 - Detail point design studies, part 1

Structures	Expand and refine trade-off studies to define (1) detail structural design concepts (2) material usage (3) design/manufacturing parameters. Generate basic structural arrangements. Perform analysis to size basic structural elements: (1) internal loads distribution analysis (2) Stress analysis for strength and stiffness (3) fatigue and fracture analysis for durability and damage tolerance (4) thermal stress analysis (5) sonic fatigue analysis. Provide preliminary basic loads Determine stiffness data for aeroeleastic analyses. Conduct structural concept tests. (Uses NASTRAN and FAMAS).
Aeromechanics	Provide (1) aeroelastic stability derivatives (2) flutter analysis (3) aeroelastic evaluation of performance requirements (4) acoustic environment (5) loads and criteria report (6) engine loads analysis (7) landing gear loads (i) design (ii) fatigue. Expand and refine trade-off studies (1) effects of C.G travel (2) detail structural design loads criteria. (Uses detailed loads programs, aeroelastic program and detailed aeromechanics programs).
Materials and producibility	Select (1) materials and processes (2) parts and equipment. Refine manufacturing breakdown. Provide producibility design support. Perform cost trade-off studies. Determine life cycle costs. Identify test requirements. Make smoothness drawings.
Model specifications	Determine (1) configuration parameters (2) Lockheed design requirements (3) Performance parameters.
Laboratories	
Engineering shop	
Flight test	
Other disciplines	Technical discipline evaluation (1) military systems - mission performance (2) human factors (3) reliability (4) vulnerability.

Figure 8: Step 4 - Detail point design studies, part 2

Customer	Give approval at end of step.
Project management	Maintain selected configuration, do design reviews, revise design parameters.
Design and systems	Refine (1) general arrangements (2) inboard profile (3) configurational peculiar items. Make detailed layouts for (1) wind tunnel models (2) mock-ups and component testing. Detailed layouts: (1) flight control system (2) power plant installation (3) structural arrangement (4) landing gear (5) crew station (6) fuel system (7) hydraulic system (8) electrical system (9) avionics systems (10) environmental control system (11) weapons system (12) miscellaneous equipment (13) mechanisms. (uses CADAM). Produce updated drawings.
Loft	Provide loft contours for mock-ups, wind-tunnel models and component testing. (uses CADAM and CALACO).
Aerodynamics	Define and direct wind-tunnel test program. Flight control system - primary and automatic. Update drag build-up per wind-tunnel results. Prepare stability and control reports. Control surface sizing, update per wind-tunnel results. Prepare performance reports. Airport performance, update per wind-tunnel results. Refine flight envelope buffet boundaries. Effect of stores, update per wind-tunnel results. Flight simulations, computer and piloted. Develop guarantees. Refine failure analysis. (Uses aerodynamic programs, transonic analysis program and ADAIS).
Propulsion	Define and conduct wind-tunnel test. Prepare engine performance reports. Finalize inlet, nozzle and nacelle location. Update installation losses per wind-tunnel results. Engine control-system models. Thrust management system. Finalize auxiliary systems requirements and definition: (1) environmental (2) anti-icing (3) auxiliary power (4) engine starting (5) vents and drains (6) thrust reverse. Detail structural temperatures and temperature gradients. (Uses propulsion programs 1, 2 and 3).

Figure 9: Step 5 - Refine selected configuration, part 1

Weights	Detail estimated weight and balance report. Define specification weight with customer/marketing. Evaluate cost/weight trade-off studies. Mass distribution per final configuration including variations in: (1) fuel (2) payload (3) distribution for critical loading. Fuel versus attitude. (Uses mass distribution program and fuel inertia program).
Structures	Continue trade-offs to define: (1) detail structural design concepts (2) materials usage (3) producibility methods. Generate detail structural arrangements. Expand and refine structural element sizing analysis (1) internal loads (2) strength and stiffness (3) durability and damage tolerance (4) thermal stress (5) sonic fatigue. Refine stiffness data for aeroelastic analysis. Continue structural tests. Plan for prototype development analysis and tests. (Uses FAMAS and NASTRAN).
Aeromechanics	Refine (1) aeroelastic stability derivatives (2) basic loads (3) flutter analysis (4) aeroelastic performance analysis (5) acoustic environment (6) loads and criteria report (7) aeroelastic optimization (8) engine loads analysis (9) wind-tunnel test program for loads. Establish structural design loads criteria. Define and conduct low-speed wind-tunnel flutter model program. (Uses detailed loads programs, detailed aeromechanics programs and airframe/ground interaction program).
Materials and producibility	Refine (1) materials and process selection (2) parts and equipment selection. Continue (1) producibility design support (2) cost trade-off studies.
Model specifications	Prepare (1) customer design requirements (2) Lockheed design requirements (3) customer peculiar configuration requirements (4) performance guarantees (5) weight guarantees.
Laboratories	Build component test rigs per engineering requirements. Conduct component tests. Design and build flutter models. Do flutter model tests. Design and build wind-tunnel models. Do wind-tunnel tests.
Engineering shop	Build mock-ups per engineering requirements.
Flight test	
Other disciplines	Technical disciplines analysis (1) military systems - mission performance (2) human factors (3) reliability (4) vulnerability (5) survivability

Figure 10: Step 5 - Refine selected configuration, part 2

Customer	Give approval and acceptance.
Project management	Prepare proposal, do customer review and contract award. Finalize design requirements. Determine modifications required. Evaluation of requirements.
Design and systems	Finalize: (1) general arrangements (2) inboard profile (3) configuration peculiar items. Complete and release prototype drawings: (1) flight control system (2) power plant installation (3) structural arrangements (4) landing gear (5) crew station (6) fuel system (7) hydraulic system (8) electrical system (9) avionics system (10) environmental control system (11) weapons system (12) miscellaneous equipment (13) mechanisms. Produce prototype drawings. (Uses CADAM).
Loft	Provide loft contours to design and manufacturing. (Uses CADAM and CALACO).
Aerodynamics	In-depth handling qualities report. Assist in planning flight-test program: (1) evaluate results (2) correlate with predictions. Finalize off design capabilities. Finalize failure analysis. In-depth performance report. Integrate simulator with prototype. (Uses aerodynamic programs, transonic analysis program and ADAIS).
Propulsion	Refine performance estimates based on flight test results. Participate in and monitor flight-test program. Prepare reports for customer data requirements. Monitor and coordinate changes with engine manufacturer. Monitor auxiliary system performance. (Uses propulsion programs 1, 2, 3 and 4).
Weights	Calculated weight and balance report Weigh first aircraft Actual weight and balance report - first aircraft Internal and customer status reports Weight and balance handbook for flight test Calculate static balance and moment of inertia of control surfaces Measure static balance and moment of inertia of control surfaces Monitor designs to target weights (Uses Master weight and fuel inertia)
Structures	Finalize structural design concepts Finalize materials usage criteria Finalize detail analysis for structural sizing (1) internal loads (2) strength and stiffness (3) durability and damage tolerance (4) thermal stress (5) sonic fatigue Finalize stiffness data for aerolastic analysis Continue structural tests Prepare data for government and customer specs: (1) stress analysis (2) test evaluations (3) final reports Provide manufacturing liaison Provide flight test liaison (Uses FAMAS and NASTRAN)

Figure 11: Step 6 - Design and build prototype, part 1

Aeromechanics	Finalize: (1) aerolastic stability derivatives (2) aerolastic performance (3) basic loads (4) Flutter analysis (5) Acoustic treatment (6) Engine loads analysis (7) Landing gear analysis Define: (1) Flight test program for loads validation (2) Ground and flight test programs for flutter substantiation In-depth loads and criteria report Aerolastic optimization Define and conduct high speed wind-tunnel flutter model program Flight test liaison (Uses detailed loads programs detailed aeromechanics programs and airframe/ground interaction program
Materials and producibility	Finalize materials and process selection Finalize parts and equipment selection Specifications and standards Commonality studies: (1) forgings and extrusions (2) parts, equipment, components Identify long lead items Design to cost program implementation
Model specifications	Finalize: (1) customer design requirements (2) Lockheed design requirements (3) customer peculiar requirements (4) performance guarantees (5) weight guarantees
Laboratories	Continue wind-tunnel tests of prototype configuration Continue component tests of prototype configuration plan and execute static tests of prototype Vehicle systems simulator Flight simulators Continue flutter model tests
Engineering shop	Revise mock-ups to prototype configuration
Flight test	Plan flight test program Execute flight test program per engineering and customer requirements
Other disciplines	Technical disciplines finalize recommendations and reports (1) military systems - mission performance (2) human factors (3) reliability (4) vulnerability (5) survivability (6) maintainability Manufacturing builds prototype (Using CADAM)

Figure 12: Step 6 - Design and build prototype, part 2

DESIGN AND SYSTEMS	STEP 1 INITIAL DESIGN PARAMETERS	STEP 2 PRELIMINARY POINT ANALYSIS	STEP 3 PARAMETER ESTIMATION TRADE-OFFS	STEP 4 DETAIL POINT STUDIES	STEP 5 REFINE SELECTED CONFIGURATION	STEP 6 BUILD PROTOTYPE
DESIGN AND SYSTEMS	baseline drawings inboard profile	general arrangements update inboard profile functional system considerations	updated layouts	updated layouts functional systems layouts	detailed layouts	finalize prototype drawings
LOFT				develop loft surface	loft contours for testing	loft contours for manufacturing
AERODYNAMICS	wing parameters thrust/weight ratio	drag data control surface sizes	manoeuverability range/fuel optimum thrust/weight ratio	control surface sizes drag build-up c.g. range, loadability	define and direct wind tunnel test	indepth handling qualities report
PROPULSION	range of cycle parameters installation criteria	performance data weight temperatures	study engine cycle and size	refine engine selection inlet and nozzle size fuel system sizing structural temperatures	define and conduct wind tunnel tests finalize inlet, nozzle and nacell location temperature gradients	refine estimates based on flight test results
WEIGHTS	approximate weight, c.g.	payload and operating equipment c.g. limits fuel-volume relationships	structural weight subsystems weight propulsion weight fuel-volume	preliminary mass distribution moment of inertia data c.g. travel analysis	detail estimated weight specification of weight with customer	calculated weight and balance report weigh first aircraft
STRUCTURES	load paths design parameters	define structural design criteria basic structural concepts	define structural component/material matrix	refine trade-off analysis basic structural arrangements size basic structural elements detemine stiffness data	detailed arrangements internal loads refine structural element sizing refine stiffness data	finalize detail structural sizing
AEROMECHANICS	provide criteria guidelines	provide parametric basic loads preliminary aerolastic assessment	parametric basic loads parametric aerolastic assessment	aerolastic stability engine loads analysis effects of c.g.travel	refine aerolastic performance analysis define and conduct wind tunnel flutter model program	finalize analysis engine loads landing gear acoustics
MATERIALS AND PRODUCIBILITY			study acquisition of production labor and tools estimate total system cost	select materials and and processes cost trade-off studies producibility report	refine materials and process selection	finalize commonality studies
MODELS				determine parameters	prepare design requirements	finalize
LABORATORIES					design and build wind tunnel models do wind tunnel tests	continue tests
SHOP					build mock-ups	revise mock-ups
FLIGHT						plan and execute flight test
OTHER			acoustics - flyover noise	military mission human factors reliability	military mission human factors reliability	finalize recommendations

Figure 13: Summary of six steps

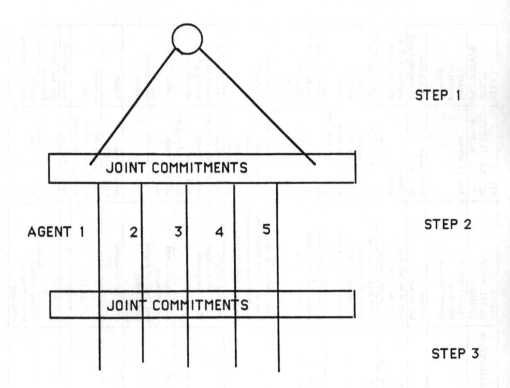

Figure 14: The concept of commitment step

Example:
approx layout
control surface size
engine weight and size
payload and c.g. limits
basic structural concepts $\longrightarrow$ structural component/material matrix
parametric basic loads

6 Design elaboration in wing design

Given the description developed so far of the organizational context, we can now describe the situation of the individual designer in the organization. For example, a designer will be in a particular department and at a particular step in the organized design process. His task is to make the next step of refinement of his model, in conjunction with designers in other departments. He uses the estimates made in the previous step, and refines his model to the point required for public commitment at the end of the current step.

6.1 The layout

The starting point is a *layout* or *configuration* for the wing section.
This has

1. first cut outside shape

2. center-line abstract spar elements

3. indication of panel geometry

4. indication of major features, such as holes, wing attachments, and wing sub-structures.

It is sometimes called an *initial sketch*. The area and stiffness requirements of the wing are also specified. The immediate source of the layout is a lead designer.

6.2 The finite element model

From the layout, an FEM model is constructed by a stress engineer. The FEM model consists of idealized panels and spars, and typically each will be treated as a separate finite element.

The following quantities are determined by FEM analysis.

1. loads to be carried in each FEM element. This is not quite the same thing as the stress in each element, i.e., the spatial deformation of the element, which can be determined by a further calculation. (Deflections are calculated but not maximum fiber stress)

2. torsional deflection

3. up-bending and down-bending

4. span-wise bending

A local FEM analysis is run on each surface skin panel, and this is used to determine:

1. the recommended spacing, height, and thickness of stiffeners to be used in each panel.

2. the skin thickness to be used

6.3   The design process

An initial specification of the spars and the panels is made. Suitable spars are chosen to be able to carry the specified loads. The main design iteration is in finalizing the panel and spar geometry, and to select and to place precisely all the fasteners needed to assemble the spars and panels into a wing section.

The design process proceeds as an interchange between the designer and the stress engineer, see Figure 15. The designer's goals are to achieve

1. geometry to fit the envelope of the configuration

2. as producible a design as possible

3. as cost-effective a design as possible

4. good interfacing to other neighboring parts being designed by other designers

These must be achieved while satisfying the stress engineer's evaluation. The stress engineer's goals are to

1. satisfy the load-carrying requirements in the spars, stringers, and the panels

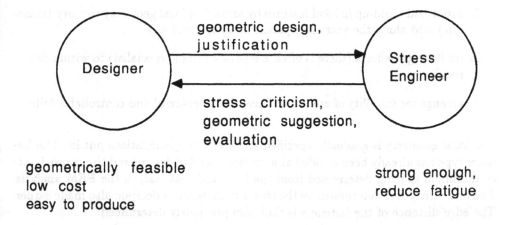

Figure 15: Cooperative relationship

2. avoid load build-up in local features by arranging local geometry to carry (transmit) load along the spars and panels in an optimal way

3. limit fatigue effects (there is often a separate fatigue specialist) to within design requirements

4. arrange for visibility of any metal breakdown (graceful and controllable failure)

The local geometry is gradually specified and fastener specifications put in. The fastener type has already been decided at a previous level of design, and the approximate or minimum spacing determined from the load and material, in the FEM analysis. The tear strength is determined by the choice of material, a decision also made earlier. The edge distance of the fasteners is thus also previously determined.

6.4 Straightforward case of fastening

In the straightforward case, with no local features, the panels are overlapped at a spar and are fastened by fasteners which are spaced uniformly along the overlap, at the determined distance from the edge.

Due to the requirement of visible failure, this is arranged to fail in the upper visible panel. This is achieved by arranging the lower panel to be thicker, say 10-20%, or stronger in some way, or for the stress level to be lower in the hidden part.

For a good producible design, the most cost-effective and best method of fabrication would be an automatic fastener machine. There must be adequate access to do the fastening operation. Usually, there is a range of throat lengths for the grip, up to a maximum length.

Several different gripper lengths may be needed for one wing section, as one large gripper length for all will not usually work adequately. Changing the gripper costs assembly time.

Automatic fastener machine currently have a fixed fastener spacing setting, so the number of different fastener spacings used should be minimized. Finally, the total number of fasteners used should be minimized, to save assembly time and also weight.

(At a higher design level, the original decision of break-up of the fuselage into panels was made. By using larger panels, one minimizes the number of joints to be made. This gives greater tolerance control, and can give weight savings. The size of the largest producible panels is often determined by the size of the largest available machine or even the size of the shop floor. In the case of the large C-17 transporter plane, Lockheed extended their machine bed from 50 to 80 feet, to allow larger panels to be formed.)

Hand fastening can also be used, but this is more expensive.

In an extreme and undesirable case, "blind" fasteners can be used, i.e., where fastening access is from one side only.

6.5   Opening geometry

The first feature encountered is to determine the detailed geometry of each opening. An opening, in this case, is an access hatch. Such doors are rarely designed to transmit stress. To transmit stress requires close fitting bolts, which require precision assembly and maintenance, and make access difficult; also replacement panels are difficult to make.

The shape of the opening is usually a compromise between the requirement of ease of access for men and tools on the one hand, and the requirement of well-formed stress transmission around the opening and fatigue resistance on the other. Fatigue resistance is best for elliptical openings, typically. The volume being accessed is usually box-shaped, hence rounded corners make it difficult to access the corners of the box. The compromise shape of a opening usually comes out as a "rounded rectangle".

There is usually an extra collar or "doubler" to allow the bolts to be fastened, to hold the hatch on. The number of bolts is already determined at a previous design phase, but their placement is decided at this stage. Using a doubler involves milling out the spar substructure. Stress analysis gives the width and the height of the doubler, the width basically coming from the opening size.

Rivets have to be sized correctly, and spaced correctly relative to each other and relative to edges. The choice of rivet type depends on the air friction tolerable as determined by aerodynamical considerations. Often, only the leading edge of the wing uses countersunk rivets, since their use provokes a thicker skin thickness due to stress requirements, and this results in greater weight as well as manufacturing and usage cost. The choice of rivet diameter depends on the load it is expected to take, and also whether it is countersunk or not, since a rivet with a head transmits stress better. The choice of rivet metal depends on stress and also corrosion properties. The spacing of rivets is basically determined by stress parameters of the material.

The initial straightforward design, as in Figure 16(a), which runs the join uniformly past the openings is criticized by the stress engineer, since the stress is not transmitted round the opening in a smooth manner, causing build-up of stress and the potential for cracking.

He indicates

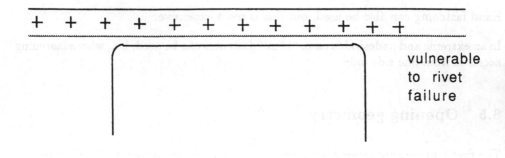

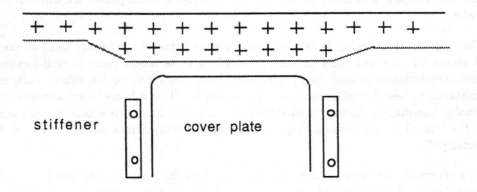

Figure 16: Opening design

1. not good stress transmission

2. suggest strengthen by greater overlap of panels.

This leads to an improved design, Figure 16(b). Here, the spar has to use a wider extrusion, and involves machining, and greater weight and material cost, so the opening causes quite a high additional cost. The angle at which the change-over from a single line to a double line of rivets occurs is usually about a 1:3 slope. This is determined by stress parameters of the material, since any greater would tear and any less would shear. Additional stiffeners must also be used at the edge of the hatch aperture to hold the hatch bolts.

An alternative design, uses a doubler which goes all round the opening. In this case, the corners of the doubler are square for easier fabrication. The spar has to have a different cross section, as shown, requiring a different extrusion or extra milling, also the rivets have to be different.

Another alternative design, of two rows of rivets all along the wing edge, was rejected, since although the chosen design requires an extra manufacturing operation to remove metal, this is not expensive, and, in the designer's judgement, the weight savings justified this expense.

7 Summary and conclusion

7.1 Summary

We described in outline how aircraft are designed in a large organization. This did not concern initial innovative design, but the ensuing main activity of design refinement/redesign.

We described some of the models used by each specialist department and the inputs and outputs among departments during the design process.

We observed that the main design choices are refinement operations on the design, and we discussed refinement.

The overall structure of the organized design process is mainly one of *coordinated refinement of models*.

We then described how the design negotiation process is controlled by an organizationally agreed sequence of commitment steps.

We discussed design elaboration in wing design.

7.2 Conclusions

1. Aircraft design proceeds by the *cooperation* of *specialists* (specialist teams or departments).

2. Each specialist has its own *model* of the design, and may use several different models or partial models for different purposes.

3. Specialists have limited ability to understand each other's models. They communicate using a *shared vocabulary*, but not necessarily shared technical knowledge.

4. Design proceeds by successive *refinement* of the models, which are coordinated and updated together.

5. The design decisions, which are acts of commitment and model refinement, are *negotiated* by the specialists among themselves.

6. One way this negotiation process is organized and controlled is by the use of *commitment steps*.

Acknowledgements

We would like to thank Dave Cannon, Bill Thompson and Dave Richardson of Lockheed Aircraft Company, Burbank, California, for discussions on wing-section design, and on collaboration in manufacturing organizations in general.

The UCLA Manufacturing Engineering Program is supported by gifts and grants from many corporations, and by the Institute for Manufacturing and Automation Research.

References

[1] Duvvuru Sriram, Robert D. Logcher, and Shuichi Fukuda. Proceedings of the MIT-JSME Workshop on Cooperative Product Development, 1989. Held at MIT, November 20-21, 1989.

[2] Alan H. Bond. The cooperation of experts in engineering design. In *Distributed Artificial Intelligence, Volume II*, pages 463–484, 1989.

Managing the VLSI Design Process

Tzi-cker F. Chiueh, Randy H. Katz, Valerie King

Computer Science Division
Electrical Engineering and Computer Science Department
University of California, Berkeley
Berkeley, CA 94720

Abstract : Ways to represent and structure data within the design environment are reasonably well-understood, and have led to a number of proposed and implemented design frameworks. Comparable support for the operational nature of design, i.e., the controlled and disciplined sequencing of CAD tool invocations, are still in their infancy. In this paper, we describe a model for managing the work of a design team within a VLSI design environment. The model is based on a *task specification language,* for encapsulating CAD tool invocations and arranging the sequencing of such invocations to accomplish specific tasks, and an novel *activity model,* which maintains the history of task invocations and serves as a focus for sharing work results in a cooperative manner. The translator of the task specification language and a prototype task manager have been implemented within the OCT CAD framework.

Key Words and Phrases: Design Databases, Process Management, Groupware, Task Specification, Activity Model.

1. Introduction and Motivation

VLSI design systems first concentrated on providing computer-aided tools for the creation and verification of the design. Because of the proliferation of design description formats, communication of design data among tools became a serious bottleneck. Design database systems, such as OCT developed at U. C. Berkeley [OCT 89], evolved to provide common formats and more structured ways of organizing design descriptions to reduce the communications problem. Design management systems were a further evolution, concerned with organizing the design across time by supporting versions and configurations. An example of such a system is the Version Server prototype also developed at U. C. Berkeley [KATZ87].

Design systems have now reached the point where design representations and data structure are reasonably well understood. The next challenge is to develop better support for the operational aspects of design. By this we mean the controlled sequencing of design activities (process management), and the allocation of resources (people, machines, etc.) to the process, coupled with the monitoring of project progress (project management). The term process, as used here, should not be confused with the usual concept of a manufacturing job shop. Rather, process management is concerned with facilitating the design work by providing supports to the dynamic aspects of circuit design. One can think of this system as a meta-CAD tool in that it helps circuit designers to make better use of conventional CAD tools.

In this paper, we shall concentrate on process management, and will propose a history model for describing and manipulating the design process. We will also describe the implementation issues of this model. The process management system basically consists of two major components: *task specification* and the *history model*.

Our history model takes a semi-structured view of the design work. "Tasks" correspond to routine CAD tool invocation sequences, and represent frequently recurring units of work whose sequence can be specified in advance. An example of a task might be the tool sequence needed to create a netlist description from a schematic. "Activities" thread these structured tasks together in a less structured way, allowing greater flexibility in the design process. They usually correspond to high-level work tasks for which the proper order of steps cannot be specified in advance, or for which a circumscribed sequence does not make sense. An example activity might be something like building the standard cell design for a datapath. Obviously such an activity involves several task invocations, probably integrates the work of multiple designers, and spans a fairly long duration. Unless the projects design style is very structured, describing *in advance* the detailed sequence of steps necessary to complete the datapath is impossible.

What activities do provide is a way of collecting history about the way a design has evolved. The model allows designers to query and browse the execution history, and to choose its sections for archive or deletion. The notions of task and activity roughly correspond to "shell-script" and directory in modern operating systems. Only the task description language allows specifying inherent parallelism in the task and the system can encapsulate tool execution by managing all the invocation details. Furthermore, the activity builds a structure into the design operation history and relates tool execution with data evolution.

The rest of this paper is organized as followed. In the next section, the previous works on this area are surveyed and the approaches are compared. Sections 3 presents the model in greater detail. In section 4 the task description language is introduced together with its implementation. The structure and implementation of the history model are discussed in section 5. Section 6 concludes this paper with the current status of the system and the future research plans.

2. Comparison with Previous Works

The earliest work that captures the dynamic aspects of VLSI design was done at Carnegie-Mellon University. Their systems, from Ulysses [DANI88] to Cadweld [BUSH89], incorporate a "script" language for describing high-level design activity in terms of low-level primitives. However, this language is non-procedural in nature because their control mechanism for tool execution is based upon the blackboard model as used in rule-based systems. The motivation is to provide an open architecture in that the scripts only specify a high-level goal and do not commit designers to use any particular tool when the scripts are "executed." When the script is invoked, the high-level goal is posted onto the "blackboard". Tools are distributed over a networked environment and those whose capabilities match the goal can volunteer for achieving that goal. Designers can select one from those qualified tools and execute, according to various performance criteria. The system is also responsible for packaging the input files and optional parameters in order to actually invoke the CAD tools. Cadweld takes a step further by adopting an object-oriented approach for embedding a class hierarchy into CAD tools, to exploit the rich structural relationships among tools.

Overall, CMU's work is geared towards supporting tool encapsulation and integration flexibility in design environment (i.e., easy to add or delete tools). They seem to focus on "intelligent" exploration of design space through artificial intelligence techniques. In this sense, their work is more of a "synthesis" flavor rather than an interaction support facility. Our system, in contrast, aims to support more flexibility for designers to explore the design space by providing a history framework for integrating design operations and design data. Their model also did not seem to address the support of "team work," which is incorporated in our model from the very beginning.

An automatic design management system called *VOV* developed by Andrea Cosotto in Berkeley addresses similar problems but with a less general scope. The central notion of VOV is called *trace*, which is represented as a bipartite acyclic directed graph in which nodes are either tools or data objects, and arcs express input-output relationships between tools and objects. A trace captures both design history as well as dependencies among design objects. Traces can thus be used to enforce the consistency of an object whenever one of its components got modified. Traces can also serve as exemplar tool execution sequences from which novice designers can benefit.

In VOV, the design history is stored in a flattening structure. There is no hierarchy built into the history, which makes it difficult to manage, both from user's and system's standpoint, the potentially enormous amounts of traces. VOV did not have any supports of tool encapsulation, which we believe is one of the most important goals of a design process management system.

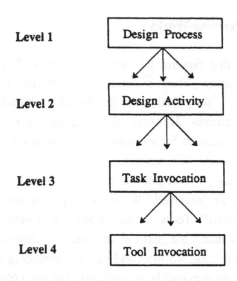

Level 1	Design Process
Level 2	Design Activity
Level 3	Task Invocation
Level 4	Tool Invocation

Figure 1 The Hierarchy of Design History

A design project consists of multiple design processes, each corresponding to the universe of work performed by a particular designer. Design processes, in turn, consist of a number of goal-oriented design activities, such as build the ALU, build the shifter, etc. A design activity is a thread of multiple task invocations, each of which is realized by actual CAD tool invocations.

3. The Hierarchy of Design History

The process management system is based on a design history data structure that records the "footprints" of the designers. The footprints include all the design operations that have been performed and the associated design objects. The history has a hierarchical structure, which is shown in Figure 1. The highest level is the *design process*. This captures a designer's entire design history associated with a project. In other words, there is a design process associated with every member in a project. A designer can be involved in more than one project, and therefore s/he may have more than one design process simultaneously.

The next level is *design activity,* which denotes the part of a design process that corresponds to a coherent unit of design operations and their associated data. More precisely, there is a goal associated with a design activity. All the operations within an activity are performed to achieve this goal. Just as a directory is used to store related files, an activity provides a "context", where designers can gather relevant data and against which relevant operations are issued. A designer usually has many activities associated with a design process. There are no explicit relationships among design activities in a design process.

The model does not place any restrictions on what could constitute an activity. Designers can create as many activities in a design process as they see fit. It should be noted, however, that the activity mechanism is meant to be used to organize design processes so the global picture of the design's evolution can be preserved. It would be therefore to the designers' advantage to create/delete activities judiciously. Tasks encode commonly-used, goal-oriented fixed tool invocation sequences, such as "create a netlist". Tasks abstract the internal tool sequences into a high-level entity. Designers thus need only to interact with tasks without getting into the peculiarities of individual tool's invocation details. This ability of separating what a tool can do from how a tool is used is called .I tool encapsulation. Complex task specifications are built up hierarchically as sequences of more primitive tasks. In the most primitive form, a task encapsulates a single design tool, describing its inputs, outputs, and default parameters required to execute that tool. We call such specifications *task templates*.

Tasks are *always* invoked within an activity. This causes a task template to be instantiated with proper inputs and parameters. Designers generally have little control over the invocation of tools except that they can customize the tasks through the choice of preferred parameter values. A design activity threads together a set of *task invocations*. There is a partial order defined over the task invocations belonging to the same activity. This order to a large extent is temporal, i.e., determined by the time of invocation. Correspondingly the activity is just a *linear* thread of task invocations. Later on we will show how designers can override this temporal ordering and create branches in the activity history.

At the bottom of the hierarchy is tool invocation, which is an invocation of a CAD tool with proper inputs and parameters. The system usually takes care of the internal details of invoking a tool such as where the tool resides, what are the inputs and outputs, and data format transformation. The sequencing of tool invocations within a task is largely predefined by the task template. Tool invocations also serve as the basic units of atomic actions. In other words, from design history's viewpoint, a tool invocation is executed either to the completion or not at all.

This history hierarchy reflects several design goals of a process management systems. Tasks hide from users the idiosyncracies of individual tools that might come from various vendors. Tasks also relieve designers of the burden of memorizing the sequence and parameter settings of frequently-used tool execution patterns. Activities provide contextual information in the form of related design operations and data. Furthermore, the structure built into the activity history greatly enhances the flexibility of design exploration. With activity in the history hierarchy, no longer a design process is just a flat collection of task invocations, but a set of internally-organized task invocation threads, each of which corresponds to a concrete design goal. The system also provides operations to manipulate (cascade, join, create and etc.) the activities so that designers can accommodate the structure of activities to reflect the dynamics of design. The notion of design process isolates a designer's work from the others. It encompasses the idea of *workspace* and provides a framework for controlled sharing in supporting team design or groupware.

4. Task Specification

4.1. The Model

Tasks are encapsulated units of work. There are two kinds of tasks: *primitive* and *complex*. They take input objects, and under the control of selected parameters, produce output objects. They can be described hierarchically in terms of simpler tasks. The specification of tasks are called *task templates*. Primitive task templates provide the information needed to invoke a specific design tools. They may be instantiated directly by the process management software, becoming part of an activity history.

Complex tasks are composed from a combination of primitive and complex tasks. Complex task templates resemble primitive tasks in their description of inputs, outputs, parameters, but include a section for *subtasks*. Subtasks are named instances of task templates, primitive or complex, with stipulated inputs, outputs, and parameter settings and arguments. *Ordering constraints*, constrain the sequence of subtask invocations. There are three reasons why pre-specified task templates are desirable in VLSI design. First, tasks help to automate some of the design steps which can be mechanized. If some of the steps involve human intervention, the specifications in task templates allow the system to navigate designers through the tool

space. Second, tasks encapsulate the internal workings of the underlying environment and therefore increase flexibility for adding tools to and deleting tools from the environment. Only the design project manager needs to know which tools are available and how they interact with others. Ordinary designers simply invoke tasks. Third, because designers are required to step through the tool space as specified in task templates, tasks provide a mechanism for enforcing certain design methodologies or even design styles, which are codified as sequences and choices of tools.

4.2. The Language

A task has a unique name, a descriptive purpose, and belongs to a class. A task's class can be primitive, complex, utility, or editing. This class information is exploited by the task manager to package the history information associated with the task. Usually a primitive task's name is the same as the tool that implements the task. But they may well be different. Often one has tools that can provide alternative functions depending on the parameter settings. For example, the same tool might map from truth tables to equations and vice versa. Such a tool could be encapsulated as two different tasks, with different parameter settings, depending on the work to be done. The fact that it is really the same software can be hidden from the user.

A task template also needs to specify the inputs and outputs of each of its subtasks. This specification establishes the data dependency relationship among the subtasks. Each of the encapsulated tools in a task can have a number of parameters. All of the parameters are command-line switches, but those of type "input" and "output" require additional information, such as whether the input is redirected from standard input or whether it comes from a file.

Let's consider the specification of a complex task to illustrate the graphical and internal forms. Normal designers only deal with the graphical form, while the LISP-like S-expression form is stored directly as OCT internal structures. The example of Figure 2a and 2b demonstrates the specification of a complex task. The task describes the process of (1)listing the terminals, (2)annotating the listing with placement information, and (3) performing the placement by running padp with the annotated list. Thus, it uses two distinct instances of the *padp* primitive task, with different parameter setting to control the tool's behavior.

The key difference between a primitive and a complex task specification are the additional properties added for the specifying the subtasks. Each subtask is given an instance name, unique to this template. A complex task's I/O are mapped onto the inputs and outputs of the subtasks. Some parameters may be hardwired within the specification to obtain a particular behavior from the subtasks. Although not illustrated by this example, a complex task template may also specify parameters and their conditional effects. These facilities can be used by users or higher level tasks.

The specification language renders great flexibility in modification of scripts, making the integration (or deletion) of new (old) tools straightforward, and allows frequently encountered sequences to be composed into new complex tasks as necessary. Task templates provide a limited form of AND-parallelism. Figure 3 shows a task template with parallelism among the subtasks. By AND-parallelism, we mean that all subtasks must be executed in the course of completing the task, and all predecessor subtasks must complete before a successor subtask can be invoked. In contrast, OR-parallelism refers to the case in which one or more alternative can proceed concurrently, but not all of them will be needed later on. OR-parallelism is achieved through independent tasks.

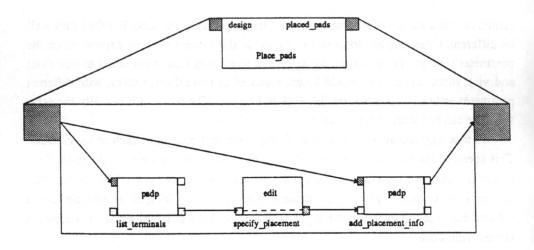

"Place_pads" Dataflow

Figure 2a - Graphical Task Specification

The Place_pads complex task is composed from three primitive subtasks. Padp (with -l) is invoked on the logic description to extract the terminals. The designer uses a text editor to annotate the terminal list with placement directives. Padp (with -D) is then invoked to perform the placement.

4.3. The Implementation of Task Management

The implementation of task management consists of three parts. A task language compiler that translates the task specifications into task templates stored in design database; a task manager that interacts with the designers and takes care of all the housekeeping work while the tasks are active; a task previewer is a debug tool for specifying tasks since the project manager (person) can use this previewer to verify the specifications by simulating the execution flow of the tasks.

The task manager is the software component with which designers interact while invoking tasks. The task manager navigates a designer through a task by comparing where he is in the current task with the task's template. At any one time, there may be more than one subtask that can be invoked next. The task manager presents the qualified subtasks and the designer can pick one of them and proceed. Once a subtask selected, the task manager will prompt for inputs, outputs and control parameters. In those cases where inputs and outputs are specified implicitly in the templates, the task manager is responsible to allocate and name these intermediates. If a designer violates the specifications by invoking a tool that is not one

of qualified subtasks, the task manager will issue a warning message. This check is useful in ensuring that designers follow the design methodology encoded in the task

```
(task
    (name Place_pads)
    (class complex)
    (input
        ((name design) (type oct_name)))
    (output
        ((name pads_placed) (type oct_name)))
    (subtasks
        (seq
            ((name padp list_terminals)
                (input pad_logic design)
                (output pad_list terminal_list)
                (parameters (l)))
            ((name edit specify_placement)
                (input edit_file terminal_list)
                (output edit_file terminal_list))
            ((name padp add_placement_info)
                (input pad_logic design)
                (input pad_specifier terminal_list)
                (output placed_pads pads_placed)
                (parameters
                    (D terminal_list)
                    (o pads_placed)))))
    (purpose
        ("Get a list of terminals and specify their placement")))
```

Figure 2b - Internal Form of Task Specification

Note the use of subtasks and sequencing clauses. Also, the complex task's inputs and outputs are mapped onto the inputs and the internal subtask instances.

templates. The task manager provides all these services through a graphical interface.

The task previewer provides a graphical interface to allow one to step through a task without invoking any tools. The person who specifies the task templates can use this tool to debug the specifications by comparing actual task behavior with the desired behavior. The previewer also allows the ordinary designers to "see what he's getting into" before invoking a task.

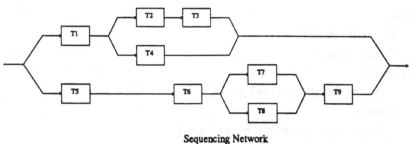

Sequencing Network

Figure 3 - Sequencing Constraint Example

The AND forks and joins impose partial orderings on the subtask invocations. For example, T1 and T5 can be simultaneously in execution, but T1 must complete before T2 or T4 can be invoked and T5 before T6. T7 and T8 must complete before T9 can commence.

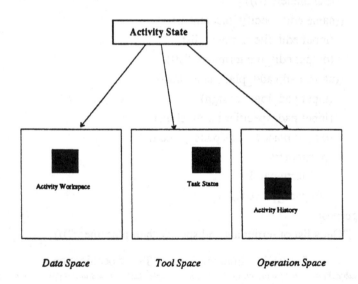

Data Space	*Tool Space*	*Operation Space*

Figure 4 The State of A Design Activity

The three components of an activity state: the collection of data objects produced and consumed by the activity, the tools related to the current active tasks, and the set of recorded invocations since the activity began.

5. The Activity Model

5.1. Conceptual View

A VLSI designer typically faces three distinct object spaces during the design development: the *Data Space*, the *Tool Space*, and the *Operation Space*. The data space is the collection of data objects that a designer has created or referenced in a design project. The tool space refers to the set of tools available in the design environment and the organizational relationships among tools. Finally, the operation space refers to the history of design operations that a designer has performed so far. A design operation represents a binding between a CAD tool and the data objects that are the I/O's of the tool invocation. An activity provides a mechanism to thread together task invocations that are issued in the same context. Furthermore, it defines an ordering relationship among task invocations. The physical contents of a design activity combines three components derived from the three spaces described above: the *Activity Workspace*, the *Activity History*, and the *Task Status*. As illustrated in Figure 4, these components open windows into the data, operation, and tool spaces, respectively. Together they form a context relating to an activity's specific design goal.

An activity workspace contains the data objects produced or consumed by the tasks within that design activity. The data can be organized along version, configuration, and equivalence dimension as in the Version Server model [KATZ87]. Since a designer can have more than one activity simultaneously, the union of a designer's activity workspaces forms his *Private Workspace*, which is the local, non-sharable database where a designer carries out the design work.

An activity history is a (possibly branching) sequence of history records. Each history record corresponds to a task invocation. Due to the hierarchical nature of tasks, a history record can also consist of other history records. Each history record logs the input objects, output objects, control parameters of a task invocation, and possibly other history records. The history records are largely ordered by the time of invocation. Between two history records (or two task invocations) defines a *design point*, which uniquely identifies the state of activity workspace right before the second task is invoked. The state of activity workspace associated with a design point is called its *data scope*.

The task status records the progress a user has made in the current set of task invocations. Since a designer can invoke more than one task within an activity or across different activities simultaneously, the task status maintains the interleaved execution status of each in-progress task invocation within an activity. This data structure makes tool navigation possible as described in the last section.

In addition, each design object also has a derivation history when it got created. A derivation history of a design object is defined to be the sequence of history records that lead to the creation of this object. Note the derivation history of an object does not cross activity boundaries. In other words, explicit input objects are viewed as "historyless" when computing the derivation history, thus limiting the history back-tracing within the same activity. The derivation history provides a basis for both the data dependency relationships among design objects, and the tool execution sequence needed to reconstruct an object when its dependees are modified.

5.2. Operational View

The following assumptions underlie the use of facilities of the activity model:

[1] Every task is invoked within a certain activity, which can be either explicitly specified or implicitly inherited from the previous invocation. Within an activity, there is a *current cursor* which is the default design point to which the history record corresponding to the subsequent task invocation is to be appended. After a new history record is appended, the current cursor is advanced. The data scope of the current cursor is the part of the activity workspace that is visible when a task is invoked. Therefor, this assumption requires that before invoking a task, a designer should make sure that he is in the proper context by selecting the appropriate design point within the appropriate activity.

[2] All the history-manipulating operations are limited to a single activity. To manipulate a different activity's history, a designer must select that activity and be positioned within it. If a designer wants to deal with two or more activities simultaneously, he would have to combine those activities into a single new activity and proceed.

[3] When a designer invokes a task template with inputs and parameters, he commits to following the prescribed sequence of operations. A user steps through the tool space under the guidance of the task manager. Thus, the system not only navigates for users, but also checks their operations, reporting errors when the prescribed sequences are violated. This supports the idea that tasks can also be used to enforce a design methodology or design style.

From user's point of view, there are two classes of design operations: *Task Invocation Operation* and *Control Operation*. The former do the real work by starting and suspending tasks, while the latter help to organize the design process. As we have already mentioned, the activity mechanism is used to impose certain structures onto their design process. The control operations allow designers to group activities in a meaningful way or to override the strict temporal ordering of task invocations within an activity. They can be further characterized as those that apply within (internal) a design activity and those outside (external).

Internal control operations are issued within a specific activity. Tasks are invoked from the current cursor of the current activity. Designers can explicitly change the position of the current cursor by internal control operations. Since the data scope of the current cursor defines the visible part of the activity workspace, changing the current cursor changes what is visible in the activity workspace. In particular, if a designer wants to restore the database to a previous state, he simply changes the current cursor to the design point corresponding to that state. Designers manipulate the history through a graphical browser, which provides a powerful operational paradigm to query history database. Furthermore, it simplifies the selection of versions. Namely, instead of specifying which versions of which objects to use, the designers just specify the appropriate design point. The system will take care of the design-point/data-scope mapping automatically. This "roll-back" capability makes it possible to explore distinct design alternatives by applying different design operation sequences on the same state of activity workspace. Note also that it is this re-positioning of current cursor that creates the branch structure in the activity history. The ordering of task invocations thus are no longer temporal but can be overridden by internal control operations.

External control operations can be issued only in the special *system activity*. External control operations are used to create new activities, compose new activities from existing ones or to change their status. Activities are either active or asleep, and a single distinguished active activity is called the *current activity*. Users can change the current activity simply by selecting among the active activities. CASCADE and JOIN operations are used to compose a larger activity from smaller activities. Designers use these control operations to interrelate activities in any way they desire. When an activity is initially created, there is nothing in its workspace. Our model allows newly-created activities to inherit workspace from some other activity. This mechanism supports the exploration of several large-granule alternatives by creating a distinct activity for each alternative. By copying the workspace from the same parent activity, the system ensures that these alternatives start from the same data set. This is what we called OR-parallelism in section 4.

The detailed list of these control operations, together with their functionalities are omitted and can be found in {CKV89}.

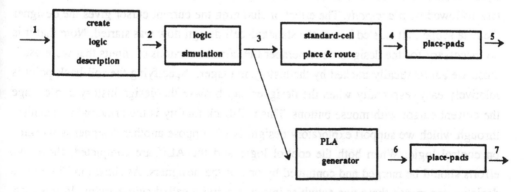

Figure 5   The Synthesize - ALU Design Activity

5.3. An Example

In this section, we illustrate the concepts and operations presented above. Figure 5 shows an example design flow, whose goal is to synthesize an ALU. First the designer creates an activity with a descriptive name, such as *synthesize-ALU* At the initial design point, the data scope is empty because nothing has yet been generated or referenced. To create the logic description of the ALU, the designer next invokes a complex task called *create logic description*. Inside this task, there are actually three subtasks: *enter-logic, format-translation*, and *logic minimization*. The task manager leads the designer through this sequence step by step. The designer is only responsible for setting proper parameters and preparing inputs when necessary.

After *create-logic-description* has completed, the designer invokes the primitive task *logic simulator*. Because the outputs of the simulation might indicate some design errors, the designer may have to reinvoke the first task to correct the errors. This is an iterative process: many invocations may be needed to get the correct logic description. However, only the final result is needed in the following design steps. The designer can issue internal control operations ITERATE-START and ITERATE-END before and after this sequence of steps to notify the history manager of the iterated nature of this task sequence. The effect is that only the objects that are actually used later on in the process flow are maintained; all the rest are garbage-collected automatically.

After the logic is finally made correct, the designer then invokes the *standard-cell-place-and-route* task, followed by the *place-pads* task (which was shown in detail in Section 4) to complete the activity. At this point the current cursor is at design point 5.

Suppose the designer is not satisfied with the result of the standard-cell approach and wishes to explore another alternative, such as an implementation in a PLA design style. He then resets the current cursor to design point 3, and invokes the *PLA-generation* task followed by *place-pads*. The effect of changing the current cursor gives the designer the data scope that existed before the standard-cell design flow was started. Note that it is not necessary for the designer to remember the correct versions of inputs that were used: these are automatically tracked by the history manager. Specifying the roll-back point is relatively easy, especially when the designer can browse the design history and change the current cursor with mouse buttons. This roll-back facility is the principal mechanism through which we support exploratory design. Now suppose another designer is working on control logic. When both the control logic and the ALU are completed, these two efforts should be merged and continued by one of the designers. As shown in Figure 6, a designer can merge these two activities into one activity called *chip activity*. In this case, the data scope of design point N is the union of the activity workspaces of these two activities. The histories of these two activities are also unioned. Moreover, this combined activity is as if it had been created by the current designer: he can roll back to any design

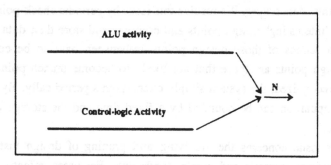

Figure 6 Merging Two Activities into One Activity

point in this new activity and modify the history structure. This facility of combining small activities into larger ones supports the hierarchical design style and promotes cooperative team work. Note that after the merging, the original activities can go on independently of the new activity. That is, any modifications made on one place won't be seen by the other. This is what we call *merge by copy* semantics. The model also allows *merge by reference* semantics in which modifications will be reflected in both places. But in general the latter could easily cause conceptual confusion and thus is less useful in practice.

5.4. Implementation Issues

The central implementation challenge is to represent the design history in a time- and space-efficient way. We use a doubly-linked list, augmented with index hash table, to store the activity history. Because of the similarity of this data structure with the threaded structure of a design activity, computing the data scope associated with each design point becomes a backward traversal from the design point to the boundary of the activity. All the objects associated with the history records that are visisted along the traversal are unioned to form the data scope. The index hash table is used to quickly locate the history record just before the design point when given the index of that design point. This history record serves as the starting point of the traversal.

Although computing data scope by backward traversal is conceptually simple, yet it is computationally expensive. This is especially true when the activity grows bigger and bigger, or when the current cursor is moved frequently. On the other hand, it seems infeasible to compute the data scopes for all design points and store them explicitly. There are two reasons for this. First of all, not every design point will be used as branch point; so it is not worthy to store the data scope of every design point. Second, since the activity history is largely a linear structure, there is a lot of redundancies between adjacent design points' data scopes. We resolve this issue by periodic check-pointing. That is, we pick those "interesting" design points and compute and store their data scopes explicitly. The data scopes of those design points in-between have to be computed. The interesting design points are those that are likely to become branch points. If no such points can be recognized, the system simply check-points periodically. By doing so, the data scope computation can be bounded by a fixed time and the storage efficiency can also be attained.

The other issue concerns the archiving and pruning of design histories. This is important both from system's and user's standpoints. For users, effective pruning can hide the irrelevant details and unimportant history, and thus presents a more informative view of the current context. For systems, effective pruning can significantly reduce the working set of the system and enhance the speed of history-manipulation operations. Due to space limitations, we refer readers to [CK90] for detailed algorithms.

6. Summary

We have presented a model for process management based on task specification and history management. Key elements for task specification are a graphical format for describing tool encapsulations and a way to create complex "tasks" from the composition of more primitive tasks. The history model is founded on the concepts of design projects, design processes, activities, and task invocations. Its key feature is the notion of an activity: the focus for collecting the history of task invocations including the consequences of such invocations in terms of the design objects produced and consumed. A primitive task manager and tool navigator is now operational and has been implemented on top of the U. C. Berkeley's OCT Data Manager. The implementation of the internal algorithms of the History Manager is also completed. We are working on the graphical user interface part.

We view design process management as a natural outgrowth of the CAD community's emphasis on design data management over the last few years. The emphasis is now shifting away from data concerns to those which are more operational in nature. Beyond process management, we see a rich area for future work in project management: that is, the exploitation of knowledge about the design process in order to better utilize the resources dedicated to completing a project in a timely fashion.

References

[BANN83] L. Bannon, A. Cypher, S. Greenspan, M. L. Monty, "Evaluation and analysis of users' activity organization," Proceedings of the CHI'83 Human Factors in Computer Systems, page 54-57, Boston, Massachusetts.

[BUSH89] M. Bushnell, S.W. Director, "Automated design tool execution in the Ulysses design environment," IEEE Transactions on CAD", Vol.8, No.3, (March 1989).

[CARD87] S. K. Card, D. A. Henderson Jr., "A multiple, virtual-workspace interface to support user task switching", Proceedings of the CHI'87 Human Factors in Computer Systems, page 53-59, Toronto, Ontario.

[CKV89] T.F. Chiueh, R.H. Katz, V. King, "Managing the VLSI Design Process," UCB/CSD 89/538, University of California, Berkeley, Computer Science Division, (November 1989).

[CK90] T.F. Chiueh, R.H. Katz, "The Design Flow Management System : A Survey and A Synthesis," in preparation.

[DANI89] J. Daniell, S.W. Director, "An object-oriented approach to distributed CAD tool control," in IEEE Proc. 26th Design Automation Conference, Las Vegas, NV, (June 1989).

[KATZ87] Katz, R. H., R. Bhateja, E. Chang, D. Gedye, V. Trijanto, "Design Version Management," IEEE Design and Test, V 4, N 1, (February 1987).

[LEBL84] D. B. Leblang, R. P. Chase, "Computer-aided software engineering in a distributed workstation environment," Proceedings ACM SIGPLAN/SIGSOFT Conference on Practical Software Development Environments, (April 1984).

[LEE 88] A. Lee, "Use of history for user support," Technical Report CSRI-212, Computer Systems Research Institute, University of Toronto.

[LINX86] C. Linxi, A.N. Habermann, "A history mechanism and UNDO/REDO/REUSE support in ALOE'" CMU-CS-86-148, Department of Computer Science, Carnegie Mellon University.

[OCT 89] OCT Manual, U. C. Berkeley EECS Department Technical Report, 1989.

Towards a Shared Computational Environment for Engineering Design

Eswaran Subrahmanian
Arthur Westerberg
Gregg Podnar
Engineering Design Research Center
Carnegie Mellon University
Pittsburgh, PA 15213

Abstract: This paper presents an outline of an architecture for shared computational environments for engineering design based on studies on the nature of engineering design conducted from cognitive and social points of view. The basic thesis of this paper is that a group of designers in performing a design task use a variety of engineering and management oriented models and that an environment that supports the design process will have to accommodate the different modeling paradigms within a single integrated framework. Further, the environment should facilitate the negotiation process that is characteristic of a multi-person design process.

1. Introduction

The critical role of engineering design in enhancing the ability to design quality products in the shortest time is widely recognized. A large body of research has addressed questions concerning theories and methodologies of design from diverse disciplinary perspectives. Recent technological advances in computer and communication technologies - such as powerful workstations, high capacity networks, database management systems, knowledge representation and inference methods among others - have spurred efforts to investigate their application for achieving greater design effectiveness. The proposed research follows this tradition with some crucial differences in the basic approach.

The primary objective of this paper is to propose a design for a shared, computer-based environment capable of supporting the co-ordination of diverse activities and the collaboration among a team of designers engaged in relatively complex engineering design projects. Our central focus will be on the preliminary design phase during which much of the structuring of the design problems takes place. We argue that this phase poses the more challenging questions in terms of providing computer-based support, mainly because we do not have a complete understanding of the preliminary design process.

The basic thesis of this paper is that designers in performing a design task use a variety of engineering-oriented models such as functional, equational, geometric models etc. and that an environment that supports the design process will have to accommodate different modeling paradigms within a single, integrated framework. This thesis, when extended to a group which typifies most real-world design projects entail, requires the capacity for facilitating not only the technical aspects of the design process but also organizational issues, project planning activities, and communication among designers. The computer-based environment is expected to evolve continually to a point at which most users (engineering designers) would acknowledge it as being ideally suited for collaborative design work especially in the area of preliminary design. We anticipate that the system would prove to be useful beyond the preliminary design stage in the overall design process. It will also serve as a test-bed for an empirical analysis of design.

The work reported in this paper was motivated by our observation of a preliminary design team at the Westinghouse Electric Corporation with the objective of identifying the computational support needs of such a group [35]. The organization of the rest of the paper is as follows. Section 2 reviews, in brief, research in the study of engineering design in the last two decades and also provides an overview of current approaches to computational support for engineering design. Section 3 provides a characterization of the engineering design process from a group or social point of view and from a cognitive view of individual designers. Based on these chracterizations of engineering design, this section also explores their implications for building computational design support systems. Section 4 provides an outline for an architecture of a support system that is based on the needs of the design process. Section 5 provides a summary of a preliminary prototype of the system built in HyperCard on the Macintosh Personal Computer. Conclusions and future work that is planned are discussed in the section 6.

2. Motivation and Previous Work

The need for organizing and rationalizing engineering design was the focus of the first conference on design methods in 1962 [16]. This led to a flurry of work over the next decade in the characterization and management of the design process [7]. The literature has dealt with different phases of the design process: conceptual design [11], embodiment and detail design [17, 25] and systems based management of design [17]. Most of these approaches were prescriptive approaches to engineering design and were deficient in their sensitivity to the practice of design and to the needs and capability of the human designers. A paradigmatic shift in the study of engineering design took place with the change in emphasis from prescriptive methods of design to attempts at the development of empirical theories of design. Empirical research into the nature of engineering design can be divided into two streams. They are: a) cognitive studies on individual designers and b) observation-based studies of groups of designers. Cognitive studies were motivated by the advent of the new field of cognitive science which provided the researchers with the methods for observing and encoding the process of an individual doing design [23]. Meanwhile, the need for understanding design in an industrial context led to studies in engineering design using observer based case studies and diverse methodologies such as decision analysis and sociological analysis [11, 14, 3]. While all of these studies are directed towards improving the effectiveness of design, a recent participant-observer study by Hales [14,15] develops quantitative and qualitative measures to capture the effectiveness of the design process. The basic conclusion reached by both cognitive and group studies of design process point to the need for development of design practice and theoretical frameworks that are directed away from prescriptive approaches towards empirically grounded theories and practice.

Study of engineering design and supporting engineering design usually have taken divergent routes even though supporting engineering design has been an active area of research. Support of engineering design, especially computer based design, has been led by technology rather than the nature of the design process. Current practice of providing design support from a computational perspective can be classified into three distinct types: geometric modeling, algebraic modeling and, logic-based modeling (meant in the wider sense of systems based on artificial intelligence techniques). All of these approaches to support are restricted by the underlying assumptions they make about the design process. Geometric modeling systems or CAD systems view the process of design as creating a geometric model of the artifact. Algebraic modeling approaches to design are based on viewing design as choice of parameters to a given set of constraints while achieving a given set of objectives. Artificial intelligence systems or logic-based systems are based on viewing the problem of design as having predetermined structural decomposition with a set of rules (heuristic and otherwise) for choosing among alternative solutions for the subproblems and combining the alternatives into a whole. The above approaches are essentially based on the assumption that stages of the design problem consist of problem formulation, analysis, synthesis and evaluation. Most current support systems are directed at the analysis and synthesis stages of well understood problems. The view of design process adopted by these systems tend to separate the problem formulation and problem solving phases and provide support for problem solving.

Apart from the above approaches, a "management" perspective to design has been directed towards developing techniques for design management in terms of tasks and schedules. Many of these techniques are embodied in the form of computational tools. In this approach, design is viewed as a sequential set of stages with their own set of tasks that are amenable to modeling as networks and performing cost and time computations over the networks. This approach is most often used in managing large design groups. Similar to the other approaches described above, this approach is also directed towards a particular slice of the design problem and with an underlying view of the design process. There are two main shortcomings that are common to all of the described approaches to design support.

Firstly all these systems view design from a single viewpoint. For example, geometric modeling systems have taken the view that the constraints in the design process are resolved in the specification of the overall shape. Attempts at expanding this view are directed towards adding other types of design and manufacturing information. Smithers et al. [34] point out that systems that encode design knowledge over geometric representations are inadequate both from the point of view of parametric computation and automatic inferencing. Equational modelling systems and artificial intelligence based systems that rely on numeric and symbolic techniques respectively are also representationally inadequate to deal with all aspects of the design problem. This is not surprising because studies on representations for problem solving point out how different representations are best suited for computationally efficient problem solving even when they (the representations) are informationally equivalent [22]. Representational and problem solving adequacy of a given representation play a crucial role in the choice of representations required to address all the diverse needs of a design task. There may exist no single representation that can possibly address the representational needs of the design process; this can only be satisfied by a collection of representations that are related to each other.

Secondly, current support systems are mostly black boxes in terms of the knowledge in them. None of these computational support systems approaches answer the following questions:

"What knowledge is used, how it is used, where it comes from, what form is it in, what knowledge is generated, why, what form this new knowledge needs to be in, what else does it get used for, how is it structured and maintained." [33]

Existing systems are based on a user getting to know the language to describe the inputs of the problem to the system. These systems, in most cases, provides an uninterpreted output as a solution. Most of these systems do not provide the underlying conceptual model of knowledge used by the problem solver to the user so as to allow for exchange of knowledge and its structure with the user.

Despite these problems current approaches have a role in the design of future computational support.

The current state of computational use in design is that of unstructured clusters of automation in the midst of human designers. To address the issue of support in a systematic manner and to improve the current state of understanding of the design process, computational systems that would best serve the design process are those that are designed based on the understanding of generation, organization, and manipulations of knowledge used during the course of design or the "knowledge process"[33]. The need to systematically integrate the computer into the design process has been observed by a study for the National Science Foundation on research needs in the area of engineering design who conclude that:

"Research is needed to understand the conceptual process of design and to integrate and expand the capabilities of computers to aid in the creative process."[27]

It is the objective of this paper to propose, based on recent empirical studies on design processes from social and cognitive perspectives, a design support environment that provides for the integration of computational tools and the needs of the human designers to manage the knowledge process that underlies the engineering design process. We also expect the proposed environment to serve as a testbed for further empirical studies on the design process.

3. Characterization of Engineering Design

Definition of a design problem varies based on the persuasions of the person defining design. Cognitive scientists, following Simon [30], in describing the structure of design problems point out that they occupy a continuum of well-structured and ill-structured problems. Where a particular problem falls is based on whether the problem has been formalized as a well structured problem. Designers on the other hand emphasize the product of the design process by describing design as the specification of an artifact that performs the functions designed for and is manufacturable [9]. More recent definitions of engineering design also include the specification of service, maintenance and disposal. To describe engineering design from the context of building support environments, we review two characterizations of design in detail. They are: engineering design as a social process [4] and as a cognitive process [16]. The latter characterization of design problem is based on identifying invariant features across prototypes of design problems based on information processing theory of human problem solving [16] while the former is an ethnographic perspective of engineering design [4]. We explore the relationship between the two views and the implications for design support.

3.1 Design as a Social Process

Bucciarelli [4] in reporting the main finding of his ethnographic study of design claims:

> ...different participants think about the work on design in quite different ways. They do not share fully congruent internal representations of the design. In this sense design at any time in the design process is more than the sum, or simple synthesis, of its participants' interpretation. In this sense it is a social construction."

In describing design as social construction, Bucciarelli identifies four inter-related aspects of design.: organization, object worlds, specification and constraints and design discourse. Design discourse is classified as constraining discourse, naming discourse, and decision discourse.

Organization: Organization of the design task is often determined by the perceived structure of the object being designed. This may be hierarchical as well as functional. An object may be dissected in more than one way depending on the criteria used. The criteria for dissecting the overall design task identifies the boundaries between subtasks. The interacting subtasks in the nearly decomposed structure are the source of ambiguity that is resolved by setting clear interface conditions between the subtasks.

The participants allocated to the subtasks operate within their own specializations. The naming of the subtasks and the interfaces between them are determined as part of the decomposition process. Organizing the design itself is a design task; more precisely organizing design is part of the overall design task.

Object Worlds: Object worlds are best characterized as worlds of specialization with their own theories, system of symbols, models, tools and other domain-specific heuristics. Every participant brings his own object world to the design process and spends some time operating purely within it. A study comparing the design problem strategies of three professionals(an academic, a consultant and a practicing engineer), designing a high rise building, points out that they structure and solve problems within their area of knowledge [Baker87]. This study measures this difference by the amount of time spent on different aspects of the design task. The results of this study support the observation that participants view and solve a design problem from their own object worlds. Groups of participants in dealing with interfaces between subsystems operate on their shared worlds together to iron out interface issues.

Specification and Constraints: Specification and constraints arise from the interests of the participants stemming from their object worlds. Constraints come in the categories of technical constraints, legislative constraints, and performance constraints. The constraints themselves are hard or soft. Technical constraints arising from physical laws are hard constraints while other technical constraints such as safety and maintenance constraints are soft constraints. The major observation here is that there is no supra(canonical)-object world that defines an unambiguous exchange between participants in the design. Hence, specification and constraints are generated through a process of negotiation among disciplines and interests of the participants. As the design process comes to a close, the ambiguities are eliminated through the negotiation.

Design discourse: Design discourse, as mentioned earlier, does not take place in a super-design language but is defined by the reconciliation between the object worlds of the participants and by agreement on the naming of the parts and functions of the design. Bucciarelli identifies three aspects of design discourse: constraining discourse, naming discourse and decision discourse. Constraining discourse is the process of generating performance specifications of the object being designed and to define a design concept that moves the design problem from an unstructured state to a relatively structured specifications stage. It is this process that constrains the discourse of design for the later stages.

Naming is an integral part of the discourse of design; the process of naming is closely related to the decomposition of the problem. In decomposing the problem the scope of the subproblem is described by naming and defining the objects by agreement among participants from different object worlds.

Decision discourse refers to the part of the discourse where the participants decide on the nature of solutions to the subproblems. Mathematical models and physical models are used to analyze the effect of a decision to varying levels of precision. In this process, for example, the interface issues between two aspects of design are not necessarily resolved; rather a decision is made based on the costs of non-resolution in terms of performance, marketability, etc.

In summary, the view of design as a social process suggests:
   1) Organizing design is an integral part of the design task; it is solved concurrently with the design problem. The resultant structure of the organization is often dictated by a functional decomposition of the product being designed;
   2) Each participants in a design team brings a personal object world (defined by their specialty) consisting of symbols systems, theories, practices, models, etc;
   3) Design discourse is characterized by constraining discourse, naming discourse and decision discourse. They deal with defining the scope of the problem, to provide means for understanding the design goal from multiple object worlds, and making decisions based on performance modeling and negotiation at the problem boundaries; and
   4) Specification and constraints are generated by the participants from their own object worlds resulting in ambiguity at the interfaces. Ambiguity in design is inevitable especially in the conceptual design stages. Ambiguity reduces as the process draws close to finalizing a design.
Pointing out the implications of this view of design in building support systems, Bucciarelli suggests:
   .., then they themselves ought to be designed to accommodate the different perspectives of users within the firm. The importance of exchange of object worlds in designing ought to be taken into account. This points to the desirability, and problem of networking participants' work through computer representations. At the same time the notion of different object worlds points to the need for

flexibility in the tool. It ought to be able to accommodate the peculiarities of the furniture of an individual users own object world. [4]

We shall address the issue of support after examining the cognitive view of design and its relationship to the social view presented here.

3.2 Invariant Structures in Prototypical Design Problems: An Information Processing Theory View

Cognitive science has generally viewed design problems primarily in terms of the structure. In describing whether a design problem is a well-structured or ill-structured problem, Simon [Simon73] points out that the description is based on the stance of the problem solver. An architect doing creative design has an ill-structured problem at hand while a person doing routine design is solving a well-structured problem. Most work in artificial intelligence based systems have been directed towards dealing with the problems that are well-structured. An argument in defense of this approach is that an ill-structured problem, once structured, becomes a well-structured problem for subsequent tasks [30]. However as Simon points out;

..there is merit to the claim that much problem solving effort is directed at structuring problems, and only a fraction of it at solving problems once they are structured.[30]

The few cognitive studies on problem structuring in design that have been done to date have concentrated on observing domain based structuring behavior of the designers [37,2,1]. They define the process within a narrow task environment that is defined by a problem statement's direct mapping onto a problem structure [16].

Recently, Goel and Pirolli, have reported a study in which they attempt to identify invariant features in prototypical design problems from within information processing theory in cognitive science [16]. They do not accept the more general view in cognitive science that design problem solving is the same as problem solving in general. Their premise in generating invariants for design problem solving is based on the observation that design as a category that exhibits prototype effects. Further, they expand the notion of task environment with respect to previous studies by including external factors and the motivations and goals of the problem solver. Based on a preliminary analysis of protocols, they propose a model of invariant features of the design task environment and in the structure(s) of the design problem space. The task environment is characterized by the following invariant features: a) Size and complexity of the problem; b) Goal statements as input and product specification as output; c) Temporal separation of specification and delivery of product; d) Delayed feedback from the world on the functioning of the product; e) Independent functioning of the product; f) Cost of action; g) No right or wrong answers but only good or bad answers; and h) Many degrees of freedom in problem statement. These invariants in the task environment drive the structure of the design problem space.

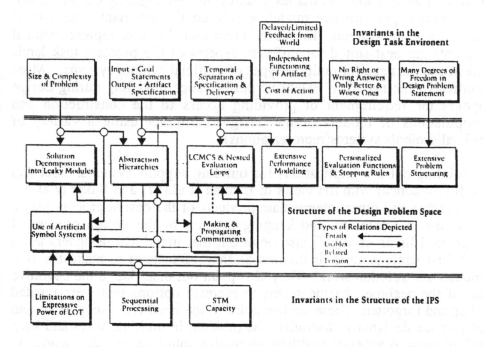

Figure. 1. Invariant structures in design problem space
(Reproduced from [16])

The invariants in design problem space as structured by the design task environment is shown in Figure 1. The invariants identified in the structure of design problem space are: 1) extensive problem structuring; 2) extensive performance modeling; 3) personalized and institutionalized stopping rules; 4) a limited commitment mode control strategy with nested evaluation cycles; 5) the making and propagation of commitments; 6) solution decomposition into leaky (or nearly decomposable) modules; 7) the role of abstractions in the transformation of goals to artifact specification and; 8) the use of artificial symbol systems. The task of extensive problem structuring is characterized by collection and clarification of information on the design problem, specification of constraints, and negotiation of constraints. The process of problem structuring is mediated by personal knowledge. This knowledge comprises of general knowledge about the world in terms of procedural knowledge, conceptual knowledge fragments that are situation specific, knowledge of patterns, and domain specific knowledge. Some of these knowledge types have consistent underlying theories while others do not. In Figure 1 we see that the invariants of problem structuring, use and creation of abstraction hierarchies, making and propagating commitments, and extensive performance modeling rely on the invariant - the use of artificial symbol systems. The observation that different representational structures are best suited for different aspects of the problem task lends credence to the need for multiple types of artificial symbol systems. More specifically, the need for extensive performance modeling during design imposes the requirement of providing access to the construction and manipulations of models of the designed product using a variety of artificial symbols systems(representations).

In pointing out the implications for building support systems, Goel and Pirolli [16] concur with the views of Ullman et al.[37] and Baker et al. [2] that sketches and other intermediate products of the design process play a major role in reminding and keeping account of the design process of designers. Ullman et al.[37] also point out that individual designers use a depth first strategy in their process as they often tend to make the first hypothesized solution work. They also point out that, due to the cognitive load of the designer, he/she seems to recreate options that were created earlier and forgotten. These studies point to the need for a support system that aids the designer to formulate the problem in multiple ways and keep track of them to generate multiple alternative solutions; in other words, to support the exploration of the design space [6].

3.3 Relating the Social and Individual Processes of Design

In the previous sections we discussed two processes of design; a single designer doing design versus a team of people involved in design. As in all fields the reconciliation of the macro versus the micro view of a process produces intense debates on the scalability or reducibility of one to explain the other. This debate is well known in the social sciences especially in economics and in the debate between sociologists and psychologists. Especially in the context of supporting the engineering design the micro view (the cognitive view) and the macro view (the social view) of the design process, we believe are not contradictory. This is not surprising because the micro view, while restricting itself to the single designer does not posses characteristics that are disjoint with the the social view. The social view encompasses the cognitive view while opening to debate aspects of the design process in the cognitive view in a group setting It is precisely this debate that transforms the design task into a social construction the vocabulary of the design and the evaluation of the design are to be negotiated through a process of agreement. In the following paragraphs, we will elaborate on the similarities and differences between the two views and illustrate how they dove-tail with each other so as to describe the nature of design environments that we believe will support engineering design.

Structure of the design problem: The structure of the design problem in both the macro and micro view requires the understanding of the design problem in order to decompose the problem. Decomposition is an important means for dealing with complexity [31]. The decomposition in the individual designers case is based on the individual knowledge, evaluation functions and the constraints of the design process. In group settings, decomposition is often negotiated. In design groups, the individual and group needs and responsibilities are reconciled in terms of the decomposition of the design task for the organization of design.

Objects worlds: Both individual and group views have object worlds arising from the variety of domains required to solve a given design problem. In a group setting, obviously, the numbers of design object worlds increases leading to the need for additional object worlds such as project planning and other organizational models besides the collection of object models brought by every individual designer in the group.

Specification and Constraints: Constraints are essential part of any design problem. Beyond constraints that are derived from physical laws, the set of constraints that pertain to subjective aspects of the designer or groups of designers are the what are commonly referred to as soft constraints or evaluative constraints. The the trade offs embedded in the evaluative (performance) constraints correspond to the goodness measure of the design solution of the designer or the group. In an individual designers case, he has to define this measure in terms of performance specifications the product should satisfy. On the otherhand, in a group the trade -offs are negotiated to achieve a set of constraints and a solution which falls within the set of solutions. This set of solutions is some acceptable intersection of goodness measures of the individuals in the group based on their perceived view of the artifact and its use. It is not usually not the case that the solution is optimal in any sense to any or all of the participants [4]. It is in this sense that design is a social construction arrived through negotiation by a group of designers.

Design Discourse: This aspect of design is explicit in a group design context while it is mostly implicit in the case of the individual. It is explicit in a group design context precisely because the three basic invariant parts of a design task, decomposition, object worlds, and constraints, are not unique across individuals. In other words, the ways in which a problem can be decomposed and the ways in which a set of constraints can be chosen and ordered for a design task is not unique. As we have argued elsewhere, we feel that an individual is not able to articulate his evaluative criteria for design prior to the start of the problem; in fact he discovers these in the process of exploration of the design space [5]. As can be expected, for design carried out in groups this process of exploration also involves negotiating: a) the language of discourse(reconciliation of naming between object words); b) constraining the nature of the discourse; and c) specification of constraints of the design problem. In essence, design in groups while possessing additional dimensions such as development of a design organization and negotiating a language for communication share the same invariant features of design task environments of individuals performing design independently.

3.4 Implications for Design of Support Systems

The characterizations of the design problem as social and cognitive processes point to the extensive problem structuring that accompanies any design problem solving. In both views, the studies reported chose to characterize design problems that fall in the category of ill-structured problems [4,16]. However, in a design problem solving situation certain subproblems in the decomposition may be well-structured. Well-structured subproblems are amenable to a variety of design methods such as optimization techniques, weak methods and other mathematical techniques. AI based systems have been demonstrated to perform well in a closed world well-structured symbolic domain that use weak methods for problem solving. To support the design task at the level of ill-structured problems that require extensive structuring, a computational support system should be directed towards aiding the invariant aspects of the problem in a given domain of design. The most crucial aspect of the invariants in both models of design are object worlds or personal knowledge. This knowledge consists of domain knowledge with its theories, form and structure, abstract conceptual knowledge that is fragmentary without a consistent underlying theory of the worldly experience and knowledge patterns. When this knowledge is formalizable as a symbol system, it is amenable to representation on the computer. This representation of symbol system for a domain should also address the construction and manipulation of abstraction hierarchies. For knowledge that is not easily formalizable facilities for expressing in textual or graphical form should be provided.

Current design systems view the use of representation systems such as geometry as a means of communication. Several studies on design problem solving point out that figures and sketches and intermediate products generated during design serve as means for focusing the design task and to augment memory [16, 37, 2]. The point that multiple representations are required to deal with design from a computational point of view was made earlier. It was also noted that intermediate products in a group design environment are used to serve as records of agreement and social exchange. The implication of this observation for support systems is that the system should provide the means to structure the different object worlds that are made up of different symbolic representational systems with or without an underlying theory of organization. Different object worlds should be allowed to co-exist in the same environment. The extent to which the object worlds are represented on the computer is based on the existence of symbol systems to represent and manipulate those worlds. Object worlds contain past experience and are reorganized with experience; current research on machine learning hopes to address this issue computationally. However, humans are the best agents we know who are able to catalogue and transfer experience from one domain to another and hence support should be provided to enhance this ability.

Performance modeling is an important invariant in both views that relies on the artificial symbols systems for description and simulation. Many of the models can be represented as well-structured problems with different levels of predictive and simulation capability. These models are operators on artificial symbol systems and very often do not share the same representational structures. Iterative use of these models in performance modelling leads to complications in their integrated use.

In summary, the main features of a support system that would aid the task of design are:
1. Models of artificial symbol systems. This allows for the creation of domain specific models and individual participant models of the design task. It corresponds to the development of representations of artificial symbol systems for problem solving as well to provide support in expressing and organizing the intermediate products of design.
2. Model of the agents participating in the design. At the individual level of support it corresponds to organizing computational agents based on the types of demands for performance modeling. In a

social context this becomes important because of the existence of both human and computational agents. Further, a model of agents and their specialization allows for the team to access and experiment with tools from the perspectives of different participants in a single environment. This model can also provide a means for communicating the underlying organization of agents, for given task to the entire group.

3. Models of tasks and task networks. All design tasks at the individual or the social level require the breakdown of tasks based on problem decomposition. This task model is hierarchically structured with higher level tasks decomposed into a set of lower level tasks. The lowest level tasks operate on appropriate models of artificial symbol systems. High level tasks are essentially directed towards managing the design project. Provision should be made for describing lower level tasks that can be integrated using a set of computational tools.

4. A knowledge management system that allows for defining and displaying specific design knowledge as needed by a human agent.

Providing such comprehensive support suggests a hypertext like model for building the support environment. The issues we have raised from the context of design support have direct relationships to the set of issues that have been identified as research directions in the hypertext literature [13]. They are: a) search and query in hypertext/hypermedia networks; b) augmenting the basic node-link model (with appropriate conceptual models of nodes and links); c) virtual structures for changing information (use of virtual structures correspond to use of multiple conceptual models for manipulating information); d) Computation over hypermedia networks (the techniques of integrating computational agents that operate over the network of hypermedia objects); e) Versioning.. (A method for recording revisions and record keeping); and f) Support for collaborative work. The issue of collaborative work is directly related how the previous issues are dealt with in terms of allowing multiple object worlds to co-exist. In the next section we propose a model of the design environment that is inspired by the work in intelligent hypertext environments in software engineering [13].

4. Towards an Architecture for an Engineering Design Support Environment

Having identified the congruence between the research issues in design support environments and in hypertext environments, we have chosen the hypertext based framework for software life-cycle management by Garg and Scacchi, described in this section, as a starting point [13]. This is reasonable because both engineering design and software engineering are prototypical design tasks. From a system design point of view, even though there are similarities between the problems, there are significant domain-based differences.

4.1 Computers in a Social Organization

The approach to the design of a computational environment in a social organization is based on identifying and integrating the different components that affect the design problem throughout the life-cycle in a unified framework termed as the "web of computing" by Scacchi and Kling [28]. In applying the notion of "web of computing" in the context of software engineering, Garg and Scacchi identify three inter-related aspects in a software life-cycle [13]. They are: a) tangible products used and generated during the life-cycle, b) the setting in which the product is developed, manufactured and maintained, and c) the process carried out in the life-cycle of development. In engineering design, the same three aspects of the life-cycle are applicable. In our previous discussions on engineering design, we identified intermediate tangible products (such as sketches) to be very useful in focusing the design task and to serve as a memory aid. In engineering design, as opposed to software design, the number of artificial symbols systems used are larger. Concomitant to this condition is the existence of a variety of computational tools to operate on them as well.

The second aspect identified in software life-cycle is the setting in which the product is developed, manufactured, and maintained. In software engineering, the physical environment of development, manufacture, use, and maintenance are the same whereas in engineering design that is not the case. However, conceptual models and performance models for manufacturing and maintenance are representable using artificial symbols systems allowing for the design environment to encompass the setting of the life-cycle.

The third aspect corresponds to the modeling of the design process, with respect to which engineering design and software design are congruent. We have pointed out that the design process is not clearly partitioned as problem formulation, analysis, synthesis, and evaluation and that actually all of those tasks are inter-leaved. A model of tasks and their interrelationships would allow for the structuring of task at different levels. The individual user should be allowed to create his own models of tasks based on his requirements. This is crucial for engineering design because different alternatives can potentially be generated and evaluated automatically by the system by the use of previous models (of task networks) created by the user (by changing a the set of assumptions). This balancing of control of task networks, especially in the case of computational tools, between the user and the system is a research issue in itself.

In the next section a preliminary architecture for an engineering design environment is proposed based on the web of computing model. As there are differences between engineering domains and software engineering, additional issues in building this system are also identified.

4.2 Architecture of an n-Dimensional Information Modeling System

A new architecture is required to support a system that models the three aspects of the web of computing and provides support for the management of these aspects. The chief components of this architecture, based on the implications for support, are:

1. A model of data objects of varied representations: text; drawings; databases; etc.

2. Support for a variety of models which span subsets of the data object base. This would include mechanisms to maintain the intermediate products of the design process.

3. A model of human and computational agents participating in the design process.

4. A model of tasks and task networks to configure and manage the design process.

5. A knowledge management system that allows for defining and displaying a user's design context. This design context is defined by the role and purpose of the representations and computational agents the user is currently employing in his task.

6. A support system that provides for configuring and controlling the design process at different levels of task networks.

A user in this system corresponds to one of the agents in the model of agents. Based on his area of responsibility the system invokes the appropriate knowledge structures (design context) relevant to his task. All the interactions with the user correspond to the modification of the hyper-object system that maintains the intermediate products of the design process. The crucial difference between software and engineering design lies in the fact that in the former context design and manufacturing are inseparable. In contrast, in engineering design distinguishes between the two not only terms of of locus of action but also in terms of object worlds. Tasks which fall outside the scope of computational models and hence have to be undertaken separately. The results of these tasks will have to be reported to the computational design environment for general dissemination and decision making. Examples of intermediate products are drawings, equational models, functional models, textual documents symbolizing commitments and agreements. In essence, intermediate products are products of the artificial symbol systems used in the design task and are not considered to be the end product of the design process.

4.2.1 Models of Data Objects in a Hypertext-Like System

In describing the implications for a support system, the representation of multiple artificial symbol systems in a single environment was identified as one of the crucial necessities. The approach adopted here is to view all representational primitives as data objects irrespective of the type of the representational structure. The most common types of representational primitives are text, sketches, geometric entities, structured data objects, etc. In engineering design, the number of representational structures required and their organization are dependent on the domain. The basic organization of the data objects into a "hyper-object" model is similar to those by Garg and Scacchi for their hypertext Document Integration Facility(DIF) [15].

The proposed system allows for browsing, managing, and using data objects created during the engineering life-cycle. These are organized into a number of basic classes: initial specifications, functional specifications, geometric specifications, equational models, manufacturing specifications, operating specifications, and, maintenance specifications. Each of these in turn are organized into a set of data object templates with associated types that are used to describe them. This organization of engineering life-cycle is easily redefinable. Different aspects of the life-cycle along with its set of data object types and their structures can be included depending on the requirements and the scope of the design project. The data objects created throughout the engineering life-cycle will be stored in a hyper-object structure. The hyper-object storage structure in its basic form consists of a node-link model where nodes correspond to the data objects and links provide a means for navigation. The data objects in the hyper-object system may contain any type of data: text, equational models, functional models, sketches, source code, geometric models, etc. Each of the nodes may be associated with support tools for editing, manipulating, and filtering data.

The basic objective in designing the system as in the Garg and Scacchi model [13] is based on providing maximum flexibility in constructing models of data objects to be stored for the engineering design situation at hand. The other objective is to provide a means for storing the data in a consistent manner to ensure completeness and precision of data. A model of data objects consists of two levels: (1) data object (information) level and (2) model level (structure of information level).

Data Object Level: The data level is the level at which data objects are stored. All data objects are typed. These include any number of text objects: memos, specification documents, computer source code; graphic objects: sketches, solid models, shop drawings; and others such as photographs, sound objects, etc. Models are also a type of data object stored in the system. Each type of data object has an associated group of agents which allow objects to be entered, modified and used.

Model Level: The model level corresponds to conceptual models of the organization of the data objects. These models allow for a description of the   product   within   a   given   modeling paradigm (Figure 2). In addition to providing a description, the availability of the explicit information structure facilitates navigation and query.

Each object world, or model type, defines a set of Links and rules for using these links to associate data objects. These model types are created by designers and are accessed from a library. Functionally, there are a limited set of link types, however, these links are further defined in the context of each representation used. For example, an ASSOCIATION link may be used to link an object in a functional decomposition model and one in an equational model. This example is an inter-model link, as it connects object descriptions of the same entity developed in two different object worlds.

Links such as IS-A and PART-OF are an integral part of some knowledge representation schemes. These links are defined in the context of the representation used. A representation whose primitive object is narrative text is organizable only in terms of the semi-structured aspects of the text. The semi-structured specification is created by the user in his organization of the project data objects. The user by creating an instance of a semi-structured object allows for its filing in a principled manner. In some representational structures links have different names for the same semantic relationship while in other cases the relationship between names and semantics are reversed. Another class of links are those created for tracking versions of an data object. These are called revision links. Revision links are associated with data objects and models. Revision links are unique and are treated as such.

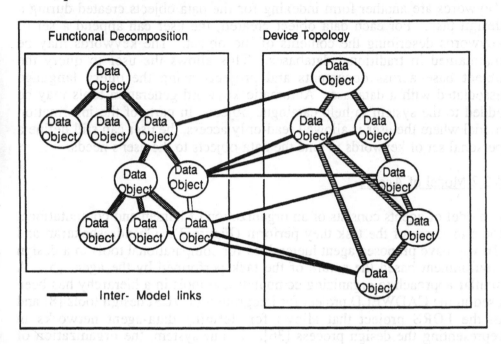

Figure 2. Two Different Information Models of Data Objects

Most of the links required for describing model type fall into one of the following categories [14,22]:

SPECIALIZATION: is_a
AGGREGATION: part_of
GROUPING: element_of
ASSOCIATION: flows_to, revision, input, output, ...

In engineering design, data objects are generated in the course of creating models of functional decomposition, device-based, and other decompositions of the product being designed Some of these models (such as functional decomposition) have well defined knowledge representation structures [38]. We call such models "principled models". Designers also use other, less well defined (or undefined) models as needed. The ability to add these models to the system as the design process progresses is an important capability. This not only enhances flexibility of the environment but also allows for new models to be shared among designers. This notion of extensibility of data models has also been identified as a requirement for design databases [10].

Keywords are another form indexing for the data objects created during a design task. For each data object created, the user can append a set of keywords describing the contents of the object. The keywords may be maintained in traditional databases. This allows the user to query the object base across documents and projects using the query language associated with a database. Automatic keyword generation tools may be added to the system to help catalogue objects. In parts of the information model where the user is allowed read-only access, the user can still define a personal set of keywords to tune the data objects to the user's needs.

4.2.2 Model of Agents

A model of agents consists of an organization of human and computational tools in terms of the task they perform (Figure 3). Chandrashekaran and Brown have proposed agent hierarchies for computational tools in a design environment based the nature of the task performed by the agent [5]. A similar approach to organizing computational tools in a hierarchy has been used in the CADWELD project for integration of VLSI design tools [8] and in the FORS project that allows for defining data-agent networks in representing the design process [36]. In our system, the organization of humans participating in the project and computational tools are integrated together in defining the model of agents.

Each of the computational agents is capable of performing a particular task or set of tasks by accepting inputs of certain types of data objects, processing, and generating outputs corresponding to the type of the output data object. Human agents are specified in terms of their area of responsibility. Their responsibilities may require carrying out several tasks. The model of agents can be used in conjunction with the task model to assign responsibilities to the agents for completion of the tasks at different levels of the task hierarchy.

4.2.3. Model of Tasks and Task Networks

Given a model of the data objects and the model of agents participating in a project, the design process is represented using task networks (Figure 4). A model of tasks is based on task classification. There are two types of tasks: a) project tasks and b) product tasks. Project tasks correspond to the tasks associated with organizing, scheduling, and staffing the project. Product tasks are further divided into actions and primitive actions. A product task is a collection of actions with precedence ordering of the actions. Actions are composed of primitive actions that operate on a specific input data object to produce output data objects of different representational types. These output data objects may be created by the action of a human agent or a computational agent performing the task.

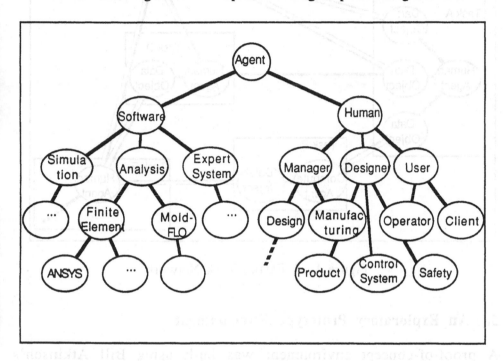

Figure 3. A Partial Model of Agents

Computational tools for project management are also represented in the model of agents and hence can be used on task networks for evaluating project status. Task networks convey a sense of fixed ordering of tasks. This is not true especially in the integrated use of computational tools. The problem of controlling these tools within a task network in itself is a research issue. A level of control that is shared by the user and system depends on the system being able to understand the intentions of the individual designer. Smithers [32] has proposed a model of intelligent control for integrating a set of AI-based tools where the system supports the user by inferring his intentions. It provides this support by explicit representation of intentions and reasoning using them. The issue of control of task networks has to be investigated further for different types of computational tools and their combinations.

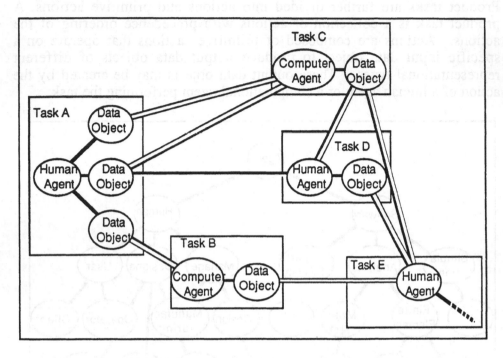

Figure 4. A Partial Task Network

5. An Exploratory Prototype Environment

A proof-of-concept environment was built using Bill Atkinson's HyperCard. This was chosen for its object-oriented approach and accessible graphics. The basic parts of the system are:

• Data Objects – which have a structured part containing name, type, author, date, and an unstructured part which may be multiple pages of text or graphics.

• Links – which have type, author, and date, and bi-directionally connect two objects. Each link, when it is created is recorded in a model.

• Model Types – which specify the valid links between types of objects. Each model type is the definition of an 'object world'.

• Models – which have type, author, and date. Each model is an instance of an model type. Models contain a set of links created by a user, simple references to objects, and references to other models. One user may create any number of models.

The system has a number of additional utilities for control, browsing, and administration. Typically, a user will create a model within which to work, assign it a type, and proceed to create and link objects. The links are recorded in the current model and are restricted to the definition of valid links within the current model type.

Currently, we have four well-developed model types: Project, Functional [38], Equational [20], and Device. Additional model types may be created by a 'super' user. Taking the Functional model type as an example, a variety of object types are defined including: Function, Flow Process, Conversion Process Element, etc.; and a variety of link types including: composed–of, converted-to, embodied-by, annotation, revised-to, etc. Object types and link types are expanded as more model types developed.

6. Conclusions and Future Work

In this paper we have examined the nature of engineering design both from the social process view and the cognitive process view to propose a design support environment. We pointed out that the social view is complementary to the social view in the sense it elaborates the design problem faced by the individual designer in a group design process. Further, we pointed out that the requirements for the design of the support environment for both the individual and cognitive view overlap in their characteristics such as the need for recording the intermediate products of design; supporting multiple models of artificial symbol system, and computational systems that operate on them. Inspired by the model of a life-cycle support environment in software engineering, we have proposed an architecture of a support environment for engineering design. We are currently implementing systems to prove and test the underlying concepts of the support system. The support environment, being a flexible tool for configuring models of information objects (object worlds), model of agents and model of tasks and task networks (depending on the design problem at hand) will require extensive testing for robustness in a variety of problems. We believe that support systems such as those proposed in this report will go a long way in helping manage engineering design projects. Experimenting with the system on large number of projects will also allow us to gather empirical information on the nature of engineering design. An empirically tested system in a given engineering domain could then serve as test-bed for training engineers to work in similar collaborative environments. Further, it is our belief that, as new and better computational tools for different well-structured parts of engineering problems are developed, they can be seamlessly integrated into the larger environment.

The support environment should also be able to provide intelligent assistance in configuring tasks based on previous design histories. Machine learning techniques (such as chunking, explanation based learning, case based reasoning that are subject of research in artificial intelligence) can be used in improving the performance of the system. The architecture presented in this paper for a design environment provides a framework for evolutionary development. The environment will also serve as a repository of organizational design memory that is easily accessible for subsequent tasks of the same type.

We have proposed an approach to the application of computer and communication technologies to engineering design based on the concept of 'informating' [39] the human designer. This enables us to focus on the less-structured aspects of the design process and to identify and integrate the diverse languages, models, and information to create a potentially comprehensive grasp of engineering design. The proposed system is expected to evolve into a learning environment in which "....(design) work itself becomes a process of inquiry, and the contributions that (team) members can make are increasingly a function of their ability to notice, reflect, explore, hypothesize, test and communicate." [39].

Acknowledgements

The authors would like to thank Joseph Davis, William Elm, Robert Coyne, Pankaj Garg, and Suresh Konda for comments on an earlier draft of the paper. This work has been supported by the Westinghouse Electric Corporation and by the National Science Foundation through the Engineering Design Research Center.

Bibliography

[1] Akin, O., Chen, P., Dave, B., and Pithavadian S., "Problem Structuring in Architectural Design", Engineering Design Research Center, Tech Report :EDRC-48-05-87,1987.

[2] Baker, N. and, Fenves, S., "A Knowledge Acquisition Study of Structural Engineers Performing Preliminary Design", Engineering Design Research Center Tech. Report: EDRC-12-19-87, 1987.

[3] Bucciarelli, L., "Reflections on Engineering Design practice", *Design Studies*, Vol.5(2),1984.

[4] Bucciarelli, L,. "An Ethnographic Perspective on Engineering Design", *Design Studies*,Vol 9, 1988.

[5] Chandrashekaran, B, and Brown, D, "Knowledge and Control in Design Problem solving", Department of Computer Science Tech Report, Ohio-State-University,1986.

[6] Coyne, R., and Subrahmanian, E., "Computer Supported Creative Design: A Pragmatic Approach", In Proceedings of the International Round Table Conference on Models of Creativity and Knowledge-based Creativity, Heron Island, Australia, 1989.

[7] Cross, Nigel, *Developments in Design Methodology*, Wiley, 1984.

[8] Daniell, J, Director, S. W., "An Object Oriented Approach to Distributed CAD Tool Control", In Proceedings of the 26th ACM/IEEE Design Automation Conference.1989.

[9] Eastman, C., "Recent Developments in the Representation in the Science of Design", In Proceedings of the eighteenth ACM and IEEE Design Automation Conference, 13-21.1981

[10] Eastman, C., et. al, "A Formal Approach for Product Specification", Tech Report, Department of Architecture, University of California, Los Angeles..

[11] French, M. J., Engineering Design - Conceptual Stage, Heinaman, London, 1971.

[12] Gregory, S. A., "What We Know about Designing and How We

Know it", Institution of Chemical Engineers, Design Congress, University of Ashton, 1979.

[13] Garg, P, Scacchi, W, "On Designing Intelligent Hypertext system for Information Management for Software Life Engineering", Proceedings of Hypertext '87, University of North Carolina, 1987.

[14] Garg, P.Abstractions Mechanisms in Hypertext, *CACM*, pp 862-870,July 1988.

[15] Garg, P, Scacchi, W, "A Hypertext System to Manage Software Life Cycle Documents", Proceedings of 21st Hawaii International Conference in System Sciences, Vol 2, pp. 337-346.

[16] Goel, V., and Pirolli, P., "Motivating the Notion of Generic Design within Information Processing Theory: The Design Problem Space", *AI Magazine*, pp. 18-47,Spring 1989.

[17] Hubka, V., *Principles of Engineering Design*, Butterworth Scientific, London, 1982.

[18] Halasz, F., "Reflections on Notecards: Seven Issues For The Next Generation of Hypermedia Systems", *CACM*, pp. 837-851, July 1988.

[19] Hales, C , " Analysis of the Engineering Design Process in An Industrial Context", Phd Thesis, Department of Engineering Science, Cambridge University, United Kingdom, 1987.

[20] Hales, C, and Wallace, K, "Preliminary Results of An Empirical Study on Engineering Design", In Proceedings of the International Conference on Engineering Design, pp.54-58,1989

[21] Jones, C., "A Method for Systematic Design", *Conference on Design Methods*, Jones. C and Thronley (ed), Pergamon Press, Oxford, 1963..

[22] Larkin, J, and Simon, H. A., "Why is a Picture Worth a Thousand Words?", Cognitive Science, Vol.11, No 1.,pp 65-100, Jan. 1987.

[23] Nadler, G., *The Planning and Design Approach*, John Wiley & Son, New York, 1981.[Newell & Simon, 1972]

[24] Newell, and, Simon, H., A., *Human Problem Solving* , Prentice Hall,

[25] Pahl, G., and Beitz, W., *Engineering Design* (English Edition) The Design Council, 1984.

[26] Piela, P, ASCEND: "An Equational Modelling System", Phd Thesis, Dept. of Chemical Engineering, Carnegie Mellon University, 1989.

[27] Rabins, M., J. et al., "Research Needs in Mechanical Systems: Summary of study from ASME Board Research to U.S. National Science Foundation", Mechanical Engineering, Vol. 108, Number 3, pp 27-43, March 1984.

[28] Scacchi, W., and Kling, R., "The Web of Computing: Computing Technology as Social Organization", *Advances in Computing*, M. Yovits(ed.), Academic Press, 1982.

[29] Scheil, U, "Abstractions Mechanisms in Semantic Networks", *SIGART Newsletter*, January 1989.

[30] Simon, H. A., "Structure of Ill-structured Problems", *Artificial Intelligence*, 4, pp. 181-201, 1973

[31] Simon, H. A., "The Architecture of Complexity", Chapter 5, *The Sciences of the Artificial*, MIT Press, 1980.,

[32] Smithers, T.,"Intelligent Control in AI-based Design Support Systems", University of Edinburgh, DAI Tech. Report no. 423, 1989.

[33] Smithers, T. et al. "Design as Intelligent Behavior: A Design Research Programme", DAI, University of Edinburgh, 1989.

[34] Smithers, T., "AI based Design Vs Geometry Based Design, or Why Design Cannot be Supported by Geometry Alone", *Computer Aided Design*, Vol 21, Number 3, pp. 141-150, 1989.

[35] Subrahmanian, E., Westerberg, A. W., and Podnar, G.,"A Proposal for a n- Dimensional Information Modelling Environment for Engineering Design", Unpublished Report, 1989.

[36] Talukdar, S, et. al, "Upgrading Design Processes", Proceedings of the Third Intl.Conference on AI in Engineering Design, Computational Mechanics, 1988.
Princeton, 1972.

[37] Ullman, J., Stauffer, L. A., and Dieterich,T., Preliminary Results of an Experimental Study of the Mechanical Design Process. Technical Report-856-30-9, Depart. of Computer Science, Oregon State Univ., 1987.

[38] "A Functional Decomposition Language", Westinghouse Internal Document, 1988

[39] Zuboff, S., "Automate/Informate the Two Faces of Intelligent Technology", *Organizational Dynamics*, Autumn 1985.

Organizing the Tasks in Complex Design Projects

Steven D. Eppinger
Daniel E. Whitney
Robert P. Smith
David A. Gebala
Massachusetts Institute of Technology

Abstract

This research is aimed at structuring complex design projects in order to develop better products more quickly. We use a matrix representation to capture both the sequence of and the technical relationships among the many design tasks to be performed. These relationships define the "technical structure" of a design project which is then analyzed in order to find alternative sequences and/or definitions of the design tasks. Such improved design procedures offer opportunities to speed development progress by streamlining the inter-task coordination. After using this technique to model design processes in several organizations, we have developed a design management strategy which focuses attention on the essential information transfer requirements of a technical project. We expect that this research will benefit not only new design tasks that have never been structured before but also long-standing, often repeated design tasks that may have drifted into poor organizational patterns over many years.

Introduction

Intense competition forces firms to develop new products at an increasingly rapid pace. This mandate places substantial pressure on engineering teams to *develop better products* and at the same time to *develop products faster*. Engineering organizations have responded to these two challenges by popularizing the concepts of "design for manufacture" and "simultaneous engineering". By exploring the nature of complex product development efforts, this research recognizes that not everything can be done concurrently and therefore design managers need some tools to help structure projects effectively.

Design for manufacture (DFM) is the adoption of a new attitude among engineers that emphasizes the relevant manufacturing issues throughout (especially early) in the product development process [11]. Simultaneous engineering is an effort to create the product design and the manufacturing process concurrently by allowing design engineers to work closely with manufacturing engineers, field service engineers, and representatives of others interested in the manufacture and use of the product [21]. While these techniques are often difficult to practice, some firms using them claim to be designing better products in less time as a result of increased coordination and awareness of broader design issues [42].

Despite these successes, complex product development efforts remain a technical and organizational challenge. The design of an automobile, aircraft, or computer can involve coordinating thousands of engineers making more than a million design decisions over several years. None of these many tasks is performed in isolation [9, 10]. Each design choice may be a tradeoff affecting many other design parameters. Facilitating the transfer of information among design groups is an essential organizational task of product design managers [2, 12, 24, 40].

For the engineers, however, the challenges of simultaneous engineering are particularly difficult when many design tasks are interdependent and cannot be performed in series or in parallel. In these cases, since many design decisions are coupled, they must be made "simultaneously", perhaps by iteration or negotiation among specialists [7]. Potentially, many engineers from various disciplines must be involved in this complex decision process [17, 33]. Strategically decoupling the major design tasks into sub-systems can reduce the sizes of the working design groups, and this can have a dramatic impact on development performance [3, 24].

Two types of design can be distinguished: design of entirely new items, for which there exists at first no organized design procedure; and redesign of existing items, such as automobiles, where there is a large investment in existing design procedures, often heavily bureaucratized. The need for aids such as proposed here is easily recognized in the first case. The benefit of this work for the second type may be just as great but harder to recognize. This is due to the fact that a "procedure" exists and seems to work well. However, it may have grown up organically and historically, without having been subjected to careful analysis. So its internal inefficiencies or irrationalities remain undetected.

Our research builds on work by Steward [35, 36] that is introduced below. We are investigating strategies for design management that can not only reduce the overall product development time, but also improve the quality of design decisions. We have found that in many industries, product development processes can be clearly mapped out in terms of the major design milestones and the minor negotiations which must take place along the way [5, 19]. Some examples can be found in aspects of automotive, computer, and aircraft design. We contend (as Simon also argues [31]) that if design procedures can be documented and studied, then they can be greatly improved. By analyzing the complex relationships among design decisions, we can identify the design drivers and the feedback paths. These concepts are central to the development of strategies to better organize a design procedure by improving coordination among the designers, which facilitates faster and better product development.

We aim to develop two major results, a computer-based analysis tool and a set of design management strategies. Together these can improve the product development process by:

1. identifying the key factors which determine many of the design results,
2. reducing both the perceived and actual complexity of design tasks,
3. sharing engineering data earlier and/or with known confidence,
4. redefining critical tasks to facilitate overall project flow,
5. forcing designers to organize their decision processes,
6. helping design managers to place emphasis on task coordination, and
7. allowing design iteration to be strategically planned.

Our approach involves mapping an existing or proposed design procedure into a simple array representing the complex inter-relationships among the many design tasks which must be accomplished. The argument for a design methodology which corresponds to the underlying structure of the design problem has been articulated by Steward [35], Simon [31], and other authors, most notably Alexander in the 1960s [1]. The analysis we will perform considers the relative importance of each design parameter to other parameters, allowing the information requirements to determine the appropriate scheduling of the decisions. The result of this analysis is an array of options for a manager or engineer to rearrange or reprioritize the tasks. Strategies include decoupling and resequencing tasks, insertion of new decision points, splitting or condensing tasks, and other schemes to improve the flow of information and decisions. .

Design Management Techniques

The design management response to the challenge of reducing product development lead time has typically been to encourage engineers to develop the product and its associated manufacturing process concurrently. This policy has two beneficial effects. First, it emphasizes the need for design engineers to be aware of production issues, and this is the focus of the popular "design for manufacturing" approach. Second, we find that designers are sharing or transferring information to their counterparts in manufacturing engineering much sooner than they had done previously.

These trends bring up many new issues in design project management. Today we find that the design procedures which have evolved over the years are being transformed into new design recipes. Engineers are now performing their standard design functions with potentially different inputs and outputs. They are expected to make use of more information than was previously available and to practice new design methodologies [6, 11, 15, 37]. This new information takes many forms, including more accurate consumer preference data and manufacturability data. Distribution of the results of their engineering efforts is also more broad in scope. Designers are now expected to work more closely with manufacturing and marketing, reporting on their progress at frequent intervals.

Engineers and managers have adopted techniques for planning, organizing, and monitoring the complex network of tasks in a large development project. These procedures require documentation of the entire design process. However, the most widely used representations do not adequately describe the design structure as we define it.

The most popular project planning tools use network diagrams to represent the precedence relationships among activities. In the PERT method [45], time estimates are given to each task, and probability of timely task completion can be computed along with the associated start times for each activity. The critical path method (CPM) performs a linear time/cost tradeoff for tasks on the critical (longest-lead-time) path. To accelerate the project, additional resources (at greater costs) are placed on critical tasks to shorten the critical path. The precedence diagramming method (PDM) [44] places the activities on the nodes of the graph, rather than the arrows, and this allows the graph to be drawn to scale, visually representing time.

All of these network techniques require that there be only one-way progression along paths, with no feedback or iteration, no feed-forward of information part-way through a task, etc. The emphasis is placed on the interactions between the tasks, not on the details within the tasks. The tendency is therefore to define tasks in the large, ignoring a multitude of engineering interactions required within each one. Furthermore these techniques are not aimed at improving the procedures but rather only at running projects as defined.

A more powerful technique is the Air Force standard IDEF project definition method [20, 29, 30], which can be used to represent some of the intra-task complexity. (IDEF was developed by Ross at Softech, Inc. in the 1970s. The technique was known as SADT until it was adopted by the Air Force as a standard representation.) Moreover, IDEF supports the concepts of "as is" and "should be" design procedures but provides no method for moving from the former to the latter. IDEF charts tend to grow rapidly for large tasks until managers can hardly see what is going on. This complexity is managed somewhat by using available software for describing and analyzing the diagrams [14]. Many firms (including US automotive and aircraft manufacturers) are using such tools.

Project management tools are generally applied to the design process on the basis of "start task/complete task" representation, ignoring the technical structure of the tasks, the information tasks need or produce, and the overall information flow network that underlies the whole effort. Also, they may document an idealized view of the process that ignores the vital, informal, and usually undocumented interactions that are undeniably essential to project success.

When a representation omits significant effects, then important system behavior remains unexplained. If we ignore the design task coupling, then we will fail to recognize the most significant challenges of the design effort. On the other hand, if an improved representation technique can include the complex task dependencies inherent within the process, then those relationships can finally be studied and exploited if possible. We propose that new approaches to managing design complexity will become practical through the use of a more accurate description of the design process.

Sequencing Design Tasks

Creating the more detailed description we seek involves explicitly mapping out the technical aspects of the design procedure. We contend that to be most useful, the design representation must include not only the sequence of the tasks but also the many technical relationships among the tasks. The description we use is based on Steward's design structure matrix. However, before presenting this method, we will illustrate some general issues in sequencing design tasks and transferring engineering information.

Consider two design tasks, labelled A and B. Figure 1 shows directed graphs (digraphs) [41] of three possible ways in which the two can be related. If task B simply requires the output of task A (or vice-versa), then the two tasks are *dependent* and would typically done in series. On the other hand, the two would be entirely *independent* if tasks A and B could be performed simultaneously with no interaction between the designers. Finally, if task A needs information from task B, and also task B requires knowledge of task A's results, then the two tasks are *interdependent*, or *coupled*.

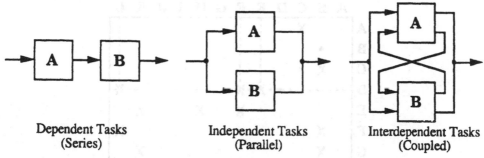

| Dependent Tasks | Independent Tasks | Interdependent Tasks |
| (Series) | (Parallel) | (Coupled) |

Figure 1. Three Possible Sequences for Two Design Tasks

Coordinating either the dependent (series) tasks or the independent (parallel) tasks is quite straightforward. Certainly with no limitation on resources, the parallel tasks can be completed more quickly. The interdependent (coupled) tasks are much more challenging to organize, often requiring much more design time and many iterations of information transfer [38].

To illustrate using a familiar theme, we can envision task A to represent a product design function, and task B to represent the associated manufacturing engineering function. Then our series model depicts the outdated "throw the design over the wall" methodology. The parallel tasks model might then represent an idyllic view of simultaneous engineering, where both design and manufacturing functions are given the same challenge, and they magically develop product and process concurrently (without complex interactions). The coupled tasks model is a more realistic diagram of simultaneous engineering, where the information transfer is essential and iteration is typical.

PERT software tools can typically analyze project sequence diagrams only if they contain no coupling (loops). The representation requires the coupled tasks to be bundled into larger design tasks. If the project planner chooses to consider the tasks separately, then the essential information coupling must be neglected. Below we present a representation which handles the complex relationships among tasks more naturally.

The Design Structure System

Steward's design structure system [35, 36] uses a representation which allows the direct coupling of any task to another. Figure 2 shows the design structure matrix in its original binary form as described by Steward, where the design tasks to be performed are each represented by an identically labeled row and column of the matrix. The marked elements within each row identify which other tasks must contribute information for proper completion of the design. For example, the marks in row **D** are in columns **E**, **F**, and **L**, indicating that completion of task **D** requires information to be transferred from tasks **E**, **F**, and **L**. We would then desire these three tasks to be performed <u>before</u> task **D**. (The diagonal elements in the matrix are essentially meaningless at this point but are included to distinguish the diagonal and the upper and lower triangles of the matrix.)

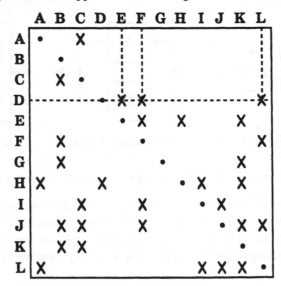

Figure 2. A Binary Design Structure Matrix, Unpartitioned

The primary goal of design structure analysis is to find a sequence of these design tasks which allows this matrix to become lower triangular. If the tasks can be sequenced so that each one begins only after it receives all the information it requires from its predecessors, then no coupling remains in the design problem. However, this rarely happens. Instead, analysis usually yields a matrix in block-angular form. Figure 3 shows the above matrix after the twelve tasks have been rearranged (partitioned) by interchanging rows and also swapping the corresponding columns to achieve a more organized design sequence.

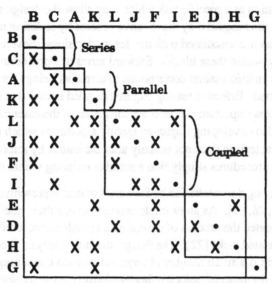

Figure 3. The Binary Design Structure Matrix, Partitioned

The partitioning process has sequenced the tasks to be performed in the order: **B-C-A-K-L-J-F-I-E-D-H-G**. The matrix shows that task C is dependent upon task B, so they are performed in the sequence B-C. Tasks A and K can be then completed in parallel (since task K does not depend upon task A). The two "blocks" encompassing the task sequences L-J-F-I and E-D-H identify two sets of coupled tasks, the most challenging aspects of this design problem. These tasks must be performed simultaneously, and the information transfer required may take the form of iteration and/or negotiation.

The partitioned matrix in Figure 3 is not unique, but rather its form depends on the algorithm used to reorder the tasks. Several schemes for identifying the blocks are available, including techniques based upon binary matrix algebra [18], a rule-based (expert system) analysis [27, 28, 33], and Steward's loop tracing procedure. Still, we have developed improved partitioning algorithms which are discussed in the appendix.

When the design structure matrix cannot be manipulated into lower triangular form, we then seek a form that minimizes the size and number of the remaining blocks on the diagonal. Collapsing these blocks into single tasks (as would be required for PERT analysis) would certainly make the project appear to be simpler. In our example, we would combine tasks L, J, F, and I into one task and then collapse tasks E, D, and H into another. We would be left with seven tasks in lower-triangular form instead of the twelve tasks as shown. However, this approach hides the real design problems and precludes any opportunity to further improve the design procedure by applying other techniques.

Since the coupled blocks in the design structure matrix represent design iteration, choosing the proper sequence to work through even these tasks is quite important. We believe that there is tremendous advantage in performing the initial "guesswork" required to start the design iteration at a specific task which may allow the design to converge quickly. This can reduce the time required by the iterative process by isolating uncertainty and increasing the confidence associated with the design decisions. Several algorithms also exist for sequencing within these blocks. Steward terms this procedure *tearing*, since guessing the unknown information corresponds to elements being torn from the matrix to get the iteration started. Effective tearing requires detailed knowledge of the problem domain so that the less important elements are torn to leave the essential ones below the diagonal. We are also developing improved tearing algorithms which are discussed in the appendix. (Note that tearing does not actually alter the matrix by removing any of the marks, rather these procedures simply find a suitable ordering within a block.)

An encouraging demonstration of Steward's matrix representation is found in recent work at NASA [27, 28, 33]. As an example problem to test their rule-based partitioning algorithm, they modeled the process of designing a complex spacecraft antenna system with over 50 interrelated tasks [22]. The design structure analysis showed that in this design problem there is a small number of large subsystems containing from 5 to 20 tasks each. These coupled groups of tasks are then performed in the sequence: actuators, sensors, structures, dynamics, controls, etc.

Extensions to the Design Structure Matrix Representation

As presented by Steward, the binary design structure matrix only represents strict precedence relations. (A task either does or does not depend upon another task.) In complex design (sub-)problems, we find that the binary matrix is often crowded with weak dependencies, and this leads to an extremely coupled design matrix.

We therefore extend the basic representation by explicitly including measures of the degree of dependence, so that we can use more sophisticated analytical procedures to further improve the design process. Figure 4 shows a numerical design structure matrix which uses values to represent the importance of each task dependency. The rules for partitioning and tearing this matrix can now consider rearranging tasks to (for example) minimize the importance of the above-diagonal elements. This would allow even the iteration within the coupled sub-systems to be minimized since the most important inter-task relationships are in the proper positions.

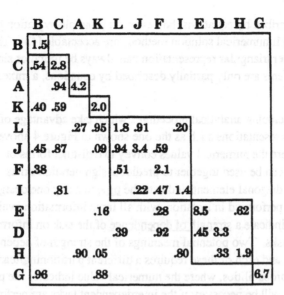

Figure 4. A Numerical Design Structure Matrix

	B	C	A	K	L	J	F	I	E	D	H	G
B	1.5											
C	.54	2.8										
A		.94	4.2									
K	.40	.59		2.0								
L			.27	.95	1.8	.91			.20			
J	.45	.87		.09	.94	3.4	.59					
F	.38				.51		2.1					
I		.81				.22	.47	1.4				
E					.16	.28			8.5	.62		
D						.39	.92		.45	3.3		
H					.90	.05		.80		.33	1.9	
G	.96				.88							6.7

The numerical values need not necessarily depict the strength of the task input dependency. Other metrics to consider include task completion time, functional coupling [26], physical adjacency, electrical or vibrational characteristics, parameter sensitivity, historical variance of task results, certainty of planning estimates, or volume of information transfer. Furthermore, each matrix element could instead be a vector of multiple measures, such as certainty and strength of dependence dependence.

For example, if a task vitally depends on information from another task but that information is known to lie within predictable limits, then the dependent task might be able to start based on a good guess of the anticipated information. Thus the dependency would be represented as weak. Similarly, if the task depends only slightly on information that is largely unpredictable, the dependency might again be judged as weak. Contrarily, needed information with large impact and large variability implies a strong dependency. (We cannot start without it, nor can we predict it well enough.) An "importance ratio" can be calculated as the basis for determining the strength of the dependency. This ratio would be similar in definition to Taguchi's "signal-to-noise" ratio used to compare the relative effects of parameters [8].

To sequence a group of coupled tasks more smoothly, we would begin with the one which is missing only information that is relatively certain. Such a strategy would reduce the number of design iterations necessary.

Developing a numerical design structure model would be quite difficult, however dependency values could be extracted from an engineering task/parameter sensitivity analysis. It is also likely that methods of constraint propagation [25, 34, 39] can be used to help write the matrix representation automatically. This is possible only in problems that are completely described by equations, however. In principle, equation problems can be resequenced at will if numerical solution methods are acceptable [43]. That is, the equivalent of a lower triangular representation can always be found or simulated in such cases. When problems are only partially described by equations, a mixed approach is required.

We are developing analytical procedures which take advantage of numerical design structure matrix representations such as the one shown in Figure 4 above [32]. We prefer to use a matrix where the numerical values convey two distinct forms of quantitative information which can be used together to predict design iteration times. In our numerical design models, the diagonal elements indicate the time that any one design activity would consume if it were performed in isolation, with all input information available. The off-diagonal elements indicate a strength of dependence of the task on information produced by each of the other tasks. Two potential meanings of the strength of dependence measure are being investigated, and each of these requires a different partitioning/tearing algorithm. The first involves probabilities, where the numerical value indicates the probability that one additional iteration will be necessary if the interdependent tasks are performed in the specified order. Each of the dependencies is assigned one such probability, and all potential orderings of interdependent tasks are investigated to identify the sequence which minimizes the expected iteration time.

The second analytical technique does not rely on a stochastic description of the design process. In this technique, the off-diagonal values measure what portion of information produced during the first iteration would need to be changed during the second iteration. In this way the design process can be seen as a series of iterations of decreasing duration.

Through either of these methods it is possible to evaluate the degree to which the coupling in the design will affect the time necessary to complete the design. Various proposed structures of the design tasks can be compared to determine which would be better from a point of view of time necessary to complete the design process. We will investigate the ability of these schemes to represent (predict) design iteration in actual procedures with coupled tasks.

Exploring Design Structure Data

We have used the design structure system to represent several product development procedures within the automotive industry. In searching for design process data, we have created two types of models: high-level task-based descriptions, where the task relationships can be studied; and low-level parameter-based descriptions which document the technical relationships among the engineering parameters. Of the two examples given here, the first shows a task-level description, and the second example demonstrates a parameter-level description of a design problem. Since we have found both types of descriptions to be necessary, but neither one to be adequate, we will in the future attempt to collect enough detailed data to create a hybrid model.

Task-Level Design Description

Figure 5 shows one portion of the matrix representation for the design of a single powertrain component. We developed this matrix by translating a set of existing IDEF diagrams which were drawn to document the "as-is" component design procedure. The IDEF modeling technique [20, 29] requires the model authors to extensively interview members of the design organization (at many levels) to characterize the relationships among the tasks. The legend in the figure identifies various task coupling labels. The marks I, C, and M represent three different types of task dependencies: input, control, and mechanism, which are defined by the IDEF methodology. We have labelled some of the above-diagonal marks F to depict the feedbacks in the design procedure which drive iteration. (Most of the F marks were originally I marks in the original IDEF model, but are explicit feedback in this particular task sequence. Finally, we have added the marks labelled A to improve the design process by providing additional paths for information flow which were not present in the IDEF model.

The design matrix in Figure 5 appears in the exact sequence documented by the IDEF data. That is, we found the design tasks to be naturally partitioned into the block-angular form shown with four tightly linked blocks representing the major (iterative) design activities, coupled through only a few tasks. One organizational structure suggested by this matrix would be four design teams, each performing one of the major activities. In fact, that is the structure which is in use at the company, perhaps having evolved to minimize the number of external feedback loops.

Parameter-Level Design Description

In other design process modeling efforts, we use a very different approach, and have found very different results. To create a parameter-level description, we document the design process by interviewing engineers only (not their managers). We ask the designers which parameters must be fixed in order to set another design parameter. By documenting all of these precedence relationships, we develop a "complete" description of the design problem. When partitioned, the model identifies the flow of information required to develop the final design configuration from the customer requirements.

Figure 6 shows the design matrix model developed through detailed study of automotive brake systems. (This work was begun in a related study by Black [4] and was continued by Smith in our group.) For the brake system model, the design parameters have names like: rotor diameter, lining material, splash shield geometry, and booster travel. The full brake system model includes more than 100 design parameters, and this large matrix is shown in Figure 6a to indicate the overall structure obtained after partitioning. The brake system matrix shows that about one third of the parameters can be determined quite simply beginning with the customer requirements. The difficult portion of the design

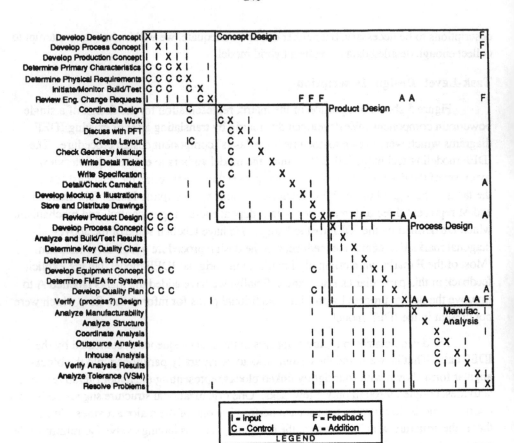

Figure 5. Component Design Task Matrix

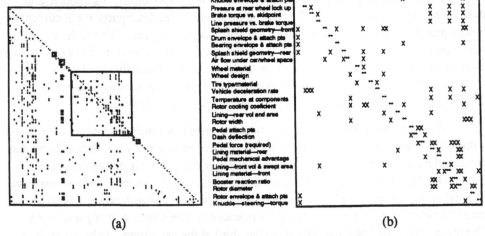

(a)   (b)

Figure 6. Brake System Design Parameter Matrix

problem is described by the large block of more than 30 tasks forming the center of the matrix. The remaining details of the design are worked out in the lower portion of the matrix, which involves little iteration.

The center block is also shown in Figure 6b to display the coupling more clearly. These parameters must be set through an iterative process, which in actual practice utilizes several computer simulations to predict brake system performance. Unfortunately this block also includes the prototyping and testing tasks, which take a considerable amount of time. (We find these tasks in the iterative design loop because certain design parameters require the test results in order to be finalized.)

Improved Design Models

The next steps in this modeling work involve developing numerical models and hybrid models. A numerical model, as described above and illustrated by Figure 4, requires numerical metrics to characterize the interactions among the design tasks. We may be able to create such a model from the parametric model above by exploring the cross-sensitivities in simulation to evaluate many of the relationships. (Mathematically, the partial derivatives evaluated at some nominal design configuration.)

In reality, both the higher-level task models and the lower-level parametric models are insufficient. The former ignore too many important technical details, while the latter lack the overall context. (For example, in the brake system model, we find that some of the most important redesign loops involve the managerial decisions that are required when key design constraints cannot be met or time and budget adjustments are needed.) We seek to create hybrid models which embody both types of features. We expect that such a model will enable the study of the important feedback marks lying far above the diagonal, linking the blocks of tightly coupled task activity. Redefining these inter-block constraints may provide new opportunities for innovative design management. We call this designing the design process, or "meta-design", discussed in the following section.

Ultimately we desire considerably more detailed design models than even the parameter-level models discussed above. If the design problem could be expressed as a set of equations and constraints, then analysis may be able to identify which iteration paths are needed for a given set of input requirements or which requirements must be relaxed. This type of analysis (design simulation) needs both the connectivity and sensitivity information embodied in the equations, thereby broadening the notion of technical structure to include both topological connectivity and analytical sensitivity.

Strategies for Designing Better Design Processes

Analyzing the technical structure of a design can identify many opportunities to improve the design process. As two examples of design improvement strategies, we present two conflicting approaches to consider: removing coupling versus adding coupling.

Decoupling Tasks To Speed Design

A loosely coupled group of tasks can sometimes be split up into two or more smaller, more tightly coupled groups by *artificial decoupling*, which involves actually removing one or more task dependencies (one or more marks) from the matrix. This can be accomplished in several ways, including the creation of an additional task to be performed earlier in the design procedure. The definition of this new task would require the parties associated with the removed dependency to agree ahead of time on the relevant task interfaces. Another approach to this artificial decoupling strategy is illustrated by the following example we obtained by comparing the design procedures in two firms developing competing products (an electro-mechanical instrument).

Designers in one firm recognize three aspects of the product (the casing, wiring, and optics) to be so tightly coupled that they must be designed simultaneously, requiring lengthy negotiation (five to ten design iterations, taking up to six months) before enough detail can be settled to build the first working prototype. The design structure matrix describing this procedure is shown in Figure 7a. The designers in the competing firm believe that a first prototype must be delivered much more quickly and that it is acceptable for the wiring inside such a prototype to be untidy. They have developed the design procedure illustrated by Figure 7b, where the wiring is absent from the design iteration loop. The design is completed more quickly (in two iterations, taking only a few weeks), and the prototype is built with crude wiring. The final wiring layout is completed for the second prototype. The wiring was artificially decoupled from the design in order to speed development.

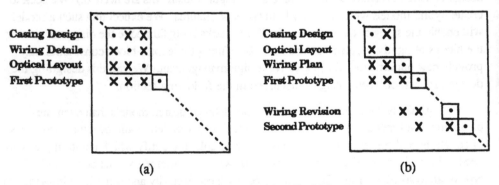

Figure 7. Instrument Design Task Matrices

Increasing Coupling to Improve Design Quality

An increased coupling strategy is the essential basis of simultaneous engineering and design for manufacture (DFM). In the traditional (sequential) design process, depicted by the matrix in Figure 8a, the product designers would perform their design tasks somewhat independently from the manufacturing engineers. In the modern (concurrent) design process, Figure 8b, the practice of DFM mandates that these two activities be performed simultaneously. This is beneficial because the production expertise is brought into the early design stages (often causing much iteration), resulting in designs which are simpler to manufacture. However, the added coupling in the design process in fact slows product development considerably. Advocates of this philosophy would argue that overall design time can still be reduced because the need for later (more lengthy) iteration is therefore lessened. This is particularly true if the feedback from manufacturing engineering to design was indeed present in the original design procedure. This feedback is shown in Figure 8a by the + marks which depict redesign activity addressing the production problems which inevitably arise.

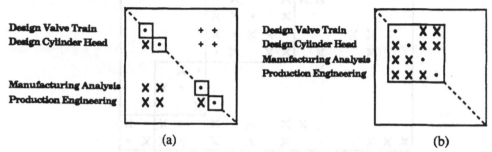

Design Valve Train
Design Cylinder Head

Manufacturing Analysis
Production Engineering

Design Valve Train
Design Cylinder Head
Manufacturing Analysis
Production Engineering

(a)   (b)

Figure 8. Sequential and Concurrent Design Procedures

Recommended Design Strategy

It has become accepted that adding coupling in a design process is helpful to improve product quality because it can provide feedback of multiple perspectives to early design decisions. However, since this strategy usually does increase iteration, causing the design process to take more time to execute, one must not implement this scheme to the extreme; too much feedback would actually stall design progress. If the matrix is full of marks because every decision is allowed to directly influence every other decision, then the design procedure may never finish! A compromise must be made to optimize the tradeoff between reducing design time and improving design quality.

Figure 9 depicts an improved design management strategy which represents a hybrid of the sequential and concurrent schemes discussed above. The example includes several major iterative blocks representing the tightly coupled sub-systems. The partitioned task matrix identifies which tasks can be done in parallel and which in series. Outside the partitioned blocks lie the most important elements of this design process: the system-level feedback. The few feedback marks that fall above the block-diagonal partitioning drive the longer iterations among the sub-systems of groups. Since these iterations may involve major development efforts, they must be chosen very carefully.

In this improved design management strategy, the design team must understand their design process and take systematic steps to improve it. Design managers can implement this scheme by following this procedure:

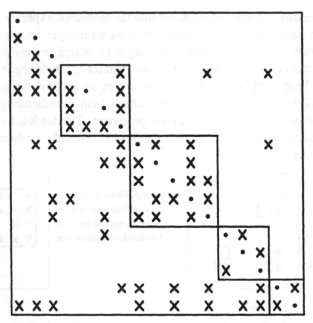

Figure 9. Recommended Design Management Strategy

1) Engage designers and engineers in a design process modeling activity. Using the matrix format to display the model builds group consensus and forms the basis for process analysis and coordination.

2) Find an appropriate set of major tasks into which the overall project may be divided. The best partitioning may not coincide with natural or traditional subsystems. Rather they may be found in other areas where many tasks are inherently tightly coupled due to the underlying problem structure.

3) Facilitate design iteration within these very tightly coupled task blocks. This may require improved channels of communication and/or changes in group organization.

4) Allow tasks to be performed in parallel where possible. This may be accomplished by encouraging all participants to identify where their needed information is generated and to collect those inputs when available.

5) Remove some of the less important task couplings which might otherwise cause wasteful iteration. These may be very difficult to recognize and would generally be a matter of conflicting opinions, however the leverage gained by streamlining a few tasks may be tremendous if this allows many others to be more productive as well.

6) Most importantly, design managers must decide strategically where to place the important iteration drivers. Some of these longer feedback loops are essential to the current design. Others are for generational learning. The key feedback elements must be preserved and these loops should be shortened where possible by performing coupled tasks closely together .

7) Direct an ongoing effort to continuously modify and improve the matrix design process model. Solicit suggestions for improvement while spreading process understanding throughout the organization.

The Potential for Design Process Improvement

We recognize that product design is difficult for several reasons: products can be technologically complex; a complete design procedure may involve millions of tasks; and all the tasks are coupled in some manner, making iteration an inherent characteristic of the design activity. We claim that the design process can be performed more successfully if it can be organized more sensibly.

Design is a process just like any other step in manufacturing, such as machining or assembly. The first step in improving a process is to model and understand it. Methods exist for modeling machining and, to a lesser degree, assembly. The design process so far lacks convincing and effective models that permit analysis and systematic development of improvements. The design structure matrix and its associated process modeling effort is a step in this direction. It assumes that the basic elements of a design process are tasks that require input information, take time to execute, and produce decisions or output information for input to other tasks. It further assumes that a major route to process improvement, other than making each task more efficient, is to resequence individual tasks or groups of tasks so that required information is available sooner and available information is used sooner. Not yet included in this paradigm but potentially useful is to redefine tasks by breaking them up and recombining them, which is a natural extension of resequencing.

Practical results of this approach take two forms. Even without applying algorithms for resequencing tasks, one can use the design structure matrix as a display of the existing design process or of the designers' view of the process. The matrix graphically displays all the existing information flows and makes it easy to see the difficulties in the form of coupling and unnecessary delays. Engineers can find their place in a large and dispersed activity. Pracht showed that even a simple directed graph was a powerful visual aid in decision making [23], and the matrix format reveals even more surprising features, including some problems that can be easily remedied. While this approach to design process improvement requires a detailed process model, this requirement is common to all past successful process improvement efforts. The resulting matrix can also be used as a management tool to redirect engineering effort to tasks involved in key iterations. Design reviews and progress assessments can be based on the matrix, with managers assuring that available information actually was used, required information actually was transmitted and received, and tasks started as soon as they could.

In the future, our research and interaction with industry will produce computer tools that permit managers to find optimum ways of restructuring more complex design tasks, exposing problems and creating unique solutions that could not be found just by manually inspecting the matrix. One can also imagine the matrix augmented with designers' names, phone numbers, electronic mail addresses, datafile names, and other information. Such information will make designers' work and communication more efficient and make the structure of engineering design databases more consistent with the needs of the design process and its information flows.

Appendix: Partitioning and Tearing Design Structure Matrices

In analyzing design structure matrices, there are two distinct mathematical problems which can be treated separately. Although the two problems are not mutually exclusive, the literature divides them into separate domains for ease of reference. The first type of analysis concerns the structure of the task interdependencies and is referred to as *partitioning*. The second level of analysis focuses on the context of the interdependencies and is referred to as *tearing*.

Partitioning identifies task sequences which maximize the availability of requisite information for each of the design tasks. In terms of the design structure matrix this corresponds to making the matrix as lower diagonal as possible to minimize the number of feedbacks encountered in carrying out the project. Partitioning identifies the loops of circular information flow which are then used to find a sequence for the tasks, placing the blocks of tasks (the loops) along the diagonal.

The goal of tearing is to work within the loops of information flow identified by the partitioning analysis. Each loop defines a set of tasks which are in a block and which must be considered simultaneously. However, a loop can be temporarily broken to initialize iteration if one or more tasks is performed without all of its necessary information. The aim of the tearing procedure is then to determine which task or tasks provide the best opportunity to initialize the loops of information flow.

Partitioning Algorithms

Partitioning analysis can be performed easily by following either of two general strategies. Both strategies partition a matrix by identifying those tasks which comprise the iteration loops and placing these tasks in blocks. The blocks and other tasks can then easily be scheduled in lower-triangular form. A description of the partitioning algorithm is given below. The two schemes differ only in how they identify the loops.

1. Schedule the tasks which are not components of any loops. Tasks with empty rows should be performed first. Task with empty columns must be performed last. Once a task is scheduled, it is removed from further consideration.
2. Identify loops by path searching or adjacency matrix analysis. Once a loop has been identified, it can be scheduled as one task.
3. Repeat steps 1 and 2 until all tasks have been scheduled.

The first of these methods is referred to in the literature as path searching [16]. To search, the information flow is traced until any task is encountered twice. All tasks between the first occurrence and the second occurrence of that task constitute a loop of information flow. Once a loop has been identified, it is temporarily collapsed into a single task while the rest of the loops are traced. When no more loops exist, the sequencing can be completed.

Figure A1 illustrates a simple example of path searching using a matrix of eight tasks. The partitioning proceeds as follows: a) Task C has an empty row indicating that it is not part of any loop. Schedule it first and remove it from further consideration. All other tasks belong to loops. b) Trace dependency starting with any unscheduled task. Task A depends on Task D which depends on Task A (loop). Collapse Task D into Task A and represent as a single task, AD. c) The composite Task AD has an empty row indicating that it is not part of any loop. Schedule it next and remove it from further consideration. d) Task E now has an empty row indicating that it is not part of any loop. Schedule it next and remove it from further consideration. e) Task H has an empty row indicating that it is not part of any loop. Schedule it next and remove it from further consideration. f) Trace dependency starting with any unscheduled task: Task B depends on Task G which depends on Task F which depends on Task B. This final loop includes all the remaining unscheduled tasks. g) The final partitioned matrix.

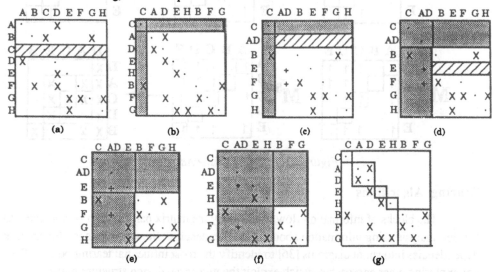

Figure A1. Matrix Partitioning

An alternative method for finding the loops of information flow is a technique which uses powers of the adjacency matrix to identify successively higher order loops [18]. The adjacency matrix contains binary information describing which nodes or tasks are connected by a directed path of information flow. If a pair of tasks is connected by such a path, they are said to be adjacent [13]. The adjacency matrix, therefore is the binary design structure matrix with no marks along the diagonal (eliminating loops of length one).

Raising the binary adjacency matrix to the n-th power using Boolean multiplication yields a higher-order matrix containing elements denoting which tasks are reachable in n steps. For example, squaring the adjacency matrix yields a matrix revealing which tasks are reachable in two steps. The third power of the adjacency matrix identifies nodes which are reachable in three steps. The powers of the adjacency matrix are useful for determining the circular flow of information because any task or node in a circular information flow must be reachable from itself. This implies that task x is reachable from itself in n steps if the adjacency matrix raised to the n-th power has a non-zero entry in the x-th element of its diagonal.

Figure A2 illustrates use of the adjacency matrices to enumerate iteration loops using a simple matrix with five elements. The second power of the adjacency matrix indicates that Tasks C and E are in a two step loop. The third order matrix reveals that Tasks A, C, and E are in a three step loop. The higher order matrices reveal no other loops in the system.

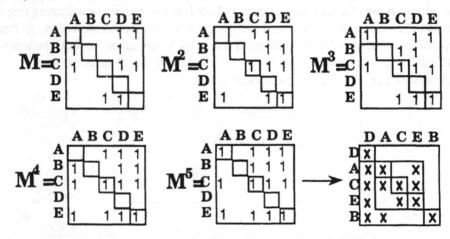

Figure A2. Powers of the Adjacency Matrix

Tearing Algorithms

The blocks of information flow revealed by the matrix partition can be subjected to further analysis using information about interdependencies. Steward maps the binary task dependencies into shunt diagrams [36] to identify the most influential tearing points. We are exploring other approaches which exploit the numerical design structure matrix.

In general our numerical tearing algorithms are specific to a particular definition of the numerical values in the matrix. One such algorithm we have implemented uses numerical matrix elements representing task repeat probabilities and task durations [32]. The repeat probabilities reflect the likelihood of repeating the task if it proceeds without a particular required input. These values are the off-diagonal elements in the matrix. The diagonal elements contain the durations of the tasks, times as if they were performed independently.

For example, in Figure A3, tasks A and B are tightly coupled; task A needs the output of task B and task B needs the output of task A. If task A proceeds without the information from task B, there is a 20% chance that task A will have to be repeated once task B does supply the requisite information. If the other option is chosen and task B is performed without the input from task A, the likelihood of repeating task B, once task A is completed, will be 40%. This matrix is then used to construct a Markov chain whose value (total expected iteration time) beginning with A or B can be computed using the repeat probabilities and the task durations. This allows each sequence to be scored and compared to other sequences on a common basis.

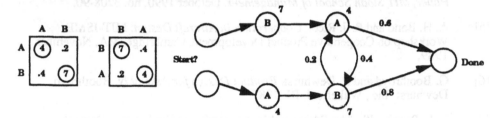

Figure A3. Expected Iteration Computed as the Value of the Markov Chain

We have also implemented several other schemes for scoring sequences of tasks within blocks. (Interestingly, we have found that coupled with a swapping algorithm, these scoring/swapping schemes can do both partitioning and tearing quite well in one single iterative algorithm.) While the above scoring technique relies upon a certain model of design iteration, other schemes make different assumptions. This work and the experimental verification of the matrix predictions of iteration are ongoing and detailed in [32].

Acknowledgment

This research is funded jointly by the National Science Foundation under Grant Number DDM-9007062, by the General Motors Corporation, and by the MIT Leaders for Manufacturing Program, a partnership involving eleven major US manufacturing firms and MIT's engineering and management schools.

The four authors are affiliated with (respectively) MIT Sloan School of Management, Charles Stark Draper Laboratory, MIT Sloan School of Management, and MIT Department of Mechanical Engineering.

Bibliography

[1]   C. Alexander. *Notes on the Synthesis of Form*. Harvard University Press, Cambridge, Massachusetts, 1964.

[2]   T. Allen. *Managing the Flow of Technology: Technology Transfer and the Dissemination of Technological Information Within the R&D Organization*. MIT Press, Cambridge, MA, 1977.

[3]   D. G. Ancona and D. E. Caldwell. "Demography and Design: Predictors of New Product Team Performance", *Working Paper, MIT Sloan School of Management*. September 1989, no. 3078-89.

[4]   T. A. Black, C. H. Fine and E. M. Sachs. "A Method for Systems Design Using Precedence Relationships: An Application to Automotive Brake Systems", *Working Paper, MIT Sloan School of Management*. October 1990, no. 3208-90.

[5]   A. H. Bond and R. J. Ricci. *Cooperation in Aircraft Design*. MIT-JSME Workshop on Cooperative Product Development, Cambridge, MA, November 1989,

[6]   G. Boothroyd and P. Dewhurst. *Product Design for Assembly*. Boothroyd Dewhurst, Inc., Wakefield, RI, 1987.

[7]   L. L. Bucciarelli. "An Ethnographic Perspective on Engineering Design", *Design Studies*. vol. 9, no. 3, July 1988, pp. 159-168.

[8]   D. M. Byrne and S. Taguchi. "The Taguchi Approach to Parameter Design", *Quality Progress*. December 1987, pp. 19-26.

[9]   K. B. Clark. "Project Scope and Project Performance: The Effect of Parts Strategy and Supplier Involvement on Product Development", *Management Science*. vol. 35, no. 10, October 1989, pp. 1247-1263.

[10]   K. B. Clark, B. Chew and T. Fujimoto. "Product Development in the World Auto Industry", *Brookings Papers on Economic Activity*. vol. 3, 1989, pp. 729-771.

[11]   J. W. Dean Jr. and G. I. Susman. "Organizing for Manufacturable Design", *Harvard Business Review*. January-February 1989, pp. 28-36.

[12]   P. F. Drucker. "The Discipline of Innovation", *Harvard Business Review*. May-June 1985, pp. 67-72.

[13]   F. Harary. *Graph Theory*. Addison-Wesley, Reading, Mass., 1969.

[14]   T. C. Hartrum, T. D. Connally and S. E. Johnson. *An Interactive Graphics Editor with Integrated Data Dictionary for IDEF$_0$ Structured Analysis Diagrams*. National Aerospace and Electronics Conference, Dayton, Ohio, May 1988, pp. 765-770.

[15]   J. R. Hauser and D. Clausing. "The House of Quality", *Harvard Business Review*. May-June 1988, pp. 63-73.

[16]   E. Kehat and M. Shacham. "Chemical Process Simulation Programs, Part 2: Partitioning and Tearing of System Flowsheets", *Process Technology International*. vol. 18, no. 3, March 1973, pp. 115-118.

[17]   T. Kitzmiller. *Avionic System Design*. MIT-JSME Workshop on Cooperative Product Development, Cambridge, MA, November 1989,

[18]   W. P. Ledet and D. M. Himmelblau. "Decomposition Procedures for the Solving of Large Scale Systems", *Advances in Chemical Engineering*. vol. 8, , pp. 185-254.

[19]   H. L. Malchow and S. R. Croopnick. "A Methodology for Organizing Performance Requirements for Complex Dynamical Systems", *IEEE Transactions on Engineering Management*. February 1985.

[20]   D. A. Marca and C. L. McGowan. *SADT: Structured Analysis and Design Technique*. McGraw Hill, New York, 1988.

[21]   J. L. Nevins and D. E. Whitney. *Concurrent Design of Products and Processes*. McGraw-Hill, New York, 1989.

[22]   S. L. Padula, C. Sandridge, R. T. Haftka and J. L. Walsh. "Demonstration of Decomposition and Optimization in the Design of Experimental Space Systems". In J.-F. M. Barthelemy, Ed. *Recent Advances in Multidisciplinary Analysis*, NASA Langley Research Center, Hampton, Virginia, 1988.

[23]   W. E. Pracht. "Gismo: A Visual Problem-Structuring and Knowledge-Organization Tool", *IEEE Transactions on Systems, Man, and Cybernetics*. vol. SMC-16, no. 2, March/April 1986, pp. 265-270.

[24]   J. B. Quinn. "Managing Innovation: Controlled Chaos", *Harvard Business Review*. May-June 1985, pp. 73-84.

[25]   J. R. Rinderle and V. Krishnan. "Constraint Reasoning in Design", *International Conference on Design Theory and Methodology*. Chicago, September 1990.

[26]   J. R. Rinderle and N. P. Suh. "Measures of Functional Coupling in Design", *ASME Journal of Engineering for Industry*. November 1982, pp. 383-388.

[27]   J. L. Rogers. *DeMAID: A Design Manager's Aide for Intelligent Decomposition User's Guide*. NASA Technical Memorandum 101575, March 1989.

[28]   J. L. Rogers and S. L. Padula. *An Intelligent Advisor for the Design Manager*. NASA Technical Memorandum 101558, February 1989.

[29]   D. T. Ross. "Structured Analysis (SA): A Language for Communicating Ideas", *IEEE Transactions on Software Engineering*. vol. SE-3, no. 1, January 1977, pp. 16-34.

[30]   D. T. Ross. "Applications and Extensions of SADT", *IEEE Computer Magazine*. April 1985, pp. 25-34.

[31]   H. A. Simon. *The Sciences of the Artificial*. MIT Press, Cambridge, Massachusetts, 1970.

[32] R. P. Smith and S. D. Eppinger. "Modeling Design Iteration", *Working Paper, MIT Sloan School of Management*. June 1990, no. 3160-90.

[33] J. Sobieszczanski-Sobieski. *Multidisciplinary Optimization for Engineering Systems: Achievements and Potential*. NASA Technical Memorandum 101566, March 1989.

[34] D. Sriram and M. L. Maher. "Representation and Use of Constraints in Structural Design", *AI in Engineering*. Springer-Verlag, Southampton, UK, , April 1986.

[35] D. V. Steward. "The Design Structure System: A Method for Managing the Design of Complex Systems", *IEEE Transactions on Engineering Management*. August 1981, pp. 71-74.

[36] D. V. Steward. *Systems Analysis and Management: Structure, Strategy, and Design*. Petrocelli Books, New York, 1981.

[37] N. P. Suh. *The Principles of Design*. Oxford University Press, New York, 1990.

[38] N. P. Suh, A. C. Bell and D. C. Gossard. "On an Axiomatic Approach to Manufacturing and Manufacturing Systems", *ASME Journal of Engineering for Industry*. May 1978, pp. 127-130.

[39] G. J. Sussman and G. L. Steele. "Constraints -- A Language for Expressing Almost-Hierarchical Descriptions", *Artificial Intelligence*. vol. 14, 1980, pp. 1-39.

[40] E. von Hippel. *Task Partitioning: An Innovation Process Variable*. MIT Sloan School of Management Working Paper no. 2030-88, June 1988 (rev. April 1989).

[41] J. N. Warfield. "Binary Matrices in System Modeling", *IEEE Transactions on Systems, Man, and Cybernetics*. vol. SMC-3, no. 5, September 1973, pp. 441-449.

[42] D. E. Whitney. "Manufacturing By Design", *Harvard Business Review*. July-August 1988, pp. 83-91.

[43] D. E. Whitney and M. Milley. "CADSYS: A New Approach to Computer-Aided Design", *IEEE Transactions on Systems, Man, and Cybernetics*. vol. SMC-4, no. 1, January 1974, pp. 50-58.

[44] J. D. Wiest. "Precedence Diagramming Method: Some Unusual Characteristics and Their Implications for Project Managers", *Journal of Operations Management*. vol. 1, no. 3, February 1981, pp. 121-130.

[45] J. D. Wiest and F. K. Levy. *A Management Guide to PERT/CPM*. Prentice-Hall, Englewood Cliffs, New Jersey, 2nd Edition, 1977.

Knowledge-Based Conflict Resolution for Cooperation among Expert Agents

Susan E. Lander, Victor R. Lesser, and Margaret E. Connell

Department of Computer and Information Science
University of Massachusetts
Amherst, MA 01003

Abstract

Cooperating human experts are able to integrate their skills and knowledge productively to achieve goals beyond their individual capabilities. Machine agents may someday increase their power similarly by working in teams of specialized experts. To do this, the systems must be able to communicate knowledge, propose solutions, resolve conflicts that occur during problem-solving, and agree on results. We describe the Cooperating Experts Framework (CEF), a generic framework that supports cooperative problem-solving among sets of knowledge-based systems. The systems solve subproblems relevant to their specific expertise and integrate their efforts using conflict resolution strategies. CEF provides scheduling and communication support for the agents, a set of conflict resolution strategies, and a set of heuristics for choosing the most effective strategy for the situation. We also describe STEAMER, a system implemented in the CEF framework, that designs steam condensers.

1 Cooperating Experts Problem Solving

There is vast potential for sets of cooperative computational agents that can work together to achieve unified goals. To realize that potential however, agents must have the capability to integrate their knowledge and skills productively. **Cooperating Expert Problem Solving** (CEPS) is a style of problem solving that allows agents to communicate and cooperate through a shared language with shared expectations about how to reach agreement when conflicts occur. CEPS both preserves the autonomy of the agents and enables appropriate interactions.

Examples of the integration of expertise through cooperation are seen in human problem-solving tasks such as design, research, business management, and human relations. To motivate the CEPS approach, consider a team of human experts working in an office who

This research was supported by DARPA under Contract #N00014-89-J-1877 and by a University Research Initiative Grant, Contract #N00014-86-K-0764.

are given the task of choosing a telephone company. The team consists of a manager and an accountant. They have the shared goal of selecting an appropriate system for their office, but each individual would like to insure that her own priorities receive top consideration. Unfortunately, many of the individuals' local goals and priorities are conflicting from a global viewpoint. For example, the accountant would like to try Cost-Company, a company with excellent long-distance rates, to save money. The manager is concerned about the quality of service and would rather choose Qual-Company, a company with a known high level of quality. How can the agents come to a decision when there are no global criteria for evaluation?

In this situation, it is very difficult to judge which solution is the "correct" solution since it depends on the criteria used to decide. In truth, there is no right or wrong answer: the company may need the level of service provided by Qual-Company, but it may also need to save on costs through Cost-Company. The agents must reconcile their differences and reach a decision, taking into account both viewpoints. Since solution correctness is an elusive concept, the experts strive for balance. A solution which is acceptable to all experts, though possibly not ideal for any one, is the best that can be hoped for.

To take this example a step farther, let us say that it is company policy to always choose the least expensive alternative when faced with an ambivalent choice situation. The company therefore does impose a global evaluation function which can be used to guide the decision. However, the manager has worked out a scenario in which Qual-Company is actually less expensive than Cost-Company because salesmen have fewer delays in placing calls, there are fewer communication errors when transmitting data, and, in general, the phone service is faster and more reliable. This theory could be tested by setting up experiments comparing phone service and productivity over some time period. However, the type of savings being talked about is not enough to justify the cost of evaluation: a global evaluation exists but it is too costly to compute.

Again, the agents must come to terms without any absolute notion of truth: it simply is not clear which is the "right" solution. There are several ways of reaching agreement on a solution however; for example, they can look for other alternatives (is there a MidQualMidCost-Company somewhere?), they can try to convince each other, or they can look at solutions to similar conflicts that occured in the past. In the end some solution must be agreed upon whether or not that solution is guaranteed to be optimal with respect to the company's policy.

One of the motivating factors in the CEPS approach is the need to find a solution when there is no strong global model of correctness or optimality. This occurs when global evaluation criteria are absent, when global evaluation criteria are too expensive to compute, or when a global evaluation is some combination of a set of locally computed evaluations [17]. The latter case occurs when the problem is decomposed in such a way that each agent has enough expertise to evaluate some part of the solution, but not all of it. To compute a comprehensive evaluation, a "super agent" would be required, yet it is not always desirable or even possible to build systems with this all-encompassing outlook.

Why is Cooperating Experts problem solving a desirable paradigm? Bringing together diverse knowledge is a source of robustness and balance which is extremely important in many real-world situations: a structural engineer and an architect work together to design and build a safe and functional building, or a pediatrician and a cardiologist consult to help an infant with heart disease. The team can solve problems that are beyond the scope of the individual experts. This is true also of machine agents: integrating knowledge has the potential for increasing problem-solving power. If we build agents that can work together even when the individuals don't fully understand the entire task, we can begin to look at problems with a whole new level of task complexity. Furthermore, the richness of combined knowledge and viewpoints from various specialties provides the potential for creative problem solving and innovation.

From a software engineering viewpoint, the CEPS paradigm allows for modular programming. No development-time consistency checking is required among the systems comprising the CEPS set, which has far-reaching implications for the degree of autonomy that can occur in system-building efforts. Each agent can be implemented, debugged, tested and maintained independently.

CEPS sets can be dynamically arranged to fit the problem solving situation. Systems can be added and deleted with minimal effort. Different sets of agents can be combined to handle different problems or customized to a particular situation. Agents can be varied according to expertise, desired inferencing techniques, or based on the amount of computational overhead that can be supported. We envision a "warehouse" of potential agents available for problem solving: for a particular problem, the user chooses the most pertinent.

2   The Cooperating Experts Framework

The **Cooperating Experts Framework** (CEF) is designed to support CEPS by providing the communication and conflict resolution structures and protocols required for cooperative interaction. CEF is implemented in the Generic BlackBoard framework, GBB [3]. Figure 1 shows the general CEF architecture.

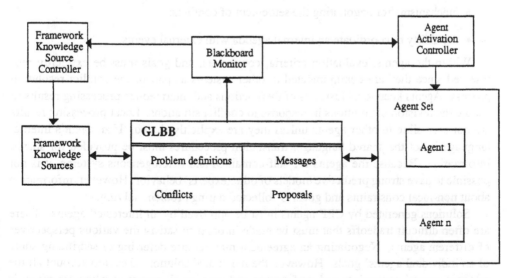

Figure 1: The CEF Architecture

The GLobal BlackBoards (GLBB) of CEF are used to facilitate communication among agents. Any information placed on the these blackboards must be represented in a common language shared by all agents. The language is defined using the object definition capabilities of GBB. There are both domain-independent and application-specific objects and blackboard structures. The domain-independent structures are supplied by the framework, for example a CONFLICT-OBJECT and a CONFLICT-BLACKBOARD will be available in any domain. Application knowledge is contained in the domain-specific objects and blackboard spaces. In the steam condenser design domain described below, examples include a MOTOR-OBJECT and a MOTOR-SPACE on the PROPOSAL-BLACKBOARD. The global blackboards for the steam condenser domain are shown in detail in Figure 3.

The CEF control shell integrates the execution of framework knowledge sources for performing high-level tasks on GLBB objects with the execution of independent agents. Although CEF is implemented as a blackboard system, it does not use traditional blackboard knowledge sources as agents. A CEF agent is a fully functional knowledge-based system which can solve problems in its limited domain independently. The agent does it own internal scheduling and has private data, knowledge, goals, and history mechanisms. Although it can operate as a separate problem-solving entity, it has specific capabilities which allow it to act as a member of a team. These capabilities include:

- a shared communication language;

- internal knowledge representations which capture sufficient goal and history information to allow for cooperative solution revision;

- provisions for sharing information in a timely manner during problem-solving;

- mechanisms for incorporating externally produced partial solutions;

- mechanisms for negotiating the settlement of conflicts;

- the ability to coordinate an internal agenda with external events.

Within the agents, evaluation criteria, constraints, and goals must be explicitly represented since they are communicated to other systems as part of the conflict resolution process. Agents keep local histories of their actions and intermediate processing results to enable the revision of solutions in response to conflict situations. Local processing results are not accessible to other agents unless they are explicitly shared. If an agent's internal language is not the shared language, translation procedures must be provided for shared information. Because the agents are self-contained and heterogeneous systems, it is not possible to have strong predictive models of other experts' behavior. However, information about non-local constraints and goals is collected during problem-solving.

Solutions generated by CEF agents must be approved by all interested agents. There are often difficult tradeoffs that must be made in order to satisfy the various perspectives of different agents. Negotiating an agreement may require deferring or sacrificing some of an individual agents' goals. However, the negotiated solution takes into account all the relevant agents' constraints and preferences and satisfies all agents to whatever extent is possible.

2.1 Conflict among Agents

Conflicts are an inevitable and positive part of the problem-solving process in CEF. Conflict serves as a catalyst for the exchange of knowledge and goals among agents. Common sources of conflict include:

- resource contention among the distributed agents;

- incomplete or incorrect knowledge;

- incompatible goals, priorities, or preferences;

- different evaluation criteria.

Conflict situations can be either direct or indirect. For example, two agents may propose solutions for the same subproblem or for two subproblems which interact directly. On the other hand, two agents may propose solutions for subproblems that have no apparent relationship, but which ultimately interact through a chain of other subproblems. Conflict sets are formed dynamically for each specific conflict situation by adding agents to the set as interactions between their subproblems are discovered. Once an agent has been incorporated into a conflict set, it will be notified of any changes that are suggested in response to the conflict.

When conflicts do occur, the conflict participants must have protocols for the resolution process. This entails both a set of strategies for conflict resolution and a set of meta-strategies for choosing one. These strategies are detailed in Section 5.2.

3 Comparison to other work

3.1 Traditional blackboards

Hearsay-II [7] provides an early model of multiple specialists working together to solve a single, complex problem; namely, the interpretation of spoken utterances. In Hearsay-II, knowledge is divided among specialists called knowledge sources (KSs) which share information through a global structure called a blackboard (BB). Cooperation occurs implicitly through the incremental extension of globally available hypotheses. Conflicts are not resolved explicitly, instead competing hypotheses coexist and vie for processing resources to improve their believability.

The expertise of a traditional blackboard system as exemplified by Hearsay-II is represented by KSs which parallel the knowledge-based systems of the CEF framework. Traditionally, KSs have some or all of the following attributes:

1. they are instantiated in response to a particular pattern on the blackboard;

2. they respond only to information that is available at the time of their instantiation;

3. they have no understanding of the problem outside of their own area of expertise;

4. they cannot be suspended during execution or reinstantiated once execution has ended;

5. they keep no history of their actions.

CEF agents, on the other hand, are fully functional systems which have the property of persistence throughout the problem-solving process. They can generate partial solutions independently and have private data, knowledge, goals, and histories of their own actions. They can reexamine earlier decisions and change results. They can suspend work on a particular task at any time and resume it when the situation seems more suitable.

Another difference between the Hearsay-II and CEF frameworks is in control strategies. Hearsay-II had a centralized scheduler which made control decisions based on the global situation represented on the blackboard. Each CEF agent is responsible for scheduling its own tasks based on both its internal problem-solving state and the information available through the global database.

3.2 Negotiation models

Relevant work on conflict resolution and problem solving models comes from two perspectives, human models and computational models.

3.2.1 Human models of conflict resolution and creative problem solving

Pruitt [16] discusses negotiation and conflict in a general way and details specific negotiation tactics. His work comes from a background of social psychology and is grounded in domains such as international relations. Human negotiation models can't be directly applied to machine cooperation. Human motivation is more complex than the state of our current understanding; often, even the disputants in a conflict don't know what they really want. However, the study of human negotiation offers tremendous insight into possible strategies for dealing with conflict and for the beneficial use of conflict as a platform for creativity.

DeBono [5] defines *lateral thinking* as a mechanism for generating innovative solutions in human problem-solving. Lateral thinking is a method in which different approaches to a problem are explicitly sought through strategies which are designed to elicit unusual connections between problem elements. Although DeBono does not speak directly to the issue of negotiation of conflicts, his work offers insight into the type of creative problem-solving that can be used to form innovative solutions.

3.2.2 Computational models of conflict resolution

Sycara [20] presents a negotiation model which integrates case-based reasoning, qualitative reasoning, and constraint propagation in a mechanical design domain. Agents have a *belief structure* that represents the importance and relationships among goals. Goal graphs include attributes of importance, feasibility, and contribution. There is also a representation of the *preference structure* of an agent which expresses the utility for each attribute in the goal graph. Case-based reasoning is used to propose "ball-park" solutions and compromises while reasoning with utilities is used in situations where case-based reasoning is not appropriate. The problems Sycara addresses in her work are very similar to those considered in the design of CEF. CEF provides a more flexible conflict resolution format, providing multiple resolution strategies and using characteristics of the conflict situation to choose one.

Klein [11] has developed a hierarchy of conflict types and conflict resolution strategies. He uses a centralized controller to determine the type of conflict and map it to its appropriate strategy. CEF does not attempt to determine the type of a conflict in the sense of its underlying cause, instead it analyzes the "symptoms" of the conflict. The mapping of symptoms to strategies is done by the agents involved in a conflict rather than by a centralized controller.

3.3 Design models

The STEAMER domain is an example of parametric design. In Dominic II [15], parametric design of mechanical components of a system is accomplished using iterative redesign. Both iterative redesign and CEF develop a model for overcoming unsatisfactory situations in the design process. Both apply strategy changes to make improvements. Dominic II defines a set of hill climbing strategies and maps them to unproductive efforts at design. Similarly, CEF defines types of conflicts which occur among experts and maps them to strategies used to resolve them.

4 An Application Domain: STEAMER

CEF is being used as the basis for a system that does parametric design of steam condensers, STEAMER. Design is the process of constructing an artifact description that satisfies a functional specification and criteria on the form of the artifact. It can be realized in its target medium and within the restrictions of the design process, and it meets performance requirements [14]. Some of the characteristics which make the design process particularly amenable to a CEPS approach are described in [10]:

- The cost, scale, and complexity of many design problems exceed the resources of a single individual or organization.

- The design process may involve diverse resources that in turn are managed by different agents.

- The process of design has been studied extensively thereby providing a basis for the implementation of knowledge-based design systems.

- Design problems can be characterized as routine, creative, or innovative with each type of problem requiring different design methodologies.

In parametric design, the general form of the artifact being designed is known, but the designer must find values for variable parameters of the artifact. STEAMER uses application knowledge from a system with the same domain but a different problem-solving methodology [13].

Figure 2 shows the general form of a steam condenser, comprising a pump, heat exchanger, motor, platform, shaft and v-belt. CEF agents produce *proposals* which

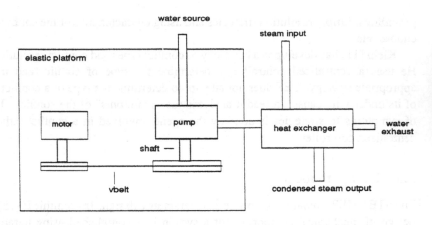

Figure 2: A Steam Condenser

represent solutions to subproblems. In STEAMER, a proposal is either a component for a condenser or a complete condenser. Each component is designed by an agent with expert knowledge and problem-solving methods that can include anything from numerical optimization to sets of heuristics. STEAMER's agents correspond to the components of a condenser, e.g., the pump agent produces pump components. There is also an agent that is concerned with characteristics of the complete condenser such as natural frequency, total weight, and total cost. The components are independent except for shared parameters which represent the interface points of the design. The values for these parameters must be acceptable to all agents that use them. For example, the parameters of a pump component include water flow rate and power. The pump and heat exchanger share the water flow rate parameter (water flows between the pump and heat exchanger) and the pump and motor components share power (the motor must deliver sufficient power to run the pump).

To begin processing, STEAMER is given a problem definition that specifies values for a set of condenser attributes. A typical problem definition is shown below:

```
Problem_definition_1
    Platform-side-length 120
    Maximum-platform-deflection .01
    Required-capacity 2000
```

The problem definition is placed on STEAMER's global blackboard (GLBB) which is accessible by all expert agents and by a set of knowledge sources (KSs) which do high level operations on GLBB objects. The blackboards are shown in Figure 3. Any agents that have work to do (whether pending or in reaction to new objects on GLBB), will execute during each processing cycle. In this case, the pump, heat exchanger, and motor agents will begin local processing based on the new problem definition. All agents in a CEF set must be able to perform a set of tasks:

1. create new proposals

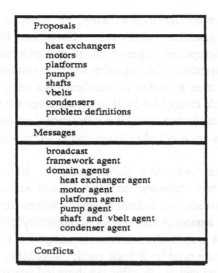

Proposals
heat exchangers
motors
platforms
pumps
shafts
vbelts
condensers
problem definitions
Messages
broadcast
framework agent
domain agents
heat exchanger agent
motor agent
platform agent
pump agent
shaft and vbelt agent
condenser agent
Conflicts

Figure 3: Global Blackboards (GLBB) in STEAMER

2. evaluate proposals

3. detect conflicts

4. respond to conflicts

In response to the problem definition, each triggered agent performs a *create-proposal* task. In this domain, problems are naturally decomposed by having each agent responsible for a particular component type: the pump agent creates a pump component, etc.

Because this is a new problem, problem-solving tends to be underconstrained. The agents work independently using whatever information is available and use default values when they must make assumptions about interface parameters. These assumptions are often unrealistic from a more global perspective, but the agents use this opportunity to put forth proposals that best reflect their own interests. It is a chance for each agent to act selfishly. As problem-solving progresses, it becomes more difficult for an agent to emphasize its own preferences, so it is important to do so early on.

Continuing with our example, the agents' newly-generated component proposals are placed on GLBB. KSs link the proposed components to a steam condenser proposal. Their compatibility is checked by doing a syntactic analysis of the parameter names and values. When incompatibilities are found, the new proposals trigger *evaluation tasks* by any agents that share parameters with assigned values.

Evaluation tasks assign a local rating to a proposal. The agents use a shared rating scale: ratings have two components: *compatibility* and *constraint satisfaction*. The *compatibility* rating provides information about whether or not the proposal under evaluation is compatible with the current local solution. An incompatible proposal is one for which the agent has produced local solutions for the same problem definition, but the current local solution(s) conflict over one or more parameters. A compatible solution is one in which all shared parameter values are equal or within acceptable ranges of some local solution.

To determine a *constraint satisfaction* rating, an agent applies all relevant local constraints to the proposal under consideration. Constraints have attributes including flexibility, preferred and acceptable ranges of values, and importance (how important it is to satisfy a particular constraint). The degree to which constraints are satisfied provides the rating, which ranges from *infeasible* to *excellent*. An infeasible proposal is one for which there are no possible compatible local solutions given the set of parameter values. Note that the constraint satisfaction rating is not dependent on the compatibility rating of a proposal. Local ratings are attached to the proposal along with the evaluating agent's name.

Local ratings are combined into a global rating for the proposal by global KSs. Global ratings comprise two attributes: *acceptability* and *satisfaction*. *Acceptability* is a function of constraint satisfaction and compatibility values from all agents and system thresholds. For example, a possible function for acceptability is that all local ratings must be compatible, must have a constraint satisfaction rating of at least fair, and the average constraint satisfaction rating must be at least good. *Satisfaction* is a combination of the local constraint satisfaction values. Possible combination functions include average and minumum.We are currently using minimum but this is still under discussion.

The result of the initial agent processing of Problem_definition_1 is the following set of proposals and ratings:

Steam_condenser_1:
  pump_1

```
        local ratings:    (heat-exchanger incompatible infeasible)
                          (pump compatible excellent)
                          (motor incompatible good)
        global rating:    (unacceptable infeasible)
```
  heat_exchanger_1
```
        local ratings:    (pump incompatible good)
                          (heat-exchanger compatible fair)
        global rating:    (unacceptable good)
```
  motor_1
```
        local ratings:    (motor compatible good)
                          (pump incompatible good)
        global rating:    (unacceptable good)
```

A framework KS does a cursory analysis of the conflict at the global level. This analysis includes the agents and parameters involved in the conflict and the depth of the solution path. This information is stored in a conflict representation object that is placed on GLBB:

Conflict_1
```
condenser:   steam_condenser_1
agents:   (pump-agent heat-exchanger-agent motor-agent)
conflicting-parameters:
  ((water-flow-rate (heat-exchanger 207.75gpm) (pump 168.28gpm))
   (head (heat-exchanger 101.6ft) (pump 71.97ft))
   (power (pump 5.17hp) (motor 8.94hp)))
depth-of-solution-path:   2
```

Each of the agents is notified of the conflict situation and uses the conflict analysis, other globally available information such as the proposal units, and local information about its own problem-solving resources and constraints to decide what action to take.

5 Conflict Resolution

We have specified a set of strategies which can be used to resolve conflicts. The choice of strategy, given a particular conflict situation, is itself a knowledge-based problem. Information which can be applied to this choice includes available problem-solving resources, the amount of effort that has already been expended in producing a solution, the solution's rating, an estimate of the amount of processing required to generate a new solution or to repair the current one, the dependency structure of related proposals, the importance of a particular component to the global solution, the number and type of conflicting parameters, the severity of the conflict, and the flexibility of agents involved in the conflict. Some strategies are more computationally expensive than others, some are inexpensive but less likely to produce promising proposals. Some can be used to "fix" existing solutions that seem promising, others can be used to jump into a significantly different part of the search space.

5.1 Identifying an Appropriate Strategy for a Conflict

We identify some problem characteristics which are useful in determining a conflict resolution strategy. A description of the strategies is deferred to the following section.

- Other equally good proposals exist or can be generated inexpensively. Not much effort has been expended in developing the current proposal. Try *Generate Random Alternatives*. This approach doesn't require any analysis of the problem. For example, scheduling a meeting: "Can't make it Monday morning? How about Tuesday afternoon."

- The proposal under consideration is close to being acceptable to all the agents involved. There are a small number of dimensions in conflict and the dimension type is numeric or there is a known ordering on potential values. None of the agents are tightly constrained on the variables in question. The problematic constraints are not highly dependent. Try *Compromise*.

- Same conditions as for *Compromise*, except that one or more of the agents is too inflexible, has a strong belief in the problematic values, or has some constraints which must be addressed. Try *Generate Constrained Alternatives*, exchanging constraints in order to bring the viewpoints closer together.

- There are a large number of conflicting parameters or there are no existing proposals which are close to being acceptable to all agents (the conflict is severe) or the constraints in conflict have many dependencies. Try *Generate Goal Alternatives*.

- There are multiple conflicting parameters and the dependencies among them are not well-understood. Improving one parameter value may cause the proposal as a whole to have a lower rating. Try *Case-Based Parameter Set Retrieval* to find a set of changes that can be applied to improve the complete proposal.

- None of the other methods have resulted in acceptable solutions or it is believed that the problem is overconstrained. Try *Revise and Merge Goals*. This is the most computationally expensive strategy.

5.2 Conflict Resolution Strategies

In this section, we describe some of the strategies that can be used to resolve conflicts that occur.

- *Generate Random Alternatives*: In some types of problem-solving, multiple solutions exist and can be generated with little extra computational overhead. For example, in a typical blackboard system, multiple solutions exist at any given time. A highly rated one is chosen as "the answer" but there may be others that are rated equally or just slightly lower.

- *Compromise*: Find an intermediate proposal that is within the acceptable range of all agents using variable value relaxations. This strategy is the typical compromise that is used in buy/sell or other numeric transactions. Numerical optimizations or techniques based on the type of dimension can result in quick and fair results.

- *Generate Constrained Alternatives*: Generate new alternatives based on constraints that are received from an inflexible agent or based on some other agent's partial solution.

- *Generate Goal Alternatives*: The original proposals are abandoned. Alternate proposals are generated by looking for alternate goal expansions. If necessary, some goals can be relaxed or relinquished. This can lead to substantially different proposals being generated at the level in which the conflict occurred. This strategy is useful for changing the focus of the system from a plateau to a new area of the search space.

- *Case-Based Parameter Set Retrieval:* Find a previous solution that succeeded in resolving a conflict involving a similar set of parameters. Make the set of changes rather than isolated modifications. This approach minimizes oscillation that occurs in the overall proposal rating when dependencies among parameter values are not well-understood.

- *Revise and Merge Goals:* Prioritize goals and relinquish unimportant subgoals. Build a new mutually-defined goal structure that incorporates the most important goals of all agents involved in the conflict. Generate a solution guided by the new structure. This approach is computationally expensive and will only be used in situations where no other technique seems promising, the system cannot produce a feasible design, or where an innovative proposal is explicitly requested by the user. It is hoped that the mutual goal structure will cause a jump into a new area of the search space which would not be explored during the normal course of problem-solving.

Conflict resolution protocols are realized as formal dialogues with specific actions that can be taken at each processing step [18, 12]. All agents know the protocols and can formulate the messages required for their role in a particular conflict situation. For example, an agent that is beginning a new *Respond to Conflict Task* first analyzes the conflict from its own point of view and suggests a particular resolution method and possibly a set of resolution values. It sends this message to all other agents involved in the conflict. It then waits for confirmation from those agents. The other agents must respond to the message, either that they accept the resolution method, they accept the suggested resolution, or that they are proposing a different solution or method. The method is sometimes changed because another agent has a local view which makes the suggested method inappropriate. For example, the originating agent may suggest using *compromise* but the receiving agent is too inflexible. The receiving agent might then suggest *generate constrained alternatives* and send its inflexible constraints to the originating agent. Sometimes the method is acceptable, but a different solution is suggested. The originating agent cannot consider the conflict resolved until all participating agents have confirmed that a suggested solution is acceptable to them.

6 System coordination

In order for CEF agents to work together in an effective way, they must coordinate their internal activities with the global problem solving situation. In much of the work that has been done on negotiation, conflict resolution occurs as a group problem-solving process or as the primary goal of the system. All agents suspend any other activities to focus exclusively on negotiating a settlement. In some circumstances, the importance of quickly finding an acceptable solution outweighs the expense of halting other operations so it is not unreasonable to do so. However, in the general case there is no reason for all activity to come to a halt because of a conflict. We describe general coordination principles which treat conflict resolution tasks as schedulable activities within a larger problem-solving context. These tasks are performed asynchronously by the systems involved in a resolution.

When a potentially conflicting proposal is detected on GLBB, the detecting system checks to see if it has already generated an interacting proposal. If so, it links the two proposals and notifies the proposal originator of its intent to evaluate the new proposal. It then schedules an evaluation of the proposal and makes sure that this is given a higher priority than any of its pending tasks which depend on its own proposal. These dependent tasks may include conflict resolutions with other systems concerning its proposal. There is no point in resolving a conflict with one system when you know that there is another system interested in the same area. It makes more sense to gather information from all the known interested parties before attempting a resolution.

If a proposal is generated in an area of interest to a system which has not yet generated an interacting proposal, that system searches its pending tasks for related generation tasks. It checks to see if it has already started working on a proposal or is planning to start. If so, it links the evaluation and generation tasks. It schedules the evaluation of the triggering proposal before its own generation task. If the triggering proposal is acceptable (or close to acceptable), it may not be necessary to generate a separate proposal or a proposal can be generated which is tailored to integrate smoothly with existing parameters.

If there are no current plans to work on a related proposal, the evaluation task is scheduled and the system which originated the triggering proposal is notified of that. Although the evaluating system may not wish to generate its own proposal in a particular area, it may have requirements that must be met in order for other proposals to be acceptable. For example, a pump designer may not wish to generate a platform proposal but might have weight constraints that are relevant to any platform proposed by another agent.

When a system communicates a partial solution, it doesn't have to wait for evaluations to come in from all interested parties since this may take a significant amount of time. In fact, it can't be guaranteed that any particular evaluation will ever arrive since the evaluation task that produces it is just one of a set of scheduled tasks and may never get to the top of the execution queue. Once a proposal has been posted however, systems that are interested in evaluating it will send a notification as soon as possible. Monitoring of interest areas is done at every cycle and notification tasks are given highest priority. However, there may be more than one notification task pending (depending on the number of proposals submitted), so it may take several cycles for all notifications to be sent and received. For the purposes of our implementation, we wait a set number of cycles for notifications and then proceed. If one should arrive very late, scheduling decisions involving that proposal may be reevaluated and if work has already been done, the work itself may have to be reevaluated.

7 Status of the CEPS Project

We have developed a prototype version of CEF that provides language definition capabilities, communication structures and protocols, conflict detection, and support for the definition and execution of agents within the structure. We are currently implementing the conflict resolution strategies and protocols.

STEAMER is partially implemented in the CEF framework. We anticipate six agents: pump, heat exchanger, motor, platform, shaft and v-belt, and condenser. Each of these will be implemented as an independent blackboard system. Three of the agents are substantially implemented (pump, heat exchanger, and motor) and we are experimenting with conflict resolution concurrently with the implementation of the other agents. We are investigating various scheduling strategies, conflict resolution strategies, and choice heuristics.

References

[1] S. Cammarata, D. McArthur and R. Steeb. Strategies of Cooperation in Distributed Problem Solving. In *Proceedings of the Eight International Joint Conference on Artificial Intelligence*, pages 767–770, Karlsruhe, West Germany, August 1983.

[2] Susan E. Conry, Robert A. Meyer, and Victor R. Lesser. Multistage negotiation in distributed planning. Technical Report 86-67, Department of Computer and Information Science, University of Massachusetts, Amherst, Massachusetts 01003, December 1986.

[3] Daniel D. Corkill, Kevin Q. Gallagher, and Kelly E. Murray. GBB: A generic blackboard development system. In *Proceedings of the National Conference on Artificial Intelligence*, pages 1008–1014, Philadelphia, Pennsylvania, August 1986.

[4] Randall Davis and Reid G. Smith. Negotiation as a metaphor for distributed problem solving. *Artificial Intelligence Journal*, 20:63–109, 1983.

[5] Edward de Bono. *Lateral Thinking for Management, A handbook of creativity*. American Management Association, 1971.

[6] Edmund H. Durfee and Victor R. Lesser. Negotiation through partial global planning. In Michael N. Huhns, editor, *Distributed Artificial Intelligence, Volume 2*, Research Notes in Artificial Intelligence. Pitman, 1989.

[7] Lee D. Erman, Frederick Hayes-Roth, Victor R. Lesser, and D. Raj Reddy. The Hearsay-II speech-understanding system: Integrating knowledge to resolve uncertainty. *Computing Surveys*, 12(2):213–253, June 1980.

[8] M.S. Fox, B. Allen, and G. Strohm. Job-shop scheduling: an investigation in constraint-directed reasoning. In *Proceedings of the National Conference on Artificial Intelligence*, pages 155–158, Pittsburgh, Pennsylvania, August 1982.

[9] Carl Hewitt. Offices are open systems. *ACM Transactions on Office Information Systems*, 4(3):271–287, July 1986.

[10] C.T. Kitzmiller and V. Jagannathan. Design in a distributed blackboard framework. In *Workshop on Intelligent CAI*, Cambridge, Massachusetts 02139, October 1987.

[11] M. Klein and S.C.-Y. Lu. Conflict Resolution in Cooperative Design. in *International Journal for Artificial Intelligence in Engineering*, in press.

[12] Thomas Kreifelts and Frank V. Martial. A Negotiation Framework for Autonomous Agents. *Proceedings of the Second European Workshop on Modeling Autonomous Agents and Multi Agent Worlds*, Paris, August 1990.

[13] Kenneth L. Meunier. *Iterative Respecification: A Computational Model for Automating Parametric Mechanical System Design*. Master's Thesis, Mechanical Engineering, University of Massachusetts, February 1988.

[14] J. Mostow. Toward better models of the design process. *AI Magazine*, 6(1):44–57, 1985.

[15] M.F. Orelup, J.R. Dixon, P.R. Cohen, and M.K. Simmons. Dominic II: Meta-level control in iterative redesign. In *Proceedings of the Seventh National Conference on Artificial Intelligence*, pages 25–30, St. Paul, Minnesota, August 1988.

[16] Dean G. Pruitt. *Negotiation Behavior*. Academic Press, 1981.

[17] Arvind Sathi, Thomas E. Morton, and Steven F. Roth. Callisto: an intelligent project management system. *AI Magazine*, 7(5):34–52, Winter 1986.

[18] John R. Searle. *Speech Acts: An Essay in the Philosophy of Language*. Cambridge University Press, 1970.

[19] Katia Sycara. Resolving goal conflicts via negotiation. In *Proceedings of the National Conference on Artificial Intelligence*, pages 245–250, Minneapolis, Minnesota, August 1988.

[20] Katia P. Sycara. Negotiation in Design. In *Proceedings of the MIT-JSME Workshop on Cooperative Product Development*, MIT, Cambridge, MA, November 1989.

Cooperative Negotiation in Concurrent Engineering Design

Katia P. Sycara
The Robotics Institute
Carnegie Mellon University
Pittsburgh, PA 15213

Abstract. *Design can be modeled as a cooperative multi-agent problem solving task where different agents possess different knowledge and evaluation criteria. These differences may result in inconsistent design decisions and conflicts that have to be resolved during design. The process by which resolution of inconsistencies is achieved in order to arrive at a coherent set of design decisions is negotiation. In this paper, we discuss some of the characteristics of design which make it a very challenging domain for investigating negotiation techniques. We propose a negotiation model that incorporates accessing information in existing designs, communication of design rationale and criticisms of design decisions, as well as design modifications based on constraint relaxation and comparison of utilities. The model captures the dynamic interactions of the cooperating agents during negotiations. We also present representational structures of the expertise of the various agents and a communication protocol that supports multi-agent negotiation.*

1. Introduction

Issues of industrial productivity are of major economic significance. To attain substantial improvements in industrial productivity the following capabilities are crucial:

- rapid reaction to changes in functional requirements of products and to new technological opportunities

- rapid transition from design concept to product

- production of high quality products at the lowest possible life-cycle (design, manufacturing, testing, operation, maintenance) cost

In order to attain these capabilities, improvements in effectiveness and speed of design are needed. Recent developments in computer science, especially in AI, large scale modeling and simulation, and information systems provide us with unique opportunities to push beyond the present level of computer-aided automation technology and to attain fundamental improvements in industrial productivity. The vision of the next generation of industrial automation technology includes:

- Computer systems for *conceptual design* and for high level design processes, where a product is designed for functionality, manufacturability, maintainability and economy.

- An infrastructure including *design knowledge bases* for products and processes that would be widely accessible to researchers and practitioners.

Besides being of major economic significance, design is a challenging task that (1) presents many opportunities for significant scientific breakthroughs in many areas of experimental computer science (e.g., AI, Numerical Methods, Human-Machine Interface), (2) can stimulate links among these computer science areas, and (3) can stimulate links among computer science and other disciplines (e.g., mechanical, electrical, chemical engineering).

The computer field is now at a point where it can provide the intellectual foundations and the technical basis for developing a science and technology of design and manufacturing that will have a dramatic impact on industrial productivity. Furthermore, by building on top of the present state of computing, and by further accelerating research and development in areas of advanced computing which can contribute to improvements in design and manufacturing (AI in particular), we can bring about major gains in industrial productivity. Our challenge is to:

- Develop computer systems that will efficiently generate solutions (autonomously or as design assistants) to a broad range of design problems.

- Represent relevant domain and control knowledge that can be readily incorporated in these systems.

- Formulate specific design problems in a manner that can lead to their efficient solution by these systems.

1.1. Design

Design is the act of devising an artifact which satisfies a useful need, in other words, performs some function. Since our world is full of artifacts, design activity is pervasive. Underlying design tasks is a core set of principles, rules, laws and techniques which the designer uses for problem solving. His expertise lies in his ability to use these techniques to produce a feasible design. The designer's expertise is a consequence of his experience and training, much of which is based on previous exposure to similar design problems. This is particularly true in our domain of interest: engineering design [15, 3, 4].

Typically, the input to the design process is a set of specifications in terms of goals and constraints of the desired artifact. The designer's task is to transform these specifications into a structural description of the artifact in a given language of design descriptions.

There are three types of knowledge that are used in design:

1. Knowledge about the domain (e.g., theories, and models)

2. Design descriptions in terms of a language of designs

3. Design specifications

Acquiring and representing this knowledge so that it can effectively guide design generation is a central concern of design research. Typically, a designer reasons in two spaces: the space of design specifications and the space of design structures. To facilitate the automated generation of designs, we must strive to represent design structures, so that parts of the artifact correspond as directly as possible to parts of specifications.

Typically, design problems have multiple interacting goals, and/or complex systems of constraints. To handle the complexity of goal interaction, a design system should be able to decompose design problems into loosely coupled subproblems in order to handle subproblem interactions and combine partial solutions. Good design decompositions are critical since "bad" choices have strong negative impact on design efficiency. Choosing good decompositions is complicated by the fact that there is no decomposition that is good under all circumstances: The goodness of a decomposition depends on the design goals.

Design systems should not only have the ability to evaluate candidate designs for a particular set of specifications, but also be able to reason from the design specifications to candidate solution structures. This reasoning evolves gradually as successive goals and constraints are identified during the design process. Consideration of a goal or constraint at some point in the design process may result in changes of previous design decisions and/or in recommendations for modification of previously considered goals and constraints. This process is especially complex since the goals and constraints could be at different levels of abstraction, pertain to different design specialties, and express different design tradeoffs (e.g., aerodynamic efficiency versus structural strength for a turbine blade).

Design systems should have the ability to: (a) represent designs in ways that facilitate solution construction, (b) represent design records so as to facilitate explanation and design reuse, (c) represent designs from multiple viewpoints (e.g., aerodynamic and structural perspective for aircraft wing design), and (d) organize large reusable design knowledge bases.

The concept of design record is of central importance in research on design and it is an area where AI can be most useful[1]. A design record includes descriptions of the problem specifications in terms of design goals and constraints, the solution to the design problem,

---

[1]A design record is very similar to a *design case* in research work that uses case-based reasoning for design.

and the trace of decisions that shows why the solution satisfies the problem specifications. The record should be structured in such a way that it can be effectively used for tasks such as explanation, redesign, and design by analogy.

Because of the complexity of the design activity, in most cases it is impossible for a single designer to carry out the whole design effort alone. As has been ascertained from field studies of design in large organizations (e.g., [1]), design is a problem solving process among cooperating specialists/perspectives[2]. In AI terms, this process can be viewed as multi-agent problem solving where each agent is a design expert who has (a) incomplete knowledge of the environment, (b) limited knowledge of the constraints and intentions of other agents, and (c) limited number and amount of resources that are required to produce a system solution. The goals and constraints of the agents are the result of their particular expertise. Thus, each agent has a limited and egocentric view of the problem. A design is a solution to reasoning about multiple conjunctive and possibly conflicting goals.

The process through which a final design is produced is cooperative. Because each expert has insufficient local knowledge to solve the problem by himself/herself, experts have to cooperate. Conflicts arise, however, because of the variety of concerns, knowledge and evaluation criteria that each specialist brings to the design process. It is not easy to resolve these conflicts due to the fact that the experts (1) do not have the same mental model of the design, and (2) they do not "speak the same language". This engenders misunderstandings and long iterations of explanation and attempts to "translate" concerns and knowledge into another's language.

Existing approaches to concurrent design have primarily been concerned with investigating architectures for communication between various perspectives [2], [9, 32] or on conflict detection [17, 19]. In this paper, we focus on modeling the process of reconciling design decisions and design proposals that arise from the different perspectives during the design process in order to form an acceptable compromise, i.e. the final design. We argue that understanding of the negotiation process in design will enable (1) the development of intelligent and efficient design support systems to aid human designers in their tasks, and (2) progress towards the development of systems that can reason from design specifications towards candidate solution structures.

The design problem has the following characteristics:
- The global system goal is to produce a design that is synthesized from

---

[2]In this paper, we use the words "specialist", "perspective", "expert", "party" and agent synonymously.

contributions of different expertise, concerns and constraints[3].

- During the design process, conflicts in the form of constraint violations could arise. If these conflicts are not resolved in a satisfactory manner, infeasible designs will occur.

- Another kind of conflict is over approaches/styles used to achieve a design goal.

- Disparate evaluations of (partial or complete) designs could surface as a result of different criteria used to evaluate designs from different perspectives. Typically, these criteria cannot be simultaneously and optimally satisfied. The design decisions that optimize one set of criteria could conflict with those that optimize another set. If these conflicts do not get resolved in a satisfactory fashion, design suboptimalities occur.

- The system goal is achieved by making the best[4] tradeoffs on conflicting design goals and constraints.

- Because of the presence of conflicting constraints, goals and possibly evaluation criteria, it is impossible for each agent/expert/perspective to optimize the overall design using only local information.

- Backtracking can be a major problem since it may result in invalidating design decisions that other agents have made. Hence the need for computationally efficient multi-agent models.

As a result of the above characteristics, the final successful design can be viewed as a *compromise*[5] that incorporates tradeoffs such as cost, ease of manufacturing and assembly, reliability and maintainability. We suspect that such compromises are commonly done implicitly by human design experts tacitly using rules of thumb (e.g.,

---

[3]It has recently been advocated that not only design and manufacturing but also marketing, subcontractors, suppliers and customers should be involved in the design process. This is what happens in Japan, where design and prototype building and testing takes more time on average than in the U.S. but debugging the design takes much less, significantly decreasing cycle time from concept to market. This design philosophy and methodology inevitably introduces into the concurrent design process even more participants each with their own goals and evaluation criteria. As a result, the design team is not only faced with possible constraint violations that must be resolved by parameter relaxation and backtracking but also with more complex conflicts involving goals and evaluation criteria.

[4]We avoid using the word "optimal" since it is not always possible to prove optimality in design. On the other hand, the system goal is not satisfied by the first design that minimally satisfies goals and constraints, but improvements in the design are sought.

[5]Pruit [16] has identified two types of negotiation which are used by expert human negotiators to seek acceptable solutions and which may be applicable to machine agents: (a) compromise negotiation where each party makes concessions on its demands to facilitate agreement, and (b) integrative negotiation where the most important goals of each party are used to form innovative solutions, relinquishing, if necessary, secondary goals. In our view, both these negotiation types result in *compromise* solutions, in other words in partial goal satisfaction. Moreover, in typical negotiations a goal of secondary importance to one agent could be of primary importance to another because of different local evaluation functions. My use of the word "compromise" encompasses both these negotiation types. For more detail on different types of negotiation solutions and strategies, and mechanisms to automatically generate them, see [22].

imprecise versions of other agents'/perspectives' evaluation functions). Typically, these implicit compromises go unrecorded making it very difficult to trace and avoid suboptimalities in the design. The proposed model allows for explicit recording of design proposals, modifications of design decisions, and associated justifications or objections.

Depending on particular decisions concerning tradeoffs, different designs will be produced. For example, the valve for a water tap could be a metallic threaded part or a plastic plug valve with a hole. There is a tradeoff between the low cost of the plastic valve and the high durability of the metal valve. Such tradeoffs can be accomplished in a rational fashion with the use of negotiation techniques. During the negotiation process, the feasibility and desirability of proposed tradeoffs is evaluated and may result in incremental design adaptations. Despite the difficulty of applying negotiation techniques, recorded goal conflicts and their resolution, namely existing designs, provide a foundation for rationalizing designs.

Negotiating an agreement involves finding a compromise solution for multiple conflicting goals. This is a complicated problem, not amenable to traditional AI planning techniques [23]. The negotiation process is dynamic and formulating it as a search problem is inadequate since there is no well-defined goal or search operators. The negotiation process itself is a search of a dynamic problem space where an agent's beliefs about another agent's beliefs over the cycle of proposals continuously changes the space being searched. What was *not* a solution at one point becomes a solution at a later point as new constraints enter the process.

A negotiation model must somehow reason about alternatives that include "suitable" values for each issue on which an agent will agree. For continuum-valued issues the available choices are infinite. Hierarchical decomposition of the problem into smaller subproblems each of which is easier to solve may not be suitable, since a compromise solution may be a "package" whose parts are strongly interconnected and interacting. These difficulties are compounded by the absence of a coherent set of constraints that alone could guide search through the space of all possible settlements.

To address these shortcomings of traditional AI and expert systems, we have integrated reasoning from previous designs, case based reasoning (CBR), symbolic and numeric constraint propagation, and the use of multi attribute utilities. In contrast to other work [35] where different perspectives propose values for a design attribute and an arbiter evaluates and selects among the proposed values (i.e., there is no interaction among the perspectives), our model captures the full complexity and dynamics of negotiation by representing and modeling the communication and interactions that occur during negotiation in design. A communication protocol that supports negotiation is presented in section 8. The negotiation model that we present can be used for negotiation at each design stage, negotiation between design teams, and negotiation involving both humans and machines.

In the framework of the Design by Hindsight project at Carnegie Mellon, we are investigating the integration of Case-Based Reasoning, Qualitative Reasoning and Constraint Propagation in the domain of mechanical design [26]. Negotiation as a method for resolving constraint violations and achieving design optimization is a part of the project. A parallel effort is the development of a Manufacturing System Architecture [27]that will allow machine and human agents in the manufacturing domain (e.g., designer, process planner, scheduler, facility layout) to communicate and negotiate in order to integrate decision making within the manufacturing enterprise.

Although the proposed model allows for automating negotiation, the interface enables human designers to participate in the process. Users can register their reaction (acceptance or rejection) to proposals, express their objections to particular pieces of a proposed design, give the reason for a particular objection, and input their utilities with respect to various issues.

The rest of the paper is organized as follows: Section 2 presents rationale for the usefulness of accessing past designs and design decisions as part of the design process. Section 3 presents requirements of a model for negotiation. Section 4 presents a simple example of negotiation in concurrent design. Section 5 presents our negotiation process model and the reasoning methods used in the model. Section 6 presents the conceptual vehicle for representing agents' goals and expertise. Section 7 presents the agents' interactions during negotiation. Section 8 presents a detailed protocol for negotiation and section 9 presents concluding remarks.

2. Use of Design Cases

From the standpoint of AI, designs can be viewed as solutions to problems with multiple conjunctive and possibly conflicting goals. In this regard, mechanical design is not different from most other design disciplines. However, in many design disciplines, such as software design and circuit design, designs can be characterized as collections of weakly interacting functional modules, each of which implements one of the functional requirements. On the other hand, good mechanical designs are often highly integrated, tightly-coupled collections of interacting components [20, 34]. A simple and obvious correspondence between specific functional requirements of the artifact and individual components in the design does not usually exist. This has the consequence that there is no obvious decomposition of the overall function into subfunctions. For example, in a can opener the circular blades perform the function of holding the can, rotating it and cutting off the top. Ironically, these are also the major functions of the entire can opener. It is not possible to identify specific features of the can opener or its blades which perform each of the functions independently.

Because of the highly coupled nature of mechanical designs, design cases that capture good working solutions to component interactions provide a good basis for performing design. Cases are very important in engineering design. In fact almost all design efforts [10] do make use of previous design experience to provide comparisons, warn of pitfalls, and sometimes furnish components or structures for the new design. But the use of this experience is limited to the individual designer's ability to retrieve and determine the relevance of past design experiences (mostly his own) to the new design problem. Cases are the primary way in which engineering students are taught to design. This is because there are no general algorithms for design. Typically, students are exposed to numerous cases and examples which illustrate how complex problems are solved. Even when an entry-level engineer joins a design office, an important part of his training involves going through the design records of previous projects. Although the engineering design community recognizes the importance of cases in problem solving, the use of precedent cases in Computer-Aided Engineering (CAE) tools has been completely ignored. This is not because the CAE research community is not aware of the ubiquity of case based reasoning in design, but because they have not had access to the right techniques.

A typical CAE tool for design includes a geometric modeling system and a standard set of analytic tools for tasks such as finite-element and boundary-element analysis. Over the last five years, design tools are being extended to include design heuristics. These heuristics come in several forms: as rules, as constraints and as recommendations. It is only very recently that a third aspect of the design process, the use of past cases, is beginning to be recognized in the Design Automation literature [11, 33], [5], [12, 14]. Almost all organizations have records- on paper or in CAD systems -of the detailed specifications and results of previous design efforts. These records have limited usefulness, however, due to the fact that they typically do not record the design decisions that led to the final design, alternatives that were perhaps considered and abandoned, or the rationale for those decisions. Design "cases" on the other hand, besides indexing designs in terms of relevant features, also incorporate memories of *design processes* including the relevant decisions and their justifications.

Using previous cases in coming up with solutions to a new problem is called case-based reasoning. The central idea of Case-Based Reasoning (CBR) is that reasoning is done by recalling previous appropriate cases rather than reasoning from "first principles". Complete solutions for conjunctive goals (i.e. previous designs and design rationale) that have been used with success in the past are stored in memory in the form of cases, so they can be accessed and used in the future. Failures and failure reasons are also stored so that they can be used to predict and avoid future failures. If features in the past situation that gave rise to a failed solution are also present in the current situation, then the failed solution should not be tried. Thus, previous failures help the problem solver avoid potential present failures. If repairs are also stored in memory[6], upon discovery of

---

[6]Repair of a failure is available either when a similar failure case is available, or via direct user feedback.

a failure, an appropriate repair can be found. In that case, the repair is stored along with the associated failure. The repair can be applied if the same failure happens or can be predicted [24].

In our model, cases are organized hierarchically in memory around important concepts in the problem domain. In order to perform CBR, cases need to be retrieved in terms of conceptual similarity. The basic idea behind conceptual similarity between two concepts is that they share *salient* attributes. Salient attributes are the ones that allow a reasoner to make inferences that will be useful for the problem solving task at hand. For example, a stool, a chair and an armchair, though different as to their structural features that are visibly prominent, are similar in that they can be used to deliver the function of "support for sitting". Although differences in attributes such as color, size and materials in the three objects may be more numerous than the similarities, they are not salient and so they are not considered in a case retrieval of designs of artifacts that can provide sitting support.

In contrast to expert systems that build solutions from scratch and discard them at the end of problem solving, in CBR the solution and solution context are integrated into the case memory so that they can be reused. Thus, learning is central to CBR. A case-based reasoner learns new design decisions during problem solving. It learns to predict failures so it can avoid them in the future. It learns repairs so that it can apply them if similar problems occur or can be predicted. As the case memory is enriched with new experiences, a case-based reasoner can refine its problem solving strategies and improve its performance. In practical terms, CBR alleviates the knowledge acquisition bottleneck that plagues expert systems since (a) experts are much better at remembering specific cases than rules, and (b) new cases are acquired as a by product of problem solving.

3. Requirements of a Model for Negotiation

Negotiation is a process in which the parties iteratively exchange proposals and proposal justifications until an agreement is reached. The final design is a "package" whose parts are strongly interconnected and interacting. The negotiation process exhibits several characteristics that give rise to various requirements for computer-assisted negotiation.

- Negotiation involving multiple agents with multiple conflicting goals/issues/assertions is usually a lengthy and iterative process. The parties start by having conflicting goals/issues/assertions and whose distance has to be narrowed gradually to zero. Therefore, a negotiation model must be *iterative* rather than *one shot*.

- After each round of proposals the agents give feedback to each other about which parts of a proposal (partial or final design) they agree or disagree on. Hence, a negotiation model needs to be able to receive and evaluate *feedback* about a proposition.

- In order to arrive at agreement, design proposals must be modified. Hence a negotiation model must have the ability to *propose suitable modifications*.

- Since final agreement is reached through narrowing the difference in the proposals of the parties, a negotiation model must have a way of *predicting/evaluating* whether each new proposal indeed narrows these differences.

- Reaching an agreement through negotiation entails that each of the parties must modify partially or totally some of their goals and proposals. A good grounding for such modifications is justifications and arguments in support of or against proposed modifications. Hence, a negotiation model needs to have a component that generates *justifications and arguments*.

In design, negotiation occurs recursively at all levels and stages of design from conceptual design through embodiment to detailing. This model of design by negotiation implies an organizational structure that emphasizes product rather than function. The design is done by a number of design teams each of which contains various specialists and is responsible for producing a part of the desired artifact. For example, a detailed study of aircraft design [1] has found that aircraft design proceeds by the cooperation of specialists, each of which have their own model of the design. Design decisions are negotiated by the specialists among themselves. In aircraft design there are many specialists each with their own technology and language. For example, there are aerodynamicists who use surface models and equations, there are maintainability engineers, concerned with access, disassembly and replacement, there are hydraulic engineers, stress engineers, and thermodynamic experts. They do not understand each other's specializations, but they have to collaborate to produce a single design acceptable to each one of them. Each team operates within constraint ranges set by other teams. Failure to reach agreement on the design of a part that is the responsibility of one team is a problem not only for the particular team but for the manufacturing organization as a whole. Such failure must be communicated to other teams and resolved by negotiation.

Negotiation enters the design process at the following points:

- When different relevant specialists have made conflicting recommendations regarding values of attributes of a design.

- When an attribute value proposed by one specialist makes it infeasible for another specialist to offer a consistent set of values for other attributes.

- When a design decision made by one expert adversely affects the decision optimality of other experts.

- When alternate approaches can achieve similar functional results.

There are two models of design by cooperating experts/perspectives: (1) one perspective generates the design and the others critique it, and (b) individual perspectives generate different partial designs which are exchanged among the participants, evaluated and "merged". Regardless of the adopted scenario, the final design is the result of a negotiation process.

4. A Negotiation Example

Consider, for example, the process of designing a turbine blade. Some of the dominant perspectives are aerodynamics, structural engineering, manufacturing and marketing. The blade design team operates within constraint ranges specified by the aircraft engine team. The blade design team incorporates various concerns. The concern of aerodynamics is aerodynamic efficiency; for structural engineering it is reliability and safety; for manufacturing, it is ease and cost of manufacturing and testing; for marketing it is overall cost and customer satisfaction. The two variables of concern in a turbine blade that we consider in this simple example are: (a) root radius, and (b) blade length. From the perspective of structural design, the bigger the root radius, the better since it decreases stress concentration. From the perspective of aerodynamics, the smaller the root radius, the better, since it increases aerodynamic efficiency. Concerning the length of the blade, from the point of view of structural design, the shorter the blade, the lower the tensile stresses; from the point of view of aerodynamics the longer the blade, the better the aerodynamics. On the other hand, if the blade is shorter, it makes for a lighter engine which is a desirable characteristic for aerodynamic efficiency. Thus, we see that the aerodynamics expert needs to make tradeoffs internal to its perspective. From the point of view of marketing, aerodynamic efficiency lowers the cost of operation of the aircraft, thus making it more attractive to customers. From the point of view of manufacturing, it is easier to manufacture shorter blades with bigger root radii.

The following is a simplified example dialogue of the various concerned perspectives in an attempt to arrive at a mutually satisfactory turbine blade design:

Aerodynamics (possibly reasoning from existing designs) suggests particular values x and y for length and root radius of the blade. The suggested x and y values are within acceptable constraint ranges.

Structural engineering evaluates these values from its point of view and suggests values x' and y' where x'<x and y'>y (i.e., shortening the length and increasing the root radius) to increase safety.

Aerodynamics says that the values structural engineering suggested would considerably decrease aerodynamic efficiency.

Structural engineering counters that shorter blade makes engine lighter, thus also increasing efficiency.

Marketing says aerodynamic efficiency sells the product since it is less costly to operate.

Manufacturing supports structural by saying it is easier to manufacture short blades with big root radius.

Aerodynamics suggests that the materials engineering expert could try to investigate new materials that make the blade lighter, thus alleviating weight considerations.

Manufacturing says that new materials take lots of time to test and debug.

Structural engineering adds that new materials may introduce safety hazards that could go undetected.

This example illustrates the exchange of proposals for values of length and radius of the blade as well as the exchange of arguments and justifications in critiquing the proposed values. The nature of the resulting design will depend on (a) the ranges of various artifact constraints, (b) which constraints can be relaxed and in what ways, (c) the relative importance of various artifact-dependent goals (e.g., aerodynamic efficiency), (d) relative importance of various artifact-independent goals (e.g., safety), and (e) the way in which particular variable values contribute to the achievement of the goals.

5. The Negotiation Process

The negotiation process consists of three main tasks: generation of a proposal, generation of a counterproposal based on feedback from dissenting parties, and communication of justifications and supporting evidence. An initial compromise is generated and presented to each expert/perspective. Each agent evaluates the proposal from their point of view and register their reactions (evaluations, objections and suggestions). The process terminates when all concerned agents accept a proposed design.

Each agent during negotiation engages in the following activities:

- **recommending design decisions**, i.e. designs that express potentially acceptable compromises and tradeoffs of the parties. In our work, we are investigating the generation of design recommendations using a combination of case-based reasoning, use of utilities and constraint propagation techniques.

- **justifying recommendations**. Often the agents, guided by their own values and criteria, cannot recognize why a proposed design may be the best under the circumstances. In order for a design proposal to become intelligible and have an increased chance of being accepted, justifications must also be communicated. These justifications help an agent assess the desirability of a design decision from his point of view. These justifications can be derived from running numerical models or accessing previous appropriate designs.

- **exploring feasible alternatives** so as to optimize the proposed compromise. A memory for past designs provides a rich repository of such alternatives.

- **modifying a rejected compromise** to make it more acceptable to the rejecting party without making it unacceptable to the party that had previously accepted it. This is done using previous cases and modification rules. A modified candidate design is evaluated using an appropriate criterion of improvement.

The input to the negotiation process is the set of conflicting goals and violated constraints of the various design agents and the context of the design (e.g., constraints that have been handed to the design team form others). The final output is either a single consistent set of design decisions that have been agreed upon by the agents, or an indication of failure if the negotiating parties did not reach agreement within a particular number of proposals. The final output is reached through iterations of the following tasks: (a) proposal of an initial set of design decisions, (b) justification and critiquing of the proposal and (c) repair and improvement of a rejected proposal. These tasks are performed using knowledge of existing designs and their characteristics, knowledge of physical laws and constraints, traces of design decisions made so far and goal graphs (see section 6) of the participating agents. The agents could have access to a common case base of previous designs but because of their specialized knowledge each one accesses and evaluates a design from a particular *view*. Use of previous design cases offer a reasoner (a) suggestions of how tradeoffs and resolutions have been made in the past, (b) failure avoidance advice (since failures are recorded in the design case), (c) possible modifications and repairs to design suboptimalities.

Figure 5-1 presents an agent's actions in the negotiation process. In the figure, the square rectangles represent the negotiation planning processes: plan generation, plan evaluation, plan presentation to the parties, communications of justifications and arguments, plan modification, and memory update (either with successful or failed cases). The "Generate Plan" rectangle is shaded to indicate that it is the starting point of the process. Each negotiation task, i.e. generation of an initial proposal, argumentation, and proposal modification recursively uses a subset of the problem solving processes, namely plan generation, plan evaluation, plan presentation to the parties, and (if needed) plan modification. The word "plan" is used to denote a set of design decisions (i.e. a partial or final design) and it applies to a different entity for each task. For proposal generation, "plan" refers to a design proposal, for argumentation, "plan" refers to a set of justifications, for proposal modification, "plan" refers to a set of design decision modifications. The rectangles with the rounded corners in figure 5-1 denote the methods, CBR or use of multi-attribute utilities (Preference Analysis), used in each process. The ellipses denote conceptual inputs to a process and the diamonds represent decision points.

Negotiation is performed through integration of case-based reasoning [8, 22]and use of multi-attribute utilities and constraint relaxation. These methods are employed in all negotiation tasks, namely in generation of an initial proposal, repair of a rejected proposal to formulate a counterproposal, and communication of justifications and objections. The

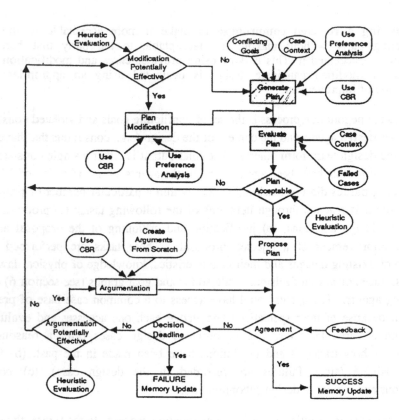

Figure 5-1: The Negotiation Process

integration of heuristic and analytic methods makes a system both robust and flexible. The problem solver does not break down when heuristic methods fail. In addition, the problem solver has the flexibility to use whichever method type is more natural to the particular problem-solving stage in which it is engaged.

5.1. Case Based Negotiation

Negotiation is a multi-agent, iterative process. Because design decisions are typically tightly coupled, modification of one design decision may necessitate undoing of previous decisions. This can have major ripple effects and render the process very inefficient. Thus, efficiency has increased importance in multi-agent systems. Reasoning from previous design cases can result in major efficiency gains in negotiating design decisions. The use of previous cases is beneficial for negotiation because:

- Negotiation is a complex process involving many steps. A case-based reasoner can learn complex sequences of negotiation steps that it can re-use rather than reason from scratch for a set of conflicting and inconsistent goals and decisions which it had resolved in the past.

- Negotiation is a process involving multiple conflicting goals. Traditional AI planners (e.g. [18, 21]) reason about each individual goal and then deal with any incompatibilities as they arise. This method, besides being inefficient, compels planners to recreate and then debug the same mistakes rather than avoid them altogether using previous experiences.

- Negotiation is an ill-defined domain with uncertain and incomplete knowledge. There are no well-specified goals and operators. Hence traditional AI planning methods cannot be used effectively.

- There is no strong domain model for negotiation. Therefore, reusing sets of decisions that have worked in the past is efficient.

- Many problems during negotiation occur with some regularity (e.g. a particular tradeoff among the same variables) Hence, resolutions of these problems can be remembered and re-used.

- Previous negotiation experiences may point out important issues that may have been overlooked in the current negotiation.

- Case-based inference minimizes the need for information exchange during negotiation, thus minimizing communication overhead.

- Anticipating and avoiding problems through reasoning from past failures helps the agents minimize the exchange of proposals that will be rejected.

- If the repair of a past failure is also stored in memory, computation by each agent is minimized.

- Cases provide successful (and failed) goal and constraint relaxations.

The case based reasoning process consists of the following steps: (1) retrieve appropriate cases (or case pieces) from memory, (2) select the most appropriate case(s) from those retrieved, (3) compare similarities and differences of the current and the retrieved cases, (4) construct a baseline solution, (5) evaluate the baseline solution for applicability to the current problem, (6) based on the evaluation, apply modifications to the baseline solution to fit the current situation, and (7) verify (if possible) the correctness of the solution. If verification fails, then debugging must be applied. The debugging process itself could also use case based reasoning to find and apply appropriate repairs. Although the case based reasoning steps have been presented as sequential, they could be interleaved. For more details on case based negotiation, see [29].

5.2. Utility Based Negotiation

Another negotiation method that is integrated with case-based reasoning is the use of utilities [7, 25] and constraint relaxations. Preference Analysis is based on Multi-Attribute Utility Theory [7]and is used in our model as the underlying formalism for portraying the parties' preferences. Utility theory models the process through which a decision maker evaluates a set of alternatives, so that he can choose the best one. It has also been used in aiding a decision maker to structure his problem in such a way that evaluation of the alternatives is easily accomplished [36, 6]. We concentrate on the ways that utility theory can be exploited in a multi-agent setting to: (1) generate potentially acceptable solutions to be proposed to the parties, (2) measure the quality of a modification to a rejected settlement, and (3) determine the effectiveness of justifications and arguments.

Each agent has a utility associated with each issue in the negotiation, i.e. a particular design decision. A design is a vector whose elements are the design attributes of concern. Each particular design alternative is a vector with specific values for each of the design attributes. Since each attribute value has an associated utility for each agent, the combination of these utilities results in an overall utility for the agent associated with a particular design proposal. An agent chooses the design alternative that maximizes the overall utility from its point of view. The utilities portray the possible tradeoffs that can be made among conflicting sets of values to arrive at an acceptable compromise. Knowledge of an agent's utilities is helpful to himself as well as other agents in making proposals for alternative design decisions. Utilities incorporate tradeoffs that could be derived from mathematical models, performance information captured by statistics and subjective judgements of the specialists. Because of the subjective elements in the utility calculations, different agents may have different utilities for the same design decision. Hence proposed design alternatives may not be immediately agreed upon by all agents.

Since many of the values that enter the calculation of a design alternative are continuous-valued, there are in general an infinite number of alternative designs. However, range subdivision of the values of the relevant attributes, application of constraints and sensitivity analysis can be used to arrive at finite sets of alternatives that designers can select from. Given a set of alternatives, various criteria can be used to determine the overall best alternative. The selection criterion most often cited in the literature (e.g., [7, 13]) is Pareto optimality. Another criterion that we have found useful for negotiation is to select the alternative that *combines Pareto optimality with equity*. In other words, the criterion maximizes the joint payoff of the agents and minimizes the payoff difference [25].

Use of utilities is particularly suited to problems involving multiple goals not all of which can be simultaneously and entirely satisfied. If an agent has some knowledge of another agent's utilities, he can model the tradeoffs that the other agent is willing to make among the many issues and goals in the negotiation and could predict which compromise the second agent will be most willing to accept. In case of proposal rejection, the payoff of possible counterproposals can be calculated. Based on such calculations, an agent can predict which counterproposal represents a relative improvement (i.e. giving an overall higher payoff) over the rejected one. Without an ability to predict which counterproposal constitutes an improvement, the negotiating agents could blindly exchange offers that could never converge to an acceptable compromise.

The criterion used in our work is that a counterproposal is an improvement if it increases the rejecting party's payoff by a greater amount than it (possibly) decreases the payoff of the parties that had previously agreed to the compromise. Upon proposal rejection, possible counterproposals are generated by modification of the rejected alternative. The criterion is used by each agent to evaluate possible counterproposals that the agent is contemplating. If a contemplated counterproposal conforms to the criterion, it is proposed. If it does not, subsequent modifications could be performed through (a) case-based reasoning, (b) constraint relaxation methods, and (c) traversal of goal graphs (see section 6).

6. Representation of Agent Goals and Expertise

The exchange of proposals and justifications lies at the heart of negotiation. It is the process used to cohere the decisions of the parties and guide the process toward solution convergence. We claim that in order to negotiate effectively, agents need the ability to (a) represent and maintain models of the knowledge and goals/beliefs of other agents, (b) reason about other agents' goals/beliefs, and (c) influence other agents' beliefs and intentions through the exchange of missing information, justifications and arguments. The information communicated is intended to "convince" the recipient agent to shift his negotiating position so as to narrow the parties' differences to achieve final agreement. In a nutshell, the process of communication of justifications and arguments can be described as follows: an agent reasons about another agent using its own (largely inexact) model of that other agent, finds as many ways as the model will allow to affect the other agent's outcomes, and uses them selectively to influence the other agent. In this section we present the representational mechanisms that are used (1) to structure the knowledge that each agent has of its own goals, constraints and utilities, and (2) to model the goals and utilities of other agents. The models of the other agents that each agent maintains and refines are used to generate inferences about potential acceptability of proposals and/or arguments that are presented to other agents. The negotiation protocol that uses the representations discussed in this section is presented in section 8.

The knowledge needed to perform generation of arguments and justifications in the design domain is (a) previous designs, and (b) an agent's *belief* and *preference* structure. The belief structure of an agent consists of a collection of goals/beliefs, goal importance, amount and feasibility as well as relationships among goals. We use the word "goal" and "belief" to indicate what is commonly thought as beliefs (e.g., that safety is a good attribute of an aircraft), abstract goals, such as increasing marketability, reducing operational costs, and also design attributes, such as length, particular material types, connections types etc. In other words, an agent's expertise is encoded as part of his belief and preference structure (to the extend that such expertise can be represented). We represent an agent's belief structure as a directed acyclic graph where each node represents an agent's goal. Edges of the graph linking two goals represent the relationship between goals in terms of how one affects (positively or negatively) the achievement of the other. For example, aerodynamic efficiency positively affects lower operation costs. Associated with each node is:

- a *sign* (+ or -) that denotes the desirability of an increase or decrease in that goal
- the *amount* by which the attribute/goal should be increased or decreased
- the *importance* that the agent attaches to the goal
- the *feasibility* as perceived by the agent of achieving the goal

The values in the goal graph are set based on the constraints on the design and company policy. For example, after an accident whose cause was traced to a defective engine, the importance of the safety goal increases for the marketing agent. Directed edges connect subgoals to the higher level goals to which they contribute. A *contribution* value is associated with each directed edge denoting the contribution of the subgoal to the higher level goal. Contribution values range from -100% to +100%. A positive value means that the subgoal supports the achievement of the higher level goal by the denoted percentage. A negative contribution value has the interpretation that the subgoal is detrimental to the higher level goal. Sink nodes[7] are the highest level goals of an agent.

Figures 6-1 and 6-2 present a partial view of the belief structure of the structural and aerodynamic perspectives. For visual simplicity we have indicated in the figure only the edges connecting particular nodes, and the appropriate sign. By traversing a goal graph one can answer the following queries:

- Which goals are supported by a set of design decisions?
- Which design decisions are justified by a set of goals?

A path from node X to node Y in a goal graph constitutes a causal/justification chain that provides an explanation of the change in Y in terms of the change in X, assuming no other change has occurred in the rest of the graph. For example, from the point of view of structural engineering, decreasing the length of the blade, Blade-Length(-), decreases tensile stresses, Tensile-Stress(-), which results in structural soundness, Structural-Soundness(+). In turn, an increase in structural soundness increases reliability, resulting in increased safety and contributing to increased marketability of the blade.

In addition to an agent's beliefs, the representation includes an estimate of its utilities for

---

[7]Sink nodes have no out-going edges

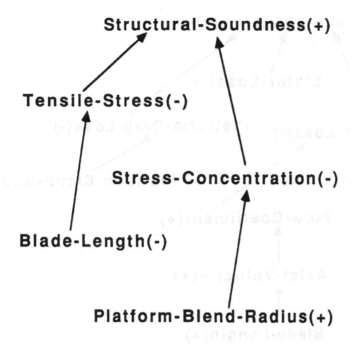

Figure 6-1: Partial belief structure of structural engineering

each attribute in the goal graph. Utilities express the *preference structure* of an agent. Moreover, utilities express the tradeoff structure among various attribute values associated with an alternative design. The (possibly nonlinear) utilities of individual attributes are combined to give an overall utility of an alternative. Being able to compare different alternatives enables a reasoner to choose the alternative that affords the maximum payoff. An integration algorithm [28] traverses the belief structure to determine which way goal values should be moved to increase payoff and thus the acceptability of a resolution. Moreover, goal graph traversal allows an agent to discover alternative design decisions that support important goals thus leading to innovative designs.

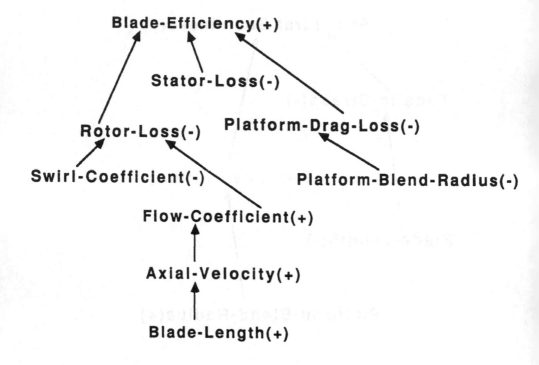

Figure 6-2: Partial belief structure of aerodynamics

7. Agent Interactions

A central task in negotiation is communication. Communication is needed in order to enable the agents to exchange information, the lack of which may have resulted in conflicts. We are currently developing an intelligent information infrastructure that manages the information needs of the interacting agents [30]. Local computation of the agents resulting in suggestions or evaluation of various design proposals is interleaved with communication to other agents of the results of local computations. Conversely, an agent uses communicated feedback of other agents as input in its local computations.

An interesting issue is the vocabulary used by the agents for communication. As has been stated in the introduction, design specialists do not share vocabulary or exact understanding of each other's models and problem solving processes. This complicates intelligible communication among them. We are currently investigating the issue of shared understanding and communication among specialists. Our hypothesis is that specialists utilize terms in an *intermediate* shared vocabulary so that they can be intelligible to others. So, although each specialist's expertise is private to him, the intermediate vocabulary is the medium for making public relevant portions or results of the expertise for intelligible communication. In the example of designing a turbine blade, although the marketing expert might not understand the concepts of Axial-Velocity or Swirl-Coefficient, (see, figure 7-1), he understands the concepts of Blade-Efficiency and Structural-Soundness and how they relate to his own high level goal of marketability. Blade-Efficiency and Structural-Soundness are examples of terms in the intermediate vocabulary used for intelligible communication among the design specialists. In Figure 7-1, the shaded portions indicate the private expertise of the aerodynamics and structural specialists, whereas the unshaded portion indicates terms to indicate goals and issues in the shared, public vocabulary.

Although we recognize that dissemination of missing information to agents who need it is a concern that must be addressed in any system that engages in automating the process of or providing decision support for negotiation in concurrent engineering, we refer the interested reader to [30] where this issue is dealt with. In the rest of this section, we describe the more sophisticated interactions that are needed to support persuasive argumentation.

The messages that the negotiating agents exchange contain the following information:
- The proposed design
- Justifications of design decisions
- Agreement or disagreement with a proposal
- Requests for additional information, such as with which issue in the proposed design the agent disagrees.
- Information that the recipient agent might have been missing
- Reasons for disagreement.
- Utilities/preferences of the agents associated with disagreed upon issues.

Since different agents evaluate designs using different evaluation criteria, the information communicated by an agent to others cannot be simply its decisions. It needs to communicate justifications of its own design decisions and proposed design changes. If challenged, an agent must communicate justifications in support of its decisions. This capability can be used to provide agent-tailored explanations and suggest alternative design decisions from the viewpoint of each agent.

Proposals and supporting justifications are used by an agent, the *persuader* as a means to dynamically change the utilities associated with various decisions and outcomes of another agent, the *persuadee*, so as to increase the willingness of the persuadee to accept

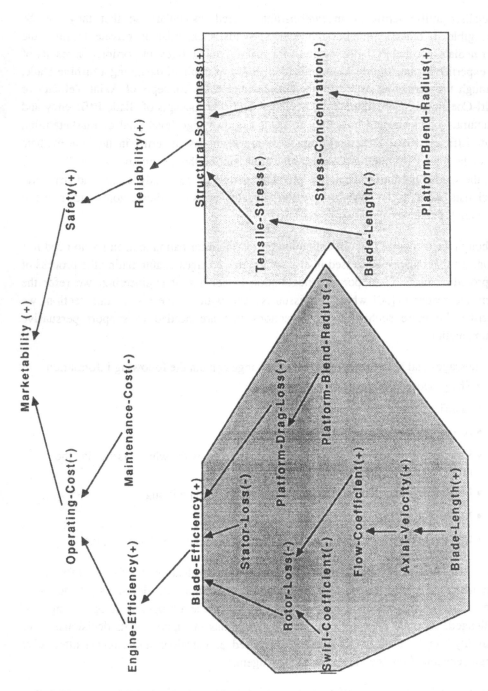

Figure 7-1: Partial view of private expertise and shared communication vocabulary

a proposal[8]. This, in turn, improves the efficiency of convergence to a global solution. By observing reactions to the proposed rationale and justifications, the persuader can update and correct its model of the persuadee, thus refining its planning and argumentation knowledge. In our work, generating proposals, counterproposals and justifications is based on integration of *goal graph search*, use of *multi-attribute utilities*, and availability of a *case memory* of experiences with similar negotiations [22].

Belief and belief modification in the model is based on the conjunctive goals of the agents and their interactions. A belief involves the correspondence between a state (a possible design) and the other agents' design decisions. Group knowledge focuses on the facts of the case: proposals, counterproposals, negotiation context etc. If agreement on a design were obtainable by inference from these facts, negotiation would be unnecessary. Such is not the case, however, since besides quantitative information available to the specialists, qualitative information involving assumptions and approximations as well as different evaluations of the assumptions and the resulting designs can be present. The negotiation process itself is a search of a dynamic problem space where an agent's beliefs about other agents' beliefs and hence feasible solutions continuously changes the space being searched. What was not an acceptable solution at one point becomes a solution at a later point as more information is generated and becomes intelligible through agent interactions possibly making some agents re-evaluate their positions.

During negotiation an agent's belief structure is updated based on his reactions to presented new information and proposals. In this way, an agent's model is refined and corrected dynamically. This functionality is important since (a) it is not possible for an agent to have a correct and detailed belief model of another, and (b) beliefs are not static but change with external circumstances and an agent's experiences.

If a reasoner decides to change another agent's beliefs, he needs guidance as to (a) what kinds of changes he wants to effect, and (b) how to do it. In addition, he needs to be able to make predictions regarding how a change in knowledge and beliefs will affect acceptability of a proposed design change.

We claim that a party's satisfaction with a proposition expresses his willingness to accept the proposition. Hence, if an agent could manipulate another agent's utilities (resulting in manipulation of that agent's payoff), he would be able to affect predictably the outcomes of the second agent. Convincing an agent to change his evaluation and increase his willingness to accept a design decision is modeled as producing a justification to increase

---

[8]In describing the behavior of multi-agent systems it is often awkward to describe agent interactions in terms of "the first agent", the "second agent" etc. We employ the terms persuader and persuadee to distinguish between the agent that is presenting a proposal, justification or argument and the one to whom the proposition is being made. Of course, during the course of the interaction, two agents alternatively may play the role of persuader and persuadee.

the payoff of the proposition. The elements of a design decision are a subset of the information that appears in the agent's belief structure. Hence, the task of a persuader can be viewed as finding the most effective justification/argument that will increase a persuadee's payoff. Since a persuadee's payoff can be approximated by a linear combination of his utilities, the payoff can be increased by either changing the importance (coefficient) the persuadee attaches to an issue, or changing the utility value of an issue.

The *argumentation goals* of a persuader express *what* in the beliefs and outcomes of a persuadee he wants to influence. To accomplish the argumentation goals, *argumentation strategies* are used. Based on a utility view of argumentation, there are two argumentation goals that could be used in the model:

1. Change the importance of a persuadee's goal/issue

2. Change the persuadee's perception of an issue's value

Changing the importance that a party attaches to an issue reflects the intuitive notion that satisfaction with a thing is a function not only of the intrinsic value of the thing, but also of the importance that one attaches to it. Changing the importance of an issue translates into changing the corresponding issue's importance in the belief structure. The change in value of a point on an individual utility curve for an issue can be interpreted as a change of the party's assessment of the value of that issue. This corresponds to changing the "amount" parameter A in a persuadee's belief structure. In the utility theory model, changing a party's assessment of the value of an issue is equivalent to changing the party's satisfaction curve at that value. Consider the situation where a designer objects to an increase of 20 inches in length of a variable as "too high". In the utility theory formulation, this can be translated as "payoff(20) = LOW". (i.e., the payoff with respect to the altered design would be some low value). In the agent's belief structure, this assessment is represented as LENGTH(+, A<20inches)[9] (i.e. the designer wants to have a length increase of at most some amount less than 20inches). Convincing the designer that this increase is not so high changes the length attribute to LENGTH(+, A=20inches). Correspondingly, this attribute change results in raising the designer's (payoff(20)>LOW).

The argumentation strategies used to accomplish the argumentation goals determine how argument generation is done. Two argumentation strategies can be used to accomplish the first goal (change the importance of an issue):

(a) indicate a change (increase or decrease) in the contribution of the present goal to a higher level goal of the persuadee. For example, the justification of a proposed decrease

---

[9]We adopt the convention of only presenting the values of goal parameters (e.g., amount, sign, feasibility) that are relevant to the discussion at hand without worrying what value the rest of the parameters have.

in turbine blade length that structural engineering could present (see section 4) is that such a design decision increases structural soundness of the blade, which in turn increases safety. This argument will be effective if the safety goal is of great importance for the organization.

(b) indicate a change in the feasibility of the proposed goal. For example, the arguments made by manufacturing (see section 4) that the development of new materials take a very long time to test and debug is meant to decrease the importance of new materials as an option for the blade design.

If a persuadee disagrees with a proposed argument, the reasons for the disagreement are analyzed for new information that could alter subsequent argumentation, such as new information about the persuadee's concerns. If the analysis reveals that the persuader had some incorrect notions regarding the beliefs and preferences of the persuadee, the appropriate *updates* are made to the persuadee's model. In addition, updates to the persuader's argumentation goals and strategies may be needed.

When the argumentation goal of the persuader is to change the persuadee's perception of an issue's value, two argumentation strategies can be used. One is to find a counterexample from past similar designs. The second is to find evidence from successful design practices of the manufacturing organization itself or competitors regarding the value of the attribute. For both strategies, the argument generation algorithm involves search of the design case memory. For example, if marketing rejects a particular design feature as costing "too high", the model could search for evidence showing that the company's competitors have successfully marketed designs with the same or more costly features. The justification for this type of argument is "appeal to prevailing practice".

The heuristic that is used to generate a persuasive argument if the persuader uses the first strategy is as follows:

Retrieve past designs with
respect to the present issue.
IF a past design is found where the persuadee's proposal
   had been implemented and was deemed a failure,
THEN point out this failure
ELSE use the second argumentation strategy

The heuristic that is used to generate a persuasive argument if the persuader uses the second strategy is as follows:

---

1. Retrieve past experiences of similar persuadees (e.g., competitors) with
respect to the same design issue.

2. Collect the ones whose value for the issue is appropriate.

3. Present them to the persuadee.

----

8. The Negotiation Protocol

We present in detail the communication protocol that supports negotiation that we are currently investigating in our work. For simplicity, the protocol is presented for two agents, agent1, who initiates an initial design and agent2, who evaluates the design and possibly generates a counterproposal. A more sophisticated negotiation protocol that also includes criteria for the order in which communication takes place when more than one agents are involved is presented in [31].

1. Agent1 communicates to agent2 a design proposal, as well as arguments and justifications in support of the proposal.

2. Agent2 uses the arguments and justifications communicated by agent1 to possibly modify its goal graph (e.g., change importance of goals, including possibly abandoning goals).

3. Agent2 evaluates the proposal from its point of view (using its constraints and utilities).

4. If the proposal satisfies agent2's local constraints and gives it payoff above a threshold, it communicates ACCEPT to agent1.

5. If not, agent2 generates a counterproposal by whatever problem solving means it has at its disposal (e.g., CBR, constraint relaxation).

6. Agent2 evaluates the counterproposal. If the counterproposal gives agent2 payoff above the threshold, agent2 communicates to agent1:
   - The PORTION/ISSUES of the proposal that have been modified
   - The REASON for modifying the previous proposal (e.g., value1 violates some of the agent2's hard constraints, a set of proposed values does not contribute enough to higher level goals of agent2).
   - The COUNTERPROPOSAL and its PAYOFF.
   - ARGUMENTS and JUSTIFICATIONS in favor of the counterproposal.

7. If the counterproposal does not give agent2 payoff above the threshold, agent2 goes to step 5.

8. If agent2 has exhausted all counterproposals it can generate through the methods of step 5, it traverses its goal graph to see whether there is another way to satisfy its higher level goals.

- If there is, it generates a counterproposal and goes to step 6.

- If there is not, it communicates FAILURE to agent1 (who now has to generate a modification and/or look for alternative ways in *its* goal graph).

9. Concluding Remarks

Design can be viewed as a multi-agent problem solving process involving multiple conjunctive and potentially conflicting goals. The agents have different expertise (e.g., mechanisms, hydraulics, assembly, testing) that propose and evaluate designs using different, possibly conflicting criteria. The process of negotiation is used to propose and examine design decisions involving various tradeoffs. Negotiation is performed recursively at all stages of design and involves different design teams. We have proposed a negotiation model based on (a) knowledge of previous designs, (b) communication of design rationale, justifications and objections to proposed design decisions, (c) constraint propagation and relaxation, and (d) traversal of goal graphs.

References

1. Bond, A., and Ricci, R. Cooperation in Aircraft Design. Proceedings of the MIT-JSME Workshop on Cooperative Product Development, Cambridge, Mass., 1989.

2. DICE: Initiative in Concurrent Engineering. Red Book of Functional Specifications for the DICE Architecture. Concurrent Engineering Research Center, West Virginia University, Morgantown, WV, February, 1989.

3. Gregory, S.A. The Boundaries and Internals of Expert Systems in Engineering Design. Proceedings of the Second IFIP Workshop on Intelligent CAD, 1988.

4. Hicks, T.G.. *Machine Design Calculations Reference Guide*. McGraw-Hill, 1987.

5. Huhns M.H., R.D. Acosta. Argo: An Analogical Reasoning System for Solving Design Problems. Tech. Rept. AI/CAD-092-87, Microelectronic and Computer Technology Corporation, March, 1987.

6. Keeney, R.L., and Nair, K. "Decision Analysis for the siting of nuclear power plants-The relevance of multiattribute utility theory". *Proceedings of the IEEE 63* (1975), 494-500.

7. Keeney, R.L. and Raiffa, H.. *Decisions with Multiple Objectives*. John Wiley and Sons, New York, 1976.

8. Kolodner, J.L., Simpson, R.L., and Sycara-Cyranski, K. A Process Model of Case-Based Reasoning in Problem Solving. Proceedings of the Ninth Joint International Conference on Artificial Intelligence (IJCAI-85), Los Angeles, CA, 1985, pp. 284-290.

9. Lander, S., and Lesser, V. A Framework for Cooperative Problem-Solving Among Knowledge-Based Systems. Proceedings of the MIT-JSME Workshop on Cooperative Product Development, Cambridge, Mass., 1989.

10. Mark, W. A Design Memory Without Cases. Working Notes of the AAAI Spring Symposium on Case-Based Reasoning, Stanford, CA., 1990.

11. Mostow, J. "Toward Better Models Of The Design Process". *The AI Magazine* (Spring 1985).

12. Mostow, J., M. Barley. Automated Reuse of Design Plans. Proceedings of the International Conference on Engineering Design , February, 1987.

13. Navinchandra, D. *Exploring for Innovative Designs by Relaxing Criteria and reasoning from Precedent-Based Knowledge*. Ph.D. Th., M.I.T., 1987.

14. Navinchandra D., D. Sriram, S.T. Kedar-Cabelli. On the Role of Analogy in Engineering Design: An Overview. In *AI in Engineering, Proceedings of the 2nd Intl. Conference, Boston*, D. Sriram, B. Adey, Ed., Computational Mechanics Publishing, U.K., 1987.

15. Pahl, G., W. Beitz. *Engineering Design*. The Design Council, Springer-Verlag, 1984.

16. Pruitt, D. G.. *Negotiation Behavior*. Academic Press, New York, N.Y., 1981.

17. Robinson, W. Towards the formalization of specification design, Master's Thesis. University of Oregon, 1987.

18. Sacerdoti, E. A structure for plans and behavior. Tech. Rept. 109, SRI Artificial Intelligence Center, 1975.

19. Sriram, D., Logcher, R., and Groleau, N. Cooperative Engineering Design. Proceedings of the AAAI-88 Workshop on AI in Design, AAAI, St. Paul, MN., 1988.

20. Suh, N.P., A.C. Bell, D.C. Gossard. "On an Axiomatic Approach to Manufacturing and Manufacturing Systems". *Journal of Engineering for Industry* (May 1978).

21. Sussman, G. *A computer model of skill acqusition*. American Elsevier, New York, 1975.

22. Sycara, K. *Resolving Adversarial Conflicts: An Approach Integrating Case-Based and Analytic Methods*. Ph.D. Th., School of Information and Computer Science Georgia Institute of Technology, Atlanta, GA, 1987.

23. Sycara, K. Resolving Goal Conflicts via Negotiation. Proceedings of the Seventh National Conference on Artificial Intelligence (AAAI-88), St. Paul, MN., 1988.

24. Sycara, K. Patching Up Old Plans. Proceedings of the Tenth Annual Conference of the Cognitive Science Society, Montreal, Canada, 1988.

25. Sycara, K. "Utility Theory in Conflict Resolution". *Annals of Operations Research 12* (1988), 65-84.

26. Sycara, K. and Navinchandra, D. Integrating Case-Based Reasoning and Qualitative Reasoning in Engineering Design. In *Artificial Intelligence in Engineering Design*, J. Gero, Ed., Computational Mechanics Publications, 1989.

27. Sycara, K., and Marshall C. Towards an Architecture to Support Integration of Decision-Making in Manufacturing. Proceedings of the IJCAI-89 Workshop on Integrated Architectures for Manufacturing, Detroit, MI., 1989.

28. Sycara, K. Argumentation: Planning Other Agents' Plans. Proceedings of the Eleventh International Joint Conference on Artificial Intelligence (IJCAI-89), Detroit, Mich, 1989.

29. Sycara, K. "Negotiation Planning: An AI Approach". *European Journal of Operational Research 46* (1990), 216-234.

30. Sycara, K., and Roboam, M. Intelligent Information Infrastructure for Group Decision and Negotiation Support of Concurrent Engineering. Proceedings of the 24th Hawaii International Conference on System Sciences, Kailua-Kona, Hawaii, 1991.

31. Sycara, K. "Modeling Group Decision Making and Negotiation in Concurrent Product Design". *Systems Automation: Research and Applications* (1991. Forthcoming.).

32. Talukdar, S., Elfes, A., and Papanikolopoulos, N. Concurrent design, simultaneous engineering and distributed problem solving. Proceedings of the AAAI-88 Workshop on AI in Design, AAAI, St. Paul, MN., 1988.

33. Ullman, D.G., T.A. Dietterich. "Mechanical Design Methodology: Implications on Future Developments of Computer-Aided Design and Knowledge-Based Systems". *Engineering with Computers 2* (1987), 21-29.

34. Ulrich, K.T., W.P. Seering. Function Sharing in Mechanical Design. Proceedings of the Seventh National Conference on Artificial Intelligence, 1988, pp. 347-352.

35. Werkman, K., and Barone, M. Evaluating Alternative Connection Designs Through Multiagent Negotiation. Proceedings of the MIT-JSME Workshop on Cooperative Product Development, Cambridge, Mass., 1989.

36. Whitmore, G.A. and Cavadias, G.S. "Experimental Determination of community preferences for water quality-cost alternatives". *Decision Sciences 5* (1974), 614-631.

Evaluating Alternate Connection Designs Through Multiagent Negotiation

Designer Fabricator Interpreter System

Keith J. Werkman
IBM Corporation/FSD
Owego Laboratory, MD 0210
Route 17C
Owego, NY 13827
U.S.A.
E-mail: keithw@owgvm0.iinus1.ibm.com

Marcello Barone
Bechtel Corporation
50 Beale Street
P.O. Box 193965
San Francisco, CA 94119-3965
U.S.A.
E-mail: marcb@zeus.ce.lehigh.edu

Stephanie J. Wagaman
E-mail: swagaman@lion.csee.lehigh.edu

John Isman Wilson
E-mail: jlw2@lehigh.bitnet

Donald J. Hillman
E-mail: djh3@lehigh.bitnet

Lehigh University
Department of Civil Engineering
Fritz Laboratory #13
Bethlehem, PA 18015
U.S.A.

Lehigh University
Department of Computer Science
and Electrical Engineering
Packard Laboratory #19
Bethlehem, PA 18015
U.S.A.

ABSTRACT

The Designer Fabricator Interpreter (DFI) is a knowledge-based system that addresses the lack of interaction among structural designers, fabricators and erectors in dealing with beam-to-column connections. Current research includes the development of a distributed problem-solving architecture in which the participants are modeled as semi-autonomous computer agents which reason from their own specific viewpoints while evaluating a connection. During the evaluation process, agents propose alternative connections for consideration which may require a negotiation process among the agents. If they cannot resolve the problem, an arbitrator agent is enlisted to help the conflicting agents reach an agreement. Potentially "better" alternate connection configurations along with reasons behind the choices are presented from the viewpoints of design, fabrication and erection.

1. Introduction

The Designer Fabricator Interpreter (DFI) project[1] is part of a comprehensive research effort intended to provide a distributed problem-solving environment which fosters communication between various participants (agents) involved in a construction project. The prototype DFI system is the result of a study of the current practices of the construction industry. Specifically, DFI is intended to address the lack of interaction among designers, fabricators and erectors with respect to beam-to-column connection design in steel framed buildings. The system gives structural designers, the intended users, the ability to check their preliminary connection designs against general fabrication and erection knowledge to determine how their initial design decisions may affect the overall fabrication and erection processes. As a result, the system presents the user with several potentially "better" alternative connection configurations along with explanations interpreted from the viewpoints of design, fabrication and erection.

This paper focuses on the distributed problem-solving aspects where agents evaluate the user's initial connection, propose alternative configurations based on issues relevant to their viewpoints, and negotiate the outcome of their proposals among the other agents in the system. The second section discusses, in part, the fragmented nature of the communications in the construction industry and how the DFI system attempts to address these problems. Included is a description of the connections database, the information flow in the system, the *DFI Relational Network*, the agent evaluation process, agent communications, agent negotiation and conflict resolution by a third-party arbitrator agent. An illustrative example is given in Section 3. The fourth section discusses the current research in DFI including the development of agent information models and enhanced forms of the *DFI Relational Network*, agent negotiation, and arbitration. A summary is given in Section 5 and a discussion of future work is given in Section 6.

1.1. Objectives

The overall objective of this research project is to provide a tool which can incorporate construction knowledge into the preliminary design stage. Connections were chosen as a focus because they are the "hot spots" for problems in structures. The Hyatt Regency skywalk collapse, a devastating failure in recent history, can be viewed as an extreme case for the need of systems like DFI to point out potential downstream (i.e., construction) problems with a design.

The research was performed in two distinct phases. The objective of the first phase

---

[1]The DFI project is one of several knowledge-based projects at the National Science Foundation sponsored Engineering Research Center, Advanced Technology for Large Structural Systems (ATLSS), at Lehigh University.

was the rapid development of a pre-prototype system to critique the geometric fit-up of beam-to-column connections [4]. This phase involved performing the following three tasks:

1. Developing a hierarchy of objects to describe a building decomposition focused on connections.

2. Identifying common mistakes or "goofs" in connection designs and representing them in a knowledge base.

3. Developing and implementing a pre-prototype system which critiques connection configurations and provides explanations and suggestions of common fabrication and erection errors.

The first phase of the research had dual purposes. Primarily, the DFI researchers were interested in showing a demonstration-of-concept or working system. In addition, the pre-prototype served as a testbed for knowledge and data acquisition.

The objective of the second phase was to build a prototype for preliminary connection design. The initial platform was rewritten to include a cooperative problem-solving scheme so agents were capable of suggesting alternative connection configurations while taking into account other viewpoints. The tasks involved in the second phase of development were:

1. Restructuring the first phase system's knowledge base into a set of constraint tables.

2. Developing a database of connection configurations using input from design, fabrication and erection experts.

3. Building models of the information each agent considers important in the satisfactory execution of their role in the design and construction process.

4. Defining a relational network for a cooperative problem-solving model.

5. Developing and implementing a system that provides a cooperative means of generating alternative Type 1 connection configurations from design, fabrication and erection viewpoints.

The second phase of development permitted the researchers to explore different areas of applied distributed artificial intelligence, specifically negotiation between agents, while expanding and refining the civil engineering domain knowledge and databases of the first phase system.

1.2. Present Practice

Construction projects frequently include several construction agents, at geographically distributed locations. A major problem is that vital engineering information is seldom communicated in a timely fashion among agents during the construction process [21]. This usually results in delays and cost overruns for the project. Typically, as problems arise at the construction site, contractors make notes on their drawings. As engineering changes are made by the designer's office and new drawings are sent to the field, the contractors rarely transfer their construction notes to these new drawings. At times, the contractor's field drawings are as many as three revisions behind the engineer's most current drawings. The communication problem is compounded as additional construction participants[2] become involved. Thus, the present practice of the industry suggests that there is a need for computer tools which act as catalysts to promote more coordination of activities.

Through the development of integrated design and construction systems, construction agents can interactively utilize data and knowledge from other agents' perspectives throughout the construction process as questions and problems arise. By integrating multiple agents' perspectives with a method of distributed problem-solving using a negotiation scheme to resolve agent conflicts, a cooperative environment of compromise can be provided. Such an environment would be quite useful for a design engineer during preliminary design when general constraints from downstream construction agents could be used to highlight potentially problematic designs. Thus, the designer could use this feedback to reconsider a design so that a new one could be proposed that might be easier and less costly to fabricate and erect.

1.3. The Design and Construction Process

When looking at the design and construction process in the U.S., one central theme runs through construction projects, "An Idea Plus Money." This can be illustrated by the following quote from [2]:

> "In construction, as in most other engineering fields, an entire series of events begins with an idea. Someone has an idea. A government wants a bridge, a sewage disposal unit, or a street lighting system; a corporation wants to improve its plant or an individual wants to place a new product on the market. However, an idea is only an illusion unless it is combined with another ingredient, money."

This section will briefly describe four stages in the design and construction process that take place as an "idea" progresses from concept to construction. The stages are conceptual design, preliminary design, detailed design, and construction. The gaps in the information flow between Architect-Designer, Designer-Fabricator, and Fabricator-Erector are also briefly discussed. Figure 1 shows the stages and agents involved at each stage along with the information gaps (shown as small black diamonds).

The stages related to Figure 1 are described below:
- **Conceptual Design:** This stage involves two principal agents: owner and architect. The agents determine the building topology (i.e. number of stories, typical floor plan) and site layout.

---

[2]These include, for example, the owner, architect, designer, fabricator, erector, and facilities manager.

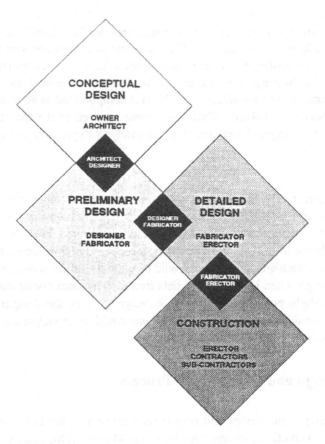

Figure 1:   Design and Construction Stages and Information Gaps

- **Preliminary Design:** This stage involves two principal agents: designer and fabricator. The building components are sized from the structural analysis and preliminary connection configurations are chosen.

- **Detailed Design:** This stage involves two principal agents: fabricator and erector. The connections are designed and detailed at this stage. Construction plans are developed for both the fabrication and erection sequences.

- **Construction:** This stage involves many different agents performing different tasks simultaneously. Example tasks include: steel erection, fire proofing, and pouring concrete.

The information gaps are described next:

- **Architect - Designer:** Misunderstanding between the architect and designer on their respective building concepts is the focus of this information gap.

- **Designer - Fabricator:** Communicating design information such that the built structure behaves similar to the analyzed structure. The designer and fabricator should strive for consistency between the preliminary component (beams and columns) design and the detailed connection design. It is desirable to evaluate the upstream design decisions to determine their effect on the downstream fabrication processes.

- **Fabricator - Erector:** Coordinating the activities required to assemble the structure are the focus of this information gap. Poor sequencing of activities could lead to excessive unproductive time on the construction site.

DFI attempts to bridge the information interface gap between design engineers and fabricators of structural steel systems. This interface was chosen because of its importance and lack of understanding and cooperation that exists between designers and fabricators on their respective tasks. A more detailed description of the stages and information gaps can be found in [3].

1.4. The DFI Approach

Computer-based methods for computer integrated construction (CIC) are intended to alleviate basic information flow problems and promote coordinated problem-solving among agents at all stages of the construction process [19, 33]. Unlike many civil engineering design knowledge-based systems which attempt to optimize structural design [14] based on one aspect, e.g., minimum steel weight, the Designer Fabricator Interpreter, similar to work done by others [24], is an attempt at developing a framework for distributed cooperative problem-solving between construction agents. The DFI system reflects the distributed nature of the construction industry by providing a multiagent architecture which models design, fabrication and erection processes. The architecture considers issues that are important to each participant in the connection design process and produces a cooperative solution, through means of negotiation. In addition, representing specialized construction process knowledge in the framework of agent models permits easier testing and maintenance as new knowledge is acquired. Finally, the modular nature of the architecture permits the addition of new agents with new construction expertise in a straightforward fashion.

The agents in the DFI system act in both a cooperative and competitive fashion. In terms of cooperative behavior, the agents work together toward a common goal by suggesting alternative connection configurations which are "similar" to that originally specified by the user. Agents also behave competitively during the proposal process by maximally improving their own positions during each proposal cycle. To provide some means of balance, an independent arbitrator agent is used to monitor the agent proposal process. The arbitrator mediates during the agents' proposal process by using an abstract level of shared knowledge about each agent's issues. The final set of alternative connections produced by the negotiated evaluation process is considered generally acceptable by all agents.

2. A Cooperative Problem-Solving System

The current version of the DFI system is a significant enhancement to an earlier version [4] which only critiqued the physical fit-up of the user's connection from fabrication and erection viewpoints. The system evaluates and suggests alternative connection designs based on multiple agent viewpoints. Each agent viewpoint is further decomposed into several unique agent issues. The issues are based on different aspects of connections such as economics, feasibility, and type of material, to name a few. The importance of an agent issue depends on which agent viewpoint one takes (designer, fabricator, or erector) within the context of a specific connection evaluation. During the proposal process, an agent will look at each connection previously proposed by other agents and evaluate any affected issues. The agent models are implemented in a frame-based knowledge representation environment developed at Lehigh University written in Quintus Prolog™. The environment also incorporates an integrated graphical user interface written in Quintus ProWindows™ running on Sun™ workstations[3].

2.1. DFI Connection Database

To make DFI more suitable for practicing professionals, a connections database was developed. In addition, the connections database acts as a constraint table on the user's input allowing the DFI to systematically guide the user to a "complete and correct" (to the degree of detail incorporated in DFI) connection configuration considered standard in light of common fabrication and erection procedures. The database is composed of a series of *Connection Information Forms* which contain all vital connection data the system needs. A typical *Connection Information Form* is seen in Figure 2 and is described in additional detail in Appendix A.2.

2.2. Information Flow

An information flow diagram of the current DFI system is shown in Figure 3. The solid boxes indicate sequential processes, the dashed box represents the iterative agent interaction process, and ovals represent input from and output to the user. The arbitrator agent resides at the logical center of the agent interaction process, monitoring all agent communication, allowing the arbitrator to assist in the problem-solving process when necessary.

Initially, the designer, as end-user of the system, reads in a description of a building and selects a floor. Then a particular column and beam are selected and a connection is

---

[3]Quintus Prolog and Quintus ProWindows are trademarks of Quintus Computer System, Inc. Sun is a trademark of Sun Microsystems, Inc.

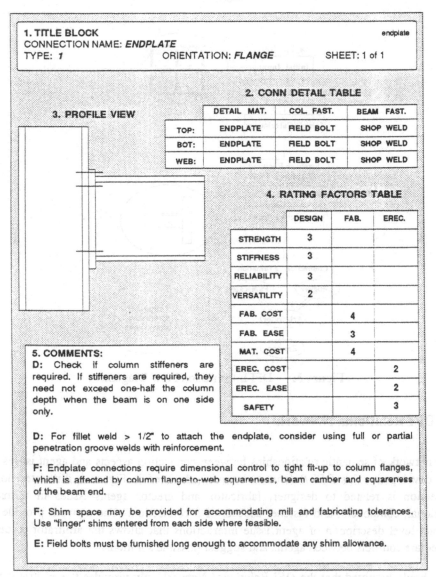

Figure 2: Example Connection Information Form

developed between the two members. Calculations are performed to determine the moment capacity of the beam and establish the required connection type. The system then provides the user with a list of connection component alternatives. At this point, the user can evaluate the connection design to see what effect it has on the fabrication and field erection processes. After the multiagent evaluation has been completed, the user is presented with the original connection configuration and three potentially different connection configurations proposed by the design, fabrication and erection agents. The user can then review the results of the multiagent connection evaluation and decide what to do.

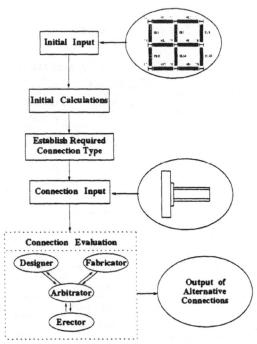

Figure 3: DFI Information Flow Diagram

2.3. DFI Relational Network

A network of semantic relationships between connection aspects and agent issues has been developed. This *DFI Relational Network*, depicted in Figure 4, illustrates how a connection is related to designer, fabricator and erector agents issues in terms of functional, component, and fastener aspects of a connection. The network provides an abstract level description of agent issue interactions that allows the arbitrator to detect immediate conflicts between agents and suggest possible solutions.

It should be noted that the *DFI Relational Network* only provides the arbitrator with an abstract level description of issues and how they relate to one another within the connection domain. This provides the arbitrator with enough information to detect interagent issue conflicts and assist in the negotiation when necessary. The arbitrator does not contain any knowledge about each agent's unique operations knowledge. In order for the arbitrator to augment a proposed solution with additional arguments, each agent has to be queried as to the reason and explanations behind the issue relationship under consideration [28]. The proposed network scheme allows for the addition of new agents to the distributed problem-solving model. Initially, each new agent must share its knowledge of relevant issues with the arbitrator so that they can be added to the network and used during negotiation.

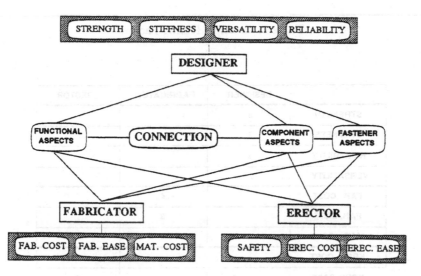

Figure 4: DFI Relational Network

2.4. The Evaluation Process

The DFI system requires the user to select a connection from the building description initially entered into the system. The user is then required to enter a "key issue," i.e., strength, fabrication cost, or safety, which forces the agents to focus their evaluation of a connection. Once this initial information is provided, the arbitrator takes control and selects the agent (design, fabrication or erection) worst affected by the user's initial connection. This is done by taking a composite or average score of each agent's issues. The agent with the lowest composite score (i.e., worst affected agent) gets to evaluate the initial connection first. Table 1 shows the Rating Factors Table from the example Connection Information Form (see Figure 2) with the composite scores computed for each agent. For this case, the Erector would evaluate the connection first with a composite score of 2.33 while the Designer and Fabricator have composite scores of 2.75 and 3.67 respectively[4].

The evaluating agent then selects the worst (lowest value) issue and attempts to improve it by suggesting alternative connection configurations[5]. Prior to selecting an

---

[4]During industry evaluation of the system, it was pointed out that the rating factor values are qualitative and performing quantitative operations may require "fine tuning" or re-evaluation based on extensive use by a wide variety of practitioners. However, agent proposals and problematic issues identified during the evaluation presented in the illustrative example in Section 3 have been identified as correct and realistic.

[5]For the example rating factors in Table 1, the evaluating agent would be the erector with the worst issue being erection cost.

Table 1: Example Rating Factors

	DESIGNER	FABRICATOR	ERECTOR
STRENGTH	3		
STIFFNESS	3		
RELIABILITY	3		
VERSATILITY	2		
FAB. COST		4	
FAB. EASE		3	
MAT. COST		4	
EREC. COST			2
EREC. EASE			2
SAFETY			3
COMPOSITE SCORE	2.75	3.67	2.33

alternative configuration, the evaluating agent must search its connection database and select all of the connections which have a greater value on the agent's worst issue and also maintain a minimum value of the key issue provided by the user. Once this set of connections is determined, the evaluating agent takes the composite score of all the connections in the set and selects the configuration with the highest value. This connection is then posted to a centralized communications area along with additional information on other possible alternatives. The additional alternative connection configuration information is used later by the arbitrator when an agent requires help in suggesting an adequate alternative.

2.5. Agent Communications

In the DFI system, agents communicate by means of a centralized communications area, called a *blackboard* [16]. The blackboard scheme in the DFI system allows agents to post messages (to who, from who, and message content) as well as read messages from other agents. The use of such a scheme allows the system to maintain a history of the agents' dialog as the proposal and negotiation process proceeds. This scheme combined with a common language of primitive interagent messages allows for an effective form of negotiation between agents which allows them to reason about the beliefs of other agents. Therefore, the interagent language must allow for the expression of agent intentions at some level of abstraction [29]. To accomplish this, a review of the work done in the area of speech act theory [1] has been performed. In particular, the communications primitives used in DFI are based on a series of speech related social actions that occur between agents [6]. The ones used in the DFI system are listed in Table 2.

Table 2: Speech Related Social Actions

Accept	Agent accepts Recipient's cause X.
Ask	Agent doesn't know Recipient's cause X.
Command	Agent wants Recipient to cause X.
Convince	Agent convinces Recipient to want X. (Makes Recipient believe he wants X)
Explain	Agent explains lack of outcome X to Recipient.
Inform	Agent informs Recipient of X (simple tell).
Refuse	Agent refuses Recipient's request.
Reply	Agent replies to Recipient's ask.
Request	Agent asks Recipient to want X.

Each social action that an agent might enter into contains a case structure (agent, recipient, additional action, objects, etc.), preconditions (necessary agent conditions), and postconditions (results of successfully performing the action). Thus, communications in terms of globally acceptable social actions provides for a plan-based approach for communication. This means that once an agent receives a specific message from a sending agent, the receiving agent will know what type and form of response message with which it is expected to reply. This makes for short explicit messages and reduces extraneous message overhead. In addition, an abstract level of an agent's intentions can be deduced by reviewing the history of that agent's proposals on the blackboard.

2.6. DFI Negotiation Scheme

A negotiation scheme has been devised for distributed problem-solving that takes place between the semi-autonomous agents in the DFI system. During the connection evaluation process, agents comment on connection characteristics based on their unique set of issues. As seen in Figure 5, each *reviewing agent* determines its best possible alternative connection configurations while maintaining or improving the value of the user's initial key issue. During the evaluation process, the *reviewing agent* evaluates the *proposing agent's* connection and determines which issue is most problematic. The *reviewing agent* then generates alternatives that enhance the worst issue and submits this list for review to the *key issue agent*. The *key issue agent* selects only the connections that meet or exceed the key issue and then returns this new list to the *reviewing agent*. In an attempt to provide a cooperative solution, the *reviewing agent* sends the list of alternatives which meets the key issue to the *proposing agent* for review. This gives the *proposing agent* a chance to order the list of alternatives based on the *proposing agent's* preferences. This *reviewing agent* then takes this ordered list and selects its best possible connection counterproposal in response to the *proposing agent's* initial proposal. The *reviewing agent* saves this specific counterproposal and performs a similar evaluation for all other agents in the system. Upon evaluating all other agent proposals, the *reviewing agent* then selects the best counterproposal from all agent specific counterproposals and proposes that connection as its response to all other agent connections currently posted on the blackboard.

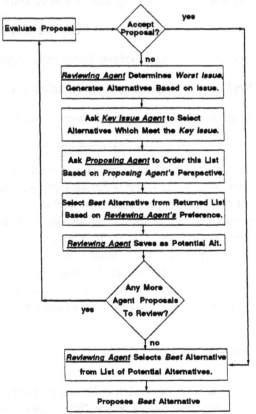

Figure 5:   The Evaluation and Proposal Process

2.7. Arbitration in DFI

At some point during the agent evaluation and negotiation process, a *proposing agent* might exceed the acceptable limits of the issues of the group. This may require an agent to concede an issue and propose an alternative in order for the negotiation to proceed. It is also possible that an agent may not be able to concede an issue because it would be too costly for that agent. In such cases, the arbitrator agent must be brought in to attempt to mediate a solution between two conflicting agents. Initially, the arbitrator monitors the current status of all agent proposals and reviews each proposal for any immediate problems that they might cause for an agent. If the arbitrator detects a problem that affects a particular agent, it warns the agent and gives control to that agent so that it has a chance to respond to the problem caused by the proposed connection.

In addition to detecting agent problems during proposals, the arbitrator also reviews the history of proposed connections to determine if a halting condition or a "deadlock" situation has occurred. The arbitrator *inform*s all agents of a *halt* of the evaluation process when two agents propose the same connection (one agent agrees with another). The resulting connections are presented to the user for review. If the arbitrator notices a "deadlock" situation (where the same proposals are being made by the same agents in response to a previous agent's proposal, also known as a flip-flop condition), the arbitrator intervenes by analyzing the situation and attempts to *convince* one agent that the other would agree if only the first agent would relax the importance of an issue or drop it altogether. The arbitrator generates the argument of which issues are relevant from abstract interagent issue relations it obtains from the *DFI relational network* as well as the history of past proposals and issues. In situations where agents still fail to agree after initial negotiation methods, the arbitrator determines the final solution given the input from both agents as to the importance of each agent's issue. This is a form of meta-level control [9] in that the final decision is based on an a priori policy of acceptance specific to the given domain of construction. If the agents' proposals do not converge after six iterations[6], the arbitrator stops the evaluation and returns control to the user. The main arbitrator control loop of the negotiation process within the DFI system is outlined in Figure 6.

The actual order of agent proposals is determined by the arbitrator, when appropriate, by utilizing shared knowledge of agents' issues and connection rating values. If the arbitrator "sees" no problem, the agents follow a predetermined default order. This scheme allows DFI to take an approach to negotiation that uses aspects of both centralized control as well as agent based control over negotiation. This differs from systems which contain fully autonomous agent control schemes where agents are totally on there own to determine what to do next [8, 10] and centrally controlled systems where one superagent maintains total control over all other agents [25].

---

[6]Given the evaluation process, this is considered to be an adequate number of iterations.

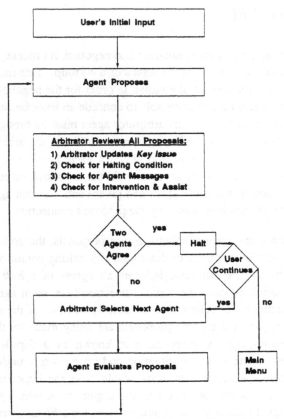

Figure 6: The Basic Arbitrator Control Loop

3. An Illustrative Example

This section contains an example of a connection evaluation with negotiated alternative proposals between the agents. Each agent has unique knowledge about connections including a standardized qualitative rating scheme for the issues related to each connection. The higher the value, the more acceptable it is. After the user enters a connection and selects the evaluate option, the user is asked for a single, most important *key issue* which is maintained by all agents during their proposal of alternate connection configurations. In this example, the user specifies an *endplate* connection with a *key issue* of *strength*. The agents will attempt to suggest alternative connections that are of the same connection type and with the same value for strength as the user's specified *endplate* connection. Initially, the arbitrator *commands* the design agent to *accept* the user's *endplate* connection proposal using *strength* as the positive supporting issue because the user is the designer in the first cycle of negotiation. The design agent then *informs* all agents of the key issue and *requests* that the proposed connection be evaluated. The designer's request is shown graphically in the *designer's window* in Figure 7.

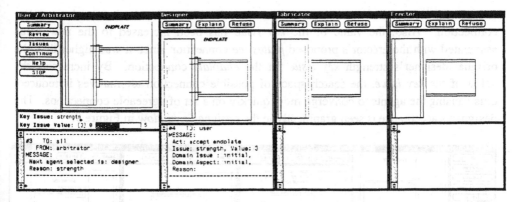

Figure 7: Designer's Initial Configuration

Before each agent's evaluation, the arbitrator reviews all proposed connections to determine which agent is most detrimentally affected and hence should go next. In this case, the erector is most severely affected by the designer's *endplate* proposal. The erector determines that the designer's proposal is unacceptable because the *endplate* connection is too difficult in terms of *erection ease*. Therefore, the erector *refuses* (objects to) the designer's connection and looks to the fabricator in hopes that it might have proposed an acceptable connection. At this stage, the fabricator has not yet proposed anything, so the erector selects a connection from the set of possible connections about which it knows. The erector *requests* the *plates-tee* because it satisfies the *erection ease* issue as well as satisfying the user specified *key issue*. This is depicted in the *erector's window* in Figure 8.

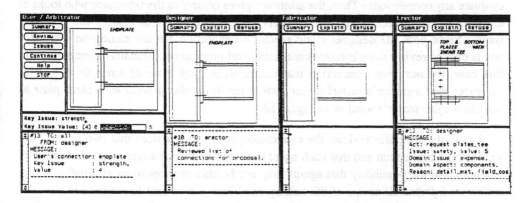

Figure 8: Erector Replies With Plates-Tee

It is important to note that the erector has directed the proposed connection back to the designer for review. The designer *accepts* the erector's proposed connection because it exceeds the *key issue* of strength as well as meets the designer's criterion for the *endplate* connection. Also, the value of the *key issue* has been increased to the new value associated with the erector's proposed *plates-tee* connection since it was higher than the original designer's strength *key issue* for the *endplate* connection. By increasing the value of the *key issue*, the search space of possible connection alternatives is reduced, thus causing the agents to converge more quickly on a set of agreeable connections. The designer's acceptance is seen graphically in the *designer's window* in Figure 9.

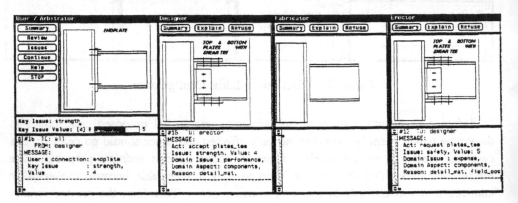

Figure 9:   Designer Agrees With Erector

Next, the arbitrator reviews the connection situation and notices that two agents have proposed the same connection. Usually, this would cause the arbitrator to *inform* all agents of a halting condition. This is not the case here because an "unfair" evaluation condition has occurred - unfair in the sense that the fabricator has not yet had a chance to evaluate any connections. Thus, the arbitrator gives control to the fabricator who looks at the designer's connection and immediately notices that *material cost* is the problem-issue. Since both the designer's and erector's connection are the same, the fabricator needs only to review the *plates-tee* connection and propose an alternative connection. In this case, the next best connection that maintains the *key issue* of strength as well as improves the fabricator's *material cost* issue is the *direct flange weld with shear plate* as seen in the *fabricator's window* in Figure 10.

Again, the arbitrator reviews the evaluation process and notices that two agents have agreed on a connection and that each agent has had a chance at suggesting an alternative. There is also the possibility that agents may not be able to propose an alternative[7]. The arbitrator *inform*s all agents of the halting condition and control is returned to the user. At this point the user can ask any agent to *explain* its proposed connection or *continue* with the evaluation. If the user *continues*, the arbitrator reviews the situation and notices that no particular agent is in "peril", and allows the agents to determine their own control

---

[7]In such cases, the agents enter into negotiation using various techniques such as logrolling [17]. In cases where the agents cannot resolve their differences, the arbitrator is consulted.

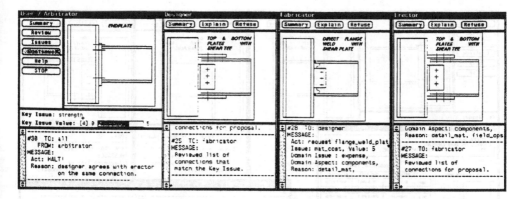

Figure 10: Fabricator Proposes Flange Weld

sequence. Whichever agent received the last message is given a chance to respond to that message. In this case, the fabricator proposed a connection to the designer. The design agent, upon reviewing this connection, notices that the fabricator's connection satisfies all issues of the designer. Thus, the design agent *accepts* the fabricator's proposal of a *direct flange weld with shear plate* as seen in the *designer's window* in Figure 11. This causes another halting condition upon where the arbitrator returns control to the user[8].

In Figure 11, the user has the option of selecting buttons from the *User/Arbitrator window*. This allows the user to obtain a *summary* of the initial connection, *review* the agent dialog of the entire negotiation process from start to finish listing each agent's proposal and related issues. Also, the user can change the overall key *issue* which focuses the negotiation, *continue* the agent evaluation, ask for *help*, or *stop* the agent evaluation and exit. Moreover, the user can select buttons from the *Agent windows* and obtain a *summary* description for each agent's proposed connection or ask the agent to *explain* its last proposal action. The explanation appears in the system's *Input/Output window* beneath the *Agent windows*, as seen in Figure 11, and includes the key issue, the connections under review, the agent's response to the reviewed connections, i.e., the acceptance or rejection of other agent's connection, the reasons for the action, and the agent's proposed connection with its justifications. Currently, the explanation of the agents' actions are in the form of keywords taken directly from the DFI relational network. Future explanations will relate to more robust user models of each agent involved in the negotiation process. At times, it is also useful for the user to be able to *refuse* (object to) and remove a connection from the evaluation process if the user knows that a particular connection is not acceptable.

---

[8]Control is returned to the user after each proposal cycle.

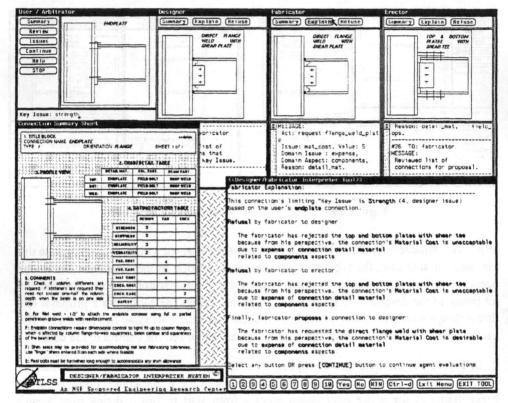

Figure 11: Designer Agrees With Fabricator After Continuing

4. Current Research

The following section describes work that has been implemented in DFI. During the development of the system, research has focused on obtaining and formalizing knowledge pertaining to beam-to-column connections. The domain research has included:

- the identification of design, fabrication and erection processes,
- the development of agent models,
- the identification of specific agent issues,
- the determination of relationships between an agent's issues, and
- the determination of both unique and shareable aspects of design, fabrication, and erection knowledge that are used during the proposal and negotiation process.

In addition, a review has been performed on negotiation strategies from the social psychology literature [17, 18, 26] as well as the distributed AI literature [5, 12, 11].

4.1. Agent Information Models

Table 3 lists the issues, subissues and characteristics used by the design agent[9] to evaluate structures. The formulation of the agent models involved the identification of various levels of information. First, the agents and their unique sets of issues (or concepts) were identified. Once identified, the issues were rated by the experts. The rating process, of course, is highly dependent on experience and, therefore, is subjective. The next level in formulating the agent's models dealt with subissues. For the DFI system to perform in a cooperative manner, there must be interaction among the subissues. The final level of decomposition used to formulated the models dealt with the characteristics (or properties) which are associated with a more detailed breakdown of the subissues.

Figure 12 graphically represents the information listed in Table 3. In this figure, the designer is linked directly to the issues. The issues are then tied to their respective subissues. Many interactions take place between the issue and subissue levels of information. This is caused by the complexity of the design process. An effective design not only considers the functional aspects of a structure, but also the labor, time and resources required for fabrication, construction and operation. Incorporating these aspects into a single design is a difficult process and requires the consideration of many issues as represented by the intersecting lines in Figure 12.

Next, the subissues are linked to the characteristics. The final level of information shown in Figure 12 are sets of metrics that could be used to quantitatively evaluate the characteristics of a connection.

4.2. DFI Relational Network - Extended

This section discusses an extended version of the *DFI Relational Network* described in Section 2.3. This scheme is based on the agent information models previously discussed and a set of conceptual relations developed in [22].

Figure 13 shows a schematic of this relational network. The connection consists of the functional and physical aspects. The aspects can be considered as databases of relationships that exist between the issues (located adjacent to each agent in grey boxes) and the subissues (surrounding the aspects). To avoid unnecessary confusion the

---

[9]Similar tables have also been developed for the fabrication and erection agents (see [3]).

Table 3: Design Issues, Subissues and Characteristics

ISSUE	SUBISSUE	CHARACTERISTICS
STRENGTH	Structural Concept	Building Topology Connection Designs
	Structural Detailing	Connection Designs Other Details
	Physical Components	Structural Members Connection Designs
	Material Properties	Strength Related Serviceability Related
STIFFNESS	Structural Concept	Building Topology Connection Designs
	Structural Detailing	Connection Designs Other Details
	Physical Components	Structural Members Connection Designs
	Material Properties	Strength Related Serviceability Related
LIFECYCLE COST	Structural Concept	Building Topology Connection Designs
	Design Methods	Design Codes Analysis & Assumptions
	Construction Procedures	Construction Schedule Field Operations
	Material Properties	Strength Related Serviceability Related
RELIABILITY	Design Methods	Design Codes Analysis & Assumptions
	Construction Procedures	Construction Schedule Field Operations
	Material Properties	Strength Related Serviceability Related
VERSATILITY	Structural Concept	Building Topology Connection Designs
	Construction Procedures	Construction Schedule Field Operations
	Physical Components	Structural Members Connection Designs
	Material Properties	Strength Related Serviceability Related

relational network does not show any level of detail beyond the subissues.

The formulation of the network involves using the agent information models to establish the links or relationships that exist within an agent and between the agents. Once these relationships were established, they were given names using some of the concepts discussed in [22]. Table 4 lists and describes a proposed set of relationship types. For example, in Table 4 an **attribute** relationship, shown on the third line of this table, links two entities where one is an attribute of another. Global relationships are used to link the agents to their issues and the issues to their subissues. The local

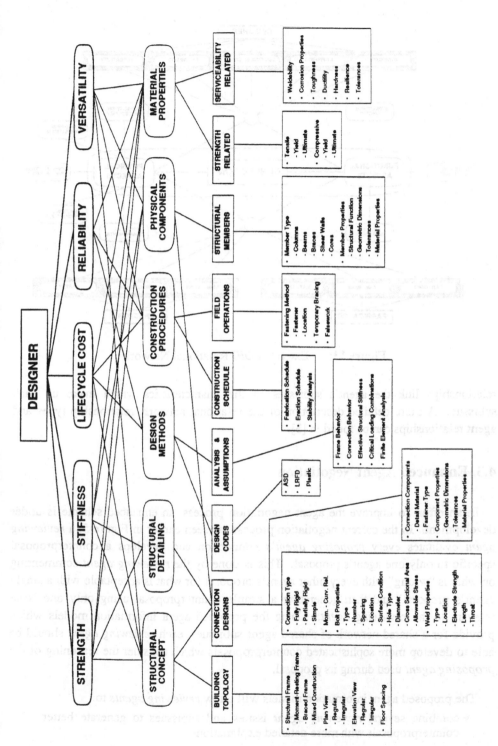

Figure 12: Designer Information Model

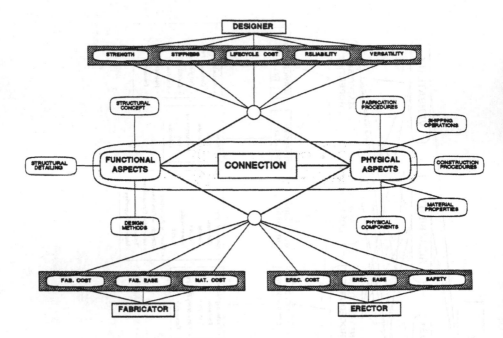

Figure 13: Extended DFI Relational Network

relationships link the agent's subissues to the characteristics which make up each subissue. A more detailed description of the relational network, relationship types and agent relationships can be found in [3].

4.3. Enhanced Agent Negotiation

In an effort to improve the agent negotiation process, an enhanced scheme is under development. In the current negotiation process, as seen earlier in Figure 5, a *reviewing agent* evaluates every *proposing agent's* connection and develops a counterproposal specific to only one agent's proposal. This is done by the *reviewing agent* commenting on what is "wrong" with every other agent's proposal (or what is acceptable with a single agent's proposal) and then generating a simple counterproposal using only one issue relevant to the *reviewing agent*. Using the proposed agent information models which provide for a shared network of shared agent subissues, each *reviewing agent* should be able to develop more sophisticated counterproposals which consider the reasoning of the *proposing agent* used during its proposal.

The proposed agent information models will allow *reviewing agents* to:
- combine several *reviewing agent* issues and subissues to generate better counterproposals with more detailed explanations,

Table 4: Summary of Relationship Types

RELATIONSHIP	TYPE	DEFINITION
needs_to_know	Global	Defines the characteristics (issues) of the structure which the agent is interested in.
influenced_by	Global	Defines the attributes (subissues) of the structure which effect the issue.
attribute	Local	Links two entities where one is an attribute of the other.
destination	Local	Links an action to an entity, towards which the action is directed.
duration	Local	Links an operation to a time-period, during which the operation takes place.
instrument	Local	Links an entity to a tool used to perform the operation.
measure	Local	Links an entity to a physical property or dimension of that entity.
method	Local	Links an operation to a way of performing the operation.
part	Local	Links two entities where one is a component of the other.

- use both shared major issues and subissues to infer some level of intention from earlier agents' proposals,

- use the inferred intentions to develop more acceptable counterproposals by inferring possible consequences of each *reviewing agent's* counterproposal.

The proposed models will allow the agents to utilize their own knowledge about their own evaluation process, as well as other agent's knowledge. This allows the *reviewing agent* to propose better alternatives based on a cooperative problem-solving view of the group. The reasoning behind each agent's counterproposal will be the product of that agent's beliefs as well as the context of the previous evaluation cycle in which a connection was proposed [27]. A discussion of the use of a simplified version of the proposed agent information models and how it influences negotiation is currently being developed and can be found in [32].

4.4. Enhanced Arbitration Scheme

A problem exists when agents cannot generate counterproposals. This is an important issue in performance and quality of the agent evaluation and proposal process. There are several reasons why an agent may not be able to generate a counterproposal. This occurs when the agent (*reviewing agent*) cannot find a connection that:

1. improves its worst issue, or

2. meets the user specified key issue, or

3. meets the *proposing agent's* conditions upon review.

The problem is addressed by an enhanced form of arbitration which takes full advantage of the knowledge contained within the system. The help of the arbitrator is enlisted when a *reviewing agent* is unable to generate a proposal that is better than its current proposal. The *reviewing agent* does this by sending a **help** message to the arbitrator specifying the *proposing agent* that is disagreeing and why.

The arbitrator responds to these requests for help in several ways. In the first case, the arbitrator suggests connections which are better than the current proposed connection based on a higher composite score. In the second case, the arbitrator suggests that the *proposing agent* consider another suitable connection with a lower key issue value which should still meet the user's initial value[10]. In the third case, where no simple solution is possible, the arbitrator looks for clues in the past negotiation dialog between the agents.

The use of the negotiation dialog allows the arbitrator to perform basic temporal reasoning. The arbitrator reviews each *negotiation cycle*[11] and attempts to use the most recent cycle that addresses the proposal problem between two agents. Initially the arbitrator reviews the current negotiation cycle that addresses the proposal problem between the two agents. The arbitrator looks within this cycle for any similar connections which the other agents approved as acceptable alternatives during their review. If the arbitrator finds a similar connection, then this connection should be considered as a proposal by the *reviewing agent*. If this is not successful, the arbitrator reviews the issues relevant to the current proposal and the objections raised by the *reviewing agent*, and suggests other issues that the agents might reconsider. This form of arbitration includes the use of *shareable perspectives* between agents and is described in detail in [32].

The reasoning behind this method of arbitration is to use the most recent, and

---

[10]Subsequent agent proposals always meet or exceed the *initial* key issue value of the user's original connection. In the case where an agent cannot meet the the user's initial value of the key issue, the arbitrator suggest a form or issue swapping (logrolling) [17].

[11]A *negotiation cycle* consists of an agent review of all other agent connections and a single counterproposal.

therefore most pertinent information before utilizing any past negotiation information. A solution is developed locally, utilizing only the issues at hand. If there is no solution for the current cycle, the arbitrator reviews the next most recent negotiation cycle and continues until all negotiation cycles have been reviewed. As the arbitrator regresses further into the negotiation dialog, there is a chance that the suggestions based on this older, possibly out-of-date information, may cause new negotiation problems. For example, similar connections found by the arbitrator in earlier negotiation cycles may have been based on different context than the most recent negotiation cycle. If the arbitrator suggests one of these connections as a possible alternative, it may cause the agents to become distracted from the issue of the current negotiation cycle. On the other hand, the arbitrator's proposal may enlighten the agents of other issues which might improve the negotiation process for the current cycle. Therefore the context of each connection proposal is important to the arbitrator's suggested solution. A detailed discussion of arbitration used to assist cooperative problem-solving can be found in [32]. Finally, if no solution is obtained, the arbitrator calls upon the user for assistance. Once control is returned to the user, the user can request explanations about the current deadlock situation, specify preferences for a connection to the *reviewing agent*, or select another key issue and *continue* the current evaluation, or restart the evaluation with a new key issue.

The arbitrator performs several other functions in addition to arbitration. These include active participation in the negotiation process when:

- its help has been requested by an agent,
- it determines that a halting condition exists,
- it notices a similar proposal/counterproposal sequence (repetitive or flip-flop condition)
- it notices that the user has changed the key issue in mid-negotiation, or
- it determines the *worst issue agent* and passes control to that agent.

In the first case, the arbitrator can respond to agent help messages. The arbitrator can also respond when the user has selected a connection to be *refused*. In this case, the arbitrator performs record keeping that prevents the connection from being used in any further evaluations. The arbitrator is *informed* by the agent who had its connection *refused*, and the arbitrator *informs* all agents to no longer consider that connection as available. In addition, the arbitrator removes the refused connection from its model of the negotiation history, thus preventing it from being suggested as a possible alternative during future requests for help.

The arbitrator also takes control when it sees certain events occurring on the blackboard. These include *halting* events, *repetitive* or *flip-flop* proposal events, and events where the user has changed the *key issue*. The arbitrator *informs* all agents of a *halt*ing condition when two agents agree on the same connection. In the case where agents produce the same counterproposals over several negotiation cycles (flip-flop proposals), the arbitrator intervenes and proceeds as if each agent failed to generate an acceptable connection. Finally, the arbitrator takes action when the user changes the *key issue* in mid-negotiation. In this case, several agents' proposals may now conflict with the new key issue. The arbitrator insures that the agents generate new proposals if they conflict with the key issue.

By enhancing the agent negotiation and arbitration process, the resulting cooperative solution, as well as the efficiency of the negotiation process (in terms of duration, computation required to generate counterproposals, number of messages sent between agents, etc), should be improved. Thus, a solution with more robust explanations in less time should be obtained as a result of implementing the proposed agent negotiation and arbitration enhancements.

5. Summary

The Designer Fabricator Interpreter (DFI) system is a step towards computer integrated construction (CIC) by initially providing a distributed problem-solving environment which allows semi-autonomous agents to work cooperatively by reasoning and negotiating about the current problem based on their expert viewpoint as well as the viewpoints of other expert agents. An arbitrator agent assists in the negotiation process when agents cannot come to an agreement. All communication is coordinated through means of a shared knowledge model and a set of communication primitives. The current domain is limited to beam-to-column connections in buildings, but can be expanded to other types of connections. The DFI architecture should be flexible enough to incorporate additional construction agents, such as an architect. One of the long-term goals of DFI is to provide an environment wherein buildings can be evaluated in a more comprehensive and consistent manner prior to the award of fabrication or erection contracts, thus resulting in a reduced number of design changes and overall project cost reduction.

In an attempt to provide better explanations, further domain research is being performed to understand additional implications of issue selection during the proposal and negotiation process. Also, a model of the user (structural designer) will assist the arbitrator direct the negotiation process. Such a model would allow the arbitrator to have access to the user's intent and could help guide the agent evaluations down a path that would be more "in tune" with what the user might expect. Finally, a more robust knowledge representation scheme is needed which will allow agents with shareable perspectives to generate better explanations to agents' queries during the negotiation process.

5.1. Industry Impact

The implementation of systems, like DFI, can provide practicing design professionals with tools to assist in designing for constructibility. DFI specifically attempts to improve the communication between designers and fabricators during the preliminary connection design process.

Integrated design and construction systems will give users the ability to predict downstream problems as a result of upstream decisions. This could lead to more economical designs which consider aspects of constructibility to reduce field rework and overall costs. These systems could integrate multiple knowledge and databases to encompass more aspects of the structure. For example, considering the recent advances in "intelligent" CAD, these systems could be combined with construction knowledge-based systems and finite element packages to facilitate a situation where the intent of what the designer is trying to accomplish can be related to field activities. The construction knowledge-based systems would be responsible for pointing out potential field problems, the intelligent CAD systems would maintain component tolerances and determine interference problems.

The present DFI prototype system is not intended for production use in industry. It does, however, demonstrate how the integration of different viewpoints during an evaluation can provide "better" connection design alternatives. DFI also provides a mechanism for sharing knowledge across various perspectives to improve the communication between designers and fabricators while allowing each to maintain a different view of the same situation.

5.2. Intellectual Contributions

The development of DFI has provided a preliminary framework for cooperative problem-solving. A systematic approach was used to represent and relate connection design and construction information across three different viewpoints.

It is suggested that the contributions of the DFI research include the following:

- Formulation and implementation of a multiagent negotiation scheme [32].

- Development of a flexible knowledge and data representation to model aspects of building information.

- Development of a practical application for conceptual graphs and relations [31, 22].

- Formulation of a structured decomposition of agent information into issues, subissues characteristics and their metrics.

DFI is a working prototype which is based on the above.

6. Future Work

The DFI prototype evaluates steel beam-to-column connections to determine if physical fit-up is possible and points out potential problems with the design and construction from the viewpoints of design, fabrication and erection. The system is capable of generating alternative connection configurations that consider the identified problems. The intent of this section is to formulate possible extensions and future work.

6.1. Extending the Connection Evaluation

The following is a list of possible extensions that would improve the current connection evaluation scheme used in DFI[12]:

- Expanding the connection database to include additional Type 1 connection configurations.
- Extending the connection database to include Type 2 and 3 connections.
- Generating a set of connection databases that group connection configurations across demographic parameters.
- Developing a testing scheme to systematically validate the rating factor values present on the connection information forms.
- Incorporating a method to dynamically generate the rating factor values for the connection information forms using the proposed agent information models.
- Developing a more comprehensive connection evaluation that uses specific agent heuristics.

The first two items would be straightforward to complete by developing more connection information forms and obtaining industry input on the values for the rating factors. The third item, generating a set of connection databases that group connections demographically, implies surveying many design, fabrication and erection firms to determine statistically what differences exist in connection configuration preference across many demographic parameters, such as, company size and geographic location. Validating the rating factor values would involve systematically testing many cases with experts to determine their correctness.

The last two items are more difficult to complete. Dynamically generating values for the rating factors would involve developing a set of rules that compile a score by looking at the quantitative information slots that make up the lowest level of issue decomposition in the agent information models. To implement a more comprehensive connection

---

[12]Research is being conducted to evaluate entire building configurations.

evaluation, specific agent heuristics would have to be formulated that could act on the issues, subissues and characteristics to evaluate potential problems associated with other agents' proposed connections.

6.2. Explanations via User and Discourse Models

As discussed in the Illustrative Example in Section 3, the explain button generates a limited explanation about that agent's prior action, and is constructed from keywords taken from the DFI relational network. It is believed that a more robust explanation facility is necessary to reflect the dynamic negotiation process. This would lend the system additional credibility by enabling the user to inspect the reasoning associated with the selection of the connections.

6.2.1. User Models

One area of explanations currently being researched is that of goal-driven explanations [15]. Simply stated, this means tailoring the phrasing of the explanation text to the (assumed) goals of the user. One way to achieve this tailoring is via a user model - i.e. a structure which represents the user's goals, beliefs, knowledge, preferences, and expertise [7].

User models can be acquired in two ways [13]:
1. Implicit model acquisition where the system builds a model as the user interacts with it; and

2. Explicit model acquisition where the model is built by direct inquiry of the user, or by coding of stereotypical information, or by a combination of both.

Since DFI currently does not support a dialog system, implicitly building a model (based only on buttons selected) would be very difficult. Therefore, building a model using stereotypical information is proposed. Some of the knowledge to be included in the model is that contained in the designer information model discussed in the previous section. By maintaining a model of the user's beliefs and goals, responses can be tailored to the designer's level of expertise.

6.2.2. Discourse Models

The user model is not complete with only stereotypical knowledge about the user. Other knowledge necessary is that relating to the particulars of the session - such as events, actions, and current topics of discussion [20]. In DFI this means maintaining a current record of the lists of connections considered, including those accepted (or rejected) by each agent. A discourse model is the proposed method of maintaining relevant session information. The discourse model is dynamic in that it changes as the negotiation process progresses [23]. It is maintained separately from the user model, but is used in conjunction with the user model. For example, if information from the discourse model conflicts with information contained in the user model, then the user model is updated [20, 30]. Also contained in the discourse model should be some form of linguistic structure used in generating the English text of the response [7]. By maintaining both a user model and a discourse model, the system can generate responses that are relevant to the session as well as geared to the goals of the user.

Acknowledgments

Grateful acknowledgment is due to Mr. Ira Hooper, P.E., Vice President of STV/Seelye Stevenson Value & Knecht Engineering Planners and Mr. Ed Becker, P.E., a professional engineering consultant and former chief engineer of Lehigh Structural Steel fabricators.

References

[1] Allen, James F. and Perrault, C. Raymond, "Analyzing Intention in Utterances", *Artificial Intelligence*, Vol. 15, No. 3, 1980, pp. 441-458.

[2] Ayers, C., *Specifications: For Architecture, Engineering, and Construction*, McGraw-Hill, New York, New York, 1975.

[3] Barone, Marcello, "Designer Fabricator Interpreter: A Step Towards Computer Integrated Construction", Master's thesis, Lehigh University, 1990.

[4] Barone, Marcello, Werkman, Keith J., Wilson, John L., and Hillman, Donald J., "A Knowledge-Based System for the Evaluation of Beam-to-Column Connections", NSF-ERC ATLSS Report 89-11, Lehigh University, Bethlehem, PA, USA, 1989.

[5] Alan H. Bond and Les Gasser, Eds., *Readings in Distributed Artificial Intelligence*, Morgan Kaufmann Publishers, Inc., 2929 Campus Drive, San Mateo, California, 94403, 1988.

[6] Bruce, Bertram C., "Belief Systems and Language Understanding", BBN Report No. 2973, AI Report No. 21, Bolt Beranek and Newman, Inc., 1975.

[7] Chin, David N., "User Models and Discourse Models", *Computational Linguistics*, Vol. 14, No. 3, September 1988, pp. 86-87.

[8] Conry, S., Meyer, R. and Lesser, V., "Multistage Negotiation in Distributed Planning", Tech. report COINS TR86-87, University of Massachusetts, 1986.

[9] Corkill, Daniel D. and Lesser, Victor R., "The Use of Meta-Level Control for Coordination in a Distributed Problem Solving Network", *Proceedings of the 8th*

International Joint Conference on Artificial Intelligence, IJCAI, 1983, pp. 748-756.

[10] Davis, Randall and Smith, Reid G., "Negotiation as a Metaphor for Distributed Problem Solving", *Artificial Intelligence*, Vol. 20, 1983, pp. 63-109.

[11] Gasser, Les and Huhns, Michael N., editor, *Distributed Artificial Intelligence, Volume II*, Pitman/Morgan Kaufmann, London, 1989.

[12] Huhns, Michael N., *Distributed Artificial Intelligence*, Morgan Kaufmann Publishers, Inc., 95 First Street, Los Altos, CA 94022, 1987.

[13] Kass, Robert and Finin, Tim, "Acquiring User Models for Tailoring Explanations", *Proceedings of the AAAI'88 Workshop on Explanation*, Sponsored by AAAI, St. Paul, MN, August 1988, pp. 51-54.

[14] Maher, Mary Lou, "HI-RISE and Beyond", *Computer-Aided Design*, Vol. 17, No. 9, November 1985, pp. 420-427.

[15] McKeown, Kathleen R., Wish, Myron and Matthews, Kevin, "Tailoring Explanations for the User", *Proceedings of the 9th International Joint Conference on Artificial Intelligence*, IJCAI, Los Angeles, CA, 1985, pp. 794-798.

[16] Nii, H. Penny, "Blackboard Systems, Part 2", *AI Magazine*, Vol. 7, No. 3, 1986, pp. 82-106.

[17] Pruitt, Dean G., *Negotiation Behavior*, Academic Press, Inc., New York, NY, 1981.

[18] Rubin, Jeffrey Z. and Brown, Bert R., *The Social Psychology of Barganing and Negotiation*, Academic Press, Inc., New York, NY, 1975.

[19] Sanvido, Victor E., "An Integrated Building Process Model- A Life Cycle Approach to Planning, Design, Construction and Operations", ATLSS Seminar Series, The Pennsylvania State University, 1989.

[20] Schuster, Ethel, "Establishing the Relationship Between Discourse Models and User Models", *Computational Linguistics*, Vol. 14, No. 3, September 1988, pp. 82-85.

[21] Simpson, G.W. and Cochran, J.K., "An Analytic Approach to Prioritizing Construction Projects", *Civil Engineering Systems*, Vol. 4, No. 4, 1987, pp. 185-190.

[22] Sowa, John F., *Conceptual Structures: Information Processing in Mind and Machine*, Addison-Wesley Publishing Company, Reading, MA, 1984.

[23] Sparck Jones, Karen, "User Models, Discourse Models, and Some Others", *Computational Linguistics*, Vol. 14, No. 3, September 1988, pp. 98-100.

[24] Sriram, D, "DICE: An Object Oriented Programming Environment for Cooperative Engineering Design", Tech. report IESL-89-03, Massachusetts Institute of Technology, 1989, Intelligent Engineering Systems Laboratory.

[25] Steeb, R., McArthur, D., Cammarata, S., Narian, S. and Giarla, W., "Distributed

Problem Solving for Air Fleet Control: Framework and Implementation'', Tech. report N-2139-ARPA, Rand Note, 1984.

[26] Strauss, Anselm, *Negotiations: Varieties, Contexts, Processes, and Social Order*, Jossey-Bass, Inc., Publishers, San Fransisco, CA, 1978.

[27] Sycara, Katia P., ''Resolving Goal Conflicts via Negotiation'', *Proceedings of the Seventh National Conference on Artificial Intelligence*, Morgan Kaufmann Publishers, Inc., St. Paul, MN, 1988, pp. 245-250.

[28] Sycara, Katia P., ''Argumentation: Planning Other Agent's Plans'', *Proceedings of the Eleventh International Joint Conference on Artificial Intelligence*, Morgan Kaufmann Publishers, Inc., Detroit, MI, August 1989, pp. 517-523.

[29] Tenney, Robert R. and Sandell, Nils R., Jr., ''Strategies for Distributed Decisionmaking'', *IEEE Transactions on Systems, Man and Cybernetics*, Vol. SMC-11, No. 8, August 1981, pp. 527-538.

[30] Wahlster, Wolfgang, ''Distinguishing User Models from Discourse Models'', *Computational Linguistics*, Vol. 14, No. 3, September 1988, pp. 101-103.

[31] Werkman, Keith J. and Hillman, Donald J., ''Designer Fabricator Interpreter System: Using Conceptual Graphs to Represent Perspectives Between Cooperating Agents'', *Proceedings of the Fourth Annual Workshop on Conceptual Graphs*, IJCAI-89, Detroit, MI, August 1989, pp. 1-5, Section 4.14.

[32] Werkman, Keith James, *Multiagent Cooperative Problem Solving Through Negotation and Perspective Sharing*, PhD dissertation, Lehigh University, 1990.

[33] Wilson, John L., ''Computer-Integrated Construction'', NSF Workshop on Construction Automation, Proceedings, Allentown, PA, April 1987.

Appendix A. Connection Information Forms

The purpose of the Connection Information Form is to provide a mechanism for information transfer and knowledge acquisition between ATLSS researchers and the industry partners associated with the Designer Fabricator Interpreter. These sheets are used to build a knowledge base wherein designers can access general fabrication and erection knowledge in the pre-bid phase of the connection design in order to help eliminate mismatch between the intent of the designer and the capabilities of the fabricator. This appendix will describe the *Connection Information Forms*, define the issues (as presented to the reviewing experts) and provide a listing of the issues used in DFI system.

1. Description of Forms

The *Connection Information Forms* were developed using the FrameMaker™ desktop publishing program running on Sun™ workstations. The author [4] developed a modular sheet format divided into five sections:

1. Title Block.

2. Connection Detail Table.

3. Profile View of the Connection.

4. Rating Factors Table.

5. Comments.

A blank template was first produced along with a connection component object library so these forms could be generated quickly and consistently. The logical, modular layout of the form was quite important because they were being faxed to the experts for comment and review. Therefore, an extremely crowded layout would be difficult to read while a more sparse layout requiring two or more sheets would take longer and cost considerably more to fax. Another feature of the development environment was that PostScript™[13] (standard graphics language) files could be generated quite easily from FrameMaker™. This allowed the researchers to write a simple postprocessing program that read the Postscript files and automatically generated a correctly formatted database for DFI from the graphic sheets. A description of each area of the connection information form is presented below, along with some example input.

1. **Title Block:** In this area the connection name, type of construction and orientation are given. The small text in the upper right corner of this block is a connection identifier for computer storage and retrieval.

   • **Connection Name:** Describes the connection configuration.

---

[13]PostScript is a trademark of Adobe Systems, Inc.

- **Type of Construction:** As described by *AISC Manual 9th Edition.*

  Type 1: Fully Rigid Moment Connection
  Type 2: Simple (Pinned) Connection
  Type 3: Partially Rigid Connection.

- **Orientation:** Describes the orientation of the connection either to the column *flange* or the column *web*.

2. **Connection Detail Table:** Here the connection (i.e., top, bottom and web) components are detailed along with the type of fastener (i.e., shop welding, field bolting) used to connect to the column and beam ends of the connection.

3. **Profile View of the Connection:** A display of the information detailed in the Connection Detail Table is presented to assist in visualization of the connection.

4. **Rating Factors Table:** The issues used to evaluate the connection are listed along with a rating on that issues from 1 to 5. The issues are grouped from the viewpoint of *design*, *fabrication* and *erection*. Notice that a specific viewpoint may not have a rating on a specific issue because that viewpoint does not have knowledge about that particular issue (i.e., the *design* viewpoint may not be familiar with the *Erec. Cost* issue).

5. **Comments:** In this area comments about the connection are listed. The letter (*D*, *F* or *E*) that precedes each comment indicates the viewpoint from which the comment is made.

2. Issues and Rating Values

The industry experts were asked to evaluate each connection on the following ten issues:

- **Strength:** The "ultimate" strength of the connection.

- **Stiffness:** The ability of the connection to resist deformation.

- **Reliability:** The ability of the connection to perform its intended function during in-service life.

- **Versatility:** The adaptability to be modified or "retrofit" when the intended use of the structure is changed from the initial design conditions.

- **Fab. Cost:** The relative shop fabrication cost based on labor.

- **Fab. Ease:** The relative ease to shop fabricate the connection.

- **Mat. Cost:** The material and delivery cost of the connection detail material from the mill.

- **Erec. Cost:** The relative field erection cost based on labor.

- **Erec. Ease:** The relative field erection ease.

• **Safety:** A relative measure on how safe the connection is to field erect.

The experts reviewed only the issues related to their particular area of expertise and were also asked to provide any comments from past experiences that should be included on each sheet.

The issues were rated using the following scale:

- • **5** = Most Desirable Condition.

- • **4** = More Desirable Condition.

- • **3** = Moderately Desirable Condition.

- • **2** = Less Desirable Condition.

- • **1** = Least Desirable Condition.

This rating scale was suggested by the industrial designer during a meeting to develop the layout of the forms. The scale was chosen to compliment the level of detail DFI uses to perform an evaluation. A more accurate scale would be in suspect since the specific details of the connection are not included on the sheet or used in the current version of DFI.

TRANSACTION MANAGEMENT IN DESIGN DATABASES*

Charles M. Eastman
Graduate School of Architecture and Urban Planning
University of California, Los Angeles

Ali Kutay
Formative Technologies Inc.
Pittsburgh, Pennsylvania

Abstract. *Databases are being increasing applied to support design and engineering, implemented on a backend file server and supporting shared access. A fundamental difference between traditional database management and design database management is that for most of the design process, integrity is partial. A management scheme, called entity state transaction management, is proposed that deals with both the partial ordering of transactions and concurrency control over shared information resources. The techniques for automatic management of integrity are described in the light of the following problems: coordinating iterated partial analyses of an engineering system, propagation of design decisions in one subsystem to other subsystems and concurrent design operations within a single subsystem. The implications of entity state management for engineering database schema definition are also explored.*

1 Introduction

Integrating the engineering design process with computer technology has been a long term goal and an important research area. It is increasingly common for engineers and designers to work at graphical workstations, connected by a network to a shared database. Controlled from the local environment will be design tools such as schematic design tools, detailed part and assembly modeling tools, analysis and other application programs. The comprehensive model of the artifact being designed will reside in the design database most probably on a backend file server, providing database support.

Design databases, like most databases, are implemented for the purpose of integrating multiple applications on a common environment. One of the main features of this integration is to maintain consistency and integrity within the model data. Developing data abstractions has been the major effort in general database research, while operation abstractions have received considerable attention only recently. The transaction concept is one that is closely related to operation abstractions. The transaction concept suggests that instead of allowing arbitrary operations on a database, these operations must be structured into sets of actions such that when each set is executed, the integrity of the database is maintained. In this way a database has complete integrity during all periods between transactions. Losses of integrity are temporary and limited to the duration of transactions upon the database. The transaction concept has led to development of different techniques to control concurrent operations on a database. These concepts fit well with most database applications, where data is to be maintained in a correct state, i.e. an integral one, for all operations.

A design is a specification for a product with adequate information for its fabrication. Designing, that is the definition of this specification, typically involves both the development of a specification and its incremental evaluation. So as to assure that the resulting product achieves various objectives and intentions, integrity of the database, then, involves both the completeness of the specification (for fabrication) and achievement of the objectives and intentions. In design, integrity does not exist within the design model until design is almost complete. Most operations have the effect of adding to or modifying the database integrity. Given this definition of design, it is apparent that a consistent *database state* where all integrity constraints are satisfied can only be reached towards the end of the design. Thus for most of the lifetime of a design database, a database state possesses only partial integrity.

In order to clearly convey this point, we develop an example engineering design application. Consider the layout of a piping system in a building or chemical plant. The objective of such a layout is to first define a piping system that connects some functional elements, e.g., a boiler or a heat exchanger, and later to define automatically the sizes of each pipe member and joint, so that they satisfy global flow, space and sizing criteria.

Piping systems are usually represented as a graph. See Figure 1. Nodes depict the point(s) where fluid is supplied (source nodes) or points where fluid must be provided (service nodes) or where pipes join (connection or intermediate nodes). Edges connect pairs of nodes and correspond to pipes.

At this point, the example consists of three transaction classes:

1. a pipe sizing program that, based on flow rates and pressure, defines the diameter of each of the pipes in the network. Obviously, flow is only possible if all nodes are connected.

2.　　　a transaction that is used in piping layout that locates a service node and defines its flow requirements, or a source or connection node.

3.　　　another transaction used for piping layout that locates a pipe by placing it between two existing nodes. When used iteratively, it provides connectivity across the graph between a service node and a supply node.

Notice that in these example transaction classes, the standard integrity requirement of a transaction is violated. In (1) full integrity does not exist. Indeed, the purpose of this transaction class is to add to the database's integrity by correctly assigning pipe diameters. Correspondingly, only partial integrity is required to invoke a transaction of this class, eg. that nodes are located and connected. After a transaction of class (1) has been executed, if a transaction of class (2) is called it invalidates the integrity of the database regarding the connectivity of the piping system. Any results of transactions of class (1) are invalidated. But after an instance of transaction class (2), a pipe sizing transaction cannot be called directly because the connectivity condition which it requires is not satisfied. A transaction of class (3), if applied to the new node, may connect it to the rest of the piping graph so that complete connectivity is achieved, allowing the sizing transaction can be meaningfully reapplied.

It is evident from this example design that the work on transactions to date has incorporated very restrictive assumptions regarding integrity before, during and after transactions:

1.　　　prior to invocation of a transaction, all the integrity conditions that apply to entities to be accessed must be satisfied.

2.　　　during a transaction, all integrity conditions that apply to a set of entities called a transaction entity set (TES) are potentially violated.

3.　　　after a transaction, all the integrity conditions that apply to its entities again are satisfied.

The practices of human designers suggest that these assumptions are not necessary. Indeed, in design databases they cannot possibly be satisfied. Specifically, assumptions #1 and #3 cannot hold because of the incomplete integrity that exists for most of the life of a design database. Full integrity need not apply to the TES of a transaction, but only a specified set of integrity conditions. Similarly, the previous example shows that the result of a transaction is not full integrity, but the alteration of specific integrity conditions. In the example cited, transaction (1) and (3) add integrity while in (2) integrity is subtracted (within the scope of the DB being considered).

In the next section, we define a revised definition of transaction as well as other concepts leading to *entity-state transaction management* [3]. In the succeeding sections, an example application of the scheme is shown for single and multiple disciplinary design. The example demonstrates the use of entity-state transaction management and outlines its information requirements.

2 Transactions in Design Databases

In order to provide a revised form to transactions in design databases the following definitions are given: A database consists of data units called *entities*. The entities of a database form a distinct set $E = \{e_1, .. ,e_n\}$. Each transaction performs its processes on a TES, which is a subset of E. A TES has two parts: a readset $\{e\}R$ and a writeset $\{e\}W$. The integrity conditions to be satisfied within a database are denoted as constraints. Here, we say, a constraint is added to the database if the database *satisfies* the constraint, else it is not part of the database. Also note for later that each constraint can be accessed by the entities it refers to. With this information a design transaction can be defined as:

A collection of actions on a database that reads entity set $\{e\}R$ and potentially writes into entity set $\{e\}W$. The integrity of the design is defined by a set of constraints $\{c_1, c_2, ...c_n\}$. Prior to invocation, the actions require that the set of integrity constraints $\{c^+\}$[1] be satisfied on the entities $\{e\}R$ and $\{e\}W$. During the transaction, the integrity constraint set $\{c\}^D$ on $\{e\}R$ and $\{e\}W$ may be violated. After successful completion of the transaction, integrity conditions on the $\{e\}W$ may have been changed. These are denoted by the sets $\{c^+\}^A$, $\{c\}^A$, where $\{c^+\}^A$ are the integrity constraints added by the transaction and $\{c\}^A$ are those that are eliminated.

The three phases of a transaction, *before, during and after,* and the corresponding constraint sets delimit:

1.   the scope of integrity required to start a transaction,

2.   the scope of integrity violations during a transaction and

3.   the effect of the completion of a transaction after it is committed.

The revised definition of transaction manages the moment-by-moment integrity of each entity within the database, using the concept called *entity state, (s_e),* which describes the degree of integrity an entity satisfies and can be represented by a set of integrity constraints in the database. A database state then can be defined as $DS = U (s_e)$. These definitions suggest that in a design database a transaction should incorporate entities together with related integrity constraints. A design transaction then takes the form of:

$$T_i: (\{e\}R, \{e\}W, \{c\}^B, \{c\}^D, \{c\}^A)$$

We refer to such a description as a *transaction class*. Thus, a transaction in a design database is an instance of a class. This definition provides control of the scope of integrity as well as consistency when there are many active transactions in a database.

By defining transactions in this way, the effect of any transaction on database integrity is fully specified. This provides several new capabilities. Transactions have the potential to check if needed preconditions (integrity conditions on entities) hold. Also, rather than managing clashes on an entity-by-entity basis, concurrency management can determine if two potentially concurrent transactions on a single entity can execute at the same time without violating the necessary integrity conditions relied upon by the other.

2.1 Concurrency Control

Concurrency control is the task of avoiding inconsistent updates in a database, when several concurrent transactions share entities. Each transaction (usually controlled by constraints and database states as in business databases), maintains the consistency of a database when it is executed alone. Thus a serial ordering of a set of transactions maintains consistency too. But when transactions are executed concurrently, the ordering of their constituent actions may not be serial but interleaved. Most techniques developed for concurrency control are based on determining a *serializable* ordering such that the final results of the execution of a set of transactions would be equivalent to a serial execution [1]. The most accepted mechanism for concurrency control, called the *locking* approach [4] is based on this model.

On the other hand, in [6], it is shown that serialization is the optimal model only when minimum information is available for concurrency control. The revised definition of transaction incorporates integrity constraints as an integral part and proposes a different concurrency control mechanism based on the entity state information [3].

3 Design Examples

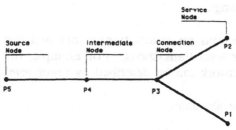

Figure 1: Piping System

In this section we provide design examples and the corresponding integrity constraints and transaction structures for two engineering subsystems. The first example is the piping subsystem introduced earlier, which is a common part in many engineering projects such as ship design, process plant design, building design, etc. The second example is a structural subsystem which is used to support the piping subsystem. First, each subsystem is considered separately and then they are integrated to demonstrate various interactions between these two subsystems. The examples are similar to the ones given in [2, 3]. Entity state transaction management is applied to both of these subsystems in the following sections. Note that we have simplified these subsystems and made some assumptions to remain in the context of transaction management.

3.1 A Piping Subsystem

Consider a simplified piping network. For a complete design of this network, we assume that the following set of transaction classes is necessary:

1. A transaction class (T_1) that defines piping system topology. It supports the definitions of source, service, connection and intermediate nodes, and the edges that connect them.

2. A flow generation transaction class (T_2) which calculates and assigns the maximum flow to each edge.

3. A pipe sizing transaction class (T_3) that defines each edge in the piping network as a pipe and assigns parameters such as diameter, material, etc., according to the flow and edge information.

4. A detail fitting design transaction class (T_4) that defines all fittings and computes the finished lengths of pipe elements.

5.　　A cost analysis transaction class (T_5) that estimates the cost of piping and the fittings.

Each of these transactions are *macro* transactions and can be represented as a combination of lower level transactions. For example, the first transaction that defines the piping network can be described by lower level transactions that:

- define node locations

- modify node locations

- merge nodes

- define edges

- delete edges etc.

Gray ([5]) and Moss ([7]) discuss the problems associated with *nested* transactions. Since such a structure is not dealt with in this paper, for simplicity we consider them as members (actions) of the transaction class T_1. See [3] for examples based on low-level transactions.

The integrity constraints for the piping subsystem also can be identified. These constraints are also combinations (or union) of lower level constraints. For the example problem, constraints are:

$$
\begin{array}{lll}
c_1 & \rightarrow & \text{"pipe topology defined"} \\
c_2 & \rightarrow & \text{"pipe flows defined"} \\
c_3 & \rightarrow & \text{"pipe size parameters defined"} \\
c_4 & \rightarrow & \text{"pipe fittings and finished lengths defined"} \\
c_5 & \rightarrow & \text{"piping subsystem cost estimated"}
\end{array}
$$

Given the transaction descriptions and the integrity constraints, the transaction classes for the piping subsystem can be formally defined as:

- T_1　:　$(\{\text{nodes, edges}\}R', \{\text{nodes, edges}\}W, \{\ \}^B, \{c_1\}^D, \{\{c_1^+\}, \{c_2^-\}\}^A)$

- T_2　:　$(\{\text{nodes, edges, flow}\}R', \{\text{nodes, edges, flow}\}W, \{\ c_1^+\}^B, \{c_2\}^D, \{\{c_2^+\}, \{c_3^-\}\}^A)$

- T_3　:　$(\{\text{nodes, edges, flow}\}R, \{\text{pipes}\}W, \{\{c_1^+\}, \{c_2^+\}\}^B, \{c_3\}^D, \{\{c_3^+\}, \{c_4^-\}\}^A)$

- T_4 : $(\{\text{pipes, flow, fittings}\}R^*, \{\text{pipes, fittings}\}W, \{\{c_1^+\}, \{c_2^+\}, \{c_3^+\}\}^B, \{c_4^-\}^D, \{\{c_4^+\}, \{c_5^-\}\}^A)$

- T_5 : $(\{\text{pipes, fittings}\}R, \{\text{piping cost}\}W, \{\{c_1^+\}, \{c_2^+\}, \{c_3^+\}, \{c_4^+\}\}^B, \{c_5^-\}^D, \{c_5^+\}^A)$

These class descriptions provide examples to the application of transactions in a design database context. The readsets marked with "*" indicate that some of the entities in their TES are conditional. For example, if T_1 is applied to null database state, it would not have any readset. But, if it is applied after T_4 is executed, it modifies the existing piping topology and therefore would include a readset. Similarly, fittings may or may not exist when transaction T_4 is executed. T_1 has no *before* conditions. The transaction graph and database states for the piping system are shown in Figure 2.

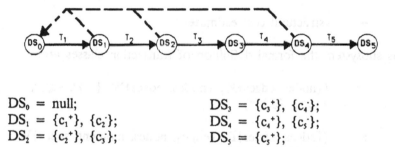

DS_0 = null;
$DS_1 = \{c_1^+\}, \{c_2^-\}$;
$DS_2 = \{c_2^+\}, \{c_3^-\}$;

$DS_3 = \{c_3^+\}, \{c_4^-\}$;
$DS_4 = \{c_4^+\}, \{c_5^-\}$;
$DS_5 = \{c_5^+\}$;

Figure 2: Transaction Graph for Piping Subsystem

3.2 A Structural Subsystem

In a similar way, transaction classes for the structural subsystem, which are used to provide structural soundness to the piping system, can be defined. Again, these are *macro* transactions, i.e. compositions of lower level transactions.

1. A transaction class (T_6) that defines the frame topology for the structural subsystem by identifying the locations of nodes and edges, and centerlines.

2. A transaction class (T_7) that defines the section modulus for individual members by identifying the moment and shear forces for the members.

3.　　A member selection and sizing transaction class (T_8) that defines the member sizes.

4.　　A detailing transaction class (T_9) that provides joint designs.

5.　　A transaction class (T_{10}) that estimates the cost of the structural subsystem.

The integrity constraints for this subsystem can be defined as:

c_6　→　"frame topology defined"

c_7　→　"moment-shears defined"

c_8　→　"member sizes defined"

c_9　→　"joints defined"

c_{10}　→　"structural cost estimated"

Then, for this subsystem the formal definition of transaction classes are:

- T_6　:　({nodes, edges}R˙, {nodes, edges}W, { }^{B}, {c_6^-}^{D}, {{c_6^+}, {c_7^-}}^{A})

- T_7　:　({edges, nodes}R, {edges, nodes, moment, shear}W, {{c_6^+}^{B}, {c_7^-}^{D}, {{c_7^+}, {c_8^-}}^{A})

- T_8　:　({edges, nodes, moment, shear}R, {members}W, {c_7^+}^{B}, {c_8^-}^{D}, {{c_8^+}, {c_9^-}}^{A})

- T_9　:　({members, joints}R˙, {pipes, joints}W, {c_8^+}^{B}, {c_9^-}^{D}, {{c_9^+}, {c_{10}^-}}^{A})

- T_{10}　:　({members}R, {structural cost}W, {c_9^+}^{B}, {c_{10}^-}^{D}, {c_{10}^+}^{A})

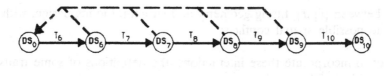

DS_0 = null;

DS_6 = $\{c_6^+\}$, $\{c_7^-\}$;

DS_7 = $\{c_7^+\}$, $\{c_8^-\}$;

DS_8 = $\{c_8^+\}$, $\{c_9^-\}$;

DS_9 = $\{c_9^+\}$, $\{c_{10}^-\}$;

DS_{10} = $\{c_{10}^+\}$;

Figure 3: Transaction Graph for Structural Subsystem

Again, the readsets marked with "*" indicate that some entities in them are conditional. For example, if T_9 is applied for the first time, its readset would not contain joints, but during an iteration it would include them.

Notice that in both examples, if an earlier transaction is applied again after later ones, it invalidates the later ones.

3.3 Integration of Subsystems

Integration of the two subsystems described in section 3.1 and 3.2 provides a common system that supports more complete management of design development. Integration is necessary if the piping subsystem requires structural support. Interaction between the two subsystems can be identified at the following levels:

1. between the piping network topology and the structural frame topology, in terms of providing shared nodes to transfer loads;

2. between pipe parameters of piping subsystem and members selected for structural subsystem, with regard to possible spatial conflicts;

3. use of the static and dynamic loads generated from the piping subsystem in the structural subsystem;

4.   between piping fitting geometry and structural joints design, with regard to possible spatial conflicts;

In order to incorporate these interactions, the definitions of some transactions must be modified. These are:

- T_7 :   ({edges, nodes}R, {edges, nodes, moment, shear}W, {{c_1^+}, {c_3^+}, {c_6^+}}^{B}, {c_7^-}^{D}, {{c_7^+}, {c_8^-}}^{A})

- T_8 :   ({edges, nodes, moments, shear}R, {members}W, {{c_3^+}, {c_7^+}}^{B}, {c_8^-}^{D}, {{c_8^+}, {c_9^-}}^{A}

- T_9 :   ({nodes, edges}$^{R^*}$, {nodes, edges}^{W}, {{c_4^+}, {c_8^+}}^{B}, {c_9^-}^{D}, {{c_9^+}, {c_{10}^-}}^{A})

T_7 requires that pipe sizes and fittings must be defined to determine their loads on the structure. T_8 defines this transaction in one of several ways, open to different policies. It treats pipe topology as given and requires structures to route around them, should conflicts occur.

These revisions define the interdependencies between the piping and structural systems, as shown in Figure 4.

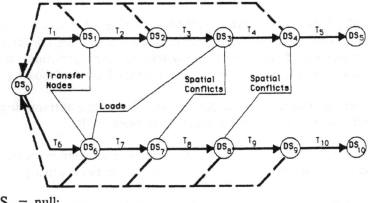

DS$_0$ = null;
DS$_1$ = {c_1^+}, {c_2^-};
DS$_2$ = {c_2^+}, {c_3^-};
DS$_3$ = {c_3^+}, {c_4^-};
DS$_4$ = {c_4^+}, {c_5^-};
DS$_5$ = {c_5^+};

DS$_6$ = {c_1^+}, {c_3^+}, {c_6^+}, {c_7^-};
DS$_7$ = {c_3^+}, {c_7^+}, {c_8^-};
DS$_8$ = {c_4^+}, {c_8^+}, {c_9^-};
DS$_9$ = {c_9^+} {c_{10}^-};
DS$_{10}$ = {c_{10}^+};

Figure 4: Integration of the piping and structural subsystems
into an integrated model

4 Transaction Management for Engineering Design

A transaction management scheme for a design database must support two important functions:

- Integrity Management

- Concurrency Control

The scheme for these functions can be developed as two separate capabilities or as a single combined one. We first describe these functions in detail according to the revised transaction definition, then define separate and joint schemes.

4.1 Integrity Management

An important advantage that the revised transaction definition introduces in the context of design databases is that it allows partial integrity. With partial integrity, the specific integrity conditions required of a transaction can be specified.

Consider the transactions defined for the piping subsystem. When a transaction instance of class T_1 is executed, it updates the database such that integrity constraints denoted as $\{c_i\}$ hold for the entities in its TES. Simultaneously, integrity constraints $\{c_2, c_3, c_4\}$ are violated due to the effects of the same transactions. In the context of business databases, such a situation indicates an inconsistent database state transformation and results in the rejection (abort) of the transaction. But for design databases, these are the required effects of T_1. Furthermore, consider a request from a transaction instance of T_3. Assume that the flows for the pipes in the TES of this transaction are not yet defined. That is $\{c_2\}$ does not hold for the entities. If T_3 is allowed to execute, it would result in failure of the transaction due to insufficient data. These features of a transaction in a design database can be formalized by the following rules about integrity management:

1. If the required $\{c\}^B$ conditions for a transaction class do not hold at any point in time, no transactions of this class are allowed to execute.

2. It is the task of a transaction to satisfy a set of integrity constraints $\{c^+\}^A$, so that other transactions which require them as $\{c\}^B$ are allowed to execute.

3. A transaction may also violate a set of constraints $\{c^-\}^A$ to indicate that other transactions should be invoked to satisfy them.

These rules suggest that integrity conditions defining partially consistent database states also define a partial ordering of transactions dictated by the constraints. This ordering is in the form of *precedence ordering* with *iteration*. The only possible ordering of transactions for the piping subsystem is shown in Figure 2.

4.2   Transaction Management Implementation Scheme

At this point, the functions of integrity management and concurrency control can be integrated to form a transaction management scheme which responds to both functions. In this way, it provides more generality and resolves the problems arising from integrity maintenance and concurrency control.

The proposed method includes three phases of information exchange between a transaction and database. These phases correspond to the integrity states of the entities of a transaction. Each entity and its state information is denoted by the doublet $<e,s>$ where:

e contains the entity name and the current value of the entity,

s_e contains the subset of all constraints $\{c_1, c_2, ... c_n\}$ that refer to entity e.

Each design application would consist of a pre-processor for executing the *before* phase and a post-processor for processing the *after* phase. Each would have coded the constraint flags characterizing the conditions expected and resulting from the application that apply to each entity retrieved. In the first phase a transaction which requires permission to execute checks whether its entities have been put into the proper state by preceding transactions. Successfully initiated transactions communicate to each other through a *transaction log*. The function of the transaction log is to identify current entity states, i.e. status of the constraints for entities that are in the TES of transactions running at a given time.

Given the integrity constraint rules and the three phase-state communication, the entity-state transaction management scheme is described as follows:

1.   When a new transaction is issued, check its $\{c\}^B$ conditions for $<e,s>_g$, where $<e,s>_g$ is the global fully committed database version. If not all $\{c\}^B$ are satisfied, reject the transaction.

2.   Check the transactions $\{c\}^B$ conditions for each $<e,s>_1$, where $<e,s>_1$ represents the current status of the relevant constraints on entities in the transaction log. $<e,s>_1$ is the current information in the log registered for each currently active (running) transaction. If all $\{c\}^B$ are not satisfied, reject the transaction.

3. If there is readset $\{c\}R$ in the transaction then read $<e,s>$, doublet for each entity in the TES to local $<e,s>_c$. That is:

$$<e,s>_c \quad <- \quad <e,s>_g$$

where $<e,s>_c$ is the local copy and $<e,s>_g$ is the global database version. Note that this can be either an assignment or a message followed by an assignment.

4. Update all $\{c\}^B$ to $\{c\}^D$ in $<e,s>_c$ so that a new transaction which conflicts with the current transaction will be rejected. For this, register the transaction into the log:

$$<e,s>_1 \quad <- \quad \{c\}^D$$

The log entry has the effect of communicating the transaction to concurrent transactions in the system. This step is the end of the *before* phase and indicates an initiating transaction.

5. Execute the actions of the transaction.

6. Search the log for all transactions that have joint entities and whose $\{c\}^B$ conditions could be affected by the current transaction's $\{c\}^A$ conditions after the current transaction commits. Send messages to such concurrent transactions for negotiating an abort. The criteria for negotiation can be precedence relations between the transactions. This is the final step of the *during* phase.

7. If not aborted then upgrade all $\{c\}^D$ to $\{c\}^A$ in all $<e,s>_1$. This step indicates the end of *after* phase.

8. Transmit $<e,s>_1$ to the database by:

$$<e,s>_g \quad <- \quad <e,s>_1$$

to denote termination of this transaction in the transaction log. Search the log for all previous transactions whose $\{c\}^B$ conditions could be affected by the current transaction. Flag these for review. This step is the end of commit.

9. Database should pass on the new values to those transactions in the log that share entities with the committed transaction.

The proposed scheme supports application-level consistency rather than serial consistency available in traditional database systems and as a result, there is a certain cost associated with it [3]. The cost of this scheme is due to:

1. Defining the relevant states of an entity is terms of $\{c\}^B$, $\{c\}^D$, $\{c\}^A$ and adding these states to a transaction class.

2. Pre-analysis of a transaction instance using $\{c\}^B$.

3. Communication between a running transaction and the log for updating constraints.

4. Communication between concurrent transactions to check the status of joint entities before committing.

The cost associated with this technique seems unavoidable since the integrity and consistency of an engineering database must be maintained either manually or automatically. Up to now, alternative management schemes integrating both (integrity maintenance and concurrency control) have not existed. However, management of integrity is a major effort in engineering design and a common cause of failures.

4.3   Application of Transaction Management Scheme

In the combined database that incorporates both piping and structural subsystems and managed by entity-state transaction management, the communication provided by database management is very helpful. Suppose that the structural engineer has defined the structural topology using T_6 and is about the analyze the elements to determine their moment and shear using T_7. This transaction will not run, in the integrated formulation, until the piping topology (T_1), flow (T_2), parameters (T_3) and fittings (T_4), have been correctly defined. Similarly, suppose after the structural sizing, the mechanical engineer finds that the layout of the piping must be altered, for example, because some new mechanical equipment has been added to the design. Both the T_2 and T_3 piping transactions and the T_7 structural transaction must be re-run. These results will occur naturally as a result of entity-state transaction management.

Because each of the transactions in this example have been defined to correspond closely to current forms of engineering application software, they each operate on all pipes or all structural members and no sharing of structural elements across multiple concurrent structural analysis is allowed. The method described here can be extended to partial analysis with the addition of nested transactions. Any iteration of an early application reverts all entities to an earlier state.

The following example shows how communication between transactions work. Suppose a T_7 transaction is currently active. It leaves in the local log a record indicating its existence and its $\{c\}^D$ constraints. Later a T_3 transaction is iterated (it was run and committed once earlier and thus $\{c_3\}$ is set). At the time of its re-initiation, its preconditions are satisfied and it begins. If it terminates with an abort, it has no effect. But if it completes before T_7, then prior to committing it searches the log and identifies that its $\{c\}^D$ state conflicts with a current transaction's $\{c\}^B$. This indicates a possible change in values of the entities referenced in T_7. Based on Step #6 of the management scheme, the iterated version of T_3 would communicate its proposed change to T_7 where it is expected that the two designers would review the effects prior to the commit of T_3 and mutually agree on the form of the change.

If T_3 was iterated and completed after T_7 was committed, then T_3 would invalidate C_4. Step #8 would flag T_7 as possibly invalidated and needing review. Each transaction only invalidates its immediate successor. It is the responsibility of step #8 of the transaction management scheme to flag successor transactions, or chains of successors. As policies, several variations of #8 could be applied. All possibly invalidated transactions could be identified earlier, in step #6, and negotiated before the commit, in order to evaluate the cost of the change. Also, one update change may propagate a review to a succeeding transaction and the succeeding transactions could propagate to others, in a cascaded chain. The complete chain could be flagged to be reviewed, if desired. Such policies could vary during design, so that early in design, changes would not be pre-evaluated or chains of changes propagated, while late in design they both would be.

5 Conclusion

Database systems that support engineering design are complex in nature and require special techniques to model both data and operations. The scheme developed for transaction management and applied to design examples in this paper, explicitly deals with the management of operations. It also presents implications for the database schema design. The doublet $<e,s>$, which provides state definitions for database entities, implies the integrated definition of entities together with their possible states. The transaction class definition, on the other hand incorporates the operations with this doublet. This representation is consistent and supportive of *object-oriented database systems* where a class encapsulates entities with the routines that manipulate them. Thus, it can be concluded that the scope and the domain of a transaction class define the level of abstraction it applies to.

Entity state management is not a constraint propagation scheme that can determine if changes must be made to specific variables in some other entities.

It is a transaction management scheme that provides integrity communication between diverse serial and concurrent applications. It does suggest, however, how constraint management might be developed in such application areas.

In this paper, it is shown that the application of the revised transaction definition provides generality and flexibility for the management of design projects. It not only allows partial integrity at database states, but exemplifies how integrity is added or eliminated by transactions in a database. It leads to a scheme where it is possible to represent and manage:

- precedence ordering

- iteration

- concurrency control

- amount of integrity satisfied

for possible transactions in a design project.

Note

This paper is an adaptation of "Transaction Management in Engineering Databases" by A. Kutay and C. Eastman, *Proceedings of 1983 SIGMOD Conference, ACM*, pp. 73-80.

Acknowledgement

This work was partially supported by a National Science Foundation grant, number DDM-8915665.

References

[1] Bernstein, P.A., Shipman, D.W., Wong, W.S.
Formal aspects of serializability in database concurrency
    control.
IEEE, Trans. Software Eng. SE-5(3), May, 1979.

[2] Eastman, C.M.
Database Facilities for Engineering Design.
Proc. IEEE 69(10), October, 1981.

[3] Eastman, C.M., Kutay, A.R.
Transactions and Concurrency in Engineering Databases.
IBS Report, CMU, 1982.

[4] Eswaren, K.P., Gray, J.N., Lorie, R.A., Traiger, I.L.
The notions of consistency and predicate locks in a shared database system.
Communications ACM 19(2): 624-633, Nov., 1976.

[5] Gray, J.
Notes on Database Operating Systems.
Operating Systems - An Advanced Course.
Springer Verlag, 1978.

[6] Kung, H.T. and J.T. Robinson
On optimistic methods of concurrency control.
ACM Transaction Database Systems 6,2 (June 1981), 213-226.

[7] Moss, J. Eliot
Nested Transactions: An Approach to Reliable Distributed Computing.
MIT Press, 1985.

A Model of Concurrent, Cooperating Transactions in an Object-Oriented Database

Andrea H. Skarra

Brown University
Department of Computer Science
Providence, RI 02192

Abstract

We describe a model of transactions and concurrency control that supports cooperative task and data sharing among users. The model augments traditional correctness criteria, such as global consistency for individual transactions and serializability for concurrent transactions, with programmer-defined correctness criteria that uniformly integrate both data and application semantics. Individual transactions are not required to maintain global consistency. Rather, transactions cooperate in groups, such that transaction groups are the units of consistency. The context for the model is an extensible object-oriented database: abstract data types define the behavior and representation of their instance objects, and each object is accessed only by way of the strict operational interface defined by its type. Applications can incrementally contribute new types to the database. The model effectively represents a transaction management system that is programmable by knowledgeable application designers. Although developed toward the needs of applications that provide computer support for cooperative activities, such as office information systems, graphical programming environments, and CAD tools for electronic or mechanical domains, the model provides a framework for any application for which the traditional transaction model is too restrictive. The model's key features are a nested framework of transaction groups that encapsulate nonserializable data sharing and a method for localized specification of semantic correctness criteria for concurrent histories of cooperating transactions.

1. Introduction

We describe a concurrency control model that supports cooperative data sharing among transactions. Traditional correctness criteria, such as global consistency for individual transactions and serializability for concurrent transactions, are replaced by programmer-defined correctness criteria that uniformly integrate both data and application semantics. The context for the model is an object-oriented database: abstract data types define the behavior and representation of their instance objects, and each object is accessed only by way of the strict operational interface defined by its type [ZW]. The model effectively represents a transaction management system that is programmable by knowledgeable application designers. Although it was developed for the needs of applications that provide computer support for cooperative activities, such as office information systems, graphical programming environments, and CAD tools for electronic or mechanical domains, the model provides a framework for any application for which the traditional transaction model is too restrictive. The model's key features are a nested framework of transaction groups that encapsulate nonserializable data sharing and a method of localized specifications for semantic correctness criteria in lieu of serializability for concurrent histories.

Traditional transactions are isolated, unrelated interactions between users and a database that preserve global consistency. Each is atomic, and concurrent executions are serializable. In cooperative applications, however, users interact not only with the database but also with each other. Data objects are commonly large, nested, and interrelated by many consistency constraints. Tasks are divided into simpler, parallel subtasks that are distributed among people and machines to reduce complexity. As a result, subtasks are commonly spanned by constraints; they are interdependent with respect to the data they access and with respect to the task of which they are subtasks. Transactions that correspond to these subtasks cannot execute in parallel under serializability. Moreover, each may have to modify an unreasonably large amount of data and violate the modularity of the subtask in order to preserve global consistency. We believe that it is not possible in general to define cooperative subtasks that are small enough to be manageable, yet large enough to be globally consistent. Atomicity and global consistency are too restrictive as the sole correctness criteria for synchronization. Furthermore, locking objects and suspending/aborting transactions are inappropriate as control mechanisms. Sessions are long, interactive, and dynamically constructed. A transaction, for example, might consist of steps taken by a designer using a graphical editor.

Section 2 discusses previous research that is either foundational to our approach or that proposes alternate solutions to the problem. Section 3 describes our model of cooperating transactions and correctness criteria, and section 4 presents an example application and its specification within the model. A summary concludes the paper.

2. Related Research

Foundational work for this model includes semantic concurrency control, nested transactions, and transaction groups. Related work includes nonatomic transaction models with improved flexibility for collaborative applications that are characterized by complex data manipulations and long design sessions. Several models include correctness criteria to supplant the traditional criteria, global consistency and atomicity.

Semantic concurrency control refers to algorithms that exploit the semantics of data, operations, and applications to define correctness and achieve higher levels of concurrency [AM, HW, S, W]. The approach is a generalization of synchronization under Read/Write semantics. Relationships between the operations defined on a type are used to produce concurrent histories under semantic atomicity. That is, the history cannot be distinguished from a serial history by operations defined by the data types. Our model uses several concepts from semantic concurrency control, like specifications over the operations of types. However, it extends semantic atomicity as a correctness criterion to allow application-specific correctness criteria.

Nested transactions extend transaction theory to a multilevel model in which transactions are contained in other transactions [M]. Each subtransaction executes atomically with respect to its parent and siblings. That is, a transaction receives the results of its subtransactions only when they commit, and the subtransactions execute under serializability. Our model provides a more flexible synchronization paradigm by allowing the specification of different criteria for correctness and synchronization on different TGs.

Earlier work on transaction groups [FZ] includes a hierarchical caching model and Read/Write locks with nonserializable semantics. We use the notion of nested groups of nonatomic transactions, and we extend the semantics to include those of arbitrary abstract types. Other models that use novel lock types include [HZ, K, SZR]. While novel lock types provide the flexibility required for cooperating transactions, they do not provide the control nor a way to specify criteria for correctness.

Another approach that provides a more flexible model of data sharing is one that supports Read-only versions [EEET, KC, KW]. Each modification of an object generates a new version. Versioning models, like novel lock types, fail to provide correctness criteria for concurrent access. Moreover, unrestrained proliferation of versions requires complex, human intervention to reconcile coexistent, parallel versions.

Other models of correctness criteria include specifications over the operations in transactions, namely semantic atomicity [G, GS] and multilevel atomicity [L]. Under semantic atomicity, transactions are grouped into compatibility sets, and the transactions in the same set are interleaved arbitrarily. Recovery is provided by countersteps or compensating transactions. Under multilevel atomicity, transactions are grouped in hierarchical sets, where there are greater degrees of interleaving at deeper nested levels. The breakpoints in a transaction where interleaving can occur is specified with the transaction. Both approaches are based on a model in which transactions are statically defined operation sequences, or at least predefined tasks. In a collaborative domain, sessions may be interactive and dynamically determined. Moreover, the correctness criteria in both approaches are fixed for all applications, and neither specification is localized to facilitate evolution and change.

[KKB] and [KS] describe a model of transactions and correctness for CAD applications. The model comprises multilevel transactions with synchronization by predicatewise two-phase locking. Each transaction maintains a set of constraints; a subtransaction's constraints are no stronger than its parent's. The set is a conjunction of constraints, and each conjunct is associated with a set of data items. A transaction observes two-phase locking for each conjunct's set of data items. Predicatewise two-phase locking is weaker than serializability, but it does not allow some of the criteria that can be defined in our model. For example, it does not allow a transaction to read several times from another that continues to modify a data item.

3. A Model for Cooperating Transactions

We describe a model of concurrent transactions that supports and controls collaborative interaction among database users in addition to interactions between users and the database. It consists of a semantic specification and control paradigm within which programmers define both transactions and the correctness criteria for concurrent histories. The database system in turn uses the specifications to control the behavior of concurrent transactions and to produce only those histories that satisfy the criteria. Unlike traditional transaction models, individual transactions in this model are not required to maintain global consistency across the database, and they are not limited to the kind of data sharing that satisfies transaction atomicity. Instead, transactions can *cooperate* in groups to achieve consistency across the data they access and the tasks they perform. Indeed, a group of cooperating transactions replaces the traditional transaction in our model as the unit of consistency.

3.1. Cooperating Transactions and Transaction Groups

A *cooperating transaction* (CT) is an initiator of operation invocations that is defined by a programmer as a member of a transaction group. It generates an operation invocation sequence that is dynamically determined, rather than statically defined. The correctness criteria for the invocations are defined by its group and supergroups.

A *transaction group* (TG) is a user-defined collection of CTs or other TGs that includes an explicit and semantic specification of a correctness criterion for the group's histories. A TG's criterion specification locally defines the extent to which the members of the TG satisfy global consistency, either individually or together, and the rules under which they share data. The criteria that an application defines for its TGs can vary from serializability to no restraint, depending on the semantics of the application's TGs and data, but in each case the TG hierarchies *encapsulate and localize* interdependent data sharing. Every user-defined TG is a member of some group: either a user-defined group or the system-defined group, G_0. G_0 is the supergroup of all user-defined TGs (i.e., the root group), and it defines and maintains global consistency across all the data in the database. Its criterion specification stipulates that each G_0 member individually maintains global consistency and that G_0 members are synchronized to preserve the atomicity of each.

3.2. Correctness Criteria

A TG's correctness criterion specification defines the correctness of the TG on the basis of its histories. A criterion describes a set of valid concurrent histories of the TG by describing the histories' content and form. The valid histories consist of operation sequences that preserve consistency within or between objects of the same or different type. A TG generates a history from the operation invocations of its members (Figure 1). In particular, a TG's history is an interleaving of the operation invocation sequences of its members who are CTs and the histories of its members who are TGs (i.e., subgroups). A TG's correctness criterion may actually comprise a number of criteria, each of which individually describes a (different) set of histories; the intersection of the individual sets constitutes the set of correct histories. A correct history satisfies all of the TG's criteria simultaneously.

In particular, a TG's history is *correct* if both of the following are true: the history satisfies the TG's criteria specification, and the subhistories are respectively correct for each of the TG's subgroups. That is, the local correctness specification of the group and those of all its subgroups are satisfied in a correct history. The operation invocations of a CT appear in the history of its group and in that of every supergroup, and for each of these groups, the CT's invocations participate in satisfying the group's criteria for its histories. If a group's history is invalidated by an invocation, then not only is the group's history incorrect, but the histories of its supergroups are also incorrect. The system history, H_0, is correct when the criteria specified by every group in the database (i.e., G_0 and all the user-defined groups) are satisfied.

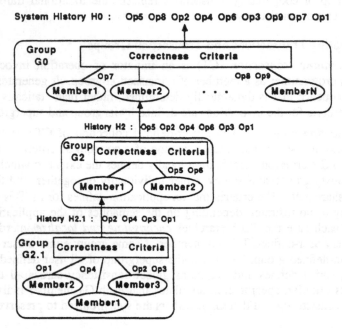

Figure 1. A TG generates a history from the operation invocations of its members. The ordering of invocations in the history is determined by the TG's correctness criteria.

3.3. Specification of Correctness Criteria

The model supports correctness criteria that are declarative descriptions of valid histories. A *pattern* criterion describes operation invocation sequences that are *required* in a correct history, and a *conflict* criterion describes sequences that are *prohibited*. Patterns and conflicts alike are defined with a construct called a *pattern machine*. A pattern machine is a finite state automaton whose power is augmented with the addition of local variables, the ability to evaluate simple predicates over operation invocations and the local variables, and the ability to perform actions such as updating the variables and sending messages. A pattern machine recognizes the operation invocation sequences that are required and prohibited by the patterns and conflicts it represents.

A history *satisfies* a TG's criteria specification when it contains all of the invocation sequences that the TG's patterns require and none of the sequences that the TG's conflicts prohibit. That is, the pattern machines that implement the patterns and conflicts parse each history in parallel, beginning in their start states, and every machine is in a final state at the end of a correct history. A history is *incorrect* when at least one machine of the group or its subgroups is in a dead state. The history is *incomplete* if a machine is in a nonfinal, but not dead, state (Figure 2).

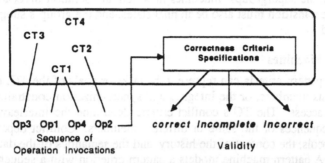

Figure 2. A hierarchical correctness specification for a collection of cooperating transactions determines the correctness of a sequence of their operation invocations.

3.4. Localization of Criteria

The model supports pattern and conflict criteria that are *localized* to the members of a single TG and to the operations of a minimal number of types in order to simplify specification for users and facilitate schema evolution. That is, each TG's criteria are defined in terms of the TG's members alone, and each criterion includes the operations of only a minimal number of types. A criterion can exclude other types in the database, even when operations are nested, such that other types access the same objects as do the criterion types. The model accommodates these localizations in its definition of the way that a history satisfies or violates a criterion. As a result, users need to define only localized correctness criteria in order to specify correct histories over multiple and arbitrary groups and types. For brevity, this document only considers the criteria of types whose operations do not access other types.

3.5. Synchronization

The database system produces only correct concurrent histories. That is, it prevents the formation of any history that violates any of the TGs' criteria. It does so by using the criteria specifications of G_0 and the user-defined TGs to synchronize group members and govern data sharing among them and to decide when groups can commit. When a group commits, its history becomes *stable* (i.e., resilient to failures in the system).

The system dynamically matches each operation invocation initiated by a CT against the pattern and conflict criteria of the CT's group and supergroups, and it prevents or delays the operation's execution if it violates any of the criteria. That is, if an operation matches an arc that goes to a dead state in one of the pattern machines, then the operation request is denied. A CT is never suspended, even if all of its operation invocations are delayed. It can continue to invoke other operations that do not depend on the suspended ones.

The system allows a TG to commit only when its commit as a member of its supergroup is correct. That is, a TG can commit only when its history maintains the kind of consistency that is prescribed by its subgroups' criteria, by its own criteria, and by its supergroup's criteria for the TG as a member. The group's pattern machines must all be in final states, the supergroups' machines in which an operation invocation of the group caused a state transition must also be in final states, and the group's subgroups must have all committed.

3.6. Pattern Machines

A TG's pattern criteria can represent the tasks or goals of the TG, the collaboration protocols of its members, or the integrity and synchronization constraints on the objects its members access. The TG's conflict criteria determine the interleaving of operation invocation sequences of the same or different members. Conflict depends on the TG's sharing protocols, the context of the history, and the semantics of the data and operations themselves. A pattern machine models a pattern criterion with a sequence of transitions from its start state to a final state for every history in which the operation invocations required by the pattern appear in the specified order. In contrast, it models conflict criteria by transitions to dead states for operation invocation orderings that are prohibited.

A pattern machine is a tuple of the form $< \Sigma, K, s, F, V, v, A, \delta, m >$, where

Σ	is the alphabet of operation invocations in the histories described by a pattern and its conflicts,
K	is a finite set of states,
$s \in K$	is the start state,
$F \subseteq K$	is the set of final states,
V	is a set of variable objects local to the machine,
v	is the initializing value assignment for the objects in V,
A	is a set of actions performed by the machine,
δ	is a transition function, and
m	is a set of group members after whose commit the criteria implemented by the machine are removed.

A pattern machine recognizes a set of histories over a set of objects, O, and a subset of a group's members, M, from an alphabet, Σ. Σ is a (not necessarily proper) subset of Σ_O, the alphabet of all possible operation invocations on the objects by the members of the group. In particular, Σ and Σ_O are described as follows, where Ops is the set of operations defined by the objects' types, $parami$ is the set of values for the ith parameter of each operation, $Op \in Ops$, and $N_{Op} \geq 1$ is the number of Op's parameters:

$$\Sigma \subseteq \Sigma_O = \bigcup_{Op \in Ops} Op \times param1 \times param2 \times \cdots \times paramN_{Op} \times M$$

Σ is an infinite set when a parameter's domain is infinite for some $Op \in Ops$. Consequently, Σ is represented in a pattern machine as a finite set of tuples in which parameter values are described by predicates. For example, a single Σ tuple, $< Withdraw (ac, amount \geq 0), M1 >$, represents an infinite number of Withdraw operation invocation tuples for a Bank_Account object, ac, a member, M1, and a nonnegative amount of money.

The transition function, δ, provides a mapping from operation invocations in Σ, states in K, and values of the local variables in V, to states in K and subsets of the actions in A. The actions can result in a new value for the local variables in V. In particular, δ is the following function, where Vi is the set of values for the ith variable in V, and 2^A is the power set of A:

$$\delta: \Sigma \times K \times V1 \times V2 \times \cdots \times VN \rightarrow K \times 2^A$$

δ is specified as a finite set of *transition tuples* of the form < Pred, s1, s2, Ac >, where

Pred   is a predicate that returns *match* for an operation invocation in Σ and a value for the variables in V, when from the machine state s1, they map to the state s2, and the actions in Ac. Otherwise, Pred returns *nomatch*.

s1 $\in$ K   is a machine state that maps to state s2 for the set of combinations of operation invocation and variable values described by Pred,

s2 $\in$ K   is a machine state to which state s1 maps for the set described by Pred, and

Ac $\subseteq$ A   is the set of actions to which state s1 maps for the set described by Pred.

Each tuple contains a predicate that describes a (possibly infinite) set of combinations for the operation invocation and local variable state. A predicate is used in each tuple, rather than a single value for invocation and local state, to allow a finite representation of δ when Σ, V1, V2, . . . , or VN is an infinite set. In particular, the transition function partitions the (infinite) set of invocation and variable combinations at each machine state, s1, with a finite number of predicates. Each predicate at s1 describes the (infinite) combinations that map from s1 to the same machine state, s2, and set of actions, Ac. The predicate, together with s1, s2, and Ac, compose a single transition tuple. If each tuple were instead to contain a single invocation and local variable state, an infinite set of tuples could be required for δ to specify the mapping.

δ contains a transition tuple, T: < Pred, s1, s2, Ac >, where Pred is matched by operation invocation O and local variable value v1, if both of the following are true: (1) T represents a mapping that is valid under the transition function from s1, O, and v1, to a state, s2, and a set of actions, Ac, and (2) s2 $\neq$ s1 or Ac is a nonempty set of actions. Transition tuples may be excluded for operations whose execution causes no change in the state of the pattern machine. An operation invocation matches at most one transition tuple predicate for a particular machine state and local variable value; it may match none.

The m field in a pattern machine designates the members of the group whose commit marks the end of that portion of the history to which the machine applies. That is, the machine implements criteria that describe only that portion of the group's history that precedes the commit of the members in m. For example, a machine that prevents the value of a member's Write() operation from being read by another member does not apply to the portion of the history that follows the first member's commit. The conflict criteria that a machine implements are effectively masked in the group's specification after the members in m have all committed.

4. An Example

A design group that prepares for a product presentation in another city defines a collection of nested TGs (Figure 3). The TGs define a variety of correctness criteria for their respective histories with patterns and conflicts over the operations of the following types:

Time — *Arrival Time*

R (t : Time) : Time_Value	*Read time and return value*
W (t : Time, new : Time_Value) : OK	*Write time and return OK*

Schedule — *Presentation Schedule*

R (s : Sched) : Sched_Value	*Read schedule and return value*
W (s : Sched, new : Sched_Value) : OK	*Write schedule and return OK*
Cmp (s : Sched) : Sched_Value	*Compact schedule (remove gaps) and return new schedule*

Slides — *Presentation Slides*

R (s : Slides) : Slide_Values	*Read slides and return value*
Pr (s : Slides) : OK	*Print slides and return OK*
W (s : Slides, new : Slide_Values) : OK	*Write slides and return OK*

Account — *Account for Travel Funds*

R (a : Acct) : Real	*Read account balance and return value*
Dp (a : Acct, amount : Real) : OK	*Deposit to account and return OK*
Wd (a : Acct, amount : Real) : OK or Insuff[1]	*Withdraw from account and return OK or Insuff*

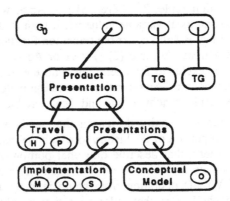

Figure 3. An application defines a TG hierarchy for the preparation of a product presentation in another city.

The TGs define different sharing protocols among their members for the types. Product Presentation synchronizes Travel and Presentations under serializability. Although both tasks must complete for consistency, travel arrangements are independent of the presentations themselves. In Travel, Hotel (H) and Plane (P) are CTs that are interdependent with respect to an arrival time, ta; hotels require notice of late arrivals. P modifies ta, and Travel allows H to read ta while P is in progress. In Product Presentations, however, Presentations cannot read ta until Travel completes because of the serializability criterion. In Presentations, both Implementation and Conceptual Model can concurrently read and write the current presentation schedule, sc, but they cannot share each other's presentation slides. Within Implementation, however, Objects (O), Messages (M), and Storage (S) can read each other's presentations concurrently.

4.1. Pattern and Conflict Criteria

The design group's TGs define their correctness criteria as patterns and conflicts over the operation invocations of their members on the types. The criteria preserve consistency across one or more objects of the same or different type, and they specify the sharing protocols. The criteria of each TG are localized to the TG's members. That is, each criterion is defined over the members of a single TG. It is independent of the TG's subgroup structure. The criteria for the design group's TGs are as follows, where the bracketed tuples are operation invocations that include the operation name, its parameters, and the TG member that invokes the operation. The designation *any* in the tuples means "any value for this field." The pattern machines that implement the TGs' criteria are described next in §4.2.

Product Presentation TG

The Product Presentation TG defines serializability as a criterion for its members, Travel and Presentations with the following type-specific criteria. Product Presentation also requires that the arrival time is read by Presentations when set by Travel.

C1: A Time object is not modified by a member after another member has read the value.
For every object t : Time and any members, T1 ≠ T2, < R (t), T1 > is not followed by < W (t, any), T2 > until after < Commit ( ), T1 > appears in the history.

C2: A Time object is not read or modified by a member after another member has modified it.
For every object t : Time and any members, T1 ≠ T2, < W (t, any), T1 > is not followed by either < R (t), T2 > or < W (t, any), T2 > until after < Commit ( ), T1 > appears in the history.

C3: A Sched object is not modified by a member after another member has read the value.
For every object s : Sched and any members, T1 ≠ T2, < R (s), T1 > is not followed by < W (s, any), T2 > or < Cmp (s), T2 > until after < Commit ( ), T1 > appears in the history.

---

[1] Account balances are always ≥ 0; Wd does nothing and returns Insuff when funds are insufficient for a withdrawal.

C4: A Sched object is not read or modified by a member after another member has modified it.

For every object s : Sched and any members, $T1 \neq T2$, < W (s, any), T1 > and < Cmp (s), T1 > are not followed by either < R (s), T2 >, < W (s, any), T2 >, or < Cmp (s), T2 > until after < Commit ( ), T1 > appears in the history.

C5: A Slides object is not modified by a member after another member has read the value.

For every object sl : Slides and any members, $T1 \neq T2$, < R (sl), T1 > and < Pr (sl), T1 > are not followed by < W (sl, any), T2 > until after < Commit ( ), T1 > appears in the history.

C6: A Slides object is not read or modified by a member after another member has modified it.

For every object sl : Slides and any members, $T1 \neq T2$, < W (sl, any), T1 > is not followed by either < R (sl), T2 >, < Pr (sl), T2 >, or < W (sl, any), T2 > until after < Commit ( ), T1 > appears in the history.

C7: An Acct object is not modified by a member after another member has read the value.

For every object ac : Acct and any members, $T1 \neq T2$, < R (ac), T1 > is not followed by < Dp (ac, any), T2 > or < Wd (ac, any), T2 > until after < Commit ( ), T1 > appears in the history.

C8: An Acct object is not read by a member after another member has modified it.

For every object ac : Acct and any members, $T1 \neq T2$, < Dp (ac, any), T1 > and < Wd (ac, any), T1 > are not followed by < R (ac), T2 > until after < Commit ( ), T1 > appears in the history.

C9: A member does not withdraw funds from an account from which another member previously deposited or withdrew funds.[2]

For every object ac : Acct and any members, $T1 \neq T2$, < Dp (ac, any), T1 > and < Wd (ac, any), T1 > are not followed by < Wd (ac, any), T2 > until after < Commit ( ), T1 > appears in the history.

C10: A modification to the arrival time object ta by Travel is read by Presentations and reconciled with the current schedule object sc.

For objects ta : Time and sc : Schedule, < W (ta, any), Travel > must be followed by both < R (ta), Presentations > and < R (sc), Presentations >.

Travel TG

Travel defines a cooperative protocol for its members and the arrival time object ta. The protocol consists of a single criterion C11 instead of the criteria C1-C2 that Product Presentations uses. Members H and P can concurrently read and write object ta, provided both members commit with the same value. Travel also defines a collaborative

---

[2]Product Presentation uses commutativity as a conflict definition. However, it does not prevent a Dp from following a Wd, because failed Wd operations do not appear in histories. Dp operations commute with previous Wd operations that completed successfully.

protocol for the presentation's travel fund account object acp. The protocol consists of criterion C12 instead of the criteria C7-C9. A member's withdrawal does not preclude other members' withdrawals, while a member's deposits are protected against another member's withdrawal only until the first member withdraws an amount greater than or equal to his deposits. For other objects, it defines the same criteria as Product Presentations, namely C1-C9.

C11: A member whose access to object ta is overwritten by another member reads ta before committing.

For object ta : Time and any members, $T1 \neq T2$, $< R (ta), T1 >$ must follow a sequence in which $< R (ta), T1 >$ or $< W (ta, any), T1 >$ is followed by $< W (ta, any), T2 >$ before $< Commit ( ), T1 >$ appears in the history.

C12: A member does not withdraw funds from account acp when another member's net deposit is positive.

For object acp : Acct and any members, $T1 \neq T2$, $< Dp (acp, amount1), T1 >$ is not followed by $< Wd (acp, any), T2 >$ until after $< Commit ( ), T1 >$ appears in the history, or until a number of $< Wd (acp, amount2), T1 >$ tuples appear in the history, such that the sum of the amount2's is greater than or equal to the sum of the amount1's.

Presentations TG

Presentations defines a cooperative protocol for the current schedule object sc. The protocol consists of a criterion C13 instead of the criteria C3-C4 that Product Presentations uses. Members Implementation and Conceptual Model can concurrently read and write object sc, provided both members commit with the same value. For other objects, it defines the same criteria as Product Presentations, namely C1-C9. The group Presentations also defines a criterion that requires that a modified Sched object must be compacted before the group commits. The criterion C14 is member-independent; one member's Compact suffices for any member's preceding Write.

C13: A member whose access to object sc is overwritten by another member reads sc before committing.

For object sc : Sched and any members, $T1 \neq T2$, $< R (sc), T1 >$ must follow a sequence in which $< R (sc), T1 >$, $< W (sc, any), T1 >$, or $< Cmp (s), T1 >$ is followed by $< W (sc, any), T2 >$ or $< Cmp (s), T2 >$ before $< Commit ( ), T1 >$ appears in the history.

C14: Object sc is compacted after modification.

For every object s : Sched, $< W (s, any), any >$ must be followed by $< Cmp (s), any >$ before $< Commit ( ), Presentations >$ appears in the history.

Implementation TG

Implementation defines criterion C15 to ensure that the group's slide handout is complete and current. It requires that there is at least one print of each member's presentation slides and that modified slides are reprinted. Members can read each other presentation slides under criterion C16, but each slides object is modified by only one member. Msl is member M's slides, Osl is O's slides, and Ssl is S's slides. For other objects, Implementation defines the same criteria as Product Presentations, namely C1-C9.

C15: The presentation slides are printed at least once, and modified slides are reprinted.

For each object sl ∈ { Msl, Osl, Ssl } , there is at least one < Pr (sl), any > before < Commit ( ), Implementation > appears in the history, without an intervening < W (sl, any), any > .

C16: Objects Msl, Osl, and Ssl are not modified by a member after another member has read or modified them.

For the object, member pair (sl : Slides, T member-of Impl) from { (Msl,M), (Osl,O), (Ssl,S) }, and a member that is not T, $\overline{T}$, < R (sl), $\underline{T}$ >, < Pr (sl), T >, and < W (sl, any), T > are not followed by < W (sl, any), $\overline{T}$ > until after < Commit ( ), T > appears in the history.

4.2. Pattern Machines

Each pattern machine is defined locally over the members of a single TG. It does not distinguish among the members of the TG's subgroups. That is, an operation invocation by member P, such as < Read (t), P >, is not distinguishable from the same invocation by member H, < Read (t), H >, for purposes of their comparison to criteria in Product Presentation. Figure 4 illustrates the machines that implement the design group's pattern and conflict criteria for a single instance of each type, namely ta :Time (arrival time), sc : Sched (current presentation schedule), Ssl : Slides (member S's presentation slides), and acp : Acct (presentation travel funds account). The machines for other instances of the types to which the criteria apply are analogous. In the case of criteria C1-C9, C11-C13, and C16, the figure shows the machine for only a single member. The machines that implement the criteria for the other members of the groups are analogous. Each transition arc in a machine is labelled with an operation invocation upon whose successful completion the arc is traversed from the current state.[3] Some arcs also carry an italicized label that indicates an action that the machine performs upon traversal of the arc. A machine no longer applies to histories of a TG after the TG member(s) in m commit(s).

The operation of the machines is illustrated by histories H1 and H2 of the TG Product Presentation. Neither history is correct for Product Presentation.

H1:   < R(ta),H >   < Dp(acp,$50),H >   < W(ta),P >   < Wd(acp,$10),P >   < R(ta),M >

C1:	s0	s1	s1	s1	s1	s1
C2:	s0	s0	s0	s1	s1	s2†
C10:	s0	s0	s0	s1*	s1*	s3*
C11:	s0	s1	s1	s2*	s2*	s2*
C12:	s0	s0	s1	s1	s2†	s2†

---

[3] A circle represents a state, an arrow head indicates the start state, and double circles are final states.

365

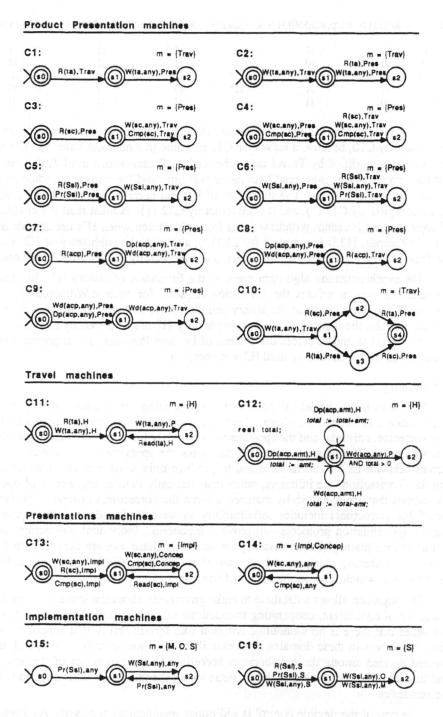

Figure 4. Pattern machines that implement the design group's criteria.

H2: $< R(ta),H >$ $< Dp(acp,\$50),H >$ $< W(ta),P >$ $< R(ta),H >$ $< Wd(acp,\$50),H >$ $Wd(acp,\$10),P >$

C1:	s0	s1	s1	s1	s1	s1	s1
C2:	s0	s0	s0	s1	s1	s1	s1
C10:	s0	s0	s0	s1*	s1*	s1*	s1*
C11:	s0	s1	s1	s2*	s1	s1	s1
C12:	s0	s0	s1	s1	s1	s1	s1

H1 is incorrect by C2, because it leaves the C2 machine in a dead state (†), and it is incomplete by C10, because it leaves the C10 machine in a nonfinal state (*). The arrival time object ta modified by Travel cannot be read by Presentations until Travel commits, and then Presentations must read both the arrival time and the current schedule object sc in order to reconcile them. The subhistory of H1 that corresponds to Travel's history is also incomplete by C11 (*), and it is incorrect by C12 (†). H must read P's modification of object ta, and P cannot withdraw funds from object acp when H's net deposit is positive. In contrast, H2 is incomplete for C10 (*), although the subhistory of H2 is correct for Travel. Presentations must read object ta as modified by Travel after Travel commits.

The synchronization algorithm prevents the formation of history H1. In particular, the database system refuses the invocation requests for both $< Wd(acp,\$10),P >$ and $< R(ta),M >$ at those points in the history and thus prevents their execution at objects acp and ta. Further, the algorithm requires that history H2 is completed by a Pres member's reading objects ta and sc before the commit of Product Presentation. It prevents Product Presentation from committing until H2 was complete.

5. Summary

We describe a model of concurrent, cooperating transactions that includes a specification and control paradigm. Application programmers specify transactions and their correctness criteria, and the specification uniformly integrates both data and transaction semantics. The database system in turn uses the specifications to control the concurrent behavior of the transactions and to produce only those histories that satisfy the criteria. Transactions are initiators, rather than statically defined sequences, of operation invocations that are dynamically matched against the correctness criteria. The range of specifiable correctness includes serializability as well as data-dependent requirements like design validation protocols that prove components. Individual transactions are not required to maintain global consistency across the database, nor are they restricted to the kind of data sharing that preserves the atomicity of each. Rather, they are defined in nested groups which serve as the unit(s) of consistency.

The approach allows a database to make guarantees about the semantic integrity and resiliency of concurrent, cooperating transactions that are specified by users. It reflects our belief that there is no monolithic criterion like serializability that supports cooperation; correctness in these domains is necessarily application-specific. Tasks and data are divided divided among the collaborators according to the semantics of the application and its data. The correctness of their transactions depends on the division, and hence on the semantics.

The cost of the flexible control is additional specification for users. As a result, the model simplifies specifications and at the same time facilitates schema evolution by supporting localized correctness criteria. Localization is particularly useful for simplifying specifications in the presence of nested operations and nested transaction groups. The criteria specifications in the model replace the specifications in traditional applications of statically defined transactions that preserve consistency, so part of the specification cost for criteria is offset by the absence of specifications for transactions. Further, we envision a persistent library of criteria specifications and support tools that facilitate their reuse. Future work includes developing a model of recovery and cooperative strategies for conflict and deadlock resolution.

6. References

[AM] J. E. Allchin, M. S. McKendry. "Synchronization and Recovery of Actions," In *Proceedings of the Second Annual ACM Symposium on Principles of Distributed Computing*, 1983.

[EEET] D. J. Ecklund, E. F. Ecklund, R. O. Eifrig, F. M. Tonge. "DVSS: A Distributed Version Storage Server for CAD Applications," Proceedings of the Thirteenth International Conference on Very Large Data Bases, 1987.

[FZ] M. F. Fernandez, S. B. Zdonik. "Transaction Groups: A Model for Controlling Cooperative Transactions," *A Workshop on Persistent Object Systems: Their Design, Implementation and Use*, The University of Newcastle, N. S. W., Australia, 1989.

[G] H. Garcia-Molina. Using Semantic Knowledge for Transaction Processing in a Distributed Database, ACM Transactions on Database Systems, 8(2), June, 1983.

[GS] H. Garcia-Molina, K. Salem. *Sagas*, Technical Report CS-TR-070-87, Department of Computer Science, Princeton University, January, 1987.

[Gr] J. Gray. "The Transaction Concept: Virtues and Limitations," In *Proceedings of the Seventh International Conference on Very Large Data Bases*, 1981.

[HW] M. P. Herlihy, W. E. Weihl. "Hybrid Concurrency Control for Abstract Data Types," In *Proceedings of the Seventh ACM SIGACT-SIGMOD-SIGART Symposium on Principles of Database Systems*, 1988.

[HZ] M. F. Hornick, S. B. Zdonik. "A Shared, Segmented Memory System for an Object-Oriented Database," *ACM Transactions on Office Information Systems*, 5(1), January, 1987.

[KC] R. H. Katz, E. Chang. "Managing Change in a Computer-Aided Design Database," Proceedings of the Thirteenth International Conference on Very Large Data Bases, 1987.

[KW] R. H. Katz, S. Weiss. "Design Transaction Management," In *Proceedings of the 21st ACM/IEEE Design Automation Conference*, 1984.

[K] H. F. Korth. "Locking Primitives in a Database System," *Journal of the Association for Computing Machinery*, 30(1), January, 1983.

[KKB] H. F. Korth, W. Kim, F. Bancilhon. "On Long-Duration CAD Transactions," Information Sciences, 46:73-107, 1988.

[KS] H. F. Korth, G. D. Speegle. "Formal Model of Correctness without Serializability," In *Proceedings of ACM SIGMOD International Conference on Management of Data*, 1988.

[L] N. A. Lynch. "Multilevel Atomicity — A new Correctness Criterion for Database Concurrency Control," ACM Transactions on Database Systems 8(4), December, 1983.

[M] J. E. B. Moss. Nested Transactions: An Approach to Reliable Distributed Computing, MIT Press, Cambridge, MA, 1985.

[S] P. M. Schwarz. Transactions on Typed Objects, Technical Report CMU-CS-84-166, Department of Computer Science, Carnegie Mellon University, December, 1984.

[SZR] A. H. Skarra, S. B. Zdonik, S. P. Reiss. "An Object Server for an Object-Oriented Database," Proceedings of the International Workshop on Object-Oriented Database Systems, ACM/IEEE, 1986.
Revised in A. H. Skarra, S. B. Zdonik, S. P. Reiss. ObServer: An Object Server for an Object-Oriented Database, Technical Report CS-88-08, Department of Computer Science, Brown University, July, 1987.

[W] W. E. Weihl. "Commutativity-Based Concurrency Control for Abstract Data Types," IEEE Proceedings of the 21st Annual Hawaii International Conference on System Sciences, 1988.

[ZW] S. B. Zdonik, P. Wegner. "Language and Methodology for Object-Oriented Database Environments," IEEE Proceedings of the 19th Annual Hawaii International Conference on System Sciences, 1986.

A PROTOTYPE OF FEATURE-BASED DESIGN FOR ASSEMBLY

by (listed alphabetically)

T. L. De Fazio

A. C. Edsall

R. E. Gustavson

J. A. Hernandez

P. M. Hutchins

H.-W. Leung

S. C. Luby

R. W. Metzinger

J. L. Nevins

K. K. Tung

D. E. Whitney

The Charles Stark Draper Laboratory, Inc.
Cambridge, MA 02139

Work supported through DARPA Contract MDA972-88-C-0027

ABSTRACT

This paper describes a prototype software system that implements a form of feature-based design for assembly. It is not an automated design system but instead a decision and design aid for designers interested in Concurrent Design. Feature-based design captures design intent (assembly topology, product function, manufacturing, or field use) while creating part and product geometry. Design for assembly as used here extends existing ideas about critiquing part shapes and part count to include assembly process planning, assembly sequence generation, assembly fixturing assessments, and assembly process costs. This work was primarily interested in identifying the information important to DFA tasks, and how that information could be captured using feature-based design. It was not intended to extend the state of the art in feature-based geometry creation, but rather to explore the uses of the information that can be captured. The prototype system has been programmed in LISP on Sun workstations. Its research contributions comprise integration of feature-based design with several existing and new assembly analysis and synthesis algorithms; construction of feature properties to meet the needs of those algorithms; a carefully chosen division of labor between designer and computer; and illustration of feature-based models of products as the information source for assembly analysis and process design. Some of its functions have been implemented approximately or partially but they give the flavor of the benefits to be expected from a fully functional system.

INTRODUCTION

Need

There is a general need for better quality designs of manufactured products and their parts. It is widely believed that 70% or more of the life cycle cost of a product is determined during the early design process and there is intense interest in developing design tools and aids that will make design more effective. At present, however, most computer tools for aiding design are directed at creation of geometry or pictures of geometry, together with some analytical capability for functional performance such as finite element analysis. Even these tools do not provide any guidance or advice to help improve the design. Little has been done to link geometric models to cost analyses, process planning for fabrication or assembly, tolerance analysis, quality analysis or other aspects of product design and manufacture. Furthermore, there are few or no computerized tools to aid these analyses.

A major consequence of the lack of tools is that those who wish to improve design by using Concurrent Design [2] must do so almost totally manually. There is no comprehensive computer-aided design environment with design for manufacturing and assembly tools that will give a designer rapid feedback concerning cost, producibility, or other important criteria. Lacking this, companies expand the design team with experts from other domains who also lack even specialized computer aided tools. Their input undoubtedly improves the design but large teams can be cumbersome, possibly defeating some of the purpose of forming them. Furthermore, since existing computer design aids focus on functional design rather than fabrication or assembly, the latter constituencies lack ammunition and credibility in the design negotiating process.

Desirable Properties of a Design for Manufacturing and Assembly (DFMA) System

What would a useful DFMA system be like and how would we create one? Ideally, it would be a workstation-like environment at which a designer could create a design in terms beyond just geometry, and have access to capabilities for design tradeoff studies, cost reduction studies, cost driver identification, producibility evaluations, design rule checking, and manufacturing and assembly evaluations and recommendations. That is, it would act like a manufacturing expert looking over the designer's shoulder, providing suggestions, comments, and information about fabrication and assembly.

To support such an environment, we must create a method of describing designs, one that can absorb the information necessary to carry out the relevant analyses. This information must be in the designer's customary vocabulary. Most important, the environment must provide an incentive for the designer to use it, such as permitting creation of designs that will stand scrutiny on DFMA and cost criteria. Our approach to this challenge is to begin with feature-based design.

Definition of Feature-Based Design (FBD) and Feature-Based Design for Assembly (FBDA)

Feature-based design is a technique that permits a designer to express design intent while creating the geometry of the product.[1] It both requires and permits the designer to think beyond mere shape and to state explicitly what portions of a part are important and why.

A "feature" is any geometric or non-geometric attribute of a discrete part whose presence or dimensions are relevant to the product's or part's function, manufacture, engineering analysis, use, etc., or whose availability as a primitive or operation facilitates the design process. Tables 1 and 2 give some examples.

TYPICAL FEATURES
Hole
Pin
Flat
Slot
Spline
Datum

Table 1. Examples of Features

TYPICAL FEATURE ATTRIBUTES
Diameter
Depth
Tolerance
Orientation (WRT part coordinates)
Used for (mating, fixturing, test,....)
Mates-with (feature # xx on part # yy)

Table 2. Examples of Feature Attributes

Recently, considerable work has been done in feature-based design, but it focused mostly on ease of part geometry creation and information for evaluating individual part fabrication, especially machining. [3-7] Since our focus is assembly, the rest of this paper describes feature-based DFA but it should be remembered that the larger challenge is to include in a feature-based approach all the other aspects of design and manufacture as well. We are developing a structure that will be expandable.

We will show that much of the information needed for DFA can be captured during the actual creation of the design geometry, through an extended feature-based modeling system. Once the design has been described in terms of features, the computer can analyze it using a variety of techniques, including heuristics, directed search, geometric reasoning, numerical analyses, and so on. These techniques gain much of their power from the designer's geometric and non-geometric information contained in the features of the parts and assemblies.

Intellectual Challenges

Implementing feature-based design poses several intellectual challenges. These include:

• what is a part that is designed using features?

This is not a trivial issue, since with currently available tools it is too tedious to design every region of a part using features. It would also defeat an important purpose of features, namely to focus attention to those few areas that need it. For these reasons, we define (for now) a featurized part as any geometric shape onto which features have been attached or portions of which have been singled out as features. This definition may be supplanted as the field matures.

• what information is really needed to support FBDFA?

We have identified two classes of data. These are part data and assembly data. Part data include all the usual functional data (geometry, mass distribution, material, dimensioning scheme) plus tolerances, feature existence, feature attributes, and feature use. Assembly data include inter-part dimensions, tolerances, clearances, feature mate type, presence of lubricants or adhesives, degrees of freedom in the mate, permission to grip or fixture on the feature, and others yet to be identified. We use this information in generating and evaluating assembly sequences, process plans, and cost estimates.

• how should feature-level information be entered?

Here there seem to be three possibilities. The computer could recognize the features; the designer could point out what collections of existing geometry constitute features; or the designer could call them forth parametrically from a library. The latter two seem to be the most likely to be useful in the long run since recognition appears to be limited to geometric information and the designer would have to add the other information anyway.

• how to deal with features at the appropriate time?

Designers are used to making a layout drawing first and then adding details to individual parts. The input is sketchy at first and becomes elaborated later. Feature-based design needs to be able to support a range of design styles; among these could be rough geometry followed by feature specifications, or feature sketches (using icons?) right from the beginning.

• how to deal with parts having "layers of features"?

"Layers of features" means having features that are obliterated during processing and replaced by other features. Forging followed by machining is an example. We raise this and the ones that follow without making specific suggestions at this time.

• how to define features that are subsets of or overlap other features?

An example is a keyway in a shaft end. Another is identification of the cylindrical part of a shaft end as a bearing-mate feature and identification of both the cylindrical part plus the flat end as a fixture-mate feature.

• what other feature-based design information is required for operation of the business, such as purchasing or production management?

Benefits

In addition to the benefits cited above for better design tools in general, FBD and FBDFA offer specific benefits. These include allowing the designer to

• operate in a high level vocabulary ("Create a countersunk 1/4-20 NC threaded hole here.")

• orient parts with respect to each other easily by referring to the features that mate (and automatically create the mating database referred to below)

• maintain dependencies between features such as correct diameters for pin and hole that will be press fit

• check adherence to design rules, such as ensuring that at least pin or bore has a chamfer or that bolt torques are appropriate to their size and material

• discover difficult mating situations based on feature attributes, materials, or tolerances

CAPABILITIES OF CURRENT PROTOTYPE

Implementation

A prototype software system has been written that embodies several of the above properties. It runs on Sun 3 workstations and employs LISP, C, and I-DEAS™ (SDRC, Inc.). A summary description follows, and subsequent sections give more detail. References 2, 6, 8-11, 13, and 14 describe the underlying theory of assembly sequence analysis and editing as well as assembly process planning, economic analysis, and assembly system synthesis. These references also contain further references to the general literature in these areas.

The particular contributions of this paper and the prototype it describes are

• integration of capabilities into an end-to-end design system not achieved before to our knowledge

• creation of assembly feature requirements based on prior research on algorithms (for assembly sequence analysis, process planning, system design, etc.) that call for information that properly designed features can provide

• observance of some distinctions between what a person can do (such as geometric analysis or judgement of assembly difficulty) and what a computer can do (sort through thousands of alternatives, create graphs, perform arithmetic, etc) with the result that the prototype described here combines a high level of credibility in its output with fairly fast response at the cost (benefit, really) of involving the human designer in the process.

The work described here was not intended to extend the state of the art in feature-based modeling but rather to show the potential for feature-based modeling in assembly process design. Most of the algorithms included are well-tested on real products and were developed based on our experience using concurrent design in industry.

Summary Capabilities

Figure 1 shows in schematic form the topics in a typical design of a product with discrete parts, after the functional requirements have been established, and highlights the capabilities and potential for feature-based design for assembly.[1]

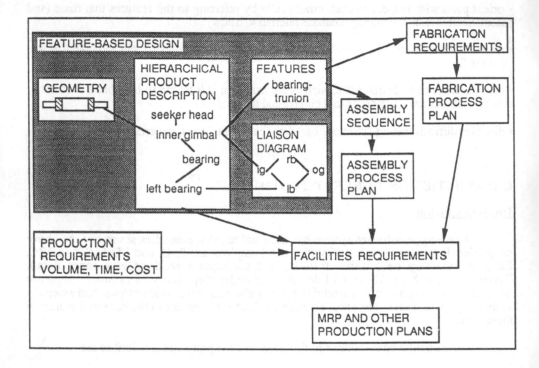

Figure 1.   Relation of Feature-based Design to the Process of Designing a Discrete Parts Product. The prototype software described in this paper includes all the entities in this figure except those dealing with fabrication and MRP.

Figure 2, shows in schematic form the design process as supported by the current prototype software. Upon starting the software, the user constructs a feature-level solid model of the product, then assembles the parts by indicating feature mates. Features and assembly information are captured in a database in hierarchical form with all the parts and their features, plus mating data in the form of a liaison diagram [8].[2]

---

[1] Of course, there may be revisions to the requirements as design proceeds. These aspects of concurrent design are not discussed here.
[2] A liaison represents a mate between two parts.

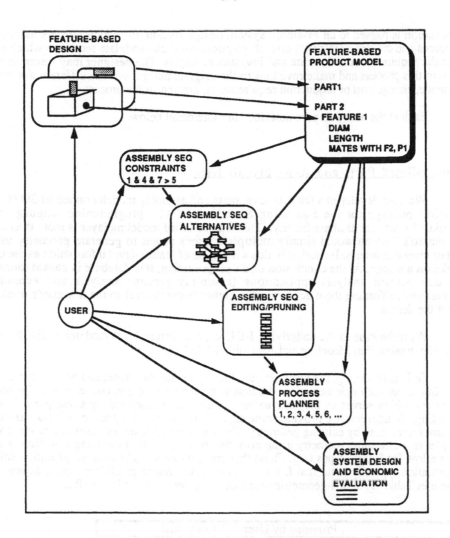

Figure 2. Sketch of the Design Process Supported by the Software

Next, the user invokes the assembly sequence generator, which uses a question-answer dialog [8] with the designer plus the geometric features to determine the legal assembly operations and generate all the feasible assembly sequences. The designer may then edit the sequences by optionally eliminating assembly states, assembly actions, assembly plans with parallel operations or with converging assembly lines, plus other explicit restrictions, until a satisfactory set of sequences is obtained.

The designer transfers these sequences to an assembly process planner which uses feature information and user input to plan assembly. The assembly plan contains information on part or subassembly orientation, size, weight, and task type. This information is passed to an assembly system design module [9] which musters assembly resources and creates a least cost assembly system for each candidate sequence which will meet the required production rate and investment targets. The designer may return to any place in this process and make revisions to the original design, select a different assembly sequence, change cost or production requirements, and repeat the process.

Each of the above steps is described in more detail below.

Feature-Based Parts and Assembly Modeler

We have developed a features-level parts and assembly modeler on top of SDRC's I-DEAS™ package for the Sun using SDRC's "IDEAL" programming language and PEARL™ relational database facility. This feature-based modeling layer is more than a set of "macro's," which would simply multiply a user's power to generate geometry using higher level commands. Instead, it builds a database of feature-level information as the user works on a design. At the conclusion of a design session, this database is passed along to the downstream analysis applications (assembly process analysis and economic evaluations), affording them access at this higher features level to the designer's thinking about the design.

As is the case in the underlying I-DEAS, our feature-level modeler is divided into two main modes: Part Modeling and Assembly Modeling.

In Part Modeling, the designer can directly create Pin, Bore, and Slot features on a part. In our current implementation, the first step for each part is to create an initial piece of geometry which serves as the base to be augmented or modified by subsequent feature modeling. In addition, we provide some capabilities for the designer to point out features that are represented by existing geometry. This capability allows for cases where it is today simpler to create some geometry using primitive solids (e.g., by Revolving a profile) as well as to allow for feature types (e.g. Flats) that are not easily made up from primitive solids. Information typically requested from the user or inferred from his/her mouse actions are shown in Table 3. All non-geometric information is stored as text in PEARL.

	Provided by User	Computed
For Parts and Assemblies	name, density, shape, size	weight, CG, inertia properties, bounding box (for process planning)
For Features	ID, description, purpose, shape, size, location on part	reference direction (for assembly analysis and process planning)

Table 3. Data About Features

Other information could be requested, such as tolerances, surface finishes, thread sizes, and so on, and used for further assembly modeling or by other software modules not included now, such as for fabrication planning.

Duplicate parts may be defined first as separate entities (e.g., 3/8" bearing), and copies (e.g., left 3/8" bearing, right 3/8" bearing) may be made as needed and included in the product. Each feature is an instance of existing feature library entries but at present the user cannot create new entries.

Figures 3 and 4 show a product comprising 18 parts that was constructed in this way. It is the mechanical structure of a generic seeker head, a component of tactical air-air missiles.

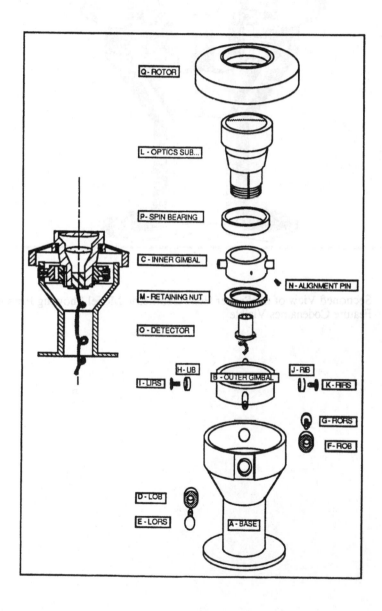

Figure 3. Generic Seeker Head Product

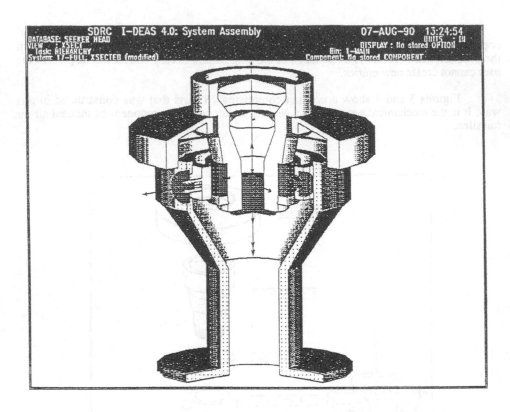

Figure 4.   Sectioned View of the Seeker Head Geometric Model Showing Parts with Some Feature Codenames Visible

When the designer is finished making all the parts, he/she may switch to the assembly modeler and model the final assembly state of the product. This is done by calling forth the parts and typing the names of the features that mate them. The software uses information in the database concerning the reference directions and locations of the features to align the parts, a technique that yields the correct positions most of the time. This method is a considerable improvement over the corresponding facility provided by I-DEAS™, which requires the user to work at the geometry level with cumbersome orientation commands. Figure 5 shows this action occurring for the base and outer gimbal of the seeker head.

Our implementation of assembly modeling via features is intended to exemplify the improvement in user-computer interaction afforded by raising the discourse to the features level. It is not complete and currently cannot correctly mate every kind of feature we can define, but there is no barrier other than programming time to such extensions.

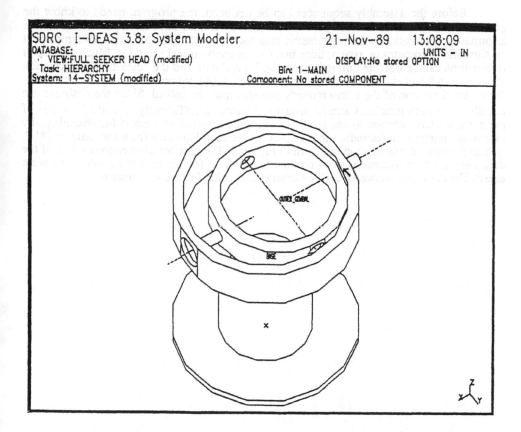

Figure 5.   Outer Gimbal Being Oriented with Respect to the Base Via Specification of the Mate Between the Pin on the Gimbal and the Bearing Bore in the Base.

During feature-based modeling, our program layer builds a database of the higher-level feature information using the I-DEAS™ PEARL™ relational database facility. At completion of modeling, the program writes out the database into a text file which is read by LISP code and converted into an object database that contains all the logical and textual information created during the I-DEAS™ session. This information includes the logical structure of the product, such as what the parts are, what mates to what and via what features, and what type of feature mate is involved. Information that can be inferred includes clearances and degrees of freedom of mates, relative extraction directions for mating features, total weight and bounding box size of the product or any subassembly, distance between two features on different parts and (in future implementations) tolerances between such features. Also possible in the future is interpretation of assembly difficulty using Boothroyd [11] or Draper [2] methods.

Assembly Sequence Constraints

Before the assembly sequences can be deduced, the program needs to know the geometric constraints on assembly. While several researchers have attempted to obtain this information automatically from geometric data such as described above, such attempts rest on simplified geometry or assumptions that do not apply to real products. Much constraint information can be obtained directly from the logical data and the "direction" information about mating features, but inevitably some complex geometry must be analyzed or a multi-dimensional version of the piano mover's problem must be solved. Since the designer can usually solve such problems almost instantly if shown a sufficiently realistic drawing[1] of the parts, we have chosen to use an illustrated question-answer method for obtaining any assembly constraint information that cannot be deduced logically from the features.[8] A typical moment in this method is shown in Figure 6. The number of questions asked of the designer varies considerably from product to product; for the seeker 58 questions were asked. The computer answered 203754 others itself using feature information.

---

[1]In this prototype, the illustrations are made separately in Sundraw™.

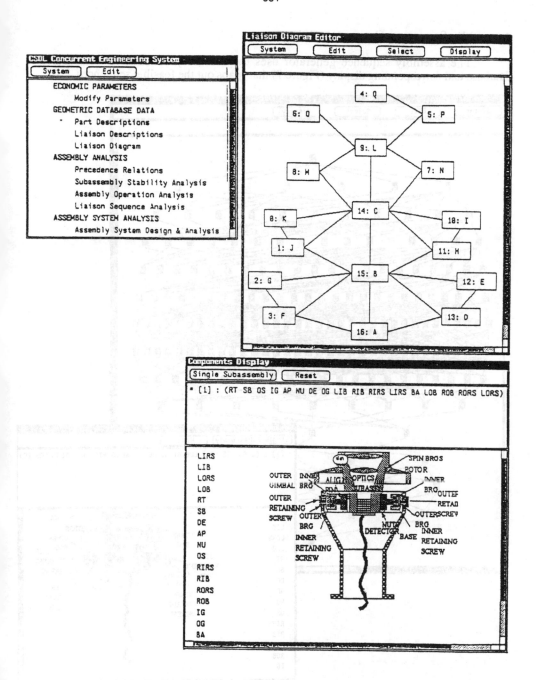

Figure 6. View of Screen During Question-Answer Session for Determining Assembly
Constraints

Assembly Sequence Generator-Editor

The assembly sequence generator uses the assembly constraints and creates a database and corresponding display (Figure 7) that maps out the feasible sequences. [10]

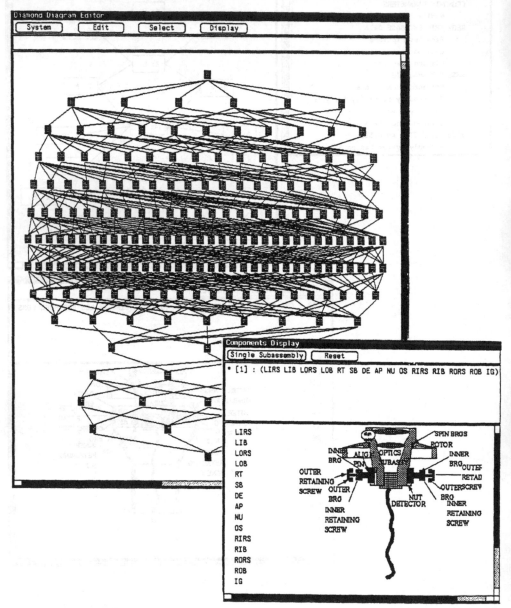

Figure 7a.   View of the Screen Showing the Feasible Assembly Sequences for the Seeker After the Designer Has Edited Out Several Undesirable Assembly States and Moves.

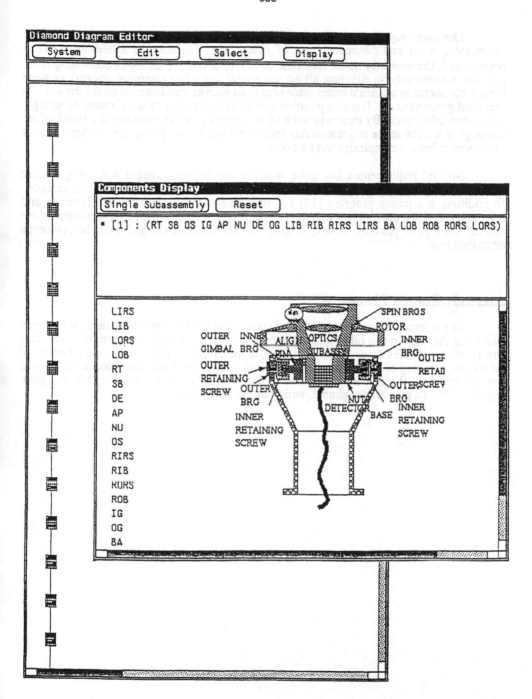

Figure 7b. View After Editing to One Sequence. Each box in the network is a state of assembly corresponding to mates that have been established. A path from top to bottom in this network is a unique assembly sequence.

The user may click on any box and see a picture of the state of assembly it represents, or on any connected pair of boxes and visualize the assembly move it represents.[1] The user may delete any state or move, or remove all states containing more than one subassembly (to eliminate all but sequential single line assembly layouts), or write logical statements to eliminate undesirable situations such as simultaneous establishment of a specified group of mates. It is also possible to require that a mate or set of mates occur right after some other mate. By means of such edits the designer can consider the possibilities thoroughly and can arrive at a reasonable sequence in less than an hour for products similar to the seeker head in complexity and part count.

Not yet implemented but quite feasible are heuristic means for using feature information to accomplish preliminary editing of mates and subassemblies for the designer. In addition, a separate program [14] has implemented consideration of fixturing and orientation options, permitting the designer to choose a sequence with as few reorientations and refixturings as possible. This capability has not yet been merged with the prototype described here.

Assembly Process Planner

The assembly sequence(s) produced above consist of a series of mates in the desired order but they lack much other information necessary to a complete assembly plan. This information includes orientation, fixturing, application of adhesives, oven curing of adhesives, torquing of bolts, and so on. The data necessary to add this information can be determined from the geometric features or from information supplied by the designer. Figure 8 shows a plan for the gimbal portion of the seeker head.

---

[1]The Sundraw™ illustrations are used here, too.

Table Window

| System | Edit | Apply |

Task	Type of Task	DoD	Mot Req	Load	Description
1	⟳ Place	2	X Y Z	0.2281	Attach SPIN_BEARING-P to pallet.
2	⟳ Assemble	3	X Y Z	1.7708	insert ROTOR-Q.
3	⟳ Automatic-reorient	1	X Y Z	4.3297	rotate pallet/trunion.
4	⟳ Assemble	3	X Y Z	2.3316	insert OPTICS_SUBASSEM-L.
5	⟳ Automatic-reorient	1	X Y Z	4.7092	rotate pallet/trunion.
6	⟳ Place	1	X Y Z	0.3794	Assemble INNER_GIMBAL-C.
7	⟳ Automatic-reorient	1	X Y Z	4.7099	rotate pallet/trunion.
8	⟳ Place	1	X Y Z	7.5E-4	Assemble ALIGNMENT_PIN-N.
9	⟳ Automatic-reorient	1	X Y Z	4.8167	rotate pallet/trunion.
10	⟳ Bolt	2	X Y Z	0.1067	insert and torque RETAINING_NUT-M.
11	⟳ Automatic-reorient	1	X Y Z	4.9439	rotate pallet/trunion.
12	⟳ Place	2	X Y Z	1	Apply adhesives to surfaces.
13	⟳ Insert	3	X Y Z	0.1272	Orient and install DETECTOR-O.
14	⟳ Place	1	X Y Z	4.9439	Oven cure.
15	⟳ Place	2	X Y Z	1	Position and attach fixture to pall
16	⟳ Place	1	X Y Z	0.6104	Assemble OUTER_GIMBAL-B.
17	⟳ Automatic-reorient	1	X Y Z	5.5693	rotate pallet/trunion.
18	⟳ Assemble	3	X Y Z	0.0149	insert R-2_BEARING-J.
19	⟳ Automatic-reorient	1	X Y Z	5.5842	rotate pallet/trunion.
20	⟳ Assemble	3	X Y Z	0.0149	insert R-2_BEARING-H.
21	⟳ Automatic-reorient	1	X Y Z	5.5983	rotate pallet/trunion.
22	⟳ Bolt	2	X Y Z	0.0058	insert and torque SCREW_2-64-I.
23	⟳ Automatic-reorient	1	X Y Z	5.5953	rotate pallet/trunion.
24	⟳ Bolt	2	X Y Z	0.0058	insert and torque SCREW_2-64-K.
25	⟳ Place	2	X Y Z	4	Position and attach fixture to pall
26	⟳ Place	1	X Y Z	3.8978	Assemble BASE-A.
27	⟳ Automatic-reorient	1	X Y Z	9.5198	rotate pallet/trunion.
28	⟳ Assemble	3	X Y Z	0.0256	insert R-3_BEARING-F.
29	⟳ Automatic-reorient	1	X Y Z	9.5455	rotate pallet/trunion.
30	⟳ Assemble	3	X Y Z	0.0256	insert R-3_BEARING-D.
31	⟳ Automatic-reorient	1	X Y Z	9.5528	rotate pallet/trunion.
32	⟳ Bolt	2	X Y Z	0.0073	insert and torque SCREW_4-48-E.
33	⟳ Automatic-reorient	1	X Y Z	9.5601	rotate pallet/trunion.
34	⟳ Bolt	2	X Y Z	0.0073	insert and torque SCREW_4-48-G.
35	⟳ Automatic-test	2	X Y Z	0.0	perform test
36	⟳ Place	1	X Y Z	9.5601	pack / unload assembly.

Figure 8.   Assembly Plan for the Seeker's Gimbal

For example, if a ball bearing is to be installed and there is no bearing retainer, then it will be installed with a shrink or interference fit, or glued in, either with epoxy or Loctite™. In the case of epoxy, an oven cure is necessary. In the case of bolt torquing, the size of the bolt usually determines the necessary torque directly. For fixturing, the feature information contains the approach direction for each mate. If we adopt the heuristic that mates should be made from above if possible, then the need for reorientation can be deduced. We also assume that the first part in a sequence must be placed on a fixture. Also, each separate subassembly built needs its own fixture.

Finally, it may happen that a part must be added to an assembly but not immediately mated to the other parts; instead it must be put on a separate temporary fixture. The need for such a temporary fixture cannot be deduced directly from the assembly sequence method described above because it presumes that each assembly step establishes at least one mate. However, it sometimes happens that interferences between parts require that parts be placed near each other, followed by the insertion of intervening mating parts; if the intervening parts were added first, then one of the other parts could not be inserted. This situation is illustrated in Figure 9.

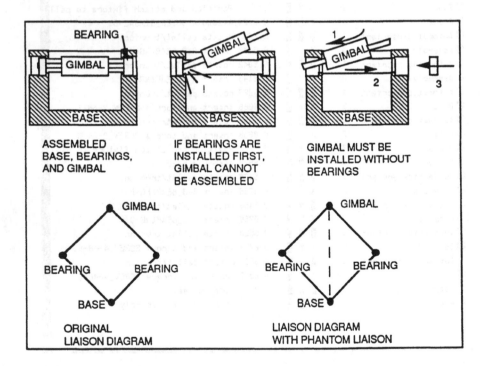

Figure 9.   Assembly of Parts That Do Not Mate Directly, Showing Use of the Phantom Liaison.

At present the designer must supply this information by adding a "phantom liaison" between the two main parts. Since establishing this liaison does not mate any parts, the temporary fixture is called for. If the phantom liaison were omitted, there would be no feasible assembly sequences.

When the software has finished making the process plan, the designer may review it and make any changes desired.

Assembly System Designer

The last step accomplished by the prototype design software is assembly system design. This step converts the assembly process plan into a list of equipment and tools together with the plan steps that each equipment will accomplish. Equipment includes manual assembly and maintenance labor, robots, and conventional fixed assembly automation. The final cost of assembly is also calculated, based on labor and equipment costs. Some non-feature information is required to provide economic and production data, such as cost of labor, desired annual production quantity, and information on investment return requirements.

Process planning is carried out heuristically using feature information such as bounding box size of subassemblies, weight of parts, and type of mate. Larger or heavier parts, or longer reach required of assembly equipment (calculated from the size of the assembly's bounding box) require more costly equipment, more assembly time, or both. Heuristics determine task difficulty based on type of mate, sizes and weights of parts, and number of features that mate simultaneously. The task difficulty score is used to rule out certain types of equipment and to determine equipment cost estimates.

The algorithm seeks to obtain the lowest unit cost of assembly, and uses equipment costs and speeds to decide which equipment to choose for each step. "Flexible" equipment such as manual labor or robots can do more than one task so the algorithm can assign several tasks to one such piece of equipment if time in the assembly cycle is available. See [2, 9] for more information on how these calculations are made.

The resulting plan is presented to the designer, who can alter it as desired. Figure 10 shows the system design for the gimbal portion of the seeker.

388

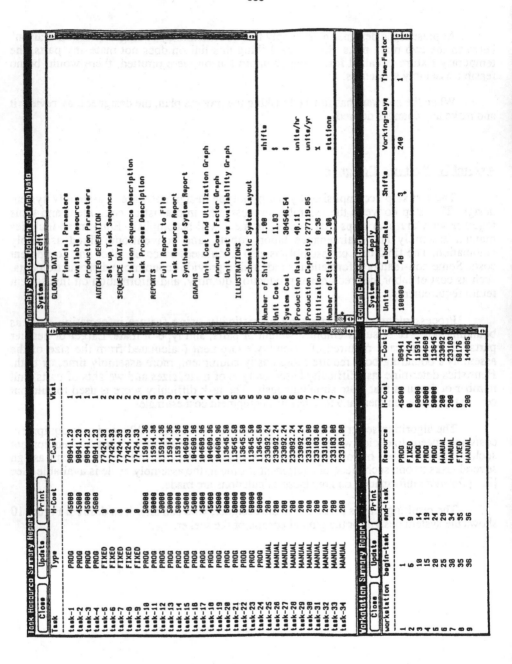

Figure 10. Assembly System Design Data for the Seeker Gimbal

CONCLUSIONS AND FUTURE WORK POSSIBLE WITHIN THIS ARCHITECTURE

The information needs of the design for assembly analyses we have investigated which can be provided through feature-based modeling are;

1. Topology of the assembly, connections between parts must be explicit and should be described as feature to feature mates. This also makes assembly modeling easier by allowing the user to position parts just by specifying the mates.

2. Interface features, knowing that a mate is composed of a spline in a through hole, as opposed to a peg in a blind hole, is important to subsequent assembly analyses.

3. Links from features to geometric database, having access to the geometry that represents a part or features, provides DFA analyses the power of both a symbolic and quantized representation.

4. Feature parameters, the parameters used to create the features, such as diameter of a hole must be stored with the feature. This allows subsequent calculation of clearances and assembly difficulty without having to parse the geometric database.

5. Tolerances on feature parameters and part dimensions will become extremely important to the more detailed DFA analyses described later.

It should be noted that a properly designed feature-based modeling system can both, meet the information needs of the downstream analyses, and yield a significant improvement in productivity of geometric modeling.

We now have the basis for feature-based design for assembly. It consists of a means for describing parts and assemblies together with the important features that describe assembly operations, plus algorithms and displays that permit a designer to explore the assembly opportunities, discover the assembly problems inherent in the design, and correct them at an early stage. Many aspects of design are not included but the basis for doing so exists. These are briefly discussed next.

Incorporation of Part-Based DFA

A wealth of information exists concerning ability to feed and insert individual parts. [11] Most of this information can be expressed in terms of part features. It should be fairly straight-forward to combine this information with the software system described here.

Critique of Part Mate Difficulty

The science of part mating is well-established and is described in reference [2]. This theory permits direct assessment of the difficulty of part mates on the basis of relative clearance, size of chamfers (if any), friction, compliance of grippers and fixtures, and accumulated position and angle errors between mating parts at the moment of assembly. A first stage assessment of difficulty can be obtained simply from the clearance, chamfer, and friction information, which in turn is found directly in the feature information. For example, a relative clearance (clearance divided by diameter) in a round peg-hole mate of less than 0.001 and friction coefficient of more than 0.2 may be judged difficult.

To complete the picture of assembly difficulty requires additional calculations involving tolerance stackup in assemblies, fixtures, and assembly equipment. One needs to know what surface on what part is being used for fixturing, plus tolerances on all the intervening parts across the features being used for mating. One also needs to know something about the accuracy and repeatability of assembly equipment. Alternatively, one can calculate the requirements on such equipment to obtain, say, "six sigma" performance. The information for making such calculations exists within the features and the assembly plan. However, due to the undeveloped state of tolerance representation in geometric modeling, additional research is needed before the addition of such calculations will be straightforward. [12]

Critique of Part Cost

As each part is designed, the designer should be given information on its fabrication cost. Such information depends on feature information, especially shapes and tolerances, as well as choices by the designer concerning fabrication methods and materials. This is a separate and active topic of research and development. There is no reason, however, why the results of such research cannot be incorporated into the system described here. [6, 7]

Critique of Assembly Automation Opportunities

The heuristic assembly system design algorithm makes numerous choices of equipment based on mating information. Such choices are not presently communicated to the designer. It would be straightforward to do so, however, permitting the designer to explore design changes that might permit more options for equipment and possibly yield lower assembly costs.

Analysis of Fixturing Requirements

At present the software makes only preliminary fixturing analyses. Additional opportunities, ranging from straightforward to challenging, include reorientations, fixture interference with parts, clamping, and tolerance stackup.

Inclusion of Testing Requirements

One may conclude from the above discussions that assembly includes much more than just putting parts together. An important element not mentioned above is testing, in particular in-process testing of partially completed assemblies. In-process testing may be advantageous because problems can be found sooner and more easily, and can be repaired more easily compared to testing only after assembly is complete.

However, there are several complications. First, some possible failures can be detected only at final test. Second, in-process tests require the presence of certain parts and completion of certain assembly steps. Third, tests at some points during assembly may be able to detect failure but be unable to determine the cause, requiring diagnosis. Consequently, planning of in-process testing depends on the choice of assembly sequence. In separate research [13] we have begun to work on the problem of determining optimum testing opportunities. Full exploitation of this aspect of assembly requires statistical data concerning likelihood of certain failures, plus the costs of test equipment, cost and time to make repairs, and information about the interaction of test capabilities and failures present.

References

1. Anon, "Requirements for Support of Form Features in a Solid Modeling System," Final Report R-85-ASPP-01, CAM-i, Inc., Arlington, TX, 19851.

2. J. L. Nevins, D. E. Whitney, editors, Concurrent Design of Products and Processes, New York: McGraw-Hill, 1989.

3. E. Kroll, E. Lenz, J. R. Wolberg, "A Knowledge-based Solution to the Design for Assembly Problem," Manufacturing Review, v1, #2, June, 1988, pp104-108.

4. M. R. Cutkosky, J. M. Tenenbaum, "CAD/CAM Integration Through Concurrent Process and Product Design," ASME Symposium on Integrated and Intelligent Design, 1987.

5. R. D. Logcher and D. Sriram, "CAE Techniques for Distributed Design," to be presented at Int'l Symposium on Building Economics and Construction Management, Sydney Australia, March, 1990.

6. S. C. Luby, J. R. Dixon, and M. K. Simmons, "Designing with Features: Creating and Using a Features Database for Evaluation of Manufacturability of Castings". Proceedings of the International Computers in Mechanical Engineering Conference of the American Society of Mechanical Engineers, Chicago IL, August 1986. Reprinted in CIME Magazine, Vol.5, No. 3, November, 1986 pp. 25-33.

7. P. London, B. G. Hankins, S. C. Luby, and M. Sapposnek, "The Expert Cost and Manufacturability Guide: A customizable Expert System", Proceedings of the International Computers in Mechanical Engineering Conference of the American Society of Mechanical Engineers, New York, NY, August 1987.

8. D. F. Baldwin, T. E. Abell, M-C M. Lui, T. L. De Fazio, D. E. Whitney, "An Integrated Computer Aid for Generating and Evaluating Assembly Sequences for Mechanical Parts," submitted to IEEE J. Robotics and Automation.

9. R. E. Gustavson, "Design of Cost-Effective Assembly Systems," SME Paper AD88-250, presented at Successful Planning and Implementation of Flexible Assembly Systems, March 29-31, 1988, Ann Arbor, MI.

10. M-C M. Lui, "Generation and Evaluation of Mechanical Assembly Sequences Using the Liaison Sequence Method," MIT SM Thesis, ME Department, May, 1988.

11. G. Boothroyd and P. Dewhurst, Product Design for Assembly, Wakefield RI: Boothroyd and Dewhurst, Inc., 1987

12. J. Turner, "An M-Space Theory of Tolerances in Solid Modeling," proceedings NSF Design and Manufacturing Systems Grantees Conference, Tempe AZ, January, 1990, published by SME.

13. S. Pappu, "A Dual Descent Algorithm for Finding the Optimal Test Strategy for an Assembly Sequence, MIT SM Thesis, Operations Research Center, May, 1989.

14. T. E. Abell, "An Interactive Tool for Editing and Evaluating Mechanical Assembly Sequences Based on Fixturing and Orientation Requirements," MIT SM Thesis, ME Department, 1989.

Feature-Based Design For Manufacturability Critique In Concurrent Engineering

Rajit Gadh
Donna Herbert
Alexander Kott
Charles Kollar

Carnegie Group Inc., 5 PPG Place
Pittsburgh, PA 15222

(412) 642 6900

1 Introduction

Most American manufacturing corporations do not spend enough time and effort in incorporating production knowledge into designs. Therefore, a large number of design iterations result, causing increased product cycle time and, as a consequence, increased costs. For example, the American automakers take sixty two months and five million engineering hours to evolve a design from concept to production, whereas the Japanese automakers take forty three months and three million engineering hours respectively [1].

To be competitive in current world markets, American industries will need to take bold steps in their search for alternative solutions to current technological practices, so that the cycle time to produce products may be reduced. One major cause of such large cycle times is the large number of product iterations required to create a design that is manufacturable and is usable for the intended function. The typical stages in the life cycle of a product, including design iterations, are shown in Figure 1. We believe that by designing products in a concurrent fashion, by bringing downstream expertise to the design table, will result in fewer design changes. Fewer design changes reduce cycle time and decrease expenses. A concurrent engineering methodology that brings the downstream knowledge to the designer will also assist in reducing downstream problems.

In a typical concurrent engineering solution, the problem is two-fold. One is defining and creating models of knowledge possessed by various experts that can, in an automatic or semi-automatic manner, critique a particular design with respect to a particular life cycle concern. Another is to control the interaction between the various experts so that the system reaches a desirable solution. One commonly cited paradigm for solving these problems is the blackboard architecture [2]. In a blackboard architecture, several experts are modeled using knowledge-based techniques and interact via a blackboard communication mechanism to create a design in a concurrent fashion. Each expert represents a life cycle concern and optimizes the design based on its concern. These life cycle concerns may be manufacturability of design [10], assemblability of design [18], analysis of design [28], etc.

Both of these problems, creating models of experts and controlling their interactions, are currently frontiers of active speculation and research. Some of the work done in the area of architectures and case studies for concurrent engineering in manufacturing are presented in [26], [8], [9], [25], [16], [4], [5], [19], [22], [3], and [6].

In the current paper, we describe an important critic in the life cycle concern : **The Manufacturability Critic.** Our solution is predicated on the blackboard architecture framework of several experts interacting to create a design in a concurrent fashion. In the current research, the life

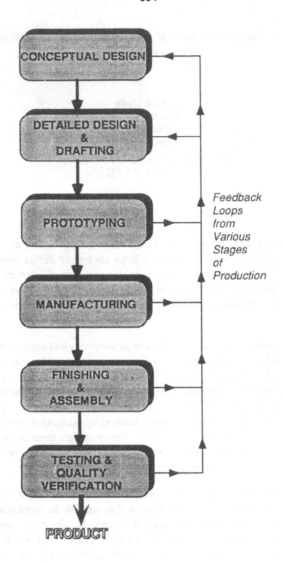

Figure 1: Typical Stages in the Life Cycle of a Product

cycle concern that we address is the manufacturability of single-piece, "shell-like" products such as those found in injection molding, casting, extrusion, and sheet metal cutting. An example of a shell-like object is shown in Figure 2, along with some typical manufacturability rules. In knowledge-intensive industries where shell-like products are produced, design iterations occur frequently. As a result, large time and monetary losses are encountered during the design and manufacturing processes. Thus, we believe these industries and products constitute an ideal domain for the application of concurrent engineering.

The manufacturability critic described in this paper is a knowledge-based system. The knowledge for the system was derived from manufacturing experts and design handbooks. From examination of these

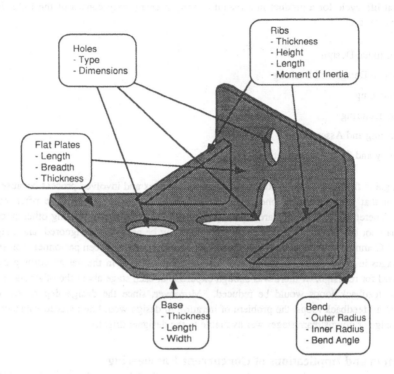

Rule 1 : Bend.Outer Radius < r1*
Rule 2 : Bend.Inner Radius < r2*
Rule 3 : Hole.Maximum Dimension < M*
Rule 4 : Rib.Thickness / Base.Thickness < x*

Figure 2: Sample Shell-Like Part: features, attributes, and constraints

sources of knowledge, we found that most of the knowledge associated with shell-like products is based on geometric or physical forms on the products known as features (Gadh [10] [11], Henderson [15]). Features and information about features are typically not available directly from most CAD systems, and thus need to be extracted from the information that is available. In the current research, we show a heuristic-based method for extracting features from a Boundary Representation (BREP) Solid Model CAD description. These features are input into the manufacturability critic, which critiques the part for various problems in manufacturing such as ejectability, shrinkage, distortion, etc.

2 Problem Addressed by Concurrent Engineering : Large Cycle Times

The manufacturing industry has evolved into a well-defined sequential set of processes such as design, manufacturing, marketing, etc. As a result there are experts for each process and a substantial number of iterations between the process steps and the various experts. Interaction of special expertise applied to decision making in a sequential process requires iterations, which results in time delays in creation of the final product.

A typical life cycle for a product in a manufacturing scenario may consist of the following stages (reference Figure 1):

- Conceptual Design
- Detailed Design and Drafting
- Prototyping
- Manufacturing
- Finishing and Assembly
- Testing and Quality Verification

However, going from stage one to stage six is a fairly complex and involved process because pieces of information that are required at one stage, developed at subsequent stages, are often not readily available. Therefore, assumptions are made by personnel at each stage regarding other stages, which may or may not be correct. There are subtleties that may be neglected or ignored, and may become important. Commonly, there is less than adequate communication between personnel representing the various stages in the product life cycle, and that frequently results in the design coming back to the design board for redesign. If there was enough expertise at each stage about the other stages, then the number of feedback loops would be reduced. Moreover, since the design department is usually involved in all feedback loops, the problem of iteration in design would be reduced substantially if all the knowledge of downstream stages was available to the designer directly.

3 Definition and Implications of Concurrent Engineering

We define concurrent engineering as "an engineering methodology used to reduce the product cycle time by concurrent application of multiple specialized perspectives". There are three important implications of this definition. First, the objective is reduction of product cycle time. Second, there are multiple perspectives, each of them being specialized in their own domain, and the requirement that each be involved in the decision making process of the design. Third, the involvement of expertise should be concurrent and not sequential.

4 A Vision for Concurrent Engineering

Our vision of the concurrent engineering paradigm (see Figure 3) is based on the commonly cited paradigm for concurrent problem solving: the blackboard architecture [2]. In this paradigm there are several expert critics that interact to create a design in a concurrent fashion. Each critic represents a life cycle concern and optimizes the design based on its concern. These life cycle concerns may be manufacturability of design [10], assemblability of design [18], reliability of design, testability of design, etc. For each critic there are constraints on design parameters, such as those represented in Figure 3 by C1 through C7. These constraints are based on criteria identified by a relevant expert. More often than not, constraints of one critic violate that of another. This is depicted in Figure 3 by the outer circle that connects the various critics.

The common bond between the various critics is the design database that is shared, accessed, and modified by the various critics. Typically, some control is exercised over the database, so that two critics can not access the same information at the same time.

Controlling the concurrent engineering environment is an "Overriding Decision Maker" (reference Figure 3), that resolves conflicts of various kinds. For example, in the case of a conflict between two

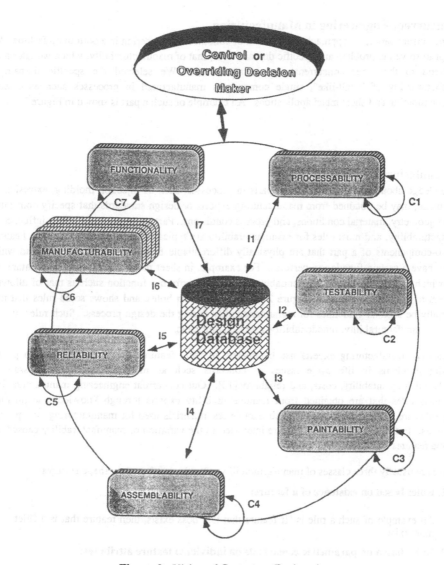

Figure 3: Vision of Concurrent Engineering

design decisions, the decision maker would use its own state of knowledge to decide the outcome. Modeling this state of knowledge is not an easy task. The overriding decision maker performs a function similar to a manager, in that it resolves disputes based on a large number of factors such as timeliness of the product, state of the market at the time the decision is to be made, monetary effects of the decision, and others factors which may be dynamic.

5 Concurrent Engineering in Manufacturing

In the current paper, we approach the problem of concurrent engineering in a bottom up fashion. We attempt to solve the problem at a specific domain level, that of manufacturability, which we later hope to extend to the other concurrent engineering issues. We selected the specific domain of manufacturability of "shell-like", single components manufactured in processes such as casting, injection molding and sheet metal applications. An example of such a part is shown in Figure 2.

5.1 Manufacturability Rules

Knowledge about manufacturability of parts in processes, such as injection molding, extrusion, or sheet metal, may be obtained from manufacturing experts or design standards that specify constraints on part geometry, material conditions, and process conditions. Part geometry has a strong influence on manufacturability, and most rules for manufacturability are typically based on part features. Features are sub-components of a part that are physically differentiable from the rest of the part, and which usually have a certain function to perform. For example, in sheet metal, an instance of a feature is a hole, which can be physically differentiable, and it may perform a function such as that of allowing fasteners to go through the part. Figure 2 shows a part with holes, and shows some rules that may potentially be used as guidelines for manufacturability during the design process. Such rules may be based on manufacturability, functionability, assemblability, etc.

Typically, manufacturing experts use parameters of form features (or shape features) to predict potential problems in life cycle issues or concerns such as manufacturability, processability, assemblability, paintability, costs, and reliability [10]. Our concurrent engineering manufacturability critic uses rules that are obtained from manufacturability experts through knowledge acquisition. These rules are based on features and their parameters, materials used for manufacturing, and process conditions. In the current research, we are interested in the variation of manufacturability caused due to shape features.

There are usually three classes of manufacturability rules that are based on shape features:

1. **Rules based on existence of a feature:**

   An example of such a rule is "if feature that is a boss exists, then feature that is a fillet must exist".

2. **Rules based on parametric constraints on individual feature attributes:**

   An example of such a rule is "Rib.thickness > R1 (where R1 is a function of material, process conditions, etc.)".

3. **Rules based on relational constraints on multiple features:**

   Examples of such rules are:

   "Rib.thickness / base.thickness < X(material, process conditions, etc.)", or

   "Hole.diameter/base.thickness > Y(material, Process Conditions, etc.)", or

   "Distance between two bosses > Z(part thickness, material, process conditions)".

5.2 Knowledge Base Requirements

Rules that are used for analyzing manufacturability are based on features, materials, and physical process conditions such as temperature, pressure, etc. Physical conditions and materials are typically available from process databases directly. Features on the other hand have to be obtained from the CAD databases. Along with the features, parameters associated with the features need to be evaluated. For example, for a rib, the thickness, height, taper, and length of the rib are required for manufacturability analysis. Relationships between features are required to analyze rules of type three mentioned above. For example, one of the relationships is "adjacent-to" which indicates that two features are touching. In Figure 2 the rib is touching the base, and this information is needed for rule one in class three of the manufacturability rules.

The other class of information that is needed is the relationship of geometry to features. This is essentially a reference from the features to the surface on the part where the feature is located. This is required for a certain class of rules that depend on local properties of features rather than aggregate properties. For example, ejecting a part from a mold requires a certain slope angle at all points on the surface of a curved rib. Since the slope angle may be different at various points on the surface, it would have to be computed at the local level. For this a reference from the feature to the surface is required.

6 Constructing Feature-Based Descriptions for Shell-Like Objects

Obtaining features from a CAD model is possible by two methods: use the CAD system to design with features directly or extract the required features from the CAD description provided. CAD systems that provide feature-based construction, can have the disadvantage however of not providing all of the features required for a certain domain or engineering perspective. This is in fact most often the case because of the specificity and finiteness of CAD systems; and even if the CAD system allows the user to create features, the CAD system does not store or even represent the user defined feature internally. Even if a system that allows feature-based construction existed, a certain amount of feature recognition may be still be needed. Therefore, we have chosen to recognize and extract the required set of features from existing BREP solid model descriptions available from the CAD system.

6.1 Feature Recognition and Extraction

Recognition of features is a complex task because there are a large number of variations within each feature class (Gadh [12]). For example, in the case of a rib, increasing its thickness slightly, changing its side surface tapers, or changing its length does not change its type. One of the biggest problems with feature recognition is the fact that instances of features are very different. Many feature recognition approaches are applicable for relatively simple parts, but when the geometry gets complex, they become computationally intractable. The current approach to feature recognition uses a specific domain specific heuristic, which is that the part thickness is approximately constant, to perform feature recognition prior.

Feature recognition has been performed by various researchers for a variety of manufacturing domains such as injection molding, casting, extrusion, machining, etc.; using a variety of methods such as filtering, search, pattern matching, volume removal, curvature detection, etc. Some of the original research in this field has been done by Staley, Henderson and Anderson [27], Henderson [13], Henderson [14], Kyprianou [17], and Woo [29]. Most of the initial research efforts have been from the point of view of demonstration of potential, but not production quality implementations. In recent years there has been a greater emphasis on real-time, robust, feature recognition systems. To this effect, we analyze a sample of recent efforts in greater detail.

Gadh [12] uses a depth perceptive filter to eliminate a large subset of the entities in a BREP solid part model, thereby reducing the space required for matching patterns. This filtered model is called the skeleton model. The filtering scheme is based on human perception in which the filtered skeleton contains a strong hint about the location and nature of each feature. Multiple filters are used to create various skeleton-types, and then a merging of all skeletons is done to create a master-skeleton. Subsequently, a rule-based mapping is performed on the merged skeleton to identify features. Finally, a facial-feature reconstruction is performed to add faces on the features of the part identified from the skeleton. The principal advantage of this method is its ability to reduce the search space by a substantial amount, at the same time preserving the feature information in the form of a skeleton. A characteristic of most existing feature recognition approaches is that they do not have sufficient computational speed to handle objects with a large number of topological entities. The depth perceptive filter handles this problem by eliminating a large number of the entities that are not necessary for describing features.

A graph grammar approach to feature recognition has been proposed by Pinilla et. al. [21]. Features are recognized by parsing the feature against the graph of the object. A topology graph that contains geometric information is used for the underlying representation. Although this approach is extremely generic for recognizing features, it has the potential of being a combinatorially explosive search problem.

Floriani [7] performs feature identification and classification based on analysis of connectivity properties of edge-face graphs within a model. The edge-face graph is a face-based topological description of the object boundary. Based upon geometric considerations and connectivity properties of the edge-face graphs, the features are extracted. The features are in the form of hierarchical graph decompositions, which partition the object boundary into components representing form features. This method is a very general method for feature recognition, as it only depends on the local geometry.

Staley, Henderson and Anderson [27] use a syntactic pattern recognition method for feature extraction. The syntactic pattern recognition is applied to hole classification from 2D cross section descriptions that are extracted from 3D solid models. The approach is generic with respect to hole shapes, however it does not address extraction of other types of features.

Sakurai and Gossard [23] [24] perform feature recognition from a BREP solid model. They search for subgraphs with the same characteristics as the shape feature to be recognized. When a shape feature is recognized, a removal of the feature from the rest of the solid is performed. Subsequently, the model left behind is analyzed for additional features. Such a recursive process is repeated until no additional features are left. One of the benefits of their approach is that they provide a simple interface to define new features of which the system has no *a priori* knowledge. The disadvantage of their approach, as the authors recognize, is that it cannot recognize generic features.

The approach used in the current research is somewhat different from the other popular approaches. We use a domain-centered, heuristics-based approach that requires *a priori* knowledge about the shapes of features. We do not strive to make it a completely generic approach at this stage, as we are striving to solve a practical problem of recognizing features in real objects with arbitrary complexity of geometry. This is a domain-centered approach and it uses knowledge specific to a class of geometry. For the current research, the class of geometry considered is the shell-like geometry such as that shown in Figure 2. The description of the geometry is in terms of a BREP solid model.

6.2 Assumptions

Since the approach is a domain-centered approach, it uses knowledge about the general classes of shapes that exist within the domain to recognize features. Therefore, currently, the approach will recognize a subset of the shape features that are found in shell-like part domains. The current approach to feature recognition is based on the following assumptions about the shapes of the input parts:

1. **Single-piece objects:** Parts are assumed to be single-piece parts for performing feature recognition. If feature recognition is to be performed for an assembly of components, the single part feature recognition process may be repeated for all the components of the assembly.

2. **Shell-like geometry:** The part is assumed to be a shell-like part such as that found in injection molding, thin aluminium castings, sheet metals, and certain types of extrusions. A shell-like part is shown in Figure 2, which has a thin shell-like base with features attached. Some features are projecting features, like the ribs, and some are depression features like the holes [11]. In any case there is one connected body, connected by the thin shell-like base with features on it.

3. **Approximately constant thickness:** The shell-like part is assumed to have an approximately constant thickness. This is because, in the processes mentioned above, constant thickness of the part implies lower costs of production and therefore, most parts are designed this way.

4. **Input part is described in a standard BREP format:** The geometric description and definition of the part is assumed to be in terms of a standard solid model, boundary representation scheme such as the one provided by PDES [20]. This is so that a single algorithm for a given representational scheme (PDES in this case) may be generated for feature recognition, thereby allowing us freedom to make the feature recognition scheme universal and optimized. If a variation of the BREP format is encountered we convert it to the standard PDES-based format.

6.3 Feature Recognition as an AI Search Problem

The feature recognition problem is modeled as an artificial intelligence (AI) search problem based on constraints and heuristics. One of the biggest problems in feature recognition is the combinatorial explosion problem of searching for the correct combination of geometry and topology that corresponds to a feature in the surface description of the part [11]. Therefore, providing an initial guess that has a high likelihood of being right is preferable to performing a blind search for features. Domain-based heuristics may be used to perform an initial assignment of some of the features in the model. This initial assignment may not always be correct, but may be verified using constraints once some of the features have been identified. To eliminate any incorrect solutions found while performing the heuristic assignment, backtracking may be utilized.

Figure 4 shows a part with some of the features which are recognized by the current method. We focus herein on the following features: Rib, Boss, Hole, Bend and Base. The heuristics and constraints used for the recognition of these and other features are as follows:

- **Shell Boundary Elements (SBE):** The Shell Boundary Element (shown in Figure 5) is a part of the side face of a shell-like object. It has four edges and two of its opposite edges have the length which is the thickness of the part. Since the part thickness is assumed to be approximately constant, this thickness is equal to the thickness plus or minus a certain tolerance amount.

  Heuristics:

  1. Has four edges

  2. Two opposite edges separated by distance which is approximately equal to the part thickness.

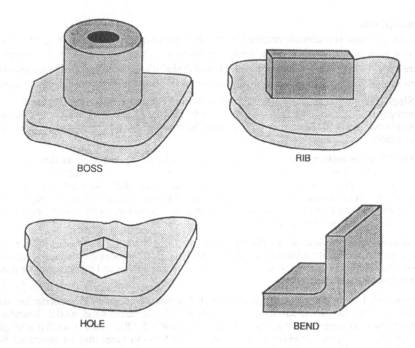

Figure 4: Features Recognized in Current Methodology

Constraints:

    1. Is not a part of a paired parallel surface.

    2. Bounded by SISC's on two sides.

    3. Bounded by two SBE's on opposite sides.

- **Shell Internal Surface Components (SISC):** Since the part is shell-like it has sides (which are SBE's) and part surfaces which are not on the boundary but are internal to the shell, which we call SISC's. A SISC is flat, and usually has features such as holes, ribs, bosses, etc. attached to or contained in it.

Heuristics:

    1. Is one of a pair of parallel paired surfaces.

Constraints:

    1. Bounded completely by projecting features, shell boundaries, bends, and holes.

- **Bend Surface:** A bend surface is either the inside or outside surface of a circular bend. For the current research, we are assuming that a bend can only have a circular cross section. This is in fact true for most bends, as they have a fillet radius provided.

Heuristics:

    1. It is a curved surface.

    2. Must have associated with it another bend surface separated by a distance which is approximately equal to the part thickness.

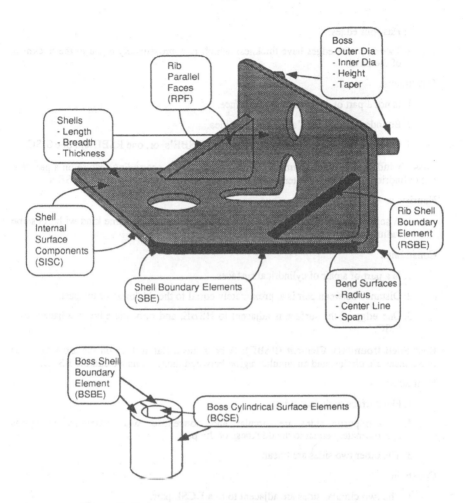

Figure 5: Features with Identifying Elements in Sample Part

Constraints:

    1. Must be connected to SISC's at two non-adjacent sides.

    2. Must be connected to two continuous set of SBE's on two sides.

- **Rib Parallel Faces (RPF):** A rib is typically a flat plate-like object protruding from the base of the part. It has two faces similar to the ones that a SISC has.

Heuristics:

    1. Is one of a pair of parallel paired surfaces.

Constraints:

    1. Bound by a connected set of non-cyclic SBE's and a SISC.

- **Rib Shell Boundary Elements (RSBE):** An RSBE is a face on the edge of a rib that is similar to the Shell Boundary Element (SBE).

Heuristics:

1. Has four edges.

2. Two opposite edges have thickness which is approximately equal to the thickness of the part.

Constraints:

1. Is not a part of a paired parallel surface.

2. Bounded by two RPF's on opposite sides.

3. On two other sides bounded by either two RSBE's, or, one RSBE and one SISC.

- **Boss Cylindrical Surface Element (BCSE):** A boss is a protruding feature on a part that has cylindrical internal and external faces. These two surfaces we call the BCSE's.

Heuristics:

1. A semi-cylindrical surface attached to another one of the same kind with the same radius on two opposite edges of the surface.

Constraints:

1. Is a part of a pair of cylindrical surfaces.

2. Distance between pair is approximately equal to the thickness of the part.

3. One edge of the surface is adjacent to BSBE, and opposite edge is adjacent to a SISC.

- **Boss Shell Boundary Element (BSBE):** A boss has a flat surface on the top which has two concentric circles, and an annular region between them. This we call the BSBE.

Heuristics:

1. Flat surface with four sides.

2. Two opposite sides are circular and concentric, with difference in radius approximately equal to the thickness of the part.

3. The other two sides are linear.

Constraints:

1. The two circular sides are adjacent to to a BCSE pair.

2. The two opposite sides are adjacent to one other BSBE (this belongs to the same boss).

The search mechanism used for feature recognition utilizes backtracking. The following is a description of the algorithm and the general steps of the algorithm are illustrated in Figure 6. First, a new surface is selected and, based upon known heuristics, a feature tag is assigned to the surface. This feature tag only provides an initial guess about the nature of the feature and is by no means a conclusive recognition of a feature. Therefore, at this point, a check of constraints is performed for the feature to which the face potentially belongs. If any of the constraints of the feature are violated, the feature label is removed, and a new feature label is assigned to the face based on heuristics, and the search proceeds. If no constraints are violated, then a new surface is selected for which heuristics are applied, a feature tag is assigned to the surface based on the heuristics, and the search continues. If all of the feature labels result in a constraint violation for a particular surface, then the system backtracks to a previous surface, assigns another feature tag, and the search continues. The heuristics aid in a reduction of the search space. In the worst case all the features may be found, but it might be very expensive from a computational standpoint.

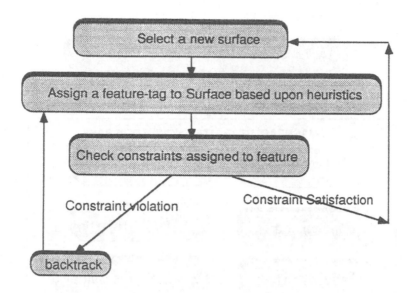

Figure 6: Backtracking Search Engine

6.4 Important Issues in the Current Approach

In this approach, heuristics provide a starting point for the search. They make the computationally expensive task of searching for features in a BREP model tractable. They eliminate a large number of permutations which most computational methods, such as a simple pattern matching, usually have to handle. A heuristic may not always be correct. If it is not correct, the error will be detected at the time of constraint checking. However, if correct, it will quickly lead to a solution.

Constraints, on the other hand, are a means of verifying that a topological entity that has been assigned to a specific feature belongs to the feature. Therefore, if a constraint is violated at any stage, it implies that the current or some prior feature assignment results in an illegal feature configuration. Constraints are a powerful means to eliminate illegal solutions.

7 System Architecture for DFM Analysis

The system architecture for the knowledge-based design for manufacturability (DFM) analysis is shown in Figure 7. The CAD database format describes the part in terms of topology and geometry. The features that are extracted from the CAD database are represented in terms of schemata and input into the manufacturability knowledge base, which contains manufacturing experts such as warping experts, deformability experts, shrinkage experts, removability experts, and breakage experts [10]. Each expert requires a different class of knowledge. Some, like the shrinkage experts (in injection molding), require knowledge about ribs and their dimensions, and some, such as removability experts (in casting or injection molding), require knowledge about the entire part geometry. Therefore, all the CAD knowledge, ranging from features to topology and geometry, is used by various experts in the manufacturability knowledge base. The common database that is used by all experts is the features information in the Features database and the geometry and topology information in the CAD database.

In the system architecture, there is a manufacturability control module that performs conflict

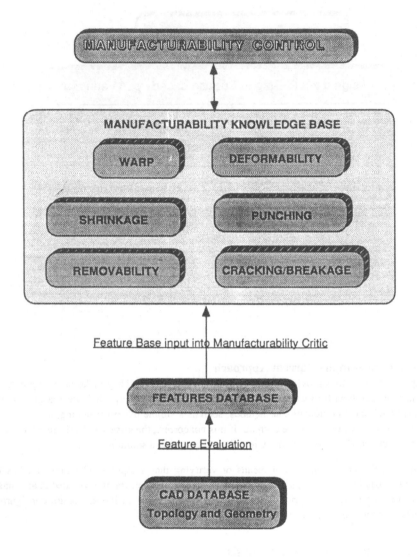

Figure 7: System Architecture For Manufacturability Critic

resolution between the various critics. Notice that the manufacturability critic itself is a single critic in the proposed multi-critic concurrent engineering vision (Figure 3).

8 Observations about Feature Recognition

1. For complex geometries, we expect better performance as compared to other computational methods such as graph matching, because the current approach narrows the search space quickly to prevent combinatorial explosion.

2. By varying heuristics appropriately, a substantial speed-up may be obtained in the feature recognition process. This is because the initial guess that is based on heuristics

ultimately determines how quickly the search proceeds. The strength of the initial guess depends on the part geometry, the nature of the heuristics, and the nature of the constraints. Further research is needed in this direction.

3. The feature recognition method has been demonstrated to work for a set of simple geometries.

4. The current method requires a certain amount of symbolic computation, which lowers the computation speed of the approach. On the whole, we believe that it is still faster than purely numerical approaches that perform pattern recognition, without initial hints, based on topology and geometry alone.

9 Extensions to Research

In the current research, we have proposed an approach to recognizing features for relatively simple object shapes. To recognize features from more complex objects requires a larger set of heuristics and constraints, which is a subject for future research.

The features that are used as input into the manufacturability critic may not be the same as those used by other critics. Research in that direction will yield a richer set of features and, possibly, a formalization or classification of features based on the nature of the critic.

10 Summary

Concurrent engineering is a desirable goal for manufacturing-based corporations as it will ultimately reduce costs and time to production, and improve quality and productivity, thereby increasing profits. Our vision of concurrent engineering is a set of critics observing and providing criticisms on the design and recommending design changes. Such criticism is provided on a single part by one critic at a time. The critics share databases, and they may be either human or computer experts in the specific product life cycle issues. Our bottom-up approach to concurrent engineering involves the creation of a manufacturability critic for the current phase, then the creation of other critics, and finally the creation of the concurrent engineering control system in the future.

The manufacturability knowledge is obtained from design rules in handbooks or from the minds of experts. The rules are based on geometric shapes of objects known as features. All features required for such analysis are not available from most CAD systems, therefore, they need to be recognized. We use a heuristics-based approach to recognize features and use them as input to the manufacturability critic.

References

[1]   Chao Nien Hua.
        Mechanical Design and Mechanical CAE/CAD/CAM.
        In EDRC Fall 1988 Design Lecture Series, AT&T BellLabs , 1988.

[2]   Charniak, Eugene, and McDermott Drew.
        Introduction to Artificial Intelligence.
        Addison Wesley Publishing Co., 1986.

[3]   Cleetus K.J., Kannan R., Londono F., Reddy Y.V.
        Software to Facilitate Concurrent Engineering.
        In *Workshop on Concurrent Engineering Design.* American Association of Artificial
             Intelligence, Detroit, MI, Aug, 1989.

[4]   Cutkosky, M. R. and Tenenbaum, J. M.
        CAD/CAM Integration Through Concurrent Process and Product Design.
        In *Intelligent and Integrated Manufacturing Analysis and Synthesis*, pages 1-10. American
             Society of Mechanical Engineers, New York, 1987.

[5]   Dixon, J. R.
        Designing with Features: Building Manufacturing Knowledge into More Intelligent CAD
             Systems.
        In *Proceedings of ASME Manufacturing International-88.* Atlanta, Georgia, April, 17-20,
             1988.

[6]   Finger, S., Fox, M. S., Navinchandra, D., Prinz, F. B. and Rinderle, J. R.
        Design Fusion: A Product Life-Cycle View for Engineering Designs.
        In *Second IFIP WG 5.2 Workshop on Intelligent CAD.* IFIP, Cambridge, UK, 19-22
             September, 1988.

[7]   Floriani, Leila De.
        Feature Extraction from Boundary Models of Three-Dimensional Objects.
        IEEE Transactions on Pattern Analysis and Machine Intelligence 11(8):785-798, August,
             1989.

[8]   Fox, M. S. and Smith, S.
        ISIS: A Knowledge-Based System for Factory Scheduling.
        International Journal of Expert Systems 1(1), 1984.

[9]   Fox, M. S.
        Industrial Applications of Artificial Intelligence.
        Robotics 2:301-311, 1986.

[10]   Gadh Rajit, Hall M.H., Gursoz E., Prinz F.
        Knowledge Driven Manufacturability Analysis from Feature-Based Representations.
        In *ASME Winter Annual Meeting, Symposium on Concurrent Product and Process Design.*
             1989.

[11]   Gadh Rajit, and Prinz F.B.
        Shape Feature Recognition Using the Differential Depth Perception Filter.
        In *To appear: In Proceedings of the International Symposium on Automotive Technology and
             Automation, Vienna, Austria.* Dec 3-7, 1990.

[12]   Gadh Rajit.
        Recognition of Shape Features for Knowledge-Based Automated Manufacturability Analysis.
        PhD thesis, Carnegie Mellon University (in progress), 1990.

[13]   Henderson, M. R.
        Extraction of Feature Information from Three Dimensional CAD Data.
        PhD thesis, Purdue University, May, 1984.

[14] Henderson, M. R. and Anderson, D. C.
Computer Recognition and Extraction of Form Features: A CAD/CAM Link.
Computers in Industry 6(4):315-325, 1984.

[15] Henderson, M. R. and Chang, G. J.
FRAPP: Automated Feature Recognition and Process Planning from Solid Model Data.
In *Computers in Engineering 1988*, pages 529-536. American Society of Mechanical
Engineers, San Francisco, CA, August, 1988.

[16] Kott, A. S., Kollar C., and Agin G.
Concurrent Engineering : Dimensions and Approaches.
Technical Report, Carnegie Group Inc., 1989.

[17] Kyprianou L.K.
Shape Classification in Computer Aided Design.
PhD thesis, Univ. of Cambridge, 1980.

[18] Matikalli R. and Khosla P.
Determining the Assembly Sequence from a 3D Model.
In *ESD/SMI Third Annual Expert Systems Proceedings*. Detroit, Michigan, April 4-6, 1989.

[19] Matsumoto Allen S., Jagannathan V., Buenzli C., Saks Victor.
Concurrent Design for Testability.
In *Workshop on Concurrent Engineering Design*. American Association of Artificial
Intelligence, Detroit, MI, Aug, 1989.

[20]
PDES/STEP Standard, National Institute of Standards and Technology, available through NTIS
as no. NIST-IR-88-4004, 1989.

[21] Pinilla, J. M., Finger, S. and Prinz, F. B.
Shape Feature Description and Recognition Using an Augmented Topology Graph Grammar.
In *Submitted to the 1989 NSF Engineering Design Research Conference*. University of
Massachusetts, Amherst MA, June 11-14, 1989.

[22] Requicha, A. A. G.
Form Features for Concurrent Engineering.
In *Workshop on Concurrent Engineering Design*. American Association of Artificial
Intelligence, Detroit, MI, Aug, 1989.

[23] Sakurai, H. and Gossard, D. C.
Shape Feature Recognition from 3-d Solid Models.
In *Proceedings of the International Computers in Engineering Conference*. American Society
of Mechanical Engineers, July, 1988.

[24] Sakurai, H. and Gossard, D. C.
Recognizing Shape Features in Solid Models.
Submitted to IEEE Computer Graphics and Applications, 1989.

[25] Smith, S. F., Fox, M. S. and Ow, P. S.
Constructing and Maintaining Detailed Production Plans: Investigations into the Development
of Knowledge-Based Factory Scheduling Systems.
AI Magazine :45-61, Fall, 1986.

[26] Sriram, D., Logcher, R. D., Groleau N. and Cherneff, J.
DICE: An Object Oriented Programming Environment for Cooperative Engineering Design.
Technical Report, Intelligent Engineering Systems Laboratory, MIT, August, 1988.

[27] Staley, S. M., Henderson, M. R. and Anderson, D. C.
Using Syntactic Pattern Recognition to Extract Feature Information from a Solid Geometric
Database.
Computers in Mechanical Engineering, September, 1983.

[28]   Suri, R.
       A New Perspective on Manufacturing Systems Analysis.
       Design and Analysis of Integrated Manufacturing Systems.
       National Academy Press, Washington, DC, 1988, pages 118-133.

[29]   Woo, T. C.
       Feature Extraction by Volume Decomposition.
       In *Proc. Conf. on CAD/CAM in Mechanical Engg.*, pages 39-45. MIT, Cambridge, MA, Mar
          24-26, 1982.

Intelligent Suggestive CAD Systems
Research Overview

Mark J. Jakiela

Department of Mechanical Engineering

Massachusetts Institute of Technology

Abstract. *Systems that make suggestions to designers are proposed as an aid to preliminary design and as a computational tool for concurrent engineering. By providing suggestions, such systems could help users obtain better design ideas and could bring information normally not considered during preliminary design to the intial design stage.*

A suggestion-making CAD system is developed that uses a feature-based representation of the design and a production rule representation of the concurrent engineering knowledge. The encoded knowledge concerns the design of parts for assembly (Boothroyd and Dewhurst, Design for Assembly - A Designer's Handbook, University of Massachusetts at Amherst, 1983). The system uses no representation of the design specifications. Because of this, the system can not autonomously design something; it can only alter a design in response to a user's design steps. This allows the system to be applicable to many classes of designs that are relevant to some concurrent engineering concern. The user builds a design with a predefined set of geometric features. The system makes suggestions by altering the design with the same set of features.

A system-user test was performed with the system configured in three interactivity modes: a mode that makes no suggestions, a mode that makes suggestions during the preliminary design process, and a mode that makes suggestions immediately after the preliminary design process. Five users were tested with each mode. All users were given the same design assignment, and all were allowed to refer to the standard book-form design for assembly information. The two user groups that received suggestions had a higher fraction of users that created high-quality designs than did the unaided user group. There was little distinction in quality, however, between the suggestions-during and suggestions-after designs. Additionally, users that received suggestions stopped using the book-form information very early in the design process and relied solely on the system's assistance. These results demonstrate that suggestion-making systems can integrate concurrent engineering information into the preliminary design process.

1. Introduction

This article is a condensation of the Phd thesis recently completed by Mark Jakiela at The University of Michigan. We hope to provide an overview of the work and outline the major results of the research. Interested readers can find significantly more detailed discussions in the thesis [Jak.1].

The thesis research was motivated by two major issues. The first is the need for a computational aid for preliminary design. Existing computer aided design systems (CAD) are most useful for *modeling* a design, that is, once a design concept has been chosen, the CAD system is used to make an accurate record of the idea. This record, or "model," can often be used to analyze the design and generate realistic graphical renderings. The systems do little (if anything), however, to help the designer conceive a better design idea; they only help to create a useful record of the designer's solution. It is reasonable to argue that analysis capabilities and realistic renderings can aid in the preliminary design process since they can provide the designer with more information about the realized design idea. The designer still must generate the original design and it is for this process that we seek to provide assistance.

The second major issue is the need for a computational framework for concurrent engineering. Often a product is designed and manufactured in a serial manner. First, product designers will create a design. This design is then sent on to manufacturing engineers who are responsible for designing and implementing the production processes for producing the design. In many cases the design idea is very difficult or impossible to manufacture because the product designers do not take into account manufacturing considerations while designing. In these cases, costly redesign and revision cycles are required that raise the cost of the final product and delay its entry into the market. In a concurrent engineering approach, all aspects of the product's life cycle, such as manufacturing, assembly, and repair, influence the initial design. Design decisions are more informed and the final product is realized at lower cost and in less time. Such an approach is presently more of an administrative issue than a technical one. Teams of designers, with each team member representing a particular life cycle aspect, cooperate to produce the initial design effort. We hope to provide a computational substitute for a particular team member. Experts are often in great demand. They cannot spend all of their time involved in design, particularly if design is performed in many different areas of an organization. By providing their input to a concurrent engineering design process computationally, their expertise is available to a larger number of designers any time it is needed. Large gains in design productivity are possible.

We propose to address these two needs by making suggestions to designers during the preliminary design process. Consider figure (1) as an example, which shows four successive steps in a CAD modeling session. In figure (1a), the user has created a block. In figure (1b), the user has subtracted a groove from the block in order to satisfy some design requirement. Assume the users's concern is to maintain the dimension indicated. The system recognizes that a feature has been added to the block and in figure (1c) graphically suggests that the groove be moved to the center of the block face. The system's concern is to alter the feature to make the entire design 180-degree symmetric about the X-axis, perhaps to facilitate later mechanical handling of the part. If the user does not understand the system's motivation, an explanatory text interactivity could be carried out on a separate terminal. In figure (1d), is shown the user's design solution. The user has widened the groove in order to both maintain the important dimension and obtain symmetry. There has been an effective mixture of human and artificial intelligence, with the human intelligence creating a design to meet specifications and with the artificial intelligence analyzing each design step and suggesting improvements relative to some previously encoded knowledge domain.

Regarding the two major issues discussed above, note first that the system is actually altering the preliminary design process of the human user. By interacting with the system during design creation, a different, better design was created. Second, note that if the suggestions embody information related to some concurrent engineering aspect, then the system is bringing knowledge about that aspect to bear on the intial design process. By providing suggestions, we hopefully will effectively address the two needs described above. It is not certain, however, that an interactivity like that described above will be effective. There are two major questions. First, will users actually be influenced by the suggstions, or will they ignore them and pursue their own ideas? Second, can knowledge concerning a single life cycle aspect be separated from the other knowledge required to carry out the design, particularly knowledge of design function? This will broaden the applicabilty if so, for the system will not be restricted to a particular class of parts. Will the

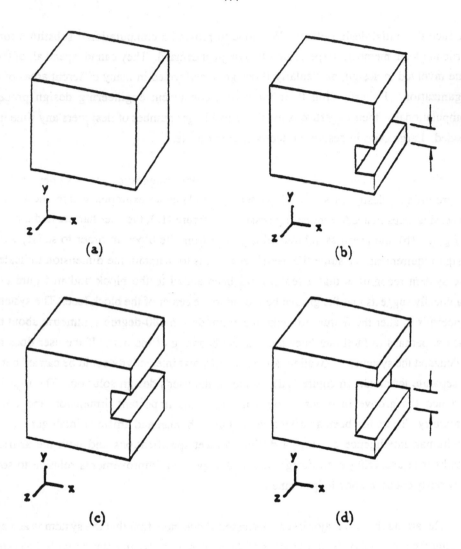

Figure (1): Proposed interactivity with the intelligent CAD program   (a) Initial design
(b) User input   (c) System suggestion   (d) Revised user input

resulting suggestions be sensible? Will they be useful to the designer? To answer these questions and determine the utility of such a system, an experimental prototype system was developed and tested with human users. The major findings from this effort are described below.

2. Background and Related Work

Recent experimental artifically intelligent CAD systems do not directly attempt to stimulate users to achieve better design ideas. Instead, they use artificial intelligence techniques to perform advanced analysis operations. A system described by Runciman and Swift ([Run.1, Swi.1]), for example, accurately predicts the costs related to a particular concurrent engineering aspect given a proposed design model. This system is much like the one described in this article in that it addresses the same design concern (design for automated assembly), and it does make simple graphical recommendations. The emphasis is, however, on the accurate prediction of subsequent costs. To evaluate their system, the authors compare the system's predicted cost to that predicted by a practicing manufacturing expert. Additionally, the recommendations are made on a planar CAD model of a drawing and alter the design in only very minor ways. In the system described here, a true three-dimensional CAD model is used and gross changes may be suggested in order to lead the user to a better design solution. A system described by Luby et al. automatically evaluates the suitability of a design for manufacture by casting [Lub.1]. This system uses an advanced graphical interface but does not make graphical suggestions. There is no attempt to graphically stimulate better design ideas.

Intelligent tutoring systems do not necessarily stimulate better creative ideas, but they do attempt to alter the user's approach to a problem by providing instruction. Sleeman and Brown have edited a collection of work in this area [Sle.1]. These systems typically operate by using two models: a model of the student that is derived from the interactivity and a model of the expert that is encoded beforehand. The two models are compared to determine pertinent differences in skill and knowledge that will guide subsequent instruction. The WEST program described by Burton and Brown, for example, coaches users on how to more effectively play a computer game [Bur.1]. Usually, the student plays against the system. A geometry tutor described by Anderson et al. provides instruction in the formulation of proofs in high-school level geometry [And.1]. Production rules are used to represent the decisions that might be made in the proof formulation. One set of productions contains the appropriate decisions and another set, the so-called "bug catalog," represents the incorrect steps. The system monitors the student and if one of their decisions is in the "bug catalog," helpful instruction is provided. Like the interactivity proposed in figure (1), these systems monitor the users and provide assistance when appropriate. In figure (1), however, there is no intention to provide instruction, although it may be a useful byproduct. In fact, if a suggestion-making system functions as we hope, there is no need for the user to learn the information embodied in the suggestions. Note also how the tutoring systems are more capable in their domains: for example, the WEST program can actually play the computer game and the geometry tutor can complete a proof. The analagous capability for a suggestion-making program would be for it to autonomously complete a design. This might be possible for a specific class of designed object, but this was not our approach. Instead, we sought to develop a system that applied more general knowledge to a wide variety of objects the designer might consider.

Some tutoring systems are more aligned with this approach. The SPADE-0 system developed by Mark Miller ([Mil.1]) attempts to promote good program planning, development, and debugging practice in the coding of simple graphics programs. This system is more concerned with the programming methodology than the program itself. It does not, for example suggest alternate portions of computer code. Closer to our idea of influential suggestions is a system described by Shrager and Finin [Shr.1]. This system will monitor a user's session with an operating system and suggest a more efficient utilization of commands. To make these suggestions, this system often must determine what the user is trying to accomplish (e.g. renaming a file by copying it to a new file with the desired name and deleting the old file). The system we propose will not have a similar capability: The system will not know the intended function of the part being designed.

Finally, some recent studies of the cognitive processes of design provide support for the idea of suggestion making systems. In a protocol analysis study (see [Eri.1]) of mechanical engineering designers, Ullman et al. found that designers tend to pursue a single conceptual design idea [Ull.1]. This idea is chosen very early in the design effort and is maintained and "patched," no matter how bad it proves to be. We hope that a suggestion-making CAD system will cause better initial ideas and promote the abandonment of bad ideas later in the design process. In another study reported by Malhotra et al. subjects were asked to design a restaurant [Mal.1]. Along with the design specifications, one group was given a list of random words. These subjects were found to produce designs that were considered to be more practical, but not more original, than the designs of the other subjects. (Refer to [Mal.1] for operating definitions of "originality" and "practicality.") The authors hypothesize that the words served as memory cues that brought more items from the user's memory into contact with the design problem. The suggestion-making systems we propose will achieve a similar, but more deliberate effect, with suggestions that are focused on a particular design domain.

3. Suggestive Systems: Previous Efforts

Prior to developing the system described here, the author made two other significant efforts at devising a useful suggestion-making program. Both of these systems consider design for automatic assembly as the concurrent engineering design domain. Specifically, the information contained on the design charts proposed by Boothroyd and Dewhurst ([Boo.1]) is used to evaluate the quality of the designs and provide a basis for suggested design improvements. This information concerns designing a part so it is suitable for vibratory bowl feeding. Typical influential part properties include various symmetries and geometrical and topological features, such as the presence of grooves or flats and surface roughness. The interested reader is directed to two of several possible references [Boo.1, Boo.2].

The earliest system provided only text suggestions [Jak.2]. The information on the design charts was reorganized into a ranked directed graph structure, with a text suggestion at each node. The user would traverse a path from the root node to a terminal leaf node by receiving text suggestions and responding yes or no. The response to a particular suggestion would determine the subsequent arc to traverse. The system had no model of the user's evolving design: the user was expected to incorporate the meaning of the accepted or rejected suggestions into a design that they were creating offline on a sheet of scratch paper. In user tests the system failed miserably. The users found the text suggestions to be too brief and uninformative and many of them requested graphical suggestions. A sample interactivity is presented in [Jak.2] and [Jak.1].

To address these shortcomings, a second system provided suggestions as text with corresponding pictures. Two side-by-side computer terminals were used. One terminal provided detailed text suggestions and the other provided a picture that was an example of the suggestion. A sample interactivity is provided in [Jak.1]. Note that these pictures were not CAD models: the system still had no model of the evolving design and the user still had to sketch their idea offline. User tests showed that most users were favorably influenced by the system. A minority of users were uninfluenced. From the observations of the interactivity sessions it was clear that suggestions presented on an evolving CAD model would be more useful. Creating and testing a system with such a capability became the doctoral research effort.

4. System Requirements, Design, and Implementation

The previous suggestive system efforts naturally point toward a system that makes graphical suggestions on an evolving CAD model. Two major requirements are evident for the implemenation of this idea. First, the system must be very easy to use so the user can actually *design* with it. The user should spend as little time as possible thinking about using the system and as much time as possible thinking about the design problem. The interface should be easy to learn and use, and should facilitate the rapid creation of design ideas. The second requirement is some means to encode knowledge needed for design analysis and suggestion generation. In order to generate suggestions, the design must first be analyzed to determine the design quality. If the design can be improved, then additional knowledge is required generate the improvement suggestions. An expert designer would similarly evaluate and redesign a part. The system must contain and use knowledge that will allow this design improvement capability.

To meet these requirements, a production rule system operating with a feature-based CAD interface was developed. Production rules naturally allow the encoding of decisions that would be made when analyzing a design and suggesting improvements. In addition, a set of production rules can grow as more design knowledge is understood and encoded. A feature-based interface will be easy to use because features are sensible geometric building blocks for designers. It is natural to think of volumetric features such as grooves, holes and chamfers, rather than more standard CAD primitives such as points, lines, and arcs. Features also often correspond to concurrent engineering design knowledge. The Boothroyd/Dewhurst system, for example, determines the quality of a design by noting the geometric features. In the architecture of the system (see [Jak.1] and [Jak.3]), the features are the data objects in the working memory of the production rule system.

To this point, the term *feature* has been used in a general sense. There are actually three different classes of data objects used. A user builds a design with a predefined library of geometric alteration steps. These alteration steps are added one at a time until the design is completed. We will refer to an alteration step created by the user as a *feature*. In this system, these are material removal features used for the Boothroyd/Dewhurst ranking: the user can remove grooves, holes, steps, and chamfers from an original block. In response to the user's actions, the system suggests design improvements using the same predefined library of geometric alteration steps. An alteration step created by the system will be called a *suggestion*. Features and suggestions are both tentative in nature and can be easily discarded from the design. When the user wishes to keep a created feature or suggestion, an *incorporation* process takes place. Incorporated features or suggestions are called *objects*.

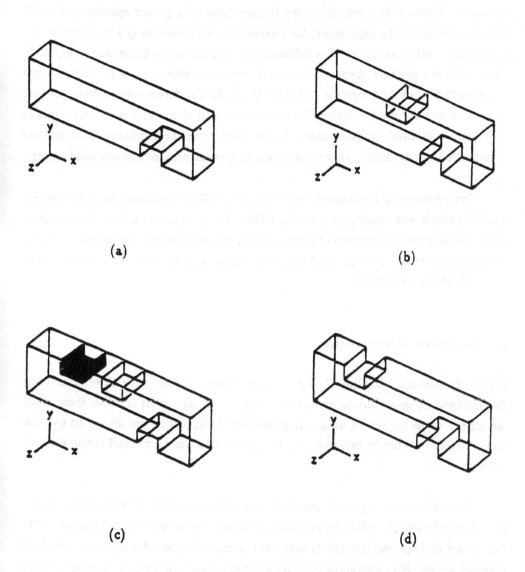

(a)

(b)

(c)

(d)

Figure (2): Clarification of definitions (a) Initial design composed of two objects (b) User's feature input (c) System's suggestion input (d) Suggestion incorporated into the design

To clarify these definitions, consider the design cycle shown in figure (2). In figure (2a), the design is shown before the user's feature input. For the purposes of this example, the design is composed of two objects: a block, and a groove opening in the -Y direction. Figure (2b) shows the user's feature input of a groove opening in the +Y direction. Note that the edge lines of the groove are not trimmed away with the input of a groove as would be expected. This indicates the tentative nature of the feature input. In figure (2c) the system's suggested improved groove is shown shaded. In the actual implementation, objects, features, and suggestions have different colors. Note how the suggestion makes the entire design 180-degree symmetric about the Z axis. This might be a design for assembly consideration. Figure (2d) shows the suggestion accepted and incorporated into the design. Note the trimmed lines to make a geometrically valid object.

The system was implemented on the Calma DDM/Dimension III CAD system ([Cal.1]) which was running on a VAX 11/780. The system was written in the Calma DAL language and is composed of approximately 370 subprograms for the feature based interface and intelligent processing. Further details on the architecture of the system can be found in [Jak.1] and [Jak.3].

5. Suggestive Interactivities

Figure (2) showed an example of what could be called a *during* suggestive interactivity. Suggestions are made *during* the design process: the user must consider them while designing. Other suggestive modes are possible and this section will disuss the two that were implemented for the user tests. All figures in this section are actual output from the system.

To clarify the *during* mode, consider first a nonsuggestive mode as shown with a flowchart in figure (3). While the user wishes to continue, the user inputs a feature. With the system as implemented, this is done with a digitizing pen directly onto the CAD graphics screen. No locations or sizes are entered through the keypad. This results in a freehand sketching style for the interface. If the user is satisfied with the feature as input, it is incorporated. If the user is not satisfied, the feature is discarded and a new feature input is possible. We will refer to every iteration through this process as a *design cycle*. The during mode, as shown in figure (4), provides suggestions regarding each feature input, as it is input. Either the feature or suggestion can be inpcorporated. The user may, of course,

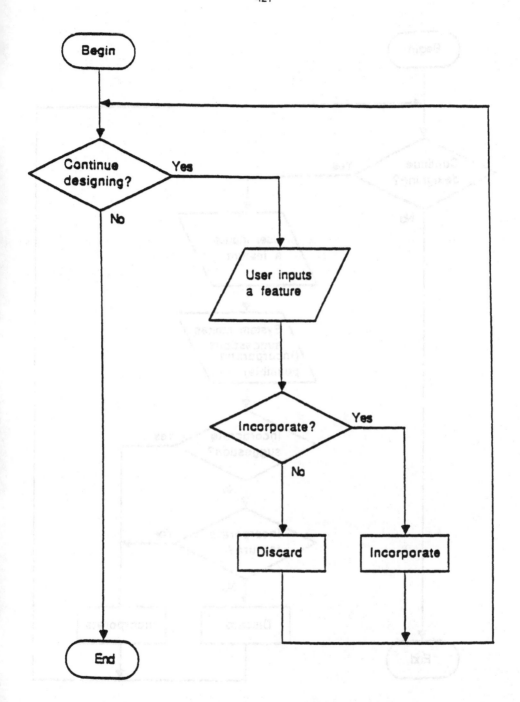

Figure (3): The nonsuggestive design process

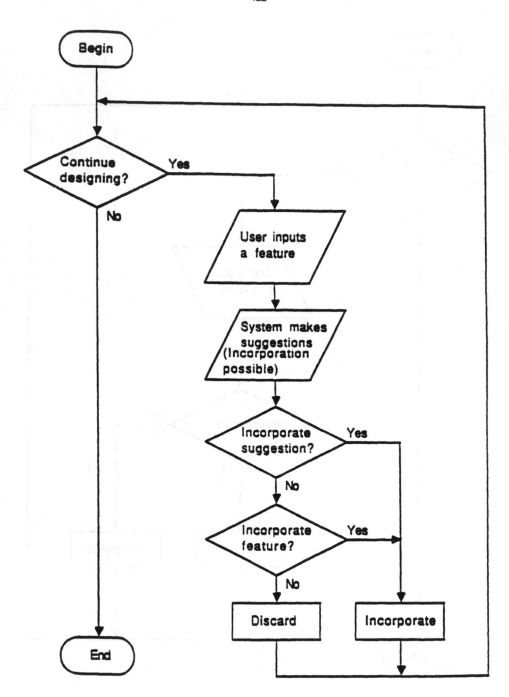

Figure (4): The *during* suggestive mode

reject both and try a new idea that was perhaps stimulated by viewing the suggestion. This mode brings the best possibilities to the user's attention during the design process. Information is given to the designer before any decisions are finalized. With such a mode, we anticipate fewer redesigns and design revisions. There is the danger, however, that the user will find suggestions during the design process obtrusive and distracting.

We present an extended example to give some idea of typical suggestions that would be generated. Note that the suggestions appear on a graphics screen and accompanying text explanations appear on an alphanumeric screen. Figures (5a) through (5i) show the first design cycle. Assume the user begins with the block shown in (5a) and then builds the groove feature in (5b). The system will analyze the design quality with the feature input and will then formulate a list of suggestions. (Refer to [Jak.1] for a discussion of the rule-based processing.) In this case, since the unaltered block was 180-degree symmetric about all three axes, the suggestions will attempt to maintain some symmetry. Figure (5c) shows how three-axis symmetry is obtained by duplicating the groove in three other locations; (5d) obtains three-axis symmetry by first moving the groove and then duplicating it in one other location; (5e) obtains symmetry about the X axis by duplicating in one other location; (5f) obtains Y-axis symmetry by duplicating once, and (5g) obtains Y-axis symmetry by moving the groove; (5h) obtains Z-axis symmetry by duplicating the groove once. Analysis of the design quality with each of the suggestions produces the interesting result that symmetry about the X axis is best, followed by symmetry about the Y axis, followed by three-axis symmetry, followed by symmetry about the Z axis. This makes (5e) the best suggestion, going against the common intuition that maintaining three-axis symmetry is optimal. This unexpected Boothroyd/Dewhurst ranking is caused by the dimensions of the overall block and illustrates the type of design suggestion that could help even a more experienced designer. Figure (5i) shows the suggestion (5e) incorporated into the design.

Figure (6) illustrates the second design cycle. Figure (6a) shows the user's feature input of a hole. Design quality analysis yields a low quality score because the orientation of the entire design is defined by the orientation of the hole, and the hole is fairly inacessible to standard filtering and orienting devices. Within the bowl feeder, the parts slide against and interact with these devices as they are put in the proper orientation. A hole facilitates this orientation process less than a groove, for example, since the hole borders two of the block faces while the groove borders three. Since the design prior to the hole feature input was symmetric only about the X axis, only suggestions that are symmetric

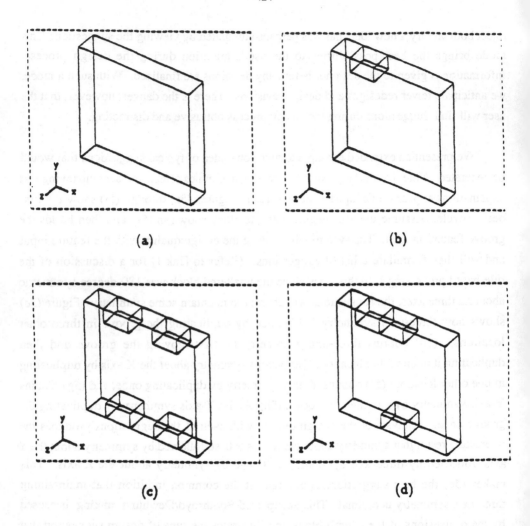

Figure (5): The first design cycle of the *during* mode   (a) The design prior to the feature input
(b) A groove feature input   (c) First suggestion to obtain three-axis symmetry
(d) Second suggestion to obtain three-axis symmetry

about the X axis or all three axes are necessary. Indeed, note that deriving a suggestion that is Y- or Z- axis symmetric, when the prior total design was X-symmetric, will yield a very poor design because two features will be required to orient the part as it moves through the bowl feeder. (These explanations may not be clear to the uninitiated reader. Space does not permit more detailed discussions. The interested reader is directed to [Jak.1] and [Boo.1].) The suggestions depicted in figures (6b) and (6c) cause an X-axis symmetric hole: (6b) by duplicating the hole and (6c) by moving the hole; (6d) provides a

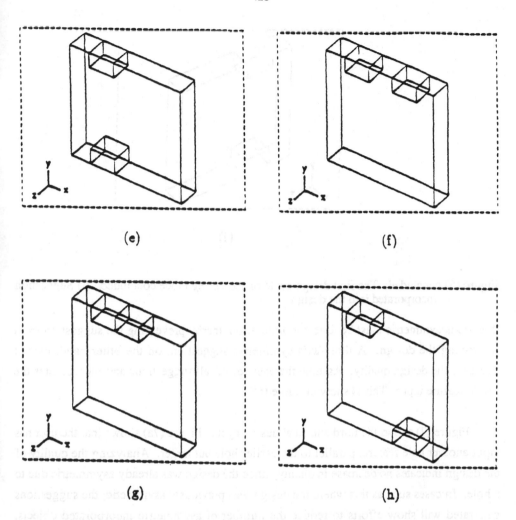

(e)   (f)

(g)   (h)

Figure (5) continued: The first design cycle of the *during* mode continued   (e) Suggestion to
obtain X-axis symmetry   (f) First suggestion to obtain Y-axis symmetry
(g) Second suggestion to obtain Y-axis symmetry   (h) Suggestion to obtain Z-axis
symmetry

three-axis symmetric hole hole by duplicating the hole three times, and (6e) by moving and
duplicating once. The suggestion of (6d) actually would not be output because two of the
holes clash with two of the grooves. When analyzing the design quality and ranking the
suggestions in situations where single-axis symmetry existed prior to the feature input, the
following heuristic is used: suggestions that cause the existing symmetry are preferrable to
suggestions that offer three-axis symmetry. A suggestion that is three-axis symmetric
within itself is a neutral addition to the design. Other incorporated objects that are not

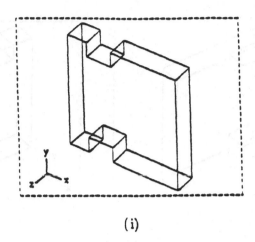

(i)

Figure (5) concluded: The first design cycle of the *during* mode concluded ; (i) Suggestion incorporated into the design

three-axis symmetric must be used for orientation, therby preventing the suggestion from improving the design. A three-axis symmetric suggestion, on the other hand, cannot decrease the design quality. Assume the user rejects all suggestions and incorporates the initial feature input. This is show in figure (6f).

Figure (7) shows the third and final design cycle. Figure (7a) shows that the user has input another hole feature, parallel to the earlier hole but larger. Analyzing the quality of the design indicates no decrease in quality, since the design was already asymmetric due to a hole. In cases such as this where the design was previously asymmetic, the suggestions generated will show efforts to reduce the number of asymmetric incorporated objects. Figure (7b) shows one possibility: moving the hole feature and decreasing its size. Figure (7c) shows the suggestion incorporated into the design.

This extended example makes evident some of the limitations of the *during* suggestive mode. Suggestions are made regarding only the feature just input. The system will not suggest that an incorporated object be moved or altered, since objects are considered to be permanent. Note also that this *during* mode emphasizes the order of feature input. The early features and suggestions can influence later suggestions. This was demonstrated by the suggestions that maintain existing symmetry. If there is any relative importance among the features, the more important ones should be created earlier.

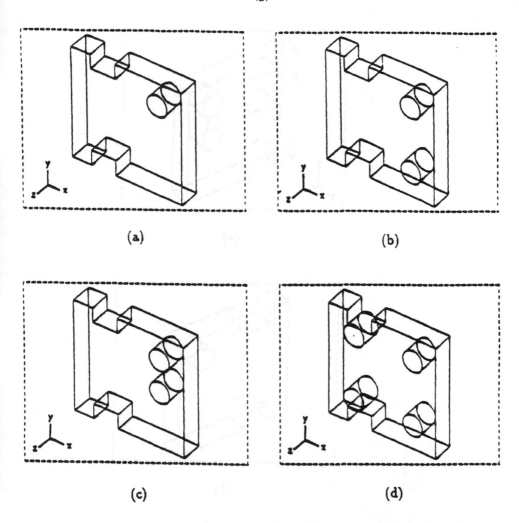

Figure (6): The second design cycle of the *during* mode (a) A hole feature input (b) First
suggestion to produce an X-axis symmetric hole (c) Second suggestion to produce
an X-axis symmetric hole (d) First suggestion to produce a three-axis symmetric
hole

In contrast to a during mode consider an *after* mode, shown as a flowchart in figure
(8). Suggestions are output only after the user has completed a nonsuggestive design
process. This is a true postprocessing approach. The users complete a design without help
and without distraction. They then receive suggested improvements and are expected to
complete at least one redesign effort. In the actual implementation, suggestions are made
regarding each object of the completed design, as if that object were the only object present
in the design. If, for example, the initial design was a block to which was added a single

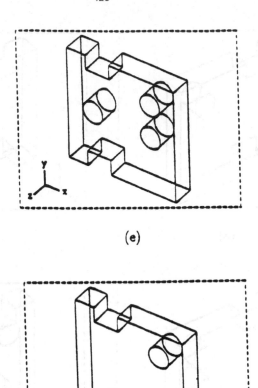

(e)

(f)

Figure (6) concluded: The second design cycle of the *during* mode concluded   (e) Second
suggestion to produce a three-axis symmetric hole   (f) Feature incorporated into the
design

groove and a single hole, suggestions would first be generated regarding the block. These
suggestions would not take into account the presence of the groove or hole. After this,
suggestions would be made regarding the groove, taking into account the dimensions of the
block (since the groove cannot exist without the block) but not the presence of the hole.
These suggestions would be similar to those shown in figure (5). Finally, suggestions
would be made regarding the hole as if the groove were not present. Each feature is
isolated when making suggestions because a completed design will often prevent the
application of many or all of the suggestion-making strategies shown in figures (5) through

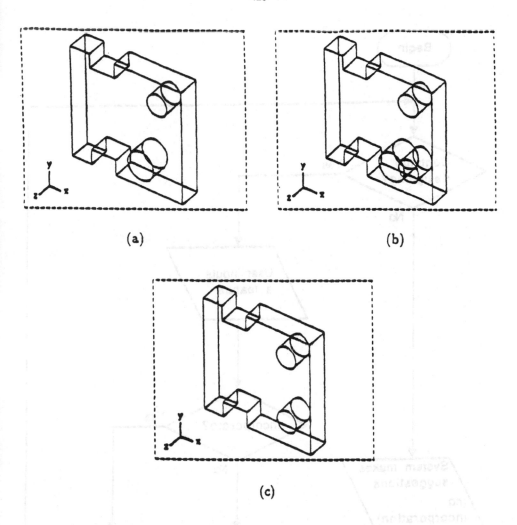

Figure (7): The third design cycle of the *during* mode   (a) A hole feature input   (b) A
suggestion to reduce asymmetry   (c) Suggestion incorporated into the design

(7).   In the case described here, for example, with the block, groove, and hole, no
suggestions will be generated from the groove if the hole is taken into account. If the hole
is still present, there will be no symmetry to maintain. Also there is no other groove to
match with the groove. The design becomes "gridlocked." We consider each feature as if
it is the only one present so we can use the same suggestion-making strategies (and the
same sets of production rules) as were used in the *during* mode. A sample interactivity is
shown in the thesis [Jak.1].

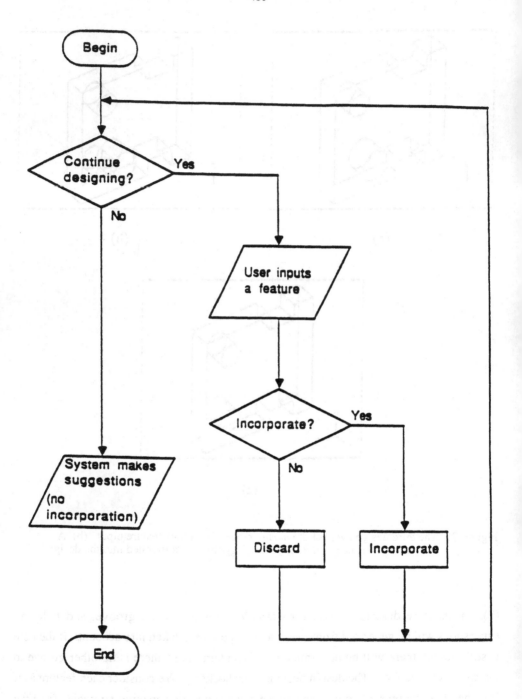

Figure (8): The *after* suggestive mode

Note that in the *after* mode the suggestions can only be viewed: none of them can be incorporated. The user is expected to view the suggestions, obtain new ideas, and complete a redesign. Although it seems natural to receive help after the design process, it is not clear if users will welcome the suggestions. With an initial design effort, users may become committed to their design idea and be unwilling to change it to accomodate the suggestive assistance. The system was configured to operate in the nonsuggestive, during, and after modes for the user tests.

6. Human Computer Interaction Studies

After the system was satisfactorily operating in these three modes, user tests were performed. The goal was to determine which mode was most effective and to gather initial findings on user behavior the system.

The experiment consisted of testing three interactivity modes with three groups of users to determine which mode helps designers create the best design solutions. Users of each mode were given the same design assignment and were instructed to pay attention to design for vibratory bowl feeding along with other concerns. The design assignment is discussed further below. All users were allowed to refer to the Boothroyd/Dewhurst charts.

The fifteen users (five for each interactivity mode) were students in the interdisciplinary "Design Laboratory" class at the University of Michigan. The course is taught at a graduate level and is composed of students from all engineering disciplines and industrial design students, who are taught in the school of art and architecture. As part of their class instruction, they were introduced to basic design for assembly ideas and were given an assignment to determine the Boothroyd/Dewhurst ranking of several parts. They knew how to use the design for assembly charts, but were not skilled with them. Additionally, they were taught how to use the feature-based CAD modeler that provided the basic interface for all of the suggestive modes. To be certain they could perform the fundamental necessary modeling operations, they were given the CAD modeling assignment shown in Appendix A. All users completed this design assignment using the nonsuggestive mode described earlier. In general, the users were enthusiastic and unbiased.

A design assignment was required that provided a very unambiguous specification of function and a very ambiguous specification of form. The users should be told to "Design something to do ...," rather than "Design one of these ...." It is important that a wide variety of geometric forms can satisfy the functional specifications. This will prevent the users from all creating similar designs. On the other hand, there should be no doubt that a design satisfies the functional specifications. The degree to which function is satisfied should not be a measure of design quality.

Unfortunately, it is more often the case that a version of a prototype is designed. Most designs seem to be redesigns, and design specifications are often in terms of form rather than function. This was clearly unacceptable for this experiment. To overcome this problem, we created an artificial design domain that is similar to the domain of digital circuit design. In the same way that each digital circuit element performs a single function (e.g. NAND gate, NOR gate, etc.), each feature in the feature-based modeler should perform a single function. This idea resulted in the "design of gauge tools" domain.

The fundamental idea is that features match each other in pairs. Consider, for example, a groove and a block. The groove gauges an upper tolerance of a single dimension of the block since if the block fits into the groove, the block is small enough. Conversely, a block gauges a lower tolerance of a groove since if the groove fits over the block, the groove is large enough. Pegs and holes are similar gauge pairs. Steps and chamfers are "gauges" in the sense that they provide a shape template to match with other steps and chamfers. A typical design problem is to configure a number of gauging features on a single, multipurpose gauge tool, given a set of gauging requirements. The design domain is more fully explained in the design assignment shown in Appendix B.

Note how there is a certainty of function with this domain. Grooves gauge blocks, holes gauge pegs, and so on. There is, on the other hand, a broad ambiguity of form. For a groove to gauge a block, for example, it is only necessary to specify the groove width. Values for other attributes, such as depth, length, location, and orientation are not needed. In this way, many designs are possible for a given set of functional requirements. Figure (9) shows a design that meets the assignment's Case A specifications. The original midlength side of the block is intended to gauge the three unit groove. The two grooves gauge the two boxes and the hole gauges the peg. Assuming that the two faces of a step are approximately equal in size, the "characteristic dimension" of a step is the approximate depth of the faces. For a chamfer, this depth is a right-angle projection of the slanted face.

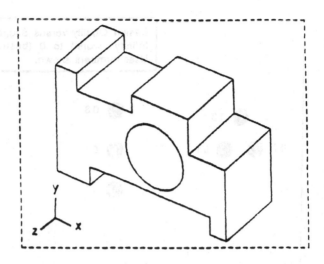

Figure (9): A design that meets the Case A specifications of the experiment assignment

The overall results of the experiment are shown in figure (10). This is a plot of design quality versus suggestive mode with each user represented by a black dot and user identifiation number. The design quality (or more appropriately "design penalty"), as interpreted from the Boothroyd/Dewhurst charts, can range from zero for the best designs to infinity for the worst designs. All users created designs with quality better than 16. These results are for Case A of the design assignment only as many of the users did not have time to start Case B in the allotted two hour time limit. The results seem to show that suggestions of some type do help. The Mode 1 and Mode 2 user groups have a higher fraction of users that created good designs, say with quality less than or equal to four, than does the Mode 3 group. There is little distinction, however, between the suggestions-during and suggestions-after groups.

Additional factors were also investigated. Recall from the example suggestive interactivity given earlier that many suggestions might be generated from a single feature. The user was required to view at least one before proceeding, but they could view all of them repeatedly. A log of program menu choices recorded the viewing of each individual suggestion. There was no correlation between the number of suggestions viewed and the design quality for either Mode 1 or Mode 2. Users were also allowed to stop work on a CAD model at any point and begin a new effort, or return to a previous effort. The log also kept track of these CAD model changes. Again, there was no correlation between number of model changes and design quality for any of the user groups.

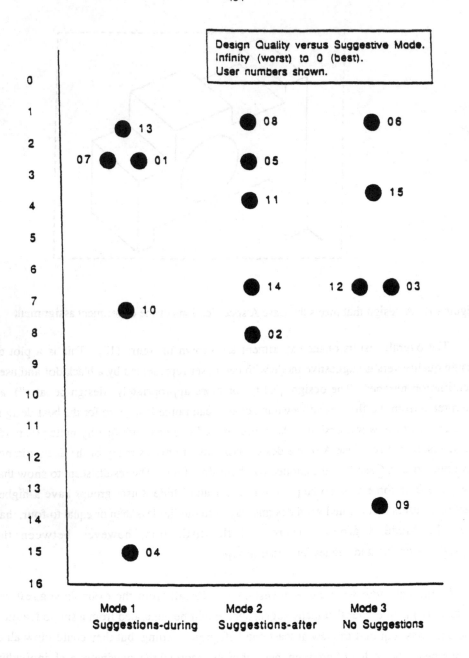

Figure (10): Design quality versus suggestive mode (Case A only)

It is also interesting to note which mode allowed the users to be most productive. One simple measure is the number of users who had time to make a serious effort at Case B of the design assignment. The suggestions-during mode is the clear winner. Four of the Mode 1 subjects made some serious attempt at Case B, compared to one of the Mode 2 subjects, and two of the Mode 3 subjects.

Regarding the efficacy of the system as a replacement for the standard charts, it was observed that users of the suggestion-making modes readily abandoned the available hard-copy charts in favor of the system's assistance. Of those 10 users that received suggestion in some form, 5 looked at the charts during design and 4 of these stopped using the charts very early in the design process. Four of the five Mode 3 designers used the charts throughout the design process.

Since the general results are not very conclusive, it is useful to consider the behavior of the individual users. The Mode 3 users (along with all others) received a quantitative indication of the the design quality at the end of each design cycle. It was possible for a user to observe the change in this figure and use it to deduce more advantageous design decisions. One Mode 3 user, user 15, made this a primary design strategy, terminating a design effort if the figure appeared to drop too far. This resulted in eleven Case A design efforts compared to two or three for the other users. A moderately good design was created with a great deal of effort. A troubling observation of the suggestions-during users was that they often chose to incorporate non-optimal design suggestions when better suggestions were available and possible. This might happen because they did not view all suggestions, but in some cases all possible suggestions were viewed. They also did not have fewer CAD model changes than the other users, which goes against our expectation. Apparently, the suggestions-during mode does stimulate some wholesale redesign ideas. The suggestions-after users had perhaps the most interesting individual sessions. Some of them seemed to adopt a cynical approach to using the system. It was clear that some initial efforts were designed only to meet the functional specifications: little or no attention was paid to design for assembly issues. With a single redesign, fairly high quality designs were created. These users anticipated the help that the system would provide and therefore did not put a great deal of effort into the initial design.

7. Discussion

At the outset, two questions were posed. Will the suggestions influence the designers? Can the concurrent engineering knowledge be segregated from the other knowledge necessary for design? The results of the experiment along with the fact that many users who received suggestions stopped using the hard-copy charts (or did not use them at all) indicate that we can answer "yes" to both questions. The results, however, are not totally convincing. The evidence that suggestions in some form do help is not very strong and the lack of distinction between the Mode 1 and Mode 2 users is particularly disappointing. This experiment should be viewed as a preliminary effort, intended to provide information regarding the testing of design advisory systems as well as information about the systems themselves. There were several problems with the experiment that could be corrected prior to further testing. Of course, it would be better to use a larger number of subjects, although it was a significant task to prepare fifteen users for this experiment. The preparation might also be altered. In the experiment as conducted, all users were familiar with design for assembly ideas and the use of the Boothroyd/Dewhurst Charts. This was done to put the no-suggestion users on an equal footing with the other two groups. In a realistic setting, the most likely users of suggestive systems are those who are totally ignorant of a concurrent engineering design concern. A test comparing the during and after modes with such users could be very revealing.

The experimental results also indicate improvements for future suggestive CAD systems. Many users would have appreciated an "undo" capability for feature input. In the terminology adopted in this article this might better be called a "de-incorporate" capability. Other researchers have already developed CAD modelers with this capability [Tor.1]. A system tailored to the cynical approach to postprocessing suggestions would also be interesting. In addition to inputting the features of the initial design, users would also specify allowable variations in the features. They might, for example, specify a required groove width and allow the groove to have a range of depths and locations on a face. The system would then take this input and automatically create an optimized redesign.

8. Conclusion

An intelligent suggestion-making CAD system was developed and tested with human users. It was found that the system can help users create better designs but that refinement and further testing are necessary. Results of the experiment indicate that suggestions provided during preliminary design can effectively and unobtrusively bring more information to bear on the preliminary design process.

9. Acknowledgements

In the early stages, this work was supported by the International Business Machines Corporation and later by the National Science Foundation under grant number DMC-86-11916. This support is gratefully acknowledged. The author also wishes to thank the Phd thesis committee and particularly Professor Panos Papalambros, the thesis chairperson, for their support and encouragement.

10. References

[And.1] Anderson, J. R., Boyle, C. F., Reiser, B. J., "Intelligent Tutoring Systems," *Science*, Vol. 228, April 1985, pps. 456-462.

[Boo.1] Boothroyd, G., Dewhurst, P., *Design for Assembly-A Designer's Handbook*, Department of Mechanical Engineering, University of Massachusetts at Amherst, 1983.

[Boo.2] Boothroyd, G., Poli, C., Murch, L., *Automatic Assembly*, Marcel Dekker Inc., New York and Basel, 1982.

[Bur.1] Burton, R. R., Brown, J. S., "An Investigation of Computer Coaching for Informal Learning Acitivities," in *Intelligent Tutoring Systems*, (eds. D. Sleeman and J. S., Brown), Academic Press, London and New York, 1982, pps. 79-98.

[Cal.1] General Electric Calma Co., *System Reference Manual for DDM & Dimension III on the VAX and Apollo*, 9805 Scranton Rd., San Diego, Calif. 92121-1765, 1983.

[Eri.1] Ericsson, K. A., Simon, H. A., *Protocol Analysis: Verbal Reports as Data*, MIT Press, Cambridge, MA 1984.

[Jak.1] Jakiela, M. J., *Intelligent Suggestive CAD Systems*, PhD Thesis, University of Michigan - Ann Arbor, 1988.

[Jak.2] Jakiela, M. J., Papalambros, P. Y., Ulsoy, A. G., "Programming Optimal Suggestions in the Design Concept Phase: Application to the Boothroyd Assembly Charts," *ASME Journal of Mechanisms, Transmissions, and Automation in Design*, Vol. 107, No. 2, June 1985, pps. 285-291.

[Jak.3] Jakiela, M. J., Papalambros, P. Y., "Design and Implementation of a Prototype "Intelligent" CAD System," American Society of Mechanical Engineers, Paper 87-DAC-51, New York, 1987, also *ASME Journal of Mechanisms, Transmissions, and Automation in Design* (to appear).

[Lub.1] Luby, S. C., Dixon, J. R., Simmons, M. K., "Creating and Using a Features Data Base," *Computers in Mechanical Engineering*, November, 1986, pps. 25-33.

[Mal.1] Malhotra, A., Thomas, J. C., Carrol, J. M., Miller, L. A., "Cognitive Processes in Design," *International Journal of Man-Machine Studies*, Vol. 12, No. 2, pps. 119-140.

[Mil.1] Miller, M. L., "A Structured Planning and Debugging Enviornment for Elementary Programming," in *Intelligent Tutoring Systems*, (eds. D. Sleeman and J. S., Brown), Academic Press, London and New York, 1982, pps. 119-135.

[Run.1] Runciman, C., Swift, K., "Expert System Guides CAD for Automatic Assembly," *Assembly Automation*, Vol. 5, No. 3, August 1985, pps. 147-150.

[Shr.1] Shrager, J., Finin, T., "An Expert System that Volunteers Advice," *Proceedings of the National Conference on Artificial Intelligence*, August 18-20, 1982, Pittsburgh, PA, American Association for Artificial Intelligence, pps. 339-340.

[Sle.1] Sleeman, D., Brown, J. S., (eds.), *Intelligent Tutoring Systems*, Academic Press, London and New York, 1982.

[Swi.1] Swift, K. G., Firth, P. A., "Knowledge Based Expert Systems in Design for Automatic Handling," *Proceedings of the Fifth International Conference on Assembly Automation*, May 22-24, 1984, Paris, France, IFS (Publications), and North-Holland, Amsterdam, pps. 117-126.

[Tor.1] Toriya, H., Satoh, T., Ueda, K., Chiyokura, H., "UNDO and REDO Operations for Solid Modeling," *IEEE Computer Graphics and Applications*, Vol. 6, No. 4, April 1986, pps. 35-42.

[Ull.1] Ullman, D. G., Stauffer, L. A., Dietterich, T. G., "Preliminary Results of an Experimental Study of the Mechanical Design Process," in *Results from the NSF Workshop on the Design Process*, (ed. M. B. Waldron), Ohio State University, Columbus, Ohio, 1987, pps. 145-186.

Appendix A: Introductory CAD Modeling Assignment

FEATURE-BASED CAD ASSIGNMENT

You task is to produce a line printer plot as shown below. Please note the following points:

1. You must do a hidden line removal in the isometric viewport (i.e. upper right box).

2. The initial block is generally long. Refer to your Boothroyd/Dewhurst handouts for a definition of "long".

3. The steps are symmetric about the X-axis of the block. (Again, refer to your handout for a definition of "X-axis").

4. All other features are asymmetric. They are not made with the symmetric feature options.

5. Just make a model with the features in the same configuration. Dont worry about precise dimensions.

What you hand in (Due 29 March 1988):

1. The plot.

2. On the plot, write the name you gave to your model (I suggest the first six characters of your last name), and your full name. Write these on the border of the plot outside the viewports.

3. On a seperate attached sheet of paper, describe any difficulties you had, and the times you will be available for a 2 hour user testing session.

Remember the log-on procedure:

1. Turn on the machine and press carriage return.

2. USERNAME: DESLAB, PASSWORD: ME516 (followed by carriage returns.)

3. DDM (carriage return)

4. 1 RETRIEVE A FILED MODEL.

5. MODEL NAME: STARTE

6. _!_ DESLABCAD

7. Remember to keep CapsLock and ask Craig   (in the back room) for any help.

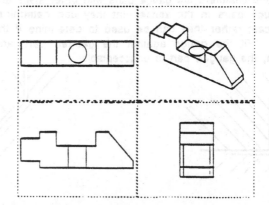

Appendix B: Experimental Design Assignment

FEATURE-BASED DESIGN ASSIGNMENT

User Number:
Suggestive program:

Introduction

Consider the idea of *gauge pairs* for tolerance. A groove and a box, for example, are gauge pairs. The groove can gauge one dimension of the box since if the box fits into the groove, the box dimension satisfies an upper tolerance. On the other hand, if the box does not fit into the groove, the box dimension does not satisfy an upper tolerance. A box of known size may similarly gauge a groove.

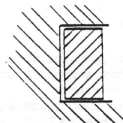

A hole and a peg are gauge pairs. If the peg fits into a known hole diameter, the peg diameter satisfies an upper tolerance. If the hole fits over a known peg diameter, the hole diameter satisfies a lower tolerance.

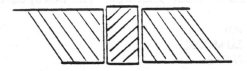

Steps and chamfers are gauge pairs with other steps and chamfers. They are not gauge pairs in the sense that they can determine if dimensions satisfy tolerances; rather they can be used to determine if the shapes of the pairs match. Fit the gauge against the gauged part, and if any light passes through, the gauged part is unacceptable.

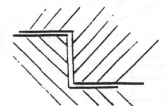
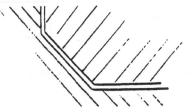

Design Specifications

Design a multi-purpose gauge tool that will gauge required clearances of other parts in a machine. This gauge tool will be fed with a vibratory bowl feeder, to be placed and stored in a larger machine where all of the gauged parts are located. A service person will later find the gauge tool when performing routine gauging service. The dimensions given below are approximate to the extent that you can estimate them while designing free hand.

Design Assignment

Design the gauge tool for the following two cases:

Case A:

The gauge tool must perform the following gauging operations. It must gauge that a groove is greater than three units wide. It must gauge two boxes. One that has a dimension of about two units, and one that has a dimension of about four units. It must gauge that a peg is less than about 2 units in diameter. It must gauge either a step or a chamfer (you choose), with characteristic dimension of about 1.5 units.

Optimize the assemblability of the tool.

Models created for Case A (in order of creation):

Case B:

The gauge tool must perform the following gauging operations. It must gauge a chamfer with characteristic dimension of about 1 unit and a step with characteristic dimension of about three units. It must gauge that a peg is less than about 1.5 units in diameter. It must gauge a box with dimension about two units.

Optimize the assemblability, minimize the volume, and minimize the number of machining operations required to produce the gauge tool.

Models created for Case B (in order of creation):

Obtain line printer plots for both cases and annotate them to explain how the design specifications are met.

A Method towards Design Intelligence Modeling

Yoshiki Kishi

Human Engineering Department
Industrial Products Research Institute
M.I.T.I.

Abstract

One purpose of design is said to think and make artificial things
that have never existed in the world. It is, however, very difficult
to make such an ideal software system currently. In this report, to
answer problems such as
-what kinds of design information to be treated
-what operations to be adopted
-how to derive numerical values
and
-how to certify the reality of results
for the ideal system, a computing model is described from
a total view of Design Intelligence, which means balanaced
thought and practice in design. It has four sequential parts, which
are (1) idea-occurring to get ideas, (2) Knowledge-binding to
modify knowledge, (3) Constraint-solving to get numerical values
and (4) Conceptual-forming to certify shapes and their movement.
Adding to this, a simple parallel approach is tested using an AND
Parallel Prolog for concurrent communications among software
modules.

1. Introduction

The currently important point in design is to analyze designer's
thinking characteristcs and to clarify the frame of intelligence from
the totality of design process. Even if individual tools for design
aids are built in elaborate ways, no relationship or cooperation
among the tools will give designers only awkwardness.

The current level has little power for building a software system
with consistent and cooperative intelligence model of design. To
break through the current level, it is necessary to propose an
experience frame of Design Intelligence (DI) in design and
investigate what methods are available for building the model as a
software system.

In this study, I make an outlook of conceptual design first. Secondly I try to pick intelligence elements for cooperative design, and thirdly build a model of design intelligence through action of each element and connection between elements.

2. Outlook of Conceptual Design

To build a frame of intelligence modeling in conceptual design, it is necessary to grip a real process of design. In this study, I discuss the conceptual design process of Laser Graphic Device (LGD) which uses laser beams instead of electric beams for information display and input.

(1) As the start, I used and tested existing graphic devices and made vague images of desirable functions and awkaward functions to deal with. This process is included in so-called marketing research. Functions in this stage, however, are merely a list of ad hoc requirements.

(2) Next I compared merits and demerits of analogous things associated with the word, 'graphic device'. In this stage, I made a matrix of demanded functions on methods of commercial products. realized mechanism and information in references, which are not all realized, and selected methods and mechanisms near to demanded functions.

If the matrix is satisfied with existing methods and mechanism systematically, the design is focused on quality improvements such as function or accuracy. One of the requirements in this case, however, demanded 'a flat and wide area display without parallax just like writing on paper with pencils'. As all existing products and methods gave no answers to this demand. I considered this was the development of a new product, and I decided to construct new concepts to solve the requirements.

(3) Then I wrote down ones near to required functions among methods and facts found in existing products or references, and thought over their applicability to the functions. Nothing suitable for the applications needs to paraphrase the functions into more detailed functions and find something applicable to make combination and fusion of functions. This process is so-called 'divide-and-conquer'. The paraphrase, however, is dependent on individual experience and knowledge of designers'.

(4) In the process to combine and fuse methods, I certified the satisfactoriness from the numerical view simultaneously. Equations used in the view are derived from methods.

(5) In addition to numerical estimation, a schematic drawing on section paper was tried. If the model is not satisfactory, I must

modify the model. After this process I got several functional models at last.

(6) After estimation of the cost and possibility of mechanical realization on the last models, I selected reasonable models.

(7) Then meetings on practical design with experts of makers' were held. Some parts of the model are replaced with another method using know-how of the maker's. The replacements are for cost diminishing relating to the demand accuracy, period reduction of production, and reliable and easy maintenance. Importance parts for functions are decided at conceptual stage, but other parts are left to the maker.

The model I adopted finally is:

"4 laser beams are scanned vertically with a motor-rotated polygon mirror and horizontally with a motor-vibrated mirror on the back of a digitizer, whose surface is attached with translucent material. On the surface, a stylus points the location or a menu and a computer controls graphic displaying after translating the pointed information to beam scan data and beam power strength. The display has 3700 x 3700 wide and 1024 x 1024 dots."

The arranged flow of the LGD design process is in Fig.1. Numbers headed at each block of the figure are mentioned in the chapter 3.

3. Views for Design

There are some kinds of views clearly to comprehend the problem in design process. Figure 2 illustrates the role of view in generic ways. The real problem is complex, but some view filter can focus on clear problem solving. A small area, say A, of the problem is supposed to be viewed through a view i and a view j. Even if it is difficult to solve in the real problem domain, we can easily solve in the filtered domain having a simple view. Although the neighbor of A is obtained as Ai through the view i and as Aj through the view j, it is supposed that the two have mutual influence accoridng to the topology originated from the real problem.

To say more precisely, the views are double folded. One is abstract thinking process derived from individual designers, and another is individual manifold thinking process based on daily practices. Experienced designers apply the abstract views to confronting daily works, in which the daily views gets reconfiguration according to the abstract views. The reconfiguration over designers' diversity is harmonically integrated through mutual interactions or

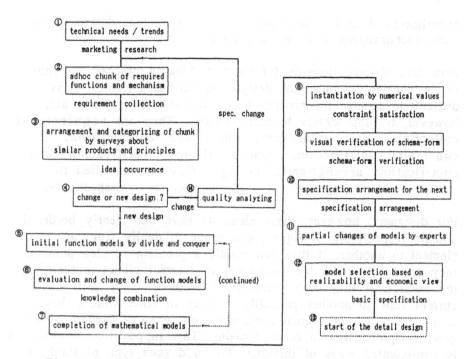

Fig.1 Outlook of conceptual design process for LGD

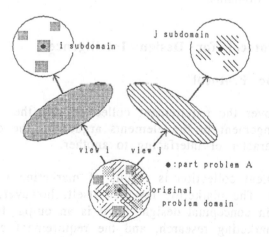

Fig.2 Problem simplification by views

experiments at each design problem, and an actual design advances with bootstrapping this reconfiguration.

Now let's discuss elements for abstract thinking process. As shown in the chapter 2, conceptual design has various activities. It is difficult to arrange the process as a sequential flow. There are, however, 6 subprocesses bordered clearly. They are **requirement collection, idea occurrence, knowledge combination, constraint satisfaction, conceptual-form verification and specification arrangement.** In Fig.1, they are classified to ① - ②, ③ - ④, ⑤ - ⑥, ⑦ - ⑧, ⑨ and ⑩   respectively.

For designers, however, these elements have not clearly bordered domain respectively. Designers can move gradually from an element to another. If they can handle a problem in idea domain, they are apt to work by themselves or interact others mutually in the domain. If they can't comprehend problems, they shift the current view to another gradually. To say in other words, they suppose that his or mutual comprehension in some domain gives good comprehension in other domains. This supposition, however, is human-oriented ways of thinking. To build such type of thinking model on a computer, it is necessary to make clear domains and interfaces among domains.

4. Semantic Protocol for Design Intelligence

4.1 On Semantic Protocol

Now let's think over the requirement collection and the specification arrangement in the elements argued in the chapter 3. These have a character of interfacing to another.

First the requirement collection is results of marketing research in conceptual design. The marketing research itself, however, is a task in business than in conceptual design. So it is an output from the process of the marketing research, and the requirement collection is a specification generated by the marketing research in a same sense. Next the specification arrangement in conceptual design is requirements for the successive stage (i.e. basic design).

This analysis leads us to a supposition that the 6 elements derived in the chapter 2 are a set of design semantic translator with interfacing to other types of design activities by the requirement collection and the specification arrangement. Moreover this supposition can include not only conceptual design but also general design process.

If this set is applied to an individual designer, this is biased according to his characteristics and experience. Now I call elements of the set as modules of a design semantic protocol. This protocol means to comprehend semantics of design from others and create new semantics of design to others.

Here I describe the content of the module programmed and experienced to now. The requirement collection and the specification arrangement are out of modeling because the information of others' interfacing is not well known. Therefore I discuss methods and implementations on the idea occurrence, the knowledge combination, the constraint solution and the conceptual-form verification.

4.2 Principle of Idea Occurrence

Human beings' idea occurrence includes information such as the discovery of analogous forms and analogous functions or thoughts, and the variation of relations acquired from experiences and observations of events happening.

In researches of invention and discovery, an origin of idea occurrence is said to be based on memory connections associated with view points caused from design environments. As models suitable for idea occurrence, a neural network [1] seems to offer a new method for modeling. The parallelism acts greater parts in processing.

In parallelism, the propagation of effects from some information to others is more important than information retrieval. Therefore the effect and the information need representations suitable for the ways of human beings'.

I suppose that idea occurrence in design is in the state of getting information relating to design requirements and idea fragments satisfactory for them. I dopted the Connectionist Model (CM), whose outlooks are illustrated in Fig.3, to realize idea occurrence process according to experiences in the LGD design [2].

This method introduces 4 nodes in the CM to consider familiarity with logical inference and knowledge expression. The kinds of nodes are:

(1) logical nodes which express logical fact predicates,
(2) class nodes which correspond to classes such as in the object progamming,
(3) individual property nodes which are properties of a class node and
(4) generic property nodes which make access to a node of (3) by activation of individual property nodes of some other classes.

The relations among the 4 nodes are shown in Fig.4, in which nodes except logical nodes allow only symbolical atoms now and logical nodes allow only single Prolog goals also. The currently implemented CM system, however, doesn't have learning methods different form usual neural networks. The reason of this is that learning in design is too generous to give an appropriate method of learning now. This method is already applied to the LGD design simulation argued in chapter 5.

4.3 Principle of Knowledge Combination

Information from the idea occurrence isn't knowledge structures but fragments related to knowledge. I suppose knowledge combination certifies the real semantics through interpreting and supplementing lacks of the information from idea occurrence. To bind them, knowledge representation by frame is fit for design. A difficulty, however, in using the frame occurs from simple listing to properties, so I adopted the case grammar [3] of a natural language-like representation so as to reflect relations among properties [4],[5]. Now about 40 cases in Fig.5 are defined, and its frame configuration is illustrated in Fig.6. This method was already applied to the LGD design simulation argued in chapter 5 and to a CAI system for the explanation of the work of fuel injection pumps of diesel engine [6], and got satisfactory results also. The aim of the method is to keep intentions of designers and knowledge engineers as completely as possible, and to realize naturally in design through making relations between design activity and daily thinking.

A complicated knowledge structure takes a long time in justification among knowledge used in design. In that case, if knowledge is constructed logically, other knowledge is deduced to be justified automatically. In design, however, especially in upper stages, knowledge is sophisticated, and it has no definite meanings but dependency on the context of its environment.

In such cases, however, designers have meta knowledge that supposing some loose decisions for the time being will cause good

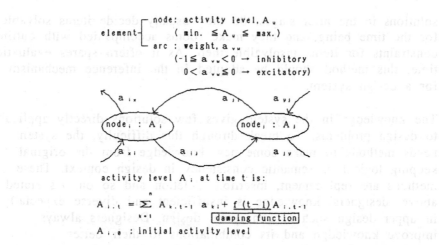

Fig.3 Principle of implemented Connectionist Model

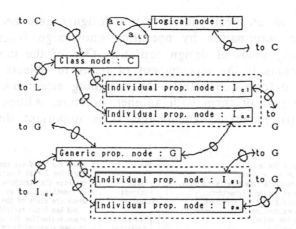

Fig.4 Relations among nodes

solutions in the after stages. So they usually decide items solvable for the time being, and they make rooms accompanied with outline constraints for items insolvalble then. As it oftern spares evaluation time, this method should be adopted in the inference mechanism for a design system.

The knowledge in the system gives few solutions directly applicable to design problems. To break through this difficulty, the system needs methods to make some new knowledge from the original keeping logical or semantic consistency in design context. These methods are replacement, insertion, deletion and so on. As stated above, designers' knowledge is insufficient and diverse expecially in upper design such as conceptual design. Designers always improve knowledge and its combinations to their better satisfaction. From this point of knowledge construction and utilization, it is needed to build formal operations getting new knowledge from the old like the Piajet's method [7].

It is supposed in practical phases that a designer gets necessary knowledge and information by operating knowledge fragments obtained in many kinds of design activities. One of the most frequent operations is the replacement of items in objects. This needs how to deform consistently the designing structures in case of replacing a part of them with another structure. Although this doesn't deny parameterized knowledge, it is important that

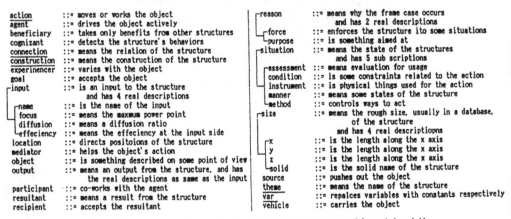

action	::= moves or works the object
agent	::= drives the object actively
beneficiary	::= takes only benefits from other structures
cognizant	::= detects the structure's behaviors
connection	::= means the relation of the structure
construction	::= means the construction of the structure
experinencer	::= varies with the object
goal	::= accepts the object
input	::= is an input to the structure and has 4 real descriptions
name	::= is the name of the input
focus	::= means the maxmum power point
diffusion	::= means a diffusion ratio
effeciency	::= means the effeciency at the input side
location	::= directs positoions of the structure
mediator	::= helps the object's action
object	::= is something described on some point of view
output	::= means an output from the structure, and has the real descriptions as same as the input
participant	::= co-works with the agent
resultant	::= means a result from the structure
recipient	::= accepts the resultant

reason	::= means why the frame case occurs and has 2 real descriptions
force	::= enforces the structure ito some situations
purpose	::= is something aimed at
situation	::= means the state of the structures and has 5 sub scriptions
assessment	::= means evaluation for usage
condition	::= is some constraints related to the action
instrument	::= is physical things used for the action
manner	::= means some states of the structure
method	::= controls ways to act
size	::= means the rough size, usually in a database, of the structure and has 4 real descriptiopns
x	::= is the length along the x axis
y	::= is the length along the x axis
z	::= is the length along the x axis
solid	::= is the solid name of the structure
source	::= pushes out the object
theme	::= means the name of the structure
var	::= repalces variables with constants respectively
vehicle	::= carries the object

c.f. A case with ___ means a frame case, and other necessary cases are used in real description.

Fig.5 Cases for frame representation

```
                    /* Variable declaration */
         (@=var,        [ConstructionName=(***)|More]).

                    /* Theme name declaration */
         (@=theme,        ThemeName).

                    /* Construction case declaration */
         (@=construction, ConstructionName
          @=size,        [@=x,           @?data, ConstructionName
                          @=y,           @?data, ConstructionName
                          @=z,           @?data, ConstructionName
                          @=solid,       @?data, ConstructionName ]
          @=using,       [@=feature,     Feature
                          @=NeededCase,  SomeInformation
                          /* Cases defined by users */  ]
          @=input,       [@=name,        InputName
                          @=focus,       @?data, ConstructionName
                          @=diffusion,   @?data, ConstructionName
                          @=effeciency,  @?data, ConstructionName
                          @=strength,    @?data, ConstructionName ]
          @=output,      [@=name,        OutputName
                          @=focus,       @?data, ConstructionName
                          @=diffusion,   @?data, ConstructionName
                          @=effeciency,  @?data, ConstructionName
                          @=strength,    @?data, ConstructionName ]
          @=has_a,       HasAName,       at,?
                    /* If more 'has_a' are needed, copy the above line */  ).

                    /* Connection case declaration */
         (@=connection,  ConnectionName
          @=object,      ConnectionObject
          @=source,      ConnectionSource,    at,?
          @=goal,        ConnectionGoal  ,    at,?
          @=reason,      [@=force,       ConnectionForce
                          @=purpose,     ConnectionPurpose ]
          @=situation,   [@=manner,      ConnectionManner
                          @=method,      ConnectionMethod
                          @=instrument,  ConnectionInstrument
                          @=condition,   ConnectionCondition
                          @=assessment,  ConnectionAssessment ]
                    /* If more 'situation' are needed, copy the case */  ).

                    /* Action case declaration */
         (@=action,      ActionName
          @=agent,       ActionAgent
          @=mediator,    ActionMediator
          @=object,      ActionObject
          @=source,      ActionSource,   at,?
          @=goal,        ActionGoal,     at,?
          @=vehicle,     ActionVehicle
          @=reason,      [@=force,       ActionForce
                          @=purpose,     ActionPurpose ]
          @=situation,   [@=manner,      ActionManner
                          @=method,      ActionMethod
                          @=instrument,  ActionInstrument
                          @=condition,   ActionCondition
                          @=assessment,  ActionAssessment ]
                    /* If more 'situation' are needed, copy the case */  ).
```

Fig.6 Frame representation format based on the case grammar

knowledge about parts doesn't exist independently on design contexts but plays its role under the control of parts relations in design contexts.

In solving logically, as logic processes problems by pattern matching, simple logic isn't sufficient to accomplish the replacement in case of meeting different functions. From this point of view, I give answers by using prototypes of design and meta knowledge which controls the usage of knowledge.

Each knowledge is represented in a frame-like form according to the case grammar, so that meta knowledge and logic control the replacement. As parts described in frame and cases are logical, the replacement is adapted to any knowledge without considering the real content of knowledge.

Now, I use 6 knowledge operations, which are **replacement, insertion, deletion, association, categorization** and **paraphrase.** Association is initially implemented with object-oriented ways using frame-like expressions, but now it has two styles. One is as same as the CM. Another is used as a property of knowledge. Categorization has two styles. One is a 'is-a' like ladder of logical relations of knowledge whose relations are apriori given. Another is a statistical method which compares properties of knowledge using the association property of knowledge and derives dynamically a new category from them. Insertion or Deletion inserts or deletes a part of knowledge to target knowledge logically consistent with the environment of the target knowledge. Paraphrase makes simply conversion of a word to another word now. Replacement, association and logical categorization are binded now. Insertion, deletion, logical categorization and association are binded also. The relations and processes of some schematic operations are illustrated in Fig.7. Their basic functions are tested in some design cases. Especially the replacement is certified in the LGD design about scanner replacement based on the fragments from idea occurrence (in chap.5). And the operations are combined to manipulate knowledge processing. In addition, these operations are implemented on the Decision Environment for Concept Inferred DEsign (DECIDE) system, which were developed from '82 till '86 by the author [8],[9].

4.4 Principle of Constraint Satisfaction

A qualitative reasoning [10] offers useful information in design. But designers in design rooms are eager to get concrete information such as dimensions, locations, and so on. They want not only

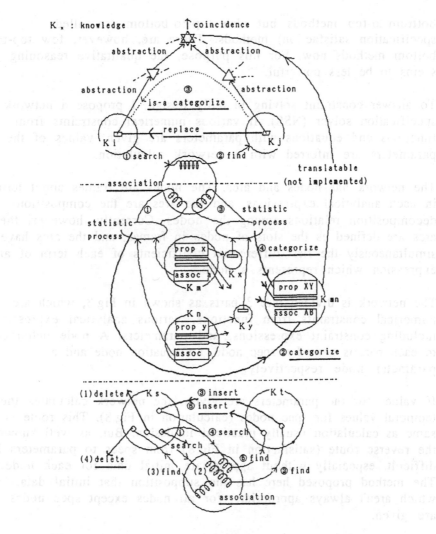

Fig.7 Some shemes of knowledge operations

botttom-to-top methods but also top-to-bottom (so-called specification satisfaction) methods. There are, however, few top-to-bottom methods now. For this purpose, the qualitative reasoning seems to be less powerful.

To answer constraint solving in daily design, I propose a network specification solver (NSS). If various numerical constraints from functions and equations with parameters are given, values of the parameters are inferred with a network calculation.

The network has nodes and arcs. The nodes are frames about terms in each analytical expressions, and the arcs are the composition-decomposition relations among the nodes. Currently, however, the arcs are defined as the slots of nodes in frames, and the arcs have simultaneously the first differential coefficients of each term of an expression which represents a node.

The network is divided into 3 parts as shown in Fig.8, which are numerical constraints from functions, various analytical expressions including constraint expressions, and parameters. A node belonging to each part is named a spec node, an equation node and a parameter node respectively.

If values for the parameters are given, the network calculates the temporal values for spec nodes (calculation in Fig.8). This route is as same as calculation usually practiced in design. But, as well known, the reverse route (satisfaction in Fig.8) from specs to parameters is difficult, especially without appropriate initial data for each node. The method proposed here has the supposition that initial data, which aren't always appropriate, for all nodes except spec nodes are given.

The principle of the reverse solving is in Fig.9. Figure 9 says that each node (the top is a spec node) puts some modification amount, which is decided by the threshold to keep the first order approximation on its current value, on just below nodes selected according to the comparison of their differential coefficients, and functional constraints are solved one by one.

The current method gives all modification amount to a node having max modification ability and min propagation arcs. If any remainder results from a just below node, the remainder is handed the next max-min node. And after putting modification amount on all nodes just below, the last remainder is returned to an upper node of each node. If a node returned the remainder from below nodes is a spec node, the remainder is ignored. And recalculation

455

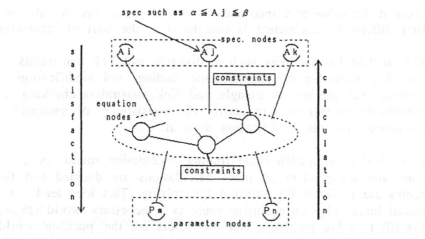

Fig.8 Scheme of Network Specification Solver

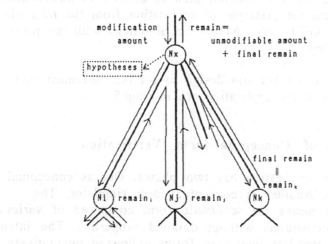

Fig.9 Modification method of NSS

starts if the value of a spec node is out of constraints. A value of first differential coefficient is calculated at the start of recalculation.

The method has facilities such as triangle and link constraints checking, exclusive calculation route finding, and modification learning and solving. In triangle and link constraints checking, a hypothesis process runs to certify the consistency of unequality constraints for the modification amount.

In exclusive calculation route finding, calculation routes for a constraint independent on other calculations are decided and the routes are preferentially selected for solving. This idea leads us to modal logic [11]. An exclusive route is a 'necessary' world (shown in Fig.10) to solve problems, and the others are the 'possible' worlds. Practically in design we use necessary worlds to meet accurately the specification in adjustment process.

With learning and solving, modification ratios by an NSS trial are accumulated and the next solving plan is derived in modification. The plan deforms the principle of calculation from the max-min order so as to prefer nodes having no affections with the previous constraint solving.

NSS is applied to a robot arm design to get the movement range of the arm. Details of the application are in chap.5.

4.5 Principle of Conceptual-form Verification

Conceptual-form verification has two phases. One is conceptual-form integrator. Another is conceptual-form simulator. The conceptual-form means the schematic form composed of various variables and constraints without detailed properties. The intention I aim at is to translate imaginary forms expressed qualitatively in such as natural language into concrete forms.
By the way, relations between solid models and programming languages have 3 types [12] such as
(1) database expressed mainly in numerals and procedural languages without knowledge,
(2) database of forms in procedural languages and knowledge in logic,
and
(3) both in logic to operate semantics consistently.

As is well known, forms have both quantitative and qualitative aspects [13]. As most researches have treated the former, a solid is mainly modeled in procedural languages. Employing the method (1), the calculation of forms is surely easy, but it is difficult to represent the semantics of forms.

Moreover it needs, according to human beings' properties, the diversity of comprehension to communicate information to others correctly and to stimulate new creative idea-occurring. The method (2) enables tø share works and solve partially this contradictory problem to diminish programming efforts. As miscommunication, however, is apt to happen because of differences between data and language, some interface is necessary to prevent it.

To handle semantics, the method (3) is necessary. By the method, meaning of forms and logic are integrated, and logic is linked to natural language also. Although an 'image' is generated logically by symbols, the generated 'image' have to find realistic meanings in design.

An answer to this is the conceptual-form integrator which integrates logically expressed linguistic relations to geometric constraints expressed in equations. And calculating geometric constraints coincident with the semantics expressed in language manages the truth maintenance of semantics. In the calculation, constraints are expressed in equations and have variables, but contradictions among conceptual forms are testable by instantiating variables with corresponding values.

This method is not suitable to the certification of detailed forms, but can offer the limit in interaction of handling detailed dimensions by converting the semantics of forms to the geometric and equational constraints.

From the above reasons, I developed a model of conceptual-forming to link linguistic expressions to geometric constraints [14].[15]. Figure 11 shows the principle of the model. As this model is logically described to details, keeping consistency is easy and the freedom of natural language remains also. My investigation is mainly concentrated on translating from conceptual-forms into linguistic expressions. So that translating linguistic expressions into conceptual-forms is fairly weak.
The developed system using a solid modeller in Prolog enables to generate new constraints from geometric constraints given in linguistic expressions. Figure 12 shows the process handling a solid with four planes. To define a new linguistic literal and to accumulate this new relation, learning semantics of forms is possible in the system. As easily noticed, 'some' meaning is defined

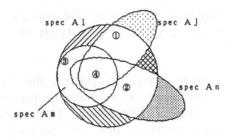

Non white subsets obtained from top-down satisfaction routes of each spec's are supposed to be
the 'necessary' worlds for a design target. If
these cases don't exist, subsets such as ①, ②,
and ③ are alternatives.

As complex subsets such as ④ are difficult to
handle, but the cpmplexity of subsets can make the
order of routes for constraint solving or satisfaction.

Fig.10 'Necessary' worlds by exclusives from routes set

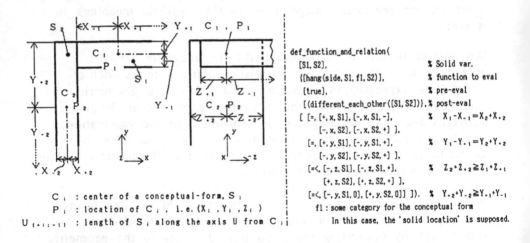

C_i : center of a conceptual-form, S_i
P_i : location of C_i, i.e. (X_i, Y_i, Z_i)
$U_{(+i:-i)}$: length of S_i along the axis U from C_i

```
def_function_and_relation(
  [S1, S2],                              % Solid var.
  [[hang(side, S1, f1, S2)]],            % function to eval
  [true],                                % pre-eval
  [(different_each_other([S1, S2]))],    % post-eval
  [ [=, [+, x, S1], [-, x, S1, -],       % X₁-X₋₁=X₂+X₋₂
     [-, x, S2], [-, x, S2, +] ],
    [=, [+, y, S1], [-, y, S1, +],       % Y₁-Y₋₁=Y₂+Y₋₂
     [-, y, S2], [-, y, S2, +] ],
    [=<, [-, z, S1], [-, z, S1, +],      % Z₂+Z₋₂≥Z₁+Z₋₁
     [+, z, S2], [+, z, S2, +] ],
    [=<, [-, y, S1, 0], [+, y, S2, 0]] ]). % Y₋₂+Y₋₂≥Y₋₁+Y₋₁
  f1 : some category for the conceptual form
       In this case, the 'solid location' is supposed.
```

Fig.11 An expression of conceptual form

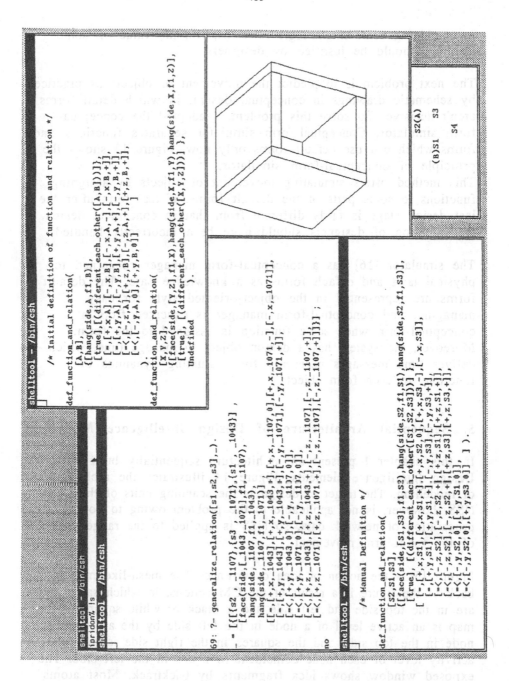

Fig.12 New relation from old ones

in combining some lingua-logic relations. But the value of 'some'
meaning should be justified by designers.

The next problem is to predict the movement of objects as practiced
by schematic drawings in conceptual design, in which detail forms
aren't decisive. To solve this problem, I adopted the conceptual-
form simulator. Conceptual-form simulator separates functions and
forms which can use default forms only now. Figure 13 shows the
principle of conceptual-form simulator.
This method offers simulating movement of objects by assigning
functions to some parts of the default forms. If real form after the
last design stage is fairly different from that in conceptual design,
the intention of designers should have been incorrectly handled.

The simulator [16] has a conceptual-form manager concerned to
physical laws and default forms as a knowledge base. The default
forms are represented in the object-oriented style for easy
managing, and conceptual-form manager is executed from a
conceptual-form when some function is assigned to the form.
Moreover, the system has a demon object to manage time, which
deliver time messages necessary for evaluating dynamics of
functions to each form object.

5. Sequential Architecture of Design Intelligence Modelling

In this chapter I present an architecture sequentially built with
Design Intelligence elements. Figure 14 illustrates the architecture
of modelling. The target of design is the scanning units of the LGD.
NSS, however, is not applicable to the problem owing to no
preparation of network data, so NSS is applied to the range design
of the robot arm movement.

Figure 15 is the action of idea occurrence. The mesh-like map in the
back of the figure is a result of the CM actions, in which same nodes
are in the top side and left side and a black or white square in the
map is an active level of a node in the left side by the arc from a
node in the top side, and the squares in the right side is the total
activity level of each node coincident to nodes in the left side. The
exposed window shows idea fragments by backtrack. Most atoms
are in Japanese, but for easy comprehension a translation table
from Japanese to English is listed.

Next, using the top fragment of idea occurrence, knowledge
combination is tried. The default knowledge about scanning is a
rotation scanner as the horizontal scanner and a vibration scanner

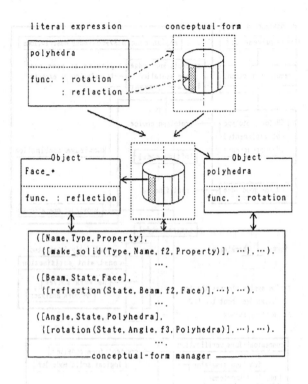

Fig.13 Scheme of conceptual-form simulator

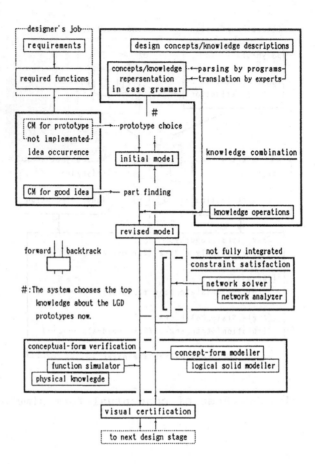

Fig.14 Sequential Design Intelligence modeling

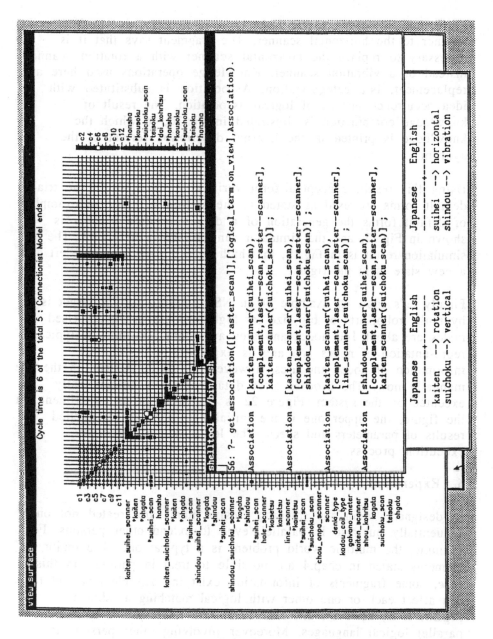

Fig.15 Example of Idea occurrence

as vertical scanner, and the laser beam goes from the vertical scanner to the horizontal scanner. The fragment says that it is necessary to replace the horizontal scanner with a rotation scanner instead of a vibration scanner. Knowledge operations used here are replacement, is-a categorization. Association is substituted with idea occurrence instead of logical association. The result of knowledge combination is illustrated in Fig.16, in which the knowledge is printed in the internal description format of the system.

Using this result, conceptual-form verification is tried. In the trial default forms are used as stated in the section 4.5. For an example of default forms the generation of a default rotation scanner is shown in Fig.17, and the simulator runs as shown in Fig.18. The simulation result is in Fig.19, in which an old state is in the left and a new state is in the right.

Finally let's show an example of an NSS application. The target is a hydraulic robot arm of big size for high load use in Fig.20. Used nodes are about 140 nodes and arcs are about 300 arcs. A typical representation of nodes and arcs is explained in Fig.21. All information of nodes and arcs, however, are to be defined in the file manually now. The process after data reading is automatically executed by the system. Figure 22 is the result of an experiment. In the figure, the upper one is the initial data and the satisfactied results of parameters and specs. The lower one is a part of execution process.

6. Experimental Approach to Parallel Model

In designers' brain and thinking, design items are treated not only sequentially but also in parallel, even to extend other persons. For example, the multiple world problem is a typical one. The major DI elements stated in chap.4 are possible to treat in parallel. In this case, some fragments of information exist in each element and they can affect each or one other with logical matching as shown in Fig.23. It is, however, difficult to make a total system by current parallel logical languages. Moreover involving other persons is colloective decision making, which is the last aim of design aid systems [17].

To certify the flavor of parallel DI, I experiment in parallel problem solving about equational expression [18]. The target is to solve simultaneous algebraic equations of the 1st degree. And a using language is a restricted and parallel Prolog (RAPP, products of Parsytec Inc.) running on 3 transputers. The number of transputers

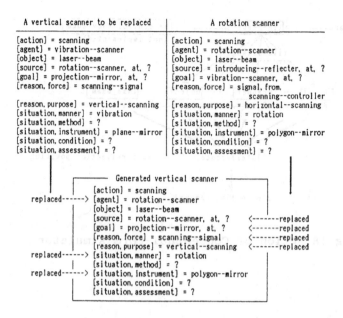

```
A vertical scanner to be replaced        A rotation scanner

[action] = scanning                       [action] = scanning
[agent] = vibration--scanner              [agent] = rotation--scanner
[object] = laser--beam                    [object] = laser--beam
[source] = rotation--scanner, at, ?       [source] = introducing--reflecter, at, ?
[goal] = projection--mirror, at, ?        [goal] = vibration--scanner, at, ?
[reason, force] = scanning--signal        [reason, force] = signal, from,
                                                             scanning--controller
[reason, purpose] = vertical--scanning    [reason, purpose] = horizontal--scanning
[situation, manner] = vibration           [situation, manner] = rotation
[situation, method] = ?                   [situation, method] = ?
[situation, instrument] = plane--mirror   [situation, instrument] = polygon--mirror
[situation, condition] = ?                [situation, condition] = ?
[situation, assessment] = ?               [situation, assessment] = ?


                    ─── Generated vertical scanner ───
                         [action] = scanning
       replaced------>   [agent] = rotation--scanner
                         [object] = laser--beam
                         [source] = rotation--scanner, at, ?    <------replaced
                         [goal] = projection--mirror, at, ?     <------replaced
                         [reason, force] = scanning--signal     <------replaced
                         [reason, purpose] = vertical--scanning <------replaced
       replaced------>   [situation, manner] = rotation
                         [situation, method] = ?
       replaced------>   [situation, instrument] = polygon--mirror
                         [situation, condition] = ?
                         [situation, assessment] = ?
```

Fig.16 Example of Knowledge Combination

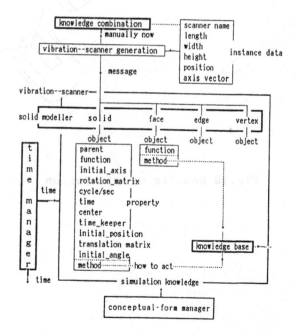

Fig.17 Architecture of Conceptual-Form simulator

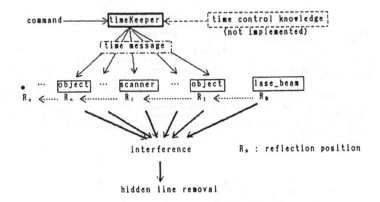

Fig.18 Action of Conceptual-Form simulator

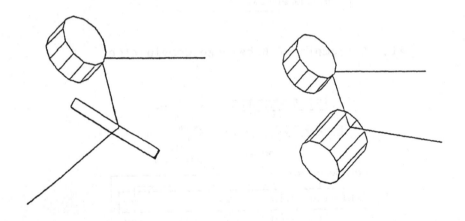

Fig.19 Results of simulation

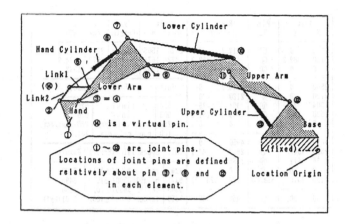

Fig.20 Schematic structure of a hydraulic robot arm of big size

```
cell_name(e6).                              % node name (presents the length from ① to ⑫ here)
inherit_key([]).                            % spec node name which controls modification propagation of this node([ ] by default)
node_switch([]).                            % regular expressions of activation condition for the node([ ] by default)
original_form(                              % regular expression of equality constraint
    sqrt((x(11)-x(12))**2+(z(11)-z(12))**2) ).
approximation_form(                         % list of the first-order approximation coefficient expressions
    [x(11), (x(11)-x(12))/e6)],             %   absolute x coordinate value of joint ⑪
    [z(11), (z(11)-z(12))/e6)],             %   absolute z coordinate value of joint ⑪
    [x(12), (x(12)-x(11))/e6)],             %   absolute x coordinate value of joint ⑫
    [z(12), (z(12)-z(11))/e6)] ).           %   absolute z coordinate value of joint ⑫
parent_arc(c6, [ql,hmax], [ql,dmax]).       % arc list to parents (which quote this node)
children_arc(                               % arc list to children (which are in the equality constraint)
    [x(11), RX11, WX11, []],                %   R** is a value of the 1st-order coefficient of a child node
    [z(11), RZ11, WZ11, []],                %   (____ is inferenced at each satisfaction trial, and same in below)
    [x(12), RX12, WX12, []],                %   W** is an arc weight to associate a node (not used)
    [z(12), RZ12, WZ12, []] ).
incremental effect([]).                     % Σ (approximation coefficient×value of this node×limit ratio of this node)
switch_arc([]).                             % arcs to nodes which are included in conditions of the node_switch
spec_value([], [], []).                     % nominal spec value, +error, -error ([ ] except spec nodes)
old_value([]).                              % value by the last satisfaction trial according to the regular expression
new_value([], []).                          % value and spec name by the current trial according to the regular expression
node_threshold(0.05).                       % limit ratio to modify the old_value (0.05 by default)
initial_value([]).                          % initial value of this node
value_range([], []).                        % upper and lower limit of value of this node ([ ] by default)
forced_value([]).                           % value to be set forcedly ([ ] by default)
```

Fig.21 Example of nodes and arcs representaion in NSS

Init		Pin	Result		Init		Cyl.	Result	
X	Y	No.	X	Y	max	min	Length	max	min
1220	0	①	1219.7	0	2520	1505	upper	2520	1518.8
-120	389.2	②	-120	389.2	2872	1675	lower	2872	1674.9
(0	0	③	0	0)	2331	1392	hand	2331	1392

Init		Pin	Result		Init	Others	Result
2500	0	④	2545.7	0			
2120	20	⑤	2120	20			
304	475	⑥	304	475	528	link1	528
-630	252	⑦	-603.4	251.8	508	link2	520
(0	0	⑧	0	0)	280	hand cyl. pr.	280 (kgf/cm²)
					100	hand cyl. dia.	101.3

Init		Pin	Result		Init	Specs, Value(Error)	Result
4650	0	⑨	4650	0			
2623	1047	⑩	2623	1047.1			
1756	979	⑪	1756	979			
0	0	⑫	0	0	8297	radius, 8400(±10)	8400
(120	1410	abs. ⑫	120	1237.3)	8471	height, 8500(±10)	8496
					5546	depth, 5650(±10)	5650
440	-430	⑬	440	-430	7850	force, 8100(±100)	8101(kgf)

```
approximation end.
incremental effect end.
Threshold is 0.05.
No. 9 depth error=0.05626982219,  value=5650.05627,  spec=5650.
No. 9 radius error=.139908696,  value=8400.139909,  spec=8400.
No. 9 height error=-4.068228772,  value=8495.931771,  spec=8500.
No. 9 force error=1.406610464,  value=8101.40661,  spec=8100.

Obtained radius is 8400 equal to the spec of 8400 by 0 .
Obtained depth is 5650 equal to the spec of 5650 by 0 .
Obtained height is 8496 under the spec of 8500 by 4 .
Obtained force is 8101 over the spec of 8100 by 1 .
```

Fig.22 Example results of satisfaction by NSS

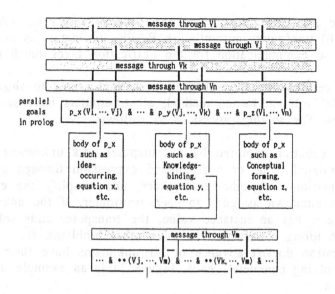

Fig.23 Problem solving scheme by AND parallel Prolog

```
        An example equation is:
             -83 + 15x + 20y + 7z = 0
              -5 +   x +  2y + 3z = 0
             -12 +  2x +  3y +  z = 0


Logging of execution
      Notation in the below is:
          pex(V) => a goal.
          [IntegerOf6Figures,Interger] => IntegerOf6figures*10**(Integer-5)
          The 3 lines below 'start' show the solution orders.
-----------------------------------------------------------------------
====> Creating output ...

Please enter the goal ! ...

? - pex(V).
start :
CPU No.2 : [[[999978, -1], 0],[[100000, 0], z]],
CPU No.1 : [[[-200006, 0], 0],[[100000, 0], x]],
CPU No.0 : [[[-299992, 0], 0],[[100000, 0], y]],
yes

V = [[x,[[200006, 0]]],[y,[[299992, 0]]],[z,[[-999978, -1]]]],

Command ?

Execute program once again  -> Space
Choose new program          -> 'l'
Terminate program           -> Any key
```

Fig.24 Example results solved by AND parallel Prolog

is caused from the limitation of experimental resources. RAPP can run on 40 transputers currently. In RAPP, unification is done in parallel, so communication for the unification takes much time.

But the result using the substitution method seems to show validity of parallel solving. In the method, all transputers have same predicates. The solving process is as follows:

First an equation captured by a transputer gets unknowns having an instantiated value or a simplified expression through unification communication with other transputers, and simplify the equation about an unknown assigned to each transputer. If the unknown on a transputer has an instance value, the transputer ends solving, and goes into idling or can start to solve other problems. If simplification doesn't advance or all unknowns have their instance values, solving completely ends. Figure 24 is an example of execution.

From this experiment, catch-and-throw of logical information among various design nodes seems to be carried out in parallel Prolog. The current information structure for catch-and-throw is by simple stacking or listing. To handle more sophisticated information such as knowledge or symbols, more refined methods are necessary.

7. Conclusions

I proposed idea occurrence, knowledge combination, constraint satisfaction and conceptual-form verification as elements of Design Intelligence. Applying these elements to practical design problems, I made a sequential model of Design Intelligence and confirmed its validity. Moreover, to make a computing model familiar with designers' way of parallel thinking, solving experiments by parallel Prolog are tested, and they seem to offer useful models.

References

[1] J. L. McClelland and D. E. Rumelhart, *Parallel Distributed Processing*, The MIT Press, Cambridge, 1986
[2] Y. Kishi and J. Yamashita, *Thinking-Aids Model for Comprehension and Generation of Functions in Design*, JSAI SIG-KBS-8803, pp.59-68, 1988.
[3] C. J. Fillmore, *Towards a Modern Theory of Case and Other Articles*, (Japanese Translation by H. Tanaka and M. Funaki),

Sansei-do, Tokyo, 1975.

[4] Y. Kishi, *Studies on Intelligent Design System Associated with Knowledge -- Knowledge Representation of Machine Organization--*, J. of the JSPE, 51, 11, pp. 2077-2083, 1985.

[5] Y. Kishi, *Studies on Concept-inferred Design System Associated with Knowledge--Representation and Inference of Numerical Design Knowledge--*, J. of the JSPE, 52, 8, pp.1412-1419, 1986.

[6] Y. Kishi and T. Kondoh, *Studies on Knowledge Representation and Function of Fuel Injection Pump with Knowledge Modelling*, Toyoda Technical Review, 14, pp.6-11, 1986.

[7] J. Piajet, *Six Etudes de Psychologie*, (Japanese Translation by T. Takizawa), Misuzu-Shobo, Tokyo, 1968.

[8] Y. Kishi and Y. Fukui, *Decision Environment for Concept Inferred Design Based on UNIX & Prolog*, Bul. of Industrial Products Research Institute (IPRI), 104, pp. 21-32, 1986.

[9] Y. Kishi, *Study on Methodology of Knowledge and Concepts Operations in Design*, Bul. of IPRI, 110, pp. 11-40, 1988.

[10] K. D. Forbus, *Qualitative Process Theory*, Artificial Intelligence, 24, pp.85-168, 1984.

[11] J. Allwood, L. -G. Andersson and O. Dahl, *Logics in Linguistics*, (Japanese Translation by T. Kimihira and K. Noe), Sangyo-Tosho,Tokyo, 1979.

[12] J. Yamashita and Y. Kishi, *An Approach to Intelligent Solid Modelling*, Proceedings of Symposium on Industrial Applications of PROLOG '88, Tokyo, pp.71-80, 1988.

[13] L. Joskowics, *Shape and Function in Mechanical Devices*, Proceedings of AAAI '87, pp.611-615, 1987.

[14] Y. Kishi and Y. Fukui, *Basic Study on Inference Method about Meaning and Structure of Solids*, Bul. of IPRI, 110, pp. 41-48, 1988.

[15] J. Yamashita and Y. Kishi, *An Approach to Intelligent Solid Modelling*, Proceeding of Symposium on Industrial Applications of PROLOG '88, Tokyo, pp.71-80, 1988.

[16] Y. Kishi and J. Yamashita, *Thinking-Aids for Comprehension and Generation of Functions in Design*, JSAI SIG-KBS-8803, pp.59-68, 1988.

[17] A. L. Elias, *Computer Aided Engineering: The AI Connection*, Astronautics & Aeronautics, pp.48-54, 1983.

[18] Y. Kishi and J. Yamashita, *An Approach to Problem Solving in Parallel Prolog*, Proceedings of the 3rd Annual Conference of JSAI, pp.303-306, 1989.

Simultaneous CAE System for
Reducing Engine Radiated Noise
- Study of a Method for Calculating
Sound-Absorbing Material
Characteristics Using Radiated Noise
Contribution Factor Analysis -

Akira Arai   *Ichiro Hagiwara*

Computer Aided Engineering Section No.3
Product Development   Systems Department
Nissan Motor Co., Ltd

Abstract

In developing new vehicle models to meet a wide variety of performance requirements, consideration should also be given to the manufacturing process and the selection of materials based on analytical simulations. Thus, simultaneous CAE has become an important issue in new model development today. Work has been advancing recently on systems that can carry out performance simulations and manufacturing process studies simultaneously. However, very little work has been done on the development of systems for conducting performance simulations and the selection of materials simultaneously.

Among the various performance requirements that cars must meet, noise radiated from the engine is one important factor affecting marketability because of its effect on vehicle interior noise and exterior noise. The type of sound-absorbing materials used has a significant effect in the resulting sound field characteristics. In this investigation, an attempt was made to conduct performance simulations simultaneously with the selection of sound-absorbing materials to be used in the engine compartment. The concept of the radiated noise contribution was introduced to a radiated noise analysis program based on the boundary element method.

This paper describes the theory behind this method and its applicatiion to an actual engine.

1. Introduction

A wide variety of materials are used in manufacturing vehicles today including various types of composite materials. In developing new vehicle models to fulfill many different performance requirements, consideration must also be given to ease of manufacture at the design stage. To complete new model development projects within a short period of time while assuring high levels of performance, it is necessary to carry out various activities concurrently. This includes the selection of materials , a process check for manufacturability and perforamence studies, all of which should be performed on the basis of analytical simulations using CAD data. For this reason, simultaneous CAE has become an important issue in new model development today.

Work has been advancing recently on simultaneous engineering capabilities for conducting performance simulations and manufactturing process studies concurrently. For example, systems are being created that can execute die and mold designs at the same time as noise and vibration performance designs, thereby making it possible to run simultaneous checks for potential problems in the stamping and casting processes for the parts involved. In developing products that suitably fulfill market needs in the coming years. It will be necessary to make use of new materials and actively design materials with the desired properties. At this point, however, very little work has been done on system that support simultaneous performance simulations and material selection. This paper presents a simultaneous CAE system for conducting analysis aimed at reducing engine radiated noise.

2. Radiated Noise Contribution Analysis

Since the noise radiated from an automotive engine affects both interior and exterior noise level, the extent to which it can be reduced has a significant impact on vehicle salesability. One way to reduce engine radiated noise is to apply sound absorbing materials to the engine compartment. Through the use of the boundary element method and other advanced analytical techniques it is now becoming possible to predict the sound reduction effect of such materials. However, there is still no direct method for determing the most effective locations for sound absorbing materials or the sound-absorption characteristics needed to reduce noise to the desired level. Such decisions have to be made on a trial-and-error basis through repreated experimentation and analytsis. In this work, an attempt was made to conduct an analytical performance simulations simultaneously with the selection of sound-absorbing materials.

Two situations can be considered for the execution of a noise reduction design based on the use of sound-absorbing materials to lower engine radiated noise. In the first siuation, the sound-absorbing materials have already been specified and the places where they are to be applied in the engine compartment are to be determined. This means performing an analysis for a design study involving predetermined materials. In the second situation, the locations where the sound-absorbing materials are to be applied have already been specified and the task is to determine what sound-absorption characteristics are required. This involves calculating the required material properties from the results of performance simulations.

In this work, a capability for conducting radiated noise contribution factor analysis was incorporated in a sound field analysis program based on the boundary element method. A study was made of methods for calculating the sound absorption coefficient and the places where sound-absorbing materials should be applied to obtain the desired effect. The aim of this study was to find a method for predicting the effectiveness of and suitable locations for sound-absorbing materials in order to reduce engine radiated noise to the desired level.

The concept of the radiated noise contribution factor is defined in Eq.(1), which indicates the noise reduction effect of a sound-absorbing material per unit area of application.

$$Ci = (| P | - | P - Pi|)/Si \qquad (1)$$

where Ci is the radiated noise contribution factor of element i, P is the sound pressure level at the measurement point. Pi is the effect of element i on sound pressure P, and Si is the surface area of element i.

3. Procedure for Determining Sound Absorption Coefficient

The first case considered was one where the location of the sound-absorbing materials was already specified. An analysis was carried out to determine the sound-absorbing charactreistics of the material needed to reduce engine radiated noise to the deired level. Figure 1 shows the calculation procedure which includes a step for determining the radiated noise contribution factor. Using Eq.(1), the required sound absorption coefficient , α_i is given as

$$\alpha_i = \alpha_0 + (P - P)(1 - \alpha_0)/(C_i \times S_i) \qquad (2)$$

where α_i is the sound absorption coefficient needed to attain the sound pressure target. α_0 is the present sound absorption coefficient. P is the present sound pressure and P is the target sound pressure level.

The results obtained where this method was applied to the simple model shown in Fig.2 are given in Fig.3. Analyses were conducted for locations having large, small and itermediate contribution factors. By rearranging the contribution factors in asceding order of magnitude as shown in Fig.4, it was possible to identify the overall tendency for the magnitude of the contribution factors. With the exception of places having a small contribution factor, the required sound absorption coefficient was obtained efficiently with a small number of iterations.

An investigation was then carried out to confirm whether the method of rearraging the order of increase in the contribution factor, which was shown to be applicable to the simple model, could be applied to a large-scale model. Figure 5 shows the model of an actual engine compartment which was used in the investigation. The contribution factors found for all the elements are given in Fig.6. Based on these results, the sound absorption coefficient needed to reduce the engine radiated noise to the desired level was found for the places having a large contribution factor. The results obtained are given in Fig.7 and they confirmed that the method is also applicable to large-scale models.

4. Procedure for Determining Effective Locations for Sound-absorbing Materials

In this analysis, it was assumed that the sound absorption coefficient was already specified and the task was to determine where the required materials should be applied to reduce the engine radiated noise to the desired level. The analysis was carried out using the two methods outlined in Fig.8.

The first method, the sound absorption coefficeint was applied to all the elements thought to require sound-absorbing materials in view of their contribution factor and then the sound pressure level and contribution factor was calculated again. This process was repeated until the sound pressure converged. With the sound method, the sound absorption coefficient was applied to one element at a time, beginning with the element having the largest contribution factor and continuing in descending order, and the sound pressure level and contribution factor were calculated again. This process was also continued until convergence was obtained.

To begin wtih, a comparison was made of the two methods by conducting an analysis using the simple model shown in Fig.2. As the results in Fig.9 indicate, convergence was obtained faster with the first method. The locations for applying the sound-absorbing materials coincided with those found with the second method. Therefore, it was decided to apply the first method to the large-scale model shown in Fig.5 and the results obtained are given in Fig.10. It is seen that that target sound pressure level was attained in seven iterations, confirming that the method is also effective in conducting analyses involving large-scale models.

The results of the foregoing analyses verified that the radiated noise contribution factor can be used effectively in finding the necessary sound absorption coefficient and locations for applying sound-absorbing materials in order to obtain the desired noise reduction.

5. Future Work

Using the radiated noise contribution factor, the authors intend to investigate a method for determining the sound absorption coefficient of several different types of sound-absorbing materials simultanesouly at multiple measurement points. In addition, a study will also be made of a finite element model automation system that can quickly modify the analytical models automatically when parts shapes are changed. It is thought that this capability will be an essential function for the efficient use of simultaneous CAE in the future.

477

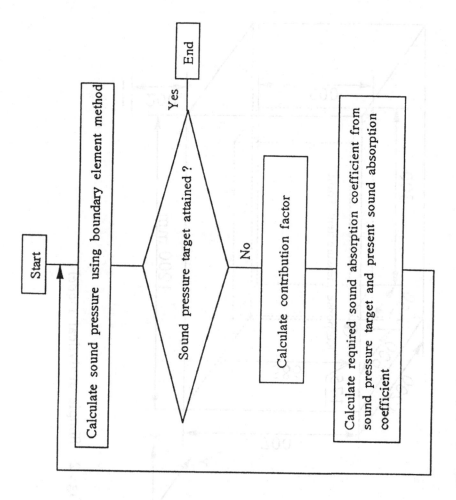

Fig . 1 Calculation procedure of sound absorption coefficient

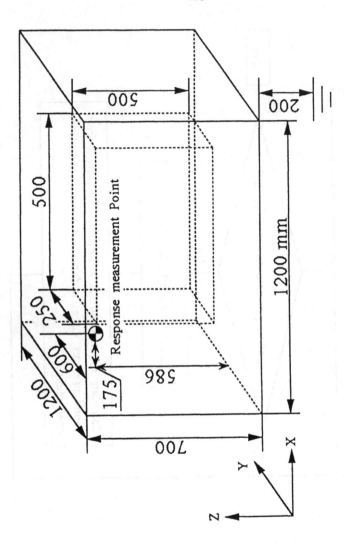

Fig . 2 Simple analytical model

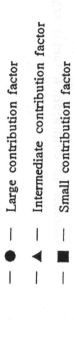

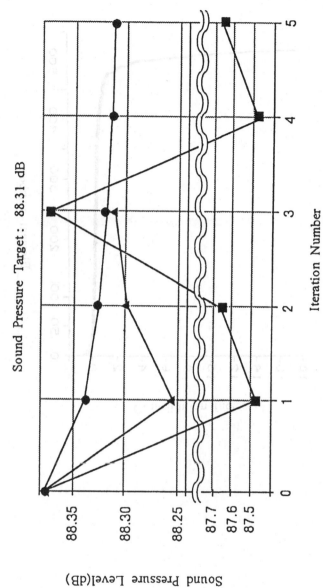

Fig . 3   Magnitude of contribution factor vs. convergence condition

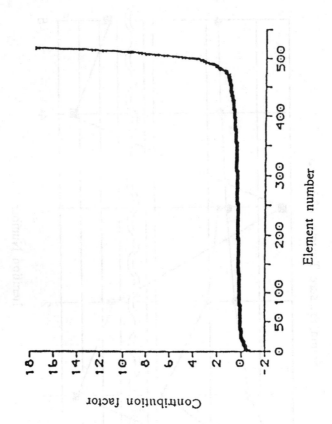

Fig . 4 Results obtained with simple model when order of increase in contribution factor was rearranged

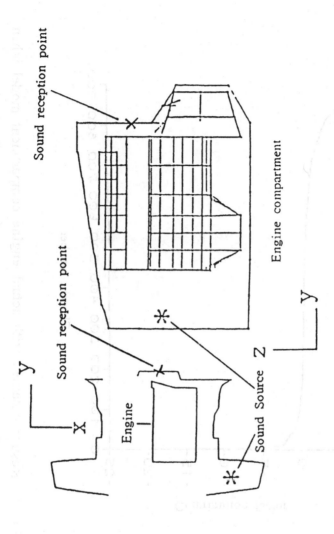

Fig . 5   Engine compartment calculation model

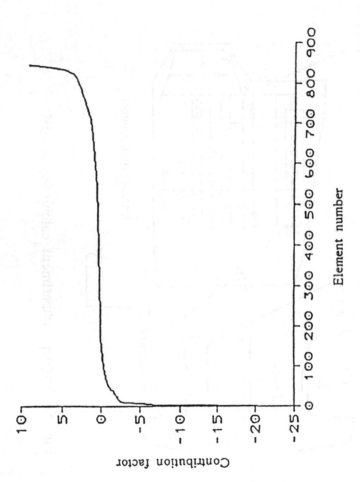

Fig. 6 Results obtained with actual engine compartment model when contribution factors were rearranged in ascending order

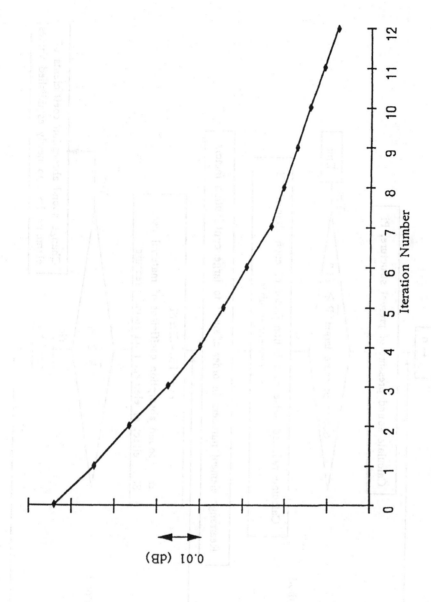

Fig. 7　Calculation results for actual engine compartment

484

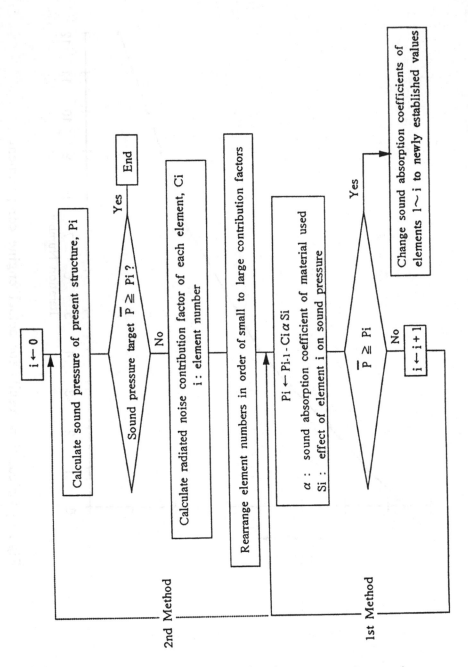

Fig. 8 Calculation procedure for locations of sound-
absorbing materials using the contribution factor

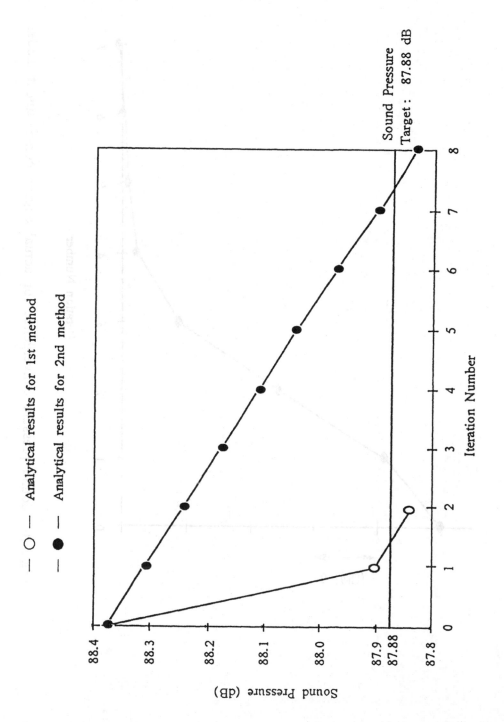

Fig . 9 Difference in convergence for two calculation methods

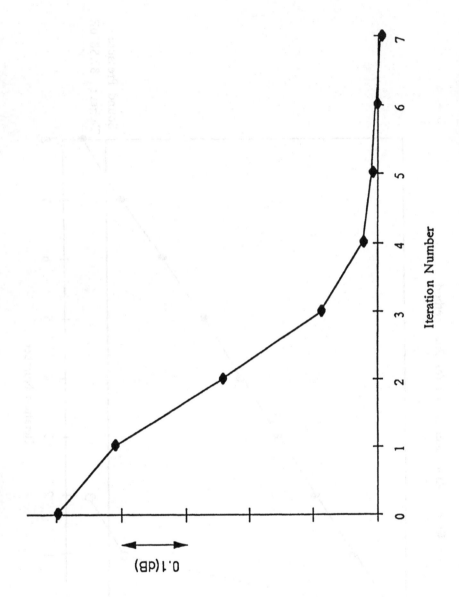

Fig . 10 Sound pressure convergence for actual engine compartment model

EXPERT R&M DESIGN SYNTHESIS
AN ENABLING TECHNOLOGY FOR CONCURRENT
ENGINEERING

James Glover Ray Rolen Tim VanBibber

McDonnell Douglas

ABSTRACT

Multi-disciplinary design teams are a critical element of concurrent engineering, and to be effective, participating functions must have commensurate technical capability. The proposed key to successful concurrent engineering is the technical ability of each design team member to productively participate. This paper describes the importance of "synthesis" software tools to integrate Reliability and Maintainability (R&M) into the early Computer Aided Design environment, thus enabling productive concurrent engineering. A newly developed expert R&M synthesis tool is described along with recent concurrent engineering experiences which lead to its development.

If participation is all that were needed concurrent engineering would have been implemented long ago. The key to effective concurrency is in the ability of the individual team members to productively contribute to the design decision process in a timely manner. Major design configuration decisions must be made before much design detail is available. Technology offers the ability to develop the engineering tools needed to discriminate between design and technology options in this early decision process thus enabling effective concurrent engineering.

INTRODUCTION

Effective concurrent engineering requires the use of multi-disciplinary design teams where each team member has both the opportunity and capability to fully participate in the design process. The concurrent engineering process requires that timely trades of system design alternatives be made as the design concept evolves. Each of the speciality groups (manufacturing, logistics, maintainability etc...) need to participate in the system design and trade study process, but; are the needed concurrent-process tools available to support early design decisions? Do each of the participating functions have commensurate technical capability? Can participants pro-actively influence design through feed-forward processes, or are they limited to reacting to design in the role of design police? Design concurrency, in our experience, is significantly dependent on having the technical analysis tools available to enable each functional group or individual to productively contribute, and in a timely enough manner to support the design decision process. The application of "synthesis" software tools that integrate R&M and Operations and Support Cost features into the early Computer Aided Design environment enables productive design participation and concurrent engineering.

This paper describes the concurrent engineering concept and a Reliability and Maintainability synthesis software tool that has been developed to improve design concurrency.

ACES (Advanced Configuration Expert-System Synthesis) is an expert system developed by the McDonnell Douglas Missile Systems Company (MDMSC) to evaluate supportability within the concurrent engineering process for use in Advanced Design. The ACES software incorporates expert system evaluation and the selection of a preferred design based on supportability criteria such as: reliability, maintainability, availability, and support costs. The ACES software program offers direct simultaneous comparison of different system designs and allows significantly faster evaluation of supportability than previously available tools. It evaluates and compares alternative missile system design and support concepts at any level from the air vehicle to individual subassemblies. Each parameter in the model can be decomposed to its smallest unit, and source of data. During this process, the user has constant visibility of how each element is calculated and the difference in value between the design alternatives. Data elements can be easily changed to allow the user to make "what if" decisions or to revise data to better represent the system under analysis. The ACES program offers easy to interpret graphics, sensitivity analyses, and text summaries. Interfaces between the ACES program and Computer Aided Design systems allow a single design loop to define configuration options, geometry models, performance, and support factors, significantly improving productivity and the concurrent design process.

CONCURRENT ENGINEERING -- A TOTAL QUALITY MANAGEMENT CONCEPT

Increasingly, "Quality" is used to describe a new management philosophy rather than a top-of-the-line product or service. Managers have discovered that, while Computer Integrated Manufacturing, Computer Aided Engineering, and Management Information Systems may integrate the technical and business systems they cannot integrate the human system. In a report prepared for the Harvard Business Review, James Dean Jr., of the Pennsylvania State University Center For The Management of Technology And Organizational Change said, "Manufacturing organizations are going through changes equal to any in history..., and that without human system integration these automation systems are little more than expensive showpieces." In a OASD(P&L) (Office Assistant Secretary of Defense (Production and Logistics)) report to The Committee on Appropriations of the United States House Representatives, quality was defined as "A dedication to shifting emphasis from bottom line profits to doing things right the first time." Quality was described as the ability to track and measure mistakes during the design and production process and correcting them as they occur. Peter Angiola, Staff Assistant, Defense Industrial Productivity and Quality Directorate said that "New quality concepts [concurrent engineering] are shifting the emphasis on making a product successful as viewed from conformance to specifications, to conformance to correctly defined specifications."

David Halberstam, in his book THE RECKONING, describes how the corporate leaders of America's three major auto manufacturers perceived that quality would be the key to combat their declining market share against the Japanese. The "ivory towers" of Detroit, as Halberstam called them, were sincere in their goals to improve quality, but naive in their attempt to provide an environment conducive to change. They made "soft" agreements with the unions with the hope that this improved management-labor relationship would result in higher production and improved quality. The concept was spearheaded by "Harvard whiz kids" who were totally consumed in business statistics. Despite their attempts, production did not improve and quality was only a slogan.

Quality experts estimate that the total cost of poor quality, or the cost of not doing things right the first time, is 20% of gross sales for manufacturing companies, and 30% for services companies. Total U.S. production of goods and services is an estimated $3.7 trillion, so our quality target, the potential for savings from quality, is a staggering $920 billion that can be saved or redirected to better uses (House Republican Research Committee).

A draft DoD Directive describes TQM as "A disciplined management process, under the leadership of the top executive, involving everyone in a cooperative effort to achieve a quality product or service through continuous process improvement combined with continuous life-cycle cost reduction to satisfy customer needs and maximize combat capability" (Quality & Reliability Assurance Committee of the National Security Industrial Association). The Directive applies to the Office of the Secretary of Defense (OSD), the Military Departments, the Joint Chiefs of Staff, and the Defense Agencies.

The Institute For Defense Analysis (IDA), a not-for-profit Federally-funded research and development center, was asked by the Assistant Secretary of Defense for Production and Logistics to assemble a a team of senior level DoD engineering personnel, academic and industry experts who could develop recommendations for defense executives concerning an acquisition policy that encouraged the principles of Concurrent Engineering. The IDA task force, consisting of approximately 100 people, met in three workshops over the summer of 1988, and resulted in a briefing to Dr. Costello and each of the Service Secretaries in November, 1988.

In a parallel effort with the IDA task force, the Pymatuning Group Inc. was contracted by the DoD to form a group of industry executives to develop insights from a cross section of industry officials to support and manage the concurrent engineering practices sought by the DoD. The Pymatuning group consists of 20 industry executives. In their Draft report to the OASD(P&L), the group stated that "Concurrent Engineering is an essential element of good design engineering management which encourages the many involved disciplines to support concurrently, and without delaying, the product design decision process." The draft report also stated that "Industry managers believe that the Defense Industrial Base could produce just as efficiently [as the Japanese] if modern structural factor changes and manufacturing innovation were emphasized by it's primary customer, the DoD, rather than the current emphasis on crippling documentation and on prohibitions to process innovation." The report said that Concurrent Engineering is an integral part of the TQM program and that CE would move quality improvements to the beginning of product development which will reduce expensive problems that would otherwise not be observed until later procurement phases.

The Pymatuning report states that CE will skew the traditional procurement funding profile with greater up-front loading of costs, which will be offset by savings during the life cycle from improved supportability, reliability etc., but recognized that well established funding procedures will need to be revised. The DoD was accused of being unable to realize the benefits of CE because of it's "stultifying and over-specified acquisition process" and was unable to define requirements for CE in early design phases. Other inhibitors to CE included technical leveling of competition by the DoD and a lack of strong systems engineering leadership in the government. Recommendations included explicit research funding, a permanent DoD CE organizational entity and development of new technology and techniques for analyzing and trading-off designs for enhanced quality and supportability.

The Draft IDA report, "The Role of Concurrent Engineering in Weapons System Acquisition," describes engineering processes used by various defense contractors that provide examples of CE principles and the resulting benefits. The report also provides recommendations for incorporating these principles in the weapons system acquisition process. The report points out that the USD(P&L) was encouraged in CE by reports from several companies, but states that favorable results in commercial ventures do not ensure similar effects in the DoD domain. The report does however, include numerous examples of significant savings and productivity improvements by major defense contractors as a result of implementing CE principles. The report includes recommendations such as: providing economic incentives for investing in CE, make process improvement a source selection criterion, and warns against making CE another specialty area.

In his paper "Designs For Producibility," James Dean (Pennsylvania State University) said that "to integrate the design and manufacturing functions, organizations as well as products will have to be redesigned." Dean describes the concepts of drawing sign-off -- providing a veto power over product design, as a heavy handed police activity which provides little creative interchange between functions and, thus, does not allow for concurrent engineering. The key consideration is the balance between leaning too heavily toward manufacturing or too heavily toward design. The need is for individuals who are able to understand and appreciate the perspectives of both worlds. Given current arrangements in the education and career paths of engineers, individuals with the required balance may be difficult to find. Dean's conclusion is that "If producibility is to be a reality, it will need to be designed not only into products, but also into organizations."

Michael Patterson, Office of the Assistant Secretary of the Army, in a concept paper titled "Too Little, Too Late For Too Much" said that he visited the National Science Foundation for tips as to where to look for the "best of the best" in design and engineering practices. NSC personnel mentioned that no such place existed in the United States, but; there were pockets of excellence and that he should see Carnegie Mellon, RPI and NYU.

CONCURRENT ENGINEERING EXPERIENCE

McDonnell Douglas Missile Systems Company (MDMSC), a major missile systems contractor, achieved significant results by implementing concurrent engineering concepts on a recent missile development competition. The competition placed high priority on Reliability and Maintainability in source selection and was one of the first implementations of R&M 2000. To meet these R&M requirements, MDMSC implemented a systems engineering or multifunctional task team approach prior to the beginning of concept definition studies. Concurrent engineering was continued throughout the competitive program and had such a significant influence on cost and system supportability that MDMSC has instituted the concept for all advanced programs.

The competition was based on results from a Phase 0, concept definition and verification effort which led to a point design of sufficient maturity to start an FSD program. The concept definition studies in Phase O investigated air vehicle configuration requirements such as sizing, propulsion, carrier aircraft/launcher integration and an optimized low cost support subsystem. Point design was focused on configuration, subsystem and technology design refinement, and verification testing.

MDMSC organized a multifunctional task team prior to the concept definition effort. This task team approach was specifically designed to bring reliability, maintainability, and logistics participation into the early design process. The team also included manufacturing and design-to-cost specialists. The task team members were co-located on the project; however, unifying this human system was a difficult task. Functional and cultural barriers existed which had to be torn down. Engineering was initially reluctant to recognize the importance of inputs from these specialty groups. This was compounded by the fact that the logistics people had little experience in the advanced design process. Basically, the traditional engineering design community did not know quite what to expect; and the maintainability/logistics people weren't quite sure of what to do.

Integration and development of a productive working relationship within this complex human system took time, but was achieved. Weekly design meetings were held to review baseline vehicle configuration candidates and discuss how each functional discipline was affected by configuration trades. The previous barriers were eradicated. A team spirit evolved within the organization at the working level. Design engineering, manufacturing, logistics, and other functions collaborated on design issues, which were participatively worked by the team.

Key design engineers began addressing maintenance and reliability issues. Designers began working supportability with the same enthusiasm as performance. For example, one engineer brought to work an elaborate functional model of a piece of handling equipment to simplify installation of missile body sections. He had designed and built the model over the weekend in his garage. This enthusiasm was spread throughout engineering. Innovative designs for reduced maintenance evolved. Attitudes characterized by comments such as "if you have a better idea..." were replaced with patented designs which dramatically improved maintainability and producibility.

Having achieved integration of the human system, it became apparent that better engineering tools would offer substantial benefits in productivity. Consequently, MDMSC initiated development of "synthesis" software tools which would facilitate rapid evaluations of design, R&M and support system trades. The tools would provide the capability to evaluate the manufacturing and R&M consequence of alternate design concepts much more rapidly than the previous fragmented analysis systems. Experience demonstrated that integration of both the human system and the various engineering tools offered dramatic improvements in productivity, product quality, and was critical to effective concurrent engineering.

Concurrent Engineering resulted in greatly simplified air vehicle design. The designed-in supportability characteristics significantly contributed to lower production cost estimates.

Unit costs associated with assembly and test were significantly less than had been expected. Concurrent design resulted in a highly producible and supportable air vehicle with no appreciable increase in development costs, and with with no performance penalty.

R&M issues, initially perceived by many engineers as "emotional requirements", were translated into identifiable and measurable design characteristics. Because of concurrent engineering, frustrating intangible requirements became specific design features. Concern for R&M and producibility became everyone's job. These concerns became real design issues which were addressed concurrently by the entire design team.

MDMSC has subsequently established a Strategic Quality Initiatives (SQI) organization, under executive management, to foster and support the implementation of quality and productivity initiatives. This effort is a key element in making the fundamental changes needed to achieve strategic business goals and continuous improvement. The SQI organization will lead the effort to build awareness and obtain commitment to Concurrent Engineering and other TQM initiatives. SQI provides the guidance and training necessary to establish continuous improvement on all active programs. SQI is also chartered with defining standard data transfer requirements and initiating improved automation technology and tools for effective utilization of digital product data. The SQI organization is creating a "factory of the future" that will provide competitive advantaged operations throughout the product cycle.

MDMSC concurrent engineering experiences have clearly demonstrated the need for both management dedication to integration of the human system and having the necessary design-tool technology available to enable concurrency. The process of participative design or concurrent engineering is a continuous improvement initiative. Improved design synthesis software tools are being developed and improved. Advances in software technology, such as expert systems, offer productivity improvements which allow concurrent engineering in a more automated environment and cover a wider range of specialty areas.

R&M DESIGN SYNTHESIS

Experience has shown that improved engineering software tools could leverage manpower resources and improve concurrent engineering effectiveness by enabling more trade studies to be conducted, covering a wider range of alternatives, and within a shorter length of time than previous methods. Additionally, improved integration among CAE design synthesis codes would further improve productivity, and provide the technical capabilities needed to dramatically influence the design decision process in the early trade study environment.

As stated in the Introduction, effective concurrent engineering requires the use of multifunctional design teams where each team member has both the opportunity and capability to fully participate in the design process. The concurrent engineering process must be such that timely trades of system parameters can be made to support early design decisions. An expert R&M design synthesis system, named ACES (Advanced Configuration Expert-System Synthesis), has been developed and implemented to improve productivity in the early concurrent engineering process.

ACES is an expert system developed by the McDonnell Douglas Missile Systems Company (MDMSC) to evaluate supportability within the concurrent engineering process for use in Advanced Design. The ACES software incorporates expert system evaluation and the selection of a preferred design based on supportability criteria such as: reliability, maintainability, availability, and support costs. The ACES software program offers direct simultaneous comparison of different system designs and allows significantly faster evaluation of supportability than previously available tools. It evaluates and compares alternative missile system design and support concepts at any level from the air vehicle to individual subassemblies. Each parameter in the model can be decomposed to its smallest unit, and source of data. During this process, the user has constant visibility of how each element is calculated and the difference in value between the design alternatives. Data elements can be easily changed to allow the user to make "what if" decisions or to revise data to better represent the system under analysis. The ACES program offers easy to interpret graphics, sensitivity analyses, and text summaries. Interfaces between the ACES program and Computer Aided Design systems allow a single design loop to define configuration options, geometry models, performance, and support factors, significantly improving productivity and the concurrent design process.

WHY AN EXPERT SYSTEM ?

Previous logistics software models required large amounts of detailed data that, in the early trade study process, were time consuming and difficult to develop or predict. Models were complex and confusing, and required dedicated people that could understand the mechanics of the model and could manually manipulate input data to perform trade studies. Timely support of trade studies was difficult because so much human interaction was needed to define data and manipulate model parameters. The need for so much human intervention in the software caused a bottleneck in the trade study process.

In sharp contrast to this conventional programming approach, an expert system could encapsulate both a data base and the knowledge and experience of several R&M experts in one flexible and easily maintained rule-based math model. Rules would reduce the amount of knowledge needed to define data and consequently speed up the analysis. The ability of the expert system to explain how each part of the model was calculated would provide the basis for a user to accept or reject the model's results. This expert system would be much easier to use than the corresponding conventional software and it would allow individual R&M analysts to perform early-design trade studies much faster than previous methods.

SYSTEM DESCRIPTION

ACES was implemented on a DEC VAXstation II with 0.9 MIPS (Millions of Instructions Per Second) of computing power and a 19" graphics monitor. Written in OPS-5, ACES is a rule-based supportability math model containing over 800 rules concerning operations, support and system configurations. It is interfaced to a CAE synthesis code to obtain data regarding the system geometry model and performance data such as component weights, materials and performance data.

OPS-5 was chosen over other languages and expert system (ES) shells for several reasons:

1) A VAX OPS-5 program can be compiled which makes the program easily transported and promotes a more widespread use of the software.

2) No new or special hardware was needed to run OPS. Other languages/ES shells required expensive hardware not common inside MDMSC. ACES will run on any VAX series computer, from the VAXstation II up to the VAX 8650.

3) The graphics interfaces for other languages/ES shells were inflexible with regard to our display needs.

While OPS is perfectly suited for use in expert systems, its rule-based nature makes it difficult to code certain functions, therefore parts of ACES are coded in FORTRAN. The coding strategy during development was to use OPS where appropriate, and employ FORTRAN where the equivalent OPS code would be too awkward or verbose. The ACES expert system has three distinct components:

1) OPS-5 missile rulebase. (approximately 650 rules)
   - Guidance rules
   - Airframe rules
   - Propulsion rules
   - Overall vehicle rules

2) OPS-5 kernel rulebase. (approximately 150 rules)
   - Factor analysis rules
   - Factor definition rules
   - Missile definition rules
   - Factor recomputation rules

3) FORTRAN routines called from within OPS-5.
- Menu routines
- Mouse input/output routines
- Workstation graphics
- VAX system utilities

ACES was verified via a two step process. First, small portions of the logistics math model, representing the condensed R&M knowledge of several experts, were prototyped using a PC-based expert system shell and tested by the same R&M experts. Second, after the prototypes were confirmed to be accurate, they were rewritten in OPS and combined to form ACES which was verified by analyzing models of existing missile systems for which there was extensive data. We found that the estimates had an excellent correlation with the real world data.

ACES has a very flexible user interface. Data provided through interfaced systems is read-in and the user is only asked for the undefined configuration factors or trade choices such as: number of missiles to be deployed, basic maintenance concept, test concept, and technology/subsystems used in guidance and target acquisition. Most of the user input is mouse-driven which permits a user to quickly select configuration options. Each time a factor or missile subsystem is defined by the user, all factors that use this new value in an equation are calculated and if there is a change in their value, this change is propagated to all other affected factors. This "chain reaction", which lasts a maximum of a few seconds, continues until all directly or indirectly affected factors have been calculated. ACES then asks for the next input from the user until the configuration options are defined.

After the design options are defined, the system displays a review screen of both configurations (Figure 1), and top-level discriminators for both missile configurations (Figure 2). Each of these factors are figures-of-merit used in the process of selecting the best missile design. The user can analyze any factor by entering its corresponding menu number. Analysis of a factor consists of displaying, for both configurations, the equation(s) used to compute the factor -- in English, and the values of it's sub-factors or terms. This process of decomposition enables the user to evaluate the difference between the two configurations as well as the factors driving support costs or other supportability issues. The first breakdown is by major subsystem (Figure 3) and then, for the selected subsystem, the top level factors are decomposed by categories of cost, reliability or maintainability. Figure 4 shows the categories of cost. The user can continue to decompose factors to a basic data element which the user may then revise. Each time a user analyzes a factor, he is essentially asking: "Why does this factor have this value ?" or "For this factor, why is there such a difference between these two configurations ?" The decomposition of factors provides the explanation that will answer these questions. These explanations allow the user to verify data accuracy and increase confidence in the trade studies' results. If a bottom-level factor requires revision, it can be immediately changed by the user. The model will automatically log the source of the data as the user and insert the user's name and the date in the data source location. If the equation used to compute a factor doesn't account for a special case, then the rule can be easily modified or an additional rule created.

CONCLUSION

Concurrent engineering can be much more effective by integrating both the human system and the various software design tools used by participating functions. Synthesis software tools can provide significant productivity benefits and allow concurrent engineering in a more automated environment. Synthesis tools enable each participating individual to productively contribute to concurrent engineering and the design decision process.

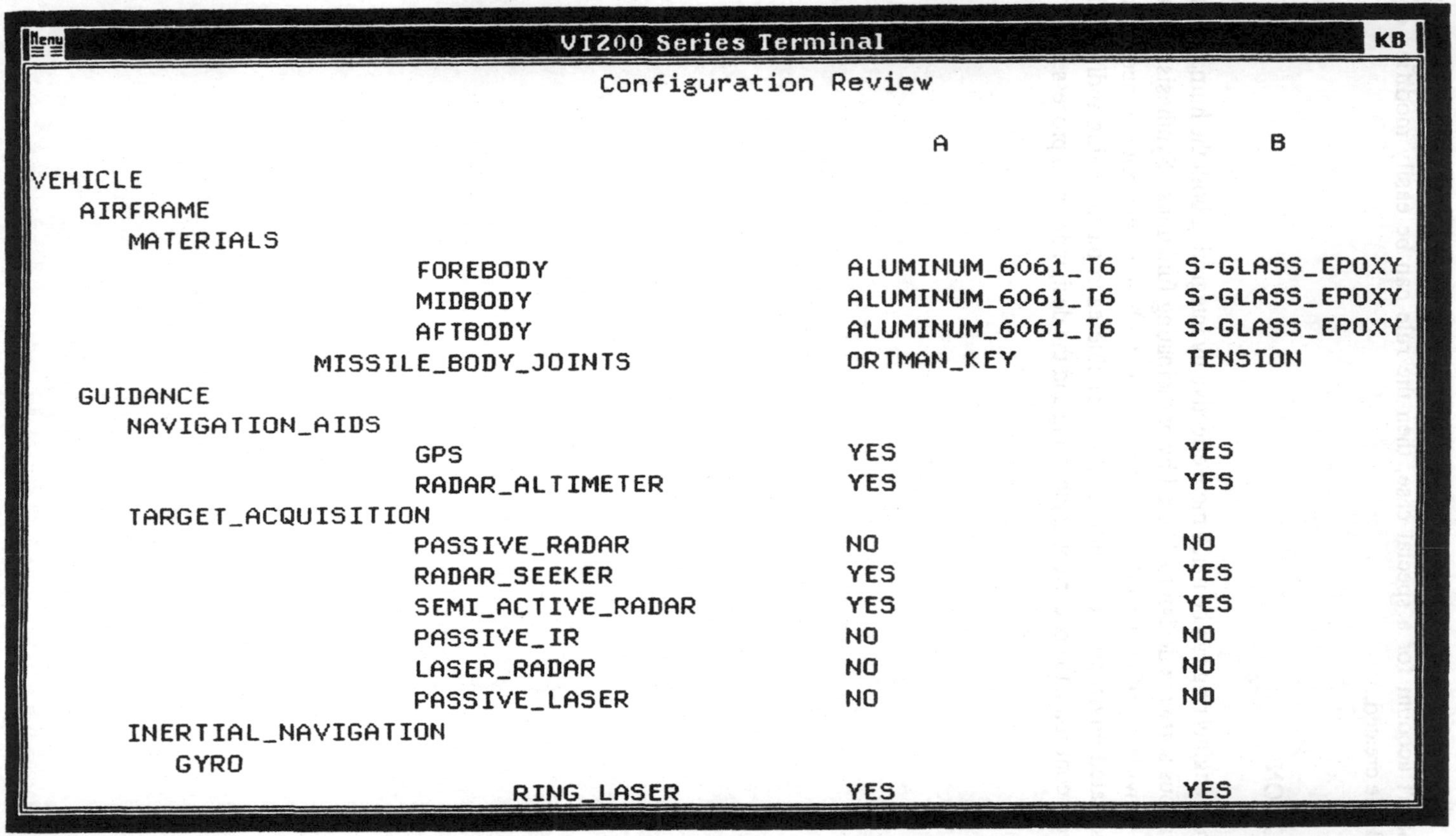

498

...for a special case, then the rules can be easily modified or an additional rule created.

CONCLUSION

```
┌─────────────────────────────────────────────────────────────────┐
│Menu≣                  VT200 series Terminal                   KB │
│                     Configuration Review                         │
│                                          A              B         │
│ VEHICLE                                                           │
│  AIRFRAME                                                         │
│   MATERIALS                                                       │
│     FOREBODY              ALUMINUM_6061_T6      S-GLASS_EPOXY     │
│     MIDBODY               ALUMINUM_6061_T6      S-GLASS_EPOXY     │
│     AFTBODY               ALUMINUM_6061_T6      S-GLASS_EPOXY     │
│   MISSILE_BODY_JOINTS     ORTMAN_KEY            TENSION           │
│                                                                   │
│ GUIDANCE                                                          │
│  NAVIGATION_AIDS                                                  │
│     GPS                   YES               YES                   │
│     RADAR_ALTIMETER       YES               YES                   │
│  TARGET_ACQUISITION                                               │
│     PASSIVE_RADAR         NO                NO                    │
│     RADAR_SEEKER          YES               YES                   │
│     SEMI_ACTIVE_RADAR     YES               YES                   │
│     PASSIVE_IR            NO                NO                     │
│     LASER_RADAR           NO                NO                     │
│     PASSIVE_LASER         NO                NO                     │
│  INERTIAL_NAVIGATION                                              │
│     GYRO         RING_LASER   YES           YES                   │
└─────────────────────────────────────────────────────────────────┘
```

Figure 1

```
Menu    VI200 Series Terminal                                              KB
Top level review of subsystem parameters.
*********************************************AAAAAAAAAAAAAAAAAA***BBBBBBBBBBBBBB
   VEHICLE                        test vehicle 1        test vehicle 2
   REVIEW
   ------------------------       ---------------       ---------------
1 OS_COST$BY_SUBSYSTEM            219,549,440.          357,463,200.
2 OS_COST$BY_COST_CATEGORY       219,549,456.          357,463,168.
3 MTBF                           10,004.7              10,155.2
4 MTTR                           2.4089                6.4063
5 OPERATIONAL_AVAILABILITY       0.9950                0.6553
6 INHERENT_AVAILABILITY          0.9995                0.9990

[ 3 ]  Enter the number corresponding to the factor you want to analyze >1
```

Figure 2

McDonnell Douglas Missile Systems Company

```
┌───────────────────────────────────────────────────────────────────────┐
│ ▤▤  VT200 Series Terminal                                          KB │
│ OS_COST(AIRFRAME) + OS_COST(GUIDANCE) + OS_COST(PROPULSION)            │
│ ********************************AAAAAAAAAAAAAAAAA***BBBBBBBBBBBBBBBBBB  │
│   VEHICLE                       test vehicle 1        test vehicle 2   │
│   OS_COST$BY_SUBSYSTEM          219,549,440.          357,463,200.     │
│   -------------------------     ---------------       --------------   │
│ 1 OS_COST(GUIDANCE)             205,667,696.          335,086,432.     │
│ 2 OS_COST(AIRFRAME)              12,430,144.           21,623,618.     │
│ 3 OS_COST(PROPULSION)            1,451,600.            753,150.0       │
│                                                                       │
│ [ 3 ]  Enter the number corresponding to the factor you want to analyze >1▮ │
│                                                                       │
└───────────────────────────────────────────────────────────────────────┘
```

Figure 3

McDonnell Douglas Missile Systems Company

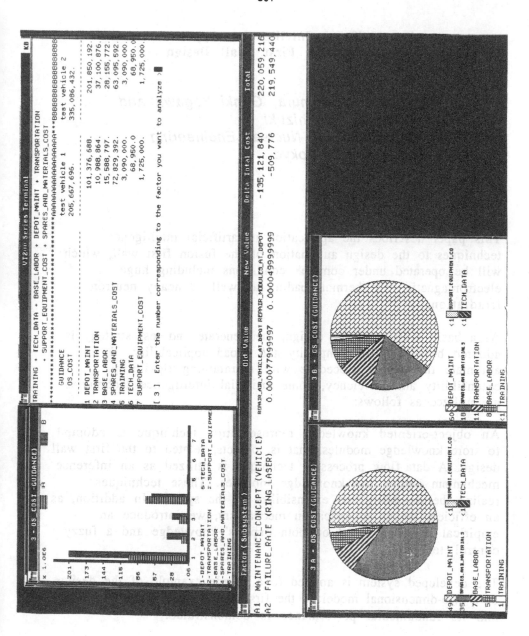

Figure 4

An Artificial Intelligence Approach to Efficient Fusion First Wall Design

Shinobu Yoshimura, Genki Yagawa and Yoshihiko Mochizuki
Department of Nuclear Engineering
University of Tokyo

Abstract

This paper describes the application of artificial intelligence techniques to the design automation of the fusion first wall, which will be operated under complex conditions including huge electromagnetic and thermal loading as well as heavy neutron irradiation.

As a basic strategy of the design, the generate and test strategy is adopted because of its simplicity and broad applicability. To automate the design procedure with maintaining flexibility, extensibility and efficiency, some artificial intelligence techniques are utilized as follows:

An object-oriented knowledge representation technique is adopted to store knowledge modules, that is, objects, related to the first wall design. A data-flow processing technique is utilized as an inference mechanism among the knowledge modules. These techniques realize the flexibility and extensibility of the system. In addition, as an efficient design modification mechanism, we introduce an empirical approach based on both experts' knowledge and a fuzzy control technique.

The developed system is applied to a simple example of the design of a two-dimensional model of the first wall with a cooling channel, and its fundamental performance is demonstrated.

Key Words

Fusion First Wall, Artificial Intelligence, Object-Oriented Knowledge Representation, Data Flow Processing, Design Modification, Fuzzy Control

1. Introduction

The first wall structures of magnetic confinement fusion reactors such as tokamaks are expected to be operated in the complex reactor environment where huge electromagnetic and thermal loading as well as heavy neutron irradiation are applied to the structure [1]. In conventional designing processes, which are mostly based on the generate and test strategy [2], a number of calculations and evaluations are carried out repeatedly to obtain an optimal design of structure. Here, the word "optimal" simply means that the structure can stand all the failure modes such as melting, yielding and fracturing. Such iterative design processes are also very complicated and time-consuming, and also require experts' empirical knowledge embedded over various engineering fields.

Recently, the accuracy and the reliability of analyses of a uni-phenomenon such as structural deformation, heat conduction or fluid dynamics have been increasing dramatically due to the progress of so-called computational mechanics techniques. In some cases, an optimal design of structure under a simple loading condition can be automatically obtained by means of mathematical optimization techniques combined with finite element analyses [3], [4]. However, those mathematical techniques are hardly applied to the shape optimization considering coupled phenomena which often appear in the fusion first wall design.

In this study, artificial intelligence techniques are utilized to automate the design process of the fusion first wall subjected to the complex reactor environment.

As a basic strategy of the design, we employ the generate and test strategy because of its simplicity and broad applicability. An object-oriented knowledge representation [5] and a data-flow processing technique [6] are adopted to kindly connect elemental calculation or evaluation processes to each other. Owing to these techniques, all the elemental design processes are kept to be independent of each other, and then the whole system succeeds in maintaining high flexibility and extensibility. In addition, as an efficient design modification mechanism, we introduce an empirical approach based on both experts' empirical knowledge and a fuzzy control technique [7].

To demonstrate the fundamental performance, the system is applied to a simple example of designing a two-dimensional model of the fusion first wall with a cooling channel which is subjected to a membrane tensile stress as well as heat loading.

2. Outline of the System

2.1 Object-Oriented Knowledge Representation

A design process of structures involves many elemental calculations and evaluations, which can be regarded as design modules. This characteristic of the design process seems very compatible to an object-oriented knowledge representation [5]. The developed system involves various types of object modules such as heat conduction analysis, elastic stress analysis with thermal effects, finite element mesh generation, evaluations of failure criteria such as melting and yielding, selection of material properties, and so on.

Figure 1 shows the schematic view of the stress analysis object, "stress_FEM" . Figure 2 shows the same object expressed by LISP. Each object consists of input/output slots and a function-call slot. The fundamental roles of the object are summarized as follows:

As soon as all the input data are prepared on the input slots and the flags of "not-ready" turn to "ready" as in Fig.2, the function-call slot sends a ready-command to the outer processor such as a finite element analysis code or a database of material properties. After the calculation or the evaluation is completed, the output data are prepared on the output slots. Each object plays a role of an expert of each elemental design process, and controls the local data stream in it. In the present system, a number of objects are stored as shown in Fig.3.

2.2 Data-Flow Processing

The data-flow processing technique [6] is utilized as an inference mechanism controlling the global data stream among objects. Figure 4 shows the schematic view of its basic principle.

Once the two-dimensional finite element mesh data, "mesh.dat(2D)", is prepared on the output slot of the object, "2D_mesh", the data is immediately sent to any objects including "mesh.dat(2D)" on input slots. In this particular example, such objects are "stress_FEM" and "3D_mesh". Next, as soon as the three-dimensional finite element mesh data "mesh.dat(3D)" is created and prepared on the output slot in the object, "3D-mesh", the data is sent to the input slot of the object, "heat_ifile". In the global data stream, the data name, "mesh.dat", itself plays a role in designating that the data is related to a finite element mesh, while the tags, "2D" and "3D" denote data attribute.

The design system based on these techniques is very suitable for complex design problems such as the fusion first wall design in which knowledge on design is renewed day by day in accordance with the progress of the fusion reactor technology and research.

2.3 Empirical Design Modification

In the generate and test strategy, design parameters are somehow modified in a permissible design space when a former design candidate does not satisfy design criteria. Such a design modification process is iterated until an optimal design is attained. This process is ambiguous, and also takes more time in accordance with the increasing number of design parameters and the spreading design space. As one of efficient techniques for design modification, much attention has been paid to mathematical approaches based on a kind of sensitivity analyses. However, the application of such approaches is limited to only simple problems such as shape optimization of simple structures subjected to simple loading.

In the present study, we propose an empirical approach for design modification based on both experts' knowledge and a fuzzy control.

(1) Empirical Approach Based on Experts' Knowledge

The empirical approach adopted here is based on the "IF-THEN" type rule. Figure 5 shows the examples of experts' empirical knowledge on design modification. These rules correspond to the example of a two-dimensional model of the fusion first wall with a circular cooling channel, which will be described in the next section in more detail.

Here, RULE 1 says that, if the maximum temperature exceeds a melting point Tm, the wall is thinned and the cooling channel is enlarged in order to increase its cooling capability. RULE 2 says that, if the maximum equivalent stress value exceeds a yielding stress σ_{ys} and a tensile stress component is dominant as well, the wall is thickened to decrease the effect of mechanical tensile loading.

RULE 3 says that, if the maximum equivalent stress value exceeds the yielding sress and compressive stress component is also dominant, the cooling capability of the wall should be increased. These "IF-THEN" type rules, which are derived based on experts' qualitative inference of physical phenomena, instruct users how to modify the design parameters, considering the reason why the former design candidate violates design criteria.

(2) Fuzzy Control of Design Modification

The "IF-THEN" type rules described previously seem suitable for the determination of the direction of design modification. However, they are not satisfactory in instructing users quantitative design modification. i.e. how much the former design should be modified. In the IF-THEN rules shown in Fig. 5, a maximum equivalent stress σ and a maximum temperature T are first evaluated, and then the design parameters, W and R are modified. The unit steps for one design modification, ΔW and ΔR are fixed in the rules. To improve the capability of the quantitative design modification, we employ a fuzzy control technique [7].

The state of the normalized maximum stress P (= σ/σ_{ys}) and that of the normalized maximum temperature Q (=T/T_m) are first labeled as:

State		Label
P(Q) is very large	$\rightarrow$	LARGE
P(Q) is large	$\rightarrow$	MEDIUM
P(Q) is a little large	$\rightarrow$	SMALL

Membership functions for those labels are shown in Fig.6. It should be noted here that the exact shapes of the functions are determined through past experience.

Using those labels, we consider the following fuzzy control rules:

F-Rule 1: If P(Q) is LARGE, then ΔW and ΔR are LARGE.
F-Rule 2: If P(Q) is MEDIUM, then ΔW and ΔR are MEDIUM.
F-Rule 3: If P(Q) is SMALL, then ΔW and ΔR areSMALL.

If the P or Q value satisfies several condition clauses of the above fuzzy control rules, the values of ΔW and ΔR are determined through the composition of the fuzzy control rules as shown in Fig7 [7].

2.4 Hardware and Software

The present system seems highly compatible to a distributed computer network system composed of various computers such as main-frame computers, 32-bit engineering workstations and 16-bit micro-computers. However, we employ the 32-bit engineering workstation (NEC EWS4800, MC68020[16MHz] & MC68881) in this study, which has the capacity of a speed of 1 MIPS, a main memory of 16MB and a disc of 180MB in order to perform a large amount of symbolic inference processing and numerical calculations on a uniprocessor machine.

The main portion of the system including the knowledge base of objects and the inference engine is written by UTILISP, and outer procedural programs such as finite element analysis are written by either FORTRAN or C.

3. Example and Discussion

3.1 Description of the Problem

To demonstrate the fundamental performance of the system, this is applied to a shape design of a two-dimensional model of the fusion first wall with a circular cooling channel as shown in Fig.8. The wall is subjected to membrane tensile loading on its edges, which might be caused by electromagnetic loading and pressure from the breeder blanket, and subjected to heat loading, Q on the plasma-side surface. The material properties used are tabulated in Table 1. An upper half portion of the wall is modeled with a finite element mesh of 195 four-noded isoparametric elements and 450 degrees of freedom. In this example, the following two design criteria are considered:

(i) Temperature criterion: $T < T_m$

(ii) Stress criterion: $\sigma < \sigma_{ys}$

For the purpose of simplicity, no safety margin is considered in the criteria.

In this problem, two design variables of the wall thickness (W) and the diameter of the cooling channel (R) are automatically designed to satisfy the design criteria of inequalities (1) and (2) for the given values of F and Q.

3.2 Design Based on Empirical Approach without Fuzzy Control

Figure 9 shows the convergence features of the design variable , (W) and (R) , starting from three different initial values. The empirical rules shown in Fig.5 are utilized in these particular examples. The bracketed numbers indicate the total number of sets of finite element calculations during a whole designing process, each set of which involves a mesh generation, a thermal conduction analysis and an elastic thermal stress analysis. A set of finite element calculations requires about 250 seconds, and the total CPU time for the whole finite element calculations takes about 95 percents in the whole designing time.

It can be seen in the figure that the convergence processes are very complicated in this kind of problems. In Fig.9, when the initial value of (W) is larger, (W) decreases and (R) increases monotonically in order to increase the cooling capability of the wall. When the initial value of (W) is medium and that of (R) is smaller, (R) increases with accompanying small oscillation of (W). This feature of convergence may be attributed to the competition between RULEs 2 and 3. When the initial value of (W) is smalller, only (W) increases to decrease a tensile effect, and then (R) increases to improve the coolant capability. Thus, it is expected that the values of the optimal design parameters that satisfy the two criteria come in a narrow region in the figure. It should be also noted that an optimal design space varies depending on the given values of F and Q.

3.3 Design Based on Empirical Approach with Fuzzy Control

Here we examine the effect of a fuzzy control technique on design modification.

Figure 10 and 11 show the convergence features of the design variables based on the membership functions 1 and 2 shown in Fig. 6, respectively. It can be clearly seen through the comparison among Figs. 9 to 11 that, although the convergence speed depends on the chosen membership function, the fuzzy control technique is still very effective to improve the convergence feature of design modiification process.

4. Conclusions

An approach to the design automation for the first fusion wall based on the artificial intelligence techniques is presented in this study.

Due to both the objected-oriented knowledge representation and the data-flow processing techniques, the system succeeds in maintaining the high flexibility and extensibility of function. In addition, the empirical approach combined with the fuzzy control technique is proposed for efficient design modification. It is clearly demonstrated through the simple example of the design of the two-dimensional fusion first wall that the present empirical approach works very well.

Acknowledgement

This work is financially supported by the Grant-in-Aid of the Administration of Science and Technology of Japan.

References

[1] G. Gasini, Fusion Engrg. & Design., 6, 95, 1982.
[2] S. Mittal, C. Dym, M. Marjaria, IEEE-Computer, 119, 102, 1986.
[3] J. A. Bennet, M. A. Botkin, The Optimum Shape, Plenum Press, 1986.
[4] S. Nakagiri and K. Suzuki, Seisan-Kenkyu, J. of Institute of Industrial Science, Univ. of Tokyo, 39, 460, 1987.
[5] R. G. Smith, Proc. of the 8th Int. Joint Conf. on Artificial Intelligence, 855, 1983
[6] J. B. Dennis, Lecture Notes in Computer Science, 19, 362, 1974
[7] L. A. Zadeh, Information and Control, 12, 94, 1968.

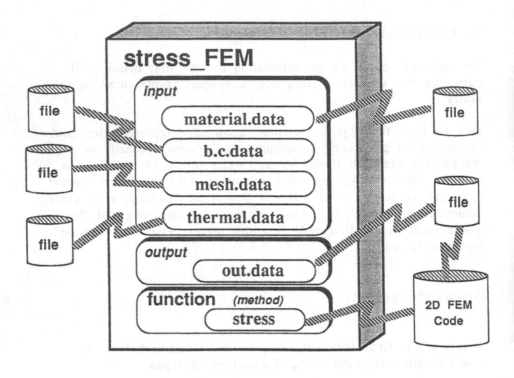

Figure 1 Schematic View of "stress_FEM" Object

```
(Stress_FEM
 (input
  (material ("material.data" file) (elstic)
   ( ) notready )
  (b.c. ("b.c.data" file) (elstic)
   ( ) notready )
  (mesh ("mesh.data" file) (2D)
   ( ) notready )
  (thermal ("thermal.data" file) (elstic)
   ( ) notready ))
 (output
  (stress_FEM.out ("out.data" file) (elstic)))
 (function
  ( "../f77/elastic/thelstic"
    (material b.c. mesh thermal)
    shell_mode))
 (group_level 10))
```

Figure 2 "stress_FEM" Object Expressed by LISP

512

heat_FEM	:	an object that performs 2D heat conduction analysis using a FEM code
stress_FEM	:	an object that performs 2D stress analysis with thermal effects using a FEM code
2D_mesh	:	an object that generates 2D FEM mesh
3D_mesh	:	an object that generates 3D FEM mesh
mp_eval	:	an object that evaluates whether the highest temperature value exceeds the melting point
ys_eval	:	an object that evaluates whether the highest equivalent stress value exceeds the yield stress
bc_prm	:	an object that produces shape parameters and boundary conditions
mat_dbase	:	an object that manages the database of material properties
heat_ifile	:	an object that creates an input data file on boundary conditions for stress_FEM object
stress_ifile_bc	:	an object that creates an input data file on boundary conditions for stress_FEM object
stress_ifile_temp	:	an object that creates an input data file on temperature values for stress_FEM object
math_design	:	an object that performs shift-synthesis on the basis of mathematical knowledge

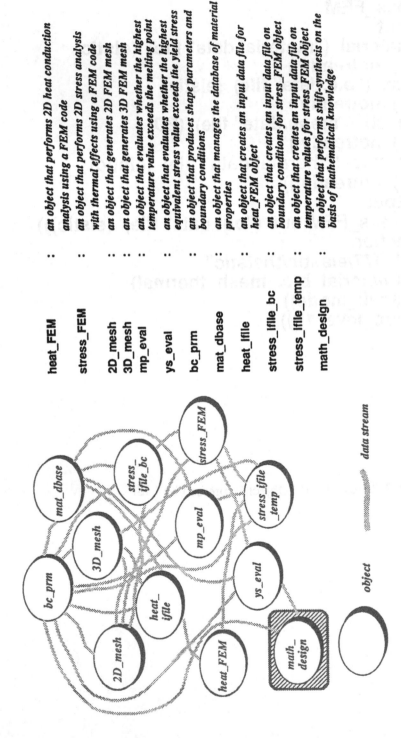

Figure 3 Object Network and Function List

513

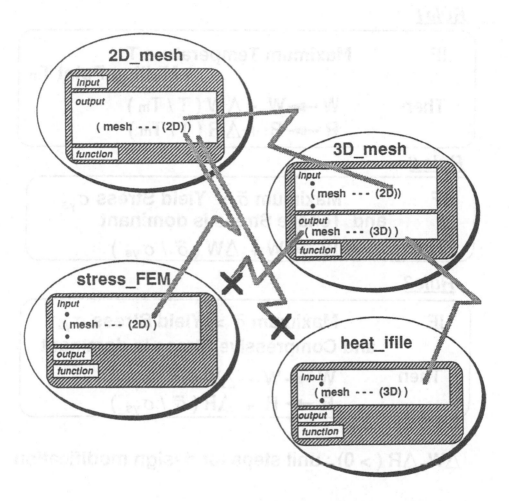

Figure 4 Schematic View of Data Flow Processing

Rule1

IF   **Maximum Temperature T**

                       > Melting Point T_m

Then $W \rightarrow W - \Delta W (T/T_m)$

              $R \rightarrow R + \Delta R (T/T_m)$

Rule 2

IF   **Maximum $\bar{\sigma}$ > Yield Stress σ_{ys}**

and Tensile Stress is dominant

Then $W \rightarrow W + \Delta W (\bar{\sigma}/\sigma_{ys})$

Rule3

IF   **Maximum $\bar{\sigma}$ > Yield Stress σ_{ys}**

and Compressive Stress is dominant

Then $W \rightarrow W - \Delta W (\bar{\sigma}/\sigma_{ys})$

             $R \rightarrow R + \Delta R (\bar{\sigma}/\sigma_{ys})$

$\Delta W, \Delta R \ (> 0)$: unit steps for design modification

Figure 5 Examples of Empirical Knowledge on
Design Modification

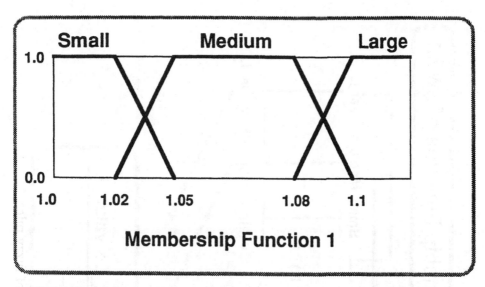

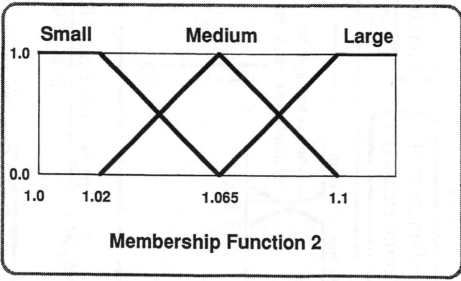

Figure 6 Examples of membership function

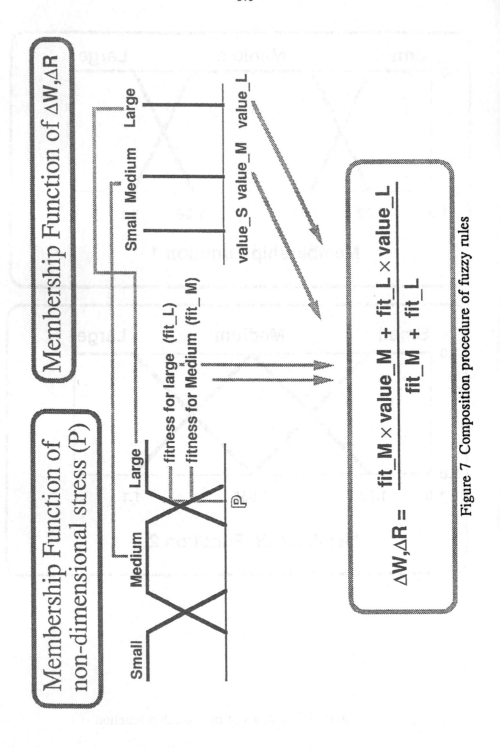

Figure 7 Composition procedure of fuzzy rules

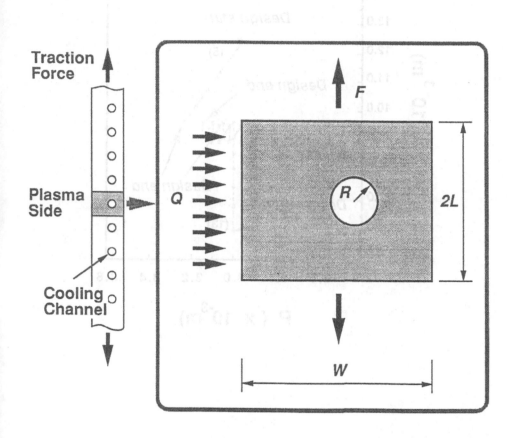

Figure 8 Two-Dimensional Model of The First Wall

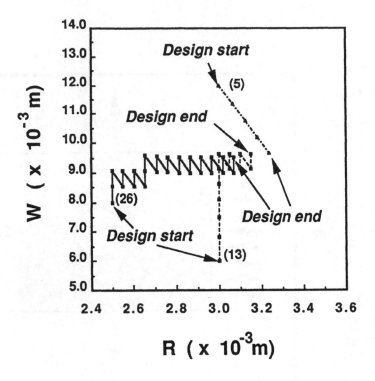

Figure 9 Convergence Feature of Design Variables Based on Empirical Approach without Fuzzy Control

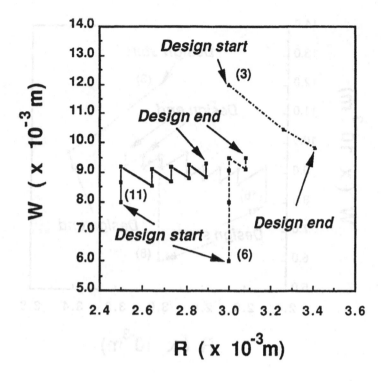

Figure10 Convergence Feature of Design Variables Based on Empirical Approach with Fuzzy Control (Utilization of Membership Function 1 in Fig. 6)

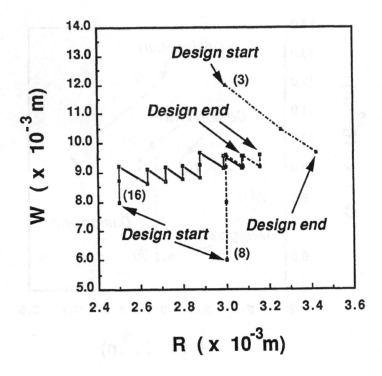

Figure11 Convergence Feature of Design Variables Based on Empirical Approach with Fuzzy Control (Utilization of Membership Function 2 in Fig. 6)

521

Table 1. Material Properties of Type 304 Stainless Steel Included in "mat_dbase" Object

	Value	Unit
Thermal Conductivity	16.338	J / (m·sec·K)
Heat Capacity	512.4	J / (Kg·K)
Mass Density	7.97×10^3	Kg / m^3
Young's Modulus	1.87×10^5	MPa
Poisson's Ratio	0.275	
Linear Expansion Coefficient	17.22×10^{-6}	1 / K
Yield Stress	150.53	MPa
Melting Point	1.5×10^3	K

An Object-Oriented Design Tool toward CIM for Shipbuilding

Ken Shimizu*   Takeo Koyama**

Abstract. *Shipbuilding is a typical example of highly cooperative product development. In this research, an object-oriented design tool was prototyped for the preliminary design of ships. Design knowledge was classified into two categories: knowledge about the design object and knowledge about the design process. A constraint oriented system with evaluation, propagation and local violation satisfaction mechanisms was used to deal with knowledge about the design object. It was helpful in detecting the conflicts and keeping consistency in a design object model. For representing a large, complex design object, in this case a ship, a part-whole hierarchy proved essential. A group of designer objects dealt with knowledge about the design process. They controlled the design process well using knowledge bases consisting of if-then rules representing human designers' know-how.*

1. Introduction

Shipbuilding is a typical example of highly cooperative product development. Each ship is custom-built for a specific use according to the requirements of her owners in a relatively short period of time from order to delivery. Furthermore, a ship is a large, complex product made of hundreds of thousands of parts. Therefore, it is inevitable that several designers must work on a project at the same time. Each designer is a specialist in a different area, such as hydrodynamics, structure, piping, engines, etc. Conflicts among those areas often occur. For example, a designer of piping might want to make a hole in a major structural part to route an essential pipe, and a structural designer might disagree because it would reduce the strength to below its critical value. Negotiation takes place when a conflict arises. In order to solve the conflict, one or both parties have to redesign.

Cooperative jobs depend upon team work. Individual tasks, such as hydrostatic calculation and structural analysis, are highly computerized. However, they are not integrated on computer systems. So the consistency must be checked by human designers. Furthermore, the designers do not provide complete instructions for manufacturing, because the high quality of assembly line workers makes it unnecessary. For example, in

---

* Advanced Craft Engineering Dept., Defense Systems Division, Mitsui Engineering and Shipbuilding Co.,Ltd., 5-6-4, Tsukiji, Chuo-ku, Tokyo 104, Japan. (currently on leave at the Center for Design Research, Stanford University)
** Professor, Department of Naval Architecture and Ocean Engineering, The University of Tokyo, 7-3-1, Hongo, Bunkyo-ku, Tokyo 113, Japan

designing a network of minor pipelines with small diameters, only the system diagrams are generated in the design section. The actual routes and fixtures are determined by the assembly staff.[1] This human network system has worked well, but it has its limitations in efficiency because precise information is often lacking. A survey showed that the assembly workers in a shipyard spent about half of their time doing "unproductive work" such as re-welding, re-cutting, looking for parts, etc., much of which is due to the lack of precise information.[2]

CIM (Computer Integrated Manufacturing) for shipbuilding is expected to resolve the above mentioned problems by efficiently producing and maintaining precise, consistent information about the product.[1],[2],[3] The total system is imagined as illustrated in Figure 1.[3] Conceptually, a centralized shipbuilding data base deals with all the information about the products. It takes care of the consistency in the product models and detects any conflict as soon as it happens. Each designer (or process planner, or any specialist involved) accesses the product model through a specific subsystem, which has a good user interface, analysis tools and knowledge-based intelligent assistance capability in the field.

The focus of this paper is the preliminary design subsystem. The purpose of preliminary ship design is to decide the ship's principal parameters, such as length, beam, depth, horse power of the main engine, etc., considering various aspects, such as weight, capacity, speed, etc.[4],[5] Since the trade-offs made in determining each parameter involves specialized knowledge from several domains, this subsystem can be seen as a miniature of the whole cooperative system.

A design tool was developed with the above considerations in mind.[17] It became a tool for generic parameter design problems rather than a specific one for the design of ships.

In order to provide a suitable framework to represent the design knowledge, it was classified into two categories: knowledge about the design object and knowledge about the design process, which are described in section 2.

More attention was paid to knowledge about the design object, because it requires a specific representation, whereas knowledge about the design process is considered relatively easy to represent using general, conventional if-then rules. In the tool which we developed, the structure and behavior of a design object are determined by a set of design parameters and a set of constraints. We took a constraint oriented approach, in which constraints play an important role in their own evaluation and propagation.[6],[7],[8] The implementation was made relatively easy by adopting the object oriented programming technique.[9],[10] The configuration and functions of the design tool are described in section 3.

The results of the application of the tool to the preliminary design of ships are described in section 4. The constraint oriented design object model worked well in automatically detecting conflicts (or constraints violations) and in assigning values to design parameters by propagation and local satisfaction mechanisms. Several designer objects were instantiated hierarchically and they controlled the design process well using if-then rules.

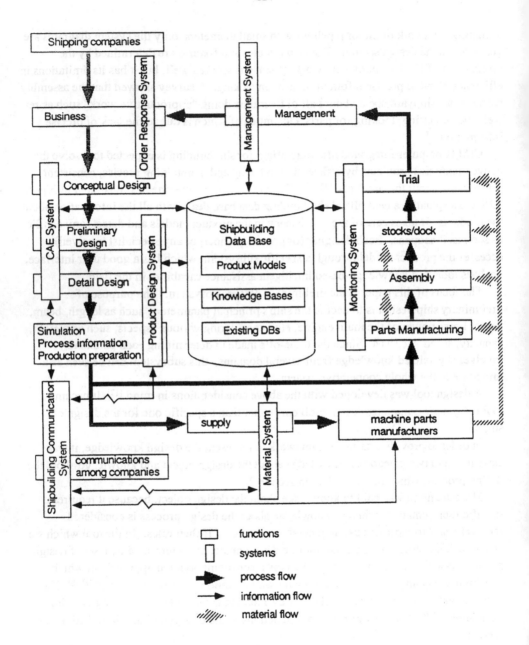

Figure 1: Image of CIM for Shipbuilding[3]

2. Classification of Design Knowledge

In order to build a sophisticated computer aided design system, the unstructured design knowledge of designers should be organized and represented clearly by a computer system. Classification of design knowledge is helpful in organizing the knowledge and in developing knowledge representation for a design tool. In this research, design knowledge was classified into two categories, i.e. knowledge about the design object and knowledge about the design process.

In design, it is necessary to clarify the design parameters and the relations among the parameters because they determine the structure and behavior of the design object. The value of each design parameter is restricted by its relations with other parameters. Those relations, or constraints, are imposed as physical laws, legal regulations, specification requirements, etc. Intricately coupled constraints make it difficult to get an optimal or a satisfactory set of the design parameter values. Therefore, the role and behavior of constraints in the design problem should be well understood.

Besides knowledge about the design object represented with the design parameters and their relations, there is another category of design knowledge: dynamic, strategic and global knowledge about the design process, such as which parameter should be set first when there are many to be set, which parameter should be changed in case of coupled constraints violations, etc. Knowledge about the design process represented as if-then rules is expected to be able to drive the design cycle of generation, evaluation and modification.[11],[12] The two kinds of design knowledge are contrasted in Table 1.

Table 1: Two Kinds of Design Knowledge

Knowledge about the Design Object	Knowledge about the Design Process
static	dynamic
status	change
feature	handling
law	know-how
existance	generation
evaluation	modification
deep knowledge	surface knowledge

3. Configuration and Functions of the Design Tool

3.1 Overview

The configuration of the object oriented design tool developed in this research is outlined in Figure 2. A *design object* and a *designer*, corresponding to knowledge about the design object and knowledge about the design process respectively, are the major objects in the tool. (Those words written in *italics* are the names of the objects in the system.) The design proceeds through message passing between the two kinds of objects.

In a *design object*, a set of *parts* and a set of *constraints* represent the structure and the behavior of the object. Constraint oriented programming,[6],[7],[8] in which declaratively represented constraints play a major role, was considered to be useful for describing knowledge about the design object, and that approach was taken in this research. In order to represent a large, complicated design artifact, a *design object* can be constructed with a hierarchy.

A *designer* in the system controls the design process using the if-then rules in a knowledge base. Because the *design object* performs constraint management, only the primary intents of design should be described in rules; resultant changes are taken care of by the *design object* itself and conflicts, if any, are detected. More than one *designer* can be instantiated in the system allowing various specialists involved in the design to be consulted together. The *designers* work cooperatively.

The structure and the behavior of each class of objects, as well as the user interface, are described in the following sections.

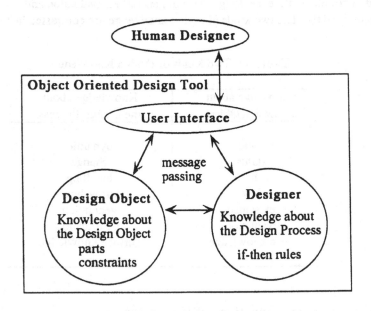

Figure 2: The Configuration of the Design Tool

Smalltalk-80[*] was used to develop the design tool. This language was chosen because:
- Object oriented programming was essential for dealing with design problems in which the overall procedure was difficult to recognize and a declarative way of describing things was desirable.
- A primitive language rather than an expert system shell (such as KEE[**]) was desirable in order to implement the constraint management mechanism.
- Compared with other primitive object oriented languages (such as C++), Smalltalk-80 had a better development environment for rapid prototyping.

3.2 Design Object

3.2.1 Configuration
A class *"Design Object"* was defined to represent knowledge about the design object. A *design object* contains a set of *parts* and a set of *constraints* as illustrated in Figure 3. The relations among the *parts* are defined by the *constraints*. Each of the *parts* has pointers to its related *constraints* and each of the *constraints* has pointers to its related *parts*.

The *parts* and the *constraints* can be added, modified or deleted easily during work with a design tool. This is important because the structure of the design object is gradually defined through the design process by stepwise refinement.

A human designer cannot deal with too many design parameters and constraints at once. In order to restrict the number of elements to be considered simultaneously, the part-whole hierarchy was introduced in the tool. Each *part* is a *design object* itself and is able to have its own *parts* and *constraints*. Each *constraint* can also be constructed with *sub-constraints* by logically combining them. The elements in the lowest level of this part-whole hierarchy are primitive *design objects* (or design parameters) and primitive *constraints*. (Figure 4)

3.2.2 Constraint Management
The following two aspects of constraints are the basis of the constraint oriented design object model developed here, which has been greatly influenced by the pioneering works in constraint oriented programming.[6],[7],[8]

    (A) status evaluation
           During the design, a designer decides what to do to by examining the constraints to see they are satisfied or violated. In order to help the activity of the designer, a constraint should be re-evaluated automatically whenever any related parameters are changed.
    (B) multi-directional propagation
           A designer not only examines the constraints but also uses them to determine the satisfactory values of the design parameters. A constraint

---

[*] Smalltalk-80 is a registered trademark of ParkPlace Systems.
[**] KEE is a registered trademark of Intellicorp, Inc.

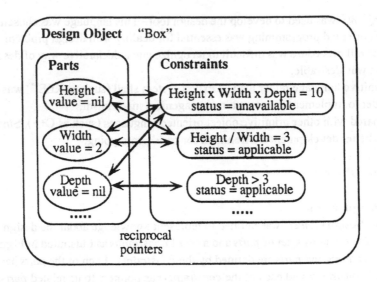

Figure 3: An Example of a Design Object

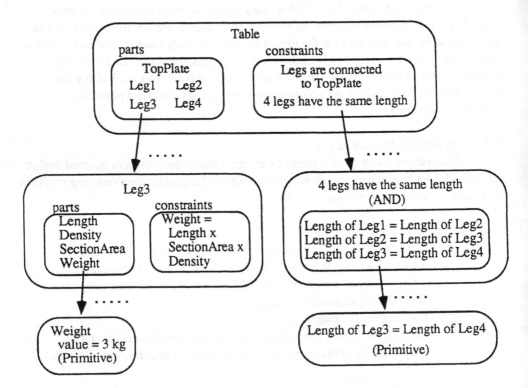

Figure 4: An Example of Part-Whole Hierarchy in a Design Object

does not define a rigid procedure to determine a related design parameter, but declares the relations among parameters. Therefore, a design tool should support the function of multi-directional propagation. For example, an equation with n parameters should be able to be used to calculate the value of any one parameter, irrespective of whether it is in the left hand side or the right hand side, when the rest of n-1 parameters are determined.

The constraint management mechanism realized in the system is described below.

A primitive *part* (or design parameter) has a value and a list of pointers to related *constraints*. Any change of value is made only by sending an appropriate message to the *part*. The message invokes a method which not only changes the value but also sends re-evaluation messages to its related *constraints* using the list of pointers, thus guaranteeing the consistency of the status of the *constraints* with the values of the *parts*. (Figure 5)

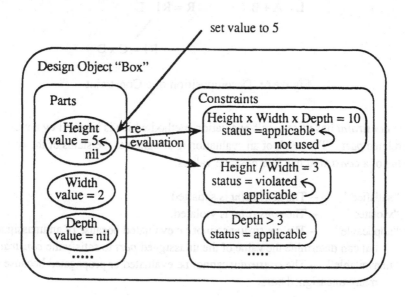

Figure 5: Setting a Value of a Design Paramter

A *constraint* contains the body of the constraint, its status, and a list of pointers to the related *parts*. *Constraints* considered in this research are:

- equations
- inequalities
- functions in the form y=f(x) and z=f(x,y), defined by the linear interpolation of user defined table values
- logical combinations of constraints

In our implementation we focused upon constraints in the form of equations. Other types of *constraints* suffer from limitations in multi-directional propagation.

A constraint expression, input as a string by a user, is parsed and decomposed into a set of primitive *constraints*; these constitute the body of the *constraint*. (Figure 6) At the same time, a list of pointers to related *parts* is generated, and a pointer to the *constraint* itself is added to the constraint list of each of its constituent *parts*, to maintain the system's consistency.

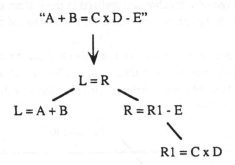

"A + B = C x D - E"

L = R

L = A + B   R = R1 - E

R1 = C x D

Figure 6: Decomposition of a Constraint

Each *constraint* has its own self-evaluation method which is invoked by a message from a related *part* . The result of an evaluation is assigned to the status of the *constraint*. The status of a *constraint* has four possible values:

"satisfied"   -- The *constraint* is satisfied.
"violated"   -- The *constraint* is violated.
"applicable"   -- The *constraint* cannot be evaluated because of an unassigned *part*, but can determine the value of the unassigned *part* to satisfy the *constraint*.
"unavailable"   -- The *constraint* cannot be evaluated or propagated because of too many unassigned *parts*.

An example of the status of a *constraint* is shown in Table 2.

Table 2: Status of a Constraint

| Values of Design Parameters | | | | | Status of the Constraint |
A	B	C	D	E	"A + B = C x D - E"
nil	nil	nil	nil	nil	unavailable
1	2	4	nil	nil	unavailable
1	2	4	5	nil	applicable
nil	2	4	5	6	applicable
1	2	4	5	17	satisfied
1	2	4	5	6	violated

The propagation of "applicable" *constraints* is multi-directional; e.g. a *constraint* "Area = Length * Width" can determine the Area from the Length and the Width, and can also determine the Length from the Area and the Width. In order to realize the function, each of the primitive *constraints*, e.g. adder, has a propagation method as in the example below.

```
propagate;
    if status = "applicable"
        if a = nil
            a := b + c
        else if b = nil
            b := a - c
        else if c = nil
            c := a - b
        end if
    end if
```

Once those primitive methods are prepared, a complicated formula, being decomposed into a set of primitive *constraints*, can propagate to any of the related *parts* depending on which is unassigned. A sequence of message passing which carries out constraint propagation is illustrated in Figure 7.

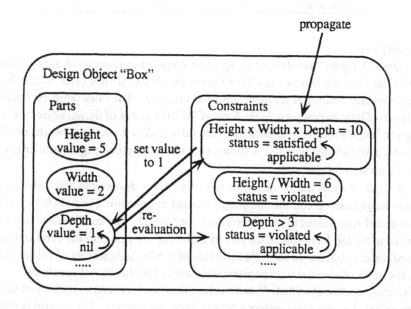

Figure 7: Constraint Propagation

A user can specify one of the related *parts* as "design advice" for the *constraint*. When a *constraint* is violated during the propagation process, the *part* specified by the design advice is recalculated automatically to clear the violation. This function is helpful in handling a group of coupled *constraints* in which the proper recalculation order in case of violations is known.

The propagation and the satisfaction of *constraints* described above may lead to confusion in the design process because they are based only on local relationships among adjacent *parts*. A flag called "activity" as shown in Table 3 was attached to each *constraint* to suppress the activity of the *constraint* to some extent. For example, a sleeping *constraint* only evaluates itself and does not propagate or satisfy itself automatically, while a wild *constraint* evaluates, propagates and satisfies itself whenever possible. The basic function of evaluation is always activated as can be seen from Table 3. The activity flags suppress only the "automatic" function of the *constraints*; even if the flag is "sleeping," a *constraint* is propagated or satisfied when explicitly specified by a human designer or a *designer*. Thus, the activity flag allows human designers and the *designer* to control the design process from a global point of view.

Table 3: Activity Flag for Constraints

activity	sleeping	active	wild
evaluation	o	o	o
propagation	x	o	o
satisfaction	x	x	o

3.3 Designer

A class "*Designer*" was defined to represent knowledge about the design process. Each object in this class contains a knowledge base consisting of if-then rules, which form an instance variable, and inference mechanisms as methods. The rules represent heuristic knowledge of human designers in the form of "If <the status of design object>, then <design/redesign action>." Modularity of the rules makes it easy to generate, modify and maintain the knowledge base.[11] A forward chaining inference engine similar to OPS 5[13] was implemented for this tool.

A *designer* is expected to replace the role of a human designer by using if-then rules in the knowledge base. It controls the design process of generating and modifying the design artifact model represented by the objects described in 3.2. The conditions to fire a rule are described in the left hand side of the rule by means of the values of the *parts* and/or the status of the *constraints*. In the right hand side of a rule, assignments of values to the *parts*, the order of constraint propagations, the order and the way of constraint satisfactions, etc. are specified. When a rule is fired and something is changed in the *design object*, the constraint system works to keep consistency. The control is returned to a *designer* to fire the next rule once the *design object* has reached equilibrium following re-evaluation, propagation and local satisfaction of all the relevant *constraints*.

More than one *designer* with different knowledge bases can be instantiated in the system to allow various types of specialized knowledge involved in the design to be applied. A *designer* can invoke other *designers* with a rule by specifying them in the right hand side.

3.4 User Interface

The design tool user interface is very important because design is essentially an interactive activity between a human designer and a design artifact model. A designer decides what to do by inspecting the temporary design artifact model, and the result of his action on the model is fed back to him to stimulate his thinking about the next action. In this research, Smalltalk-80 provided a good environment to develop a user friendly system with its built-in window and menu management system.

Figure 8 shows a "design object inspector" with which a user can generate, inspect and modify *design objects*. The top pane of the window displays the name of the *design objects*. The lower left panes display the names and values of the *parts* Each of the *constraints* is displayed in one of the four panes in the lower right corresponding to their status (satisfied, violated, unavailable and applicable, clockwise from the top left). The status of the *constraint* "L * B * D = V" in Figure 8 is "unavailable" because all of the four related *parts* have no values yet. A user can give values to the *parts* by selecting "set value" from the pop up menu in the part pane. A *constraint* moves to the appropriate pane, e.g. the "applicable" pane in the bottom left, when its status is changed as a result of a change of a *part's* value, as shown in Figure 9. The four pane system of constraints visually helps a user to recognize the present status of the *design object*. A user can also control the propagation and satisfaction of *constraints*. By manipulating the *parts* and the *constraints* as described above, a user can represent her knowledge about the design object interactively.

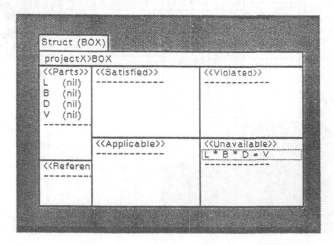

Figure 8: Design Object Inspector

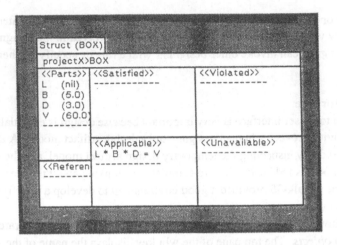

Figure 9: Change of Constraint Status

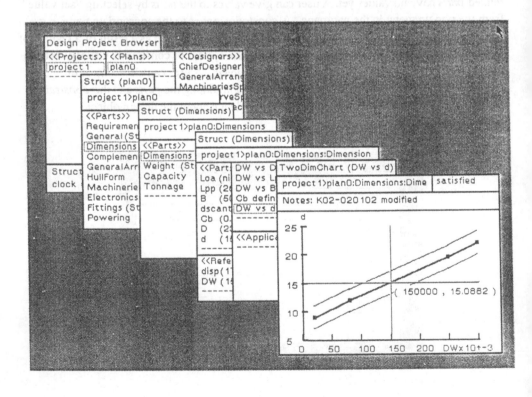

Figure 10: Inspecting a Chart under Hierarchy

A user can go down in the part-whole hierarchy of a *design object* by picking a *part* and selecting the "inspect" menu, and also can go up in the hierarchy by selecting the "inspect whole" menu. Figure 10 shows the windows opened to navigate in the part-whole hierarchy. The figure also shows how a table-defined *constraint* can be inspected graphically.

The tool can be used without any *designers*. In fact, in the first use of the tool in a given field, it is appropriate to do the design without *designers* ; a human designer is better. During the design process conducted by a human designer, some patterns of design actions (e.g. the way a violated constraint is satisfied) may be found. Then, this knowledge about the design process can be written down as if-then rules using the rule set browser shown in Figure11. A knowledge base can gradually grow up in this way.

There are a number of other important interfaces such as a "design project browser" with which a user controls the design process by generating and activating *designers* as shown in Figure 12 and a "history" menu for *design objects, constraints* and *designers* as shown in Figure 13.

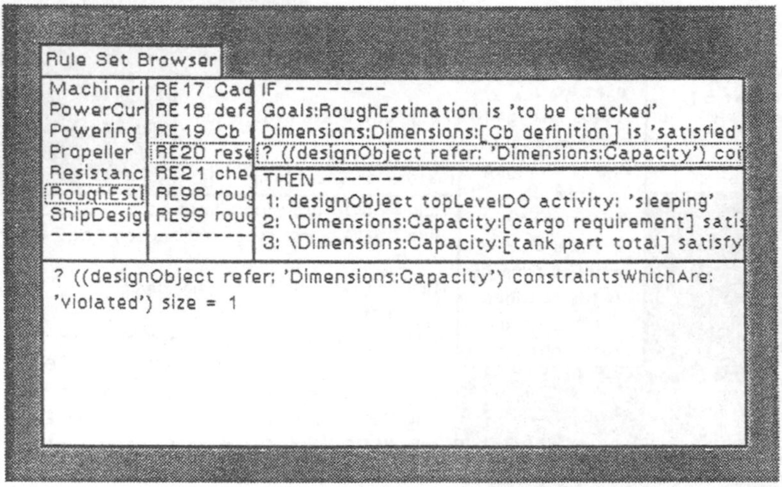

```
Rule Set Browser

Machineri  RE17 Cac  IF ---------
PowerCur   RE18 defi  Goals:RoughEstimation is 'to be checked'
Powering   RE19 Cb   Dimensions:Dimensions:[Cb definition] is 'satisfied'
Propeller  RE20 rese  ? ((designObject refer: 'Dimensions:Capacity') cor
Resistanc  RE21 che
RoughEstl  RE98 roug  THEN -------
ShipDesig  RE99 roug  1: designObject topLevelDO activity: 'sleeping'
--------   --------   2: \Dimensions:Capacity:[cargo requirement] satis
                      3: \Dimensions:Capacity:[tank part total] satisfy

? ((designObject refer: 'Dimensions:Capacity') constraintsWhichAre:
'violated') size = 1
```

Figure 11: Rule Set Browser

Design Project Browser

<<Projects>>	<<Plans>>	<<Designers>>
project 1	plan0	ChiefDesigner
-----------	----------	GeneralArrangement
		MachineriesSpecialis
		PowerCurveSpeciali
		PoweringSpecialist
		PropellerDesigner
	reset	

Struct
clock = 119

Figure 12: Design Project Browser

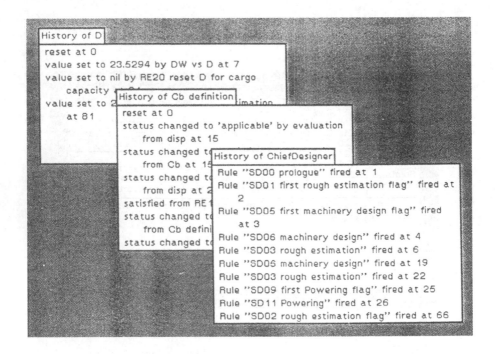

History of D

reset at 0
value set to 23.5294 by DW vs D at 7
value set to nil by RE20 reset D for cargo
    capacity
value set to 2   imation
    at 81

History of Cb definition

reset at 0
status changed to 'applicable' by evaluation
    from disp at 15
status changed t
    from Cb at 1
status changed t
    from disp at 2
satisfied from RE
status changed t
    from Cb defini
status changed t

History of ChiefDesigner

Rule "SD00 prologue" fired at 1
Rule "SD01 first rough estimation flag" fired at
    2
Rule "SD05 first machinery design flag" fired
    at 3
Rule "SD06 machinery design" fired at 4
Rule "SD03 rough estimation" fired at 6
Rule "SD06 machinery design" fired at 19
Rule "SD03 rough estimation" fired at 22
Rule "SD09 first Powering flag" fired at 25
Rule "SD11 Powering" fired at 26
Rule "SD02 rough estimation flag" fired at 66

Figure 13: Histories

4. Application

4.1 Design Objects

The part-whole hierarchy of the *design object* for the preliminary design of ships is shown in part in Figure 14. The general constraints to be satisfied in the design object were collected from books.[14],[15] There were various types of constraints, such as definitions (e.g. displacement = dead weight + light weight), physical laws (e.g. ship weight = water density × ship volume under water), legal regulations (e.g. a collision bulkhead must be located between 5% and 8% of the ship length from the bow), and empirical statistic relations (e.g. an initial estimation formula of the hull steel weight taking length, beam and depth of the ship as parameters). The *design object*, which was basically defined by the part-whole hierarchy and the constraint network but does not have any specific requirements or values of the design parameters, was saved as a prototype. The design specifications for each individual design were represented as *constraints* in the *part* named "Requirements." The *part* named "Goals" was a special *part* for the design process control which were referred to by *designers*.

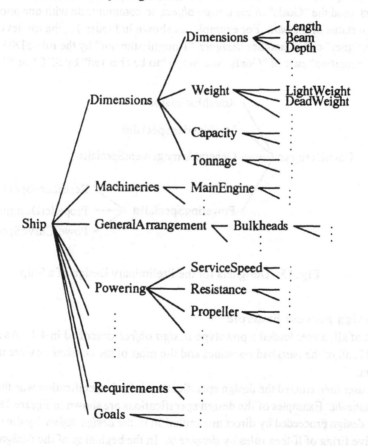

Figure 14: Part-Whole Hierarchy for the Preliminary Design of a Ship

4.2 Designers

Knowledge about the design process was acquired as if-then rules during the interactive operation with the constraint system. The acquisition was more difficult than that of knowledge about the design object which was acquired from design handbooks etc. One of the reasons is that the knowledge is not recognized explicitly by human designers themselves. They may not be able to describe their design knowledge in an organized manner, but will remember an appropriate piece of knowledge when they encounter a particular situation. The constraint oriented design object representation was useful in the acquisition of knowledge about the design process because human designers could easily see the current situation of the design, such as the values of the design parameters and the status of constraints, with the help of the system.

Several *designers* with different knowledge bases were instantiated reflecting the various specialized fields involved in the design. The *designers* generated in the application are shown in Figure 15. A *designer* in a higher level in the hierarchy invoked *designers* in a lower level. A "called" *designer* returned the control to the higher level "calling" *designer*, when the part of the design for which it was responsible was finished. *Designers* used the "Goals" in the *design object* to communicate with one another about the design status of the *part*. For example, as shown in Figure 16, the top level *designer* "ChiefDesigner" called another *designer* "RoughEstimator" by the rule SD03 when "RoughEstimation" *part* of "Goals" was set to "to be checked" by SD01 or SD02.

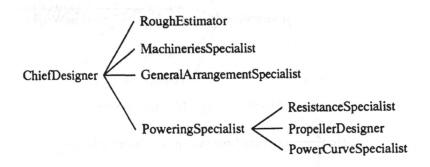

Fig.15: Designers for the Preliminary Design of a Ship

4.3 Design Process Example

First of all, a user loaded a prototype *design object* described in 4.1. As shown in Figure 17, all of the *parts* had no values and the most of the *constraints* were unavailable at that point.

The user then entered the design specifications. Each specification was then generated as a *constraint*. Examples of the design specifications are shown in Figure 18.

The design proceeded by direct manipulation of the *design object* by the user or by successive firing of if-then rules by *designers*. In the beginning of the design, many of the *parts* were assigned values by the propagation of applicable *constraints*. SD03 in Figure 16

SD01 first rough estimation flag
IF   Goals exists
        Goals:RoughEstimation is nil
THEN   \Goals:RoughEstimation setValue: 'to be checked'

SD02 rough estimation flag
IF   Goals exists
        Goals:RoughEstimation is 'ok'
        &D subGoal Goals [self lastModified > (self refer: ':Goals:RoughEstimation') lastModified]
        %subGoal is 'ok'
THEN   \Goals:RoughEstimation setValue: 'to be checked'

SD03 rough estimation
IF   Goals exists
        Goals:RoughEstimation is 'to be checked'
THEN   "initiate free propagations"
                designObject activity: 'wild'; evaluate.
     "and invoke RoughEstimator"
                designObject topLevelDO whole getDesigner: 'RoughEstimator' go.

.....

RE07 draft estimation
IF   Goals:RoughEstimation is 'to be checked'
        Dimensions:Dimensions:d is nil
        Dimensions:Dimensions:[DW vs d] is 'applicable'
THEN   \Dimensions:Dimensions:[DW vs d] propagate

.....

RE19 Cb reset
IF   Goals:RoughEstimation is 'to be checked'
        Dimensions:Dimensions:[Cb definition] is 'violated'
THEN   \Dimensions:Dimensions:[Cb definition] satisfy

RE20 reset D for cargo capacity
IF   Goals:RoughEstimation is 'to be checked'
        Dimensions:Dimensions:[Cb definition] is 'satisfied'
        ? ((designObject refer: 'Dimensions:Capacity') constraintsWhichAre: 'violated') size = 1
        Dimensions:Capacity:[cargo requirement] is 'violated'
THEN   designObject topLevelDO activity: 'sleeping'
        \Dimensions:Capacity:[cargo requirement] satisfy
        \Dimensions:Capacity:[tank part total] satisfy
        \Dimensions:Dimensions:D setValue: nil
        \Dimensions:Capacity:[tank part estimation] propagate
        (designObject topLevelDO) activity: 'wild'; evaluate

RE21 check cargo capacity
IF   Goals:RoughEstimation is 'to be checked'
        Dimensions:Capacity:[tank part estimation] is 'satisfied'
        Dimensions:Capacity:[SBT estimation] is 'satisfied'
        Dimensions:Capacity:[tank part total] is 'violated'
THEN   designObject topLevelDO activity: 'sleeping'
        \Dimensions:Capacity:CargoCap setValue: nil
        \Dimensions:Capacity:[tank part total] propagate
        (designObject topLevelDO) activity: 'wild'; evaluate

Fig. 16: Examples of Rules

is a rule which initiates free propagation of applicable *constraints* and invokes another *designer*. RE07 is a rule which simply controls the propagation of a particular *constraint*.

As the values were assigned to the *parts*, conflicts occurred. These conflicts were detected as constraints violations and displayed in the violated constraints pane in the inspector windows. A user or a *designer* specified the order and the way in which constraints should be satisfied. RE19, RE20 and RE21 in Figure 16 are examples of rules for a violated constraint satisfaction.

A design plan was finished when all the *parts* got their values and no *constraints* were violated. (Figure 19)

After several runs of the design, during which if-then rules were captured, it became possible to perform the whole process of design with the *designers*. At this stage, the human designer only had to put in the design specifications and then begin by activating the ChiefDesigner.

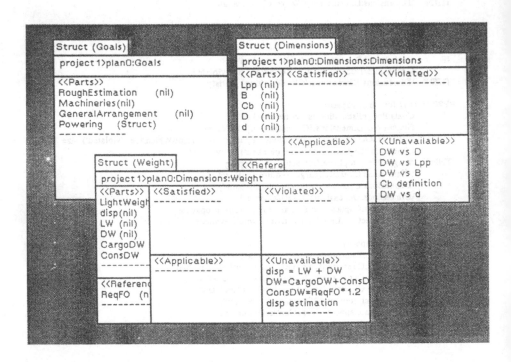

Figure 17: Initial Design Plan

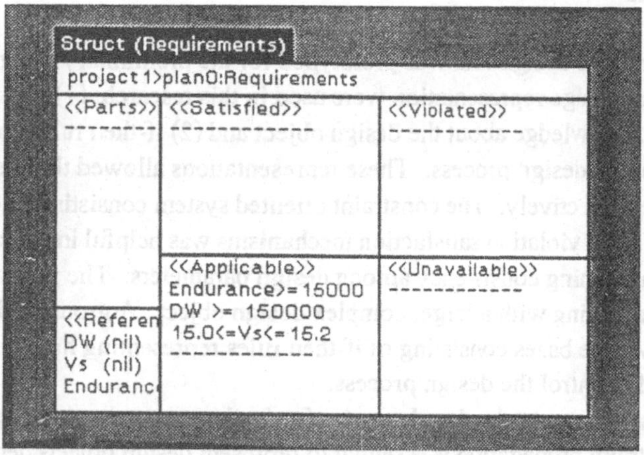

Figure 18: Design Specifications

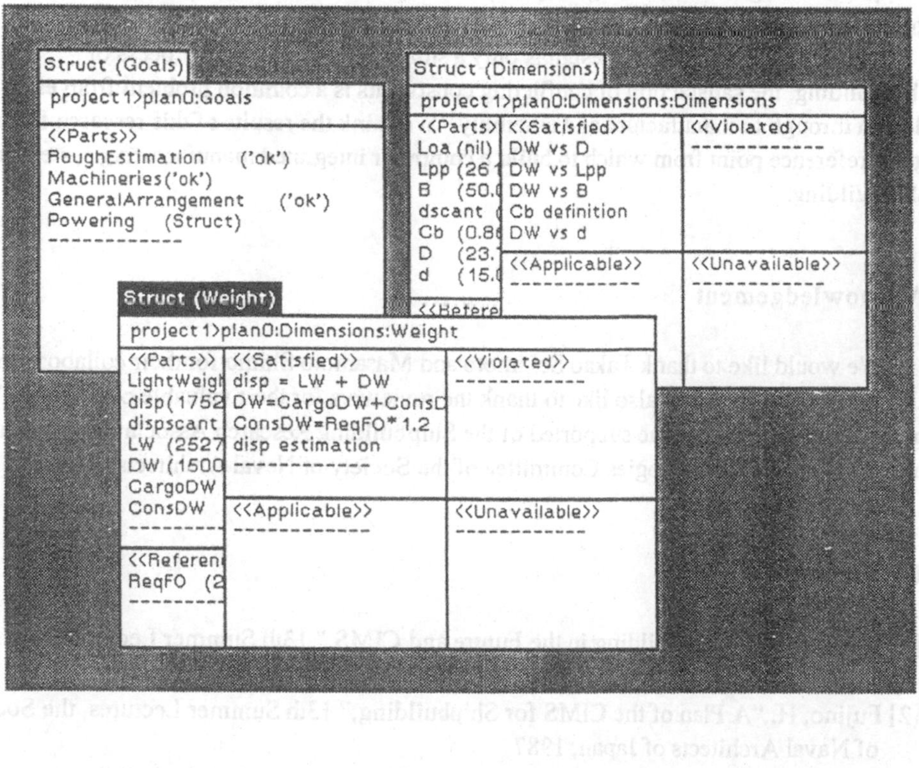

Figure 19: Completed Design Object

5. Conclusions

An object-oriented design tool was prototyped for the preliminary design of ships. Two kinds of knowledge representation were used in this research: (1) constraints corresponding to knowledge about the design object and (2) if-then rules corresponding to knowledge about the design process. These representations allowed the design knowledge to be manipulated effectively. The constraint oriented system consisting of evaluation, propagation and local violation satisfaction mechanisms was helpful in detecting the conflicts and maintaining consistency among design parameters. The part-whole hierarchy was essential for dealing with a large, complex design object. A group of designer objects, which had knowledge bases consisting of if-then rules representing human designers' know-how, could control the design process.

Some points were recognized as the topics for further research. Although multi-directional constraint propagation is essential to represent design objects declaratively, the control of the design process became harder when the constraint network became larger and more complicated; it would be nice to introduce a systematic way, such as an application of graph theory, to control the constraint propagation.[15] In order to represent the forms and the spatial arrangements of design objects, not only arithmetic constraints but also geometric constraints should be implemented in the tool.

Although the preliminary design is only a small part of the whole process of shipbuilding, the satisfaction of conflicting constraints is a common problem from early design through to manufacture and assembly. We think the results of this research form a good reference point from which to build a computer integrated manufacturing system for shipbuilding.

Acknowledgement

We would like to thank Takao Sekimoto and Masamoto Shiino for their collaboration in this research. We would also like to thank the reviewers for their valuable comments. We gratefully acknowledge the supported of the Shipbuilding Research Association of Japan and the Systems Technologies Committee of the Society of Naval Architects of Japan.

References

[1] Koyama, T., "Shipbuilding in the Future and CIMS," 13th Summer Lectures, the Society of Naval Architects of Japan, 1987
[2] Fujino, H.,"A Plan of the CIMS for Shipbuilding," 13th Summer Lectures, the Society of Naval Architects of Japan, 1987
[3] Report of the investigation and the study on the new generation shipbuilding systems, the Shipbuilding Research Association of Japan, 1989

[4] MacCallum, K. J., "Understanding Relationships in Marine Systems Design," Proc. of First IMSDC, 1982

[5] Akagi, S., Fujita, K., "Building an Expert System for the Preliminary Design of Ships," AI EDAM, Vol.1. No.3, 1987

[6] "Mechanical design systems leap to Intelligent CAD," special issue on Nikkei AI, Nikkei McGraw-Hill, 1987

[7] Borning, A., "The Programming Language Aspects of ThingLab, a Constraint-Oriented Simulation Laboratory," ACM Trans. on Programming Language and Systems, Vol. 3, No. 4, 1981

[8] Sussman, G. J., Steel, G. L. Jr., "CONSTRAINTS - A Language for Expressing Almost-Hierarchical Descriptions," Artificial Intelligence, Vol. 14, 1980

[9] Suzuki, N., Obujekuto Shikoh, Kyoritsu shuppan, 1987

[10] Goldberg, A., Smalltalk-80: the interactive programming environment, Addison-Wesley, 1984

[11] Hayes-Roth, F., Waterman, D. A., Lenat, D.B. (ed.), Building Expert Systems, Addison-Wesley, 1983

[12] Shimizu, K., "An Expert System for Subdivision Design of Tanker," the Journal of the Society of Naval Architects of Japan, vol. 164, 1987

[13] Cooper, T., Wogrin, N., Rule Based Programming with OPS 5, Morgan Kaufman Publishers, San Mateo, 1988

[14] Shibata, K. et. al., Fundamentals of the Design of Merchant Ships. Seizan-do, 1979

[15] Kansai Shipbuilding Association, Shipbuilding Design Handbook, Kaibun-do, Tokyo, 1983

[16] Serrano, D., Gossard, D.,"Constraint management in MCAE," Artificial Intelligence in Engineering: Design, J.S.Gero (ed.), Elsevier, Amsterdam, 1988

[17] Sekimoto, T., Shimizu, K., Koyama, T., "On The Object-Oriented Ship Basic Design System," the Journal of the Society of Naval Architects of Japan, Vol.164, 1988

Using Design History Systems for Technology Transfer

David C. Brown

Rahul Bansal †

AI Research Group
Computer Science Department
Worcester Polytechnic Institute
Worcester, MA 01609, USA

Knowledge Integrated Tools & Systems
Digital Equipment Corporation
333 South Street
Shrewsbury, MA 01545, USA

Abstract: This paper presents the concept of a Design History System (DHS), and describes a protoype DHS called the Process Technology Transfer Tool (PTTT) which was designed to aid in transferring process design information between Advanced Development and Manufacturing.

1. INTRODUCTION

Before the use of computers became common it was always customary to keep notes of the decisions made during design in an Engineering Notebook. This practice is still in use. There is a strong need for an electronic alternative to notebooks. Since the development of CAD tools, CIM, and Engineering Data-Bases, the possibility has started to exist for a record of design decisions to be kept using a computer. However, this opportunity has not yet been well explored.

More recently, Design Expert Systems make it possible for us to consider the automatic generation of design histories [Brown & Chandrasekaran, 1989] [Dixon et al, 1984] [Mittal and Araya, 1986] [Maher, 1985]. Such a system can keep a record of the trace of its action, keeping a record of the active plans, goals, strategies, and knowledge. It has already been shown that such systems can generate useful explanations of their decisions [Kassatly & Brown, 1987] [Chandrasekaran et al, 1988].

---

† The implementation team at DEC consisted of Dr. H-J. Fu (Team leader), Rahul Bansal, and Chuck Haggerty, with some assistance from Alice Lin, and support from Paul Posco.

A **Design History** is the result of "the *explicit* recording of design information in the form of design problems, alternative solutions and the evaluations or arguments leading to the choice of a particular alternative" [Freeman, 1975, p. 544]. Such a history should also refer to the sources of information used during decision-making, such as journal articles, technical reports, handbooks, images, and other human experts. The history should provide an explanation for the decisions. It should be time stamped so that the state of the design at any particular time can be determined. The dependency of one decision on another should also be recorded.

We will refer to a computer system that enables the acquisition, manipulation, and presentation of design histories as a **Design History System (DHS)**. Such a system should also provide support for the checking of suggested modification to the design. We make no presumptions about the level of automation in such a system. Clearly each function of the system (e.g., modification checking) might be done either automatically or manually.

2. TECHNOLOGY TRANSFER

In this paper we will present a prototype DHS called **PTTT**, the Process Technology Transfer Tool ‡. The PTTT systems operates in the domain of what DEC Shrewsbury calls **Technology Transfer**. This is an activity involving *recording* the results of the *decision-making* of the source group about some manufacturing processes, and *transferring* those results to another group, the target group, in such a form that they can easily *use* and *modify* that information. We will refer to the decisions made as a *design*. The goal of the PTTT project is to produce a software system that will aid in the technology transfer process.

2.1. The Ingredients of Technology Transfer

Decision Making: The source group is involved in decision making. Whatever computer support is provided should aid, and not hinder, their problem-solving processes. The system(s) should enhance their normal use of the computer, and should assist with their normal daily activity. It must be convenient to access the required information. It is worth noting that the target group is also involved in decision making, but on a more limited scale.

Recording: The results of the decisions made, and any intermediate decisions, should be recorded. They can be used to support decision making in both groups. There must

---

‡ A version of this system, known as MIKIS, was presented in [Fu et al, 1990]. The first author (Brown) was the consultant to the project.

be a way of recording the history of the decisions made, as well as the actual decisions. The generation of reports should be easy. The recording of the results of experiments and design decisions should be easy.

Transfer: Transfer of computerized information need not entail actual transfer of information, merely transfer of access to it. Often, only the information that the source group thinks that the target group needs is recorded and transferred.

Use: Indexing of information is going to be a key issue †. For example, TIME, PROCESS, and PERSON are the indices used in non-computer mode. These should be included in the DHS if we want the designers to use the system.

If the transfer of information to the target group remains restricted, there must also be a convenient way of gaining access to complete data about the decision making. However, care must be taken to ensure that the target group gets a full history of the decision making only when needed. It must be convenient to access the required information.

Modification: The target group has different design goals, different constraints, and different facilities than the first group. As a consequence the design they are given to use may not be totally suitable. That is, modifications are likely.

In order to confidently modify the decisions made by the source group the target group will need to understand the reasons for those decisions. That is, the "justifications" or "dependencies" must have been recorded along with the decisions. The target group's modifications, in turn, should have their justifications recorded, and should also be related in some way to the original decision, so that the design history can be maintained.

3. THE TECHNOLOGY TRANSFER PROBLEM

3.1. The Problem

Technology is advancing at a rapid pace. Product life cycles have been shortened. Manufacturers have a limited time frame to introduce new products otherwise they lose market share. The success of new product startup depends on the technology transfer process between Advanced Development and Manufacturing. The transfer time impacts manufacturing ramp-up time and the time to market.

In an organization, technology is transferred at two levels. On a geographical level it is transferred among different plants and geographically separated groups. On a plant level it is transferred whenever employees are trained, reskilled, or whenever they need information.

---

† Pun intended.

Efficient archival and accessibility of design histories are vital to technology transfer. Each organization specifies templates and guidelines to document information. However these specifications are not sufficient. They do not specify how to store the information so as to be accessible to others. The information (experiments, reports, process sheets, trouble shooting knowledge, decisions, rationale, and motivations) is stored in private repositories like engineering notebooks. It is scattered, fragmented, and unorganized. Technology receivers often waste time and resources by repeating experiments and searching for information.

3.2. Key Issues to be Addressed

It is clear that any system built to solve this Technology Transfer problem will probably need some to address several key issues. Some of these issues are listed below.

- **Appropriate Knowledge Structures:** The PTTT system supports the acquisition of expert knowledge, i.e., Knowledge Acquisition (KA). A key KA issue is how well the knowledge representation structures provided by the tool match the information which the expert is trying to convey [Buchanan et al, 1983] [Chandrasekaran, 1984] [Gruber & Cohen, 1987]. This is an issue that must be addressed by the PTTT system.

  In our domain, the process designers use a variety of representations of types of knowledge when making their decisions, such as:

  > *Process Sheets,*
  > *Process Diagrams,*
  > *Process Descriptions,*
  > *Reports,*
  > *Experiment Descriptions,*
  > *Experiment Results,*
  > *Test Results,*
  > *Images.*

  Transfer must be in terms of these types.

- **Hypertext:** The types of knowledge used in our domain have distinct patterns of relationships.

  At any particular time a cluster of types are connected by different types of links (eg. a Process Diagram refers to a Process Description), and represent the current state of the process. Other chunks of knowledge act as explanations of 'why' it is the way it is. One contribution to that explanation is a method of finding a description of the previous state. This provides history.

It is clear that a DHS must reflect those relationships, and allow easy following of paths between types of knowledge. Hypertext systems have these qualities [Conklin, 1987].

- **Levels of Abstraction:** There is a clear need for the ability to express levels of abstraction in process diagrams. Any "supporting knowledge" about any of the processes should be similarly organized.

- **Multiple Experts:** As large design projects have decisions being made by more than one person at a time, a DHS should provide the ability to record knowledge from more than one expert. However, the problem of acquisition from multiple experts is well known in the field of Expert Systems. Most texts advise that the possibility for conflicting knowledge and different strategic knowledge make the use of more than one expert inadvisable [Wolf, 1989] [Mittal & Dym, 1985].

- **User Interface:** The DHS must present information to the user in the form in which he or she normally uses it. For example, in our domain, Process Description Charts are in flowchart form. Consequently, the graphical representation of processes will be a key component in the system.

  In addition, the user interface is of great importance for all interactive systems [Shneiderman, 1987]. For Expert Systems, and other knowledge intensive systems, such as PTTT, a good interface with the user will help to enhance the the impression of intelligence (See [Hendler, 1988], and the other papers in that volume). The interface also has a major impact on the user's acceptance of the system (see below).

- **Design Histories:** A Design History System should provide all the qualities described in Section 1 above. In addition, a form of **version control**, for the decision **dependencies**, will be be important too. In that way an engineer can record what the latest version of some process description, but also go back to earlier ones.

- **Reports:** The DHS system should generate appropriate reports about the stored knowledge.

- **User Acceptance:** One of the major issues in a DHS project is motivating the users to *want* to capture their knowledge. They have to have a short-term payoff, as well as a long term payoff, otherwise they will not be motivated to change their existing practices. Learning new procedures, and using them, is hard work, and disruptive.

  It is best to provide a tool to enhance existing computer use. For example, provide users with a better method of editing text, or sending mail. In addition, the tool could provide an integral report generating system, based on the user's own standard reporting forms.

This approach has some intrinsic benefits. First, it minimizes the change to the user's modes of work. Second, knowledge can be captured at the same time as the system is making their lives easier. If the key attributes of the main "objects" that they deal with and report on can be understood, then we can provide them with forms tailored to what they want to report (e.g., an experiment, a process). These completed forms can be both printed and stored in the system.

- **Security & Access Control:** Technology transfer involves sensitive information. Therefore, for commercial reasons, there is need for security. For data integrity, access control is important in order to control who is allowed to make updates to the design.

4. DESIGN HISTORIES

4.1. In Engineering Design

It has been recognized for a long time in Engineering that the history of design must be maintained if that design is to be successfully changed in the future. There are a number of engineering design history projects in progress [Kellogg et al, 1989] [Lakin et al, 1989] [Chen et al, 1990] [Thompson & Liu, 1990] [Sivard et al, 1989], but few results as yet [Mittal et al, 1988].

4.2. In Software Design

In the world of computer programming, researchers have been considering for some while the possibility of computerizing the recording of the steps taken during the design and implementation of a program. In 1971, Wirth discussed the *stepwise refinement* approach to programming, using "a sequence of design decisions concerning the decomposition of tasks into subtasks" [Wirth, 1971]. Building on that concept, Freeman discussed "the need for for knowing the reasoning behind decisions" [Freeman, 1975, p. 543], This process he termed *design rationalization*.

4.3. In Protocol Analysis

Researchers studying the design process have recently turned to a tool from Psychology -- Protocol Analysis [Ericsson & Simon, 1984]. In both engineering design and software design, researchers have used videotapes and audiotapes to record the actions of a designer when solving a design problem [Ullman et al, 1989] [Waldron et al, 1989] [Adelson, 1989].

While these protocols certainly are a form of design history, they are so detailed and complete, maintaining records of failures for example, that they are both too long and too confusing for regular use. They are also difficult to enter into the computer.

5. THE SOLUTION -- THE PTTT SYSTEM

5.1. The Architecture of the PTTT System

PTTT is a distributed, multimedia information archival and retrieval system used to capture product design history and trouble-shooting knowledge. It was developed at Digital's Northeast Technology Center at Shrewsbury, Massachusetts. It is based on the hypertext paradigm although it is not built on any commercial hypertext system.

PTTT captures the process flow as a hierarchical graph. Each level of the graph represents a flow between processes at that level. The higher levels represent an abstraction of the more detailed process steps at the lower levels. For example, a disk head manufacturing plant might have the graph of process flow shown in Figure 1.

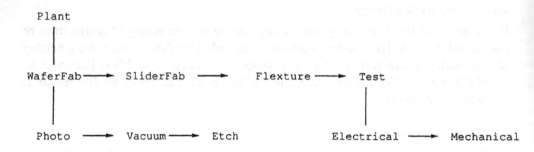

Figure 1: A Graph of Process Flow

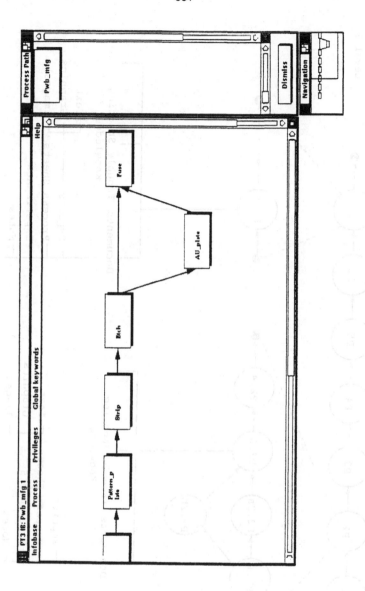

Figure 2: A Process Flow Chart in PTTT

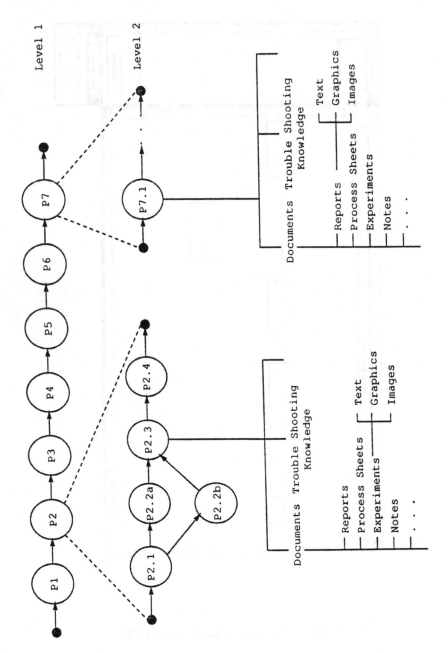

Figure 3: Documents Organized by Process

The user's interface to PTTT that provides access to a portion of a Printed Wire Board Manufacturing (Pwb_mfg) process flow chart is shown in Figure 2. The diagram represents flow of materials through processes. The hierarchy can start at any level of abstraction and can go down to any depth. Only one level of the hierarchy is presented at a time.

All information is displayed in a consistent form using DECwindows ®. There are three sub-windows. They show a portion of the current layer of the process graph, an indication of where the currently displayed portion is in the whole process graph (Navigation), and a record of those process nodes which have been expanded to get to the current level (the Process Path).

If a process node can be expanded into more detail at a lower level it is marked. Process nodes can be selected using the mouse-controlled cursor, in order to expand them and switch to the next level. Other actions include moving back up a level, or modifying the process graph. A pop-up menu which appears next to the selected node assists with this process.

Pull-down menus allow access to the major actions. It is possible to switch to another Infobase (i.e., a stored record of the development of a process plus all the associated documents), to change the process graph or the part of the process graph being inspected, to access and change the privileges of a user, and to access and use Keywords.

PTTT organizes information by chunking (associating and relating) documents. A document can be an experiment, a report, a justification [Lin, 1990], a decision, a note, a technical paper, a process sheet, or trouble-shooting knowledge. Documents are stored as "Compound Documents", allowing a combination of text, graphs, and images. Images can be annotated.

Figure 3 shows how each node in the process flow graph is associated with chunked information — the documents relevant to that process step. Therefore information is organized by processes rather than by people who created the information. Clearly, most of the information will be attached to the most detailed process nodes. However, information can be attached to any node. Thus, information can be stored about more general design decisions.

Associative links relate documents both within and between process steps. For example, if the cause of a Vacuum experiment is a Photo experiment they can be linked. So a user can browse through the information base looking for causes. Associative links may be used in either direction.

Keyword searching is another capability provided by the system to support navigation through an information base. Each document is associated with a set of keywords. Some of these are automatically assigned whenever documents are created or modified. The rest are added by the users. Each document is time-stamped and author-stamped. The users can query the information base for documents. The query can include logical operators and wildcards. For example,

process1 AND (vacu* OR (process3 AND Rahul AND NOT David)) AND process2

PTTT keeps a history of all documents. Each document is version stamped. Whenever a user modifies a document she has to enter a note justifying it. These notes store the essence of the process development history. All versions of a document are kept. A user can leaf through the various versions to understand the motivation behind certain changes. PTTT also keeps different versions of an information base. Each version represents a major stage in product development.

PTTT is a distributed application based on the DECnet ® and DECwindows ® client and server model. Information bases and the points of access are distributed and transparent to the user.

Security is extremely important for this DHS because new process development involves company confidential information. PTTT provides a flexible security system that can be made as tight as the users wants. This is under the control of a project leader. It allows different engineers to be the owners of different parts of the process design, in order to maintain quality and consistency. The owner of a process is automatically the owner of all subprocesses of that process. An example of the interface with the security module of PTTT is shown in Figure 4.

Access to the windows shown is triggered by using the Privileges pull-down menu in the Process Flow Chart window. A user is selected from the list of names given in the List Of User Names window. Using the Add, Modify or Delete buttons, the project leader can elect to change a user's privileges, or can give or remove privileges for the selected user.

The User Privileges window provides the ability to describe, delete or add those paths through the process graph which are accessable by the selected user. The user's "global" privileges are set here too. The user can be assigned special privileges for each path. This is done using the Privileges For A Process Path window. It is possible to set those privileges to automatically apply to all the subprocesses of a path, in order to reduce the amount that needs to be specified.

Human factors and user-interface design were important considerations in the design of the system. PTTT is layered on DECWindows. We involved our users early in the design phase. The final screens resulted from many iterations with users and human interface experts. An extensive feedback mechanism gives pertinent and immediate feedback to the user. The error messages not only explain what is wrong but also suggest a way of correcting the error. Context-sensitive help is also available. Use of jargon is avoided as much as possible. All dialog boxes are labeled. Ample instruction is given in each dialog box.

One of the issues considered during the design of the implementation was the speed of the system. Several techniques were used, such as the use of hash tables to quickly access the documents associated with each process, and the use of a binary search for keywords. We were also very concerned with maintaining flexibility of information storage, as it was clear that we could not anticipate all the combinations of information to be stored in the system. In addition, because of the wide variety of users, the system is designed to be somewhat customizable. For example, it is possible to select which editor to use during a user's PTTT sessions.

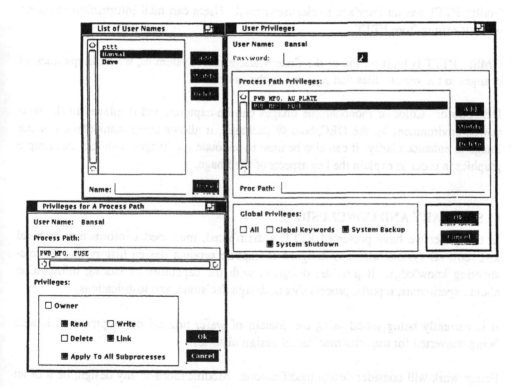

Figure 4: The Security Interface in PTTT

5.2. System Integration

PTTT was designed to use standard Digital software, such as DECwindows, CMS, DEC-net, DECwrite, DECskill and DECphoto. Some of these systems are described below.

Diagnostic Knowledge Based Systems: Process trouble shooting knowledge is an integral part of any manufacturing information system. PTTT is integrated with a tool called DECSkill ® for building knowledge-based diagnostic systems [Bansal & Posco, 1989]. A diagnostic session executed from within PTTT can identify a process problem and display a Standard Operating Procedure (SOP). This SOP can point to the stored information (experiments, process sheets) used to develop the process step.

Compound Document Editors: PTTT cuts down the time spent by engineers on writing reports. It can be integrated with a compound document editor called DECWrite ®. DECWrite is a WYSIWYG editor which makes report writing easier. Users can include pictures and graphs in their reports. For example, the pictures could display visual defects or equipment. The graphs could display results from statistical analysis. At present PTTT can refer to RS/1 ® graphs and tables.

Mail: PTTT has an interface to electronic mail. Users can mail information to others without exiting from PTTT.

CMS: PTTT is built on top of the Code Management System ®, which keeps track of changes to the various files that are used by the system.

DECphoto: Color or monochrome images can be captured and displayed in the windowed environment by the DECphoto ® package. It allows some manipulation of the image to enhance clarity. It can also be used to annotate the images with text and simple graphics in order to explain the key aspects of the image.

6. SUMMARY AND CONCLUSIONS

In this paper we have presented PTTT, a distributed, multimedia information archival and retrieval system which is designed to capture product design history and trouble-shooting knowledge. It provides designers with the capability of storing information about experiments, reports, process sheets, design decisions, and justifications.

It is currently being tested using the domain of wafer process development. It is also being converted for use with mechanical design histories.

Future work will consider design modifications. Modifications to any design, be it of an object or a process, can only be made if the effects of those changes on the performance/quality of the resulting design can be determined. This will be especially true in a system where existing decisions are associated with their justification [Lin, 1990]. We will be investigating the possibility of automatic checking of design modifications by checking for consistency with past justifications.

It is clear that Design History Systems will be a vital tool for Technology Transfer, as they will allow information of higher quality to be passed from Advanced Development to Manufacturing. This should result in faster and more accurate transfer of information, leading to a better product.

Acknowledgements: We acknowledge the support and contributions of Paul Posco, who was Manager of the KITS group at DEC, as well as the other members of the PTTT team and the KITS group.

7. REFERENCES

B. Adelson (1989) Cognitive Modelling: Explaining and Predicting How Designers Design. *Preprints of the NSF Engineering Design Research Conference* , Amherst, pp. 1-14.

R. Bansal & P. Posco (Aug. 1989) Knowledge Acquisition Tool: Promulgating Expert Systems in a Manufacturing Environment. *Eleventh International Joint Conference on Artificial Intelligence, Workshop on Knowledge Acquisition.*

D. C. Brown & B. Chandrasekaran (1989) *Design Problem Solving: Knowledge Structures and Control Strategies* . Morgan Kaufmann.

B. Buchanan, D. Barstow, R. Bechtel, J. Bennett, W. Clancey, C. Kulikowski, T. Mitchell & D. Waterman (1983) Constructing an Expert System. *Building Expert Systems* , Hayes-Roth, Waterman & Lenat (Eds.), Addison-Wesley, pp. 127-168.

B. Chandrasekaran (1984) Expert Systems: Matching Techniques to Tasks. *Artificial Intelligence Applications for Business* , W. Reitman (Ed.), Ablex, pp. 41-64.

B. Chandrasekaran, M. Tanner & J. Josephson (1988) Explanation: The Role of Control Strategies and Deep Models. *Expert Systems: The User Interface* , J. A. Hendler (Ed.), Ablex, pp. 219-248.

A. Chen, B. McGinnis, D. G. Ullman & T. G. Dietterich (1990) Design History Knowledge Representation and Its Basic Computer Implementation. *The 2nd*

International Conference on Design Theory and Methodology, ASME, Chicago, IL, pp. 175-185.

J. Conklin (Sept 1987) Hypertext: A Survey and Introduction. *IEEE Computer*, Vol. 20, No. 9.

J. Dixon, M. Simmons & P. Cohen (1984) An Architecture for Application of Artificial Intelligence to Design. *Proc. 21st Design Automation Conf.*, IEEE, pp. 634-640.

K. Ericsson & H. Simon (1984) *Protocol Analysis*, MIT Press, Cambridge, MA.

P. Freeman (1975) Towards Improved Review of Software Designs. Proc. Nat. Comp. Conf., In: Freeman & Wasserman (Eds.), *Tutorial on Software Design Techniques*, IEEE Comp. Soc., 1983, pp. 542-547.

H-J. Fu, R. Bansal, C. M. Haggerty & P. Posco (August 1990) Hyperinformation Systems and Technology Transfer. *Sysmposium on Engineering Data Management, Proc. ASME Int. Computers in Engineering Conf.* Boston, MA, pp. 121-129.

Gruber & P. Cohen (1987) Design for Acquisition: Principles of Knowledge Systems Design to Facilitate Knowledge Acquisition. *Int. Jnl. of Man-Machine Studies*, Vol. 26, No. 2, pp. 143-159.

J. Hendler (1988) Introduction: Designing Interfaces for Expert Systems. *Expert Systems: The User Interface*, J. A. Hendler (Ed.), Ablex, pp. 1-14.

A. Kassatly & D. C. Brown (Aug 1987) Explanation for Routine Design Problem Solving. *Proc. 2nd Int. Conf. on the Appl. of AI in Engineering*, Computational Mechanics, pp. 225-239

C. Kellogg, R. Gargan, W. Mark, J. McGuire, M. Pontecorvo, J. Schossberg, J. Sullivan, M. Genesereth & N. Singh (1989) The Acquisition, Verification, and Explanation of Design Knowledge. *SIGART Newsletter*, ACM, No. 108, pp. 163-165.

F. Lakin, L. Leifer, J. Wambaugh, D. Cannon & C. Sivard (1989) The Electronic Design Notebook: Performing Medium and Processing Medium. To appear in a special issue of *Visual Computer: International Journal of Computer Graphics*.

A. H-H. Lin (August 1990) *JPS : A Justification Posting System*. M.S. Thesis, Computer Science Dept., WPI, Worcester, MA.

M. L. Maher (1985) *HI-RISE: A Knowledge-Based Expert System for the Preliminary Structural Design of High Rise Buildings.* Tech. Rpt. R-85-146, Department of Civil Engineering, Carnegie-Mellon University.

S. Mittal & A. Araya (Aug 1986) A Knowledge-Based Framework for Design. *Proc. 5th Nat. Conf. on AI*, AAAI, Philadelphia, pp. 856-865.

S. Mittal, D. Bobrow & J. de Kleer (1988) DARN: A Community Memory for Diagnosis and Repair Tasks. *Expert Systems: The User Interface*, J. A. Hendler (Ed.), Ablex, pp. 57-80.

S. Mittal & C. Dym (1985) Knowledge Acquisition from Multiple Experts. *AI Magazine*, Vol. 6, No. 2, pp. 32-36

B. Shneiderman (1987) *Designing the User Interface: Strategies for Effective Human-Computer Interaction.* Addison-Wesley.

C. Sivard, M. Zweben, D. Cannon, F. Lakin, L. Leifer & J. Wambaugh (Jan 1989) Conservation of Design Knowledge. *Proc. AIAA'89, 27th Aerospace Sciences Meeting,* American Institute of Aeronautics and Astronautics.

J. B. Thompson & S. C-Y. Liu (1990) Design Evolution Management: A Methodology for Representing and Utilizing Design Rationale. *The 2nd International Conference on Design Theory and Methodology*, ASME, Chicago, IL, pp. 185-191.

D. Ullman, S. Wood & D. Craig (1989) The Importance of Drawing in the Mechanical Design Process. *Preprints of the NSF Engineering Design Research Conference*, Amherst, pp. 31-52.

M. Waldron, K. Waldron & T. Herren (1989) Empirical Study on Generation of Constraints Which Direct Design Decisions in Conceptual Mechanical Design. *Preprints of the NSF Engineering Design Research Conference*, Amherst, pp. 15-30.

N. Wirth (April 1971) Program Development by Stepwise Refinement. *CACM*, pp. 221-227.

W. A. Wolf (April 1989) Knowledge Acquisition from Multiple Experts. *SIGART Newsletter*, ACM, No. 108, pp. 138-140.

ThingWorld:

A Multibody Simulation System With

Low Computational Complexity

Alex P. Pentland[1]

Vision and Modeling Group, Room E15-387, The Media Lab
Massachusetts Institute of Technology
20 Ames St., Cambridge MA 02138

ABSTRACT. *The ability to simulate complex physical situations in near-real-time is a critical element of many engineering and robotics applications. Unfortunately the computation cost of standard physical simulation methods increases rapidly as the situation becomes more complex. The result is that even when using the fastest supercomputers we are still able to interactively simulate only small, toy worlds. To solve this problem I have proposed changing the way we represent and simulate physics in order to reduce the computational complexity of physical simulation, thus making possible interactive simulation of complex situations. A prototype system, called ThingWorld, that makes use of these new representations has been implemented for UNIX computer systems and has demonstrated $O(n)$ computational complexity (linear scaling of computational cost with increasing model complexity) for multibody dynamic simulations.*

1 Introduction: The Problem

The ability for real-time physical simulation is critical for solving many important engineering and robotics problems. For instance, concurrent design (design employing coordinated teams of designers, engineers, and life-cycle planners) requires requires being able to quickly simulate the physical situation [3,4,5], so that the shared CAD database can detect conflicts between the viewpoints of the different users. Similarly, in robotics the problem of planning in dynamic environments requires predicting the physical consequences of each action, which in general requires the ability for real-time physical simulation.

More popularly, the idea of a computer-simulated environment — a *virtual world* — that users can view, move around in, and interact with has long excited both the computer graphics community [1,2] and the scientific population at large. Constructing such a virtual world, of course, requires the ability to quickly and accurately simulate the physics of complex, multibody environments.

---

[1]This research was made possible by ARO Grant No. DAAL03-87-K-0005

To date such simulated environments have been quite simple, containing only a few objects with negligible dynamics. To move beyond such toy worlds we must confront the problem of performing real-time simulation of physics in complex environments. Although the mathematics of such simulation is reasonably well-understood, there are great practical problems in achieving real-time performance with the sort of computers that we are likely to have in the next century or two — even if computer speed keeps increasing exponentially!

The primary difficulty is the *computational complexity* of accomplishing such simulations: The computational resources (e.g., FLOPS[2] and words of storage) needed to solve problems such as collision detection, dynamic simulation, and constraint satisfaction increase rapidly as the complexity of the environment increases. As a consequence, simply designing faster, larger, or more parallel computers will not allow us to build realistically complex simulated worlds.

Before such worlds can be built we must first invent algorithms for dynamics, collision detection, and constraint satisfaction that scale linearly (or better!) with increasing problem size. In particular, I see four areas that are critical in achieving complex, near-real-time multibody simulations. These are:

- **Rendering**. This is an area that has already received much attention. Z-buffer type algorithms currently dominate hardware in this area, because of their simplicity and parallelism, and because their computational complexity scales linearly with both polygons and pixels. A large amount of attention focused on this problem has produced quite satisfying results; therefore, I consider the rendering problem to be well in hand and will not discuss it further in this paper.

- **Dynamics**. For many applications we want objects to react to external forces in a physically-correct manner. The standard method of achieving this is via the finite element method (FEM), which requires $O(n^3)$ calculations [3] and $O(n^2)$ storage locations where n is the number of vertices on an object. For example, an object defined by 1000 vertices (a number appropriate when modeling either smoothly curved surfaces or rough, irregular objects) requires $O(10^9)$ calculations to come to equilibrium in response to a static load, and also requires $O(10^6)$ storage locations.

We can translate $O(n^m)$ complexity figures into estimates of Mflops and MWords by arbitrarily assuming that each operation requires one hundred floating point operations per second to be "real time," and that each storage location is a single word. This assumption is perhaps overly optimistic, however the point is

---

[2]FLoating point OPerations per Second.

[3]The notation $O(x)$ is read "order of x" and means that to complete the computation in question requires a number of serial machine instructions that is proportional to the value of x. For instance, to find all instances of the symbol "p" in an unordered list of length x requires $O(x)$ operations, because each element of the list must be examined. In this paper the computational complexity cited for a given operation is the one appropriate for general-purpose implementations; often there are special cases which have lower complexity. Further, in the interests of brevity, I have not described all the possible hybrid computational strategies, most of which are useful only in special situations.

not to present precise numbers but to give a feel for the magnitude of the numbers involved. Using this rule we discover that it would require a computer with roughly 100,000,000 Mflop performance and 1,000 MWord storage to handle the dynamics of a world with 1,000 moving objects in real time.

- **Collision Detection.** Physical objects do not interpenetrate, and so we must calculate collisions between objects at each time step. For *coarse* collision detection it is possible to trade storage complexity against calculation complexity. For instance: a typical octree scheme allows collision detection in $O(\log m)$ operations and $O(m^2)$ storage locations, where $1/m$ is the spatial resolution of the collision detection. However most programmers have preferred to use bounding boxes rather than octrees, because although the bounding box comparison requires somewhat more calculation it is only $O(m)$ in storage.

  Unfortunately neither algorithm performs the sort of precise collision detection and characterization needed for simulating physics. In a polygon-based system checking for collision between two non-convex bodies with n polygons each requires comparing all polygons against all polygons, at a cost of $O(n^2)$ rather expensive calculations. As an example, if we had 1000 objects, each intersecting the bounding box of 10 others, and each object had 1000 vertices then contact calculation would require roughly 10^{10} calculations. Consequently, it would require a computer with roughly 1,000,000 Mflops to obtain real-time performance. For those that think this is overstating the case, it may be enlightening to look at (for instance) table 8 in reference [12].

- **Constraint Satisfaction.** Constraints are useful for controlling the geometry and behavior of a complex system, and for replacing detailed physical interactions (e.g., a hinge) with the equivalent behavior. Constraint systems commonly used in AI research are linear in their complexity but are very limited in the type of interactions they can deal with [1,2,6,7]. Physically-based constraint systems suggested for use in computer graphics [8,9] have $O(lk^2)$ calculation complexity[4] and $O(lk)$ storage complexity, where k is the number of constrained parameters and l is the number of constraints. For a world with 1000 objects, each of which has ten constraints involving ten parameters (imagine designing a car engine, for instance), it may require 10^{12} calculations and 10^8 storage locations to satisfy all the constraints. Consequently it would require a computer with roughly 100,000,000 Mflops performance and 100 MWords storage to solve this size of constraint satisfaction problem in real time.

The goal of the above discussion is not to precisely pin down the computational complexity of each operation and to explore every hybrid, special-purpose computation strategy. There are, for instance, many special cases in which things are better than as described above. Rather the point of these examples — which involve only 1,000 objects — is to make it clear that *something* must be changed if we are to have near-real-time simulation for worlds of realistic complexity and generality. Faster

---

[4]This is being generous. A more typical complexity is probably $O(lk^2 + k^3)$.

COMPUTER POWER NEEDED FOR REAL-TIME PERFORMANCE		
Problem:	**Standard Methods**	**ThingWorld**
Dynamics	100,000,000 Mflops, 1,000 MWords	100 Mflop, 1 MWord
Contact	1,000,000 Mflops, 1 MWord	1,000 Mflops, 1 MWord
Constraints	100,000,000 Mflops, 100 MWords	10,000 Mflops, 100 MWords

Figure 1: Computational resources required by ThingWorld compared to resources required when using standard methods in order to achieve near-real-time performance for the example described in the text

computers *will not* solve the problem for us because even if computers continue to double their speed every few years we won't see workstations with the required performance for more than a century.

My suggestion, therefore, is that we rethink our representations for geometry and dynamics, and our goals for generality and precision, in order to avoid the problems of computational complexity. I believe that this rethinking is the only way in which we can hope to obtain near-real-time simulation of complex worlds on the sort of computers that will be available before the year 2000.

2   Thingworld's Solutions

How are we to escape from the seemingly-intractable problems of computational complexity? There are two general approaches: One, find a representational system that is better adapted to the problems at hand, and two, see if the problem can be redefined in a way that improves its computational complexity. I have adopted both of these approaches in building a prototype multibody simulation system called Thing-World [10,18], which has the desirable property of scaling much better than standard methods for each of the above problems.

The solutions adopted in ThingWorld are:

- Accept small, controlled errors in the dynamics calculations. This allows selected high-frequency, low-amplitude vibrations to be discarded in order to achieve linear scaling with increasing object complexity.

- Represent geometry using implicit functions, that is, using analytic primitives that have an inside-outside function. This allows linear complexity contact detection and more precise contact characterization.

- Restrict constraints to be either quadratic energy functions for "soft" or inexact constraints, or to be linear holonomic for "hard" or exact constraints. By restricting the class of constraints to those that are quadratic energy functions (e.g., springs) or holonomic (e.g., nailing down degrees of freedom already in the system) we can take advantage of standard numerical techniques to increase system performance. In particular, by expressing these types of constraints in terms of their natural parameterizations we can guarantee that the constraint matrices will be both diagonal and well-conditioned, which leads to an algorithm with linear computational complexity.

These strategies can have a very large effect on the size of computer required to achieve near-real-time performance, as the comparison shown in Figure 1 illustrates. This figure assumes the 1,000 object simulated world described in the preceding examples, and compares the computer resources required to achieve near-real-time performance using first the standard methods for simulation, and then using the techniques employed in the ThingWorld system. As can be seen, by changing the problem and representation slightly we can achieve very great savings. For larger worlds the savings would be larger, for smaller worlds the savings would be less.

The following sections contain overviews of the ThingWorld dynamics, collision detection, and constraint systems, and explains how the savings shown in Figure 1 are achieved.

2.1 Dynamics: Technical Details

Most simulation systems for complex, multibody situations use only rigid-body dynamics, as the calculations for rigid-body dynamics are especially simple and efficient. However the need for describing non-rigid behavior can be seen even in the simplest examples of interacting physical objects: the duration of contact when a cylinder collides head-on with a plane, for instance, depends entirely on how long it takes the resulting wave of non-rigid compression to travel the length of the cylinder. And, of course, the non-rigid properties of materials are even more important when considering contact surfaces or friction: in rigid body schemes contact force equals mass times velocity divided by the time step, so that the force goes to infinity as the time step decreases!

We have, therefore, adopted a version of the finite element method (FEM) for simulating non-rigid multibody object dynamics. In particular, we have adopted a technique known as modal analysis in order to achieve linear scaling of the computational cost with increasing object complexity. In the modal method the basis functions over which object dynamics are calculated are chosen to be the free vibration modes of the object. This basis set diagonalizes the mass, stiffness, and damping matrices so that object dynamics may be described by linear superposition of independent vibration modes.

By examining the vibration frequency of each mode we can discard the high-frequency modes that typically have small amplitude, thus obtaining large efficiency gains at little cost in error. Perhaps even more importantly, by chosing a fixed number of modes one avoids the poor scaling behavior of the normal finite element method, obtaining a method that scales linearly in the number of vertices. The error caused by discarding the high-frequency modes can be checked by comparison against the full set of equations, so that a controlled level of error can be maintained.

Of considerable interest is the fact that rigid-body methods are simply a special case of the modal approach, the case where one discards all modes except the six translation and rotation modes. Thus the advantages claimed for rigid body techniques — mainly efficiency, stability, and simplicity — are also characteristics of the modal approach when using a small, fixed number of modes. The major difference is that by using the modal approach one may control the level of simulation accuracy, and thus can model phenomina such as object-to-object contact to the level of accuracy required. This is a critical advantage for a general-purpose simulation system because, as mentioned earlier, rigid-body methods are unable to calculate even gross collision characteristics such as duration and force profile.

2.1.1 Background: The Finite Element Method

The finite element method (FEM) is the standard technique for simulating the dynamic behavior of an object. In the FEM the continuous variation of displacements throughout an object is replaced by displacements at a finite number of so-called nodal points. Energy equations (or functionals) are then derived in terms of the nodal unknowns, and the resulting set of simultaneous differential equations are then iterated to solve for displacements as a function of impinging forces. These equations may be written:

$$M\ddot{u} + C\dot{u} + Ku = f \tag{1}$$

where u is a $3n \times 1$ vector of the (x, y, z) displacements of the n nodal points relative to the objects' center of mass, M, C and K are $3n$ by $3n$ matrices describing the mass, damping, and material stiffness between each point within the body, and f is a $3n \times 1$ vector describing the (x, y, z) components of the forces acting on the nodes. This equation can be interpreted as assigning a certain mass to each nodal point and a certain material stiffness between nodal points, with damping being accounted for by dashpots attached between the nodal points. The damping matrix C is normally taken to be equal to $s_1 M + s_2 K$ for some scalars s_1, s_2. When $s_1 \neq 0$, $s_2 \neq 0$ this is called Raleigh damping, for $s_2 = 0$ it is called mass damping, and for $s_1 = 0$ stiffness damping.

Perhaps the major drawback of the FEM is its large computational expense, because the matrices M, C, and K are quite large: for instance, an object whose geometry is defined by 100 points produces 300×300 matrices, corresponding to the 300 unknown coordinates of the 100 nodal points, (x_i, y_i, z_i). In most situations, therefore, hundreds or thousands of very large matrix multiplications are required for each second of simulated time. Furthermore, for 3-D models the computation scales as $O(n^3)$ as the number of points n defining the object geometry increases.

2.1.2 Modal Dynamics

In the modal approach an object's behavior is described in terms of its natural *strain* or *vibration* modes, rather than in terms of point-by-point displacements. The modal method is equivalent to the FEM in expressiveness and accuracy, but has the additional virtue that it separates non-rigid object behavior into independent modes of

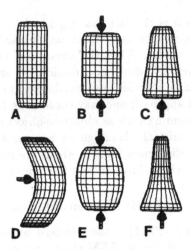

Figure 2: (a) A cylinder (b) a linear deformation mode in response to compression (c) a linear deformation mode in response to acceleration (d) a quadratic mode in response to a bending force (e) superposition of both linear and quadratic modes in response to compression (f) superposition of both linear and quadratic modes in response to acceleration

deformation, each of which may be separately analyzed and (often) solved in closed form [5,10,11]. This in turn can lead to a much more efficient and stable computational scheme.

An object's strain modes may be found by simultaneously diagonalizing $\mathbf{M}$, $\mathbf{C}$, and $\mathbf{K}$. Because these matrices are normally positive definite symmetric, and $\mathbf{C}$ is a linear function of $\mathbf{M}$ and $\mathbf{K}$, Equation 1 can be transformed into $3n$ independent differential equations by use of the *whitening transform*, which is the solution to the following eigenvalue problem:

$$\lambda\mathbf{\Phi} = \mathbf{M}^{-1}\mathbf{K}\mathbf{\Phi} \tag{2}$$

where λ and $\mathbf{\Phi}$ are the eigenvalues and eigenvectors of $\mathbf{M}^{-1}\mathbf{K}$.

Using the transformation $\mathbf{u} = \mathbf{\Phi}\bar{\mathbf{u}}$ we can then re-write Equation 1 as follows:

$$\mathbf{\Phi}^T\mathbf{M}\mathbf{\Phi}\ddot{\bar{\mathbf{u}}} + \mathbf{\Phi}^T\mathbf{C}\mathbf{\Phi}\dot{\bar{\mathbf{u}}} + \mathbf{\Phi}^T\mathbf{K}\mathbf{\Phi}\bar{\mathbf{u}} = \mathbf{\Phi}^T\mathbf{f} \quad . \tag{3}$$

In this equation $\mathbf{\Phi}^T\mathbf{M}\mathbf{\Phi}$, $\mathbf{\Phi}^T\mathbf{C}\mathbf{\Phi}$, and $\mathbf{\Phi}^T\mathbf{K}\mathbf{\Phi}$ are diagonal matrices, so that if we let $\bar{\mathbf{M}} = \mathbf{\Phi}^T\mathbf{M}\mathbf{\Phi}$, $\bar{\mathbf{C}} = \mathbf{\Phi}^T\mathbf{C}\mathbf{\Phi}$, $\bar{\mathbf{K}} = \mathbf{\Phi}^T\mathbf{K}\mathbf{\Phi}$, and $\bar{\mathbf{f}} = \mathbf{\Phi}^T\mathbf{f}$ then we can write Equation 3 as $3n$ independent equations:

$$\bar{M}_i\ddot{\bar{u}}_i + \bar{C}_i\dot{\bar{u}}_i + \bar{K}_i\bar{u}_i = \bar{f}_i \quad , \tag{4}$$

where $\bar{M}_i$ is the ith diagonal element of $\bar{\mathbf{M}}$, and so forth.

What Equation 4 describes is the time course of one of the object's *strain* or *vibration modes*. The constant $\bar{M}_i$ is the generalized mass of mode i, that is, the inertia of the ith vibration mode. Similarly, $\bar{C}_i$, and $\bar{K}_i$ describe the damping and spring stiffness associated with mode i, and $\bar{f}_i$ is the amount of force coupled with this vibration mode. The ith row of Φ describes the *deformation* the object experiences as a consequence of the force $\bar{f}_i$, and the eigenvalue λ_i is proportional to the natural resonance frequency of that vibration mode.

To obtain an accurate simulation of the dynamics of an object, one simply uses linear superposition of these modes to determine how the object responds to a given force. Either explicit, implicit, or (in simple situations) closed form solution techniques may be used to calculate how each mode varies with time. Non-linear materials may be modeled by summing the modes at the end of each time step to form the material *stress state* which can then be used to drive nonlinear plastic or viscous material behavior.

Figure 2 illustrates the some of the first and second order modes of a cylinder. Figure 2(a) shows the cylinder at rest, (b) shows the cylinder experiencing a linear deformation in response to a compressive force, (c) shows the cylinder experiencing a linear shear deformation in response to an accelerating force, (d) shows a quadratic deformation in response to a centrally-applied (bending) force, and (e) and (f) show how both the linear and second order deformations can be superimposed to produce a more accurate simulation of the object's response to the compressive and accelerating forces shown in (b) and (c).

In most applications the large cost associated with solving for the eigenvectors has been thought to make modal solutions techniques impractical. However the key observation used in the ThingWorld system is that for any fixed set of CAD building blocks the solution can be precomputed and stored away, to be used later as needed. Thus by noting that the most expensive parts of the computation need to be performed only once, beforehand and off-line, we have been able to radically improve the interactivity and efficiency of simulations in the ThingWorld system.

2.1.3 Number Of Modes Required

The modal representation decouples the degrees of freedom within the non-rigid dynamical system of Equation 1, but it does not by itself reduce the total number of degrees of freedom. Once decoupled, however, we can separately analyze the various modes in order to determine which ones are required in order to obtain an accurate description of an object's non-rigid dynamic behavior.

The most important observation is that modes associated with high resonance frequencies (large eigenvalues) normally have little effect on object shape. This is because on average:

- The displacement amplitude for each mode is *inversely* proportional to the *square* of the mode's resonance frequency. Thus higher frequencies typically have small amplitudes.

- Damping is proportional to the mode's resonance frequency. Thus higher frequency vibrations dissipate quickly.

- Frequencies are excited in proportion to the frequency content of the input force. The force generated by simple collisions typically have a roughly Gaussian time course, so that an individual resonance frequency f receives energy proportional to $e^{-f^2/\sigma}$. Thus low frequencies typically receive more energy than high frequencies.

The combination of these effects is that high-frequency modes have very little amplitude, and even less effect, in most situations. Experimentally, I have found that most commonplace multi-body interactions can be adequately modeled by use of only[5] rigid-body, linear, and quadratic strain modes [5,10,11]. For instance, in the next section Figure 3 shows a example of a simulated non-rigid dynamic interaction using only linear and quadratic modes.

Although discarding high-frequency modes generally has little effect on accuracy, it can have a profound effect on computational efficiency. The most obvious effect of discarding modes is to reduce the number of equations, with the result that only $O(n)$ operations and $O(n)$ storage locations are required (where n is the number of nodes defining the object geometry), as opposed to the $O(n^3)$ operations and $O(n^2)$ storage locations required when using standard methods. Indeed, when n is large the major cost of a low-frequencies modal approach is collecting the point forces into modal forces by computing $\bar{\mathbf{f}} = \Phi^T \mathbf{f}$, and then translating the modal displacements into point displacements by computing $\mathbf{u} = \Phi \bar{\mathbf{u}}$.

Further, because of Nyquist considerations, when using a low-frequencies modal approach we can also employ a much larger time step. In a problem involving 100 nodal points, for instance, the modal method (using 30 modes) will be roughly *two orders of magnitude* more efficient than the standard finite element approach, and yet will typically have roughly the same accuracy. In the ThingWorld system we have found that, using a Sun 4/370, approximately eight non-rigid objects can be simulated in real time, including simulation of collisions and inter-object constraint satisfaction. This performance is described in more detail below.

Another equally important benefit of using only low-order modes to describe object deformations is that they change very slowly as a function of object shape. Consequently the same modes Φ may be used for a *range* of different — but similar — undeformed shapes without incurring substantial error. This allows the modes to be precomputed, avoiding the expense of solving for Φ at run time.

2.2   Collision Detection: Technical Details

One disadvantage shared by any point-wise or polygonal representation of shape, such as used by either the FEM or the simple modal method, is the expense of calculating the distance between 3-D points (e.g., points on other objects, sensor data) and the modeled surface. When using a polygonal representation of shape one must integrate over the entire surface of the object in order to detect a collision.[6]

---

[5]Note, however, higher-order modes are required to accurately model objects whose dimensions differ more than an order of magnitude.

[6]Simpler algorithms are, of course, available for convex objects, however many — and likely *most* — of the interesting things in our environment are non-convex.

Thus the computational complexity of collision detection is $O(Nn)$ where N is the number of 3-D points that pose a collision hazard and n is the number of nodes defining the object's geometry.[7]

As a consequence, when simulating collisions between rough, irregular objects, or between objects with smoothly curving surfaces (whose surfaces require a large number of nodal points to define them accurately) the cost of collision detection and characterization is often the *majority* of the total computational cost. See, for example, table 8 in reference [12]. Clearly, this situation is something one would like to improve upon.

One method of reducing the cost of detecting and characterizing collisions is to use implicit functions to represent shape, that is, to define the object geometry by use of an inside-outside function $f(x, y, z) \leq d$. The most common example of such an implicit function is a sphere, where the inside-outside function is $f(x, y, z) = \sqrt{x^2 + y^2 + z^2} = d$, and the sphere is defined as all of the points (x, y, z) such that $f(x, y, z) \leq 1.0$.

When such an inside-outside function exists, one can determine whether or not a collision has occurred by simply substituting points (x, y, z) into the inside-outside function $f(x, y, z)$ to calculate the "distance" d. When d is less than the threshold used to define the surface (usually 1.0, as in the sphere example above), then there has been a collision. When object geometry is defined using an inside-outside function, therefore, the computational complexity of checking for collision between the object and N potential hazards is $O(N)$ — a significant improvement over the $O(Nn)$ cost when using polygons. A more subtle but perhaps equally important advantage of this approach is the ability to characterize the collision surface analytically, and usually in closed form. This advantage becomes extremely important when simulating multibody collisions.

Normally the disadvantage of such an approach is the limited range of shapes that have inside-outside functions associated with them. However by combining volumetric primitives — like spheres, superquadrics, or cubes — with analytic approximations to the modal deformations described above we can overcome this limitation. Alternatively, when dynamic simulation is not required, simple "bump mapping" techniques [13,14] applied to volumetric primitives can be used to provide inside-out functions for most objects (those whose points can be described by displacements along the normal vectors of some volumetric primitive).

2.2.1 Combining modes and volumetric primitives

The modal representation of shape can be combined with analytic shape primitives by first describing each mode by an appropriate polynomial function, and then using global deformation techniques [15] to warp the shape primitive into the appropriate overall form. The polynomial deformation mappings that correspond to each of the modes are determined by a linear regression of a polynomial with m terms in appro-

---

[7]It is possible to improve this somewhat by using an octree method, however this is only useful for coarse, initial pruning because the octree method has poor space complexity and must be continually recomputed for moving or deforming objects.

priate powers of x, y, and z, against the n triples of x, y and z that compose ϕ_i, a $3n$ x 1 vector containing the elements of the ith row of Φ:

$$\alpha = (\beta^T \beta)^{-1} \beta^T \phi_i \quad , \tag{5}$$

where α is an m x 1 matrix of the coefficients of the desired deformation polynomial, β is an $3n$ x m matrix whose first column contains the elements of $\mathbf{u} = (x_1, y_1, z_1, x_2, y_2, z_2, ...)$, and whose remaining columns consist of the modified versions of $\mathbf{u}$ where the x, y, and/or z components have been raised to the various powers, e.g.,

$$\beta = \begin{pmatrix} x_1 & x_1^2 & x_1 & x_1 & \cdots \\ y_1 & y_1 & y_1^2 & y_1 & \cdots \\ z_1 & z_1 & z_1 & z_1^2 & \cdots \\ x_2 & x_2^2 & x_2 & x_2 & \cdots \\ y_2 & y_2 & y_2^2 & y_2 & \cdots \\ z_2 & z_2 & z_2 & z_2^2 & \cdots \\ \vdots & \vdots & \vdots & \vdots & \end{pmatrix} . \tag{6}$$

The question of which polynomial powers are appropriate for a particular column of Φ can normally be decided by inspection (noting that the order of the deformation is related to the associated eigenvalue). The result is a polynomial model of the unit amplitude deformation associated with mode i. The effect of the ith mode on the overall object shape is then captured by simply scaling the ith polynomial deformation according to the mode's amplitude $\bar{u}_i$.

By linearly superimposing the various deformation mappings one can obtain an accurate accounting of the object's non-rigid deformation. In the ThingWorld modeling system the set of polynomial deformations is combined into a 3 by 3 matrix of polynomials that is referred to as the modal deformation matrix. As mentioned before, the low-order modes change very little as a function of object shape. Therefore the same modal deformation matrix can be used for a range of similar shape primitives without incurring substantial error. This allows the matrix to be precomputed, avoiding the expense of computing the polynomial deformation mappings at run time.

The ThingWorld system makes use of the family of superquadrics [16,17] as the basic volumetric primitive. Superquadrics are a generalization of the equation of an ellipsoid $((x/a_1)^2 + (y/a_2)^2 + (z/a_3)^2 = 1)$, but rather than using only powers of two, a superquadric allows fractional powers, e.g.,

$$((x/a_1)^{2/\epsilon_1} + (y/a_2)^{2/\epsilon_1})^{\epsilon_1/\epsilon_2} + (z/a_3)^{2/\epsilon_2} = 1$$

. The variables x and y are grouped together to allow separate control of the $x - y$ profile and the $z - (xy)$ profile via the shape parameters ϵ_1 and ϵ_2. The shapes generated by various values of ϵ_1 and ϵ_2 are a superset of the standard constructive solid geometry (CSG) modeling primitives. If one requires that the distance d computed by the inside-outside function be the usual Euclidian distance norm, however, then one must restrict oneself to using only spheres as the basic primitive. This is not a disadvantage, however, because by combining the basic sphere shape with an appropriate set of modal deformations, one can achieve a great range of expression and still maintain an $O(N)$ computation of distance.

In this volumetric-primitives-and-modal-deformations framework, the basic operation for collision detection is to calculate the distance between a point and the object surface. Given a point (x, y, z) this distance is calculated by first applying the inverse of the modal deformation matrix to obtain the undeformed coordinates (x^*, y^*, z^*), and then calculating $d = f(x^*, y^*, z^*)$. If d is less than 1.0, then there has been a collision, otherwise not. If an estimate of the actual Euclidian distance between the point and surface is required then (assuming that a spherical primitive has been employed) the calculated $d = f(x^*, y^*, z^*)$ must be scaled by the magnitude of the modal deformation matrix's Jacobian in the direction (x^*, y^*, z^*).

2.3 Constraint Satisfaction: Technical Details

In so-called energy or physically-based constraint satisfaction systems [1,2,8,9] one builds an l by k matrix C which relates k object parameters to potential functions defined by the l constraints. One then attempts to minimize the system energy by use of gradient or momentum minimization methods. For purposes of discussion I will take the conservative figure of $O(lk^2)$ as being the complexity of this minimization, as this is the number of operations needed to solve l linear equations in k variables ($l \geq k$, equations assumed to be consistent). When the system of equations is overconstrained and inconsistent (as is perhaps more typical) the complexity is $O(lk^2 + k^3)$, as forming the squared matrix $C^T C$ requires $O(lk^2)$ operations, and solving to find the pseudoinverse requires $O(k^3)$ operations.

Because "general" constraint satisfaction is equivalent to general-purpose equation solving, it is easy to see that no efficient, general-purpose solution method is possible. We must restrict the class of constraints used in order to reliably obtain a solution. There are two ideas that lead to the constraint satisfaction mechanism in ThingWorld: one, keep the system of equations linear, and two, try to make the system of equations diagonal and well-conditioned. Both of these points are critical for achieving reliable, efficient constraint satisfaction.

The first idea, that of keeping the system of equations linear, appears at first glance to be quite restrictive. It means that the only constraints we can use are those expressible by either quadratic energy functions (i.e., springs) or by linear holonomic constraints (i.e., linear equations of the form $f(\mathbf{u}) = 0$, where $\mathbf{u}$ is the vector describing the nodal displacements, as above). However limiting oneself to springs and linear holonomic constraints, as it turns out, is not very restrictive at all.

Spring constraints, for instance, can be used to express virtually any physical constraint. The main disadvantage of spring constraints is that they are "soft" rather than "hard" constraints, i.e., they cannot be used to enforce a constraint *exactly*. For hard constraints, therefore, the ThingWorld system uses linear holonomic constraints. This class of functions allows us to constrain any linear function of the state variables to be zero. For instance, such functions can be used to constrain the volume of a model to be constant, or "glue" two flexible models together. Because ThingWorld allows only *linear* holonomic constraints, constraint satisfaction is fast and reliable — in fact, adding constraints can increase the speed of a dynamic simulation, because it removes degrees of freedom.

The second idea, that of trying to make the constraint matrix diagonal and well-conditioned requires using *natural parameters* of the energy functions. A variable x is a natural parameter of the energy function $E(x)$ if $\partial E(x)/\partial x = 1$.

For example, if one wants to constrain three points to be at a certain fixed distance d^* from each other, one could go about it by defining an energy function $E = (e_1, e_2, e_3)$, where $e_i = \sqrt{(x_i - x_{i+1})^2 + (y_i - y_{i+1})^2 + (z_i - z_{i+1})^2}$, which is a function of the point positions $\mathbf{x} = (x_1, y_1, z_1, x_2, y_2, z_2, x_3, y_3, z_3)$. To minimize this energy, one constructs a 3 x 9 Jacobian matrix with entries $\mathbf{J}(i,j) = \partial e_j/\partial x_i$, and then computes parameter increments by

$$d\mathbf{x} = (\mathbf{J}^T\mathbf{J})^{-1}\mathbf{J}^T\mathbf{E} \tag{7}$$

The major cost in this process is usually the matrix inversion. Furthermore, the process of inverting the Jacobian often entails severe numerical problems.

Alternatively, one could define new *natural* parameters d_i, defined as the distances along the vectors connecting each pair of the points, and try to minimize the errors via an energy function $E = ((d_1 - d^*)^2, (d_2 - d^*)^2, (d_3 - d^*)^2)$. The parameter increments for the d_i can be calculated directly, and are by definition well-conditioned. After calculating the distance increments they are projected back onto the vectors connecting the three points to produce a 9 x 3 array $\mathbf{D}$ containing the nine parameter increments suggested by each of the three constraints.[8] Conflicts between these suggestions are resolved by picking the parameter increments that give the best root mean square improvement, as follows:

$$d\mathbf{x} = (\mathbf{D}^T\mathbf{D})^{-1}\mathbf{D}^T\mathbf{E} \tag{8}$$

The major advantage of this approach is that, unlike the matrix $(\mathbf{J}^T\mathbf{J})$, the matrix $(\mathbf{D}^T\mathbf{D})$ is guaranteed to be diagonal so that one need only calculate the diagonal elements. Similarly, full matrix inversion is not required, only inversion of the diagonal elements. As a consequence the algorithm requires only $O(lk + k)$ operations, rather than the $O(lk^2)$ or $O(lk^2 + k^3)$ operations required when using a standard approach.

2.4 Examples of Physical Simulation

Figure 3 shows a linked ball and cube being simulated on Sun 4 computer. The ball and cube are linked together with a spring constraint and the top of the ball is nailed in place with a position constraint. At each time step, the linkage and body deformations are computed and updated. The ball and cube are quite large and spongy, and therefore stretch and compress in response to gravity and internal inertial forces. The simulation requires 0.24 seconds of CPU time per second of simulated time, or 0.12 seconds of CPU time per object per second.

---

[8]In this case each constraint produces only six suggested increments.

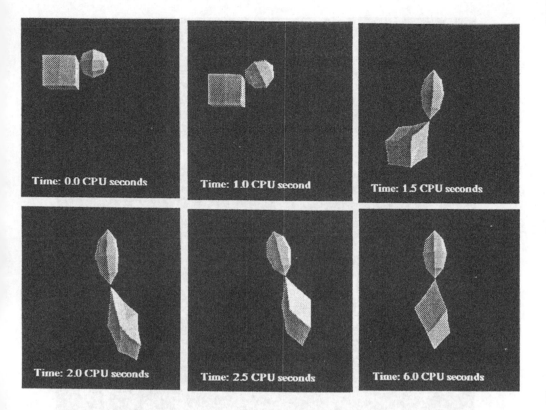

Figure 3: A large, spongy ball and cube are linked together by energy constraints, and then gravity is turned on. Total simulated time is roughly 24 seconds, requiring 6 CPU seconds.

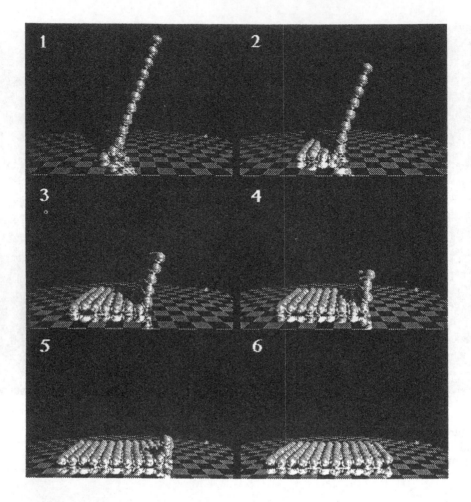

Figure 4: Sheet of balls dropping, a dynamic simulation with constraints

Another example of constraints and modal dynamic simulation is given in Figure 4. In this example, 96 balls (with 100 polygons each) are hooked together with 172 constraints to form a sheet. The sequence of images shows the sheet folding as it hits the floor then comes to rest. The simulation took six seconds per time step. This simulation also requires only 0.12 seconds of CPU time per object despite the large number of object collisions and constraint interactions, demonstrating that computational costs in the ThingWorld simulation system scale linearly with increasing scene complexity — a critically important improvement over standard simulation techniques.

3 The Thingworld Modeling System

Although the ability for near-real-time physical simulation on engineering workstations is critical for exploratory design and other engineering applications, from a design standpoint the user interface characteristics of the ThingWorld system are equally important. In particular, the ability to quickly model objects, the ability to add finer surface detail to objects via a *detail modeler*, and the ability to automatically recover models from the outside world are important to the achieving a system that is generally useful. In this section we will illustrate some of these functional subsystems, and give examples of physical simulations for small "virtual worlds" that illustrate these concepts.

3.1 The Modeling Interface

ThingWorld is a real-time, physically-based solid modeler which was developed with a dual purpose: first, to provide a solid modeling design interface which is intuitive — making it easy for naive users to quickly create, modify, and interact with complex designs — and second, as a testbed for reasoning about and simulating the physical properties of objects.

For a computer to have such an "intuitive" interface and to really understand about solid shape it must have many of the same capabilities that we do; that is, it must be able to obtain, describe, and manipulate information about shape in a manner analogous to the way people do. Similarly, the ability to reason about and simulate physical situations is critical for solving many important engineering and robotics problems.

Unfortunately, little is known about how people represent and reason about shape. We do know, however, that people are intimately familiar with physical processes, and so computer analogies to physical processes have long been considered the most promising metaphors for modeling systems [13]. Perhaps the most attractive of these physical analogies is *sculpting in clay*, as clay is widely considered to be the fastest traditional modeling medium. In part, this is because clay sculpting is an almost ideal example of the iterative design process, starting with *roughing in*, where lumps of clay are coarsely shaped and combined, and ending with *detailing*, where small surface features are carved and shaped.

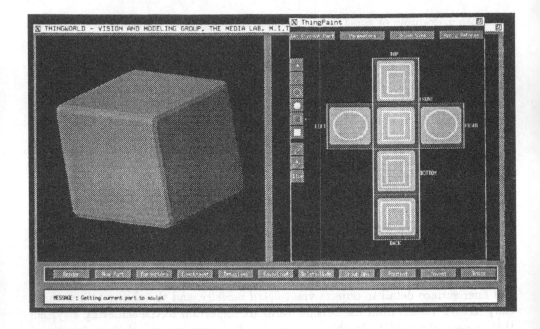

Figure 5: Using ThingPaint to paint texture details onto a solid

These observations have motivated the design paradigm used in the ThingWorld modeling system. The system presents the user with virtual lumps of clay, and allows the user to apply virtual forces in order to form them. The resulting parts may then be combined to form larger objects, or used as "virtual knives" to cut holes in other parts. The surfaces may then be blended and detailed with various sculpting tools to produce the final shape.

Besides providing an intuitive interface, an important advantage of this approach is that it builds into the system the ability for near-real-time simulation and analysis. Thus structures can be built, tested, and redesigned without leaving the computational environment. Thus ThingWorld attempts to support both the creation and analysis of design within the same framework.

3.2   The Detailing Interface

After roughing in a design, additional detailing may be required. For this task Thing-World uses an interface that is similar to the familiar computer paint programs. Figure 5 shows how a user "paints" on a set of 2-D elevation maps of the surface, with brighter shades of grey producing peaks and ridges, and darker shades producing valleys and pits. As with other paint tools, the user can paint, draw lines, boxes or circles onto the elevation map. The resulting *displacement map* allows us to add fine detail to the underlying deformed solid. The coordinates of the displacement map correspond approximately to the lines of principal curvature on the surface, so that

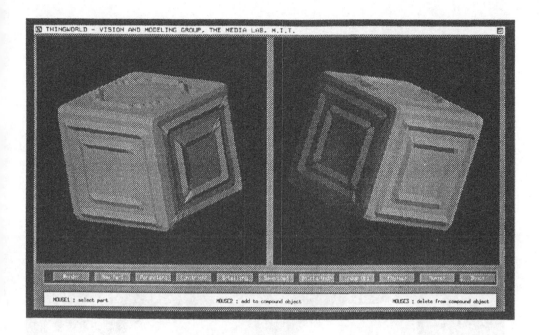

Figure 6: Resulting details

it is easy to produce details that blend naturally with the overall shape of the object. The solid produced by the painting in Figure 5 is shown in Figure 6.

Displacement maps are similar to the offsets used for B-splines in that they allow for local and fine-detail control over the shape of the surface. In the context of analytic functions like those used in ThingWorld, displacement maps function by offsetting the analytic surface of the solid along its surface normals. The advantage of this approach to detailing is that collision detection remains simple and inexpensive even for complex shapes.

Displacement maps can also be used to control local surface "offset" to satisfy tangency or other geometric constraints. One important application of this capability is blending surfaces together. ThingWorld's blending operation, similar to Blinn's [20], takes the analytical solids' inside/outside functions and uses them as energy functions. Depending on the type of joint desired, the energy functions can be either added or subtracted to allow for the full range of Constructive Solids Geometry (CSG) operations. Figure 7 shows two parts combined via CSG operations (first column) and the resulting blends (second column).

3.3 Automatic Modeling and Machine Vision

In some situations we have measurements from a real object, and would like to automatically create a 3-D model of that object. In ThingWorld this is accomplished by generating artificial forces that deform an initial computer model to fit the measured

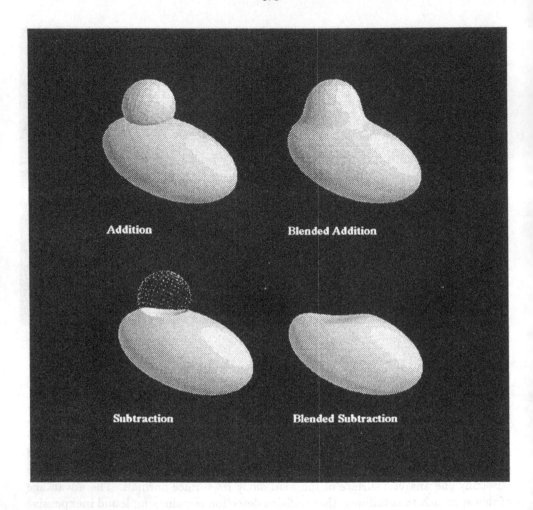

Figure 7: Solid Blending

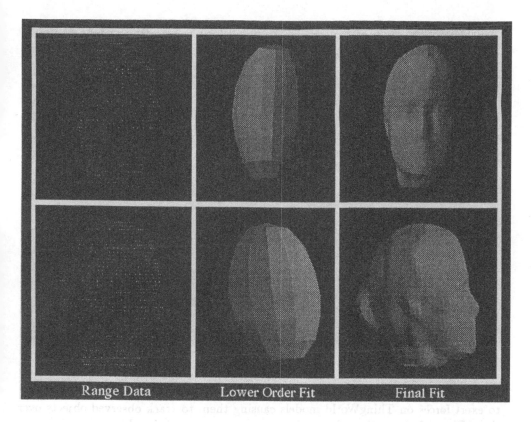

| Range Data | Lower Order Fit | Final Fit |

Figure 8: Solid model of human head automatically produced from laser rangefinder data

points, much as a human would mold a clay model. To create a model the user interactively places a ThingWorld model in approximate position, and then the error between the model and measured point data is numerically minimized producing a 3-D model that closely fits the measured points.

The head model shown in Figure 8 was produced in this manner, using data from a laser rangefinder. Front and side views of the raw range data are shown in the first column. Views of a model recovered using only low-order deformation modes are shown in the middle column. Finally, a displacement map is computed to account for the fine surface detail. The final recovered head model is shown in the last column of Figure 8. The low-order fit is most convenient for database operations such as shape comparison and recognition, while the displacement maps are required for graphical display and dynamic simulation. Total time required to fit 2500 range points was approximately 10 CPU seconds. For more details see reference [19].

ThingWorld's modeling framework is also being used for tracking articulated and/or non-rigid motion and deformation. Given a image sequence, a optical flow field is computed using standard machine vision techniques, and the flow field is used

Figure 9: Tracking the non-rigid motion of an articulated model

to exert forces on ThingWorld models causing them to track observed objects over time. Figure 9 shows three frames from an image sequence in which a jumping man was automatically tracked by an articulated ThingWorld model. Approximately 10 seconds of CPU time were required per frame.

3.4 Physical Simulations for Virtual Environments

The various modeling tools provided in ThingWorld are meant to enable users to build and interact with their designs in a physically meaningful way — in real time. The system can be used to design *virtual worlds* incorporating both objects brought into the computer from outside (by automatic model creation) and those designed from within. It is intended that this combination of real and imaginary objects can interact with each other in physical simulations, with ThingWorld serving as the computational foundation.

One example of such a virtual environment is *MusicWorld* — a real-time instrument modeling environment. Figure 10 shows a set of drums modeled within this framework. Using a 3-D sensor attached to sticks, the user can hit the drums and produce sounds. By modifying the instrument's geometry and size, the user can vary the sounds the instruments make. The ability to perform this sort of real-time physical simulation opens up a whole new range of possibilities for interactive design environments.

Figure 10: MusicWorld, a real-time instrument modeling environment

4 Conclusion

To move beyond toy-size multibody simulations researchers will have to confront problems of computational complexity, that is, the rapid rate at which the computational cost grows as problem complexity increases. For standard algorithms this rate of growth is such that simply designing faster, larger, or more parallel computers will not allow us to build realistically complex simulated worlds. Thus we are forced to make fundamental changes in our representations and algorithms for physical simulation.

In the ThingWorld system I have explored three possible solutions to these scaling problems, with the result that the system's computational complexity scales linearly with increasing world complexity. These solutions are:

- Accept small, controlled errors in the dynamics calculations, so that we may use modal dynamics to trade accuracy for speed.

- Represent geometry using implicit functions, e.g., analytic primitives that have an inside-outside function.

- Restrict constraint systems to linear and linear holonomic constraints using natural parameterizations.

By combining these solutions into an integrated system, ThingWorld has achieved linear computational complexity for complex multibody simulations, including contact detection and characterization and constraint satisfaction. The ability to obtain linear scaling of computational costs makes it appear that within the next decade, as workstations become faster and faster, we will be able to achieve near-real-time simulation of even quite complex physical models. This ability, I believe, will radically change the character of design.

Note: ThingWorld software is available for a nominal handling charge to degree-granting institutions. Please write to the author for more information.

REFERENCES

[1]   Sutherland, I., (1963), Sketchpad: A Man-Machine Graphical Communications System, in Interactive Computer Graphics, in *1963 Spring Joint Computer Conference,* reprinted in H. Freeman, ed., IEEE Comp. Soc., 1980, pp. 1-19.

[2]   Borning, A., (1979), Thinglab – a constraint-oriented simulation laboratory. SSL-79-3, Xerox PARC, Palo Alto, CA.

[3]   Tennenbaum, J., Pan, J., Glicksman, J., Hitson, B., Cutkosky, M., and Brown, D., (1989) Toward a Computer-Integrated Enterprise, *Proceedings of the MIT-JSME Workshop on Cooperative Product Development,* November 20-21, Cambridge, MA,

[4]   Tomiyama, T., Kiriyama, T., and Yosshikawa, H., (1989) A Model Integration Mechanism for Concurrent Design, *Proceedings of the MIT-JSME Workshop on Cooperative Product Development,* November 20-21, Cambridge, MA.

[5]   Pentland, A., and Williams, J., (1989) Virtual Manufacturing, *NSF Engineering Design Research Conference,* pp. 301-316, June 11-14, Amherst, MA.

[6]   Gosling, J. (1983) Algebraic Constraints, CMU-CS-83-132, Ph. D. Thesis, Computer Science Dept., Carnegie-Mellon University, Pittsburgh, PA.

[7]   Steele, G., and Sussman, G. (1978) Constraints, Technical Report, M.I.T. AI Memo 502.

[8]   Witkin, A., Fleischer, K, and Barr, A., (1987) Energy Constraints on Parameterized Models, Proceedings of SIGGRAPH '87, *Computer Graphics,* Vol. 21, No. 4, pp 225-231.

[9]   Barzel, R., and Barr, A., (1988) A Modeling System Based on Dynamic Constraints, Proceedings of SIGGRAPH '87, *Computer Graphics,* Vol. 22, No. 4, pp 179-188.

[10]   Pentland, A., and Williams, J., (1989) Good Vibrations: Modal Analysis for Graphics and Animation, *ACM Computer Graphics,* (Siggraph 89) Vol. 23, No. 4, pp. 215-223

[11]   Anderson, J. S., and Bratos-Anderson, M., (1987) Solving Problems in Vibrations, Longman Scientific and Technical Publ., Essex, England.

[12]   Hahn, J., (1988) Realistic Animation of Rigid Bodies, Proceedings of SIGGRAPH '88, *Computer Graphics,* Vol. 22, No. 4, pp. 299-308.

[13]   Pentland, A. (1986) Perceptual Organization and the Representation of Natural Form, *Artificial Intelligence Journal,* Vol. 28, No. 2, pp. 1-38.

[14]   Blinn, J.F., and Newell, M.E., (1976) Texture and Reflection in Computer

Generated Images, *Comm. ACM*, Vol. 19, No. 10, pp. 542-547.

[15] Barr, A., (1984) Global and local deformations of solid primitives. Proceedings of SIGGRAPH '84, *Computer Graphics 18*, 3, 21-30

[16] Gardiner, M. (1965) The superellipse: a curve that lies between the ellipse and the rectangle, *Scientific American*, September 1965.

[17] Barr, A., (1981) Superquadrics and angle-preserving transformations, *IEEE Computer Graphics and Application, 1* 1-20

[18] Pentland A., Essa I., Friedmann M., Horowitz B., Sclaroff S., and Starner T., The ThingWorld Modeling System, in *Algorithms and Parallel VLSI Architectures*, E.F. Deprettre (ed.), Elsevier Press, 1990.

[19] Pentland, A., Automatic Extraction of Deformable Part Models, *International Journal of Computer Vision*, 107–126, 1990.

[20] Blinn J., A Generalization of Algebraic Surface Drawing, *ACM Transactions on Graphics*, 1(3):235–256, July 1982.

A Study on Visualization of Control Software Design

Michitaka Hirose [1]   *Haruo Amari* [2]
(1) The University of Tokyo
(2) Tokyo Electric Power Company

Abstract

Virtual environment for software visualization are discussed. Visual representation plays an important role in coordinating or managing large scale system developments. First, the problem of software design for large scale control systems such as the control system for the distribution of regional electric power is discussed from a "needs" point of view. It is emphasized that the conventional methodology is no longer sufficient for recent large and complex computer system designs. Second, the use of visualization technology is introduced as a solution to the software crisis mentioned above. A method of mapping from an originally logical representation into a visual representation is proposed. Finally, implementation of the idea is discussed from a "seeds" point of view. By using this so called "virtual environment" technology, we could develop a non-text based programming environment.

1. Problems in Large Scale Software Development

In developing a large-scale software control system, such as the control system for the distribution of regional electric power,it is necessary to consider the integration of many computer systems as well as the control components. In addition, the ability of large numbers of software programmers to collaborate with each other uder an overall system design is desirable. We believe that there are currently many problems concerned with cooperative technology in the field of large-scale software design.

A schematic diagram of the complex regional power supply system in Tokyo documents the organization of a system consisting of 3 nuclear power plants (10,000,000 KW), 29 thermal power plants (26,000,000 kW), 156 water power plants (6,000,000 KW), 1300 substations and up to 18,000 kilometers of power lines (Fig.1). To supply power with high reliability and efficiency at minimum cost, much of the optimization needs to be computerized. The goal for the near future is to have the entire power distributing system controlled automatically by a vast computer networking system. In order to realize that goal, however, we need to find ways to solve the problems which arise in developing such a large and complicated software scheme.

This type of "conglomerate networking" is not only limited to power supply systems but is a general problem in advanced computer systems. Two basic types of problems associated with the different levels of the networking environment are pictorialized in Fig.2. One type of question might be : "How do I program each computer?" (This is called programmming in the small). Another might be : "How do I coordinate many computers?". (This is called programming in the large). Much research has been dedicated toward solving the former, more conventional problem. However, little research has been done toward the latter, since large scale networking has developed only recently.

Since the programming environment itself is built on "algorithmic" or "logical" characteristics, it is convenient to use text representation. In fact, many text-oriented environments have been proposed by various researchers. With text, we can eliminate much ambiguity. However, text alone becomes limiting and insufficient in the case of "programming in the large" where the most important factor in the field concerns total configuration design rather than detailed logic design. In other words, the field includes not only "logical" or "exact" problems, but also "broad-scoped" or "general" problems. Thus a more global methodology is needed to correct for faults in the overall system design, even though each individual subsystem may be correctly designed. These types of faulty global design will be criticized as being a "narrow-sighted".

Visual representation is different from text representation. Although images can be ambiguous, we are often able to understand the total image of the system by using human pattern recognition. It has a "broad-minded" attribute which can compensate for the problems of conventional programming methods. Therefore, in "programming in the large", researchers believe that visual representation could play an important role in the intuitive understanding of software and a combination of text and that visual environments will provide the best solution. Also by separating problems into two subparts, the programmer no longer needs to solve both at the same time and confusion between "programming in the large" and "small" can be avoided.

2. Effectiveness of Visualization

Naturally, an important consideration will be how to visually represent the originally amorphous software. In other words, how should this mapping from logical representation to the visual representation be accomplished.

Of course, visual representation is not a well-defined concept. We can imagine a variety of visual representations (Fig.3). Realistic drawings would have a maximum emphasis on morphology while other kinds of visual representations would emphasize topology or more logical semantics.

A fractal diagram pictorializes a metaphor of what the author want to emphasize (Fig.4). If we look at the figure from a distance, we can see its global structure. If we come closer, we can see more details of the diagram. Information compression is automatically done by using characteristics of three dimensional space. The authors believe that will be the most important feature of visual representation.

Most current visual languages place too much emphasis on topological characteristics. Based on the above reasoning, the authors wanted to use more morphological aspects of visual representation.

3. 3D Visual Representation

After much experimental investigation, a 3D visual representation was decided upon. Often, a network diagrams are given as 2D representations, known as block diagrams (Fig.5). The block diagram holds geometrical and topological information about a distributed computer network.

We conducted a simple experiment to show that 2D representation are better than 1D. Two representations were compared. In the first case (a), nodes indicating computer sites are arranged in one line (1D). In the second case (b), nodes were arranged in a 2D area (Fig.6 (a), (b)). When we assigned subjects a task (such as finding a message loop through a given set of nodes), the task completion time in the 2D arrangement was twice as fast than in the 1D arrangement. By seeing the 2D representation, subjects were better able to realize that there is a loop through site 2-4-3 and site 1 connected to all of other sites. It is easier to generate rough images of such relationships through 2D representations. The greater the number of nodes, the greater the differences between the two representations become.

Therefore, a 2D representation is considered a minimum requirement to express the static characteristics of a network system. However, if the description of a real-time control program is required, such as in the synchronization of several control processes, the time dimension should also be taken into consideration. Thus the concept of the 3D visual representation is called for (Fig.7). If we map the 3D representation onto the xy plane, it will be a conventional block diagram. If we map onto the plane normal to xy plane, it becomes a time chart. Using the full 3D representation, the programmer can intuitively grasp the state of concurrent processes.

In the 3D visual representation, the geometrical shape used to represent program flow of successive message passing is also important. The shape itself indicates the type of information exchange. Sometimes the programmer can handle the software entirely based on its shape (we might call this programming style as shape-based programing). The greater the number of processes, the greater the advantages of 3D representation, presumably due to characteristics of human cognitive processes.

4. Implementation of 3D Environment

To make use of 3D representation, we need to handle virtual 3D object (3D representation) quite easily. (like a pictorial representation of futuristic 3D programming concept shown in Fig.8). Several years ago such an idea was unrealizable due to the limitations of computer capabilities. We need a new technology able to incorporate real-time 3D animation, stereo displays, 3D input devices, and other aspects of the virtual 3D work-space. Recent rapid advances in computer hardware and consequently of the man-machine interface enable us to make 3D virtual programming environments. M.Mcgreevy and S.Fisher introduced the first virtual workstation using the HMD (Head Mounted Display) and gestural input devices [1]. The HMD supplies a computer-generated virtual 3D space around the user. By using a gestural input device, the user can handle virtual objects in the virtual space with sensation.

However, the current resolution of the author's HMD (300x300 pixels) is not enough to display objects having complicated geometrical shapes such as in the visual representation of software [3]. So, the authors have substituted the HMD by a 3D CRT monitor

(Stereographics CrystalEyes System), which generates 3D images by using a high speed (120 Hz) right and left view switching system and eyeglasses with a LC (Liquid Crystal) shutter. By adding a head movement detector (Polhemus 3D tracker), a partial "look-around" effect can be implemented.

As a gestural input device, the authors used a VPL DataGlove which can measure the joint angles of each finger by sensing the amplitude change of light emitted by optical fibers aligned on the fingers, and also the position and rotation of the palm by using the Polhemus sensor. By using input from the DataGlove, a virtual hand can be generated in virtual 3D space as an actuator.

The current hardware configuration of the virtual 3D workstation includes two sub-workstations. One of them (an HP9000SRX) is used for generating the virtual 3D image and handling I/O devices. Another (a Sun 3) is used for text handling. In other words, the first one is for "programming in the large", and the second is for "programming in the small" (Fig.9).

Basically, our programming environment employs the methodology of so called "object oriented programming". Concept of "succession" is also important. "Succession" is a succesive message passing through several objects. One succession corresponds to one function of distributed computing over the network.

The procedure for making the transition from 'programming in the large" to "programming in the small" is as follows;

"Programming in the large" corresponds to defining specifications of "objects", its "methods", "messages" and relationships among other objects. A 3D visual representation of complete software can be constructed by using the virtual 3D environment to be mentioned later. The virtual 3D representation can be considered as a kind of "source code" (Fig.10).

By decomposing the representation, objects and templates for their methods can be extracted automatically. After that, the user can concentrate on defining the contents of each method, namely "programming in the small" because the consistency among the objects has already been solved by "programming in the large". In the case of message passing, the "method" of the object is automatically activated by the receiving message. It provides a relative time concurrency control. For absolute time concurrency, timer objects can provide time message at the specific time. Since the message passing is a very strong synchronization mechanism, no other synchronization mechanism such as semaphore is needed.

Basic part of implementation of our visual programming environment has already been completed. The implementation displays the message flow between processes in virtual 3D space (Fig.11). One small box represents an "object" (sometimes it can be a process, sometimes it can be a processor). Several new concepts, such as 3D windows and cursors, are also used.

Using a virtual hand which works as a 3D pointer and a kind of "action menu" which detects gestures, the programmer can handle virtual objects (such as "objects" and "messages"..) in the virtual 3D world. The meaning of the commands corresponding to each gesture are listed in Fig.12. Currently, the environment has two modes, called "world mode" and "succession mode".

World mode is mainly for observing whole shapes of the software. Succession mode is used for editing message passing among objects. Each mode still has its own action menu selected by the gesture "GRABH". The relationships between modes and action menus are illustrated in Fig.13.

As an example, consider the case of adding a new object to an existing succession. First, the object is defined. By pointing to the succession (POINTH), the mode is changed to "succession mode". By using the EDITH gesture, the action menu is activated. By selecting NEW_OBJECT, a new object appears in the virtual 3D space. Also, a small text window opens for defining its name and other specifications, at the same time. Next, the message passing is defined. By pointing to a specific object, a message arrow is extracted from the object. (like a rubber band in 2D graphical tools). The destination of the message is determined simply by doing NULL gesture (opening the hand). Finally, the "method" is defined. Making second EDITH gesture calls up the action menu and selecting NEW_METH accomplishes the definition of the "method" name (message name) corresponding to the message just defined. These will be a typical procedures of the visual environment.

Of course, the configuration is still preliminary. Further investigation is needed concerning the design of objects handling in virtual 3D space. Questions which need to be addressed include whether we need modes at all in virtual reality and if so, what kind of modes should be designed, etc ..

Several tools are still under implementation:

+*Virtual Measure/Ruler* :   Tools to measure the exact
relationship among virtual objects. This tool is definitely needed to
check very strict timing of concurrent software.

+*Critical Path Finder* :   Tool to find and display the critical
path which determines the total network throughput for a given
network task. This tool runs in the background of the environment.

+*Network Simulator* :   Tool to simulate message passing and
data processing on each computer. Using this tool, a programmer
can check for interferences among several network tasks. This tool
includes a database of specifications of networked computers, data
links among computers, configuration of networks, and other
relevant information about the network.

+*Network Planner* :   Tool to update information about the
network configuration. This tool works with Network Simulator.

5. Assessment on the 3D Enviroment

Several microprocessor programming tasks were assigned to
subjects. The target system is supposed to be 3-4 networked
personal computers. Completion time with and without the
environment was measured. Roughly   speaking, completion time
with the 3D environment was shorter than that of the conventional
methodology.   In addition, using 3D lowers the variance over the
variety of programming tasks we have studied (Fig.14).; This also
indicated that simple but troublesome careless error were
eliminated, a finding confirmed by our personal experience.

The author believes that the concept of 3D visual representations
has proven to be effective even in the simple environment already
implemented. A far greater impact can be expected in a more
sophisticated environment as the most case of software
environment. For example, Smalltalk80 is highly values for its
concept of "object oriented" programming, but its environment is
valued much more than the concept itself. The authors consider this
kind of practical effort will be indispensable. From a practical point
of view, however much effort will be needed to prepare and
accumulate effective tools for this new environment.

6. Future Aspects and Conclusion

A 3D environment provides a more natural man-machine interface. Its programming style is based on familiar perceptions and is suitable for generating an understandable total system image for everyone. The authors believe that such an environment gives us an effective method to design very-large-scale systems; its imprecision or fuzziness is balanced by its robustness to error.

However, we need to consider the reason why we use codes such as text in the first place. By using strongly formalized representations such as text, we can largely abstract and compress information, removing redundancy and consequently obtaining efficiency instead of robustness.

Robustness and efficiency are both important from a software engineering point of view. Thus we need to make a trade-off between the two factors. Even a further abstraction process might be helpful in the proposed visual environment. Finding the optimum point between much abstraction and little abstraction will be an interesting and open-ended problem.

References

[1] S. Fisher and M. McGreevy, *Virtual Environment Display System*, Prep. ACM 1986 Workshop on Interactive 3D Graphics, 1986.

[2] M. Hirose, Yu Dong, M. Koga and T. Ishii, *A Study on Remote-Operation System in Three Dimensional Space*, Proc. 3rd Human Interface Symp. , pp.383-388 , 1987 (in Japanese).

[3] M. Hirose, M. Koga and T. Ishii, *Development of Head Mounted Display System for Artificial Reality*, Prep. Symp. on Graphics and CAD, pp.55-60, 1988   (in Japanese).

[4] M. Hirose, H. Amari, T. Sasaki, T. Myoi and T. Ishii, *A Study on Visual Expression of Control Software*, Proc. 4th Human Interface Symp. , pp. 45-50, 1988   (in Japanese).

[5] M. Hirose, Y. Ikei and T. Ishii, *Software Environment for Holonic Manipulator*, 2nd USA-Japan Symp. on Flexible Automation, pp.317-324 , 1988.

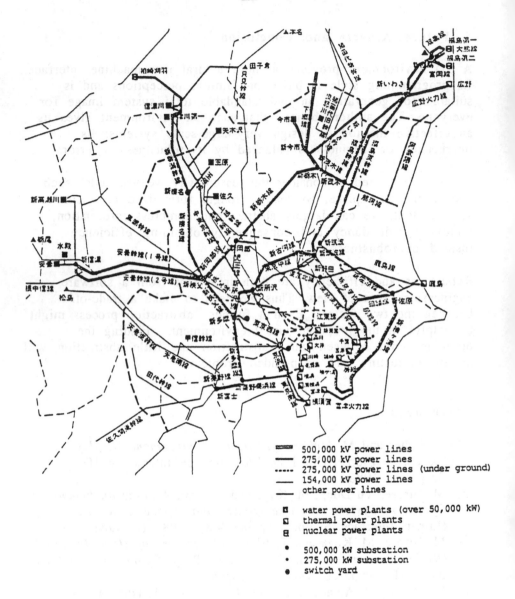

	500,000 kV power lines
	275,000 kV power lines
	275,000 kV power lines (under ground)
	154,000 kV power lines
	other power lines

▫	water power plants (over 50,000 kW)
◪	thermal power plants
◨	nuclear power plants

•	500,000 kW substation
·	275,000 kW substation
●	switch yard

Fig.1 Schematic diagram of regional electric
power supply system in Tokyo

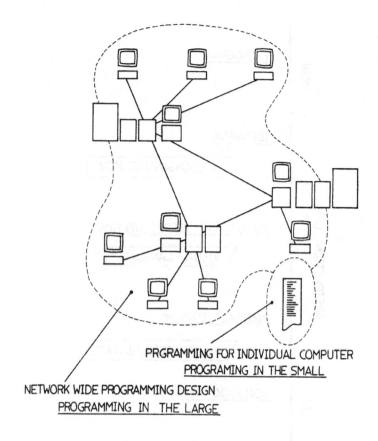

PRGRAMMING FOR INDIVIDUAL COMPUTER
<u>PROGRAMING IN THE SMALL</u>

NETWORK WIDE PROGRAMMING DESIGN
<u>PROGRAMMING IN THE LARGE</u>

Fig.2 Two basic types of problems associated with the
different levels of the networking environment

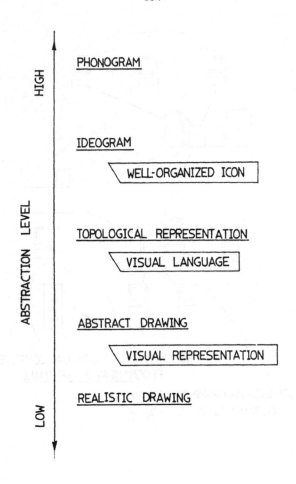

Fig.3 Variety of visual representation

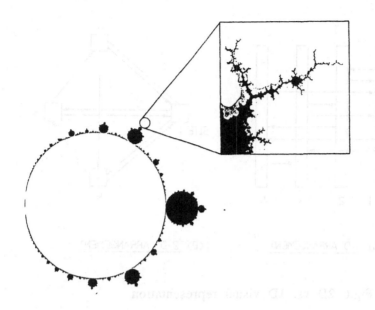

Fig.4 An example of fractal diagram

BLOCK DIAGRAM   TIME CHART

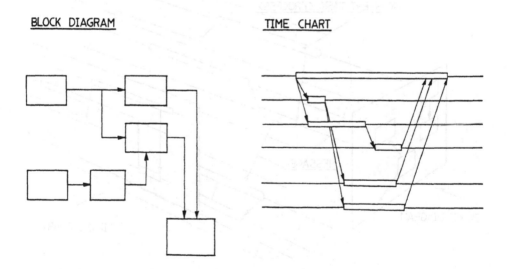

Fig.5 Block diagram and time chart

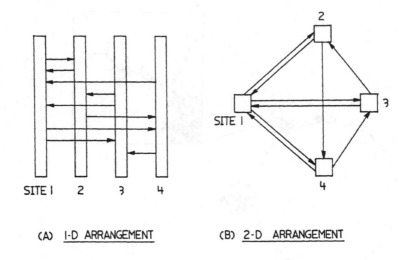

(A) I-D ARRANGEMENT   (B) 2-D ARRANGEMENT

Fig.6 2D vs. 1D visual representation

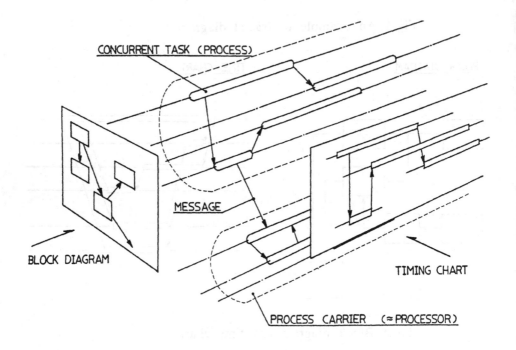

Fig.7 Concept of 3D visual representation

Fig.8 Pictorial representation of futuristic 3D programming

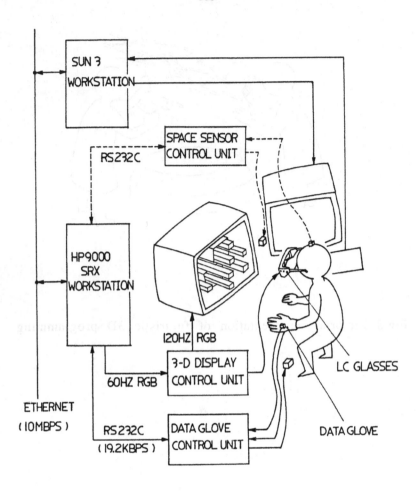

Fig.9 Hardware configuration of the virtual 3D workstation

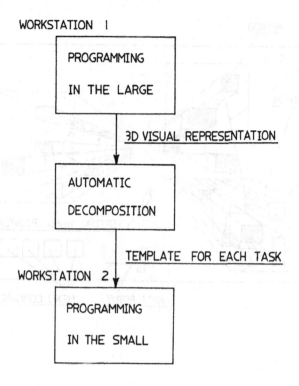

WORKSTATION 1

PROGRAMMING

IN THE LARGE

3D VISUAL REPRESENTATION

AUTOMATIC

DECOMPOSITION

TEMPLATE FOR EACH TASK

WORKSTATION 2

PROGRAMMING

IN THE SMALL

Fig.10 From "programming in the large"
to "programming in the small"

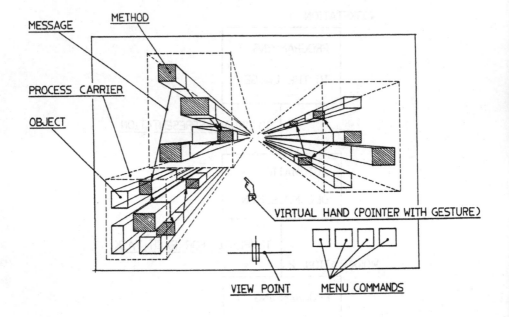

Fig.11 Example of visual 3D programming environment

GESTURE	NAME	ICON	MEANING / FUNCTION	
			WORLD MODE	SUCCESSION MODE
	GRABH		MOVE OBJECT/ METHOD BY GRASPING	MOVE OBJECT EXTRACT MESSAGE FROM METHOD BY GRASPING
	POINTH		ENTER SUCCESSION MODE BY POINTING METHOD	CHANGE PARAMETERS BY POINTING OBJECT/ METHOD
	EDITH		DISPLAY MENU	DISPLAY MENU
	CUTH		—	DELETE METHOD

Fig.12 Meaning of gestures

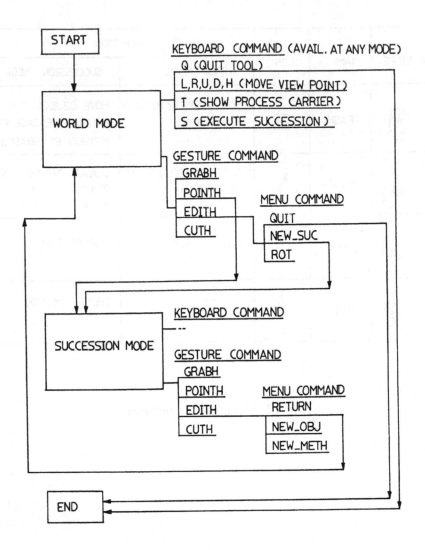

Fig.13 Relationship between modes and action menus

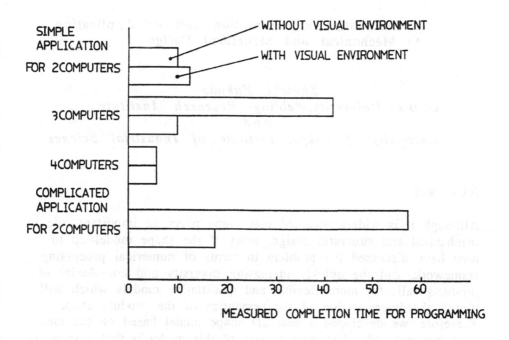

Fig.14 Results of preliminary assessment of the 3D environment

Coded Shape Representation and its Application to Mechanical and Structural Design

Shuichi Fukuda
Osaka University, Welding Research Institute
and
University of Tokyo, Institute of Industrial Science

Abstract

Although it is widely accepted that shape plays an important role in mechanical and structural design, most of the shape models up to now have discussed the problem in terms of numerical processing framework. But the quickly increasing diversity and complexity of products calls for more flexible and qualitiative models which will permit the interpretation of the semantics of the product shape. Therefore, we developed a new 2D shape model based on the idea of directional code. The main feature of this model is that a shape is represented in the form of a list so that all shape minipulations can be reduced to list operations . Hence, semantic meanings can be easily added and the form features can be extracted without any difficulty.

Key Words

Mechanical and Structural Design, 2-dimensional Shape Model, Directional Code, List Expression, Qualitative Model

1. Introduction

It is well known that in the field of mechanical and structural design, shape plays an important role in defining its functions. This is the large difference from the CAD in the field of electronics. Therefore, to realize collaborative design in this field, shape is one of the most important problems to be solved.

With the increasing diversity of products, it becomes more and more important to make appropriate decisions at more upstream stages, because as we go downstream, the number of combinations to be examined increases very rapidly. And as we go more and more upstream, the decisions become more and more qualitative in nature. Thus, what is really needed is a qualitaive evaluation of a shape. A designer has to know what will come out if he modifies his design plan to another in terms of manufacturability, constructibility, etc.

In mechanical CAD, the concept of form feature has appeared recently and is drawing wide attention [1]. This may also be interpreted as one of the moves to make up for the missing qualitative discussion in the conventional CAD systems. This concept, however, originates from the geometrical models and these geometrical models were developed with such applications as generating NC paths, etc where numerical processing occupies the dominant role.

What are the problems of the present technology of form feature are

(1) The present geometric model poses too much load on a computer.
(2) It cannot process the rough sketches properly. although the concept of form feature are quite important.

A rough sketch here means such a simplified drawing that is part of a real image or figure. Every engineer utilizes this kind of a rough sketch to convey his intention. It is simplified based on his engineering view so that it is none other than the representation of his expertise.

The present CAD and CG geometric models were developed with chief attention paid to the true reproduction of the original shape. Therefore, these models are not fitted to process such simplified drawings.

But if we are going to achieve the collaborative design, it seems more important to develop a mechanism that would more effectively reflect such a simplification process or the transformation from the real image to the rough.

It should not be misinterpreted that what we denote as rough is not the rough lines or curves but the simplified drawings. Rough lines or curves might be processed using, for example, such a technique as digital image processing.

What we would like to point out here is that we have to interpret the semantic meaning of a structural shape and that we need some interpretation mechanism. Of course, there are approaches from the knowledge engineering side toward the realization of collaborative design. But we feel that the present works seem to put too much emphasis on the improvement of inference mechanism. We think more attention should be paid to the problem of shape.

In fact, we are producing tons and tons of outputs of numerical analyses. But we don't have any appropriate means to re-utilize these results. Computer speed are getting faster and faster. So engineers do not worry too much about the reutilization of their outcomes because they can re-analyze them in an instant.

If we are concerned with the detailed design alone, the re-analysis will be all right, but if we wish to achieve the collaborative design, we have to develop a mechanism that will permit the reutilization of these outcomes at the earlier stages. In fact, these results are precious pieces of our experience and we need a mechanism that will extract a qualitative knowledge from such a numerical-based knowledge.

It should be noted that the majority of mechanical and structural designs are processing continuum bodies. That is a major difference from the electronics field. In the electronics field, the elements are defined and named after their functions. But a continuum body behaves differently if the conditions of topology, loading, constraints, etc differ. Thus, their names does not necessarily correspond to their functions. Furthermore, it the shape becomes quite complicated, we do not generally have any names for it.

At present, there seems to be no appropriate technique, at least to the author's knowlegde, to discretize the shape of such a continuum body to fit into the framework of knowledge processing. Indeed, there are techniques such as finite element mesh generators. But these techniques are developed to reproduce the original shape as true as possible and these discretized data are very difficult to be interpreted semantically.

If we could develope such a technique that will discretize the continuum shape and represent it as symbols, then it is expected that we could attach proper semantic meaning to the present data representation of numerical processing.

Most of the present approaches to the realization of collaborative design seem to be top down. A designer's intention is symbolized and interpreted to make it more substantial or concrete. But what we are trying to do in our work is the other way around. what we have in our mind is something which might be called an intelligent graphical editor or a visualization tool. A designer substantiates his idea or goal by using this tool. As he draws a rough sketch, he knows what would be the problem and what would be better alternatives. He finds his goal by trials and errors and in this process we believe a drawing will play a very important role. He draws his idea by talking with a computer. Thus, we think our approach is bottom up.

Certainly some design problems may be solved top down but we believe there are a great number of problems that need bottom up approaches. Therefore, both approaches seem to be necessary in order to realize collaborative design. They will complement each other. That is the motivation for this work.

2. Coded Shape Representation : The Fundamental Idea

The new shape representation technique we have developed is basically based on directional codes which was originally proposed by H. Freeman [2]. He asserted in his paper the advantage of great reduction of memory space if we use his concept of chain codes. But if we look at the chain codes from another angle, it is none other than the representation of shape in the form of a list. If we regard the chain codes as a list, we can attach a semantic meaning to it, and describe and process the features more easily. Further, it will facilitate not only shape processing but also the manipulation of the relationship among shape, loading and constraints. And we can easily correspond the operations of lists to those of manufacturing, etc.

The large difference between Freeman's method and ours is that Freeman was interested in raster data while we are concerned with vector data. Freeman discussed problems in the context of digital image processing. We take note of a continuum body or a polygon and are concerned with the vector data that constitute the polygon just as is done in the field of CAD.

If we adopt such an idea, a triangle can be expressed as shown in Fig.1. Of course the list is permutative. Thus, an arbitrary polygon can be expressed as pairs of edge length and its directions. If the two figures have the same edge length and directional code lists, then these two are identical and if only the directional code lists agree between two figures, they are similar. We call this type of shape representation Coded Shape Representation (CSR).

In the following we focus our attention to the mechanical behavior as one of the functions of a product to simplify the discussion. To discuss the problem of mechanics, not only shape but its mechanical environment are important. Therefore, we define directions in plane coordinates. For simplicity, we consider only four directions. In other words, we discuss the problem on the basis of four neighbourhood instead of Freeman's eight neighbourhood. But we can transform Freeman's data to ours without any difficulty. i.e., rastor data can be transformed to vector data straightforwardly so that the mechanical meaning of rastor data can be more easily interpreted. We call such type of shape representation Coded Boundary Representation (CBR).

In the CBR technique, directions are defined in terms of plane coordinates but we do not argue the absolute locations of vertices. We only pay attention to the relative location of vertices. The directional codes are defined as shown in Fig.2 and the fundamental shape primitive is defined as shown in Fig.3. It is assumed that the inside of the body lies on the left side of a vector. If we have to discuss the geometrical structure, we add an edge length list such as [10.0, 20.0, 10.0, 20.0].

As Fig.4 shows, the CBR technique may be regarded as a 2 dimensional B-reps expressed in the form of a list.

3. Manipulations of a Shape

A complex shape can be composed from the primitives and it can be decomposed into simpler ones by means of list operations. Reference [3] contains the details about the list operations for composition, decomposition, rotation and mirror image. What should be stressed here is that the topological operations can be easily performed as list operations.

4. Form Features

Let us consider the problem of extracting the form feature of convexity and concavity. Whether a figure contains a convex part or concave part can be judged if it contains in its CBR list such a sublist as shown in Fig. 5. Of course, these two correspond to the cases of convex upward and concave downward. Other cases can be described by appropriately changing the directional codes.

It should also be noted that the figures in Fig. 5 is an open or partly drawn figure. But if we express the figure in terms of a list, we can easily attach a mechanics name to it if the loading and constraint conditions are given. This will be discussed later .

If successive elements in an edge list contain the same values, we can shrink them to a single value as shown in Fig.6. Such an operation of shrinkage makes the determination of a mechanics name easier.

5. CBR and Structural Analysis

It is well known that finite element analysis (FEA) played a very important role for the advancement of structural analysis. In fact, it is not too much to say that detail designs cannot be carried out without it. Especially this is true if the shape is very complex.

But recently it has become more and more clear that FEA still needs more refinements. Fig.7 shows a model of structural analysis [4]. Before the advent of FEA, engineers developed a mechanics model at first and foresees the structural response. With this in mind, he then goes on to the process of developing a numerical model. Thus, engineers could interpet and evaluate the numerical outcomes when they used the analytic approach.

Fig.8 illustrates the difference between the analytic approach and FEA with a cantilever problem as an example. In the analytic approach, an engineer starts with the recognition of the shape of an object. In this example, an engineer recognizes the object as being a bar by comparing the length of edges. And then he examines the directional relation between the axis of the bar and the loading and concludes that the problem can be solved by using a beam theory. He further examines the condition of loading and constraints and finds out that this is a particular beam called a cantilever.

In this way, a mechanics model was developed. And once such a mechanics model can be developed, an engineer can derive an appropriate mathematical formula. The knowledge required for these steps are mostly qualitative. He enters numerical values at the final stage when he has to evaluate quantitatively and needs a numerical solution.

On the other hand, FEA proceeds quantitatively all the way from the beginning to the end. That is why FEA is so flexible and versatile. It processes everything all alike in the world of numbers without any classification as is done in the analytic approach. It solves a numerical model directly, skipping the process of constructing a mechanics model. The judgement on such matters as whether the numerical model, the result, etc are appropriate or not are completely left to a human. The situation being as such, it becomes more and more difficult even for a richly experienced engineer to make an appropriate judgement about the results of FEA because products are getting more and more diversified and complicated.

Thus, in FEA, engineers often produce inadequate solutions without knowing it. In fact, the present day FEA does not tell the difference between tensile and bending stresses. To make up for such shortcomings in FEA, we have to attach the mechanism of modelling and evaluation. If a mechanics model is developed within a FEA system, an engineer is expected to be able to evaluate his numerical outcomes properly.

In the analytic approach, the problems are solved by classification. Why such an approach was superseded by FEA is considered to be because we do not have an appropriate pattern classification tool up to now. But today we have such a powerful and flexible computer environment for classification, we may be able to classify the problem into suitable categories, even though the shape might be quite complex. What we need for that is a suitable shape model that will permit us to interpret the syntactic data of FEA semantically. This is one of the motivations why the CBR technique was developed. If we can interpret the meaning of FEA data in terms of mechanics, we can feedback the knowledge obtained by the numerical analysis or detailed design to the earlier stages of design, and prevent the repetitive numerical work for evaluating the similar cases.

If we use the CBR technique in the FEA mesh generation, we will be able to discrimate one pattern from another. The interior edges become non-directional in the process of mesh generation and the exterior or boundary edges remain as directional so that the shape can be classified into patterns as Fig.9 shows. The loading and constraints are placed on the nodes so that we can identify the similar problems by checking the list elements of a shape and those of the loading and constraints.

Fig.10 illustrates this discussion with a cantilever as an example. If an engineer generates a mesh and defines the loading and constraint conditions as shown in the figure, then the system will be able to identify the problem as being that of a cantilever by following the illustrated procedures.

If the shape is complex, we could use, for example, such a similarity index as is defined by the ratio of the number of successfully pattern-matched elements between two lists. If the index is one, then the shape is identical. The degree of similarity decreases with the decrease of an index number.

6. Processing of Rough Sketches

As is already discussed, another motivation and advantage of the CBR technique is to permit the processing of rough sketches. Fig.11 shows the procedures for interpreting the rough sketch of a cantilever as an example.

7. Prediction of a Mechanical Behavior

In the present FEA, mesh generation is carried out on the basis of the comlexity of a shape and its relation with the loading and constraints are not duly taken into account. But to a designer, the system that will let him see the overall mechanical behavior of a product easily, may it be quite rough, is more useful than the one that will provide its detailed description. What he really needs is an information that will assist him to make an appropriate decision. Therefore, qualitative information is more called for.

Another advantage of the CBR technique is to allow the user to predict roughly the mechanical behavior of a product. The fundamental idea behind this is a force line. We divide the object into meshes by extending the lines originated from loading, constraints and boundaries as shown in Fig.12 - Fig.14.

Let us consider the case of Fig.12. Most FEA mesh generators will divide the corner parts into finer meshes as shown in (b). But if we wish to evaluate the overall deformation behavior of this product, we can simplify it to the model shown in (c). This can be further simplified to (d) if we so desire. These simplification processes are based on the principle of force line as described above. Fig.13 and Fig.14 are other simplification samples.

Simplification is important for another reason. If such a simplification can be made, we can feedback the experience of numerical analyses to the earlier stages of design. Thus, we expect that this simplification process will provide us with a first step toward re-utilizing the outcomes of our numerical analyses and constructing a data or knowledge base for the mechanical behavior of a product with a complex shape. That would bridge the gap between the preliminary and detailed designs to some extent.

8. Some Samples of Preliminary Design

Finally we will discuss about the applications of the CBR technique to the prliminary design.

Fig.15 and Fig.16 show such examples. Fig.15 shows that if we wish to make a box beam stiffer, we had better change the locations of ribs from inside the wall to the outside. As far as the mechanical behavior is concerned, both plans are the same, but if we wish to improve the workability, it will, of course, be far better if we install the ribs on the outside. If a designer inputs a design plan of (a), then the system will find the better altenative from the knowledge base and show the plan (b) to a designer. This modification is carried out as a process of turning the inside out, which is realized by interchanging the lists of the initial and the terminal nodes.

Fig.16 shows another example for improving the design for better manufacturability. If we are to build up a boxbeam as shown in (a), then we have to position it four times if we will weld it flatly and twice if horizontally. But if we modify the design to (b), then we only have to position it once and we can weld it horizontally. The task of positioning takes not only time and trouble, but what is more important is that it might deteriorate the quality of a product with the increase of the number of its repetition. Thus the less the number of positioning is, the better. To a designer, these two plans do not differ very much. But to a welding engineer, plan (b) is far better than (a).

Fig.17 and Fig.18 are another example where sequence is a problem. Suppose we wish to butt-weld small plates into a large one. To eliminate distortion, welding is usually carried out from the center of a product to the outward and symmetry is taken into account. Such a heuristic knowledge can be utilized if we use the CBR technique.

From the inputs about its topology, the system infers that the edge qr is none other than the axis of symmetry because the element A and B constitute the mirror image relation and the edge qr is non-directional and the edges il and no are directional. Thus the system first produces the sequence plan as shown in Fig.18 (a). But in this plan, the start and stop locations of weldlines are identical so that there is a large possibility of the deterioration of a welded joint there. So the system backtracks and generates a better plan of (b).

What we should like to stress here is that if a little more attention is paid to the topological features, then we can improve the design in terms of manufacturability, constructibility, etc for better quality. Indeed the great portion of the knowledge for securing quality is qualitative and can be related to topological features. Thus, we believe the description of topological features is a very important task for realizing cooperative design.

9. Summary

Although it is widely accepted that shape plays an important role in mechanical and structural design, it seems that most of the past approaches to process shape are made as the extension of CAD geometric models. But these models are oriented more toward numerical processing.

The point we would like to stress in this paper is that we need another approach from the symbolic processing side. Although there are many papers on how to improve the inference mechanism, it seems, at least to the author's knowledge, not much work is carried out on how to process shape symbolically. If we wish to realize cooperative design, the processing of not only the drawings of the complete shape of a product but also its rough sketches are important, because they convey the expertise of the engineer who draws it.

If we can represent shape as symbols, then it is expected that we can process such simplified sketches more easily and in addition can interpret the semantic meaning of the syntactic representation of the data in the present day mechanical and structural design and analysis.

Therefore, we attempted to develop a shape model based on a list expression. This work is quite preliminary. In fact, we have dealt with only simple figures composed from rectangles so far. But if we introduce such mapping or transformation techniques as used in the boundary fit method in FEA, we will be able to process more complex shapes. Thus, we believe that this work serves as a first step toward our goal.

Acknowledgement

The part of this work is financially supported by the Grant for the Scientific Research, Minsitry of Education, Japan for which the author would like to express his deep gratitude.

614

References

[1] J. R. Dixon, *Research in Designing with Features,*
Special Issue "Intelligent CAD", Computrol, No.25,
pp.112-117, 1989 (in Japanese).
[2] H. Freeman, *Computer Processing of Line-drawing Images,*
Computer Survey, 6-1, pp.57-97, 1974.
[3] S. Fukuda, *Reliability Design Expert System,*
Maruzen , 1990 (in Japanese).
[4] G. M.Turkiyyah, and S. J. Fenves, *Knowledge-based Analysis
of Structural Systems, Knowledge Based Expert Systems in
Engineering: Planning and Design* (D. Sriram, and R. A. Adey,
editors), pp.273-284,
Computational Mechanics Publications ,1987

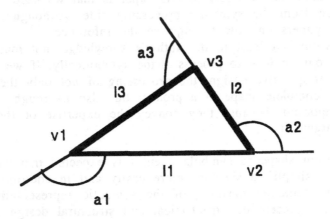

edge_list [l1,l2,l3].
edge_length-list [54.0,33.0,48.0].
vertex_list [v1,v2,v3].
direction_list [a1,a2,a3].

**Fig.1 Triangle representation by
coded shape representation (CSR)
technique**

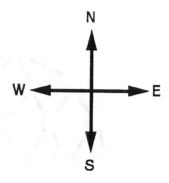

Fig.2 Directional codes

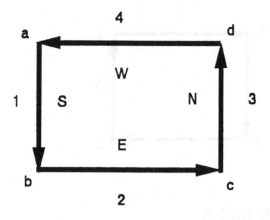

edge_list [1,2,3,4]
edge_length_list [10.0,20.0,10.0,20.0]
vertex_list [a,b,c,d]
initial_node_list [a,b,c,d]   (=vertex_list)
final_node_list [b,c,d,a]
direction_list [S,E,N,W]

Fig.3 Shape primitive in coded boundary
representation (CBR) technique

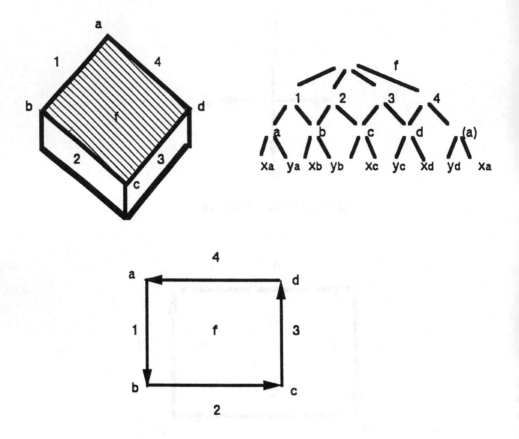

edge_list [1,2,3,4]
vertex_list [a,b,c,d] (=initial_node_list)
coordinates_list [(x_a,y_a),(x_b,y_b),(x_c,y_c),(x_d,y_d)]

Fig. 4 Coded Boundary Representation and B-rep

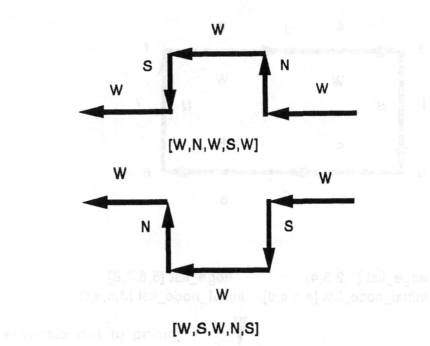

[W,N,W,S,W]

[W,S,W,N,S]

Fig.5 Extraction of convexity and concavity

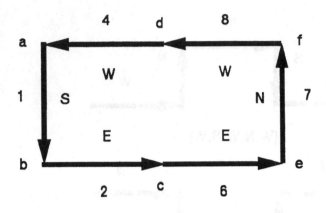

edge_list [1,2,3,4]　　　edge_list [5,6,7,8]
initial_node_list [a,b,c,d]　initial_node_list [d,c,e,f]

▼　joining of two elements

edge_list [1,2,6,7,8,4]
initial_node_list [a,b,c,e,f,d]
direction_list [S,E,E,N,W,W]

▼　shrinkage of
　　direction_list

direction_list [S,E,N,W]

▼　shrinkage of
　　edge_list and
　　initial_node_list

edge_list [1,2,7,8]
initial_node_list [a,b,e,f]

Fig. 6 Shrinkage operation

619

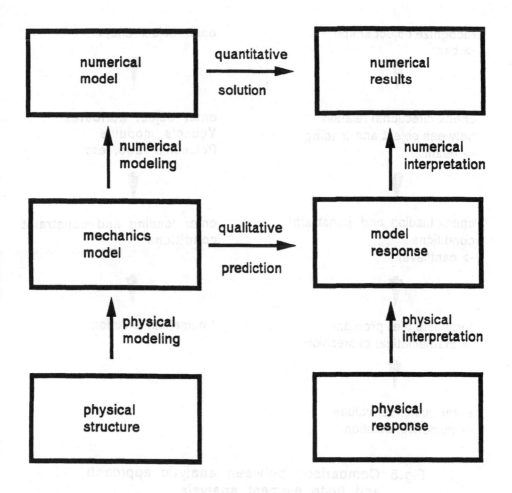

Fig. 7 Flow of structural analysis

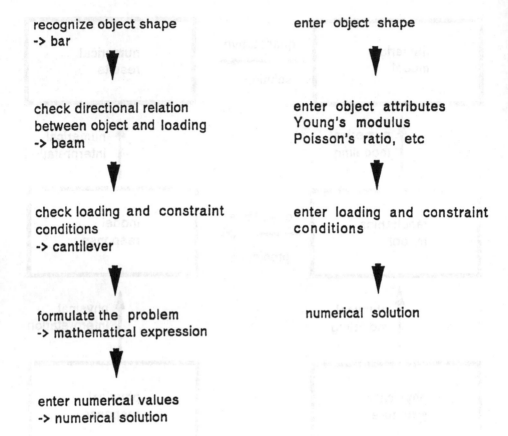

recognize object shape
-> bar

enter object shape

check directional relation
between object and loading
-> beam

enter object attributes
Young's modulus
Poisson's ratio, etc

check loading and constraint
conditions
-> cantilever

enter loading and constraint
conditions

formulate the problem
-> mathematical expression

numerical solution

enter numerical values
-> numerical solution

Fig.8 Comparison between analytic approach
and finite element analysis
(cantilever problem as an example)

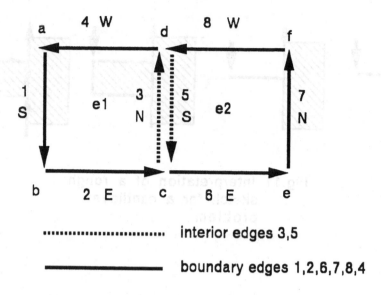

interior edges 3,5

boundary edges 1,2,6,7,8,4

Fig. 9   Interior and boundary edges

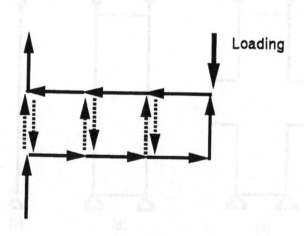

Fig. 10   Cantilever problem

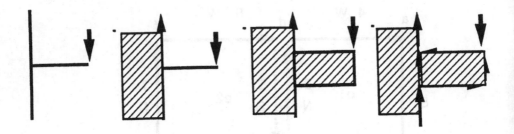

Fig.11 Interpretation of a rough
sketch for a cantilever
problem

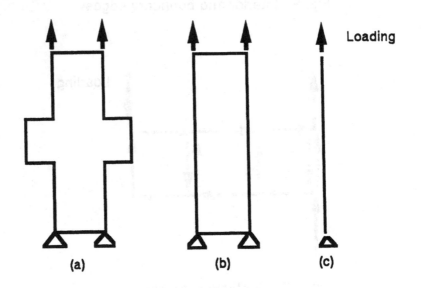

(a) (b) (c)

Loading

Fig. 12 Model simplification

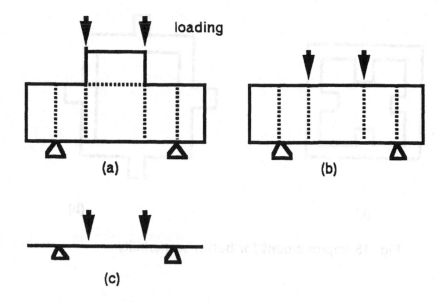

Fig. 13 Simplification of a T joint

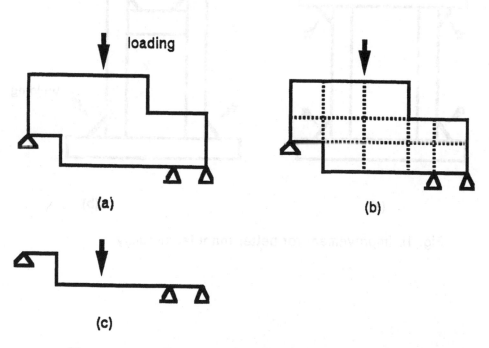

Fig. 14 Simplification of a complex case

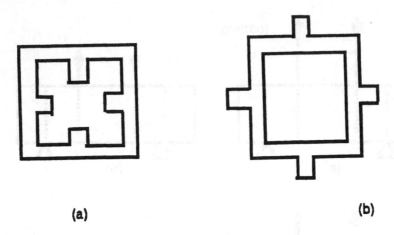

(a)   (b)

Fig. 15 Improvement for better workability

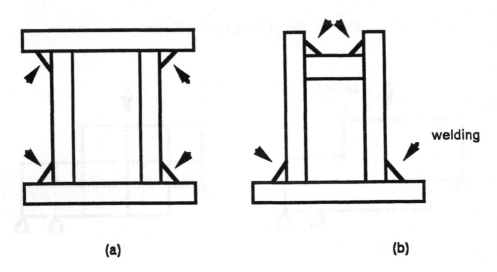

(a)   (b)

Fig. 16 Improvement for better manufacturability

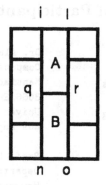

Fig.17 Butt-welding of small plates
into a large plate

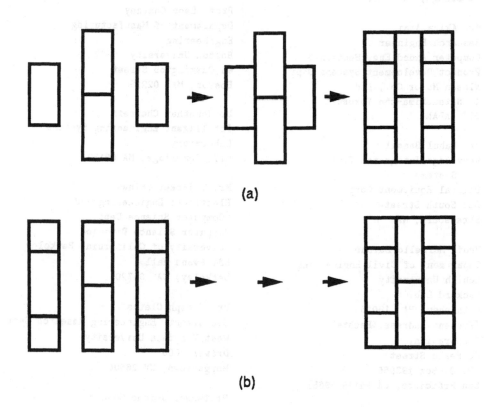

(a)

(b)

Fig. 18 Welding sequence problem

Appendix: List of Participants at the Workshop

Mr. Shamim Ahmed
Graduate student
Intelligent Engineering Systems
Laboratory
Department of Civil Engineering
MIT, Cambridge, MA 02139

Mr. Leonard Albano
Graduate Student
Department of Civil Engineering
Room 1-238, M.I. T.
77 Massachusetts Ave.
Cambridge, MA 02139

Mr. Akira Arai
Research Engineer
Computer Aided Eng. Section 3
Product Development Systems Dept.
NIssan Motor Co., Ltd.
1, Natsushima-cho Yokosuka
237 JAPAN

Mr. Rahul Bansal
Knowledge Integrated Tools
and Systems
Digital Equipment Corp.
333 South Street
Shrewsbury, MA

Prof. Marcello Barone
Department of Civil Engineering
Lehigh University
Packard Lab.
Bethlehem, PA 18015
[Present Address: Bechtel
Corporation,
50 Beale Street
 P. O. Box 193965
San Francisco, CA 94119-3965]

Dr. Alan Bond
Computer-Aided Design Laboratory
Manufacturing Engineering Program
3066 Engineering 1
University of California
Los Angeles, California 90024

Prof. David Brown
Department of Computer Science
Worcester Polytechnic Institute
100 Institute Road
Worcester, MA 01609

Prof. Leon Charney
Department of Manufacturing
Engineering
Boston University
44 Cummington Street
Boston, MA 02215

Dr Jonathan Cherneff
Intelligent Engineering Systems
Laboratory
MIT, Cambridge, MA 02139

Mr. Tzi-cker Chiueh
Electrical Engineering and
 Computer Science Dept.
Computer Science Division
University of California, Berkeley
531 Evans Hall
Berkeley, CA 94720

Dr. Joseph Cletus
Concurrent Engineering Research Center
West Virginia University
Drawer 2000
Morgantown, WV 26506

Professor Jerome Connor
Department of Civil Engineering
M.I.T.

77 Massachusetts Avenue, Room 1-353
Cambridge, MA   02139

Dr. Dan Corkill
Department of Computer and
nformation Science (COINS)
University of Massachusetts
Amherst, MA   01003

Prof. Mark Cutkosky
Dept. of Mechanical Engineering
  Design Div.
Stanford University
Terman 551
Stanford, CA   94304

Prof. Charles Eastman
Graduate School of Architecture
  and Urban Planning
University of California Los Angeles
405 Hilgard Avenue
Los Angeles, CA   90024-1467

Professor Steven Eppinger
Sloan School of Management
M.I.T.
77 Massachusetts Avenue
Room E53-347
Cambridge, MA   02139

Prof. Steven J. Fenves
Department of Civil Engineering
Carnegie-Mellon University
Pittsburgh, PA   15213

Dr. Shuichi Fukuda
Osaka University
Welding Research Institute
11-1, Mihogaoka, JAPAN

Dr. Rajit Gadh
Carnegie Group Inc.
5 PPG Place
Pittsburgh, PA   15222

Professor James Garrett
Department of Civil Engineering
Carnegie Mellon University
Pittsburgh, PA 15213

Mr. James Lee Glover
Engineer Technology
Computer Aided Technology
McDonnell Douglas Astronautics Company
Missile and Defense Electronics Division
B107 L3/1063463
P.O. Box 516
St. Louis, MO   63166-0516

Dr. Mike   Goodside
Intellicorp
125 Cambridge Park Drive
Cambridge, MA   02140

Professor David Gossard
Department of Mechanical Engineering
M.I.T.
77 Massachusetts Avenue
Room 3-449
Cambridge, MA   02139

Prof. Michitaka Hirose
Univ. of Tokyo - (but presently at)
c/o Prof. L.W. Stark
School of Optometry
Univ. of Calif. - Berkeley
481 Minor Hall
Berkeley, CA   94720

Mr. Shingo Kamiya
NTT Data
Kowa Kawasaki Nishiguchi Bldg.
66-2 Horikawa-cho, Saiwai-ku
Kawasaki-shi, Kanagawa, 210, JAPAN

Mr. Kenichi Kasai
Senior Researcher, 3rd Dept.
Mechanical Engineering Research Lab.
Hitachi, Ltd.
502, Kandatsu-machi, Tsuchiura-shi
Ibaraki-ken, 300, JAPAN

Dr. Yoshiki Kishi
Human Engineering Department
Industrial Products
Research Institute
Agency of Industrial Science
and Technology

628

M.I.T.I.
1-1-4, Higashi, Tsukuba Science City
Ibaraki, 305, JAPAN

Dr. Simon Kim
Construction Engineering Research
Laboratories
Interstate Research Park
P. O. Box 4005
Champaign, IL 61820-1305

Prof. Steven Kim
Department of Mechanical Engineering
MIT, Knowledge System Lab.
77 Mass. Avenue
Room 35-237
Cambridge, MA 02139

Dr. Ted Kitzmiller
Advanced Technology Center
Boeing Computer Services
MS 7L-64
P.O. Box 24346
Seattle, WA 98124

Ms. Susan Landers
Dept. of Computer and Information
Science
University of Massachusetts
Amherst, MA 01003

Prof. Robert Logcher
Co-technical Director
Intelligent Engineering Systems
Laboratory
Dept. of Civil Engineering
MIT, 77 Mass. Avenue, Rm. 1-253
Cambridge, MA 02139

Prof. Victor Lesser
Department of Computer and Information
Science (COINS)
University of Massachusetts
Amherst, MA 01003

Mr. Keng Lim
Graduate student
Intelligent Engineering Systems
Laboratory

MIT, Cambridge, MA 02139

Richard Mace
Bell Atlantic
Knowledge Systems, Inc.
145 Fayette Street
Morgantown, WV 26505

Prof. Tom Malone
Sloan School of Management
MIT, 50 Memorial Drive
Room E53-333
Cambridge, MA 02139

Mr. Charles Marshall
Advanced Systems and Tools Group
Intelligent Systems Technology
Digital Equipment Corporation
290 Donald Lynch Blvd.
DLB5-2/E2
Marlborough MA 01752

Dr. Shinji Matsumoto
Construction Engineering Research
Department
Construction management Group
Institute of Technology
Shimizu Corporation
4-17, Etchujima 3-Chome
Koto-Ku, Tokyo 135, JAPAN

Mr. Naoto Mine
Senior Research Engineer
Construction Engineering Research
Department
Construction Management Group
Institute of Technology
Shimizu Corporation
4-17, Etchujima 3-Chome
Koto-Ku, Tokyo 135
JAPAN

Mr. Hiroshi Nakata
Assistant Manager
Engineering Administration Dept.
Engineering Center
Komatsu Mec Corporation
1--9, Minamidai Kawagne-city
Saitawa-Pref, 350, JAPAN

Dr. D. Navinchandra
Intelligent Systems Laboratory
Robotics Institute
Carnegie-Mellon University
Pittsburgh, PA 15213

Dr. Jim Nevins
Robotics and Assembly Systems Division
The Charles Stark Draper Laboratory
555 Technology Square
Cambridge, MA 02139

Mr. Shunji Okuno
Project Manager
Engineering System Group
Information Systems Division
Komatsu Ltd.
Komatsu Bldg. 236, Akasaka
Minatoku, Tokyo 107, JAPAN

Prof. Wanda Orlikowski
Sloan School of Management
MIT, 50 Memorial Drive
Room E53-329
Cambridge, MA 02139

Prof. Alex Pentland
Dept. of Architecture
Civil Engineering and Media Lab.
MIT, 77 Mass. Avenue, Room E15-410
Cambridge, MA 02139

Dr. Steven Poltrock
Advanced Technology Center
Boeing Computer Services
MS 7L-64
P.O. Box 24346
Seattle, WA 98124

Mr. David Powell
ESB-209
GE Corp. Research and Development
P.O. Box 8
Schenectady, NY 12065

Dr. Ravi S. Raman
 Bell Atlantic
Knowledge Systems, Inc.

145 Fayette Street
Morgantown, WV 26505

Prof. Y. V. Ramana Reddy
Director
Concurrent Engineering Research Center
West Virginia University
Drawer 2000
Morgantown, West Virginia 26506

Mr. Ken Shimizu
Visiting Scholar from Mitsui Eng.
 and Shipbldg.)
Center for Design Research
Stanford University
Building 530, Duena St.
Stanford, CA 94305-4026

Dr. Andrea Skarra
ATandT Bell Labs
600 Mountain Ave.
Room 3D-551
Murray Hill, NJ 07974
[Previously with Brown University]

Dr. N.S. Sridharan
FMC Corporation, Central Eng. Labs.
1205 Coleman Avenue
Santa Clara CA 95052

Prof. D. Sriram
Co-technical Director
Intelligent Engineering Systems
 Laboratory
Dept. of Civil Engineering
MIT, 77 Mass. Avenue, Rm. 1-253
Cambridge, MA 02139

Prof. George Stephanopoulos
Department of Chemical Engineering
MIT, 77 Mass. Avenue, Rm. 66-562
Cambridge, MA 02139

Dr. Katia P. Sycara
Robotics Institute
Carnegie-Mellon University
Pittsburgh, PA 15213

Mr. Mark Silvestri

Prime Computers
14 Crosby Drive
Mail Stop 5-1
Bedford, MA   01730

Prof. Sarosh Talukdar
Engineering Design Research Center
Carnegie-Mellon University
Pittsburgh, PA   15213

Prof. Jay Tenenbaum
Department of Mechanical Engineering
Stanford University
Stanford, CA   94305

Prof. Tetsuo Tomiyama
The University of Tokyo
Faculty of Engineering
Department of Precision Machinery
7-3-1, Hongo, Bunkyo-Ku
Tokyo, 113
JAPAN

Dr. Siu Tong
General Electric Co.
Corporate Research and Development
1 River Road
P.O. Box 8
Bldg. ES, Room 209
Schenectady, New York   12301

Dr. Keith Werkman
Computer Science and Elec. Eng.
Lehigh University
Packard Lab.
Bethlehem, PA   18015
[Currently with IBM Corp, Owego Lab.
MD 0210, Route 17C, Owego, NY 13827]

Mr. Albert Wong
Graduate student
Intelligent Engineering Systems
Laboratory
MIT, Cambridge, MA 02139

Dr. Daniel Whitney
Robotics and Assembly Systems Division
The Charles Stark Draper Laboratory
555 Technology Square

Cambridge, MA   02139

Dr. Shinobu Yoshimura
The University of Tokyo
Faculty of Engineering
Department of Nuclear Engineering
7-3-1, Hongo, Bunkyo-Ku
Tokyo, 113
JAPAN

Prof. Stan Zdonik
Department of Computer Science
Brown University
Providence, R.I.   02912

Lecture Notes in Computer Science